DESTINIES

CANADIAN HISTORY SINCE CONFEDERATION

R. DOUGLAS FRANCIS/RICHARD JONES/DONALD B. SMITH

Holt, Rinehart and Winston of Canada, Limited
Toronto

Canadian Cataloguing in Publication Data

Francis, R.D. (R. Douglas), 1944-
  Destinies: Canadian history since Confederation

Companion volume to: Origins: Canadian history to
Confederation.
Bibliography: p.
Includes index.
ISBN 0-03-921706-X

1. Canada – History – 1867-   .   I. Jones,
Richard, 1943-   .   II. Smith, Donald B.,
1946-   .   III. Title.

FC164.F73 1988   971.06   C87-094453-3
F1033.F73 1988

Cover: Imtek Imagineering/Masterfile.

Publisher: Susan Lilholt
Editor: Tessa McWatt
Publishing Services Manager: Karen Eakin
Editorial Co-ordinator: Edie Franks
Copy Editor: Wendy Jacobs
Cover and Interior Design: John Zehethofer
Typesetting and Assembly: Q Composition Inc.
Printing and Binding: Metropole Litho Inc.

Printed in Canada
1 2 3 4 5   92 91 90 89 88

Preface

Origins and *Destinies* sketch the history of Canada from the beginning of
human occupation to the present. The purpose of both volumes is to
outline how this immense country (the second largest in the world) came
to be, to explain how its regions developed, and to relate the common
history of its diverse population. Throughout our two volumes we have
paid attention to Canada's various regions while keeping the country as a
whole the central focal point of the study.

This project began in 1983, when we, as professors of Canadian history,
felt the need to synthesize and supplement the older texts conceived and
written in the 1940s and 1950s, many of them still in use. We wanted a
full and up-to-date introduction for first year university and college students, one which incorporated the new historical findings of the last quarter
century—the social as well as the political and economic accounts of our
past.

Origins, our first volume, tells the history of pre-Confederation Canada—
the native people, the coming of the Norse, the Portuguese, the Spanish,
the Basques, and particularly the French and the British, who eventually
established permanent European settlements. Anyone seeking to understand our diversity today must look at the pre-Confederation era when
our present regional personalities were first formed in Atlantic Canada,
the St. Lawrence River valley, the Great Lakes, the Red River, and on
the Pacific Coast.

Destinies, our second volume, takes the story of the British North American colonies from 1867 to the present day. We show how Canada came
to take the transcontinental form it did, and how the various groups within
its boundaries came together to form one country. We have pointed out
the various regional, ethnic, and social tensions in our nation's history, as
well as the means by which these differences have been resolved in the
past.

The text is designed with the student of introductory Canadian history in mind. Each chapter treats a major topic, theme, or period, and includes subsections to aid students in organizing the material. Through the use of fully documented quotations from works by Canadian historians and up-to-date annotated bibliographical references at the conclusion of each chapter, we identify the major historical writings on the events covered. As well, we have provided a "Related Readings" section at the end of each chapter. This section indicates useful articles in the second edition of R. Douglas Francis and Donald B. Smith, eds., *Readings in Canadian History*, Volume I: *Pre-Confederation*, and Volume II: *Post-Confederation*.

Publisher's Note to Instructors and Students

This text book is a key component of your course. If you are the instructor of this course, you undoubtedly considered a number of texts carefully before choosing this as the one that will work best for your students and you. The authors and publishers of this book spent considerable time and money to ensure its high quality, and we appreciate your recognition of this effort and accomplishment.

iv

If you are a student, we are confident that this text will help you to meet the objectives of your course. You will also find it helpful after the course is finished, as a valuable addition to your personal library. So hold on to it.

As well, please don't forget that photocopying copyright work means the authors lose royalties that are rightfully theirs. This loss will discourage them from writing another edition of this text or other books, because doing so will simply not be worth their time and effort. If this happens, we all lose—students, instuctors, authors, and publishers.

And since we want to hear what you think about this book, please be sure to send us the stamped reply card at the end of the text. This will help us to continue publishing high-quality books for your courses.

Acknowledgements

In the preparation of *Origins* we have benefited enormously from the advice and suggestions of many Canadian historians. We would like to thank Gratien Allaire of the Faculté Saint-Jean, University of Alberta; Phillip Buckner of the University of New Brunswick; Jean Daigle of the Université de Moncton; Olive Dickason of the University of Alberta; John Dickinson of the Université de Montréal; Robin Fisher of Simon Fraser University; Gerald Friesen of the University of Manitoba; James Hiller of Memorial University of Newfoundland; Douglas Leighton of the University of Western Ontario; Ken Munro of the University of Alberta; Colin Read of the University of Western Ontario; and Phyllis Senese of the University of Victoria; who each read and provided us with criticisms of individual chapters within their respective research areas. On several specific issues we benefited from the comments of: Michel Granger of Brooks, Alberta (on the Acadians); James Helmer of the University of Calgary (on recent archaeological findings); Ingeborg Marshall of Portugal Cove, Newfoundland (on the Beothuk); Bea Medicine of the University of Calgary (on the native peoples' view of their origins); Dale Miquelon of the University of Saskatchewan (on recent historical writing on the economic impact of the conquest of New France); Keith Regular of Elkford, B.C. (on Newfoundland); Daniel Richter of Dickinson College, Carlisle, Pennsylvania (on the Iroquois Confederacy).

For *Destinies*, we would like to thank the following people, who read chapters of the manuscript and offered valuable criticism and advice: Douglas Baldwin of Acadia University; Gail Cuthbert-Brandt of Glendon College, York University; John English of the University of Waterloo; Gerald Friesen of the University of Manitoba; Jim Miller of the University of Saskatchewan; William Morrison of Brandon University; Howard Palmer of the University of Calgary; Margaret Prang of the University of British Columbia; John Thompson of McGill University; Keith Walden of Trent University; and William Westfall of York University.

The following historians read the entire manuscript for Holt, Rinehart and Winston. Although they did not always agree with our approach and interpretation, they offered very valuable suggestions for improving the final manuscript.

For *Origins*, we wish to thank Joseph Cherwinski of Memorial University of Newfoundland, Douglas Leighton of the University of Western Ontario, Olive Dickason of the University of Alberta, and Phyllis Senese of the University of Victoria.

For *Destinies*, we thank William Acheson of the University of New Brunswick, Thomas Socknat of the University of Toronto, Donald Swainson of Queen's University, and Eric Sager of the University of Victoria.

All errors and omissions, of course, remain our responsibility.

For making these volumes possible we warmly thank Tony Luengo, formerly of Holt, Rinehart and Winston, who first accepted the proposal, and to Tessa McWatt for seeing it to completion. We are also indebted to Edie Franks, Editorial Co-ordinator, and to Wendy Jacobs, our copy-editor, as well as all the others at Holt, Rinehart and Winston involved in the production of *Origins* and *Destinies*.

The office staff of the Department of History at the University of Calgary performed the heroic task of typing up many of the numerous drafts of the manuscript. Our thanks to Liesbeth von Wolzogen, Olga Leskiw, Marjory McLean, Jodi Steeves, and Joyce Woods, and to Barbara Nair for preparing the index for *Origins*.

Douglas Francis wishes to thank Pat Kates and her staff in Secretarial Services at York University for typing drafts of his chapters of the manuscripts during his sabbatical year, and the staff at McLaughlin College, York University, for providing him with office space and a pleasant atmosphere during that year.

To our wives, Barbara, Lilianne, and Nancy, for their support during this project, we owe debts too enormous to describe.

vi

For our children:

Marc, Myla, and Michael Francis
Marie-Noëlle, Stéphanie, Serge-André, and Charles-Denis Jones
David and Peter Smith

A small part of Canada's future

List of Maps

Contents

CONTENTS

x

xiv

CONTENTS

xvi

CHAPTER ONE

Canada: Dateline, 1867

On November 7, 1867, Governor General Lord Monck congratulated *1* Canada's first Parliament on laying "the foundation of a new nationality." Brave and hopeful words these were as the country embarked upon a bold new experiment in nation building. The Dominion of Canada had officially come into existence five months earlier, on July 1, amid doubt rather than jubilation. The Fathers of Confederation had risked a complete re-organization of British North America to solve several immediate problems: the political deadlock in the United Canadas (Ontario and Quebec), the railway debt, and the fear of an American invasion. The new nation lacked a common identity and even the most elementary sense of a shared experience among its four provinces—Ontario, Quebec, Nova Scotia, and New Brunswick. Looking back to the fragmented and uncertain Canada of 1867, it was miraculous that the colonies had united and that, within a decade, the country would expand westward from the Atlantic to the Pacific and northward to the Arctic Ocean.

Population

In 1867, the year of Confederation, three of the four groups that would make up Canada's multicultural society were well established—the native peoples, the French, and the British. Still to arrive in significant numbers were non-British and non-French immigrants from continental Europe and Asia. They migrated in large numbers at the turn of the century (see chapter 6), although there were already some German, Dutch, and American Black settlements in several districts of the new dominion.

The population figures reflect the influence of the ethnic groups that made up the small nation of just over three million people. The North American Indians within the borders of the new nation numbered approximately thirty thousand (about 1 percent of the population), with half of them in Ontario. They could be distinguished by tribal affiliation: the three largest groups were the Ojibwa, in Ontario; the Iroquois, in Ontario and Quebec; and the Micmac, in Nova Scotia and New Brunswick. Although Indians practiced their native religion, each major Christian denomination claimed converts as well. The Indians came under the federal government's jurisdiction. Section 91 (subsection 24) of the British North America (BNA) Act gave the federal government responsibility for "Indians and lands reserved for Indians."

People of French descent made up roughly a third of the total population, a percentage that remained constant until the mid-twentieth century. (In 1981 approximately 27 percent of Canadians were of French ethnic origin.) The great majority—more than 85 percent—resided in the province of Quebec, and had been in North America for two centuries and more. Approximately 93 000 or 8 percent of the French-speaking population consisted of Acadians in New Brunswick and Nova Scotia. Only 3 percent of Canada's francophones lived in Ontario, mainly in the eastern areas of the province.

People of British descent accounted for 60 percent of the Canadian population in 1867 (in contrast to 40 percent in 1981). They formed the majority of the population in Ontario and the two Maritime provinces, and were an influential minority in Quebec. They were a diverse group. Some were Loyalists who had come after the American Revolution to settle in British territory, but most were descendants of British immigrants who had come to British North America in the nineteenth century. The more recent arrivals divided into sub-groups of English, Highlander and Lowlander Scots, Protestant and Catholic Irish, and Welsh.

The remaining population—less than 10 percent—were Europeans or descendants of American Loyalists of European ancestry. This group included roughly 65 000 Blacks, the majority of whom arrived as fugitive slaves before the American Civil War. They had followed the North Star on the Underground Railroad (a loose network of abolitionists who aided slaves) to reach freedom. They established such settlements as Wilberforce and Elgin in Canada West (Ontario). Dawn, now Dresden, Ontario, was the best known because Josiah Henson—believed to be the model for "Uncle Tom" in Harriet Beecher Stowe's *Uncle Tom's Cabin* (1851)—lived there.

POPULATION DISTRIBUTION

Population distribution favoured the central provinces of Ontario (Canada West) and Quebec (Canada East). Ontario had nearly half of the dominion's population, with more than 1.5 million people. Quebec was close behind, with about a half-million less than Ontario, which had received the majority of British immigrants in the mid-nineteenth century. Even during the 1860s, when this migration levelled off, Ontario's population increased 16 percent. Quebec's population, on the other hand, increased only 7.2 percent in the same decade, and this from a high birth rate rather than from immigration. Indeed, many French-speaking Canadians in Quebec left the province for factory jobs in New England; English-speaking Quebeckers also went south and west. As the available farmland in their province rapidly disappeared, many Ontarians also left to farm in the American Midwest. The other fifth of Canada's population resided in the Maritime provinces. Nova Scotia had roughly 400 000 people, of which a significant number were recent Scot and Irish immigrants, and New Brunswick nearly 300 000, the majority being the descendants of Loyalists, Acadian French, and the newly arrived Irish.

In all three areas of the country—Ontario, Quebec, and the Maritimes—ethnic groups lived together in separate settlements. For example, Acadians resided on New Brunswick's northeastern shore, Scots on Cape Breton, Irish in Quebec City, and German-speaking Mennonites in Ontario's Waterloo county.

3

The two outlying British colonies that were eventually incorporated into Canada (see chapter 2) had even smaller populations. Newfoundland had 150 000 inhabitants and Prince Edward Island only 94 000, or roughly the population of the city of Montreal at the time. Rupert's Land, roughly defined as that area of British North America whose rivers flowed into Hudson Bay, had perhaps as many as 100 000 inhabitants, all of whom (with the exception of 1000 Scots in the Red River colony at present-day Winnipeg) were native people. On the West Coast 10 000 recent white immigrants lived among an estimated 30 000 Indians.

Politics

John A. Macdonald, the Attorney-General West in the United Canadas from 1854 onward virtually to Confederation, was chosen by Lord Monck as interim prime minister of the new country in May 1867, until the first federal election could be held. He had been instrumental in bringing about Confederation, as a result of which he had been knighted. He was first elected to the Assembly of the Canadas in 1844 to represent his home constituency of Kingston, and served for nearly half his life. A man with warm personal charm and a sense of humour, he shunned philosophical debate. A pragmatist, he never felt comfortable talking about politics in the abstract. He was best at swaying an audience on the political hustings or in Parliament with speeches delightfully mixed with conviction and humour. A masterful politician, he remained in the prime minister's office, with the exception of a five-year Liberal interlude in the mid-1870s, until his death in 1891. Quite rightly the late nineteenth century is often referred to as the Macdonald Era.

Macdonald benefited from the advice of George-Etienne Cartier, his able French-Canadian lieutenant. The prime minister once referred to Cartier as "my second self," and in some respects he was. Cartier, like Macdonald, was a conservative who believed in the possession of property as a necessary condition for public office, admired the British parliamentary system (particularly the monarchy), and distrusted American republican values such as the secret ballot and universal suffrage. As a young man, Cartier had taken up arms against Britain in the rebellions of 1837/38, but as an older man he craved British social status and cultivated a taste for British life and a close association with the British elites. In many respects, the older Cartier, although French Canadian by birth, became more British than many English Canadians, including Macdonald. He also was a successful Montreal businessman, with heavy investments in the Grand Trunk Railway, and served as director of several banking, insurance, and transportation companies. From 1867 until his death in 1873, Cartier was second only to Macdonald in the Conservative party. After Cartier, Hector Langevin and then Adolphe Chapleau became the party's leaders in Quebec, helping to return a bloc of Quebec seats to Ottawa for the Conservatives.

POLITICAL CONVENTIONS ESTABLISHED

One Canadian political convention dates back to the Confederation years. The alliance of an English Canadian and a French Canadian leader (a practice which actually pre-dated Confederation) ensured French Canadians an important voice in national politics. This practice, particularly in the Liberal party, meant that the national political leaders would most likely come from central Canada. As the Conservatives did not follow the tradition of altering English- and French-speaking leaders, their national political leaders come most often from the West as well as Atlantic Canada. The second held that national political leaders would most likely come from central Canada (although among Conservative leaders there were several important exceptions). In a political system based on representation by population and on the single-member constituency, the greatest number of seats naturally went to those provinces with the largest populations. Thus central Canada—Ontario and Quebec—dominated Parliament, a situation that created considerable discontent in the hinterland regions of the Maritimes and, later, in the West.

Confederation allowed for a new beginning in politics. The various political factions and parties that existed prior to Confederation—the Tories and the Clear Grits (or Reformers) in Canada West, the *Bleus* and the

Rouges in Canada East, the conservative and reform factions in New Brunswick and Nova Scotia—coalesced into two major parties, the Conservatives and the Liberals (Reformers), with representation and, eventually, a party machinery throughout the dominion.

Initially, these two national parties had genuine differences in ideology and party platforms. The Conservatives were, for the first thirty years of Confederation, the party of nation building. They had been instrumental in purchasing Rupert's Land in 1870, and in bringing Manitoba (1870), British Columbia (in 1871), and Prince Edward Island (in 1873) into Confederation. The Conservatives also launched the idea of a transcontinental railroad and of the "National Policy," the high protective tariff of 1879 (see chapter 3). The Conservatives under Macdonald also supported a highly centralized and powerful federal government. In 1867 and for a generation thereafter, the Liberals represented those Canadians who favoured expansion at a slower pace and who opposed Macdonald's high tariff and his centralist view of Canada.

5

FIRST FEDERAL ELECTION

The Conservatives won the first federal election in November 1867. To Macdonald's delight his arch-rival, George Brown, who had temporarily united the Clear Grits behind Macdonald's and Cartier's party into a "Great Coalition" to work for Confederation, lost his seat. Macdonald had spent money freely in Brown's riding and, obviously, to good effect. Brown's defeat (by a mere ninety-six votes) caused him to resign as Liberal leader and ended his active political career. Nevertheless, as editor and owner of the Toronto *Globe* and as a senator after 1873, Brown continued to influence his party.

In the election of 1867 Canadian voters (who consisted of male property holders only) had to declare their party preference openly, since there was no secret ballot. This system of open voting led to all kinds of abuse. Street brawls occurred at election time as emotions ran high on both sides. Candidates openly bribed voters and employers coerced employees to vote "the right way." Bars remained open at election time and bribes were given to swing votes to certain candidates. Elections were held at different times in different areas of the country, greatly influencing electoral results. These abuses would only be corrected by the Liberals once in power in the mid-1870s.

Macdonald chose his first cabinet carefully. Anxious for his party to appear national, he established what might be termed a third Canadian political convention. He chose representatives from the country's different regions and interest groups: Maritimers, Quebeckers, and Ontarians; Protestants and Catholics; Irish, Scots, English and French Canadians; busi-

National Archives of Canada (C2500).

The first Parliament of Canada, November 1867, by C.W. Simpson.

nessmen, farmers, fishermen, and, occasionally, even a representative of working people. The Conservatives also created the first federal bureaucracy to carry out the responsibilities assigned to the federal government under section 91 of the BNA Act which concerned national or interprovincial affairs. This meant jobs, or rather rewards, for party faithful. Most of the approximately five hundred positions went to former civil servants from the United Canadas and only a few token positions went to Maritimers.

Nature of Confederation

What was the "new nationality" that Lord Monck had alluded to in his Throne Speech opening the first Parliament on November 7, 1867? George-

Etienne Cartier, who had a vital interest in the subject as representative of the French Canadians, had given his views during the Confederation debates in 1865:

> Shall we be content to remain separate—shall we be content with a mere provincial existence—when, by combining, we could become a great nation? We will form a new nationality, a political nation, with which neither the national origin nor the religion of any individual can interfere.

Unity in diversity became the goal of the Fathers of Confederation. They sought to establish domestic peace between the two founding national groups, English- and French-speaking Canadians, and between Protestants and Catholics by creating a political nationality that recognized and protected ethnic and religious differences.

Despite the laudable intentions of Canada's founding fathers, friction was built into the political structure. By combining the American federal and the British parliamentary forms of governments, the new Canadian system resembled a carriage pulled simultaneously by two horses moving in different directions. Some Canadian politicians had wanted a Canadian equivalent of the British unitary state, one with a strong central government and weak municipal governments. John A. Macdonald had looked at the United States rent by civil war in the early 1860s, and to prevent a similar occurrence in Canada, he favoured a legislative union.

French-speaking Canadians and many Maritimers felt that was impossible. Understandably, French Canadians refused to be ruled by a predominantly English-speaking government. Furthermore, many areas of the Maritimes lacked municipal governments, a fact that made the centralization of all powers from Ottawa totally impractical from an administrative point of view. The Fathers of Confederation thus chose a federal union, one which divided political power between a central government with authority over matters of general and common interest, and provincial governments with authority over matters of local concern.

DEBATE OVER THE MEANING OF THE CONSTITUTION

For more than a century historians, political scientists, and legal experts have endlessly debated the intentions of the Fathers of Confederation. Did they favour a centralized or a decentralized form of government? Those who believe in the wide-ranging authority of the central government point out that the BNA Act delegated precise and very circumscribed powers to the provincial governments. In contrast, the dominion government obtained major economic and taxation powers along with the right to make laws for the "peace, order and good government of Canada" in relation to all matters not exclusively assigned to the provincial legislatures.

Centralists contend that the phrase "peace, order and good government of Canada," and the phrase "regulation of trade and commerce," incorporated all powers not exclusively given to the provinces, and therefore the residuum of powers lies with the federal government. Furthermore, the lieutenant governors of the provinces (all of whom were appointees of the dominion government) held the right to reserve and disallow provincial legislation.

Advocates of provincial rights argue, in contrast, that as the colonial leaders themselves established the union, Confederation is a compact made between their political jurisdictions. They also point to the general phrase "property and civil rights in the province," in section 92 of the BNA Act, which deals with the constitutional rights of the provinces, as proof of the intent to give broad powers to the provinces. Furthermore, they note that the provinces were given a structure of government similar to that of the federal government, implying that the provinces had an association with the Crown similar, not subordinate, to that of the dominion. Finally, they direct attention to legal tradition. The Judicial Committee of the Privy Council, the highest court in the British Empire, consistently in the late nineteenth and early twentieth centuries interpreted the constitution in favour of the provinces (see chapter 4). This constitutional court believed that the BNA Act gave wide powers to the provinces. Today, as in 1867, these differing interpretations of federal and provincial powers remain.

Canadian-British-American Relations

Did nationhood mean independence in 1867? Not for the majority of Canadians, both English- and French-speaking. George Brown wrote in the Toronto *Globe*:

> We deny that the introduction of the federal principle is in any sense a step towards independence. ... Our object is to find a system of government which shall be just and equitable to all who live under it. ... The result can best be secured while we maintain, for at all events a very long time to come, our connection with the grand old British Empire intact and unimpaired.

His political colleagues, with the exception of the minority *Rouge* faction in Quebec who opposed Confederation and favoured French-Canadian independence, concurred. In Canada in 1867 nation and empire were one and the same; the imperial connection was considered the best means for Canadians to fulfil their national destiny.

Equally evident in 1867 was anti-Americanism. The desire to be independent of the United States was one of the reasons the colonies had united. Most Canadians believed themselves to be a people different from—and better than—the Americans. British North Americans regarded the

American republican form of government as inferior to British parliamentary government. They disliked, too, the extreme form of American democracy evident in universal male suffrage, which they believed led to corruption in politics. Yet, as historian Frank H. Underhill pointed out, Canadians were becoming more American.[1] Federalism itself was an American, not a British, form of government. In becoming more egalitarian, Canadian society was also coming closer in its composition to American than to British society. The lack of an established church and the beginnings of a non-sectarian education system were also American—not British—traditions.

The Economy

The Canadian economy in 1867 rested on the nation's major natural assets: land, sea, and forests. More than 80 percent of the Canadian population worked in the primary industries—farming, fishing, or lumbering. Fishing the abundant waters of the Atlantic occupied the majority of Nova Scotians in the small fishing villages that dotted the coastline. Neighbouring New Brunswick seemed an immense forest broken only by the numerous streams that carried the logs to sea and by pockets of agricultural settlement. Only the Ottawa valley, with its massive red and white pines, rivalled New Brunswick for the timber trade, though in Quebec lumbering also was important. Softwood trees such as pine, spruce, and tamarack were ideal for ships and for construction in Britain and in the New England states.

The shipbuilding industry was closely allied with fishing and lumbering. In 1878 Canada could claim the fourth-largest merchant marine in the world, behind only the fleets of Britain, the United States, and Norway. In 1865 alone, the Maritimes turned out more than six hundred vessels. The ports of St. John, Halifax, Yarmouth, Quebec, and Montreal were major shipowning centres.

As steel ships replaced wooden ones and steam replaced sails as the source of energy, the era of wood, wind, and sails—or as the Maritimers preferred to call it, the era of wooden ships and iron men—ended. Some Maritimers equated the close of their "golden age" with the joining of Confederation and they resented union. Stephen Leacock best expressed this feeling: "the shades of night were falling, and the night was called Confederation."[2]

FARMING

The family farm was the mainstay of the Canadian economy in 1867. In Nova Scotia farming was important, especially in the Annapolis Valley,

9

and in New Brunswick farmers made up more than half the labour force. In Quebec, wheat farming had given way to mixed farming, especially to dairy production. As a result of intense cultivation over the previous two centuries and overpopulation of the seigneuries, the central farmland in the St. Lawrence lowland had become exhausted. Few Quebec farmers produced more than enough to feed their families. Some moved to the Eastern Townships (previously occupied by English-speaking farmers) and to the Canadian Shield country to the north, particularly the Saguenay–Lake St. Jean region, the Laurentians, and Témiscamingue in the upper Ottawa valley. Here the "colonist farmers" had to clear the land of forests before breaking ground. Even then, farming was marginal because of poor soil, short frost-free periods, and long distances from market centres. As the joke went, the northern farmers raised two crops: one stone, the other snow. Tens of thousands of French Canadians chose the easier course of action, and left the province for factory work in neighbouring New England. Emigration was a serious problem for French-Canadian leaders, who feared the rapid anglicization of French Canadians outside Quebec.

10

Wheat farming was the backbone of the Ontario economy, "the engine of economic growth,"[3] according to the economic historian John McCallum. At the time of Confederation the best agricultural land lay in Ontario, where 60 percent of the provincial population farmed. Coarse grain or flour made up half of all exports from Ontario at mid-century. By the time of Confederation, the peak of wheat production had been reached, with the good farmland having been occupied and some of the older districts becoming exhausted. Fortunately for Ontarians, just as they faced an agricultural crisis, the federal government acquired the vast agricultural hinterland of the Northwest for settlement. During the Confederation debates, George Brown, whose Clear Grits represented Canada West farmers, had reminded Canadians of the potential of the prairies, those "vast Indian territories ... greater than the whole soil of Russia."

TRANSPORTATION

Staple trade required efficient transportation, but in 1867 Canada's roads left much to be desired. Grain, livestock, and lumber had to be transported over what were little more than dirt tracks or wagon trails. Some widely used trails had been upgraded to "macadamized" roads, that is, roads built by placing layers of successively smaller stones and gravel upon one another. These roads were costly. Tollgates were placed every eight kilometres or so to extract tolls from farmers, salesmen, or anyone else using the road to help pay for them. A favourite sport of the time was "running the toll gate," or crashing through without paying. Plank roads (ten-centimetre-thick planks of white pine covered with fine gravel or pitch and laid across and spiked to two logs placed parallel to one another in the roadbed) began replacing macadamized roads by the 1840s and 1850s. They were less costly and provided, according to reports of seasoned stagecoach travellers at the time, a most comfortable, smooth ride.

Boats and trains made transportation more efficient. Steamboats sailed the Atlantic coast, the St. Lawrence, and the Great Lakes. A network of canals enabled small vessels to reach the Great Lakes by the St. Lawrence River. Water travel was the most efficient mode of transportation in the 1860s, but it had disadvantages: the shipping season was short; the risk of damage due to storms was great; the cost of building and maintaining canals was high; and only those living close to the waterways could benefit.

Railways opened up inland areas previously inaccessible to settlement year round and revolutionized transportation. The British North American colonies had realized the potential of railways for trade and had embarked in the 1850s on an ambitious building scheme. By the time of Confederation, 3330 km of track had already been laid. Railway building had *11* been one of the chief reasons behind Confederation. The BNA Act included the promise of a railroad linking Ontario and Quebec with the Maritimes, and implied, in its reference to a transcontinental nation, the possibility of a future transcontinental railway from coast to coast.

Most trains were about as fast as a horse and carriage, but on good track, like that between Toronto and Montreal, they could reach a speed of fifty kilometres per hour. In summer the wood-burning locomotives often caused forest fires as sparks flew from the smokestack, in spite of a wide-flanged spark-catcher and screen over it. In winter the iron rails occasionally split, derailing the train, and during snowstorms passengers had to shovel snow from the tracks. Then, too, railway building was costly, more likely to end in debt than to make a profit. Still, railroads were indispensable for trade and for industrial capital and were a stimulus to the manufacturing industries. For these reasons, Canadian politicians were prepared to subsidize them with public money.

EXTERNAL TRADE RELATIONS

Canada's trade patterns entered an era of transition in 1867. Until the mid-nineteenth century the bulk of British North American trade had been with Britain. During the 1840s, however, the mother country abandoned the mercantile system of preferential trade with its colonies in favour of free trade. The British North American colonies in turn sought an alternative and found it in free trade in natural products with the United States under the Reciprocity Treaty of 1854. But the treaty had been rescinded in 1866 by a protectionist American Senate, forcing British North Americans to look increasingly to internal (domestic) trade. Confederation formalized the association and provided the means for the colonies to trade together (although trade with Britain and the United States was still important after 1867).

In 1867 Canada's economy remained essentially underdeveloped, serving the more mature industrialized economies of Britain and the United States. Canadians produced raw materials and imported manufactured goods: textiles, textile fibres, agricultural products, consumer goods, and iron products. Nevertheless, industrialization had begun. Economic historian O.J. Firestone sees the 1860s as the turning point to a modern industrial society.[4] He points to the fact that 20 percent of the Canadian gross national product (GNP) came from manufacturing, a dramatic increase from the previous decade. Manufacturing employed nearly 200 000 Canadians in roughly 40 000 establishments. Most of these were small family businesses—blacksmith shops, sawmills, gristmills, and distilleries, in particular—attached to the owner's residence and employing only a few people doing jobs by hand. They supplied only local needs on a custom or repair basis. Mechanization, however, had come to the agricultural implements industry. Daniel Massey, a farmer in Newcastle, just east of Toronto, had been manufacturing first-class ploughs, harrows, reapers, and other simple horse-drawn instruments since 1849. The firm of Alanson Harris of Beamsville, just south of Hamilton, shipped farm equipment all over British North America. In 1890 these two rival firms amalgamated to form Massey–Harris (later Massey–Ferguson), at the time Canada's largest manufacturer of farm implements.

Specialization had begun in Canadian shops and factories in the large urban centres of Montreal, Toronto, Quebec, Hamilton, St. John, and Halifax. Quebec shipbuilding used techniques adapted from the British industrial revolution, as did the boot and shoe industry of Toronto. In Hamilton, iron smelting and steel production had begun. By 1867 manufacturing was concentrated in the Montreal area and in the vicinity of Toronto, as well as in a belt at the western end of Lake Ontario from Hamilton westward to the Grand River valley.

URBANIZATION

Urbanization was also underway in 1867, although only one in five Canadians lived in urban centres (communities with a population over 1000). More than 105 000 people lived in Montreal, Canada's largest city. Next largest was Quebec City at 60 000, and then Toronto at 50 000. Six other cities had populations of over 10 000: two were in the Maritimes (St. John and Halifax), and four in Ontario (Hamilton, Ottawa, Kingston, and London). A host of smaller towns in the range of 1000–5000 dotted the Canadian landscape. These urban centres serviced a limited rural hinter-

12

land accessible by road. Only the larger cities, thanks to their extensive rail connections, could service a region that went beyond the adjacent rural area. Montreal's hinterland, for example, included the rural areas of Quebec as well as eastern Ontario.

St. John and Halifax grew slowly compared to urban centres in central Canada. The Maritime economy was still thriving, but there were already warning signs of decline on the horizon. Many of the manufacturers in these two port cities faced hard times as they lacked a large local market and faced competition from the wealthier businessmen in central Canada. In 1877 fire destroyed the business district of St. John, along with most of its waterfront and its residential area. Halifax became the Maritimes' leading commercial centre; its merchants and urban promoters succeeded in attracting more factories, railways, and trade than did St. John. In the long run, however, neither Halifax nor St. John could compete with the volume of shipping in the larger port of Montreal.

13

Social Life

What was life like for the rural and urban inhabitants of Canada in 1867? Most Canadians lived and worked on their own farms, as close to neighbours, kin, and their own ethnic group as possible. In Quebec, the most urbanized province, more than 80 percent of the population lived on the land. Quebec farmers belonged to two classes: the landowners, and the rural tenants who worked for a landlord. The parish formed the main social unit of rural Quebec. Within the parish, the church remained (and still does in many small Quebec communities) the geographical centre. Families were large, and all members contributed to the family's livelihood. Limited financial means made consumer goods a luxury. The village's elite consisted of the *curé*, the doctor, the notary, and the local merchants. In Quebec City and Montreal the French-Canadian population lived amid a substantial English-speaking population, the latter making up roughly one-third of Quebec City's population and one-quarter of Montreal's. This English-speaking population contained the great majority of the province's commercial and business elite, who were among the most powerful businessmen in North America.

Next door in Ontario, most of the population were recent immigrants or children of immigrants. The majority were freehold farmers who had obtained land only within the last generation. Ontario farmers tended to be better off economically than their Quebec counterparts, since they owned larger farms that were newly cultivated and subsequently more productive. But they lacked the social and religious cohesion of Quebec society. People lived farther apart and were divided in their religious denominational affiliation. Socializing took place at loggings, stumpings, or barn-raising bees. According to Susanna Moodie, an upper middle-class English immigrant in the 1830s, these meetings were "noisy, riotous, drunken."

In the pioneer communities the taverns also served as a source of news. More sober talk occurred at the workplace, the gristmill, general store, or the blacksmith shop in the local village or hamlet. Local agricultural societies also brought people together. As in the United States, fraternal organizations, such as the Oddfellows, the Independent Order of Foresters, and, for the Protestants, the Orange Lodge and the Masons, were very popular. The most important centre for social life, however, was the church.

Great physical mobility characterized life in Ontario. A study of several townships along Lake Ontario near Port Hope in the 1860s revealed that within a five year span more than half of the people had been recent occupants. David Gagan's study of Peel County at mid-century substantiates these startling statistics, as does Michael Katz's study of mid-century Hamilton. Clearly, Ontario had a migrant population. Physical mobility, however, did not always mean social mobility, although the incentive for moving was often to better one's life.

In the two Maritime provinces, life was largely rural and small-town in nature. With sparse populations, poor roads, and a topography that encouraged settlement along the coast, communities often lay many kilometres from each other. Also, the diversified economy of the Maritimes— fishing, lumbering, mining, and farming—separated people according to interests and livelihood. Maritimers in 1867 still identified with their particular locale; they lacked a sense of regional consciousness.

THE INDUSTRIAL CITY

Canadian cities in 1867 were, with the exception of Montreal, pre-industrial. Rich and poor lived in close proximity, with social distinctions being marked by a person's location on a street, or by the location of a particular street in a district. In Montreal, however, urban congestion had already led to the formation of predominantly working-class districts in the city core and along the St. Lawrence and the Lachine Canal. Well-to-do families were leaving the city centre to live in the spacious, clean, and airy districts of the west end, with its numerous parks and good public services. The modern industrial segregated city had, in Montreal at least, made an appearance in 1867. By 1914, it was commonplace throughout the country (see chapter 8).

In the urban centres of Ontario, Quebec, and the Maritimes, the upper classes lived well, in houses with high-ceilinged rooms, wide verandahs, and big front lawns, and gas lighting, running water, and inside toilets. Furnaces were not in use until the 1880s, so each room was heated by a fireplace. Bathtubs had just been introduced. Servants cleaned the house, cared for the children, and cooked the meals. A typical mid-day meal might consist of cold soup as an appetizer, followed by a broiled trout or salmon, roast pigeon or chicken and a joint of beef, with a meat pie, pork chops, or sausages on the side and fresh vegetables. For dessert there was a choice of hot biscuits, fruit pie, and cake. The beverage consisted of wine and tea or coffee.

Working-class families in the city lived an entirely different existence. A typical family had one or two rooms in a tenement house—shared with five or more other families—with poor ventilation, no lighting or running water, no yard or indoor toilet. The daily diet contained no fresh vegetables, and only small quantities of meat and dairy products. Disease, poverty, and death were ever present. Newborn children of the poor were almost as likely to die as to live; in Montreal in 1867, two out of every five children died before reaching the age of one, most often from intestinal diseases caused by unpasteurized milk. (Pasteurization became common in North America only in the early twentieth century.) Children lucky enough to survive the first year had to avoid smallpox, the major cause of infant death. Among adults, especially women, tuberculosis was the leading killer. Besides disease and death, working-class families lived a life of endless poverty. Wages were abysmally low, especially for women and children, and working conditions notoriously harsh.

15

WOMEN

Women faced many disadvantages in 1867. They lacked the franchise, economic status, and legal rights. They were defined by their role in the "domestic sphere," as wife and mother at the service of husband and children. Their daily tasks consisted of cleaning house, cooking, sewing, weaving, and making butter, the rhythm broken only by church services on Sundays. The change of seasons only varied the pattern slightly.

Marriage appears to have been motivated by economic rather than romantic concerns. Although it is difficult to answer such personal questions as why people married in the eighteenth and nineteenth centuries, romantic courtship could hardly have existed or survived in rural or urban working-class Canada. Surviving women's diaries from the eighteenth and nineteenth centuries attest only to the drudgery of life and speak little of love and romance.

In the factories, a woman received half the wages of a man doing a similar job. Female employees were sought after, particularly as unskilled workers in such industries as clothing, tobacco, and footwear, not because of their skills or abilities but simply because they were cheap labour. In the workplace, women had no alternatives to low wages, unhealthy working conditions, and exploitive male employers; there were no unions to represent them.

TRADE UNIONS

Few workers belonged to trade unions in 1867. Few trade unions existed, and those that did were restricted to a particular locale or a specialized trade, such as typesetters, shoemakers, and moulders. These unions represented skilled workers only. In the 1860s the first unions for non-skilled workers appeared in shops using modern technology, a development that threatened to make unskilled jobs obsolete. But in 1867 there was no central labour organization to unify these unions or to act as a political force. Unions were illegal, in fact, until they were granted the right to exist by the federal government in 1872 (see chapter 8). The struggle to secure full union recognition continued into the mid-twentieth century.

16

Religion and Education

In 1867 the Christian churches had important social roles. They gave spiritual comfort, moral guidance, and often social assistance to pioneering settlers. They provided a place where people could meet socially. Almost all Canadians in 1867 belonged to the Roman Catholic or one of the numerous Protestant churches. The Catholic church, the largest Canadian church in 1867, had 40 percent of the Canadian population as members, and in Quebec, 85 percent of the population. In that province the church controlled the Catholic education system by supplying the teachers and deciding the curriculum. The female religious orders taught in the schools, administered the hospitals, and ran the charitable institutions. The number of nuns in Quebec increased tenfold between 1850 and 1900, from 600 to more than 6500. This growth in the number of nuns reflected perhaps an alternative for Quebec women to marriage, spinsterhood, factory work, or emigration with one's family. Female religious communities allowed their members to obtain an excellent education and to use their training as teachers, as nurses, and as social workers.

In Protestant Canada no one church dominated to the extent that the Catholic church did in Quebec. Anglicans, however, constituted, by a slight majority, the largest Protestant group. Even within a single denomination, there were divisions and distinct groups, such as the several varieties of Methodists, Presbyterians, and Baptists. These Protestant religious groups generally favoured voluntarism—the legal separation of church and state—because their Sunday schools provided religious instruction. (The Catholic church relied on the daily school system to provide religious as well as regular instruction.) This meant the abolition of denominational schools in favour of public or state schools that would nevertheless provide a moral and religious education. Protestant groups particularly opposed separate Catholic schools, seeing them as evidence of undue religious influence in education. In Ontario (Canada West), the "voluntarists" under Egerton Ryerson, the first superintendent of education in the province, succeeded in creating a non-denominational public school system. This system later became the model for education in the western provinces.

SCHOOLING

Schooling, however, was not a high priority in Canada in the 1860s. Children fortunate enough to go to school occasionally had to attend classes in corners of warehouses, blacksmith shops, stores, tanneries, or in private homes. In Owen Sound, Ontario, for example, the school was in an abandoned prospector's shack. Sometimes teachers had little more education than the children they taught, the most important requisite being a willingness to work for low salaries and to enforce discipline. Some teachers had to be satisfied with board and lodging only. Local school boards expected male teachers to help with outdoor chores, and female teachers to mind the children, help prepare meals, and sew and darn. Children, especially in rural areas, rarely went beyond the basic 3 "Rs"—"reading, 'riting, and 'rithmetic." Students in English-speaking Canada read the Bible or, if they were fortunate enough to have textbooks, from British or American texts that described experiences alien to them.

Higher education was the privilege of the middle and upper classes. In Ontario, wealthy parents paid for their children to attend grammar schools (later renamed by Ryerson in 1871 as high schools) and collegiate institutions. In the former, the students learned English, commercial subjects and natural science, especially agriculture, and in the latter they studied the classics in preparation for university. In Quebec, bourgeois families sent their sons to classical colleges to become lawyers, doctors, and priests. Universities were even more exclusive. Most were affiliated with a religious denomination, but by 1867 there were a few exceptions—the University of Toronto, Dalhousie College in Halifax, and the University of New Brunswick after 1859. Within the university curriculum, the faculties of arts and theology were dominant. The arts course was traditional, with an emphasis on classical languages, mathematics, and philosophy. Natural science was just beginning to assume importance.

The new Dominion of Canada at the moment of Lord Monck's address was a rural, predominantly farming, frontier society. Social distinctions divided the rural population and physical distance separated communities.

The National Gallery of Canada, Ottawa.

Robert Harris, who was raised in Prince Edward Island, became one of Canada's most famous artists in the late nineteenth century. In 1885 Harris completed *A Meeting of the School Trustees*, one of his best-known paintings. It shows the quizzical, sceptical Scottish pioneers of Prince Edward Island questioning a young, sincere rural school teacher.

In the few towns and cities, social classes were evident but segregation by social districts was only beginning. The upper classes lived comfortably, while the poor struggled to survive. The Canadian economy was still largely pre-industrial, with manufacturing beginning only in a few larger urban centres. Commercial trade consisted of staple products of wheat, timber, and fish for external markets—Britain and the United States. Politically, the new nation was experimenting with a new two-party system and with a new constitution that left much to be resolved in the field of dominion-provincial relations and the actual working of the parliamentary system of government. The country lacked a sense of nationalism. The prime minister, John A. Macdonald, reminded Canadians that Confederation, "now in the gristle," needed to "harden into bone."

NOTES

[1] Frank H. Underhill, *The Image of Confederation* (Toronto, 1964), pp. 11–12.
[2] Quoted in Underhill, *Confederation*, p. 6.
[3] John McCallum, *Unequal Beginnings: Agriculture and Economic Development in Quebec and Ontario Until 1870* (Toronto, 1980), p. 5.
[4] O.J. Firestone, *Canada's Economic Development 1867–1953* (London, 1958), p. 230.

BIBLIOGRAPHY

For overviews of Canada in the 1860s and interpretative essays on Confederation, students should consult Donald Creighton's "The 1860's," in J.M.S. Careless and R.C. Brown, eds., *The Canadians: 1867–1967* (Toronto, 1967), pp. 3–36; and his introductory chapter to *Canada's First Century, 1867–1967* (Toronto, 1970); F.H. Underhill, *The Image of Confederation* (Toronto, 1964); W.L. Morton, *The Critical Years* (Toronto, 1964); and Ramsay Cook, *Canada and the French-Canadian Question* (Toronto, 1966) and his *The Maple Leaf Forever: Essays on Nationalism and Politics in Canada* (Toronto, 1971). 19

Portraits of Canada's first prime minister are available in Donald Creighton, *John A. Macdonald: The Old Chieftain* (Toronto, 1955) and P.B. Waite, *Macdonald: His Life and World* (Toronto, 1975). On Macdonald's political philosophy, see P.B. Waite, "The Political Ideas of John A. Macdonald," in *The Political Ideas of the Prime Ministers of Canada*, edited by Marcel Hamelin (Ottawa, 1969) pp. 51–67. For studies of George-Etienne Cartier, see Alastair Sweeney, *George-Etienne Cartier: A Biography* (Toronto, 1976), and Brian Young, *George-Etienne Cartier: Montreal Bourgeois* (Montreal, 1981).

On the Canadian economy at the time of Confederation, the best study is Michael Bliss, *Northern Enterprise: Five Centuries of Canadian Business* (Toronto, 1987). For the traditional "staples approach," see W.T. Easterbrook and H. Aitken, *Canadian Economic History* (Toronto, 1956). On industrial development see O.J. Firestone, *Canada's Economic Development 1867–1953* (London, 1958). For an overview of economic history of Quebec, see P.-A. Linteau, R. Durocher, and J.-C. Robert, *Quebec: A History, 1867–1929* (Toronto, 1983).

John Warkentin and R.C. Harris, *Canada Before Confederation* (Toronto, 1974) provides an overview of regional societies in Canada in the mid-nineteenth century. Quantitative studies of class and social structure of two areas of Ontario are available in M. Katz, *The People of Hamilton, Canada West: Family and Class in a Mid-Nineteenth Century City* (Cambridge, 1975), and David Gagan, *Hopeful Travellers: Families, Land, and Social Change in Mid-Victorian Peel County, Canada West* (Toronto, 1981). For a study of Montreal see Bettina Bradbury, "The Fragmented Family:

Family Strategies in the Face of Death, Illness, and Poverty, Montreal, 1860–1885," in *Childhood and Family in Canadian History*, edited by Joy Parr (Toronto, 1982), pp. 109–128, 204–209.

Religion and education are reviewed in W.L. Morton, "Victorian Canada" in his edited collection, *The Shield of Achilles* (Toronto, 1968), pp. 311–34; John S. Moir, "Religion," in *The Canadians: 1867–1967*, (above), pp. 586–605; and J. Donald Wilson, Robert M. Stamp, and Louis-Philippe Audet, eds., *Canadian Education: A History* (Toronto, 1970).

Political parties at the time of Confederation are discussed by F.H. Underhill, "The Development of National Political Parties in Canada," in his *In Search of Canadian Liberalism* (Toronto, 1960), pp. 21–42. For a discussion of Canadian-British-American relations around the time of Confederation, see C.P. Stacey, *Canada and the Age of Conflict: A History of Canadian External Relations, Vol. 1: 1867–1921* (Toronto, 1977), and J.B. Brebner, *The North Atlantic Triangle: The Interplay of Canada, the United States and Great Britain* (New York, 1945; reprinted 1966).

CHAPTER TWO

Three Oceans, One Country: 1867–80

In 1867 Canada was a nation in name only. Nova Scotia, a reluctant partner of Confederation, called for the union's repeal. The Americans threatened Canada, and their congressmen talked openly of acquiring the Northwest. On the East Coast, Newfoundland and Prince Edward Island wanted better terms before consenting to join Confederation, while on the West Coast, British Columbia was isolated from other British North Americans by a vast, undeveloped territory. John A. Macdonald, the prime minister, attempted to hold together this fragile creation and to round it out by purchasing the Northwest from the Hudson's Bay Company and by bringing both British Columbia and Prince Edward Island into the union.

The Nova Scotia Repeal Movement

Nova Scotia had opposed Confederation from the beginning. Charles Tupper, the premier of Nova Scotia since 1863, refused to hold a referendum on the Confederation issue, or even to debate it in the Assembly. A report in the *Novascotian* on the celebration of Confederation indicates its unpopularity: "Dr. Tupper was burned in effigy here on Monday night last. We are only sorry it was not in person."

When Nova Scotians did have a chance to vote in September 1867, they elected anti-confederates to eighteen of the nineteen federal seats; only Tupper won for the confederates and even then by a slim ninety-eight vote majority. Provincially, they sent to Halifax thirty-six anti-confederates and only two pro-confederates. In the first meeting of the provincial legislature, the anti-confederates presented repeal resolutions to end the "bondage" of Confederation.

Joseph Howe, Nova Scotia's popular and seasoned politician, the "Father of Responsible Government in Nova Scotia," and premier from 1860 to 1863, led the Anti-Confederation League (formed in 1866) which had been founded to fight Confederation. He represented a generation of Nova Scotians who remembered with pride the colony's vital role in the triangular trade with Britain, the Maritimes, and the West Indies. A dedicated British imperialist, he wanted to strengthen the colony's ties with the British Empire, not weaken them through union with the other British North American colonies. After the stunning victories for the repealers in the election of 1867, the veteran politician headed a committee to London in early 1868 to obtain the Colonial Office's sanction for Nova Scotia to withdraw from Confederation. The Colonial Secretary refused even to meet with Howe. Britain wanted to lessen, not increase, its obligations in British North America.

Other repealers favoured independence or annexation to the United States. The latter course was particularly popular among the business interests in the province. After Britain had adopted free trade in the 1840s, Nova Scotians had found lucrative trade with the United States through the Reciprocity Treaty of 1854, but the treaty had been rescinded in 1866 by a protectionist American Senate. In 1867 many Nova Scotians preferred a renewal of reciprocity with the United States over union with Canada.

Howe faced a dilemma once the Colonial Office refused his request to reintegrate Nova Scotia in the Empire. Although he opposed Confederation, he also rejected both independence or annexation to the United States. John A. Macdonald now saw Canada's opportunity. The prime minister promised Howe a Cabinet position and offered better terms for Nova Scotia—an increased debt allowance, and a 25 percent increase in the federal subsidy to finance provincial programs (to $82 698 a year for ten years). Howe's opponents accused him of betraying his province for "eighty cents a head," the amount per person upon which the increased federal subsidy was based. Nevertheless, Howe won a by-election, thanks to very generous campaign funds (estimated at $30 000) supplied jointly by the federal Conservative government and by central Canadian businessmen. Nova Scotia's most vocal opponent of Confederation then joined the federal Cabinet.

Howe's conversion to Canadian federalism undermined the repeal movement. Only the annexationists remained a viable force. In June 1869 the Anti-Confederation League formally changed its name to the Annexation League. The timing could not have been poorer: their annexationist manifesto, advocating closer relations with the United States, coincided with a brief period of prosperity that undermined their economic grievances. By the early 1870s annexationist sentiments had subsided and the repeal of Confederation movement was silenced, although the bitterness towards Confederation remained.

Canadian Acquisition of Rupert's Land

Along with the unrest on the East Coast, Macdonald and his Conservative government faced more serious troubles in the Northwest. American sen-

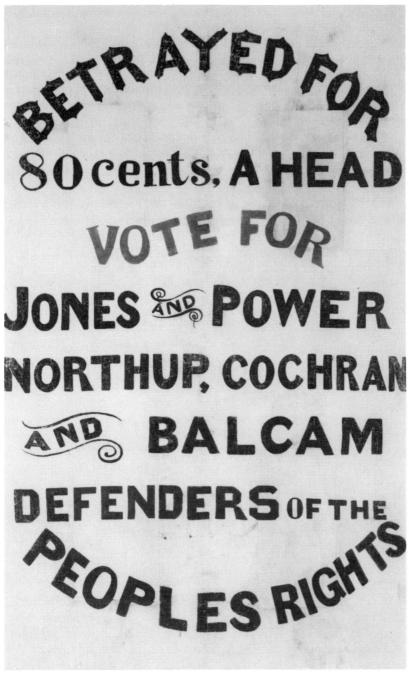

23

Public Archives of Nova Scotia.

This 1867 election banner, made out of bedsheets, captures Nova Scotians' feeling of betrayal about Confederation.

ators and congressmen talked openly of annexing the region, while American promotion agents were active in the Red River colony. Traders in Minnesota carried on active trade with the Red River colonists, who saw the Americans as their natural trading partners. In 1864 the U.S. Congress granted a charter for the construction of the Northern Pacific Railway to be built from St. Paul, Minnesota to Seattle, Washington, and to run close to the international border in order to capture the trade of the British territory. Canada's efforts to acquire the Northwest predated Confederation. In 1864 George Brown and the Clear Grits made possession of the area one of their conditions for joining the Great Coalition, a union of Clear Grits, Tories and *Bleus*, to bring about Confederation (see chapter 1).

In 1868 John A. Macdonald sent William McDougall, who had replaced Brown as the chief western expansionist in Parliament, and George-Etienne Cartier to begin negotiations in London with members of the British government and the Hudson's Bay Company to acquire Rupert's Land. The agreement they reached in 1869 proved to be one of the largest real estate deals in history. For an area ten times the size of what was then Canada, the dominion government agreed to pay the Hudson's Bay Company a cash sum of £300 000 (approximately $1 500 000), and to allow the company one-twentieth (roughly 2.8 million ha) of the land of the "fertile belt" (the area along the North Saskatchewan River) as well as the land immediately surrounding their trading posts. The company first had to transfer the land to the British government which, in turn, turned over the territory to Canada.

24

ADMINISTERING THE NORTHWEST

At the same time the Canadian government made preparations to administer the area. In June 1869 Parliament passed the Act for the Temporary Government of Rupert's Land and the Northwest Territories, which proposed a direct colonial system of government similar to that in the British North American colonies prior to the granting of local assemblies. Representative and responsible government—and provincehood—had to await sufficient population.

In preparation for the date of transfer, December 1, 1869, the federal government dispatched a survey crew to the Red River settlement. Macdonald also appointed William McDougall as the first lieutenant governor. McDougall set off for the Red River colony via St. Paul, Minnesota, but he never reached his destination. A group of Métis under Louis Riel, a twenty-five-year-old Métis from a well-known Red River family who had been educated in Montreal, had worked in a Montreal law office, and was bilingual, drove out the survey crew and stopped McDougall and his

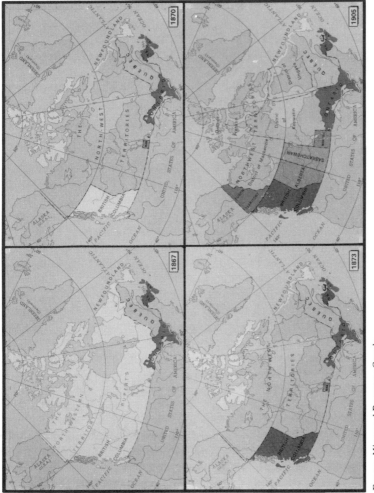

Energy, Mines and Resources Canada.

The territorial evolution of Canada from the original nation of four provinces in 1867 (Ontario, Quebec, Nova Scotia and New Brunswick), to five in 1870 (Manitoba), seven by 1873 (British Columbia and Prince Edward Island) and nine by 1905 (Alberta and Saskatchewan).

25

entourage at the American border. As the Hudson's Bay Company had given up its right but still had not yet transferred Rupert's Land to Canada the new Dominion had no legal authority in the Red River in late 1869.

MÉTIS RESISTANCE OF 1869-70

During the negotiations for the transfer of Rupert's Land no one had consulted the roughly 25 000 Indians and 15 000 mixed-bloods in the prairie West. The mixed-bloods in the Red River colony consisted of two groups: approximately 4000 Country-Born, the descendants of Indian women and British traders; and 6000 Métis, descendants of Indian women and French voyageurs. The Métis resented the Hudson's Bay Company selling their homeland to a distant state without their approval.

The aggressive actions and haughty attitude of Dr. John Christian Schultz, a sometime medical doctor and merchant, and a small group of Canadian expansionists in the Red River colony had aggravated the situation. In their newspaper, *The Nor'Wester*, these men ridiculed the Métis and proclaimed Canada's right to take control of the Northwest as part of its manifest destiny. The Métis, in response, had gathered around Louis Riel. On November 2, 1869, Riel and his followers occupied Fort Garry and, hence, gained control of the colony without firing a shot. Then they established a provisional government to fill the power vacuum.

William McDougall, not waiting for the announcement of the transfer of the Red River to Canada, forged a royal proclamation to which he attached Queen Victoria's name. On the evening of November 30, McDougall crossed the border to proclaim in the dark that the region was Canada's. What he did not know was that the Canadian government had refused to take over the territory on December 1 until the dispute was settled.

At this time Macdonald agreed to negotiate with the Métis. He realized that he would have to wait until summer before sending an armed expedition to the Red River, and by that time the region could be lost to Canada forever. He fired McDougall and asked Bishop Alexandre Taché of the Red River colony to return from Rome, where he had been attending the Vatican Council, to help reach a settlement with the Métis. Macdonald also requested the Hudson's Bay Company's Donald A. Smith to negotiate for Canada with the Red River settlers.

Riel's provisional government had drawn up a Bill of Rights in November 1869 outlining Métis grievances that became the basis for Smith's discussions. At two public meetings attended by one thousand people, held in freezing weather on January 19 and 20, Smith calmed the Métis' fears about the Canadian government's intentions, and promised better terms, to be decided by negotiations between a three-man committee of Métis and the Canadian government. Shortly afterwards the Red River colony decided to send a delegation to Ottawa. To this point Riel had achieved a great deal.

Schultz and his Canadian party, which opposed Riel's provisional government, had kept up their struggle against it. They used Schultz's general store as their headquarters. The Métis raided the store and imprisoned the Canadians, although Riel released in January those prisoners who promised either to leave the colony or to obey the provisional government. A few, like Schultz, refused to comply. Instead, he escaped by using a knife, hidden in a pudding by his wife, to cut the ropes on the windows and to lower himself out. The escapees then prepared an ill-fated attack on Fort Garry during which the Métis captured members of the raiding party, including Thomas Scott, a boisterous Protestant Irishman, a member of the Orange Lodge, and a vehement anti-Catholic.

Riel then made an error of colossal proportions. While held at Fort Garry, Scott proved a difficult prisoner. Not hiding his contempt for his prison guards, he insulted and provoked them, and threatened to kill Riel. A Métis court, organized by the provisional government, voted to execute Scott. Riel agreed, in order "to make Canada respect us." (Some historians argue that, to keep control of the Métis, Riel complied with the court order.) A firing squad shot Scott on March 4. This act would ultimately lead to Riel's own execution.

27

THE MÉTIS RESISTANCE BECOMES A NATIONAL CRISIS

With Scott's execution, a distant western struggle now became a national crisis. In Protestant Ontario, Scott became a martyr. When a group of Scott's Red River associates arrived in Toronto, throngs of supporters listened to their message:

> It would be a gross injustice to the loyal inhabitants of Red River, humiliating to our national honour, and contrary to all British traditions for our Government to receive, negotiate or meet with the emissaries of those who have robbed, imprisoned and murdered loyal Canadians, whose only fault was zeal for British institutions, whose only crime was devotion to the old flag.

In Roman Catholic Quebec, Riel became the valiant protector of the French-speaking Métis against an aggressive Ontario population intent on destroying their way of life. The spirit of conciliation existing between English- and French-speaking politicians at the time of Confederation seemed to have vanished.

Then John A. Macdonald struck a compromise. To please the Métis and the French Canadians of Quebec, his government passed the Manitoba Act in May 1870 (based on the negotiations between the Red River's three-man delegation and the Canadian government) by which Red River could enter Confederation. The Act contained most of the demands in the Bill of Rights drawn up by Riel's provisional government, including provincehood. To satisfy Ontario, the prime minister agreed to send an armed

RED RIVER
OUTRAGE.

A Public Meeting of the inhabitants of Hullett, Morris and Wawanosh will be held in the

Village of Blyth,

ON

WEDNESDAY, 20th APRIL,

AT 4 O'CLOCK, P. M.

To afford Loyal People an opportunity of expressing their deep indignation at the vile crimes committed in Rupert's land, by imprisoning and murdering British and Canadian subjects. The honor of England was never outraged with impunity, and never will be. Let Canada not be degraded, the honor of the country must be maintained, the blood of the Martyred Scott must not cry in vain for vengeance. Let Canada speak out now, and let the assassin Riel feel that a Canadian must be like an ancient Roman, free from injury wherever he goes. The men that went to Magdalla can go to the Red River. Come all Loyal Men to the meeting, this is the common cause of all Canadians.

DISTINGUISHED SPEAKERS WILL BE IN ATTENDANCE.

HURRAH FOR CANADA.

A ROPE FOR THE MURDERER RIEL!

GOD SAVE THE QUEEN!

Printed at the *New Era* Cheap Job Printing Establishment, Clinton.

Provincial Archives of Manitoba.

Emotional support for the Ontario Orangeman, Thomas Scott, executed by Louis Riel in 1870, ran high in Protestant Ontario, as shown by this circular for a public forum held at Blyth, Huron County, Ontario.

force to the Northwest and later banished Riel from Canada for five years (1875-80).

THE MANITOBA ACT

The territory of the new province of Manitoba as incorporated in the Manitoba Act included only the twelve thousand inhabitants and the 35 000 km^2 in the immediate area of the Red River settlement and Portage la Prairie. The rest of the area became the Northwest Territories.

Ottawa granted the province local self-government, with a governor, a legislative council, and an assembly, four federal MPs and two senators. But Manitoba was denied control over its own public lands and natural resources, unlike the other provinces in Confederation. These remained under the federal government's control to be used "for the purposes of the Dominion."

29

The Manitoba Act addressed the important question of linguistic and educational rights of French Canadians throughout Canada. In 1867 the Fathers of Confederation had been silent on the rights of French Canadians outside the province of Quebec and had made no provision in the BNA Act for constitutional rights for French Canadians in new provinces as they joined Confederation. Thus Manitoba, as the first new province to join, became a test case of whether French would be recognized as an official language and whether separate schools would be permitted in provinces with a sizeable Roman Catholic population at the time of union with Canada. The Manitoba Act provided those constitutional guarantees. It recognized French as an official language and provided provincial money for separate schools for the Roman Catholic mixed-blood population, the majority of whom were French-speaking in 1870. It can therefore be argued that the Fathers of Confederation intended to create a bicultural and bilingual nation where French Canadians could feel at home anywhere in the country.

The question of French-Canadian rights outside Quebec has generated considerable debate. Historian Donald Creighton has argued that a "dictatorial Riel" pressured Macdonald into making these "concessions" to the French-speaking population in Manitoba.[1] He contends that if the prime minister had failed to act quickly at this time, Canada might have lost the Northwest to the Americans. Creighton points out that the Temporary Act of Rupert's Land, drawn up in the spring of 1869, was more reflective of Macdonald's and the Canadian government's views. It contained no reference to separate schools.

In a rebuttal to Creighton, historian Ralph Heintzman emphasizes the temporary nature of the 1869 act.[2] He looks to the Manitoba Act as being more representative of the Canadian government's views. In legal terms, Heintzman argues, the Act reflected the spirit of Confederation in 1867 which continued as the nation expanded.

THE WOLSELEY EXPEDITION

Manitoba's entry into Confederation did not end the tension in the region. Once spring opened the rough pioneer road from Lake Superior to the Red River, Macdonald sent Lieutenant Colonel Garnet Wolseley and a force of British regulars and Canadian militia to the Red River. According to the public announcement, it went as an expedition of peace. But Wolseley and his troops thought otherwise. After marching for three months through the wilderness, the soldiers demanded that Riel be lynched. As the troops approached, Riel fled. Upon finding Fort Garry abandoned by Riel, Wolseley reported: "Personally, I was glad that Riel did not come out and surrender, as he at one time said he would, for I could not then have hanged him as I might have done had I taken him prisoner when in arms against his sovereign."

30   Riel had left convinced that he had achieved a victory for his people, with provincial status, and land and cultural rights secured. The victory proved short-lived, however. After Manitoba's entry into Canada an influx of land-hungry settlers, chiefly from Ontario, began. Soon the Métis lost much of the 600 000 ha reserved for their children.

In a symbolic act, a group of Ontarians in 1871 seized Métis land on the Rivière aux Ilets de Bois and renamed the adjacent river the Boyne, after William of Orange's great victory in Ireland over the Roman Catholics. The Ontarians soon dominated the political, economic, and social life of Manitoba, and worked to eliminate the cultural rights of the French-speaking population. Feeling ill at ease in their former homeland, many of the original inhabitants migrated farther west. Within fifteen years the Métis in the South Saskatchewan River valley would fight a second battle with the Canadians (see chapter 4).

British Columbia Enters Confederation

Having obtained the Northwest, Canadians could now seriously approach British Columbia. On the West Coast, Indians constituted the majority of the population, but they were denied the vote and in general lived apart from the white settlers. Two separate colonies had grown up, one on Vancouver Island and the other on the mainland. In 1866 they united into a single colony. Three choices were open to the Pacific colony: remain a British colony, join the United States, or unite with Canada.

Annexation to the United States seemed a real possibility. On the mainland Americans predominated, many of them being gold diggers who had come north from California during the Fraser Valley and the Cariboo gold rushes. Furthermore, this isolated colony, with a staple economy (similar to other British North American colonies at the time of Confederation) based mainly on fishing, agriculture, and, to a lesser extent, mining, did most of its trade with the Americans to the south. British Columbia's business firms were often owned by Americans and were branches of American establishments. Communications with the outside world went through the United States. American vessels provided the only regular steamship service. Even postal service went via San Francisco, thus requiring both local and American stamps on letters abroad. When railroads made transcontinental travel feasible, it was the American Union Pacific (completed in 1869) that first provided British Columbia with connections to the Atlantic seaboard. By contrast, the colony had no link with the British North American colonies to the east and only limited contact with Britain by sea around the tip of South America.

Despite the strong American influence, British Columbia remained a loyal British colony. The Royal Navy provided protection, while politically the British tradition prevailed, with parliamentary government and a predominance of British politicians from the governor to the majority in the Legislative Council. By contrast, the Americans had little political influence in the colony.

British Columbia had few links with Canada, since few Canadians resided in the colony. Nevertheless, those who did were influential and vocal. Amor de Cosmos, who became premier in 1872, and John Robson, a leading Reformer, both Canadians by birth, headed the Confederation movement in the Assembly. The proposal to join Canada came at a propitious time, as Britain no longer wished to maintain a separate colony on the West Coast, far from British naval protection and vulnerable to American expansionist ambitions, especially after the United States purchased Alaska from Russia in 1867.

The Colonial Office wanted to lessen its commitment to British Columbia without losing the colony to the United States, since Britain valued British Columbia as a link in its "all red route to the Orient"—a worldwide imperial trading network tying Britain to India and China through British territory. Gladstone, Britain's prime minister (1868–1874), argued that Victoria, as "the San Francisco of British North America," could achieve greater commercial and political position as part of Canada than would be attainable "by being the capital of the isolated colony of British Columbia."

The Canadian government wanted British Columbia to join the dominion. Prime Minister Macdonald corresponded with pro-Confederation politicians in the colony. He also intervened to have the British government appoint Anthony Musgrave, the governor of Newfoundland and a known supporter of Confederation, after the incumbent governor died suddenly in June 1869. Musgrave became the first governor of British Columbia to travel overland across the continent. From New York he went to San Francisco on the Union Pacific, and then by steamer to San Francisco. The trip made Musgrave very conscious of the importance of a railway to unite a transcontinental nation.

31

THE CANADIAN GOVERNMENT NEGOTIATES

Once in office, Musgrave appointed a three-member delegation to meet with representatives of the Canadian government to discuss a British Columbia resolution in favour of Confederation. The resolution agreed to union if the following terms were met: assumption of the colony's $1 million debt, implementation of responsible government, a public works program, and completion of a road to link British Columbia with the rest of Canada.

The delegation met an extremely receptive audience in Ottawa. A committee headed by George-Etienne Cartier had just completed drawing up the terms for bringing Manitoba into Confederation. Without qualification, the committee agreed to the delegation's demands. Ottawa would assume the provincial debt, request Britain to implement responsible government, and undertake a public works programme that included underwriting a loan to build a dry-dock and to maintain the naval station at Esquimalt. Unlike Manitoba, British Columbia would enter Confederation with control of its Crown lands. Cartier also assured the British Columbians that the Canadian government would construct not just a road but a railway, to be begun within two years of British Columbia's entrance into Confederation and completed in ten. The United States, with ten times the population, had only recently and with great difficulty built its first transcontinental railroad. How could Canada possibly do the same?

What the delegation had expected to bargain hard for came without any struggle, so anxious were Macdonald and Cartier that Canada reach the Pacific. The promise silenced the talk within the colony of annexation with the United States. Unanimously, the B.C. Legislative Council ratified the terms of settlement.

Cartier then ran into opposition within both the Conservative party caucus and Parliament, where he was challenged to justify such generous terms. Undeterred, the Conservatives used their majority in Parliament to push the bill through. A great banquet was held in Ottawa on April 10 to celebrate the occasion. At the festivities, Joseph Trutch, a member of the B.C. delegation, rose from his place under a banner reading "Westward the march of Empire makes its way" to make a public statement: "I am sure you will find that British Columbia is a pretty intelligent community, which will be apt to take a business view of the matter." He was referring to the promised railroad, to which British Columbia indeed took a hard-nosed "business view" after it joined Confederation.

On July 20, 1871, the Dominion of Canada reached the Pacific. This was the very year that, by the Treaty of Washington (see chapter 5), Britain and the United States confirmed the borders between the two countries, ending the threat of an American seizure of lands above the 49th parallel.

32

An Unwilling Newfoundland and a Reluctant Prince Edward Island

Only Newfoundland and Prince Edward Island remained as potential new provinces. Of the two, Newfoundland seemed the most likely to join Confederation. Although the colony had not sent representatives to the Charlottetown Conference, held on September 1, 1864, it did send two representatives—Frederick B.T. Carter, leader of the opposition, and Ambrose Shea, Speaker of the House of Assembly—to the Quebec Conference a month later. Both men became converts to Confederation, especially after learning of the generous financial terms that Macdonald and the other representatives from the Canadas had promised Newfoundland in union. Nevertheless, neither they nor the prime minister of Newfoundland, H. W. Hoyes, could persuade a dubious public, especially the merchants in St. John's and the Roman Catholic population.

33

OPPOSITION TO CONFEDERATION IN NEWFOUNDLAND

In the 1860s Newfoundland was an independent-minded outpost of the British Empire with little association with the other British North American colonies. To Newfoundlanders, their island's destiny lay to the east, to the Atlantic Ocean and Britain, not to the west and a transcontinental nation. Its economy rested solidly on cod fishing and sealing. Eighty percent of the island's working population earned its living from the sea. Trade was with Europe, the West Indies, and Brazil, not with British North America. Thus, Newfoundlanders remained uninfluenced by arguments about a transcontinental nation, railways, tariffs, or American annexation. Only the promise of benefits to their fishing economy swayed them. On this fundamental issue, many Newfoundlanders saw problems in union with the other British North American colonies. A petition that merchants, fishermen, and other Newfoundlanders sent to Britain summed up the majority viewpoint:

> The inhabitants of this colony would desire to see this island always retained separately by Britain, as its ocean fortress and military outpost in this part of the world, whatever might be the future destiny of the colonies of the mainland. ... The colony has no community of interests with Upper or Lower Canada, and little with the other maritime provinces.

Newfoundland Catholics feared Confederation would offset their favourable situation in the colony. They had their own state-funded schools which they feared might be threatened in a union with "Protestant Ontario." Also, Irish Catholics saw Confederation as analogous to the unfavourable union of Ireland and England, the root of much of Ireland's plight. They were not prepared to risk another union with a dominant British population.

Still, Confederation had much support in the colony. Before his appointment to British Columbia, Governor Anthony Musgrave persuaded the Liberal government, led by the pro-Confederationist F.B.T. Carter, to draft a bill stating the terms of union with Canada for debate in the Assembly. Despite considerable opposition, the bill passed.

THE NEWFOUNDLAND ELECTION OF 1869

In the election of 1869, the terms of union became the campaign issue. Charles Fox Bennett, a St. John's merchant, headed the anti-confederation faction. He warned of dire consequences to the Newfoundland economy, with Canadian taxes on boats and fishing gear, and exploitive competition from the mainland. He also made effective use of the concurrent repeal movement in neighbouring Nova Scotia and of a strong dose of local Newfoundland nationalism. As one contemporary folk song ran:

34

> Would you barter the rights that your fathers have won?
> No! Let them descend from father to son,
> For a few thousand dollars Canadian gold,
> Don't let it be said that our birthright was sold.
> Newfoundland's face turns to Britain
> Her back to the Gulf.
> Come near at your peril
> Canadian wolf!

Pro-confederationists appeared on the defensive. They presented Confederation as a necessary alternative to Newfoundland's depressed economy rather than as a bold and positive move. Furthermore, an improved sealing and fishing season in 1869 worked against them. In the end, Newfoundlanders rejected Confederation again, with nineteen seats in the Assembly going to anti-confederates and only eight to confederates. That defeat ended the Confederation debate in Newfoundland for the next twenty-five years.

OPPOSITION TO CONFEDERATION IN
PRINCE EDWARD ISLAND

Initially, Prince Edward Island was even more opposed than Newfoundland to Confederation. Its representatives at the Charlottetown and Quebec conferences had questioned the Canadian delegates the hardest on the possible negative effects of Confederation for the Atlantic colonies. In this, their views simply reflected the opinion of the island population. Even imperial pressure through the Colonial Office failed to persuade the islanders to join Confederation.

The prospect of economic union with the United States proved more appealing. In 1868 Congressman Benjamin Butler visited Charlottetown to negotiate a reciprocal trade agreement. The islanders had encouraged a close association with the United States by allowing Americans to fish in their territorial waters even though this went against the Anglo-American accord of 1818. Now they hoped to reach a formal trade agreement that would allow their natural products into American markets duty free in return for the continued right of American fishermen to fish in island waters. To many islanders, the prospect held out the possibility of returning to the prosperity of the period of the Reciprocity Treaty (1854–66).

Fear of losing Prince Edward Island to the Americans prompted the Canadian prime minister, John A. Macdonald, to reopen negotiations with the islanders. Late in 1869 he extended a second invitation to join Confederation. He promised more generous financial terms than in 1864 and gave guarantees of communication and transportation links with the mainland and assistance in buying off the remaining absentee proprietors who owned much of the land. Still the islanders resisted, because their economic situation, although poor, was not desperate.

By the early 1870s financial problems made Confederation compelling. A coalition government headed by J.C. Pope had embarked in 1871 on an ambitious railroad-building scheme that was rapidly leading to bankruptcy. The railroad contractors could not sell their government debentures at par at the island banks to finance the cost of construction; in 1872 they ceased construction. The Union Bank of Prince Edward Island, which held large numbers of the railway debentures, feared a financial crisis and appealed to London financiers for assistance, who replied that the Island would be in a better negotiating position if it joined Canada.

This time Prince Edward Island approached the Canadian government in early 1873. The Canadian government renewed its offer of five years earlier: assumption of the island's debt, payment of the annual interest on a $800 000 imperial loan and a special annual subsidy of $45 000 (granted in lieu of the absence of Crown lands) to buy out the absentee landowners and thus bring all land under provincial control, agreement to take over the railway guarantee, and the establishment and maintenance of an efficient all year steamer service between the island and the mainland.

In the election in April 1873 islanders had an opportunity to vote on the offer, which was presented in the form of two alternatives: Confederation or increased taxes. The islanders chose to join Confederation, and the island legislature unanimously agreed to the terms of union which, ironically, did not differ all that much from those initially offered in 1864.

35

In the end it was provincial debt and railroads that were the "Fathers of Confederation" in Prince Edward Island.

On July 1, 1873, Prince Edward Island joined the Dominion of Canada as its seventh province. The Charlottetown newspaper, the *Patriot*, recorded the public's listless response:

> On Tuesday, July 1st, whether for weal or woe, Prince Edward Island became a province of the Dominion of Canada. At 12 o'clock noon, the Dominion Flag was run up on the flag staffs at Government House and the Colonial Building, and a salute of 21 guns was fired from St. George's battery and from HMS *Spartan* now in port. The Church and city bells rang out a lively peal, and the Volunteers under review at the city park fired a *feu de joie*. So far as powder and metal could do it, there was for a short time a terrible din. But among the people who thronged the streets there was no enthusiasm.

36   With the exception of Newfoundland and the Arctic Archipelago, the joining of Prince Edward Island in 1873 completed the consolidation of British North America. On the basis of the early journeys of Martin Frobisher, John Davis, and William Baffin, as well as the British naval expeditions in search of Sir John Franklin (whose party of more than one hundred had disappeared in the mid-1840s in a vain search to find the Northwest Passage), Britain had a strong claim to the Arctic islands. In 1880 it transferred that claim to Canada, thus giving the new dominion its third coastline. Three oceans, one country—in just thirteen years Canada had become the second-largest country in the world.

Canada underwent rapid territorial expansion in the first decade after Confederation, adding three new provinces and a vast amount of land. Fear of American encroachment was a factor in the rapid expansion, but so, too, were internal economic pressures, such as the need for the Northwest for agricultural development, internal trade, and a growing railway-building program. By 1873 Canada had been rounded out. Now came the task of creating a viable economic policy for the new nation and providing transportation and communication systems to its people.

As new provinces joined Confederation, the question of dominion-provincial relations and of regional differences became more complex and strained. The challenge ahead for Canadian leaders was to find satisfactory solutions that would unite and serve to keep its different regions together.

NOTES

[1] D.G. Creighton, "Macdonald, Confederation, and the West," in *Towards the Discovery of Canada: Selected Essays* (Toronto, 1972), p. 234.
[2] Ralph Heintzman, "The Spirit of Confederation: Professor Creighton, Biculturalism, and the Use of History," *Canadian Historical Review*, 52 (1971): 267–68.

Related Readings

Four essays in R. Douglas Francis and Donald B. Smith, eds., *Readings in Canadian History: Post-Confederation*, 2d ed. (Toronto, 1986) are very useful for this topic: Donald F. Warner, "The Post-Confederation Annexation Movement," pp. 3–10; Donald Swainson, "Canada Annexes the West: Colonial Status Confirmed," pp. 64–81; Walter N. Sage, "British Columbia Becomes Canadian, 1871–1901," pp. 11–20; and F.W.P. Bolger, "Long Courted, Won at Last," pp. 21–43.

37

BIBLIOGRAPHY

Students interested in the Nova Scotian resistance to Confederation should consult R.H. Campbell, "The Repeal Agitation in Nova Scotia, 1867–1869," Nova Scotia Historical Society, *Collections*, 25 (1942): 95–130; George Rawlyk; ed., *The Atlantic Provinces and the Problems of Confederation* (St. John's, 1979); and Colin D. Howell, "Nova Scotia's Protest Tradition and the Search for a Meaningful Federalism" in *Canada and the Burden of Unity*, edited by D.J. Bercuson (Toronto, 1977), pp. 169–91. Joseph Howe's views are presented in J. Murray Beck, *Joseph Howe*, Vol. 2: *The Briton Becomes Canadian, 1848–1873* (Montreal, 1983), and his Canadian Historical Association booklet, *Joseph Howe: Anti-Confederate* (Ottawa, 1965).

Alvin C. Gluek, *Minnesota and the Manifest Destiny of the Canadian Northwest: A Study in Canadian-American Relations* (Toronto, 1965) examines American annexationist sentiments towards the Canadian Northwest. On the Riel resistance, see W.L. Morton's introduction to *Alexander Begg's Red River Journal* (Toronto, 1956); also George Stanley, *The Birth of Western Canada* (London, 1936; reprinted Toronto, 1960), and his *Louis Riel* (Toronto, 1963). Hart Bowsfield's *Louis Riel: The Rebel and the Hero* (Toronto, 1971) is a short popular biography. On Manitoba's entry into Confederation, see W.L. Morton, *Manitoba: A History* (Toronto, 1957), Donald Creighton, "John A. Macdonald, Confederation and the Canadian West," *Historical and Scientific Society of Manitoba*, 3rd series, no. 23

(1966–67), and reprinted in D. Creighton, *Towards the Discovery of Canada: Selected Essays* (Toronto, 1972), pp. 229–37, and Ralph Heintzman, "The Spirit of Confederation: Professor Creighton, Biculturalism, and the Use of History," *Canadian Historical Review*, 52 (1971): 245–75.

On British Columbia and Confederation, see Margaret Ormsby, *British Columbia: A History* (Toronto, 1958), and her "Canada and the New British Columbia," *Canadian Historical Association Report*, 1948, pp. 74–85. W. George Shelton's *British Columbia and Confederation* (Victoria, 1967) is a worthwhile collection of essays.

On Newfoundland's resistance to Confederation, see James Hiller, "Confederation Defeated: The Newfoundland Election of 1869," in *Newfoundland in the Nineteenth and Twentieth Century: Essays in Interpretation* (Toronto, 1980), pp. 67–94, and the relevant section in Frederick W. Rowe, *A History of Newfoundland and Labrador* (Toronto, 1980). Francis Bolger reviews Prince Edward Island's decision to join Canada in *Prince Edward Island and Confederation* (Charlottetown, 1964), while Ronald Tallman, "Annexation in the Maritimes? The Butler Mission to Charlottetown," *Dalhousie Review*, 53 (1973): 97–112, shows the American influence, which almost caused Prince Edward Island to reject Confederation.

CHAPTER THREE

A "National Policy"

"The future of Canada depends very much upon the cultivation of a   *39*
national spirit." This single statement by Edward Blake, the leading Liberal Party politician in 1874, neatly summarized Canada's dilemma. So
many problems faced the nation: reconciling the emerging national feeling
of English Canadians with that of the French Canadians in Quebec, and
overcoming regional differences or at least reconciling them. In the late
1870s the Conservatives under Sir John A. Macdonald believed that the
way to cultivate a national spirit lay in a dominion-wide economic policy
with a national tariff to protect native industries, a transcontinental railway
to tie the sections of the new dominion together, and a developed West
to foster east–west trade.

An Emerging English-Canadian Idea of Canada

In the spring of 1868 five intellectuals met in Ottawa to launch the Canada
First movement. Young and enthusiastic, they sought to identify and
promote a national spirit for the new Dominion. One member, Robert
Haliburton, a Nova Scotian lawyer, described Confederation as a hum-
drum, commonplace occurrence that "created as little excitement among
the masses as they would feel in the organization of a joint stock company."
The members were concerned with the lack of myths, symbols, and a
spirit of nationalism that, they were convinced, all nations must possess.
The Canada First movement, so called because they wanted to inculcate
a feeling of Canadian patriotism above all else, set out to create them. Its
members believed that Canada's greatness lay in its northern climate and
rugged landscape that had combined to create a superior Anglo-Saxon
race; Canadians were the "Northmen of the New World."

No French Canadians or native peoples belonged to the Canada First
movement, for ultimately Canada First meant Ontario First and its

Canadian nationalism meant English-Canadian nationalism. The members showed their true intentions by their support of Dr. John Schultz and his group of nationalistic Canadians in the Northwest. Together they wanted to bring in the Red River colony as a new Ontario. Their brand of nationalism was divisive, pitting French Canadians against English Canadians and natives against whites. These Canada Firsters refused to concede that in Canada there were several nationalisms, not one.

The Canada First movement also tried to transform Canadian politics. Its members believed that Canadian parties lacked principles; as parties of compromise, they stood for nothing and were puppets of the dominant interest groups that controlled them. Acting on its convictions, the movement ran candidates in the election of 1874. Its promise of party principles aside, the Canada First's electoral programme proved as vague and inconsistent as that of the two major parties. The influential Goldwin Smith, a former professor of history at Oxford who came to live in Toronto in 1871 and who served as a journalist and political commentator, joined the movement under the illusion that "Canada First" meant independence. Yet the first plank in their eleven-point party programme read: "British connection, consolidation of the Empire—and in the meantime a voice on treaties affecting Canada." The other planks were equally vague—an income franchise, reorganization of the Senate, pure and economic administration of public affairs, and a tariff for revenue while also encouraging local industry—thus illustrating the difficulty of establishing parties with principles in a nation as large and diverse as Canada.

The Canada First candidates fared poorly in the election. By 1875, the movement had ended, leaving the fate of English-Canadian nationalism in the hands of the well-established Conservatives and Liberals.

Rise of the Ultramontanes in Quebec

While the Canada First movement sought a British and Protestant Canada, an important group of French Canadians wanted their nation to be French and Catholic. After the abortive rebellions of 1837–38 Quebec became more French and Catholic than it had ever been since New France. The province cultivated closer ties with France under Napoleon III, especially after the French helped to protect the papal lands in central Italy against Giuseppe Garibaldi's army fighting to unify Italy. Quebec sent a contingent of five hundred volunteer soldiers, the *Zouaves*, to fight as "mercenaries of the Lord"—for seven cents a day.

Ignace Bourget, the influential Bishop of Montreal, and his disciple, Louis-François Laflèche, second Bishop of Trois-Rivières, became the chief spokesmen of what has been called the ultramontane movement. Laflèche set down the basic principles of its nationalism in 1866:

40

A nation is constituted by unity of speech, unity of faith, uniformity
of morals, customs, and institutions. The French Canadians possess
all these, and constitute a true nation. Each nation has received from
Providence a mission to fulfill. The mission of the French-Canadian
people is to constitute a centre of Catholicism in the New World.

The French-Canadian state and church had to unite, Laflèche declared,
to resist the Protestants, as well as Quebec's free-thinking French-Canadian liberals—those who wanted to subordinate religion to civil authority.
Ultramontanes believed that the State should be subordinate to the Church
and that it should not be permissible for a people to have laws contrary
to the laws of the Church. They also looked to Rome for guidance.

In Quebec, resistance to the ultramontanes was centred in the Institut
Canadien. In the mid-1840s a group of young French-Canadian professionals who had been influenced by the writings of such French liberal
thinkers as Voltaire, Rousseau, Montesquieu, and Blanc, and such British
liberals as Bentham and Mill, formed the Institut. It served as a literary
society and a debating club. Soon a hundred similar clubs were established
throughout the province. The Instituts encouraged free thought and the
establishment of libraries free of church censorship, and welcomed people
of all languages and faiths. They represented the new liberalism then
sweeping over Europe, one which endorsed the separation of church and
state as one of its principles. Many Institut members had given political
support to the *Rouges* in the 1850s and had become Liberals in the Confederation period.

Bourget attempted to silence the opposition. The church had sought to
eliminate liberalism, insisting upon its own role as the divinely appointed
guardian of men's morals and minds. As Bourget advised his followers in
a private circular of 1876: "Let us each say in his heart, 'I hear my *curé*,
my *curé* hears the bishop, the bishop hears the Pope and the Pope hears
Our Lord Jesus Christ.' " He placed a number of "irreligious" books in
the Institut's library on the Papal Index as forbidden reading. Then he
announced that no Institut member could receive the sacraments.

41

THE GUIBORD AFFAIR

This act proved mild, however, compared to Bourget's reaction when
Joseph Guibord, a former vice-president of the Institut, died in November
1869. The church refused Guibord's widow's request for a Christian burial.
She took her local *curé* to court with the blessing and support of the Institut,
since the case addressed the larger issue of civil or ecclesiastical supremacy.
As the case went through the various appeal courts, Guibord's coffin rested
for six years in a vault in Montreal's Mount Royal cemetery. The Judicial

National Archives of Canada (C13558).

This stone coffin was built to preserve Guibord's grave. When it proved impractical, concrete was poured into his grave instead.

Committee of the Privy Council ruled in 1875 that burial was a civil right, and therefore Guibord should be allowed burial in the consecrated section of the Roman Catholic cemetery.

The court's ruling, however, did not end the difficulties encountered in giving Guibord a proper burial. During one attempt, a rowdy crowd of nearly one thousand—throwing stones and brandishing clubs—met the funeral procession at the cemetery gates and forced it back. Then Guibord's widow, Henriette, died and was peacefully buried in the family plot in the Catholic cemetery. Friends who wanted Guibord to join his wife in their final resting place tried again, this time with an escort of more than twelve hundred militiamen and regular soldiers. They succeeded, with Guibord's coffin resting (in poured cement to prevent vandalism) on top of his wife's. Immediately, however, Bourget desecrated Guibord's plot, although his wife, only several centimetres beneath him, remained in a state of grace. Guibord still lies in Montreal's Côte des Neiges cemetery (by today's Université de Montréal) under a massive slab of unmarked granite in unconsecrated soil.

The ultramontanists created a political movement, and in 1871 issued a declaration of their principles, the *Programme Catholique*. They believed absolutely that the church had the right to direct the Roman Catholic electorate how to vote. They instructed Catholics to vote for the *Bleus*

(Conservatives), blest with the colour of heaven, and not for the *Rouges* (Liberals), who were damned by the colour of the fires of hell. They favoured candidates who endorsed the church's views on marriage, education, and social order. Some French-Canadian politicians, including such Conservatives as George-Etienne Cartier, made known their disgust at this crude mixing of religion and politics.

By 1870 two conflicting nationalisms had surfaced in both English- and French-speaking Canada that defined the nation in cultural terms, and not as a political nation-state uniting English- and French-speaking Canadians.

Liberal Rule: 1873–78

The Conservatives won the elections of 1867 and again in 1872. But just one year later, a political scandal that had emerged during the election of 1872 plagued Canada's first governing party. Macdonald and Cartier had accepted upwards of $300 000 campaign funds from Sir Hugh Allan, whose Canadian Pacific Railway Company was a major contender for the government charter to build the transcontinental railway promised to British Columbia. The money had been used to support Cartier in his home riding of Montreal East. Ironically, however, Cartier was defeated and had to seek re-election in Provencher, Manitoba. (It was arranged for him to be elected by acclamation.)

An American railway tycoon, angry at having been left out of the new consortium, supplied the Liberal opposition with the incriminating evidence that uncovered the "Pacific Scandal." The Liberals accused the Conservatives of immorality and corruption. Macdonald denied involvement—"these hands are clean," he assured the House, in one of the best speeches in his political career. But fearing a loss-of-confidence vote, he announced the resignation of his Conservative government. The governor general asked the Liberals to form a government, which they did without an election being held. Then in January 1874 the new prime minister, Alexander Mackenzie, dissolved Parliament and called an election, which the Liberals won.

LIBERAL LEADERSHIP

Alexander Mackenzie lacked Macdonald's dynamic personality, but made up for it with honesty and high principles. A poor farmer's son, Mackenzie had been born in Perthshire, not far from Macdonald's own birthplace in Glasgow, Scotland. He had come to Canada at the age of twenty and worked as a stone-mason. Later he became a builder at Sarnia, Canada

These hands are clean!

SEND ME ANOTHER $10,000

PRO ROGATION AND SUPPRESSION OF THE INVESTIGATION

PARTY

CANADA

WHITHER ARE WE DRIFTING?

from *A Caricature History of Canadian Politics* (Toronto, 1886).

"These hands are clean," John A. Macdonald assured the electorate during the election campaign of 1872. A year later the Pacific Scandal broke.

West, prospered, and entered politics as a Clear Grit, a staunch ally of George Brown. Mackenzie projected a poor public image as hard, inflexible, and dry. The acerbic Goldwin Smith once remarked that if Mackenzie's strong point as prime minister consisted in his having been a stone-mason, his weak point consisted in his being one still.

Mackenzie inherited numerous political problems. For one thing, the Liberal party had little internal unity; rather than a party, it was more a free-wheeling coalition of factions—*Rouges*, Clear Grits, and Liberal Reformers—who had come together less out of a sense of common philosophy or a unified party platform than out of a common dislike for the Conservatives and their programme. The Liberals deeply distrusted "big business interests," idealized rural life, and believed in the superiority of the self-reliant farmer. They favoured free trade over protection of the national economy and provincial rights over a strong central government.

The Liberal party needed a strong leader to pull its divergent groups together and to provide direction. George Brown had been such a leader—at least for English-speaking Liberals—but he had resigned after his defeat in the election of 1867; Alexander Mackenzie was not. The fact that a number of influential party members challenged Mackenzie's leadership compounded the problem. Brown lurked in the background; Richard Cartwright, a Conservative defector who left after Macdonald denied him the post of minister of finance, wanted a senior post; Antoine Dorion led the party's *Rouge* faction and sought the role of Mackenzie's Quebec lieutenant. Finally, there was the enigmatic Edward Blake, miscast as a politician due to his indecisiveness. The former premier of Ontario (1871–72) and a brilliant parliamentary debater, he stood out as the obvious party leader but could never make up his mind whether or not to stay in the party. His indecisiveness was a constant irritant for the prime minister.

45

LIBERALS' POLITICAL PROBLEMS

Mackenzie took office just as Canada's economic fortunes turned. Two months earlier, the financial boom of the 1860s and early 1870s in London and New York had broken. As trade declined, so did the gross national product, and the federal debt increased sharply. Mackenzie responded by slowing down and even trying to avoid implementing the railway building scheme inherited from the Conservatives. For this, Mackenzie and the Liberals were branded as anti-nationalists by the Conservatives.

They were not anti-nationalists; instead they channelled their energies into constitutional and political questions. They established the Supreme Court in 1875, as a national appeal court for the provincial and territorial courts. Final appeal still rested with the Judicial Committee of the Privy Council in Britain (and would continue to do so on civil matters until 1949), but this was the first Canadian court whose purpose was to review Canadian laws. The Liberals also restricted the powers of the governor general, Britain's representative in Canada, by withdrawing his right to disallow legislation without consulting the Canadian Parliament—all measures which advanced Canada on the road to nationhood.

In the political realm, the Liberals introduced the secret ballot, standardized election dates and proceedings across the country, and closed the taverns on election day to reduce the possibility of buying votes for drinks. They took the trial of controverted elections out of the political arena and into the courts, extended the franchise effectively to all males whether they held property or not (although not to women or native people), and ended the system of dual representation that had allowed an individual to represent simultaneously a federal and a provincial seat. These were important constitutional and political changes, but not the kind of policies that excited an electorate or ended an economic depression.

The National Policy of John A. Macdonald

Almost a decade after Confederation, the dominion had two choices for its economy: developing a predominantly north–south or an east–west trade relationship. If the United States ended its protectionist policies and opened its markets, Canada could have free trade; this north–south option was favoured by the Liberals.

Since Confederation, Canada had tried frequently to negotiate reciprocity with the United States. In 1874 George Brown persuaded Hamilton Fish, the American secretary of state, to draft a treaty similar to the Reciprocity Treaty of 1854, allowing for free trade in natural products between Canada and the United States. The American Senate, however, defeated the bill, leaving the Liberals without a commercial policy.

The Conservatives, who were not opposed to reciprocity, prepared to accept the alternative. On the eve of the election of 1878, a lobbying group of the Canadian Manufacturers' Association convinced John A. Macdonald that Canada would benefit from a high import duty. By keeping cheaper American manufactured goods out of the country, an import duty would promote Canadian manufacturing. Canadian politicians knew that highly effective import duties had assisted Britain and the United States in achieving advanced industrial development. They hoped that the same would happen in Canada: that industrialization would lead to national power. Industrial workers needed food that could be supplied by farmers in the west, who in turn needed Canadian manufacturers' agricultural equipment and other manufactured goods, thus creating east–west trade for the new transcontinental railway and uniting the country's disparate regions.

This policy of nation building—the "national policy," as Macdonald called it—rested on three essentials: a high tariff, completion of a transcontinental railway, and settlement of the West. In 1879 the first of the three-part programme was put in place when the Conservatives, after winning the 1878 election, raised the existing tariff by 10 to 30 percent on textiles, iron and steel products, coal, and petroleum products entering the country. In their budget speech, the Conservatives referred to the tariff as the National Policy, an integral part of the larger "national policy" of nation building. By calling the protective tariff a National Policy, the

Conservatives argued that all Canadians would benefit and that Canada would become a nation more than in name only.

DEBATE OVER THE NATIONAL POLICY

The Liberals, who were staunch free traders, opposed the tariff, which they saw as a fiscal barrier erected around the country. "National" in name, they saw it as regional in interest, serving the needs of central Canadians, more specifically the manufacturers and industrialists of the urban centres of Ontario and Quebec who could live off the bounty of the government. The tariff would serve only to heighten divisions between the various regions of the country, pitting the Maritimes and the West against Ontario and Quebec. Furthermore, it would put the burden of national unity on these hinterland regions, which became the suppliers of raw materials for the prosperous metropolitan centres of Central Canada— the same subservient relationship that the national policy was designed to overcome on an international level. In social terms, the same inequality would develop since workers, farmers, and fishermen would have to pay the high price for consumer goods that would result from the tariff. The Liberals drove home the point in a pamphlet they published in 1882:

47

> The farmer starting to his work has a shoe put on his horse with nails taxed 41 percent; with a hammer taxed 40 percent; cuts a stick with a knife taxed 27 1/2 percent; hitches his horse to a plough taxed 30 percent; with chains taxed 27 1/2 percent. He returns to his home at night and lays his wearied limbs on a sheet taxed 30 percent, and covers himself with a blanket on which he has paid 70 percent tax. He rises in the morning, puts on his humble flannel shirt taxed 60 percent, shoes taxed 30 percent, hat taxed 30 percent, reads a chapter from his Bible taxed 7 percent, and kneels to his God on a cheap carpet taxed 30 percent ... and then he is expected to thank John A. that he lives under the freest Government under heaven.

Opponents of the high tariff have since offered additional arguments. Some historians and economists have maintained that the policy fostered an artificial climate for industrial growth that sheltered Canadian industries from competition. Too often protection has served to conceal outmoded business practices and to foster inefficiency. Furthermore, the National Policy did not create the Canadian industries that it was intended to create—instead, it provided an incentive for American companies to establish branch plants in Canada as a means to get around the tariff. (Both the Conservatives and the Liberals favoured the establishment of branch plants at the time). Although in the short term these local industries did inject American capital into the Canadian economy and did provide jobs for Canadian workers, the long-term effects were not so salutary. Far from developing as an independent and self-reliant nation, Canada in the twentieth century became economically dependent on the United States. Macdonald's policy, some historians and economists have argued, was *un-national*.

The advocates of the National Policy, in turn, replied to their critics that a protective tariff was necessary to divert trade from a north–south to an east–west axis so as to create an economically viable second transcontinental nation in North America. The tariff was intended, in Macdonald's words, to "make this union a union in interest, a union in trade, and a union in feeling." It would provide Canadians with their own national market, thus reducing their dependency on the United States, whose policies fluctuated between protectionism and free trade. The resulting stability would ensure a more orderly process of national growth. H.R. Ives, a Montreal foundryman, articulated this pro-tariff position at the time of implementation of the National Policy of 1879: "It was a mistake to think that people will have to pay much more for goods manufactured by us than heretofore. Under the present tariff, we have a security never felt under the old tariff, which will enable us to employ improved machinery, and reduce the cost of manufacture." Furthermore, Canadian manufacturers promised more jobs for Canadian workers, technicians, and managers.

Since 1879 pro-tariff and pro-Macdonald advocates have argued that the national policy with its programme, of protectionism was essential for nation building; without it, there might not have been a Canadian nation, or at least one with a visible economic underpinning. They further argue that no realistic alternative policy existed at the time. It is well and good to talk about the benefits of free trade but the truth of the matter was that the protectionist American Senate was not prepared to negotiate a free trade deal. Finally, National Policy supporters point to its political popularity. The Conservative government stayed in power for the next seventeen years on their protective tariff policy, while the Liberals only succeeded in achieving power once they abandoned free trade and adopted their own version of the Conservatives' National Policy. Clearly, then, the policy appealed to the electorate at the time—and since, some might add.

Building the Canadian Pacific Railway

A transcontinental railroad, an indispensable part of nation building, was the second component of the national policy. Without it, east–west trade and western settlement were impossible. Settlers wishing to go from Toronto to Manitoba via British territory in the 1870s, for example, had to go by steamer on the Great Lakes, with wagon journeys at the portages, by steamboat over eastern Manitoba's lakes and rivers, over the newly

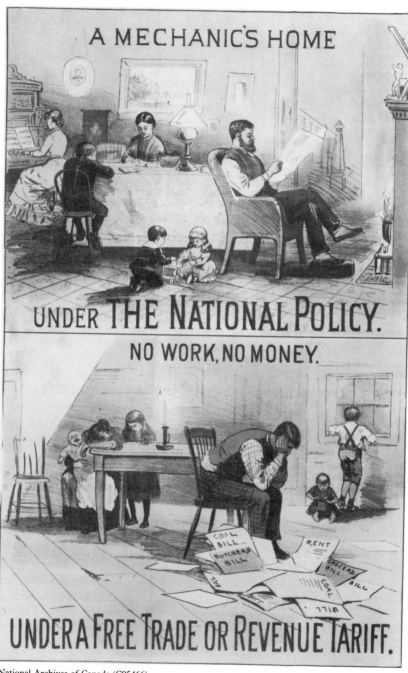

49

National Archives of Canada (C95466).

A circular prepared for the federal election of 1891. According to the National Policy's supporters, protectionism meant jobs and prosperity for the working man; free trade meant unemployment and poverty.

completed Dawson Road to Winnipeg, and finally by wagon to their destination. The alternative was through the United States, where many potential immigrants succumbed to the salesmanship of American immigration agents, who tried to persuade these Canadians to settle in the American West. Furthermore, British Columbia's entry into Confederation depended on the "trail of iron," as the only means to link this isolated colony to central Canada. Finally, a transcontinental railway, it was felt, would permit Canada to compete with the United States as a great North American nation and to become a worthy member of the British Empire. Railways meant power in the nineteenth century, and power meant influence.

GOVERNMENT INVOLVEMENT IN RAILWAY BUILDING

50   The Canadian government had a long history of involvement in railway building prior to the construction of the Canadian Pacific Railway. In the 1840s and 1850s the government of the Canadas was deeply involved in the building of the Grand Trunk Railway and other colonial lines. As part of the Confederation agreement, the Canadian government extended the Grand Trunk line from Rivière-du-Loup, the eastern terminus, to Halifax. Disagreement had arisen as to the best route to follow—along the north shore of New Brunswick and Chaleur Bay, or southward through the St. John valley. The north shore route won out thanks to the lobbying of federal cabinet ministers George-Etienne Cartier of Quebec and Peter Mitchell of New Brunswick, who both favoured a northern route as a colonization road for eastern Quebec and northeastern New Brunswick. Sandford Fleming, the chief engineer, also favoured the more circuitous northern route for military and strategic reasons because of its greater distance from the American border. The railway, which ran through large wilderness areas, cost the Canadian government an estimated $34 million, adding substantially to the new dominion's debt.

Despite these expensive projects, the newly returned Conservative government embarked on the even more ambitious and risky Pacific railway. In its boldness of conception, the transcontinental railway was as startling as Confederation itself. This line (which would be two-thirds longer than any other single line then existing in the world when completed) was to run through five thousand kilometres of precambrian shield (one part muskeg to two part rock, according to one surveyor), prairies, and mountains to link together three and a half million people scattered over vast distances. "An act of insane recklessness," protested Alexander Mackenzie at the time—although his administration reluctantly continued the project. The building of the CPR took on the dimensions of a national dream, and at times the qualities of a political nightmare.

Why did Canadian politicians agree to undertake this mammoth project?

There were several compelling reasons. The United States in the past had threatened to annex the Northwest and was in a position to do so, especially after the completion of the Union Pacific Railway in 1869. In addition, the purchase of Alaska left the Northwest directly in the middle of American territory. Only with a Canadian railroad could the dominion secure effective control over the region. Canadian leaders also had good reason to believe in the great potential of this vast territory. Two scientific expeditions into the Northwest, the British Palliser and the Canadian Hind expeditions in the late 1850s, reported that the Northwest contained millions of hectares of fertile land. This was attractive, particularly to politicians in land-hungry Ontario and Quebec. Moreover, the promise to British Columbia of a railroad within ten years of the province's entry into Confederation obliged even the Liberal government to build it. The Red River Métis' resistance in 1870 (see chapter 2) also made the Canadian government conscious of the need for quick military access to the region.

51

THE SEARCH FOR A PRIVATE COMPANY

Macdonald's Conservative government favoured a private company to undertake the project. The government would provide assistance in the form of both land grants and loans. Before the depression of the mid-1870s two companies competed for the contract: the Interoceanic Company of Toronto, headed by Senator David Macpherson and backed by British financiers; and the Canadian Pacific Railway Company of Montreal, a consortium under Sir Hugh Allan, President of the Bank of Montreal, with American financial backing. The two companies reflected the rivalry between the two metropolitan centres of Toronto and Montreal, and between British and American interests. Macdonald favoured a merger of the two companies, but neither Macpherson nor Allan would agree, each fearing that a merger would work to his opponent's advantage. The government awarded the contract to the Canadian Pacific Company in return for generous financial contributions on Allan's part to the Conservative campaign fund in the election of 1872. The resulting Pacific Scandal forced the Macdonald Conservative government to resign and ended the short-lived Canadian Pacific Company.

The new Liberal government favoured the railway but wanted to build only those sections where settlement warranted construction and only as public money became available, relying on waterways and even American lines to fill the gaps. Given the commercial depression of 1873, shrinking governmental revenues, and the failure of a private company to undertake the project, this made sense, although some Liberals opposed even this much involvement. Luther Holton, an MP from Montreal, for example, described the project as "our Elephant," while Edward Blake, who had resigned from the Cabinet but remained within the party, preferred releasing British Columbia from Confederation to finishing the railroad according to the terms of entry.

To move slowly meant exempting the Liberal government from the Conservative promise of completing the railroad to British Columbia in ten years. Mackenzie chose J.D. Edgar, a young Liberal lawyer from Toronto, to visit Victoria early in 1874 and to negotiate a longer period for completion of the railway than in the original terms of union. Edgar described British Columbians as "a population of peculiar intelligence"— no doubt a reaction to the British Columbian premier's rude response to his mission. Premier George Walker refused to discuss any delay on a railroad that he considered a binding promise and insisted on "the bond and nothing but the bond."

Lord Carnarvon, the Colonial Secretary, agreed to act as an arbitrator between the two sides. He devised a compromise by which the British Columbia government agreed to extend the time limit for completion of the Pacific railway to the end of 1890 in return for the federal government's guarantee to proceed with the railway survey, to spend at least $2 million annually on construction of the line, and to build the Esquimalt and Nanaimo railway on Vancouver Island. But Carnarvon's terms never received parliamentary consent before the Liberal government's defeat in 1878.

The Conservatives resumed office ready to move ahead rapidly. Their return to power coincided with an upturn in the economy that enabled them to find a private company interested in building the railway. A new Canadian Pacific Railway company (CPR) was formed by a group of men with heavy investments in the Bank of Montreal: George Stephen, R.B. Angus, Donald Smith, and several other financiers. The syndicate agreed to build the railway from Callander (near North Bay) to Port Arthur, and from Winnipeg to Kamloops by May 1, 1891. The government, in turn, offered the new company $25 million and twenty-five million acres (ten million hectares) of land consisting of alternate sections not already sold on a belt nearly forty kilometres wide on both sides of the track across the Prairies. In addition, the CPR obtained the sections of the line already completed or under construction, which amounted to nearly twelve hundred kilometres of track worth an estimated $31 million. All construction materials were exempted from duty, and CPR property and its capital stock would be free from taxation. Its grant of ten million hectares of land was also tax exempt for twenty years or until sold. Finally, the government agreed to a monopoly clause: no competing line could be built south of the main CPR line until 1900.

These generous terms aroused tremendous opposition in Parliament. The Liberals and even some Conservative backbenchers argued whether the terms were necessary. The two-month debate that followed was one of the longest and bitterest in the history of the Canadian Parliament. As popular historian Pierre Berton has commented, over a million words were spoken, more than the Old and New Testaments combined.[1] Yet Macdonald held his party together, and the Conservatives voted down the twenty-five amendments proposed by the Liberal opposition.

THE CPR ROUTE

One of the new company's first decisions was to alter the route from along the North Saskatchewan River and through the Yellowhead Pass to the prairie route through Swift Current, Calgary, and the Kicking Horse Pass. A number of reasons explain the company's sudden shift. First, the company feared that the Northern Pacific, a new American transcontinental, would syphon off the trade of the southern prairies, bringing the region within the American sphere of influence. Second, Elliott Galt, the son of Alexander Galt, a Father of Confederation, had discovered coal deposits near Lethbridge that could be exploited as a source of fuel for the locomotives on the southern route. Third, John Macoun, a botanist and recent leader of a scientific expedition in the West, reported that the southern prairies were not the desert that Palliser had earlier claimed them to be. (Macoun had visited the area during the wettest decade in more than a century, and Palliser had seen it in the 1850s, one of the driest periods.) Most important of all, the company hoped through the sudden switch to bypass speculators who had bought up land along the proposed northern route, and were as John Macoun commented, "as numerous as sands on the sea shore." When speculators attempted to do the same along the southern route—guessing where divisional points and stations might be— the company arbitrarily changed its plans and placed stations and divisional points at spots not originally intended. In this way the CPR, not the speculators, profited.

53

Once the route was established, speed of construction was the greatest concern. Investors demanded it, as did the rapid construction of the competitive Northern Pacific. The syndicate hired in 1881 William Cornelius Van Horne, a robust, impetuous, and experienced American engineer, as general manager to oversee the entire construction. Very confident and talented, this self-made railway man knew all the aspects of the business. He oversaw the building of the line, while George Stephen, another self-made man, obtained the capital.

Van Horne was tireless and ruthless; he drove his men without mercy, the way he drove himself. He boasted that his construction gang, which at one time had 5000 workers and 1700 teams of horses, could lay five hundred miles (eight hundred kilometres) of prairie track in one year. As surveying parties moved westward to establish the exact route, horse-drawn plows and scrapers followed to etch out the road bed. Next came

54

Dept. of cartography, cégep de Limoilou, Que.

The all-Canadian route of the CPR when completed from Montreal to Vancouver in 1886.

the boarding and construction cars bringing the men and equipment to lay track. Locomotives brought cars laden with ties, rails, and spikes to the end of track, while horse-drawn wagons hauled the ties along the graded section, dropping them at regular intervals. Work gangs then laid them in place. So it went, kilometre by kilometre, across the prairie in rhythmic pattern. The line reached Calgary in August 1883. When asked the secret of his success the hard-boiled Van Horne replied: "I eat all I can; I drink all I can; I smoke all I can and I don't give a damn for anything."

Still ahead lay the difficult mountain terrain. Surveyors had chosen the Kicking Horse Pass through the Bow River valley, despite its steep incline, as the best route through the Rockies, but it was only late in the summer of 1882 that Major A.B. Rogers, an experienced railway surveyor, discovered the pass through the Selkirk range that allowed the CPR to cross the mountains at this point. He insisted it bear his name. Difficulties abounded—laying track along the side of mountains, blasting tunnels through rock, bridging swift mountain rivers. This all took time, money, and too often the lives of a number of the thousands of Chinese hired as cheap labour.

The construction costs were enormous for Van Horne insisted on the best materials to ensure long-term use. He also persuaded the company to build along the north shore of Lake Superior instead of relying on the inefficient waterway system or competing American lines. Although the decision was a wise one, it was also costly—up to nearly $200 000 per kilometre of track. The company had to blast through what Van Horne called hundreds of kilometres of "engineering impossibilities": precambrian rock. In addition, the company secured eastern lines to connect the Pacific line with Toronto and Montreal. When Van Horne was asked about the prospect of not having sufficient funds to complete the mountain section, he replied: "If we haven't got enough, we'll get more, that's all about it." The money did come—from investors, from the sale of stock, and from bank loans. When these sources proved inadequate, the company turned to the only other source: the government.

In the summer of 1883 the syndicate needed an estimated $22.5 million—an enormous sum, almost one entire year's revenue for the federal government. Pressed by opposition within his own party to make further concessions, Macdonald replied that the company might as well ask for planet Jupiter; Cabinet would never consent. Moreover, it would break the party if they did. But the shrewd J.H. Pope, Macdonald's secretary, reminded his leader: "The day the Canadian Pacific bursts, the Conservative Party bursts the day after." The money was forthcoming, but only after the Canadian Pacific Company agreed to mortgage the whole main line, all the rolling stock, and everything else connected with the railway. Macdonald also insisted that the railway become even more political, with the CPR making political appointments to jobs, secretly backing some

55

Conservative newspapers, and constructing a terminus at Quebec City to please French-Canadian voters. Even then, the bill just barely passed the House of Commons. That money kept construction going through 1884, but by the end of that year, the company again plunged towards bankruptcy.

On the evening of March 26, 1885, George Stephen met with Macdonald to appeal for more government financial assistance. Macdonald turned him down. He knew that he could never get his party to agree to another loan. A dejected Stephen returned home convinced the railway would, after all this, go under. "I feel like a man walking on the edge of a precipice," he claimed in regards to the CPR. Then in the morning came the extraordinary news: the Métis had rebelled under Louis Riel and had defeated the Mounted Police in a battle near Duck Lake in the Northwest Territories. Macdonald's luck had saved him once again. The uprising justified the railway. That day in Parliament, the government voted to send troops out on the railway to fight Riel and the Métis. It also introduced a bill to finance the remaining section of the railroad in the mountains.

56

On November 7, 1885, Donald Smith drove in the last spike at Craig-ellachie, a small hamlet in the Selkirks—a proud moment for all involved in the project. The American-born Van Horne remarked: "To have built that road would have made a Canadian out of the German Emperor." He also boasted that a train could make the trip from Montreal to Vancouver in a mere eighty-five hours. But the cost of such national pride was high. The Pacific railway cost the Canadian government 10.4 million ha of the best prairie land, an estimated $63.5 million in public funds and govern-ment loans of $35 million. Whether the project was worth the effort and extra expense were questions Macdonald was saved from having to answer by the Rebellion of 1885.

The Dominion's Strategy for the Northwest

Development of the West was the third component of Macdonald's na-tional policy. Without a populated West there was no need for a trans-continental railway; without a railway, there could be no east–west trade. And without national trade, the National Policy of tariff protection was meaningless.

Preparations for settlement of the Northwest had begun even before Canada had acquired the region. The Canadian government had prema-turely begun surveying the land in September 1869, before the land had been legally transferred to Canada. The Canadian government divided the land into townships similar in size to those in the American West because this pattern was familiar to American immigrants. Each township six miles square (15.6 km^2), consisted of thirty-six sections that were one mile square (2.6 km^2) square and contained 640 acres (256 ha). Sections were sub-divided into more manageable quarter-sections of 160 acres (64 ha).

Not all land was available for settlement. The Hudson's Bay Company had received "one twentieth of the land of the fertile belt" as part of the agreement of 1869–70 when the Company sold the land to the Canadian government (see chapter 2). In Manitoba, the Canadian government appropriated, as part of the Manitoba Act of 1870, 1.5 million acres (600 000 ha), or one-seventh of the new province, for the benefit of the Métis. The Canadian Pacific Railway Company received 25 million acres (10 million hectares) by its charter granted in 1881, and other railway companies also received land as part of their contracts until the practice ended in 1894. Additional land was set aside for schools. The remaining land belonged to the federal government, which could either sell it directly or turn it over to private land companies to sell.

To encourage settlement, the government passed the Dominion Lands Act in 1872, which provided to each head of family or male twenty-one years of age 160 acres (64 ha) free if he paid a ten-dollar registration fee, resided on the land for three years, cultivated 30 acres (12 ha), and built a permanent dwelling. If he met his obligations on that first quarter-section, it was his, and he could pre-empt a second quarter-section at a moderate sum of money. The government believed that even free land would pay for itself by bringing in immigrants who would need consumer goods, which in turn would generate manufacturing and trade.

57

ESTABLISHING LAW AND ORDER IN THE NORTHWEST

In preparation for peaceful settlement, the federal government quickly established an effective system of law and order. In place of the Hudson's Bay Company's courts, which ceased to have any jurisdiction after 1870, the federal government established its own territorial courts and a Northwest Territories Council to try cases. It also organized a federal police force, the North-West Mounted Police, to ensure law and order.

The Mounties have become an integral and colourful part of western Canadian and, by extension, of Canadian history in general. They embodied Canadian ideals, at least in mythology if not in reality. The myth is that tough, courageous, honest, and peace-loving men put aside personal gains for justice and humanity. The three hundred Mounties worked against insurmountable odds in administering British law to the native peoples, whiskey traders, and early settlers in an area larger than western Europe. Their success lay in what they represented: their red tunics and white helmets symbolized British law and tradition, a collective as opposed to individual (as in the United States) authority. As the writer Wallace Stegner pointed out: "One of the most visible aspects of the international border [in the West] was that it was a colour line: blue below, red above, blue for treachery and unkept promises, red for protection and straight tongue."[2]

The Mounties began their work in the Northwest in 1874 after their long, difficult march across the southern prairies. They divided into two detachments along the way, with part of the expedition going north to Fort Edmonton and the rest to Fort Whoop-Up (within a few kilometres of present-day Lethbridge), the centre of the whiskey trade. Mounted Police posts soon dotted the southern prairies; the most important were Fort Macleod on the Old Man River, Fort Walsh in the Cypress Hills, and Fort Calgary at the junction of the Bow and the Elbow rivers.

The Mounties assumed numerous tasks. They controlled the whiskey trade in present-day southern Alberta and Saskatchewan by stopping American vigilantes who crossed the border to sell cheap whiskey to Canadian Indians. Also, they helped prepare the Indians for the dramatic changes in their lives with the coming of white settlers by winning their confidence, and finally, they ensured peaceful relations—initially between Indians and settlers, and later between ranchers and homesteaders.

58

INDIAN TREATIES

Before settlement could proceed, the federal government had to negotiate treaties with the Indians. Its aim was to place Indians on reserves and then to work to assimilate them into Canadian society. The Canadian government adhered to the Royal Proclamation of 1763 which prohibited settlers from occupying territory the Indians had not surrendered to the Crown. Ottawa recognized that before settlement could legally proceed on the Plains, Indian land must first be purchased by the Crown. (The Canadian government also made treaties to avoid the Indian wars that had occurred in the United States.) The federal government acquired legal control of the land in return for certain concessions to the Indians. This led to confusion, as many Indians had no real understanding of the British land-holding system. The whites maintained that they had purchased the land, whereas some Indians believed that the white man's "gifts" were in exchange for temporary use of the land only. In the first five numbered treaties which were signed with Indian bands in present-day northwestern Ontario, Manitoba, and parts of Saskatchewan between 1871 and 1875, the federal government promised annuities, reserves, and the liberty to hunt on Crown lands.

In 1876 the treaty commissioners came farther west to negotiate Treaty Six with the Cree of present-day central Saskatchewan and Alberta. They came at a time when the Cree were vulnerable. Epidemics had seriously reduced the number of Plains warriors and the tribes stood divided among themselves, with the Cree fighting the Blackfoot and the Assiniboine antagonistic to the Sioux. Few chiefs recognized the need to form a common alliance against the whites. Even individual tribes had divisions among themselves; the Plains Cree considered themselves distinct from, and superior to, the Woods Cree.

The Canadian government also benefited from the Indian wars south of the border. The Canadian Blackfoot Confederacy, for example, could not count on their fellow tribesmen in Montana in any fight with Canadian authorities because they had already come under the control of the American army. Finally, the Plains Indians faced starvation as the buffalo, the mainstay of their way of life, had almost vanished by the mid-1870s.

In Treaty Six signed with many of the Cree in 1876 the government promised to supply aid and rations in the event of "any pestilence" or "general famine," along with a "medical chest" to be kept by every Indian agent. Big Bear, the most noted Cree chief on the plains, refused initially to sign Treaty Six, seeing it as an end to Plains Cree independence. In 1877 the Blackfoot Confederacy had signed Treaty Seven, which covered present-day Southern Alberta. With the buffalo herds gone in Canada in 1879 and in Montana in 1881, even Big Bear succumbed in 1882.

The means to implement the reserve system was through the Indian Act of 1876, as amended in 1880, which consolidated all existing Indian legislation. The Act placed the Indians in a distinct legal category, as minors or special wards of the federal government, who did not have the privileges of full citizenship. The federal government also established a separate Department of Indian Affairs and appointed Indian agents to carry out the new department's directives. These agents attempted to "Canadianize" the Indians by promoting the elimination of their culture and religion. They worked to prevent the Plains Indians' sun dances, or religious celebrations, and the Pacific Coast Indians' potlaches and dances. They also sent Indian children away from their parents to church-run boarding schools to learn English and (in Quebec) French, to become Christians, and to be taught how to farm.

The goal of the Indian Department was to promote enfranchisement, or the relinquishment of Indian status, and the gaining by the "civilized" Indians of full citizenship. Adult Indian males, deemed of good character, free of debt, and fluent in English or French, could (after a probationary period of three years) apply to give up their treaty and statutory rights under the Indian Act, and their right to live in the reserve community. They gained in return British citizenship with all legal privileges and the right to vote. They also took with them their share of band reserve lands and funds. Despite the federal government's encouragement, however, an insignificant number of Eastern Canadian Indians (initially Western Canadian Indians were excluded from this procedure as the government apparently considered them still too "uncivilized") applied for enfranchisement in the late nineteenth and early twentieth centuries. Even among the bands most familiar with the ways of the new dominant society few male Indians wanted to abandon their reserves and disappear into the general society. The Indian females who married non-Indians (whites, Métis, or Indians who were not under the Indian Act) had no choice as they automatically lost their full Indian status under the Indian Act when they married (see chapter 16).

RANCHING

Ranching was the first major occupation in the newly surrendered western lands. For a short period, beef became the major staple of trade. The foothills region and the southern grasslands, with its short grass, numerous coulees and streams for waterholes for livestock, and the winter "chinook" winds that regularly melted the snow and exposed the grass for winter pasture, were ideal for cattle ranching.

60

Initially, ranching was a small-scale operation. A few Mounties bought small ranches after their three-year enlistment terms expired. They knew the terrain, were used to western living, and had already established contact with the Indians. They supplied the beef used for the local Indian tribes' rations after the disappearance of the buffalo, and for the local police force.

This era of small-scale ranching was shortlived, however. During the 1880s, "the golden age of ranching," a few wealthy gentlemen ranchers from Ontario, Quebec, and Britain established large ranches—the Cochrane Ranch, the North West Cattle Company, the Walrond Ranch, and the Oxley Ranch Company—which quickly monopolized the business. The coming of the Canadian Pacific Railway in 1883, the establishment of a government embargo on live cattle imports from the United States, and a generous land lease system that allowed ranchers to lease up to 100 000 acres (roughly 40 000 ha) for twenty-one years at the modest rate of two cents a hectare all worked to the benefit of the big ranchers.

THE RISE OF A WESTERN CANADIAN CONSCIOUSNESS

By the late 1880s or early 1890s, a settler society with its own regional consciousness was taking shape in the West. The Northwest Territories, severed from Manitoba in 1875, had a local government consisting of a lieutenant governor, council, and (after 1888) an elected assembly. Wheat farming was already profitable, and wheat was a major staple in the Canadian economy, especially after the introduction of Red Fife wheat developed by David Fife of Peterborough County in Ontario in 1876. This hardy wheat withstood early frost, matured two weeks earlier than previous strains, and produced a bountiful and better-quality kernel that made wheat farming profitable on the prairies.

Along the CPR line arose small communities—Brandon, Pile of Bones (later Regina), Moose Jaw, Medicine Hat, and Calgary. Merchants and professional people moved westward to these towns and to others away from the "steel," like Edmonton, Battleford, and Prince Albert, which became regional commercial and social centres for the surrounding farm communities.

The growing western consciousness in the early 1880s placed the region in opposition to Central Canada and in particular to the federal government. Many Indians now perceived the treaties as the Canadian government's theft of their lands. The Métis also feared the end of their way of life with the encroachment of the Canadians. Already thousands of Ontario farmers had replaced them in the Red River. Antagonism among the settlers arose as well. Many farmers in Manitoba, where settlement was more advanced, complained about unfair grading at local elevators, high *61* freight rates, the CPR monopoly, and low prices for wheat on the open market. These recent immigrants from eastern Canada saw the "enemy" as the federal government, which they thought catered too much to Central Canada at the expense of the outlying regions. A tradition of western protest had begun, led by the original inhabitants and joined by the white settler population.

By the mid-1880s the main features of the Conservatives' nation-building scheme—based on a national policy of tariffs, railways, and western settlement—were in place. But there arose considerable opposition to the federal government's centralizing activities from the provincial leaders and from neglected interest groups in the outlying regions of Canada.

NOTES

[1] Pierre Berton, *The National Dream* (Toronto, 1970), p. 363.
[2] Wallace Stegner, *Wolf Willow: A History, a Story, and a Memory of the Lost Plains Frontier* (New York, 1966), p. 101.

Related Readings

The relevant articles from R. Douglas Francis and Donald B. Smith, eds., *Readings in Canadian History: Post-Confederation*, 2d ed. (Toronto, 1986) for this chapter are Craig Brown, "The Nationalism of the National Policy," pp. 45–51, and John Dales, "Canada's National Policies," pp. 52–62.

BIBLIOGRAPHY

The nationalism of the Canada First movement is discussed in the chapter "The First Fine Careless Rapture," in F.H. Underhill, *The Image of Confederation* (Toronto, 1964), and in David Gagan, "The Relevance of 'Canada First,' " *Journal of Canadian Studies*, 5 (November, 1970): 36–44. On the rising French-Canadian nationalism in the 1870s, see Jean-Paul Bernard, *Les Rouges: libéralisme et anti-cléricalisme au milieu du XIXe siècle*, (Montréal, 1971); Nive Voisine and Jean Hamelin, eds., *Les ultra-montains canadiens-français* (Montréal, 1985); Arthur Silver, *The French-Canadian Idea of Confederation, 1864–1900* (Toronto, 1982); Mason Wade, "Growing Pains: 1867–96," in his *The French Canadians: 1760–1945* (Toronto 1955), pp. 331–92, and "The Clerical Offensive," in S.M. Trofi-menkoff, *The Dream of Nation: A Social and Intellectual History of Quebec* (Toronto, 1983), pp. 115–31.

Dale Thomson's *Alexander Mackenzie: Clear Grit* (Toronto, 1960) gives a good portrait of Canada's second prime minister. On Edward Blake, see F.H. Underhill, "Edward Blake," in *Our Living Traditions*, edited by C. T. Bissell (Toronto, 1957), pp. 3–28, and Joseph Schull's two-volume biography, *Edward Blake: The Man of the Other Way* (Toronto, 1975) and *Edward Blake: Leader in Exile* (Toronto, 1976). The ideas underlying Canadian liberalism in the 1870s are examined by F.H. Underhill, "The Political Ideas of the Upper Canadian Reformers 1867–1878," in his *In Search of Canadian Liberalism* (Toronto, 1960), pp. 68–84, and by W.R. Graham, "Liberal Nationalism in the 1870's," *Canadian Historical Association Report*, 1946, pp. 101–19.

On the national policy, see Ben Forster, *A Conjunction of Interests: Business, Politics, and Tariffs, 1825–1879* (Toronto, 1986); D. Creighton, *British North America at Confederation* (Ottawa, 1939); R.C. Brown, *Canada's National Policy, 1883–1900: A Study in Canadian-American Relations* (Princeton, 1964); and John Dales, *The Protective Tariff in Canada's Development* (Toronto, 1966). An issue of the *Journal of Canadian Studies*, 14 (Autumn, 1979) is devoted to "The National Policy, 1879–1979." Pierre Berton's two-volume popular study, *The National Dream: The Great Railway, 1871–1881* (Toronto, 1970) and *The Last Spike: The Great Railway, 1881–1885* (Toronto, 1971) describes the building of the Canadian Pacific Railway.

On the development of the Canadian West in the 1870s and 1880s, see Gerald Friesen, *The Canadian Prairies: A History* (Toronto, 1984). Also useful is L.G. Thomas, ed., *The Prairie West to 1905: A Canadian Source Book* (Toronto, 1975) for an introduction to such topics as government and politics, law and order, the ranching frontier, and the development of transportation and communications. On settlement patterns in the West, see Chester Martin, *Dominion Lands' Policy* (published in an abridged form, Toronto, 1973). For a discussion of the mounted police, see R.C.

Macleod, *The North West Mounted Police and Law Enforcement 1873–1905* (Toronto, 1976), and on ranching, see David Breen, *The Canadian Prairie West and the Ranching Frontier, 1874–1924* (Toronto, 1982).

Indian policy is reviewed by Brian Titley in the first chapter of his *A Narrow Vision. Duncan Campbell Scott and the Administration of Indian Affairs in Canada* (Vancouver 1987), pp. 1–22. Richard Price, ed., *The Spirit of the Alberta Indian Treaties* (Montreal, 1979) contains valuable essays and transcripts of interviews made in the mid–1970s with Indian elders. Several excellent biographies of important Plains Indians chiefs have been completed by Hugh A. Dempsey: *Crowfoot* (Edmonton, 1972), *Red Crow* (Saskatoon, 1980), and *Big Bear* (Vancouver, 1984).

63

CHAPTER FOUR

The Fragile Union: The Resurgence of Regionalism

64   In the 1880s and 1890s regionalism and "racial" nationalism challenged Canada's fragile unity. In Ontario, Premier Oliver Mowat led a provincial rights movement in opposition to Macdonald's centralism. In the Maritimes and the Northwest, discontent arose against perceived central Canadian domination. Within Quebec, French-Canadian nationalists debated the destiny of Quebec society. Outside of Quebec, French-speaking Canadians faced bitter disputes with English-speaking Canadians over their religious, educational, and linguistic rights. These forces undermined the Conservative domination of the country and contributed to the Liberal victory of 1896.

The Provincial Rights Movement in Ontario

Opposition to John A. Macdonald's centralist view of Confederation was long-standing. The Maritimes, Quebec, and in Ontario, the Clear Grits, had resisted at the time of Confederation the idea of a legislative union, or highly centralized government with very weak local governments (see chapter 1). The Fathers of Confederation had settled on a federal model, where power was more evenly distributed between the central and the local or provincial governments. After Confederation the relationship between these two jurisdictions now had to be worked out in practice.

Two opposing views of federal-provincial relations emerged in the first years of Confederation. Macdonald's Conservative government maintained that major power should reside in the federal government. In contrast, the provincial premiers (most often Liberals) argued that the provinces were the main source of power and that they had voluntarily delegated only a portion of it to a central government.

Oliver Mowat, premier of Ontario from 1872 to 1896, has the best claim to the title of Father of Provincial Rights. Raised as a Conservative, Mowat had as a young man switched to the Reform (later the Liberal) party. The fact that Mowat had articled as a lawyer in the Kingston law office of John A. Macdonald and then changed his political allegiance, added a personal touch to his political disagreements with the prime minister. Mowat believed that the provinces should have full sovereignty in their own areas of jurisdiction. He endorsed the concept known as the compact theory — a belief that Confederation was a compact entered into by the provinces of their own volition, and one that could be altered only with their consent.

THE ONTARIO BOUNDARY DISPUTE

As Ontario premier, Mowat continued the policy of Edward Blake, his predecessor, of making the province dominant within the dominion. One opportunity came over the question of the boundary line between Ontario and Manitoba. The origins of this dispute dated back to pre-Confederation days, when the Hudson's Bay Company administered Rupert's Land. No precise boundary line had ever been established between Rupert's Land and the colony of Upper Canada (Ontario), even after Canada purchased Rupert's Land in 1870 and created the province of Manitoba. Compounding the problem was a desire on the part of Macdonald to keep the provinces weak and subordinate to Ottawa, and therefore incapable of posing a serious challenge to the federal government. Thus, the prime minister opposed the proposal to extend Ontario's boundary.

65

Mowat argued that Ontario's boundary should at least run due north from the source of the Mississippi River, which was slightly west of the Lake of the Woods. He referred to western explorations during the French regime to justify his claim for a boundary line west of Rat Portage (present-day Kenora). (Some of his supporters went even further and claimed that Ontario should extend as far as the forks of the Saskatchewan River.) In contrast, Macdonald and the federal Conservatives argued that the boundary should be drawn near Port Arthur on Lake Superior.

The issue was unresolved when Alexander Mackenzie and the federal Liberals came to power in late 1873. The following year the two Liberal governments quickly agreed to establish an arbitration board, which promptly accepted all of Mowat's claims; Ontario appeared to have won the struggle. Before the board's decision became law, however, the Liberals were defeated in 1878, and the newly elected federal Conservatives refused to ratify the arbitrators' award.

Unilaterally Macdonald in 1881 awarded to Manitoba the disputed territory (from the Lake of Woods eastward to Thunder Bay), thereby introducing that province into the controversy. Since the federal government continued to control Manitoba's natural resources this arrangement al-

Energy, Mines and Resources Canada.

For years, the Canadian, Ontario and Manitoba governments disputed over the boundary line between the provinces of Ontario and Manitoba. This 1882 map shows the area being contested.

lowed Ottawa to keep the land and the mineral rights to the disputed area. Despite Ontario's protests, the prime minister began to grant land and timber rights. Finally, after two years of legal chaos, both governments agreed to submit the issue to the Judicial Committee of the Privy Council in London, the supreme legal authority in the British Empire. Mowat himself pleaded Ontario's case against D'Alton McCarthy for the federal government, and won. In 1884 the Judicial Committee upheld the arbitrator's award of 1878, fixing the western limits of Ontario at the northwest angle of the Lake of the Woods (the present boundary). Mowat triumphed, yet John A. Macdonald still refused to yield. Until ratified by legislation the decision was not binding, and despite Ontario's formal request, the federal government delayed implementing the Judicial Committee's advisory decision. Only in 1889 did the Conservative government finally confirm Ontario's new boundaries and the province's full rights to the natural resources within the disputed territory.

POWERS OF THE LIEUTENANT-GOVERNOR

Mowat's triumph on the boundary question coincided with a series of victories over the powers of the lieutenant governor and the federal power of disallowance. According to the BNA Act, lieutenant governors were appointees of the federal government, which also paid the salaries of the office. They received instructions from Ottawa and could be dismissed by the federal government anytime. Macdonald had favoured the subordinate position of the lieutenant governor as a means of keeping provincial policies in harmony with national objectives.

Mowat believed otherwise. He argued that the lieutenant governor should have the same relationship with the province as the governor general had with the federal government, thus making the provinces co-ordinate sovereignties with the federal government. Once again the Judicial Committee of the Privy Council upheld Mowat's position in a legal dispute over whether the province had the right to appoint Queen's Counsels, an honorary title given to provincial lawyers. In 1892 the Judicial Committee ruled that a lieutenant governor "is as much the representative of Her Majesty, for all purposes of provincial government, as the Governor-General himself for all purposes of the Dominion Government."

67

The Ontario premier also advanced provincial interests on another front. He argued that the provinces had certain legal powers before Confederation which they retained after 1867; one was the right to issue liquor licences. In 1884 the Ontario government passed the Act Respecting Licensing Duties, which the federal government immediately disallowed. Ontario took the dispute to court in the case of *Hodge v. the Queen*, in which the Judicial Committee upheld Ontario's position, arguing that liquor licensing was a local matter. The provinces, the committee ruled, had full authority in their own realm of legal jurisdiction. With decisions similar to that of *Hodge v. the Queen*, the committee contributed greatly to the strengthening of the provinces' powers.

Protest in Atlantic Canada

Mowat had allies in his fight with Macdonald and "Empire Canada." In Atlantic Canada the anti-confederate sentiments of the 1860s re-emerged in the 1880s as Maritimers became increasingly dissatisfied with their perceived inferior position in the new dominion. For example, the custom of flying flags at half-mast on July 1, which first began in 1867, continued in many Atlantic communities.

Difficult economic conditions heightened the tension. During the 1880s the Maritimes underwent profound economic change. The high tariff under the National Policy of 1879 had been countered by the Americans with a duty on Maritime fish, resulting in a staggering 75 percent drop in fish and lobster exports. Shipbuilding also declined, as iron steamers were more reliable and more economical than wooden sailing ships. Yarmouth, once a thriving centre of Nova Scotia's shipbuilding industry, built only six vessels in 1880, four in 1884, and none in 1887. Nova Scotians, many of whom relied on fishing, shipbuilding, and shipping for their livelihood, faced hard times; a substantial number left the province. Nova Scotia's population increased only by ten thousand in the 1880s, well below the former rate of increase. The province's ruling Conservative party in 1878 –84 appealed in vain to its federal counterpart in Ottawa for financial assistance; but Macdonald's priority was the building of the CPR, to which he had committed the government's financial resources. Consequently, the Liberals came to office in Nova Scotia in 1884 on a wave of anti-Confederation sentiment.

68

SECESSION THREATS IN NOVA SCOTIA

W. S. Fielding, the new Liberal premier, also attempted to extract larger subsidies from Ottawa to help Nova Scotia out of its depression. When his tactics proved no more successful than those of his Conservative predecessor, he introduced a resolution in the Nova Scotia Legislature in 1886 favouring Nova Scotia's withdrawal from Confederation. The premier appealed to the other Maritime provinces to secede and to create an independent Maritime nation. If Maritime union proved unfeasible, then Nova Scotia favoured a return to its original status as a British colony.

Secessionist sentiment developed no further. New Brunswick declined Nova Scotia's offer, seeing it as a political ploy to benefit Halifax. Furthermore, New Brunswick had just received federal financial support for a rail line to St. John. Prince Edward Island resisted Maritime union, believing it would result in the loss of control over the island to a "distant" mainland. Then Fielding retreated. Despite a stunning victory of twenty-nine of the thirty-nine seats in the 1886 election, Fielding's attempt to take Nova Scotia out of Confederation was unsuccessful. At the same time his pressure tactics seemed to have worked, for the federal Conservative government lowered freight rates and offered generous financial assistance for railway building in the province. Once again the threats of secession subsided in Nova Scotia.

NEWFOUNDLAND CONSIDERS JOINING CONFEDERATION

In Newfoundland, major economic changes contributed to support for union with Canada. The dominant fishing industry, which by 1885 employed nine out of ten of the island's work force and accounted for nearly all of its exports, experienced a serious slump. Between the early 1880s and the late 1890s export prices for salt cod fell by 32 percent, total production declined by 20 percent, and industry earnings fell by 36 percent. This decline was partly because of the Washington Treaty, a treaty negotiated between Britain and the United States that affected Canadian fisheries (see chapter 5). More serious were the marketing problems experienced by merchant exporters in St. John's, who were faced with increasingly vigorous competition from other fishing nations, such as Norway. The steep decline in output from the once-prosperous seal hunt also put many Newfoundlanders out of work, and a number chose to emigrate.

The Newfoundland government successfully negotiated a reciprocity agreement with the United States in 1890. This agreement, however, alarmed the Maritime provinces, which saw their own fishing industry in jeopardy. The Canadian government intervened and protested to Britain, and the Colonial Office vetoed the agreement.

On the wake of the collapse of Newfoundland's reciprocity treaty came the bank crash of 1894. When the newly elected Whiteway government of 1895 faced default on interest payments on its loans, the Newfoundland premier approached the Canadian government about union. Although only a few years earlier the Conservative government in Ottawa had offered Newfoundlanders terms of union even more attractive than those proposed in 1869, including an annual subsidy of $1.25 million for railway construction, the political climate had changed. Mackenzie Bowell, the new prime minister, feared that better terms for Newfoundland would reopen appeals from other provinces. Then, too, Whiteway found little enthusiasm for union within his own colony. Had not Canada scuttled Newfoundland's reciprocity negotiations with the United States? The talks broke down and Newfoundland waited another half-century before joining Confederation (see chapter 15).

The Northwest Rebellion of 1885

The Macdonald government faced opposition in the northwest as well. In Manitoba, discontent arose in the 1880s over discriminatory freight rates. Since the publication of the Canadian Pacific Railway's first freight-rate schedule in 1883, western settlers complained that they paid more to ship their goods than central or eastern Canadians (estimated for wheat to be three times for that of comparable distances) because of the lack of transportation competition in the West to keep rates down. The monopoly clause, by which no competitive lines could be built in the region for twenty years after the completion of the CPR, gave the railway free rein on the prairies to charge what the market would bear.

The Manitoba Conservative government under John Norquay responded by chartering provincial competitive lines to the American border to take advantage of American railways. The federal government disallowed these provincial charters on the grounds that they went against the national interest. As Sir Charles Tupper, the federal minister of railways, put it: "Are the interests of Manitoba and the North-west to be sacrificed to the policy of Canada? I say, if it is necessary — yes." Thus an economic problem became a constitutional and political dispute. Norquay protested loudly but gained no substantial concessions from Ottawa.

Then in 1888 he was defeated by Thomas Greenway, a Liberal. Greenway immediately embarked on the building of a railway from Winnipeg to Emerson. He warned that if opposed, he would solicit American financial — and, if he need be, military — support. The federal government gave in, abandoned its policy of disallowance, and bought out the CPR monopoly. The new railway, run by the American Northern Pacific Company, initially lowered rates but soon put its own profits ahead of a concern for competition with the CPR. The issue did, however, rally western support against the federal government.

70

DISCONTENT IN THE NORTHWEST TERRITORIES

A more serious challenge arose farther west. The Indians, particularly the Crees in the Treaty Six area, felt betrayed by the federal government's failure to keep its treaty promises. The government had never anticipated the demise of the buffalo in Canada within three years and hence had been willing to insert the "famine clause" in Treaty Six in 1876, by which it promised to provide food rations to Indians in time of scarcity (see chapter 3). Despite its promise, the debt-ridden federal government did little, aside from supplying insufficient amounts of second- or third-class quality food to the starving Indians. The prospect of a Western Canadian Indian uprising seemed real.

Anticipating trouble, Edgar Dewdney, the Indian commissioner for the Northwest Territories, reneged on the treaty promise of allowing the Indians to establish reserves where they wished. Contrary to the agreements, the commissioner prevented a large concentration of reserves first in the Cypress Hills area and then around Battleford. No large Indian Territory would be permitted, as this would constitute a military threat to Canadian rule in the Northwest. According to historian John Tobias's recent reinterpretation of developments in the early 1880s, Dewdney also used his control over rations to convince all remaining bands still refusing to sign the treaties to adhere.[1]

The Métis in the Prince Albert area, near the forks of the north and south branches of the Saskatchewan River, also felt antagonistic to the federal government. They disliked Ottawa's handling — or, more precisely, lack of handling — of their land claims. Many of the Métis had moved to the South Saskatchewan River valley, around the village that became known as Batoche, shortly after the Red River resistance of 1869–70 (see chapter 2). They had left a Manitoba crowded with settlers from Ontario. For several years they had been able to participate in the Saskatchewan buffalo hunt, until the extinction of the great herds in the late 1870s. Once again, the Métis' livelihood was threatened as settlers moved into the Northwest Territories in anticipation of the coming of the CPR. The Métis in the Batoche area had long petitioned Ottawa to recognize their land claims and to allow them to keep their river lots instead of having to conform to the rectangular plan imposed elsewhere in the territories. Delays and confusion followed, without the local Métis receiving any firm assurance from Ottawa that their river lots would be respected. By the end of 1884 Ottawa had still not responded to their petitions.

Many of the white settlers at Prince Albert, northeast of Batoche, also resented their treatment by the federal authorities. Ottawa's sudden decision to reroute the promised railroad through the southern region (see chapter 3) left them hundreds of kilometres away from quick transportation to eastern markets. Furthermore, they felt isolated from the centres of political and economic power, and they believed that theirs was a hinterland area ruled by indifferent eastern politicans in a distant Ottawa. The most politically active settlers demanded responsible government and representation in the federal Parliament.

RETURN OF LOUIS RIEL

The Métis, with the support of a group of white settlers in the Prince Albert area, brought back Louis Riel to lead their protest against the federal government. In June 1884 Gabriel Dumont, the Métis leader in the Batoche area, and three other mixed-bloods rode to Montana to ask Riel to return to Canada. He agreed.

For the most part, Riel had lived in exile since the arrival of Wolseley's troops in the Red River in 1870. He had wandered back and forth across the international border, and even ran for Parliament in the by-election in Provencher, when the seat became vacant after George-Etienne Cartier's death in the summer of 1873, and twice more after that, winning each time. He had gone to Ottawa and signed the members' register, but fled when identified. In 1875 Lord Dufferin, the governor general, granted Riel a general amnesty on the condition that he remain in exile for another five years.

During his years in exile in the United States, Riel experienced religious visions. He became convinced that God had chosen him "prophet of the New World," who was responsible for creating a reformed Roman Catholic state on the Prairies. Not comprehending his religious ideas, his French-

Canadian relatives brought him back to Montreal and committed him to a lunatic asylum, first at Longue Pointe near Montreal and then at Beauport, near Quebec. He was released in 1877, and in 1881 returned to the United States to settle in Montana, where he taught at a mission school. There the "prophet of the New World" waited for his divine mission to commence. He saw his return in 1885 as part of God's plan.

Initially, Riel used peaceful means to deal with the problems at hand. Riel's ally, Will Jackson, the white secretary of the radical farmers' union at Prince Albert, sent a petition to Ottawa on December 16, 1884 on behalf of the settlers and the Métis. It called for more liberal treatment for the Indians, a land grant for the mixed-bloods, responsible government for the Northwest Territories, western representation at Ottawa, reduction of the tariff, and the construction of a railway to Hudson Bay, as an alternative to the CPR. The federal government acknowleged receipt of the petition, but for several weeks did nothing more. Finally in February they promised to appoint a commission to investigate problems in the Northwest. Apart from making a list of mixed-bloods, however, Ottawa promised no specific action, and failed even to mention the Métis grievances.

Subsequently, in mid-March Riel took matters into his own hands. He established a provisional government with himself as president and Gabriel Dumont as adjutant general. He then armed his supporters at Batoche and attempted to duplicate the successful resistance at the Red River in 1869–70. But Riel underestimated how the situation had changed in fifteen years. A federal police force was now stationed in the Northwest along with thousands of Canadians, while a newly completed railway tied the region to central Canada. Moreover, this time the Roman Catholic church openly opposed him. Riel's unorthodox religious views, and his radical political stand lost him the support of the clergy, who denounced him as a heretic throughout the South Saskatchewan River valley, at St. Albert (near Fort Edmonton), in the Qu'Appelle valley, and in other areas of large Métis settlement. By insisting that the Indians be included in the protest movement, Riel had also lost the support of almost all the white settlers in the Prince Albert area, who feared the Indians' involvement. They remembered the Sioux uprising in Minnesota in 1862, when five hundred whites were killed and the Sioux's killing of George Custer and his entire detachment of two hundred at Little Big Horn in 1876 — a defeat inflicted on the Americans after they invaded the Sioux's hunting grounds.

MILITARY CAMPAIGN

On March 26, Dumont and a group of Métis clashed with a group of about one hundred settler volunteers and North-West Mounted Police at Duck Lake. After Dumont's victory the police abandoned Fort Carlton

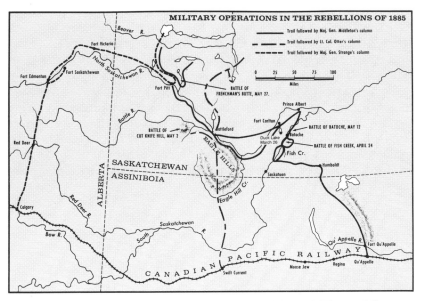

MILITARY OPERATIONS IN THE REBELLIONS OF 1885

73

from P.G. Cornell, *et al. Canada: Unity in Diversity* (Toronto: Holt, Rinehart & Winston, 1967), p. 289.

A map showing the route followed by the three columns in 1885—a first to Batoche under Major-General Middleton; a second to Battleford under Lieutenant-Colonel Otter; and a third, the Alberta Field Force under Major-General Strange.

and retreated to Prince Albert. Success at Duck Lake encouraged two Cree Indian bands to join the rebellion. Poundmaker's band of Crees besieged Battleford, while militant warriors in Big Bear's band murdered nine people near Frog Lake.

The federal government immediately dispatched troops to the Northwest. Within a month, it had sent nearly three thousand troops under the command of General Frederick Middleton on the nearly completed Canadian Pacific Railway. They joined about five thousand volunteers and Mounties in the West. Middleton organized the troops in three columns at Qu'Appelle, Swift Current, and Calgary. He confronted the Métis at Fish Creek south of Batoche on April 24. The battle ended in a stalemate — for the Métis and Indians, while poorly-equipped, were superb fighters and knew the terrain. Lieutenant-Colonel William Otter successfully relieved Battleford, but was defeated by Poundmaker at Cut Knife Hill on May 2. Major General Thomas Bland Strange led the improvised Alberta Field Force from Calgary by way of Edmonton and the North Saskatchewan River into action against Big Bear at Frenchman's Butte in late May. As at Fish Creek, the encounter proved a draw, with both sides retreating at the same time.

The main battle took place at Batoche, Riel's headquarters, beginning on May 9. For three days, skirmishes occurred; then Middleton's troops, frustrated at their general's caution, charged the Métis. The defenders, now out of ammunition, gave way. Riel surrendered on May 15, while Dumont and others fled to the United States. The Indians continued to resist until Poundmaker gave himself up on May 23 and Big Bear on July 2.

Remembering its broken treaty promises, the Canadian government had prudently sent by rail huge amounts of rations westward to the starving reserve Indians. As a result, only about 4 percent of the Plains Indians took up arms against the Crown. If the Plains Indians and the other Métis communities had joined the uprising, the settlement of the West would probably have been postponed at least another decade by the ongoing guerilla warfare.

RIEL'S TRIAL

Riel was tried for treason in a Regina courtroom before a jury of six men, all of British background. Riel pleaded not guilty. His lawyers wanted to fight for acquittal on the grounds of insanity, but he refused to comply. Two doctors — James Wallace of Hamilton and Daniel Clark of Toronto — examined Riel at the trial. Both concluded that Riel was sane, that he could distinguish right from wrong. In a minority judgement, Dr. François Roy, who had treated Riel at the Beauport asylum, testified that Riel was in no condition "to be master of his acts."

Riel's speech in English to the jury eloquently summarized his role in the rebellion:

> No one can say that the North West was not suffering last year . . .
> but what I have done, and risked, and to which I have exposed
> myself, rested certainly on the conviction I had to do, was called
> upon to do something for my country. . . . I know that through the
> grace of God I am the founder of Manitoba. . . . Even if I was going
> to be sentenced by you, gentlemen of the jury, I have the satisfaction
> if I die — that if I die I will not be reputed by all men as insane,
> as a lunatic. . . . Gentlemen of the jury, my reputation, my liberty,
> my life are at your discretion.

The jury deliberated for an hour before reaching a verdict: Riel was guilty of treason. The perceived injustice of that decision has made Louis Riel in the 1970s and 1980s one of Canada's best-known historical figures.

EXECUTION OF RIEL

Only the federal Cabinet could grant a pardon. Appeals for clemency came in to Ottawa from all parts of Canada and the United States, from Britain,

Glenbow Archives, Calgary.

One of the most dramatic moments in a Canadian courtroom—a photograph of Louis Riel taken during his trial in Regina. He spoke in his own defence in leading the resistance of 1885 against the Canadian government.

and France. But in Ontario, Orangemen demanded Riel's execution in revenge for his killing of Thomas Scott fifteen years earlier. Public opinion was divided. Macdonald hesitated and twice postponed the execution; the second time he appointed a medical commission to re-examine the question of Riel's sanity. The commissioners concurred with the earlier report that Riel was sane. A new execution date was set for November 16. On that clear and chilly morning, Riel mounted the gibbet at Regina. The executioner placed the rope around Riel's neck, the priest gave the last rites, and then the trap door was sprung. A Canadian martyr was born.

It has been argued that Macdonald had decided (in words attributed to him) that "Riel must swing" in order to keep Ontario loyal to the Conservative party. He gambled that Quebec would continue to support the party. His French-Canadian lieutenants, Hector Langevin, Adolphe Caron, and Adolphe Chapleau, did stand by their leader. As Quebec mourned Riel, these three politicians were denounced as traitors to their "race." Their leader, Sir John A. Macdonald, was burnt in effigy in the streets of Montreal. Riel's execution was one factor contributing to the demise of the Conservatives in Quebec in the 1890s and the rise of the Liberals. Wilfrid Laurier, a young Liberal politician, declared at a rally of more than forty thousand people in Montreal: "If I had been on the banks of the Saskatchewan, I too, would have shouldered a musket."

The Rebellion of 1885 began in hope but ended in failure for the Métis at Batoche. They felt that Ottawa had ignored their grievances and their distinct way of life had been threatened. The uprising was a tragedy for which, through its tardy response to the Métis claims, the federal government must bear much of the responsibility. On a national scale, the Rebellion revealed the tenuous nature of the native–white relations in Canada and accentuated the rising nationalism of both English- and French-speaking Canada.

Rising French-Canadian Nationalism

For more than a century two ideas have characterized French Canadians' attitudes about Canada beyond the St. Lawrence valley. These two strains of French-Canadian nationalism had emerged at least as early as the 1830s and 1840s: for example, in the differing views of Louis-Joseph Papineau, leader of the rebellion of 1837, and Louis-Hippolyte La Fontaine, leader of the French-Canadian moderate reformers after 1838, to the 1841 Act of Union uniting Upper and Lower Canada. French Canadians who felt that French Canada would be strengthened by union with the English-speaking Canadians followed La Fontaine. Those endorsing Papineau in the late 1840s sought to keep the St. Lawrence valley — the French-

Canadian homeland — as a separate unit and opposed union with the English-speaking outsiders, because they believed that French Canadians would be placed in an inferior position.

MERCIER'S PARTI NATIONAL

The Riel controversy not only intensified the debate but it also led to a desire on the part of some French-Canadian leaders, who saw Quebec as "l'état," or the only government that represented French-Canadian interests, to guard that stronghold through provincial autonomy. They equated French-Canadian nationalism with provincial autonomy. Honoré Mercier, 77 leader of the Quebec wing of the Liberal party after 1883, became the spokesman of this Quebec nationalist position in the 1880s. At the same rally in Montreal, on Sunday November 22, 1885, at which Wilfrid Laurier declared his support for the Métis, Mercier denounced the federal Conservative politicians who had been responsible for Riel's execution: "Riel, our brother, is dead, victim of fanaticism and treason — of the fanaticism of Sir John and some of his friends, of the treason of three of our people who sold their brother to keep their portfolios."

Mercier appealed to his fellow Quebeckers to form an exclusive French-Canadian party, a *parti national*, that would put French-Canadian interests first: "We felt that the murder of Riel was a declaration of war against Quebec; and that, therefore, French Canadians had a duty to cease their fratricidal quarrels and unite in a crusade to preserve the nation in Quebec from encroaching federal power." Only a few days earlier on November 17, Montreal's *La Presse* had declared: "Henceforth there are no more Conservatives, nor Liberals, nor Castors. There are only *Patriots* and *Traitors* — the National Party and the Party of the Rope."

Mercier succeeded in winning support from dissident Conservatives, from ultramontanists (who saw his brand of nationalism as close to their own), and from the provincial Liberals. His party won a narrow victory in the provincial election of 1886. The newly elected premier then endorsed a theory of provincial rights that complemented Oliver Mowat's compact theory of some fifteen years earlier. T. J. J. Loranger, a provincial court judge, best expressed the provincial autonomy position in his *Letters upon the Interpretation of the Federal Constitution known as the British North America Act* (1884). He argued that each level of government, federal and provincial, was sovereign in its own area of jurisdiction, and that the federal government had only limited power to deal with transprovincial concerns.

THE FIRST INTERPROVINCIAL CONFERENCE

Appealing to the other provincial premiers to assist him in challenging Ottawa, Mercier called an interprovincial conference in 1887, the first of its kind, and one held exactly twenty years after Confederation. Two provinces declined the invitation — British Columbia and Prince Edward Island (both provinces with Conservative governments) — while five accepted. The federal Conservative government, also invited to attend, chose to ignore the conference, dismissing it as a partisan session of provincial Liberal governments.

The premiers drew up twenty-two resolutions that summed up two decades of provincial complaints. They demanded larger federal subsidies, abolition of the federal power of disallowance, a better method to determine federal and provincial constitutional jurisdictions, Senate reform to strengthen provincial power, provincial control of the franchise, and the recognition that all public lands belonged to the provinces.

78

Macdonald refused to meet the premiers to discuss their complaints, and he lost much political support because of the meeting. From this time onward, the prime minister was cautious about using the federal power of disallowance. He capitulated on the Manitoba railway legislation disallowance issue in 1888, which allowed Manitoba to build provincial rail lines in the province, for example; and a year later he conceded the Ontario boundary question. By 1890 Canada had become a federal state in practice as well as in theory.

Wilfrid Laurier best expressed the French-Canadian nationalism that was an alternative to Mercier's and one that included French Canadians across the country. Initially, the future prime minister did not hold such a position. In the 1860s he was a member of the *Rouges* and in 1867 had opposed Confederation. Laurier only became reconciled to union in the early 1870s, when he won election to the House of Commons and began a brilliant career that made him the federal Liberal leader in 1887. As Mercier became more embittered towards English-speaking Canadians and more separatist in orientation, Laurier withdrew his support from the provincial leader, fearing an ethnic polarization of the country. While he blamed the federal government for neglecting the Métis' grievances, he appealed for moderation on both sides. He warned Mercier that "it would be simply suicidal for the French Canadians to form a party by themselves. . . . We have only one way of organizing parties. This country must be governed and can be governed only on questions of policy and administration."

Cultural and Religious Feuds

Laurier's appeal for unity between English and French Canadians seemed to go unheeded in the racially and religiously intolerant atmosphere of the

Ontario Archives C-11583.

The first interprovincial conference held at Quebec City in 1887. Premier Oliver Mowat of Ontario chaired the meeting. Seated from the left are the other premiers present: A.G. Blair (New Brunswick), Honoré Mercier (Quebec), W.S. Fielding (Nova Scotia) and John Norquay (Manitoba). Absent were the Conservative Party premiers of British Columbia and Prince Edward Island. Prime Minister John A. Macdonald boycotted the meeting.

79

late nineteenth century. Two issues — the Jesuit Estates Act and the Manitoba Schools Questions — revealed just how bitter English- and French-Canadian relations had become.

JESUIT ESTATES CONTROVERSY

The dispute over the Jesuit Estates began in 1888 when the Mercier government introduced an act designed to compensate Roman Catholic claimants for property taken from the Society of Jesus after the order was temporarily disbanded by the pope in the 1770s. The land became provincial property in 1800 and was used for educational purposes. Roughly thirty years after the pope re-established the Jesuits as a world order in 1814, Bishop Bourget re-introduced them to Quebec. Once re-located, they appealed to the provincial government either to have their property returned or to receive financial compensation. Mercier agreed to give the various claimants $400 000 (a sum well below the actual value of the land), to be distributed among the various Catholic groups on the basis of a papal decision. He awarded a further $60 000 to Protestant post-secondary education institutes in Quebec.

Protestant Ontario reacted vehemently to the idea of consulting the pope. D'Alton McCarthy, who had been the federal government's lawyer in the Ontario Boundary dispute, and was also a fiery anti-Catholic, Conservative MP from Ontario, insisted that the pope had no right to meddle in Canadian affairs and moved a resolution in the House of Commons to have the act disallowed by the federal government. His twelve supporters became known as "the noble thirteen" or "the devil's dozen," depending on one's perspective. They considered the Jesuit Estates Act the latest in a series of attempts by French Canadians to dominate Canada. The Conservative party was to blame, they maintained, for giving in to Quebec's demand in return for votes. McCarthy appealed to English-speaking Canadians to insist upon one common Canadian nationality based on one language (English) and one culture (British). He believed that Confederation would never succeed until the country had one strong unified nationality. But as Prime Minister John A. Macdonald refused to intevene in this provincial matter, McCarthy and his followers — "the McCarthyites" as they might well be called — lost, for the present at least. The battle was far from over; however: racial and religious tension now centred on the school question.

The Manitoba schools question had its origins in the Manitoba Act of 1870 (see chapter 2) and to a degree, in the Confederation agreement of 1867. At stake was the broad question of English- and French-Canadian relations but, more specifically, the linguistic and educational rights of

NOW'S A CHANCE FOR JOHN A. TO USE HIS **DISALLOWANCE** GUN IN THE PUBLIC INTEREST
BUT **WILL HE DO IT?**

Grip, April 30, 1887.

This *Grip* cartoon captured the prevailing English-speaking Canadians' view of the Jesuit Estates controversy: a domineering and sinister Catholic Church held Quebec firmly in its grasp. The Toronto journal insisted that John A. Macdonald disallow the legislation.

French-speaking Canadians and Roman Catholics outside the province of Quebec.

NEW BRUNSWICK SCHOOL QUESTION

The only previous dispute over denominational schools since Confederation occurred in New Brunswick. The BNA Act recognized denominational schools that existed *by law* before the union in the four original provinces. Denominational schools existed by custom in New Brunswick before the union, but not by law. In 1871 the New Brunswick government proposed legislation to amend the Schools Act to introduce a non-sectarian school system, which would deny public support to "separate" parish schools teaching French and providing religious instruction. To New Brunswick's Roman Catholics, both Acadians and Irish, this legislation meant depriving them of a right that they had enjoyed, if not precisely "by law," at least in fact at the time of Confederation. They requested the federal government to intervene to disallow the act under the power given to it by the BNA Act. Section 93 included the right to intervene to protect the educational rights of a minority.

The federal Conservative government refused to interfere. As minister of justice, Sir John A. Macdonald argued that the act was within the competence of the provincial legislature, since Roman Catholics did not lose any rights they had *by law* at the union or had acquired since. Macdonald did not see a reason for disallowance, or for remedial action under section 93. Furthermore, the prime minister was reluctant to intervene in an area — education — that was clearly, by the BNA Act, under provincial jurisdiction. The federal government did make a strong appeal to the New Brunswick legislature to consider minority rights but went no further.

The New Brunswick school question was the only precedent for the courts and the politicians when the Manitoba schools question arose, but because it dealt with educational rights in a founding province of Confederation whose rights had been written into the original BNA Act, it applied only in part. On the matter of what were to be the rights, linguistic and religious, of minorities in new Canadian provinces, the Fathers of Confederation had been silent, preferring to deal with the problem when the situation arose, which it did in 1870 when Manitoba entered Confederation.

82

MANITOBA SCHOOLS QUESTION

Manitoba became a significant test case because in 1870 it had an almost equal number of French- and English-speaking, Roman Catholic and Protestant inhabitants. The French-speaking Roman Catholics, who in 1870 were almost all Métis, had had the right to establish denominational schools in their own language (see chapter 2). The Manitoba Act of 1870 and the Northwest Territories Act of 1875 (as amended in 1877) conferred language and school rights on French and English, Roman Catholics, and Protestants.

By 1890, however, the situation had changed in Manitoba. The French-speaking, Roman Catholic population, as a percentage of the total population, had not grown as rapidly as the English-speaking Protestant community, and many French-speaking Métis left the province. The English-speaking Protestant population increased tenfold by 1890. This imbalance might have caused a controversy over separate schools on its own, but well before it arose, interference came from the outside.

In August 1889, D'Alton McCarthy gave an emotional speech at Portage la Prairie against denominational schools in Manitoba. Only a few months earlier, he had supported the Equal Rights Association, which claimed in its platform to stand for "equal rights of all religious denominations before the law, special privileges for none," by which was meant a single language — English — and a single system of public schools. To McCarthy and his followers, Canada's minorities, especially the French-Canadian and Métis Catholics in the West, deserved no "special concessions." He attacked the French language, separate schools, and provincial rights as evils that would undermine the future greatness of Canada. For McCarthy the only important question was whether the country would be English or French.

On the same platform as McCarthy at Portage la Prairie stood Joseph Martin, attorney general in Manitoba's Government. This recent Ontario immigrant liked McCarthy's speech and immediately pledged his government's support in abolishing the dual school system as well as French as an official language in Manitoba. In the 1890 session of the legislature, the Manitoba Liberal government passed school legislation establishing a provincial Department of Education and a system of non-sectarian public schools that alone would receive the provincial grant for education and that all ratepayers would be obliged to support. Denominational schools were still allowed to exist but would not be given government funding. Those contributing to such schools would have to do so in addition to their public school taxes. The same session of the Legislature, contrary to section 23 of the Manitoba Act, abolished French as an official language.

83

MANITOBA CATHOLICS FIGHT SCHOOL LEGISLATION

Discontented Catholics had three avenues of recourse open to them: to appeal to the federal government to use its right of disallowance of provincial legislation; to take the issue to the courts to have the legislation declared *ultra vires* or unconstitutional; or to appeal to the federal government to intervene on behalf of the minority as set out in section 93 of the BNA Act. Eventually, they tried all three options.

Macdonald was reluctant to use the federal government's right of disallowance. Based on his past failures to disallow a number of provincial laws, he feared that such action could end up strengthening the power of the provincial governments. He also saw it as a volatile political issue that could harm his party electorally, so he favoured court action and even agreed to the government paying the legal costs of the appellant. The case, known as *Barrett v. the City of Winnipeg*, went through the courts to the Supreme Court of Canada (the latter upholding the right of the Roman Catholic minority to have state-supported separate schools). Then, in an appeal to the Judicial Committee of the Privy Council, the Committee reversed the Supreme Court's decision and favoured the Manitoba government's position. Macdonald did not live to hear the decision (he died in office in 1891).

The Manitoba Roman Catholics had one final course of action: to appeal to the federal government for remedial action under section 93 of BNA Act. The courts had to determine now whether the federal government had the legal right to intervene on behalf of a minority under provincial legislation that had been found by the Judicial Committee to be *intra vires* or valid. Sir John Thompson, who replaced John Abbott, Macdonald's immediate successor as prime minister in 1892, initiated court proceedings. In the case of *Brophy and Others v. the Attorney-General of Manitoba*, the court ruled in the affirmative: the federal government had the constitutional right to intervene on behalf of the minority even though the Manitoba law was valid, or *intra vires*. Thompson, however, never heard the court's verdict — he died in 1893 on a visit to England. His successor, Mackenzie Bowell, an active Orangeman, had to act on the ruling.

REMEDIAL LEGISLATION

84

In 1895 Bowell summoned the federal Cabinet to act as a judicial tribunal to hear the appeal of the Manitoba Catholics. The Cabinet favoured remedial legislation to restore the lost school privileges. It drew up a Remedial Order, as an Order in Council approved by the Cabinet and by the governor general, promising a Roman Catholic separate school system. A nine-member board would run the separate school system, to be supported by the Roman Catholics' own tax monies. These schools would also share a portion of the provincial educational grant. To insure proper standards the separate schools would be inspected regularly and money withheld if they were judged inefficient. Clearly, the remedial order favoured the Catholic position.

The Conservatives introduced a bill based on the remedial order in Parliament in January 1896, but Parliament was dissolved on April 23, with the bill still on the books. Four days later, Bowell resigned as Conservative leader after having to face a Cabinet revolt and the impending resignation of some of his ministers over his inept and delayed handling of the schools questions.

THE ELECTION OF 1896

The Conservatives entered the federal election of 1896 with a new leader, Charles Tupper — the fifth leader in five years — and a divided party. The Manitoba schools question was only one of several contentious issues in the election, although an important one. In Quebec the Conservatives stressed the positive features of remedial legislation for the Manitoba Catholics and reminded the Quebec electorate that it was the Conservatives who introduced the bill. In English-speaking Canada, Conservative candidates emphasized that the bill was not, and might never become, law. Some English-speaking Conservatives even spoke openly against the party position. Outside of Quebec, the Conservatives were also on the defensive over their tariff policy and were blamed for the country's continuing weak economy.

The Conservative party had mixed opportunities in the election campaign. In Quebec the Roman Catholic hierarchy issued a pastoral letter appealing to parishioners to vote for candidates who promised to support remedial legislation. But many of the French-Canadian Conservatives who were knowledgeable of the internal split within the party refused to work during the campaign. Adolphe Chapleau, the party's leading figure and lieutenant governor of Quebec, sat quietly in Quebec City refusing to intervene. Israël Tarte, a one-time Conservative organizer, had already defected to the Liberals.

The Liberals were in an enviable position. As the opposition, they could denounce the Tories without having to offer concrete alternative policies. On the controversial schools question, for example, Wilfrid Laurier had not taken a strong stand during the stormy parliamentary session of 1896. During the election campaign, the Liberal leader promised that a Liberal government, if elected, would end the dispute through compromise with the Manitoba Liberal government, in a way that would respect provincial rights: "If it was in my power," he said during a speech at Morrisburg, Ontario in October 1895, "and if I had the responsibility, I would try the sunny way." To voters weary of the wrangling between the federal government and the provinces, the "sunny way" seemed appealing. In Quebec, the Liberals also had the advantage of a French-Canadian Catholic leader. Israël Tarte, who worked faithfully for Laurier in the province, reminded Quebeckers that if they turned Laurier down, they would never live to see a French-Canadian prime minister in Ottawa.

85

The Liberals narrowly won the election of 1896. They tied the Conservatives in the number of seats won outside of Quebec, and obtained forty-nine, or two-thirds of Quebec's own sixty-five seats. Quebec, which had ceased to be a Tory stronghold, was instrumental in putting the Liberals in power.

LAURIER-GREENWAY COMPROMISE

Immediately Laurier opened negotiations with Thomas Greenway, Manitoba's premier. They struck a compromise: there would be no state-supported denominational schools, but religious instruction would be allowed in the public schools for half an hour at the end of each day. Catholic teachers could be employed in urban schools with forty Catholic pupils or in rural districts with twenty-five. On the language question, it was agreed that when 10 of the pupils in any school system spoke the French language or any language other than English as their native language, the teaching of such pupils shall be conducted in English and that other language, "upon the bilingual system."

The French-Canadian Catholic minority in Manitoba would have obtained more under the Conservatives' remedial legislation. The compromise allowed religious instruction but led to the abolition of the state-supported separate school system. French was retained when sufficient population warranted it; but it lost its status of equality with English, as had been the case in the Manitoba Act of 1870. Instead it became a language like any other in Manitoba, all of which were unofficial except English. (In 1916, at the height of World War I, even the bilingual clause of the Laurier-Greenway compromise was abolished making English the only language of instruction in the province's schools.)

The agreement with Manitoba did not silence the opposition, however. The Roman Catholic hierarchy in Canada accused Laurier of capitulating to the English-Canadian Protestants. Some Canadian bishops sent a delegation to Rome to appeal to the pope to intervene on behalf of the Manitoba Catholics. Laurier argued that the agreement was the best that could be hoped for, given the Catholics' minority position. To try to win greater concessions would only lead to "a holy war." Confused by the conflicting messages, the pope sent an adviser, Monsignor Merry del Val, to investigate so that the Vatican could better judge how to respond. In the end, the pope condemned the Manitoba Schools Act of 1890, declared the Laurier-Greenway compromise unsatisfactory, but appealed to Catholics to accept the situation. Laurier had won.

In the 1880s provincial rights became an influential political force. Regional protest had arisen in the Maritimes, the West, and Quebec, to the point where the two national parties could ignore such discontent only at their political peril. In addition, social and religious controversies over the execution of Louis Riel, the Jesuit Estates Act, and the Manitoba schools question left English- and French-speaking Canadians deeply divided. These disputes contributed to undermining the political strength of the Conservative party and to the election of the federal Liberals, considered the champions of provincial rights, regional protest, and minority rights.

NOTE

[1] John L. Tobias, "Canada's Subjugation of the Plains Cree, 1879–1885," in *Readings in Canadian History : Post Confederation*, edited by R. Douglas Francis and Donald B. Smith (Toronto, 1986), pp. 107–8.

Related Readings

The topics in this chapter can be examined in greater depth in the following articles from R. Douglas Francis and Donald B. Smith, *Readings in Canadian History: Post-Confederation*; 2d ed. (Toronto, 1986): George Stanley, "Louis Riel: Patriot or Rebel?", pp. 82–102; John L. Tobias, "Canada's Subjugation of the Plains Cree, 1879–1885," pp. 103–27; W. L. Morton, "Confederation, 1870–1896: The End of the Macdonaldian Constitution and the Return to Duality," pp. 103–46; and J. R. Miller, "Unity/Diversity: The Canadian Experience, From Confederation to the First World War", pp. 147–56.

BIBLIOGRAPHY

For an overview of dominion-provincial relations in the late nineteenth century, see P. B. Waite, *Canada, 1874–1896: Arduous Destiny* (Toronto, 1971), and the *Report of the Royal Commission on Dominion Provincial Relations*; Book 1 (Ottawa, 1940).

The provincial rights movements in Ontario is discussed in J. C. Morrison, "Oliver Mowat and the Development of Provincial Rights in Ontario: A Study in Dominion-Provincial Relations, 1867–1896," in *Three History Theses* (Toronto, 1961), and Christopher Armstrong, *The Politics of Federalism: Ontario's Relations with the Federal Government, 1867–1942* (Toronto, 1981). On political protest in Atlantic Canada in the 1880s, see T. W. Acheson, "The Maritimes and 'Empire Canada'," in *Canada and the Burden of Unity*, edited by D. J. Bercuson (Toronto, 1977), pp. 87–114; E. R. Forbes, *Aspects of Maritime Regionalism, 1867–1927* (Ottawa, 1983); and George Rawlyk, ed., *The Atlantic Provinces and the Problem of Confederation* (Halifax, 1979). Rawlyk also deals with developments in Newfoundland in the 1880s and 1890s, as does Frederick W. Rowe, *A History of Newfoundland and Labrador* (Toronto, 1980).

On western Canada, see T. D. Regehr, "Western Canada and the Burden of National Transportation Policies" in *Canada and the Burden of Unity*, edited by D. J. Bercuson (Toronto, 1977), pp. 115–41.

The most authoritative account of the Northwest uprising is Bob Beal and Rob Macleod, *Prairie Fire: The 1885 North-West Rebellion* (Edmonton, 1984). Hugh A. Dempsey explains the participation of Big Bear's band in *Big Bear* (Vancouver, 1984). On Louis Riel, see the readings cited for chapter 2 as well as Thomas Flanagan, *Louis 'David' Riel: 'Prophet of the New World'* (Toronto, 1979), and his *Riel and the Rebellion: 1885 Reconsidered*, (Saskatoon, 1983).

Quebec's views on dominion-provincial relations are analysed in R. Cook, *Provincial Autonomy; Minority Rights and the Compact Theory, 1867–1921* (Ottawa, 1969), and in Arthur Silver, *The French-Canadian Idea of Confederation, 1864–1900* (Toronto, 1982). See as well Mason Wade, *The French Canadians: 1760–1945* (Toronto, 1955), pp. 331–446, and S. M. Trofimenkoff, *The Dream of Nation: A Social and Intellectual History of Quebec* (Toronto, 1982), pp. 150–66.

J. R. Miller's *Equal Rights: The Jesuit Estates Act Controversy* (Montreal, 1979) deals with that subject in depth. On the Manitoba school question, consult Paul Crunican, *Priests and Politicians: Manitoba Schools and the Election of 1896* (Toronto, 1974); Lovell Clark has compiled a collection of sources in *The Manitoba School Question: Majority Rule or Minority Rights* (Toronto, 1968). On D'Alton McCarthy's role in the controversy, see J. R. Miller, "D'Alton McCarthy, Equal Rights, and the Origins of the Manitoba Schools Question," *Canadian Historical Review*, 14 (1973): 369–92.

88

The politics of the 1890s are discussed in the following: John T. Saywell's introduction to *The Canadian Journal of Lady Aberdeen, 1893–1898*, (Toronto, 1960); Lovell Clark's "Macdonald's Conservative Successors, 1891–1896," in *Character and Circumstance: Essays in Honour of Donald Grant Creighton*, edited by John Moir, (Toronto, 1970), pp. 143–162; H. B. Neatby and J. T. Saywell "Chapleau and the Conservative Party in Quebec," *Canadian Historical Review*, 37 (1956): 1–22; and H. Blair Neatby, *Laurier and a Liberal Quebec: A Study in Political Management* (Toronto, 1973).

CHAPTER FIVE

Imperialism, Continentalism, and Nationalism, 1867–1909

After Confederation, the new dominion faced three choices in terms of its   *89*
position in the world: it could seek greater unity with Britain, closer
economic or political association with the United States, or increased independence. All three possibilities—imperialism, continentalism, or independence—were, in their own way, forms of Canadian nationalism, since
each was debated in light of the advancement of Canadian interests. In
the end, Canadians blended all three, evolving a close relationship with
both Britain and the United States, while maintaining a degree of autonomy. This became the basic convention of Canada's foreign policy for the
next half-century.

North Atlantic Triangle

In the early years of Confederation Canada's stability was threatened by
the United States. The North had just won the Civil War. During that
conflict Britain had allowed the South to purchase ships and ammunition
for the Confederate cause. One such ship, the *Alabama*, inflicted heavy
losses on American merchant shipping, and the North demanded compensation from Britain after the war. British ships, such as the *Trent*, had
also carried Confederate envoys to England. As a final irritant, on one
occasion, Canada had become a base for Confederate soldiers to attack the
North.

The Americans, in turn, had contributed to the tension with Canada.
After the Civil War they had allowed the Fenian Brotherhood, a radical
group of American Irishmen who hoped to capture Canada for use as a
bargaining tool for Irish independence, to make raids across the border.
The Fenians continued their attacks until 1871. Furthermore, prominent
American leaders talked openly of annexing Canada as part of their "manifest destiny" to control the North American continent. After the United

States purchased Alaska from Russia in 1867, many Americans expected to acquire British Columbia. Congress also cancelled the Reciprocity Treaty in 1866, and some Congressmen assumed that economic collapse would follow, causing the British North American colonies to seek union with the States. Many Americans believed that Canada was like a ripe pear— ready to drop on its own into the lap of its southern neighbour.

Canada's continued independent existence from the United States depended on Britain's support. Both English- and French-speaking Canadians wanted an association with Britain and welcomed the fifteen thousand British troops stationed in the new dominion in 1867. It was the British government (anxious for economy), not Canada, which insisted on their withdrawal in 1871. The army's departure left Canada with only a poorly trained and inadequately equipped home militia to defend its borders. Fortunately by this date the Americans had agreed to respect the integrity of Canada's borders.

90   At the same time, Canadians desired greater control over their external affairs and recognition that Canada was a nation with interests different from those of Britain and the United States. Canadian leaders pressed for greater control over domestic matters, especially as they became aware of Britain's willingness to sacrifice Canada in the interests of Anglo-American harmony.

The Treaty of Washington

The Treaty of Washington reflected the intricacies of Anglo-Canadian-American relations. British and American leaders agreed to call a conference in Washington in 1870 to settle outstanding disputes between the two countries resulting chiefly from the Civil War, in particular the *Alabama* claims. The United States also wanted the right to fish in the territorial waters of the Maritimes provinces and Newfoundland and to use their ports, rights that had been denied them since 1818, except during the term of the Reciprocity Treaty of 1854–66. On the Pacific, a clear boundary line between Vancouver Island and the American mainland had not yet been determined. Canada hoped to use the fisheries question as leverage to force the Americans to renew the Reciprocity Treaty. It wanted as well compensation for damages caused by Fenian raids.

The Washington negotiations illustrate just how difficult the triangular relationship was for Canada. For the first time a Canadian, Prime Minister John A. Macdonald, attended an international conference as a participant. Although he spoke for Canada, he was officially one of the three-member British delegation and therefore was expected also to represent Britain. This dual role placed him in an awkward position, as Macdonald himself realized: "If things go well my share of the kudos will be but small and if anything goes wrong I will be made the scapegoat at all events so far as Canada is concerned."

To Macdonald's disappointment, the British were all too willing to bargain away Canadian interests for a lasting Anglo-American peace. With the unification of Germany and of Italy, potential rivals in Europe, Britain was seeking a close, friendly relationship with the United States.

The Americans did well in the settlement. They succeeded in keeping off the conference agenda the question of compensation to Canadians for the Fenian raids. They also obtained the right to fish in Canadian territorial waters in return for a cash payment (subsequently agreed upon by an arbitration committee to be $5.5 million) and free navigation in perpetuity on the St. Lawrence. By the treaty, the German emperor was asked to arbitrate the location of the Canadian-American boundary through the Gulf Islands between Vancouver Island and the United States and to judge as well the *Alabama* claims. The kaiser confirmed the U.S. claim to the Gulf Islands southeast of Victoria, including San Juan, and also awarded a $15.5 million cash settlement for the *Alabama* claims.

The Canadians received very little of a concrete nature: the right to free navigation on three remote Alaskan rivers and the import of Canadian fish into American markets duty free. Yet in one respect Canada did well: the treaty gave Canada official U.S. recognition of its existence as a separate transcontinental nation in North America, ending the danger of American annexation. Canada no longer needed the British military garrison, as its borders had been recognized.

Macdonald returned from Washington conscious of the need for a greater Canadian voice in deciding imperial policy. The prime minister later appointed Alexander Tilloch Galt, who had briefly served as the dominion's first finance minister in 1867, as high commissioner for Canada in London in 1880. Only reluctantly did the British government approve the new quasi-diplomatic post. Galt's tasks included the promotion of Canada's exports to Britain, the fostering of British investment, and the encouragement of British emigration to the Canadian Northwest.

Continentalism

Canadian-American relations were a central issue in Canadian politics in the 1880s and 1890s. Generally speaking, the Liberals more than the Conservatives favoured stronger continental ties during this period. Closer ties between the two countries could take many forms. Freer trade, for example, was a possibility and one that appealed particularly to the staple producers—fishermen, lumbermen, and farmers—anxious for American markets for their natural products. Some Liberals simply wanted a return to the Reciprocity Treaty of 1854 or a restricted reciprocity agreement on natural products only. Others favoured unrestricted reciprocity or free trade in some manufactured goods as well as in natural resources; still others proposed commercial union or an integrated economic union with a free interchange of all products, a sharing of internal revenue taxes, and a common tariff policy against other countries (somewhat like the present-day European Common Market). At the extreme end of this spectrum was political union.

All of these positions naturally depended on the Americans' openness to some kind of association. In the 1870s protectionists dominated the Senate, and the Republican governments turned down Canadian offers to renegotiate a reciprocity treaty. The situation was more promising in 1884 with the victory of the Democratic candidate Grover Cleveland as president. He pledged to reduce the tariff and made it a major issue in his 1888 re-election campaign. He lost, however, to the Republican candidate, Benjamin Harrison. The Republicans rescinded a Democratic fisheries treaty negotiated by Cleveland and passed the McKinley Tariff Act in 1890, which raised duties to an even higher level.

THE TRADE QUESTION AND THE ELECTION OF 1891

Nevertheless, in Canada support for lower trade barriers persisted. In the general election of 1891 the Liberals favoured closer Canadian-American ties, although they were divided on how best to achieve them. Goldwin Smith, the outspoken historian cum journalist, advocated political union. He wrote *Canada and the Canadian Question*, a political tract for the election campaign. In it the former Oxford University history professor argued that Canada was an unnatural country economically, geographically, and culturally; political expedience alone held it together. Its natural destiny lay in a larger North American nation. The volume has been called "the most pessimistic book that has ever been written about Canada."[1] Smith looked towards continental union as the means to assimilate the troublesome French Canadians, to open up the natural north–south trade axis, and to achieve a federation of North America's English-speaking people.

Richard Cartwright, former minister of finance in the Mackenzie government, saw a customs union between the two countries with a common tariff against outsiders, as being in Canada's best interest. Commercial union received a boost when Samuel J. Ritchie, an American businessman with interests in Canadian mines and railways, and Erastus Wiman, a New York financier who was a Canadian by birth, founded (with Goldwin Smith's support), Commercial Union leagues in Toronto and other parts of Ontario. These leagues worked closely with provincial farm groups, and supplied speeches and literature on the virtues of unrestricted reciprocity with the United States. Edward Farrer, an editorial writer for the

Toronto *Globe*, wrote a pamphlet for limited private circulation during the election campaign in which he tried to convince Americans that unrestricted reciprocity would force Canada into annexation. The Conservatives got hold of the proofs of the pamphlet and used them as evidence of the Liberals' supposedly treasonous position.

Edward Blake, leader of the federal Liberal party in 1881–87, opposed unrestricted reciprocity as a threat to national interests. He was pressured into silence until after the election, when he publicly denounced unrestricted reciprocity in an open letter to his constituency of West Durham (immediately east of Toronto) to explain his stand on the free trade question. Caught in the middle was Wilfrid Laurier, the Liberal leader. Commercial union appealed to him in principle but was too extreme for a party platform, and he committed the party to unrestricted reciprocity instead.

Initially, Sir John A. Macdonald, now seventy-six years old, refused to denounce limited reciprocity. Instead, he argued that a Conservative government could best achieve that goal. He referred to his government's recent attempts in 1891 to make Canada part of the trade agreement being negotiated between the United States and Newfoundland.

93

When James Blaine, the American secretary of state, repudiated Macdonald's position, the prime minister reversed himself to endorse protectionism and closer ties with Britain. For several years Canadian manufacturers had pressured the Conservatives by publishing a manifesto in 1887 indicating that reciprocity would adversely affect the infant industries of Canada that were still struggling under the National Policy to survive a recession. Thus, midway through the election campaign the Conservatives came out strongly for protectionism. The prime minister claimed unrestricted reciprocity threatened Canada's independence, as it would lead to political union with the United States. He maintained that protectionism was the means to uphold the British connection and declared his loyalty to the British flag: "A British subject I was born, and a British subject I will die."

THE 1891 ELECTION RESULTS

The Conservatives won the election of 1891, but only by a narrow majority of twenty-seven seats. They lost seats to the Liberals in close votes in Ontario and Quebec. In both provinces the Liberals won seats in the rural areas with their policy of unrestricted reciprocity, while the Conservatives won the urban vote on the National Policy. In Quebec the Conservatives also had the clergy on their side. Archbishop Edouard Fabre of Montreal and other members of the church hierarchy published pastoral letters warning that a vote for the Liberals and unrestricted reciprocity was a vote for annexation to the United States.

94

THE OLD FLAG, THE OLD POLICY, THE OLD LEADER.

McCord Museum, Montreal.

During the election of 1891, the Conservatives championed continued association with Britain under "the old flag," the "old policy" of national protection, and the "old leader." By implication the Liberals offered close association with the United States, and free trade, under an unknown and untried leader (Wilfrid Laurier).

Even with this clerical support, the Conservatives won five fewer Quebec seats than in the 1887 election. The Conservatives made their gains in the outlying provinces—"the shreds and patches of Confederation," as a disgruntled Cartwright called them. They won in all three Maritime provinces on the loyalty issue and returned fourteen out of a possible fifteen seats in the West. With the open backing of the CPR, they had won every seat but one (in Manitoba) along the railway's main line from Vancouver to Montreal. When asked about that one loss, Cornelius Van Horne, director of the CPR, replied that must have been a case of pure oversight on the CPR's part!

The election of 1891 defeated unrestricted reciprocity. The Liberals now dropped the issue, and it was nearly two decades before they again championed "continentalism."

Imperialism   95

Many English-speaking Canadians favoured the British connection through greater imperial unity. Canadian imperialism flourished in the depressed and racially charged 1880s and 1890s. After 1875 British attitudes to empire had changed. Benjamin Disraeli's statement in the 1850s that colonies were "millstones around the neck of the British" had given way to a new imperialism in the late nineteenth century. Ironically, Disraeli, the Conservative prime minster, came to appreciate the importance of colonies to maintain Britain's military and economic supremacy. They were increasingly more important as Germany and Italy emerged united and powerful and as the United States became a world power after the Civil War. These latecomers to imperial rivalry joined France as Britain's major competitors for colonial possessions in Asia, Africa, and the Pacific.

The resulting rivalry meant competition for colonial markets and for world trade, which gave an economic base to imperialism. The cry from imperialists "trade follows the flag" led both British manufacturers and many in the working class to support imperialism in the late nineteenth century. Acute depression in England during the 1880s and 1890s, along with competition from abroad, also strengthened the new movement.

Imperialism, however, was more than trade, tariffs, and guns; it was an intellectual and spiritual force. Imperialists believed implicitly in the superiority of the Anglo-Saxon race. Applying Charles Darwin's theory of evolution in the animal kingdom to society, race theorists argued that some races were born superior—were better fit to survive—than others, that in Britain and in colonies settled by whites the Anglo-Saxons were the elite. Charles Dilke, later undersecretary of the Foreign Office, wrote *Greater Britain* (1869) as his "conception, however imperfect, of the grandeur of our race, already girding the earth, which it is destined, perhaps, eventually to overspread." Imperialists argued that this superior position made it imperative for Anglo-Saxons to spread their "virtues"—their Anglo-Saxon values and Christian beliefs (the two were seen as synonymous)—to the less fortunate "infidels" of Asia, Africa, and the Pacific islands. This was "the white man's burden," as Rudyard Kipling expressed it.

IMPERIALISM AS NATIONALISM

Canadian imperialists believed that Canada had much to offer the Empire in the way of trade, military assistance, and common spiritual values. In turn, the Empire could elevate Canada's status; in this sense, as historian Carl Berger has written, "imperialism was one form of Canadian nationalism."[2] These imperialists thought that Canada was destined to become in the near future the seat of the British Empire; throughout history, they pointed out, all great races had come out of northern climates. English-speaking Canadians were the last group of Anglo-Saxons to struggle in a cold, rugged, northern climate, and this struggle "in the true north, strong and free" had strengthened their will to survive and prepared them to assume the mantle of imperial grandeur as it passed from British hands. While Canadians aided the Empire, they would also be helping themselves. Canadian imperialists envisioned imperial unity as a means to free Canada from economic depression, ethnic tension, provincialism, and threatened American annexation, enabling it to reach greater heights—"a sense of power"—in the world.

Imperialism drew its greatest support in Canada from a small English-speaking social and political elite (mainly Protestant ministers, lawyers, teachers, and politicians) whose status in the new industrial society appeared threatened by the rise of the *nouveaux riches*. They formed the Imperial Federation League in 1887, a branch of the British organization by the same name which had been established three years earlier. Descendants of United Empire Loyalists joined in large numbers, giving the league its greatest support in Ontario and the Maritimes.

In contrast, French Canadians in Quebec were unsympathetic to the "Anglo-Saxon race" ideology underlying English-Canadian imperialism and, if they were interested in any empire, wanted an empire of faith based on the dominance of the Catholic church. Farmers and the working class in English Canada saw the imperial tie as a deterrent to free trade with the United States.

LEADERS OF THE CANADIAN IMPERIAL FEDERATION LEAGUE

The League attracted some colourful individuals. In Toronto, Colonel George Taylor Denison was the most visible member. A descendant of a long line of enthusiasts of the British military tradition, Denison wanted to follow an army career, although he was educated as a lawyer. A supporter of the Confederacy in the American Civil War, he hated the North, especially its materialism. In 1866 he fought against the Fenians.

As a young man he tried a number of unsuccessful careers. Finally, his connections secured him the post of police magistrate in Toronto. Apparently speed not justice was his main concern; Denison prided himself on once trying one hundred and eighty cases in three hours—an average of one a minute. He was by the 1880s ready to commit himself to a new cause, and the Imperial Federation League provided the opportunity.

Denison saw the League as a military organization. His book on the League, *The Struggle for Imperial Unity* (1892), could have been entitled, in the words of one reviewer, "How I Saved the Empire." John S. Willison, editor-in-chief of the *Globe*, chided Denison publicly for saving Canadians from their enemies even when they did not recognize they were being threatened. Willison was one of the few able to tease this ardent imperialist, for Denison had an explosive temper that could be triggered at the slightest provocation. For thirty years, from 1880 to 1910, the fiery magistrate was Canada's most vocal spokesman for imperial unity. 97

Two other "Georges," George Munro Grant and George Parkin, belonged to the Imperial Federation League. Unlike Denison, they gave the movement intellectual respectability. Grant became a Presbyterian minister after his schooling at Pictou Academy in Nova Scotia, his native province. He attended Glasgow University in the 1850s, when Scottish clerics were debating the social function of Christianity. At university he became convinced of the need for a ministry that reached out to society and became an advocate for social change. In 1877 he was appointed principal of Queen's University, a position he held for a quarter-century until his death in 1902.

Grant's imperialism was an outgrowth of his religious fervour. He saw imperial unity and Christian unity as one and the same thing, for British imperialism embodied Protestant Christian values. He admonished Anglo-Saxons to sacrifice themselves to save the Empire in distant corners of the globe, to allow others to benefit from the virtues of the "Anglo-Saxon race." The British Empire, he believed, was an instrument for the betterment of mankind.

George Parkin was a more fervent champion than Grant for the humanitarian side of imperialism. John S. Ewart once described the native New Brunswicker as "the prince of Imperialists and their first missionary." Parkin never became a minister but found an outlet for his missionary zeal in education. The youngest of thirteen children of a poor family, he began teaching high school in his native province. In the 1880s the school teacher joined and became a leader of the Imperial Federation Movement, about which he wrote three books. He served from 1895 to 1902 as principal of Upper Canada College in Toronto, until he left to become organizing secretary for the Rhodes Scholarship Trust, an educational fund begun to honour Cecil Rhodes, the British South African arch-imperialist. The scholarship sent gifted students from the Dominions to Oxford University.

As a member of the Imperial Federation League, Parkin toured the Empire on a meagre salary to spread the gospel of imperial federation. His *Imperial Federation: The Problem of National Unity* (1892) set out a vision of a single British imperial nation that would unite all Anglo-Saxons in the world into one cultural entity. The incentive behind imperial unity for Parkin was a sense of religious mission—"to assume vast responsibilities in the government of weak and alien races." In his view the British Empire was an instrument for the betterment of mankind providing freedom from ignorance and advancement for the non-white races.

Stephen Leacock was one of the younger members of the Imperial Federation League and later of the British Empire League, as the organization became known after 1896. Born in England in 1869, he grew up on a farm near Lake Simcoe in Ontario where his family lived after 1876. After schooling at Upper Canada College and the University of Toronto, he became modern-language master at Upper Canada College in 1891. He never enjoyed teaching, which he described as "the only trade I could find that needed neither experience nor intellect," and so left in 1899 to study economics and political science at the University of Chicago. In 1903, with his Ph.D. in hand, he joined the staff at McGill, where he taught economics and political science for thirty-five years.

Best remembered as one of Canada's finest humorists, Leacock had a serious side that was expressed in his writings on imperialism. He wanted Canada to play a greater role in imperial affairs so as to elevate the country beyond the role of a small provincial nation. The Empire was Canada's means of achieving greatness—a "Great Canada," to use the title of one of his imperialist writings.

These men—Denison, Grant, Parkin, and Leacock—led the imperial movement in Canada in the pre-World War I era. Their writings and public speeches emphasized Canada's interest in distant imperialist wars and in British affairs. They argued for closer links with the mother country through a transatlantic cable and through the penny post. While large segments of the middle-class English-speaking population listened, many in Canada could not accept the new imperialism—French Canadians, Métis, Indians, and the growing number of non-Anglo-Saxon immigrants. Thus Canadian imperialism in the end divided and threatened the country rather than united it.

QUEEN VICTORIA'S DIAMOND JUBILEE
AND IMPERIALISM

British imperialism peaked in the 1890s. Joseph Chamberlain, appointed to the Colonial Office in 1895, personified the imperial spirit. Two years later, Queen Victoria celebrated her Diamond Jubilee (sixty years as the ruling monarch) in a spectacular celebration to show the world the splendour and the might of the British Empire. Representatives from all the colonies, including Canada's new prime minister, Wilfrid Laurier, joined in the military parades and reviews, assemblies of school children, patriotic speeches, unveiling of monuments, and numerous banquets. Special commemorative stamps were issued, among them a Canadian stamp showing a map of the world splashed with red for all the British possessions. The inscription read: "We hold a greater empire than has been."

99

The South African War

The South African or Boer War was part of this imperial grandeur. Fighting had broken out between Britain's Cape Colony and the two Afrikaner, or Boer, republics—the Transvaal and the Orange Free State. The Boers were descended from the original Dutch settlers in South Africa. Chamberlain, the British colonial secretary, saw the war as an opportunity for Britain to display its imperial unity through a token contribution of military force from its various self-governing colonies.

Canadian newspapers, especially in Toronto and Montreal, whipped their readers into an emotional frenzy in support of the British position in South Africa. They ran the biased reports issued by the South African League Congress, a front organization for the interests of Cecil Rhodes, the imperial enthusiast and mining magnate. Colonel Sam Hughes, an Ontario Orangeman, offered to lead a regiment or brigade of volunteers for South African service. At the same time, Lord Minto, the governor general, and Major General Edward Hutton, commander of the Canadian militia, worked out plans for a Canadian contingent, without informing Laurier. Then on October 3, 1899, the *Canadian Military Gazette*, a non-governmental but respected publication, announced that in the event of war the Canadian government would offer troops. This announcement coincided with a cable from Joseph Chamberlain thanking Canada for its "offer to serve in South Africa." His thanks were premature, since the Canadian government had not yet made an official statement of support.

Prime Minister Laurier refused to dispatch troops to fight in a distant war without Parliament's consent. He stated his views to reporters of the Toronto *Globe* on October 4, 1899:

There is no menace to Canada, and although we may be willing to contribute troops, I do not see how we can do so. Then again, how could we do so without Parliament granting us the money? We simply could not do anything. In other words we should have to summon Parliament.

The South African War aroused a strong nationalist response in Quebec. French-Canadian newspapers reported the war as an example of imperial aggression. If French Canadians sympathized with anyone in the struggle, it was with the Boers, whom they regarded as a kindred cultural minority fighting a common oppressor. Israël Tarte, Laurier's leading Quebec minister, opposed Canadian participation without the dominion obtaining a voice in the British councils; his view was: "Not a man, not a cent for South Africa."

100

THE CANADIAN COMPROMISE ON THE SOUTH AFRICAN WAR

For two days Laurier's Cabinet met to find a solution. Tarte threatened to resign if Canada authorized troops, while Ontario's William Mulock, the postmaster general, who supported Britain, stormed out of the meeting in protest at the government's delay in sending volunteers. On October 13, 1899, Laurier devised a compromise solution. He proposed that "in view of the well known desire of a great many Canadians who are ready to take service under such conditions," the government would equip and transport a volunteer force of one thousand men for service on the British side. Once in South Africa, however, the troops would become the British government's responsibility. Laurier reminded imperialists and French Canadians alike that this action should not be "construed as a precedent for future action." In the end, Canada sent 7300 men to South Africa. Of this total, 245 died overseas, more than half from disease.

Nevertheless, English-speaking imperialists were unhappy. John Willison, editor of the *Globe*, wanted Canada to assume full responsibility for Canadian troops in South Africa. In Montreal, McGill students attacked the offices of the anti-war French-language newspapers— *La Patrie, Le Journal*, and *La Presse* —and fought street battles with French-Canadian university students in Montreal. Also in Montreal, Margaret Polson Murray, a native of Scotland and a longtime resident of Canada, founded the Imperial Order of the Daughters of the Empire (IODE), an organization whose motto "One Flag, One Throne, One Country" declared its members' support for a united empire. It sought to promote Britain and British institutions in the schools.

In Parliament, Henri Bourassa, a young politician and a brilliant orator like his grandfather the legendary Louis-Joseph Papineau, accused Laurier of yielding to the fanatical imperialists. Bourassa resigned his seat on October 18, 1899, in protest, only to be re-elected by acclamation six months later. He argued that the mere fact of sending troops had established a dangerous precedent, since Britain would expect support every time the country got entangled in a foreign war.

Joseph Chamberlain, hoping to capitalize on the imperial sentiment generated by the South African War, called a colonial conference in 1902. "The time has come," Chamberlain noted, "when the defence of the Empire, and its military and naval resources, have become the common concern of the whole Empire and not of the Mother Country alone, and that joint action, or at least joint organization, with regard to this subject should be organized on a permanent footing."

Laurier, however, acting cautiously on the imperial question in light of the divisions caused by Canada's involvement in the Boer War, refused to accept a consolidated imperial defence force. He agreed that Canadians must contribute to their own defence but assured Parliament on the eve of the colonial conference that he would not "bring Canada into the vortex of militarism which is the curse and blight of Europe."

101

BOURASSA'S AND LAURIER'S VIEWS OF IMPERIALISM

The basic disagreement between Laurier and Bourassa originated in their views of imperialism. Laurier saw the British Empire as the leading protector of liberal values of liberty and justice. As historian Blair Neatby notes he had "a sincere respect for the British political system, and for British political ideals, and even for British society."[3] Thus, Laurier could uphold imperialism without supporting imperial federation, because the Empire he envisioned respected the rights and autonomy of the nations within it. Bourassa, however, equated imperialism with militarism and commercialism. He condemned the British Empire "not because it is British, but because it is Imperial. All Empires are hateful. They stand in the way of human liberty, and true progress, intellectual and moral. They serve nothing but brutal instincts and material objects."

Although Bourassa opposed imperialism, he avoided advocating independence, at least in 1902. Like journalist Goldwin Smith, he believed that Canada was unprepared for independence. With such great internal divisions between English- and French-speaking Canadians, independence might lead to American annexation. Bourassa's ideal was a Canada eventually independent in which both linguistic groups would respect one another.

GROWING FRENCH-CANADIAN NATIONALISM

Bourassa's opposition to imperialism increased his political influence in Quebec, particularly among youth. The immediate result of the popularity of Bourassa's views was the founding of a nationalist organization, the *Ligue Nationaliste* in 1903 and of a newspaper, *Le Nationaliste*, in 1904. The organization had a three-point programme: Canadian autonomy with an informal British connection; provincial autonomy within a federal state; and the advancement of Canada intellectually and economically.

Coincidental with the rise of the *Ligue Nationaliste*, other nationalists formed the *Association catholique de la jeunesse canadienne-française* (ACJC) in 1904. This group drew its largest following from the classical colleges of the Montreal region. Under the guidance of Catholic leaders, most notably the abbé Lionel Groulx of Valleyfield, the group's nationalism had a religious overtone similar to that of the ultramontane nationalists a few decades earlier (see chapter 3).

102

ACJC members found inspiration in the writings of Jules-Paul Tardivel, a Franco-American born in Kentucky who came to Quebec in 1868 to study French and then took up the causes of ultramontanism and nationalism. In his newspaper, *La Vérité*, and in *Pour la Patrie* (1895), a futuristic novel, Tardivel proposed Quebec's separation from Canada.

In an exchange published in 1904 in their respective newspapers Tardivel and Bourassa outlined their conceptions of French Canada. Tardivel distinguished between his exclusive French-Canadian form of nationalism and Bourassa's broader Canadian nationalism: "Our own nationalism is French-Canadian nationalism. . . . For us our fatherland is—we do not say precisely the Province of Quebec—but French Canada; the nation we wish to see founded at the hour marked by Divine Providence is the French-Canadian nation."

Bourassa replied with his opposing views on nationalism and that of the *Ligue*:

> [It is] a Canadian nationalism founded upon the duality of races and on the particular traditions which this duality involves. . . . For us the fatherland is all Canada, that is, a federation of distinct races and autonomous provinces. The nation that we wish to see develop is the Canadian nation, composed of French Canadians and English Canadians, that is of two elements separated by language and religion, and by the legal dispositions necessary to the preservation of their respective traditions, but united in a feeling of brotherhood, in a common attachment to the common fatherland.

In this interchange lies the essence of two currents of twentieth-century French-Canadian nationalism, one leading to separatism, the other to a bilingual and bicultural country.

Alaska Boundary Dispute

At the turn of the century a major border dispute led to growing support among English-speaking Canadians for Canadian control over its foreign policy. John Bartlet Brebner, a historian of Canadian-American relations, describes the Alaska boundary dispute as "the most unfortunate single incident, the worst setback to reasonable understanding in Canadian-American relations since the War of 1812."[4]

The origin of the dispute dated to the Anglo-Russian Treaty of 1825, which had established an ambiguous boundary line running north from Portland Channel "to follow the summit of the mountains situated parallel to the coast," in the words of the treaty, but not to exceed ten marine leagues from the sea. The problem was that the territory encompassed many mountain chains and an uneven coast.

The Americans inherited the Russian position on the border when they purchased Alaska in 1867. They sought a continuous border along the coast, and after 1871, when British Columbia joined Confederation, they denied Canada's claim to several fiords with access to the Yukon. The news that gold had been discovered in the Yukon (the big strike had come on August 16, 1897, at Rabbit Creek, a tributary of the Klondike River) made the boundary question of utmost importance. Prospectors crossed the mountain passes into the Yukon, and by the summer of 1898, Dawson City had a population of more than twenty thousand people, making it temporarily the largest Canadian city west of Winnipeg. In June 1898 the federal government made the Yukon a separate territory with its own commissioner, to help prevent the area from becoming a *de facto* part of Alaska.

103

Both the Canadians and the Americans, along with the British, agreed to settle the issue through a joint high commission. Britain, which had sovereign control over Canada's foreign policy, made the appointments and named five Canadians to the six-man Anglo-Canadian commission. It appeared at first as though a quick settlement could be reached, but negotiations broke down as each side refused to compromise. The commission ceased to meet after February 1899.

In Canada, underlying the border dispute were deeper issues, such as long-standing anti-Americanism and a jingoistic outlook; both were the result of the country's involvement in the South African War and Canada's new found economic prosperity. Americans saw the dispute as part of their manifest destiny, a belief originating in the early nineteenth century that the United States had a God-given right to control the North American continent. Theodore Roosevelt, the new U.S. president, refused to consider any decision short of a complete victory on the Alaskan question. As with the Washington Treaty of 1871, Britain wanted only a settlement that would keep the United States as a possible ally in the event of a future war with Germany.

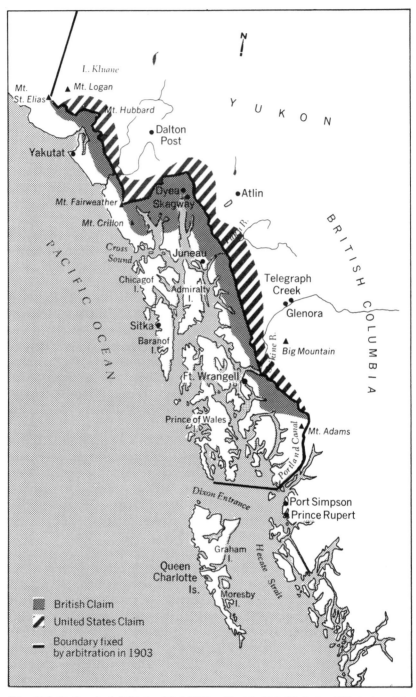

Edgar McInnis, *Canada: A Political and Social History* (Toronto: Holt, Rinehart and Winston), p. 468.

Alaska Boundary Dispute, 1903

After much discussion, the U.S. and Britain, along with Canada, agreed in 1902 to appoint a six-member tribunal (three from each side) to review the problem through the courts and not, as the Canadians had hoped, by arbitration. The American appointees—Secretary of War Elihu Root and Senators Henry Cabot Lodge and George Turner—far from being impartial, were determined to secure the full acceptance of the American claim. Furthermore, Roosevelt confidentially informed the British that should they fail to win the American case, he would "run the line as we claim it." Britain appointed a British judge and two Canadian lawyers.

In the end, Lord Alverstone, the British member, sided with the Americans. He accepted the American position that the boundary line should be around the heads of the inlets, giving the United States territorial control of them. He also agreed to the equal division of the four islands at the mouth of Portland Canal. By a vote of four to two, the commission voted in favour of this settlement. Both Canadian commissioners voted against, and refused to affix their signatures to, the award of the tribunal.

105

Whether Alverstone's decision was strictly for diplomatic reasons has been debated ever since by Canadian historians. Most recent writers tend to argue that the Canadian position was actually the weaker of the two, at the same time as the Americans showed poor taste in their bellicose handling of the issue.

Regardless of the merits of Alverstone's decision, many Canadians, including the prime minister, considered it "one of those concessions which have made British diplomacy odious to Canadian people." The Alaska boundary dispute conveyed a lesson to many English-speaking Canadians, one that brought them one step closer to French-speaking Canadians: Canadians needed greater control over their own affairs, since Britain could not be relied upon to safeguard Canadian interests.

After the contentious Alaska boundary question had been resolved in 1903, Canadian-American relations improved. One controversial issue that remained, however, concerned disputes relating to the use of boundary waters between the two countries. The Boundary Waters Treaty of 1909 provided that interference or diversions on either side of the border that caused injury on the other side would, in the words of the treaty, "entitle the injured parties to the same legal remedies as if such injury took place in the country where such diversion or interference occurs." The treaty also created an international joint commission to decide future boundary waters disputes. What is most significant about the Boundary Waters Treaty is that it was largely shaped by Canadian policy makers and reflected English-speaking Canadians' desire for a greater degree of independence.

For more than a quarter of a century after Confederation, Canadian leaders had debated the nation's destiny. Many politicians and critics felt that Canada was incapable of being an independent nation and sought some form of association with either Britain in an imperial federation or the

United States in a continental association as the means to enhance Canada's national status. Gradually, however, as the nation prospered and its population expanded rapidly, many Canadians felt confidence in Canada's survival as an independent nation, an idea that gained widespread support during World War I.

NOTES

[1] Frank H. Underhill, *The Image of Confederation* (Toronto, 1964), p. 27.
[2] Carl Berger, *The Sense of Power: Studies in the Ideas of Canadian Imperialism, 1867–1914* (Toronto, 1970), p. 259.
[3] H. Blair Neatby, "Laurier and Imperialism," in *Imperial Relations in the Age of Laurier*, edited by C. Berger (Toronto, 1969), p. 3
[4] John Bartlet Brebner, *North Atlantic Triangle: The Interplay of Canada, The United States and Great Britain* (Toronto, 1966), p. 264.

BIBLIOGRAPHY

The most comprehensive survey of Canada's relations with Britain and the United States is C. P. Stacey, *Canada and the Age of Conflict: A History of Canadian External Policies*, vol. 1: *1867–1921* (Toronto, 1977). On the North Atlantic Triangle relationship in the late nineteenth century, see John Bartlet Brebner, *The North Atlantic Triangle: The Interplay of Canada, The United States and Great Britain* (New York, 1945). W. L. Morton discusses the Treaty of Washington in *The Critical Years: The Union of British North America, 1857–1873* (Toronto, 1964).

Canadian-American relations in the late nineteenth century are dealt with in C. C. Tansill, *Canadian-American Relations, 1875–1911* (New Haven, 1943). Goldwin Smith's *Canada and the Canadian Question* (Toronto, 1891; reprinted 1971) is an interesting contemporary statement. Also of importance are W. R. Graham, "Sir Richard Cartwright, Wilfrid Laurier and the Liberal Party Trade Policy, 1887," *Canadian Historical Review*, 33 (1952): 1–18; and F. H. Underhill, "Edward Blake, the Liberal Party and Unrestricted Reciprocity," *Canadian Historial Association Report*, 1939, pp. 133–41; and P. B. Waite, *The Man From Halifax: Sir John Thompson, Prime Minister* (Toronto, 1985). Norman Penlington's *The Alaska Boundary Dispute: A Critical Appraisal* (Toronto, 1972), and John Munro's *The Alaska Boundary Dispute* (Toronto, 1970) cover this issue in Canadian-American relations; the latter is a collection of primary and secondary sources.

Carl Berger's *The Sense of Power: Studies in the Ideas of Canadian Imperialism 1867–1914* (Toronto, 1970) analyses the beliefs of English-Canadian imperialists. Norman Penlington's *Canada and Imperialism, 1896–1899*

(Toronto, 1965) discusses Canadian imperialism in the context of the South African War. See as well Robert Page, "Canada and the Imperial Idea in the Boer War," *Journal of Canadian Studies*, 5 (February, 1970): 33–49. Carl Berger's edited collection of essays, *Imperial Relations in the Age of Laurier* (Toronto, 1969), is also useful.

French-Canadian views on imperialism and nationalism during this era can be found in M. Wade, *The French Canadians, 1760–1945* (Toronto, 1955), pp. 447–535, and in S. M. Trofimenkoff, *The Dream of Nation: A Social and Intellectual History of Quebec* (Toronto, 1983) pp. 167–83. Joseph Levitt's *Henri Bourassa on Imperialism and Bi-culturalism* (Toronto, 1970) and his Canadian Historical Association pamphlet, *Henri Bourassa, Catholic Critic* (Toronto, 1976) summarize the ideas of this French Canadian thinker.

107

CHAPTER SIX

Immigration and Western Settlement

"Over these great plains the wave of immigration is rolling today—a wave about 500 miles long, lapping each year another ten miles in width." That was how Reverend George Lloyd, a founder of Lloydminster, Saskatchewan, in 1908 described the tens of thousands of immigrants arriving each year to settle on the Canadian prairies. They came from diverse countries—Britain, Denmark, Sweden, Norway, Germany, the Netherlands, Russia, the Austro-Hungarian Empire, Italy, and the United States—as well as from central and eastern Canada, but they had one thing in common: they were beginning a new, and, they hoped, better life in the Canadian West. They established homesteads, and gradually cleared the sea of buffalo grass that had stretched almost unbroken across the prairies until the late 1890s. They built churches and schools, provided work for tradesmen and business for merchants and professionals, and became, often reluctantly, the backbone of the central Canadian economy.

A populated West made Sir John A. Macdonald's national policy possible. The new settlers required the goods produced in eastern factories and manufacturing centres. In turn, they provided the food, especially wheat, for the growing urban population of central Canada and for export to foreign markets. A "ribbon of steel," the Canadian Pacific Railway provided the means for trade and was the lifeline connecting east and west. By 1914 Canada was an integrated country with a strong east–west economy based on western settlement.

The Pre-1896 Era

In the first thirty years after Confederation, the population of the Canadian West grew more slowly than the central Canadian nation-builders had hoped. Despite the Canadian government's generous offer of 160 acres (almost 65 ha) of free land to any prospective homesteader over twenty-one, relatively few immigrants came (although by 1885 the settler population on the Prairies already outnumbered the native peoples), preferring instead to settle in the American West. So many Canadians went south that the dominion barely maintained its population.

Nevertheless, small settlements were scattered throughout the Canadian prairies. French- and English-speaking Métis lived around Winnipeg, in the Qu'Appelle valley, around Batoche on the south branch of the Saskatchewan River, and along the North Saskatchewan River. In the 1870s so many Ontarians had settled in Manitoba that the region acquired the nickname of Ontario West. Maritimers and English-speaking Quebeckers joined them. These English-speaking Canadians had established, and by the 1880s politically and socially controlled, the new West. After the suppression of the 1885 rebellion, the Indian agents and the missionaries worked through the newly built schools to turn the Indians into self-reliant Christian farmers.

109

LOW FRENCH-CANADIAN IMMIGRATION TO THE WEST

The Roman Catholic church in the West, run by French-speaking clergy, attempted to attract French Canadians. Thousands came in the 1880s but in numbers significantly smaller than the anglophones. Distance was the church's major obstacle. New England was located on Quebec's doorstep, and almost everyone in Quebec had relatives there. Furthermore, Quebeckers could find jobs as factory workers or as labourers—work they considered much easier than farming.

In 1900 more than one million French-speaking Quebeckers lived in the United States, chiefly in New England. By contrast, the Northwest was separated from Quebec by Protestant Ontario. Moreover, railway rates were much higher for Quebeckers than for immigrants from Britain or Europe, who were allowed special reduced fares (often only one-half of the regular price). Finally, the Quebec clergy discouraged emigration, preferring instead to see the colonization of northern Quebec, where French Canadians could remain in Quebec and under the influence of the Quebec clergy. Only after intense pressure from the French-speaking Roman Catholic clergy in the Northwest did the Quebec bishops encourage westward migration, and then just among French Canadians who had already moved to the United States.

EARLY IMMIGRATION TO WESTERN CANADA

Few immigrants from outside of Canada entered the Northwest in the late nineteenth century. The first to come were Mennonites. Descendants of the radical Anabaptists of the Reformation era and followers of Menno

Simons (1496–1561), the Reformation leader in the Netherlands, they left their homes in southern Russia from fear of the intense Russification policy in the schools and the introduction of universal conscription, which went against their pacifist beliefs. The Canadian government provided travel assistance of thirty dollars per adult to "Mennonite families of good character."

Once in Canada, they were promised the right to settle in street villages or *strassendorf* (as they had known in Russia), religious freedom, and exemption from military service. The seven thousand Mennonites who came in the 1870s settled on two reserves, one southeast and the other southwest of Winnipeg. The latter reserve was on open prairie, and the Mennonites were the first of the post-Confederation European immigrants to farm prairie land.

In the mid-1870s two thousand Icelanders left their homeland with its limited supply of fertile land and a declining fishing trade to settle on the shores of Lake Winnipeg. They named their settlement "Gimli," meaning paradise, for to them Canada's agricultural and fishing conditions were ideal. They set up a democratic government and adopted a constitution for what they called the Republic of New Iceland. Difficulties beset them from the beginning, however. Grasshopper plagues and inadequate food drove them to the brink of starvation. A smallpox epidemic in 1876–77 carried off one hundred members of the community. The province of Manitoba responded to the epidemic by quarantining the Icelanders at gunpoint. Then floods in 1879 and 1880 forced many to resettle in Manitoba and in the Dakotas. Despite these setbacks, the original settlement prevailed and was even prospering by the 1880s.

Jews came in significant numbers to western Canada in the 1880s. Sir Alexander Galt, Canada's High Commissioner in London, joined the Archbishop of Canterbury and several titled English gentlemen in aiding victims of Russia's pogroms (or the massacres of Jews) and offered Manitoba as a refuge. The Canadian government encouraged them to farm, and they established rural farming communities. The most famous was New Jerusalem, near Moosomin in present-day southeastern Saskatchewan, begun in 1884. Few remained in the rural areas, however, choosing instead to become small shopowners, merchants, or labourers in prairie urban centres, particularly Winnipeg. The adjustment to the prairies, and even to Winnipeg, proved difficult for some. In a letter back home, one immigrant wrote:

> I know not in what to dip my pen, in the inkstand before me, or in the flow of tears running from the eyes of the unfortunates who have come here with me, in order to describe their lamentable conditions. One hears nothing but weeping and wailing over the prospect of wasting one's youth and spending it vainly over the desolation known as Winnipeg.

110

Some Germans, Scandinavians, and Americans also arrived in this early period of immigration. The Mormons were the largest single American group to arrive prior to 1896. Charles Ora Card, a religious leader, entrepreneur, and colonizer from Utah, first led them northward in 1887 to establish farms at Lee's Creek (later changed to Cardston in honour of their leader) in present-day southern Alberta. The Canadian government welcomed them because of their experience in dryland farming in Utah, which was necessary for farming in the arid Palliser's Triangle of southern Alberta and Saskatchewan. Some settlers in the area opposed the Mormons' practice of polygamy, sanctioned by their religion until 1890, when the church suspended it. After 1890 the North Western Coal and Navigation Company of Lethbridge arranged with the Mormon church in Utah to provide land and salaries for labourers willing to settle and irrigate the semi-arid land east of Cardston in the present-day townsites of Stirling and Magrath. Between 1887 and 1911 more than ten thousand Mormons came to Canada.

111

An Immigration Boom after 1896

Until the late 1890s the prairies had a small population. Along the railway line were isolated settlements. Farmers were few; the open spaces were a vast ocean of prairie grass. Then, in 1896, 17 000 immigrants arrived in Canada. By 1899 the figure almost tripled to 45 000 and, by 1905, reached 150 000. Many of them went directly to the prairies. A speaker to the Canadian Club in Winnipeg predicted: "In 40 or 50 years Canada will have a population of 40 to 50 million, and Saskatchewan and Alberta will be greater than Ontario in population and Winnipeg will have surpassed Toronto and Montreal." Wilfrid Laurier, prime minister during these years of large-scale immigration, predicted confidently in 1904 that the twentieth century would belong to Canada, just as the nineteenth had been that of the United States.

"PUSH" AND "PULL" FACTORS IN WESTERN SETTLEMENT

What had changed by 1896 to account for this tremendous influx of immigrants? Both "push" and "pull" factors caused many to leave their native land for Canada. The push factors varied as did the migrants themselves. Many left because of limited prospects in their homeland. The industrial revolution in Europe had raised the birth rate and decreased the death rate, which led to a larger population. In the countryside, particularly in eastern Europe, relatively poor agricultural land was being

Immigrants 1890-1914

Years	Numbers
1890	75,067
1891	82,165
1892	30,996
1893	29,633
1894	20,829
1895	18,790
1896	16,835
1897	21,716
1898	31,900
1899	44,543
1900	41,681
1901	55,747
1902	89,102
1903	138,660
1904	131,252
1905	141,465
1906	211,653
1907	272,409
1908	143,326
1909	173,694
1910	286,839
1911	331,288
1912	375,756
1913	400,870
1914	150,484

from David J. Hall, "Room to Spare," *Horizon Canada*, number 76 (1986), p. 1803.

divided into smaller parcels to provide for more people. In Galicia, the northeastern province in the Austro-Hungarian Empire, each peasant needed about seven hectares to provide for his family, yet most farms were only half that size, and some families had to get by on less than a hectare. A new class of landless peasants appeared.

In the cities, working-class people lived in cramped quarters in slum areas. The Canadian government's promise of 160 acres (64 ha) of good farmland offered an escape. The risk was better than the drudgery they now faced. For others, the move was an adventure, a chance to strike out on their own and to become self-sufficient. This was particularly true of Americans who moved north and the prosperous British immigrants who came on the advice of friends or relatives already in Canada.

For still others, like the Mennonites, Hutterites, and Doukhobors, religious persecution was the motivating force; they hoped that in a new

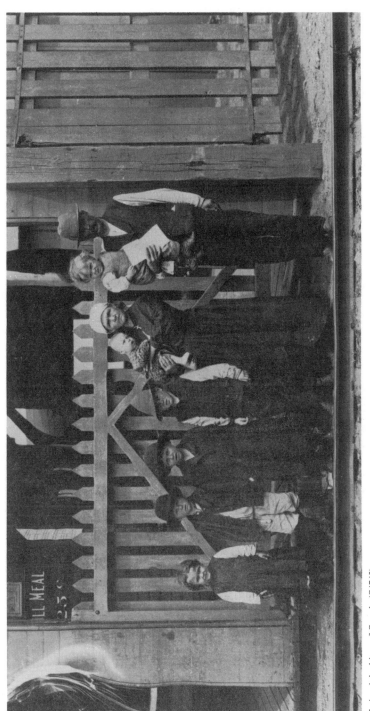

National Archives of Canada (C4745).

Hundreds of thousands of immigrants, like this Ukrainian couple with their six children, entered Canada in the years 1896 to 1914 bound mainly for "the last, best West."

homeland they could worship in peace and live free from outside interference. The Slavs and the Jews from Galicia faced ethnic persecution in the Austro-Hungarian Empire. Asians came to work on the railroads or simply to have a better way of life. Many immigrants were single men who hoped to make sufficient money either to return home prosperous or, if married, to bring their family to Canada.

The pull factors were equally varied and related to world conditions in general and to the Canadian West's attractions. The more rapid growth of international trade after 1896 meant more jobs and greater opportunity to save sufficient money to make the trip. Prosperity also increased demand for raw materials, especially food for the growing urban population. For western farmers willing to grow a crop, a ready market and a high price for Canadian wheat existed. Increased prosperity also meant declining interest rates and lower freight rates, which in turn resulted in higher profits and greater opportunity for farmers to borrow money for expansion. Most important of all, Canada benefited from the closing of the American frontier after 1890. When the best land—especially well-watered land—in the American West was gone, the Canadian West became the "last best West."

114

Improved farming conditions made the West more attractive, too. Better strains of wheat such as Marquis (discovered by the Canadian plant breeder Charles Saunders, in 1909) matured earlier than Red Fife, commonly used before Marquis was available. This meant that wheat could now confidently be grown in Alberta and Saskatchewan without a great risk of frost damage. The price of wheat quadrupled between 1901 and 1921, while production increased twentyfold in the same period. Better machinery, such as the chilled steel plow (introduced from the United States), improved harrows and seed drills, tractors and threshers, all aided farmers.

By World War I the West was experiencing a mechanical revolution. More hectarage could be brought under the plow in less time and with less effort. During the first decade of the new century, farming expanded beyond the fertile belt into northern areas such as the Peace River district and into the southern semi-arid region of the Palliser's Triangle. Other primary industries such as coal and lumber production also began. Secondary industries, such as building and railway construction, led to the development of manufacturing, particularly in Winnipeg, the largest centre on the prairies.

Clifford Sifton as Minister of the Interior

At the age of thirty-five, Clifford Sifton became minister of the interior in Wilfrid Laurier's Cabinet. The six-foot-tall lawyer was the most prominent Liberal politician in the West. Born and educated in Ontario, Sifton joined the thousands of Ontarians in the 1880s migrating to Manitoba.

He set up a law firm in Brandon, Manitoba, with his brother, Arthur, who eventually became premier of Alberta. Clifford worked hard and expected the same from those under him.

From the beginning of his career, Sifton had political ambitions. In 1888 he ran for the provincial Liberal party in Brandon and won the seat, thus beginning a political career that lasted twenty-three years. In 1891 Thomas Greenway, the Manitoba premier, appointed Sifton his attorney general, with the responsibility of defending the Manitoba Schools Act. In 1905 he resigned from Laurier's Cabinet, allegedly over the Autonomy Bills, which were intended to reinstitute separate schools in the newly created provinces of Saskatchewan and Alberta (see chapter 7). In the three years after his resignation as minister of the interior, three major scandals in his department under his ministry came to light. Whether he benefited personally from these spurious activities remains uncertain, but Sifton, who had started with nothing, left government with a personal fortune the equivalent of $20 million today.

115

SIFTON PROMOTES THE WEST

When Sifton joined the federal Cabinet in 1896 he had one major objective: to populate the West. The new minister of the interior became the driving force behind the greatest immigration scheme in Canadian history. Sifton had a definite idea as to the type of immigrant best suited to the Canadian West—"only farmers need apply." To him, agriculture was the backbone of the Canadian economy and everything else depended on its success. The best European agriculturalists, he believed, came from northern areas—Britain, Scandinavia, western or eastern Europe, while the least desirable came from the south.

A one-time Methodist lay preacher, Sifton viewed himself as a missionary for the country and promoted it to prospective immigrants. First, he completely reorganized his department, bringing it under his direct control. He dismissed previous Conservative appointees, including the deputy minister, and replaced them with Liberal supporters and loyal personal friends. Then he pressured the Hudson's Bay Company and the Canadian Pacific Railway to sell lands that had been reserved for them at reasonable rates to prospective settlers. He discontinued the practice of using land grants as incentives to railway promoters. Next he simplified the procedure for obtaining a homestead and encouraged settlers to buy up an adjacent section, if available, by allowing them the right to pre-empt such land, i.e., make an interim claim, and to purchase it at a reduced rate later from the government.

Having made these preparations, Sifton and the interior ministry then embarked on an ambitious advertising campaign, with such pamphlets as

116

The Canadian government issued millions of pamphlets, extolling in both pictures and words the virtues of the Canadian West. These pamphlets described a prosperous, happy West for all those willing to come and settle there.

The Wondrous West; Canada: Land of Opportunity; Prosperity Follows Settlement; and *The Last Best West.* His department in 1896 sent out sixty-five thousand pamphlets, and four years later the figure had reached one million. Practically every farmer in northern Britain and the American prairies received pamphlets and brochures. He advertised in thousands of newspapers, paid popular writers to set their romantic novels in the Canadian West, arranged for lecture tours and for promotional trips for potential settlers (particularly Americans), and offered bonuses to steamship agents that were based on the number of immigrants they brought to Canada. Sifton's goal was to saturate the United States and Europe with propaganda about the Canadian West.

Immigrant Experiences

Most European immigrants began their journey to western Canada by travelling first to the great ocean ports: Liverpool and London in England; Hamburg and Bremen in Germany; and Trieste, the Austro-Hungarian Empire's major port on the Adriatic. At the port of departure, medical inspections took place. Hawkers also descended upon the immigrants, *117* trying to cheat them out of their meagre funds. Next came the 10–12 day ocean crossing, often beset by raging storms on the North Atlantic. Conditions varied from ship to ship and according to class of accommodation. Steerage passengers were crowded into tiered bunks in the holds of outdated vessels. Third-class travellers had better sleeping quarters and sufficient food. Those travelling first- or second-class had luxurious cabins with the services of a steward, and they ate meals comparable to those of fine restaurants. Few deaths occurred at sea and epidemics were rare—a sharp contrast to mid-nineteenth century immigrant voyages.

Most immigrants landed at Halifax, Quebec City, Montreal, or St. John. Once inspected a final time, they were left to find their way to their destination. Some fell prey to vendors who charged exorbitant prices for food and sold the newcomers fake travel tickets. To prevent such exploitation, federal authorities directed new immigrants to immigration sheds, where they stayed until railway cars were available to take them out west. These "colonist cars" had wooden seats that converted into small berths and crowded kitchen facilities at one end. Here immigrants of all nationalities were crowded together for the long trip west. Few had any idea what to expect after their journey. Many had chosen their destinations at random, or on the recommendation of land speculators, or, if they were lucky, on the advice of relatives of friends who had gone before them.

Once at their destinations the immigrants could apply for a homestead. After purchasing supplies in the local town they would go to find their 160 acres (roughly 65 ha), marked by iron stakes bearing their section number. Very often there were no other settlers near them, and this empty land became home. Many could not cope with the loneliness and hard work, gave up, and settled in towns and cities; others persevered, living in a tent or a tar-papered shack or a sod hut until they could build a real home.

London Illustrated News, November 24, 1888. Glenbow Archives, Calgary.

The familiar means for immigrants to reach their destination was by train on colonist cars. These coaches had seats, berths, and limited cooking facilities at one end. This artist's sketch for the *London Illustrated News* shows space was at a premium.

British Immigrants

The immigrants' adjustment to Canada varied. For British immigrants, it was relatively easy, without a new language or radically different customs to learn. Some were fairly prosperous. They arrived on their own but generally settled in areas where other Englishmen or relatives and friends from Britain already lived. British homesteaders without farming experience had a difficult time adjusting; many who failed drifted into the booming prairie towns. Others first learned how to farm as hired hands.

Not all Englishmen received a warm welcome. Resentment grew against a certain type of upper- and middle-class Englishmen who came expecting special treatment in the "colony." Employment ads in western newspapers often included the words "No English Need Apply." In 1905, H.R. Whates, a London reporter covering the immigration boom for the London *Standard*, was bluntly told by Canadians: "The Englishman is too cocksure; he is too conceited, he thinks he knows everything and he won't try to learn our ways." Many Englishmen resented the pressure to assimilate, to conform. Like other immigrants, they preferred their old ways and accustomed traditions; they wanted to remain Englishmen in Canada, not become "real Canadians." Those who adjusted, however, fitted comfortably into the polyglot society of western Canada. They moved quickly into prominent positions in local politics, social clubs, and farm and labour organizations.

Poorer English immigrants arrived with the assistance of charitable societies anxious to rid England of paupers and to offer them a new start in the colonies. The Canadian government later deported many of these destitute and inexperienced would-be farmers back to Britain; in 1908, for example, 70 percent of all deportations from Canada were recent British immigrants. Among the destitute were the "home children"—paupers, waifs, and orphans from charitable homes in England. Between 1867 and 1924, one hundred thousand British children came to Canada, where they were placed in foster homes ranging across the country. The sponsoring organizations preferred rural placements, with most boys sent to apprentice as agricultural labourers and girls sent to smaller towns or rural homes to work as domestic servants. Life was lonely and in most cases difficult for these child immigrants, since they were treated as cheap labour. Many left farming and the rural areas soon after their indenture was completed, and they sought employment in service, manufacturing, logging, and mining. Few became rich or famous, but most enjoyed financial security, a comfortable life, and an opportunity for their Canadian-born children to do better.

119

BARR COLONY

One attempt was made to establish a British settlement. The Reverend Isaac Barr, a Canadian-born Anglican clergyman who wanted to save Canada for the British Empire, and George Lloyd, another Anglican clergyman who had lived in the Canadian West, advertised for hardy Englishmen willing to farm the virgin prairie soil. Their advertisement read in part: "Let us take possession of Canada. Let our cry be 'Canada for the British.' ... If you are honest and brave and intend to work hard, if you propose to lead the temperate and strenuous life, then come and cast your lot with us and we will stand together and win." More than two thousand Englishmen responded; most of them, unfortunately, were Londoners with no farming experience. "Very few had the remotest conception of what conditions actually were or what difficulties would have to be overcome," one colonist recalled, "but trusted blindly to our leader and all his promises." Later these followers dubbed themselves "Barr's lambs."

Trouble developed from the beginning, since Barr was a terrible organizer. Poor food, inadequate sleeping accommodations, and stormy weather made the journey to Canada a desperate one. To protect himself from the irate colonists, Barr had to lock himself in his cabin for most of the journey. Eleven days later, the weary travellers arrived at St. John, New Brunswick, to await innumerable delays and endless baggage inspections—for the colonists had brought all their worldly possessions; these included pianos, furniture, books, and even bathtubs. Finally, they boarded three trains for the long overland journey to Saskatoon. One colonist complained: "I can only say that the 3rd class carriages on the English railways are a king to the filthy cars we were huddled into. No sleeping accommodation, and as to the lavatory arrangements they were simply a disgrace to civilization."

More disasters followed in Saskatoon, because Barr had failed to make adequate arrangements for their arrival. The immigrants lived in a tent city for two weeks before setting out to their new homes. Merchants charged them exorbitant prices for supplies. With no guides to lead them, they made the 300 km wagon trip alone through Battleford to the large reservation of land just east of the present-day Saskatchewan–Alberta border. The overloaded wagons kept getting stuck in the mid-April mud. The women and children walked most of the way. Some discontents returned to Saskatoon; others remained in Battleford, the halfway point. Those who pushed on arrived to find an empty tract of land recently scourged by a spring fire.

At a mass meeting in Battleford the colonists deposed Barr, who next moved to the United States and then to Australia, where he continued into his ninetieth year to spin out dreams of settlement in the distant corners of the empire. The remaining colonists elected Lloyd, after whom Lloydminster was named in 1903, to lead the colony. He became head of a twelve-man committee, which quickly became known as the "Twelve Apostles." The colony survived and by 1908 prospered, thanks to Lloyd and to the handful of Barr colonists who remained.

American Immigrants

American immigrants were high on Sifton's list of desirable settlers. He spent more than one-quarter of his department's budget to convince Americans to come to Canada. Experienced farmers, already established, came north. They sold their farms at home at a high price and bought at a low price in Canada; for example, one Iowa farmer sold his old homestead for $250 per ha and bought good land in Manitoba for $18 per ha. Many who came were ex-Canadians. About one-third were newcomers from Europe—Germans and Scandinavians who had initially settled in the American West but now wanted better land for their children.

American colonization companies were allowed to buy tracts of land at low prices which they then turned around and sold for a handsome profit. In 1902 the Saskatchewan Valley Land Company, the largest and most controversial of these companies, purchased 336 000 ha of land at sixty-one cents per hectare and then sold the land five years later for $3.20–$4.80 per ha.

Americans came in the tens of thousands and outnumbered the British-born two to one in Alberta and Saskatchewan. In 1905 in both the new provinces they were the largest immigrant group. Most Canadians welcomed the Americans enthusiastically. The *Lethbridge Herald*, for example, wrote:

> This class of immigration is of a top-notch order and every true Canadian should be proud to see it and encourage it. Thus shall our vast tracts of God's bountifulness ... be peopled by an intelligent progressive race of our own kind, who will readily be developed into permanent, patriotic, solid citizens who will adhere to one flag—that protects their homes and their rights—and whose posterity ... will become ... a part and parcel of and inseparable from our proud standards of Canadianism.

Although not British, the majority were of Anglo-Saxon extraction; and because they already spoke English, they mixed easily with their Canadian neighbours and participated fully in their new communities.

121

The Americans brought with them many new populist political ideas, such as the referendum on controversial questions, the recall of elected representatives who failed to serve their constituents, and the idea of local initiative—a citizen's right to demand that politicians address certain issues. Americans took positions of leadership in farm organizations and developed an ideology of agrarian protest. They contributed to the formation of new political movements, most notably to the United Farmers of Alberta and later the Progressive Movement.

In this racially conscious age, American Blacks were not welcome in Canada. To discourage them from emigrating, Canadian agents stressed the rigorous climate as being too severe. The same agents, however, told white Americans how mild and healthy the climate was. When a group of well-to-do and agriculturally experienced Blacks from Oklahoma crossed the border in 1910, local newspapers, especially the Edmonton *Journal* (since Edmonton was reported to be their destination) warned of an "invasion of Negroes." Canadian immigration authorities' efforts to limit Black immigration were effective: between 1901 and 1911, the peak period of immigration, fewer than 1500 Blacks immigrated to Canada.

European Immigrants

The Canadian government had little success in attracting large numbers of western Europeans. France, for example, had a low birth-rate and a well-balanced economy that provided ample work for its population. For those with a desire for adventure, France had its own colonies, such as Algeria. Other western Europeans preferred the United States to Canada. The government did little to encourage the French to come, and thus few

French-speaking immigrants supplemented the limited French-Canadian population on the prairies.

Some Germans and Scandinavians came directly from their home country, although more significant numbers came via the American West. By the turn of the century, Germany prohibited immigration agents and fined steamship lines for carrying emigrants. The Scandinavian countries were equally unco-operative in arranging emigration schemes, fearing the negative result of such migration, especially of skilled workers, on their own economy.

To overcome these obstacles, Clifford Sifton allowed W.T.R. Preston, Canada's immigration inspector in London, to set up in 1899 a clandestine organization of European shipping agents. The North Atlantic Trading Company brought emigrants from western European countries having emigration quotas. The agents received five-dollar bonuses for any man, woman, or child over twelve who were bona fide farmers. The company acted as a screening agency, since it was to receive payment only for healthy immigrants with farming experience. This illegal scheme ended in 1905 after public allegations that unknown European agents profited from the scheme at the Canadian government's expense. During its operation, however, the company brought in thousands of emigrants from western Europe.

IMMIGRANTS IN "SHEEPSKIN COATS"

Sifton also encouraged eastern European immigration. The minister of the interior considered them hard-working, obedient, agricultural people: "I think a stalwart peasant in a sheepskin coat, born on the soil, whose forefathers had been farmers for ten generations, with a stout wife, and a half-dozen children, is good quality."

The Ukrainians were the largest group to come from central and eastern Europe. Dr. Josef Oleskow, a Ukrainian professor of agriculture, attempted to arrange in 1895 for the emigration to Canada of the best farmers, the most educated and productive. His scheme failed, but eventually 170 000 Ukrainians came to Canada during the great wave of immigration at the turn of the century. They were a cross section of Ukrainian rural society but they came with one common expectation—*vilni zemli* or free land.

The first group of four thousand Ukrainians or Galicians, as the immigration agents called them, settled together in Alberta at Star and Josefberg, sixty-five kilometres east of Edmonton. This forested area assured them an abundant supply of wood, a scarce commodity back home. Soon the tightly knit communities grew into villages of timber and whitewashed clay houses with thatched roofs and distinctive churches with onion-shaped domes. The Ukrainian Catholic or Orthodox churches became the centre of community life. These women and men opened up much of Alberta's and Saskatchewan's parkland. They helped build the railways, mine the coal, cut the timber, and do various jobs in the towns and cities. Their industriousness and their willingness to work for low wages made them invaluable to the business community, which pressured the government to encourage unlimited numbers of such immigrants.

At the same time, the fact that the Ukrainians kept to themselves, communicated in their own language, and encouraged their children to wear their national dress, made them suspect among Anglo-Canadians, who wondered whether the Galicians could be assimilated. Many felt they could not, including the future social reformer J.S. Woodsworth. In *Strangers Within Our Gates* (1909), he wrote: "No more figures are needed to show what an important factor the Galicians are in the West, and how difficult is the problem of Canadianizing them, even without the influx of another immigrant."

123

THE DOUKHOBORS AND HUTTERITES

Another eastern European minority group that faced discrimination were the Doukhobors. These "spirit wrestlers," as their tormentors called them, had broken away from the Russian Orthodox church in the eighteenth century in opposition to church ritual. As pacifists, they opposed war and refused to swear allegiance to earthly rulers. Both beliefs went against tsarist state philosophy and led to their persecution. These same beliefs, along with their simple and communal lifestyle, appealed to Leo Tolstoy, the great Russian novelist who, with Peter Kropotkin, a leading Russian anarchist, arranged for their emigration. Professor James Mavor, a professor of political science at the University of Toronto and a friend of Kropotkin's, offered to help these people settle in Canada. In 1898, 7400 Doukhobors arrived and settled in two colonies near Yorkton, Saskatchewan, and in another near Saskatoon. They held land communally, in a special arrangement agreed upon by the Canadian government, and lived in communal villages. Often the men worked on the railways to supplement their meagre income while the women of the fundamentalist wing of the group, which opposed worldly possessions, plowed the fields. Occasionally, they pulled the plows themselves in teams of twenty-four women.

All was peaceful until a radical wing calling itself the Sons of Freedom marched towards Winnipeg in search of Christ and a new earthly paradise, and in expectation of the arrival of their leader, Peter Veregin, who had been in captivity in Russia. Six months later, the group walked naked through the Doukhobor villages in a quest for a state of purity akin to that of Adam and Eve before the Fall. The newspapers sensationalized these activities, which resulted in the first overt public opposition to the Doukhobors. The protests also provided an excuse for Frank Oliver, founder of the *Edmonton Bulletin* and Clifford Sifton's successor as minister of the interior (1905–11), to confiscate half of the Saskatchewan land on the grounds that the Doukhobors had refused to cultivate quarter-sections or to swear allegiance to the Crown. (The federal government had exempted them from these conditions in 1898). In protest, five thousand Doukhobors abandoned their prosperous farms in Saskatchewan and trekked to the Kootenay district near Grand Forks, B.C., where Peter Veregin had purchased private land. Here they remained, isolated from the outside world, until internal dissension and further nude marches and arson by the Sons of Freedom once again aroused opposition.

The Hutterites, like the Mennonites, were descendants of the Anabaptists and followers of Jakob Hutter, who organized disparate groups in 1528 in central Europe. These German-speaking immigrants left Russia in the 1870s to escape persecution and settled in South Dakota. Pressures to assimilate and persecution during World War I persuaded them to move again in 1917–19, chiefly to southern Manitoba and southern Alberta. The Canadian government assured them of exemption from military service if they immigrated.

The Hutterites held the land collectively, lived communally, and shared their possessions. Their way of life was simple and their dress plain black and white, with the women wearing bright coloured kerchiefs on their heads. They did not, however, reject such conveniences as modern farm equipment, and their farms in southern Alberta and southern Manitoba prospered and expanded rapidly. Once a colony reached a maximum of 100–150 families, it split and a new one was formed. Opposition to the Hutterites' collective farming practices surfaced among the independent farmers in the region where these colonies were located. Otherwise, they were left to pursue their own religion and customs, and they were even allowed to establish community schools, taught by outside teachers.

Although he could tolerate eastern European immigrants as potentially good farmers, Sifton disdained southern Europeans as migratory labourers who would settle in the urban centres. "I don't want anything done to facilitate Italian immigration," the minister of the interior warned his assistants. When, for example, in May 1898 a railroad car of Italians from New York arrived to work on the Crow's Nest Pass railway line, Sifton sent them all back. He faced strong opposition from business interests, however, who wanted Italians as cheap labour, especially for the railroads and in the mines. *Padrones*, or employment agents, illegally worked with shipping companies and employed sub-agents abroad to bring in unskilled Italian workers. Without any legal protection these young men worked for low wages. Labour unions resented them for taking jobs away from union workers, while Canadians in general saw them as a threat to society.

124

Asian Immigrants

Due to the larger numbers of Chinese and Japanese that had settled there, British Columbia became the centre of anti-Asian sentiment. Asian immigration had steadily increased since the first Chinese arrived in the 1850s during the gold rush era. They came to this land of opportunity despite a head tax (money to be paid on entry) of $50 in 1885 that increased to $100 in 1900 and went as high as $500 in 1903. Employers often paid the head tax or brought in Asians illegally to build the railways and work the mines, because they were industrious and cheap labour. The fifteen thousand Chinese who worked on the CPR between 1880 and 1885 saved the company an estimated $3.5 million. In 1911 nearly 11 percent of the province's population was Asian.

As a result of a combined temporary recession and an exceptional annual jump in Asian immigration from two thousand to twelve thousand, xenophobia reached an acute point in 1907. In August an Asiatic Exclusion League formed, and one month later it organized a protest march through Vancouver's Chinatown. During the ensuing riot the mobs damaged buildings and assaulted Asians.

125

This overt opposition forced the Canadian government to re-examine its immigration policy for Asians. Japan posed a special problem because it was a military ally of England and a major trading partner of both Canada and Britain. China, too, was an allied nation, while India belonged to the Empire. Nevertheless, the Canadian government negotiated an agreement with Japan to restrict immigration to four hundred Japanese annually. It made a similar agreement with China which, however, was never honoured.

Canada could not reach an agreement with the Indian government. Tensions were heightened in May 1914, when British Columbia refused entry into Vancouver harbour of the *Komagata Maru*, with 376 Indian passengers aboard. For two months the ship anchored offshore, while government officials deliberated and British Columbians jeered. H.H. Stevens, a Conservative MP, demanded that Canada be "pure and free from the taint of other people." In the end, the *Rainbow*, one of Canada's naval vessels, escorted the Indian vessel out to sea amid cries of "White Canada forever" and refrains of "Rule Britannia."

Nativist Attitudes

With the arrival of immigrants in large numbers at the turn of the century, a hierarchy of ethnic groups developed among Canadians that was based, as the ethnic historian Howard Palmer notes, on each group's "physical and cultural distance from London (England) and the degree to which

Vancouver Public Library (7641).

These Sikh lumber workers were a few of the South Asians allowed into Canada in the pre-World War I era. Many were turned back, like the shipload of Indians on the *Komagata Maru* who were prevented from docking at Vancouver harbour. Once here, South Asians met racial discrimination by the dominant Anglo-Canadian population.

their skin pigmentation conformed to Anglo-Saxon white."[1] Not surprisingly, the British and Americans, who for the most part were white Anglo-Saxon Protestants, were at the top of the list of desirable immigrants. Then came the northern and western Europeans, particularly the Scandinavians, Germans, and the Dutch, who were considered to have many qualities of the Anglo-Saxons and hence were easily assimilable. To English-speaking race theorists, the French, while a desirable nation, posed a problem in that they did not easily assimilate. After the "chosen races" came the central and eastern Europeans, generally respected as industrious people and good agriculturalists. Sifton, for one, believed that they would eventually be "nationalized" through their experience on the land. Among these groups, the Ukrainians and Doukhobors were least tolerated because of their exclusiveness. Lowest among the Europeans came the Jews and the southern Europeans; they were considered both difficult to assimilate and poor farmers.

Ranked well below the Europeans were non-whites: Blacks and Asians (Japanese, Chinese, and South Asians). If the question regarding eastern and southern Europeans was whether, once admitted, they would make good farmers and assimilate, the question regarding Blacks and Asians was whether they should be allowed into the country at all.

Canadians at every level of society almost universally held racist views. *127* Many expressed them blatantly. T.S. Sproule, a Conservative MP, claimed: "Canada is today the dumping ground for the refuse of every country in the world." The Calgary *Herald* questioned whether Sifton was handing the Canadian West over to "dirty hordes of half-civilized Galicians who were lacking everything but dirt." Canadians in general feared that these new immigrants with different languages and customs would create a polyglot nation lacking cohesion and unity. One newspaper believed Canada was becoming a nation along "the lines of the Tower of Babel, where the Lord confounded the language so that people might not understand one another's speech."

The schools and the churches, English-speaking Canadians believed, had to make these "foreigners" into good Canadians. J.S. Woodsworth, a social reformer, spoke for many English-speaking Canadians when he noted in his book, *Strangers Within Our Gates* (1909): "If Canada is to become in a real sense a nation, if our people are to become one people, we must have one language." But English-speaking Canadians also expected the schools, besides teaching English, to inculcate British-Canadian beliefs in citizenship, democracy and the Protestant work ethic. The fight over the school question—in Manitoba in the 1890s and in 1905 when Saskatchewan and Alberta became provinces—centred on the belief that one language of instruction and a state-controlled school system could achieve that objective.

What type of society did Anglo-Canadians envision for the West? Some wanted a replica of British and Ontarian society with a dominant British population and Anglo-Celtic values. As the Methodist Missionary Society explained in 1910: "Our objective on behalf of European foreigners should be to assist in making them English-speaking Christian citizens who are clean, educated, and loyal to the Dominion and to Great Britain."

Others envisioned a "new West," one superior to that of the rest of

Canada and even Britain, through an amalgam of a new land and a new and varied population. These theorists—particularly early western Canadian writers such as Ralph Connor, Nellie McClung, and Robert Stead—favoured more of an ethnic mix than the Anglo-conformists, in which the finer qualities of all new westerners would surface to create this superior "race." Still, this new West, while not a replica of Britain or eastern Canada, was supposed to be decidedly Anglo-Celtic. Neither group believed that the "foreign" immigrants had anything constructive to contribute to western Canadian society. Outsiders like the Indians and the Métis were expected to conform and to assimilate. Yet, as historian Howard Palmer points out, there was a basic contradiction in Anglo-Canadian attitudes towards ethnic minorities: "Non-Anglo-Saxons were discriminated against because they were not assimilated, either culturally or socially, but one of the reasons they were not assimilated was because of discrimination against them."[2]

128

By World War I British, American, European, and Asian immigration had transformed Canada, and particularly western Canada, into a polyglot society. Prairie population grew from 400 000 in 1901 to 2 million by 1921. All areas of the West, including the park and forest belt to the north and the Palliser's Triangle to the south, were open to settlement. Most immigrants homesteaded, but a significant number moved first into urban centres or later, after an unsuccessful attempt at farming. While these immigrants contributed to the West's economic growth, they also bore the brunt of ethnic discrimination, resulting in tension within the region. Clearly, though, the Prairie West had emerged by World War I as a dominant fifth region to challenge the established regions of Ontario, Quebec, the Maritimes, and British Columbia.

NOTES

[1] H. Palmer, "Reluctant Hosts: Anglo-Canadian Views of Multiculturalism in the Twentieth Century," in *Readings in Canadian History*, edited by R. Douglas Francis and Donald B. Smith, 2d ed. (Toronto, 1986), p. 187.
[2] *Ibid.*, pp. 190–91.

Related Readings

The following articles from R. Douglas Francis and Donald B. Smith, eds., *Readings in Canadian History: Post-Confederation* 2d ed. (Toronto, 1986), are very useful for further study of this topic: G. Friesen, "Immigrant Communities 1870–1940: The Struggle for Cultural Survival," pp. 158–84; and Howard Palmer, "Reluctant Hosts: Anglo-Canadian Views of Multiculturalism in the Twentieth Century," pp. 185–201.

BIBLIOGRAPHY

Good overviews on immigration to western Canada are available in R.C. *129*
Brown and R. Cook's chapter "Opening up the Land of Opportunity,"
in *Canada: 1896–1921: A Nation Transformed* (Toronto, 1974); and in
Pierre Berton's *The Promised Land: Settling the West, 1896–1914* (Toronto,
1984).

On immigration to western Canada in the pre-1896 era, see Norman
Macdonald, *Canada: Immigration and Colonization, 1841–1903* (Toronto,
1966). Clifford Sifton's role in promoting immigration to the West is
examined in D.J. Hall, "Clifford Sifton: Immigration and Settlement
Policy, 1896–1905," in *The Settlement of the West*, edited by Howard Palmer (Calgary, 1977), pp. 60–85, and in Hall's two-volume biography,
Clifford Sifton, vol. 1: *The Young Napoleon, 1861–1900* (Vancouver, 1981),
and vol. 2: *The Lonely Eminence, 1901–1929* (Vancouver, 1985).

The immigration of British home children is the subject of Joy Parr's
Labouring Children: British Immigrant Apprentices to Canada, 1869–1924
(Montreal, 1980) and Kenneth Bagnell's *The Little Immigrants* (Toronto,
1980). On American farmers' immigration to western Canada see Carl
Bicha, *The American Farmer and the Canadian West*, 1896–1914 (Kansas
City, 1972), and Harold Troper, *Only Farmers Need Apply* (Toronto,
1972). European immigration is discussed in *'Dangerous Foreigners': Eu-
ropean Immigrant Workers and Labour Radicalism in Canada, 1896–1932*
(Toronto, 1979). George Woodcock and Ivan Avakumovic's *The Doukhobors* (Toronto, reprinted 1977) deals with this important group. The European immigrants' perspective can be obtained from John Marlyn's novel,
Under the Ribs of Death (Toronto, 1971) and from R.F. Harney and H.
Troper's *Immigrants: A Portrait of the Urban Experience, 1890–1930* (Toronto, 1975).

Black immigration to western Canada is covered in Robin W. Winks,
The Blacks in Canada: A History (New Haven, 1971). On Asian immigration to British Columbia in the pre-World War I era, see Peter Ward,

White Canada Forever: Popular Attitudes and Public Policies Towards Orientals and British Columbia (Montreal, 1978), and Hugh Johnston, *The Voyage of the Komogata Maru: The Sikh Challenge to Canada's Colour Bar* (Delhi, 1979). On nativist attitudes see Howard Palmer, *Patterns of Prejudice: A History of Nativism in Alberta* (Toronto, 1982).

The history of the western Canadian Indian in the early twentieth century is reviewed by E. Brian Titley in his chapter, "Senseless Drumming and Dancing," in *A Narrow Vision: Duncan Campbell Scott and the Administration of Indian Affairs in Canada* (Vancouver, 1986), pp. 162–183. For an account of one native person's experiences in Southern Alberta in the early twentieth century, see Hugh A. Dempsey, *The Gentle Persuader: A Biography of James Gladstone, Indian Senator* (Saskatoon, 1986).

CHAPTER SEVEN

Laurier, Borden, and the Politics of Prosperity

Surprisingly, the national policy proved more successful for the Liberals *131* than it had been for the Conservatives who put it in place. Wilfrid Laurier, the country's first French-Canadian prime minister, came to power in 1896 just as the international trade recession lifted. With increased revenues, the federal government took on additional responsibilities. It aided an ambitious railway-building scheme, assisted immigration, and increased foreign trade, especially with Britain. By 1905, however, after ten successful years, the Laurier coalition began to disintegrate. In 1911 French-Canadian nationalists in Quebec allied with English-Canadian imperialists in Ontario to defeat Laurier and the Liberal party and the Conservatives returned to power under a reform-minded Robert Borden.

A Party Transformed

Wilfrid Laurier led the Liberal party for the last nine of its eighteen years in opposition (1878–96). His role as opposition leader had perfected his political skills. From observing his political opponent, John A. Macdonald, he had first learned the art of successful politics in Canada. "Reforms are for Opposition," Sir John had once commented. "It is the business of governments to stay in office." Staying in office meant satisfying as many divergent interest groups in the country as possible. To achieve this objective, he transformed the Liberals into a middle-of-the-road party.

A MODERATE QUEBEC LIBERALISM

Significantly, Laurier made his peace with the Catholic church. In a famous address on political liberalism delivered at Quebec City in 1877, Laurier identified his party with the moderate and respectable British political liberalism of Fox, Russell, Mill, and Gladstone rather than with the papally condemned European variety. More reluctantly but equally decisively, he moved the party away from an economic policy of unrestricted reciprocity with the United States, which in the election campaign of 1891 had tainted it with the charge of annexationism (see chapter 5). At the party's first national convention in 1893, Laurier convinced the party to adopt a moderate policy of protectionism. In essence, therefore, the Liberals after 1896 resembled the Conservatives both in style and in policies. In the words of one critic, Frank Underhill, little now distinguished the two parties except that one happened to be in office and the other out.

LAURIER'S FIRST CABINET

Laurier's first Cabinet reflected the party's re-organization. The long-serving Sir Richard Cartwright, the obvious choice for the senior post of finance minister, was passed over because of his support for unrestricted reciprocity. W.S. Fielding, the former Nova Scotian premier and a protectionist, obtained the post. Two other powerful ex-provincial premiers joined Fielding in the Cabinet: Oliver Mowat of Ontario, the great champion of provincial rights, and A.G. Blair of New Brunswick. Their presence symbolized closer dominion-provincial relations. Laurier excluded the Quebec *Rouge* element, with the exception of Sir Henry Joly de Lotbinière who, like Cartwright, was given a junior Cabinet post. Instead, he gave Israël Tarte, the former Conservative who had worked hard on Laurier's behalf, a ministry. From the Northwest, Clifford Sifton entered as the new minister of the interior, the most powerful post in the Cabinet. Laurier's Cabinet reflected a new Liberalism shorn of its past Clear Grit and *Rouge* radicalism.

The Liberals' National Policy

The Liberal government, seeing the impossibility of reaching a trade agreement with the protectionist Republicans in office in Washington under President William McKinley, sponsor of the McKinley Tariff of 1890, adopted the Conservatives' National Policy of high tariff protection. Fielding introduced the Liberals' first protectionist tariff in his 1897 budget. For business, it maintained the high duties on imported goods, such as textiles and iron and steel products coming from the United States and other countries that restricted the entry of Canadian goods. At the same time, the new policy lowered tariffs to any country admitting Canadian goods at a rate equal to the minimum Canadian tariff. As Britain already did so, the policy became known as the "British preference." Subsequently, Anglo-Canadian trade increased, winning the Liberals much support from Canadian imperialists.

During the Laurier years (1896–1911) immigrants came in even greater numbers (see chapter 6). One million people settled on the prairies. This expansion increased the demand for greater railway service, especially to remote areas not serviced by the CPR.

TWO NEW TRANSCONTINENTAL RAILWAYS

Politicians and promoters both believed so strongly in Canada's potential that they built rail lines on faith that tomorrow the land would be settled and its natural resources exploited. Railway building and nation building were considered synonymous.

133

Two Ontario-born entrepreneurs, Donald Mann and William Mackenzie, built up a railway empire in the West by buying up near-defunct charters from rival companies which often included substantial land grants (a policy discontinued during the Laurier era) and by building new lines. By 1901 their Canadian Northern Railway Company had sufficient mileage to apply for federal financial assistance to complete the long section eastward from Port Arthur (at the western end of Lake Superior) to Montreal. It had also won the hearts of many westerners, who saw it as a rival to the CPR and as a western-based railway. One railway official described it as "the West's own product, designed to meet the West's own needs."

At the same time, the Grand Trunk, an eastern-based railway, decided to obtain by 1902 a share of the prairie grain traffic. This was an opportune moment for the Canadian Northern and the Grand Trunk to co-operate. Both companies, however, feared that the other would dominate in any joint venture. Unfortunately, Laurier refused to force a merger. Instead, he backed the Grand Trunk, while at the same time encouraging Mackenzie and Mann to pursue their scheme on the unrealistic assumption that the country could support three transcontinental railways. As Laurier told Parliament:

> To those who urge upon us the policy of tomorrow, and tomorrow, and tomorrow; to those who tell us, wait, wait, wait; to those who advise us to pause, to consider, to reflect, to calculate and to inquire, our answer is: No, this is not a time for deliberation, this is a time for action. The flood tide is upon us that leads on to fortune; if we let it pass it may never recur again.

The Liberal government provided the Grand Trunk Railway with a generous final offer. It agreed to build the 2880-km-long eastern section of the railway at government expense, through northern Ontario and Quebec

THE GROWING TIME FOR TRANS-CONTINENTAL RAILWAYS.
The Premier: "The People pay for and give you the Railways, and make you a present of the country: but what do they get as a quid pro quo?"
Chorus: "The People as represented by the Government—will get—er—our vote and influence, you know."

The Laurier era was a time of frontier railway building with two new transcontinental railways built. Too much, as this cartoon by J. W. Bengough humorously suggests.

to Moncton, New Brunswick. This section, known as the National Transcontinental, would be leased to the Grand Trunk for fifty years at a modest annual rate of 3 percent on construction costs, and with the first seven years of operation rent free. The western section from Winnipeg to the Pacific would be built by a new company, the Grand Trunk Pacific, a subsidiary of the Grand Trunk, with bond money guaranteed up to 75 percent by the federal government.

The Canadian Northern Company continued to plan its transcontinental line, convinced that Ottawa would bail it out in hard times. Often in the West these competing lines ran parallel to each other and sometimes within sight of each other. As historian T.D. Regehr noted: "a short distance west of Portage la Prairie, a traveller going north could cross eight parallel east–west lines within the space of 55 km."[1]

THE IMPACT OF RAILWAY BUILDING

The Liberal party based its railway policy on politics rather than on economics. "The $200 million vote-catcher," was how the Tories described Laurier's railway-building scheme, "designed to carry elections rather than passengers." Even O.D. Skelton, Laurier's biographer, had to admit that the Grand Trunk was "the most corrupting single factor since Confederation." The railway historian G.R. Stevens summed up the fate of the Canadian Northern: "Given honest and dynamic administration and a measure of good luck, it had a bare chance of success; under the dead weight of party politicians, greedy contractors and arrogant managers, it had none."[2] The two railway companies did add eighteen thousand additional kilometres of prairie railway (six times more than the first CPR line), opened up lucrative mining areas in northern Ontario and Quebec, and provided employment for thousands, but all this was at an enormous cost—estimated at a quarter-billion dollars, the equivalent of four billion dollars today—to the Canadian taxpayer. On the eve of the outbreak of World War I, Canada had more railways per population than any other country in the world.

The railroad mania symbolized the new confidence Canadians had in their country. The mood of depression and uncertainty that dominated in the late nineteenth century had vanished. The Liberal government took advantage of this new optimism, reminding Canadians of their nation's vast size and potential wealth. Often it linked prosperity and the Liberals together, as in the election campaign of 1908 when Laurier joked: "Providence has used us to bestow its blessings upon the Canadian people just as, earlier, it used the Conservatives to punish this same people." The Liberals won easily in 1900 and in 1904, but by 1905 the great coalition Laurier had assembled showed signs of breaking up.

135

The Autonomy Bills and an Educational Crisis

The school question in the West again became pressing during Laurier's third term in office (1904–08). Nearly ten years earlier the prime minister had weathered the volatile Manitoba schools question (see chapter 4); in 1905 he had to face a similar issue over the creation of two new provinces, Alberta and Saskatchewan. The schools question arose as a result of a growing population and the decision of the government of the Northwest Territories (comprising the districts of Assiniboia, Saskatchewan, Alberta, and Athabaska) to request provincial status.

CREATING THE PROVINCES OF ALBERTA AND SASKATCHEWAN

Originally, discussion between the federal and the territorial governments had centred on the creation of three provinces—Alberta, Saskatchewan, and a northern province, Athabaska, as well. Another idea favoured by Frederick Haultain, leader of the Assembly of the Northwest Territories, was to create just one prairie province. But the federal government opposed, arguing that one political unit would be too large and would upset federal-provincial relations. Haultain also proposed that the new provinces be allowed to control their own natural resources like all other provinces (except for Manitoba). Laurier turned down the suggestion because he believed the federal government needed to maintain control over settlement and the development of the region at this critical time of expansion.

In 1905 Laurier introduced autonomy bills to create two new western provinces. The proposed boundaries had little to do with the region's physical geography. British Columbia already extended to the 60th parallel, so it became the northern boundary of the two new provinces as well. The 110th meridian was chosen for the east–west boundary because it divided the area into two provinces of roughly equal size.

136

THE SCHOOL CONTROVERSY IN ALBERTA AND SASKATCHEWAN

The Autonomy Bills represented Clifford Sifton's views, except for a controversial school clause. Charles Fitzpatrick, the minister of justice and a Quebec Catholic, and Henri Bourassa had drafted the clause while Sifton was out of the country. The original ordinances of the Northwest Territories Act of 1875, as amended in 1877, had provided that, as in Ontario, both Protestant and Roman Catholics could establish schools and share in public funds for education. Also, both French and English could be used as languages of instruction.

In the early 1890s, however, French-language instruction had been drastically curtailed. The territorial government made English the official language of instruction in the Roman Catholic school system, the use of French being permitted only in the primary course (the first two to three years of school) for French-speaking children. In 1901 the territorial government passed new educational ordinances that established a territorial board of education, but with separate schools under government supervision. Religious instruction was restricted to the last half-hour of the school day.

Fitzpatrick's and Bourassa's educational clause would have restored the system to that of 1877 by permitting the free establishment of Roman Catholic and Protestant schools as well as the use of French in the school system. Upon his return to Ottawa, Sifton was incensed at the alterations. Openly, he denounced the educational clause as thwarting the wishes of the Northwest as expressed in the ordinance of 1901. In protest, he resigned as minister of the interior.

In federal politics Laurier always tried to find the middle road, seeking compromise between the two linguistic and religious communities. Again he sought unity and allowed Sifton to redraft the educational clauses, although he did not invite him back into the Cabinet. Sifton's revised clause restricted the rights of the French-Canadian Catholic minorities to those limited concessions granted in the ordinance of 1901. Apart from some face-saving phrases, few features of the separate school system were restored. Nevertheless, to keep his party together, Laurier accepted the "honourable compromise," as he described the Sifton amendment, and urged his Quebec colleagues to do the same.

Bourassa denounced the new clause, arguing that it infringed on rights previously enjoyed by French Canadians in the West, whose language had received official recognition in the amendments made in 1877 to the Northwest Territories Act of 1875. These amendments had given English and French equal status in the territorial council and the courts, and guaranteed the right to organize Roman Catholic schools in which French could be the teaching language. Moreover, Bourassa argued that French-Canadian Catholics in the West should surely enjoy the same rights as did English-Canadian Protestants in Quebec. Despite his protests the Sifton amendment became law.

137

The educational crisis hurt Laurier's coalition. It lost the prime minister his most powerful English-speaking minister, Sifton, while further alienating Bourassa at the other end of the political spectrum. Laurier also failed to make any significant gains for the French-Canadian Catholics in the West. At the same time, Laurier's "compromise" had contributed to the growth of a French-Canadian nationalism in Quebec contrary to his own. Nationalist representatives in the House of Commons now demanded bilingual stamps and currency. Laurier, anxious to keep harmony between the "races," opposed these proposals, which in turn increased the nationalists' determination to fight for French-Canadian rights.

The Naval Crisis

The political damage of the Autonomy Bills was minor compared to that of the naval crisis of 1909–10. Shortly after the end of the Boer War and the Colonial Conference of 1902 (in which Laurier had successfully resisted attempts to formulate a common imperial policy) (see chapter 5), the British Liberals came to power. No more anxious for imperial solidarity than the Canadian Liberals, the British government retreated from Chamberlain's imperialist policies.

In the early twentieth century, Canada gained increased autonomy. In 1904, at Britain's request, Canada assumed responsibility for the British-controlled ports of Halifax and Esquimalt (near Victoria, B.C.). Then in 1907 Joseph Pope, formerly private secretary to Sir John A. Macdonald and after 1896 undersecretary of state, recommended the creation of a

Department of External Affairs to deal with foreign affairs in a uniform way. Laurier agreed, and the department was established in 1909.

Meanwhile political tension escalated in Europe. In 1908 an alarmed British press alerted public opinion to Germany's naval build-up. British Conservatives demanded that the British government begin immediate construction of eight more super battleships or dreadnoughts. This led to a new domestic crisis in Canada as English-Canadian imperialists appealed for a Canadian contribution to imperial naval defence. The *Montreal Star* noted in 1909: "The British Empire cannot be imperilled without bringing menace to the peace, prosperity and independence of Canada."

Another divisive national debate arose over what the nature of this involvement should be. The Liberals and the Conservatives eventually agreed that Canada's best *long-range* policy was to build a Canadian navy rather than contribute funds regularly to the British Admiralty. The two parties differed on the best *short-term* policy, however. Conservatives favoured an emergency direct cash contribution in the present crisis, while Liberals wanted the immediate establishment of a Canadian navy under Canadian command (but to be used by Britain, if the Canadian Parliament approved, in the event of war).

138

Laurier introduced the Naval Service Bill in January 1910. The prime minister proposed that Canada construct five cruisers and six destroyers, all to be manned by a volunteer force, and also establish a naval college to train Canadian officers. Although the force would be under the control of the Canadian government, it could, "in case of war," be placed under imperial control with the approval of the Canadian Parliament. In response to a question as to whether the bill's phrase, "in case of war," referred to war anywhere in the Empire or in Canada only, Laurier gave the following reply, which he later regretted:

> War everywhere. When Britain is at war, Canada is at war; there is no distinction. If Great Britain, to which we are subject, is at war with any nation, Canada is exposed to invasion; hence Canada is at war.

OPPOSITION TO THE NAVAL SERVICE BILL

The bill's ambiguous proposal for creating a Canadian navy that would be subject to British control in wartime appealed to Laurier as a suitable compromise. But it annoyed his opponents. On the one hand, imperial-minded Conservatives (both federal MPs and provincial premiers) denounced this "tin-pot navy," as they described it, as a disgrace to Canada's role in the Empire. The *Montreal Daily Star* wrote on November 2: "Now if the Empire—including Canada—were at war, and the Canadian Navy were to refuse to go into action, how would that action differ from cowardice on the field of battle—from betrayal of a brother people—from treason to the King?"

On the other hand, Bourassa and the *nationalistes* opposed the naval bill because it went too far; this navy could be used to fight imperial wars of no interest to Canada. "It is the most complete backward step Canada has made in half a century," Bourassa declared. "It is the gravest blow our autonomy has suffered since the origin of responsible government." Bourassa favoured a navy for home defence but not one that would involve Canada in the "whirlpool of militarism." He questioned whether Canada needed a navy at all, since the only threat to the country could come from the United States, with whom Canadians had enjoyed a century of peace.

RISE OF THE *NATIONALISTES* IN QUEBEC   *139*

Since 1907 Henri Bourassa's attacks against Laurier had become more strident. He left federal for provincial politics, where he could concentrate his energy and bolster his influence. In 1910, he established his own daily newspaper, *Le Devoir*. That same year, the *nationalistes* ran a candidate against the Liberals in a by-election in the "safe" seat of Drummond-Arthabaska. Laurier, who had represented the district in the Quebec legislature, campaigned personally on behalf of the Liberal candidate, only to see the *nationalistes* win. Proudly, Bourassa told a crowd of well-wishers outside his *Le Devoir* office on the election night: "I say to you French Canadians that we have today done a great work. We have taught Sir Wilfrid Laurier that he is not omnipotent."

The Quebec Conservatives had openly supported the *nationalistes* against the Liberals in Drummond-Arthabaska. Badly split on the naval issue, the national Conservative party had favoured a temporary direct financial contribution to imperial defence, but the Quebec Conservatives, led by F. D. Monk, insisted on no commitment until a referendum could be held to decide the people's wishes. It was this "unholy alliance" of Quebec *nationalistes* and Conservatives that defeated Laurier in the election of 1911.

The Reciprocity Issue

In 1911 Laurier and the Liberal party also faced a revolt in Ontario over the issue of reciprocity with the United States, which had angered manufacturers in the country's leading industrial province. The Liberal party's decision to adopt reciprocity, a policy it had abandoned in 1896, stemmed largely from agrarian discontent in Ontario and especially in the West.

Western farmers felt unfairly treated in Confederation and insisted that the unjust economic system be revised to suit their needs. They demanded the Liberals reduce freight rates to the lower levels applied in central Canada. Wheat farmers wanted an end to the domination of the grain trade by the major eastern-owned grain elevator companies, an increase in the CPR's boxcar allotment for grain shipment, and a new railway to Hudson Bay as an alternative to the CPR. They also called for the establishment of stable pricing in a volatile open-market system. One grain dealer concluded cynically that western farmers believed "all wheat's No. 1 Hard, all grain buyers are thieves, and that hell's divided equally between the railways and the milling companies."

At the turn of the century Ottawa granted western farmers some of their demands. The Liberal government passed the Crow's Nest Pass agreement in 1897, by which the CPR agreed to reduce eastbound freight rates on grain and flour and westbound rates on a list of manufactured goods used by settlers. In return, the CPR received a government subsidy to assist in building a branch line from Lethbridge through the Crow's Nest Pass to Nelson, British Columbia, allowing the company to exploit the mining fields of southern Alberta and British Columbia. The government also passed the Manitoba Grain Act in 1900, which improved the storing of western grain at loading platforms and warehouses. Then, in 1902, the Territorial Grain Growers' Association took the CPR to court in the famous Sintaluta case (named after the town where the legal challenge arose), over the company's inadequate provision of boxcars for grain shipment at peak periods. The court ruled in the farmers' favour and demanded that the CPR increase its railway car allocation.

These limited victories left the fundamental problems unsolved, however. The same economic structures remained in place, most notably the tariff, which for western farmers symbolized the inequity of Confederation. Farmers resented having to buy their agricultural implements and materials in a closed protected market and to sell their wheat in an open competitive market. The tariff, they felt, worked against their best interest and should be repealed. Like the Macdonald Conservatives, the Laurier Liberals refused at this stage to abandon protection—the keystone of their national policy.

RISE OF FARMERS' CO-OPERATIVES IN WESTERN CANADA

The farmers began to organize. They realized that, in a political system influenced by effective lobbying tactics, they had to exert pressure through effective political channels. "The day has gone by for remaining scattered, unbanded communities, a tempting bait to the ambitious design of others,"

W.R. Motherwell, a founder of the Territorial Grain Growers' Association, reminded farmers in 1902.

Farm leaders familiar with co-operative methods in Britain, Europe, and the United States, assisted western farmers in organizing. Western farmers also drew on the experience and support of established eastern agrarian organizations such as the Grange and the Patrons of Industry, both of which had begun in Ontario in the 1870s. In 1906 E.A. Partridge, the energetic and erratic visionary, organized and ran the Grain Growers' Grain Company (later the United Grain Growers), formed to convince farmers to own and operate an independent grain buying and selling system. Two years later, he founded the weekly *Grain Growers' Guide*, a newspaper that became "the Bible" for western farmers. Under the editorial guidance of George Chapman and with Arch Dale's superb editorial cartoons, it became the voice of prairie farmers and a forum for such social reformers as J.S. Woodsworth; Edward Porritt, a free trade advocate and author of *Sixty Years of Protection in Canada* (1913); and Frances Beynon, the women's page editor.

141

These western accomplishments were followed by the formation in 1909 of the Canadian Council of Agriculture, a national farm organization. It served as a clearing house for information concerning agrarian problems and acted as a national political pressure group.

Laurier learned of western discontent during a three-month western tour in the summer of 1910. Everywhere he stopped on his scheduled tour, farmers presented demands for tariff reform. One Saskatoon farmer asked: "In 1896 you promised to skin the Tory bear of protection. Have you done it? If so, I ask you what have you done with the hide?" Shortly after Laurier returned to Ottawa, more than eight hundred farmers—five hundred from the West, three hundred from Ontario, and a handful from Quebec and the Maritimes—came together for a "siege on Ottawa" to demand lower tariffs.

NEGOTIATING RECIPROCITY WITH THE UNITED STATES

By 1910 the prospects for tariff reform were much better than the farmers realized. In the summer of that year, the Canadian and U.S. governments drafted a reciprocity trade agreement. Surprisingly, the initiative came from the Americans who to this point had supported protectionism. President Howard Taft, who came to office in 1909, favoured lower tariffs. The negotiating team he sent to Ottawa openly admitted that the rapidly expanding American industries badly needed more Canadian raw materials. A jubilant W.S. Fielding, the finance minister, announced to the House of Commons on January 26 a reciprocal trade agreement that in effect renewed the popular Reciprocity Treaty of 1854. The proposal

Provincial Archives of Manitoba.

This cartoon by Arch Dale from the *Grain Growers' Guide* in 1915 conveys the western farmers' view of the Canadian political and economic reality.

142

provided for the free entry of Canadian natural products into the United States, while American manufacturers benefited from a lower Canadian duty.

In contrast to the Reciprocity Treaty of 1854, however, free trade came into effect through concurrent legislation passed by the two governments rather than by treaty. This arrangement enabled Canada to avoid seeking British approval. The Americans approved the legislation in July 1911, and it remained only for the Canadian Parliament to give its approval.

To Canadian politicians in both parties, the agreement seemed ideal. The Liberals enthusiastically endorsed free trade, convinced that it was the issue that would keep them in office; the Conservatives feared that it would keep them out of office.

OPPOSITION TO RECIPROCITY

Then came the opposition. The first blow to Liberal complacency came from within the party. Clifford Sifton, who had resigned as interior minister in 1905, quit the Liberal party altogether over the issue. Now a well-established Ontario businessman, Sifton opposed reciprocity, feeling the country was better off without it. In Parliament on February 28, 1911, he voiced his protest: "These resolutions, in my judgment, spell retrogression, commercial subordination, the destruction of our national ideals and displacement from our proud position as the rising hope of the British Empire."

At the same time as Sifton's defection, a manifesto signed by eighteen prominent Toronto manufacturers, industrialists, and financiers led by Zebulon Lash and Sir Edmund Walker argued that ratification of the trade agreement would "weaken the ties that bind Canada to the Empire ... and make it more difficult to avert political union with the United States." A weakened business community, they argued, would mean a weakened nation. This Ontario business group helped form the Canadian National League to fight reciprocity and published a pamphlet, *The Road to Washington*, with supposed evidence that the United States intended to absorb Canada economically and politically.

Inopportune statements by imprudent American politicians aided the anti-reciprocity lobbyists. Champ Clark, Speaker-designate of the House of Representatives, said of reciprocity: "I am for it, because I hope to see the day when the American flag will float over every square foot of the British North American possessions clear to the North Pole." President Taft himself noted that "Canada stands at the parting of the ways." By this he meant that Canada had to choose between remaining an isolated country or trading freely with the Americans, but anti-American proponents interpreted the phrase to mean Canada had to choose between Britain and the United States. Emotional arguments about loyalty and nationalism replaced economic ones. *143*

The Conservatives capitalized on this wave of emotion. Party leader Robert Borden allied himself with Sifton, arguing that free trade would lead to commercial union and, eventually, political annexation with the United States. He also gained the support of Sir James Whitney, the new Ontario Conservative premier, who opposed reciprocity and was willing to allow the national party to make use of the Ontario Conservative machine to fight reciprocity.

THE ELECTION OF 1911

Laurier had Parliament dissolved and appealed to the country for another mandate. In Ontario, the reciprocity issue predominated; in Quebec, the naval question. Imperialists in Ontario accused Laurier of being a continentalist; French-Canadian nationalists branded him an imperialist. "I am neither," Laurier protested during an election campaign rally in St. Jean, Quebec in August, 1911, "I am a Canadian. I have had before me ... a policy of true Canadianism, of moderation, of conciliation." The Conservatives supported the imperialists in Ontario and favoured the *nation-alistes* in Quebec. All that united the Conservatives and the French-Canadian *nationalistes* was a common determination to defeat Laurier and the Liberals. In this alone, the joint alliance succeeded.

The Liberals lost the election of 1911, winning only thirteen of the eighty-six seats in Ontario and barely half (thirty-eight of the sixty-five seats) in Quebec, their stronghold. In the Maritimes the two parties essentially split the vote, while in the West the Liberals did well in Saskatchewan and Alberta, as did the Conservatives in Manitoba and British Columbia. The Conservative victory was greatest in Ontario. Even without any support from Quebec, the Conservatives had a five-seat majority in the House of Commons.

A Reform Conservative Government

144

Robert Laird Borden, the eighth prime minister of Canada, lacked his predecessor's flair. Bruce Hutchison, a political commentator, has noted: "He lacked any talent of self-advertisement, any loveable eccentricities, any gift of speech."[3] A self-made man, this Nova Scotian believed the highest qualities of a leader to be duty and sacrifice. In the words of one acquaintance, Borden was "preeminently the businessman of Canadian politics."

Like Laurier before him, Borden had acquired his political skills over a decade as the federal opposition leader. A schoolteacher who later became a highly successful Halifax lawyer, Borden first ran for the federal parliament in 1896. While he found the life of a Conservative backbencher lonely and frustrating, he did make important political contacts, including an acquaintance with Henri Bourassa. In 1901, when Sir Charles Tupper stepped down as leader of a badly divided party, the Tory caucus, on Tupper's recommendation, chose Borden. The new leader worked to rebuild his party and to establish a reform policy—the Halifax Platform of 1907, which called for civil service reform and increased public ownership.

BORDEN'S FIRST CABINET

Borden's Cabinet reflected his temperament and beliefs. No one minister stood out as dynamic or memorable, with the possible exceptions of Colonel Sam Hughes, minister of militia and defence, and Sir George Foster, minister of trade and commerce. Yet collectively they ran an efficient government. Limited French-Canadian representation in the Cabinet was the most obvious weakness.

The alliance with the *nationalistes* broke down almost immediately after the election. Henri Bourassa refused a cabinet position while F.D. Monk, the Conservative leader in Quebec, held only the lesser ministry of public works. Monk's hesitancy to make decisions and his failure to act as a liaison between Quebec and Ottawa weakened further the Conservative government's tenuous relationship with Quebec. Borden's two other French-Canadian cabinet ministers received portfolios mainly as compromise candidates of the Conservative and *nationaliste* factions.

CONSERVATIVE REFORMS

Civil service reform was high on the government's list of priorities. Borden believed in good, efficient, and honest government—principles that he thought the Liberals had compromised during their long years in office. The prime minister appointed a commission to investigate the civil service with a view to "securing increased efficiency and more thorough organization and co-ordination of the various departments." The commissioners found little proof of corruption and graft, but much evidence of incompetence and inefficiency. They made two major recommendations: that ministers concern themselves less with day-to-day departmental operations and more with broader political concerns; and that competitive examinations, as well as tighter controls over appointments and promotions, be introduced.

145

The Borden government passed two minor amendments to the Civil Service Act in 1912; one provided for a higher grade of private secretaries for ministers, the other for a third civil service commissioner. More substantial changes met with resistance from the Cabinet and the party. The winners, after fifteen years in opposition, wanted to enjoy the fruits of office and the advantages of patronage.

The Borden government also reformed the grain trade. It passed the Canada Grain Act of 1912, which established the government-regulated Board of Grain Commission to supervise, inspect, and regulate grain sales. It also permitted the government to own and operate grain terminal elevators in an effort to satisfy western farmers' complaints of malpractice in the inspecting and grading of wheat. Other measures introduced to aid farmers included free mail delivery, construction of a railway to carry grain to a port on Hudson Bay, funds to the provinces for upgrading agricultural education, and support for provincial highway construction. To satisfy those Canadians who still believed that the country's strength came from its strong agrarian base, some of these reforms were aimed at stemming rural depopulation, occurring at an alarming rate during the downswing in the economy in 1913–14.

THE CONSERVATIVES AND THE NAVAL DISPUTE

The naval question was the most contentious issue facing the new Conservative government. The *nationalistes'* opposition to Laurier's naval bill had contributed to the Liberal's decline in Quebec. Borden now faced the difficult task of formulating his own naval policy. Convinced that a state of military crisis existed in Europe, the new prime minister favoured a direct emergency contribution to the British navy; he believed this contribution would encourage Britain to grant the Dominions a greater voice in deciding imperial foreign policy.

Quebec Conservatives disagreed with Borden, however. Monk argued that an emergency naval contribution should be made only when the time warranted it and that no crisis existed. The Quebec Conservative leader also resisted Canada having a voice in imperial foreign policy, seeing this as a ploy to get the country embroiled in foreign wars of no interest or concern to Canadians.

146

The prime minister introduced a Naval Aid Bill in December 1912. It provided for a direct cash contribution of $35 million to Britain to build three dreadnoughts. Monk found the decision unacceptable and resigned, but some French-Canadian Conservative backbenchers did support the bill. The Liberals attacked Borden's bill as a sham and as an inadequate alternative to Laurier's naval program. In the end, the Conservatives—for the first time in Canadian history—imposed closure to cut off debate. Then, in an unprecedented move, the Liberal majority in the Senate defeated the bill. Shortly afterwards, the issue died when military experts began questioning the efficiency of dreadnoughts. Thus, on the eve of World War I, Canada had neither made a contribution to the British navy nor built up a navy of its own.

In 1914 many Canadians had achieved a level of prosperity unforeseen half a century earlier. The national policy, adopted by both major political parties, was firmly in place. The West and its rapidly growing population was being integrated into the nation by the three transcontinental railways servicing the region. Wheat exports had become Canada's single most important export commodity.

Yet in these good years, from 1896 to 1914, lay the roots of discontent and dissension. French-speaking and English-speaking Canadians were pursuing different goals for the nation—the former generally appealing for increased autonomy, while an influential elite among the latter urged closer ties to the Empire. Farmers and industrialists were also divided on whether to continue the National Policy or negotiate a reciprocity treaty with the United States. It was a difficult country to govern. The Great War would briefly unite Canadians but, ultimately, divide them even further.

NOTES

[1] T.D. Regehr, "Triple Tracking," *Horizon Canada*, number 7 (1986), p. 1878.
[2] Quoted in R.C. Brown and R. Cook, *Canada 1896–1921: A Nation Transformed* (Toronto, 1974), p. 153.
[3] Bruce Hutchison, *Mr. Prime Minister, 1867–1964* (Toronto, 1964), p. 147.

BIBLIOGRAPHY

An overview of the Laurier era is available in R.C. Brown and R. Cook, *Canada, 1896–1921: A Nation Transformed* (Toronto, 1974). Biographies of Laurier include O.D. Skelton, *Life and Letters of Sir Wilfrid Laurier*, 2 vols. (Toronto, 1921; reprinted 1965); Joseph Schull, *Laurier: The First Canadian* (Toronto, 1965); Richard Clippingdale, *Laurier: His Life and World* (Toronto, 1979); and Réal Bélanger, *Wilfrid Laurier: quand la politique devient passion* (Québec, 1986).

On railway building during the Laurier years, consult T.D. Regehr, *The Canadian Northern Railway: Pioneer Road of the Northern Prairies 1895–1918* (Toronto, 1976), and G.R. Stevens, *Canadian National Railways*, 2 vols. (Toronto, 1960). Treatment of the school question in Alberta and Saskatchewan can be found in Manoly R. Lupul, *The Roman Catholic Church and the North-West School Question: A Study in Church-State Relations in Western Canada* (Toronto, 1974). On Sifton's role in the controversy see D.J. Hall, *Clifford Sifton*, vol. 2: *The Lonely Eminence, 1901–1929* (Vancouver, 1985).

The debate over naval defence is discussed in C.P. Stacey, *Canada and the Age of Conflict: A History of Canadian External Relations, vol. 1: 1867–1921* (Toronto, 1977). For the conflicting views in Quebec, see Mason Wade's chapter, "Nationalism vs. Imperialism: 1905–11," in *The French Canadians: 1760–1945* (Toronto, 1955), pp. 536–607. The issue of reciprocity in the 1911 election is analysed in L.E. Ellis, *Reciprocity, 1911: A Study in Canadian-American Relations* (New Haven, 1939). Paul Steven, ed., *The 1911 Election: A Study in Canadian Politics* (Toronto, 1970) is a compilation of primary and secondary sources.

The fortunes of the Conservative party are discussed in R.C. Brown, *Robert Laird Borden: A Biography*, vol. 1: *1854–1914* (Toronto, 1975), and in John English, *The Decline of Politics: The Conservatives and the Party System 1901–20* (Toronto, 1977).

147

CHAPTER EIGHT

The Rise of Urban and Industrial Canada, 1880–1914

By 1914 the predominantly rural and agricultural Canada of 1867 had become an urban and industrial society. This transformation occurred as a result of greater prosperity, increased immigration, large-scale invest-ment, and a new attitude towards business. Not all regions of the country, though, advanced at the same rate. The Maritimes grew slowly, while the West experienced phenomenal expansion. As the national policy intended, most urban and industrial growth occurred in highly populated central Canada (Ontario and Quebec).

Along with growth and prosperity came new social problems: slums, unhealthy working conditions in factories, underpaid women in the work-place, industrial accidents, and infant mortality. How to deal with these problems—and, indeed, deciding who should be responsible for dealing with them—became contentious issues.

Canada's Economic Expansion

The turn of the century was the springtime of Canadian industrialization. The long international trade recession of the 1870s and 1880s finally ended by 1896. Britain, the United States, and Europe, all had healthy industrial economies, and needed Canadian wheat, timber and minerals.

Canadians felt confident about their country's future. The *Canadian Courier*, a popular English language weekly magazine, captured the new optimism in a 1909 editorial:

> Hundreds and thousands of Canadian boys can hope to trip over a fortune one of these days in the Canadian wilderness. Pots of gold lie hidden there more truly than at the end of rainbows. ... Golden opportunities lie all around; and we can never tell that the lad who plays on the street before us will not some day be a railway builder,

a bank president, a mighty financier. ... Canada is a perpetual Christmas Tree with a present for every son of the house.

GROWTH IN SECONDARY INDUSTRY

The national policy was working, at last. Growth in farming, fishing, lumbering, and mining increased the demand for secondary industries, particularly road construction, rail transportation, and shipbuilding. Within Canada itself, industry and manufacturing greatly expanded. The CPR and the new railways brought hundreds of thousands of immigrants westward, and took away the Northwest's natural resources. Equally, a growing rural population in the West further increased the demand for eastern manufactured goods. Every new homesteader was a potential buyer of, for example, agricultural implements as well as the usual household items.

149

The increase in demand for such goods meant more jobs. Workers were needed in central Canadian boot and shoe factories, iron and steel foundries, agricultural implements works, textile industries, machine shops, railway yards, and in a host of other smaller manufacturing plants that supplied consumer goods. Service industries, as well as governments (national, provincial, and municipal), became major employers.

FINANCIAL INVESTMENT

With abundant natural resources and an increasing population, Canada became an inviting field for investment at the turn of the century. The federal government provided direct investment as well as indirect financial assistance to private companies. The Quebec, and especially Ontario, governments became large investors, too, each seeking to take advantage of the potential within its provincial boundaries. They offered bonuses, subsidies, and guarantees to industrialists to locate new plants within their borders. Ontario in particular ignored the formation of trusts and monopolies, sought out foreign investment, and even nationalized industries (with the help of Ontario businessmen) deemed to be in the "public interest."

Banks provided another source of internal revenue. The three largest Canadian banks—the Bank of Montreal, the Royal Bank (also with its headquarters in Montreal), and the Toronto-based Bank of Commerce—centralized their operations, invested in new industries, and provided capital for entrepreneurs. Banks and life-insurance companies offered interim financing and underwrote securities. Bond and stock dealers marketed securities.

Foreign investment increased as well. Britain continued to provide money for railways, construction, and business, chiefly in the form of indirect portfolio investments (i.e., loans in the form of bonds). In contrast, American businessmen, who preferred ownership to indirect investment, continued to build branch plants in Canada to avoid tariff restrictions. They also invested heavily in mining and in the growing pulp and paper industry.

The rise of mass industrial production necessitated large sources of capital. To encourage investment beyond that of a single individual or of small groups of individuals, the concept of limited liability was adopted by Canadian businesses. The investor contributed only a portion of the necessary sum, and if the company failed, lost only what was contributed and no more.

The introduction of limited liability opened up the investment field. Large corporations—"immortal beings" in terms of commercial law—became the rule. In 1902, there were a handful of consolidated companies; by 1912, there were nearly sixty. These mergers involved nearly 250 smaller companies and had a combined total capitalization of almost half a billion dollars, or roughly eight billion in later values.[1] Especially noteworthy were Dominion Canner Limited, which in 1910 amalgamated thirty-four smaller canning factories; Canada Cement, a consolidation of eleven cement companies in 1909; and Stelco (the Steel Company of Canada), formed in 1910 out of several small Ontario and Quebec iron and steel mills. The latter two were the work of the young New Brunswick financier Max Aitken (later to become Sir Max and eventually Lord Beaverbrook). "I created all the big trusts in Canada," he once boasted. (Aitken was so skilled at mergers that one friend commented at the time of his death in 1964 that he could now "set about merging heaven and hell.")

150

ROLE OF GOVERNMENT IN THE ECONOMY

Most politicians defined the responsibilities of government quite narrowly at the turn of the century: the government was best that governed least. Ottawa did nothing to regulate the monopolies, apart from passing the Combines Investigation Act of 1910, introduced by William Lyon Mackenzie King, the new minister of labour. This act allowed for governmental investigation of monopoly price-fixing, but during its entire nine-year lifespan, the investigation board dealt with only one case. Business thus had a free hand in the boom years before World War I.

Some state participation in the economy occurred, usually with the blessing and support of business. Private businesses enthusiastically supported publicly–financed corporations that could do the same job as a private company much more cheaply and without heavy private investment. Ontario Hydro was a prime example, as were the utility companies of the prairie provinces.

In the case of Ontario Hydro, public ownership occurred when businesses in Toronto and in other southwestern Ontario towns and cities needed cheap energy. When it seemed likely that the tremendous energy power of Niagara Falls might be harnessed by only a small privileged business group, other businessmen rallied behind Adam Beck, a manufacturer of cigar boxes and a Conservative member of the Ontario Legislature for London, to force the Ontario government to nationalize the industry. "From the outset," the historian H.V. Nelles notes, "the crusade for public power was a businessmen's movement; they initiated it, formed its devoted, hard-core membership, and, most importantly, they provided it with brilliant leadership. By the phrase 'the people's power,' the businessmen meant cheap electricity for the manfacturer, and it was assumed that the entire community would benefit as a result."[2] Many ordinary consumers agreed. Ontario Hydro was an example of state capitalism, not state socialism.

151

A NEW MENTALITY TOWARD BUSINESS

The new industries necessitated a new managerial class and a more skilled labour force. In many ways the primary schools became the children's training ground for the workplace. In factory-like institutions, the young were taught the values of punctuality, obedience, thrift, and self-discipline—values essential for an industrial society. Workers in factories were expected to follow the rhythm of machines and, indeed, to become like machines. Schools prepared them for that task.

Governments pressured educational institutions into providing technical and scientific training. Girls studied domestic science, while boys learned mechanical skills or acquired a business education. In 1903 Ontario set up grants for manual training and domestic science courses. Under the Industrial Education Act, schools were established for the basic trades and for specialized industries. The Quebec government also established secondary technical education schools in Montreal and Quebec City. Nova Scotia opened the Technical University of Nova Scotia in 1907, a post-secondary trades college.

Since education was a provincial concern, the federal government intervened in the area of technical education reluctantly and gradually. In 1910 it established a Royal Commission on Industrial Training and Technical Education, which made a thorough investigation of the current state of Canadian education at the time. Four years of war intervened before the federal government acted on the report. Then in 1919, the federal

Technical Education Act established a fund of $10 million for technical education over the next decade.

Canadian society at the turn of the century prized those who succeeded in commerce. At the top of the social order stood the businessmen, enshrined as national heroes. In a poll taken in 1908 by the *Canadian Courier*, the public named among "Canada's Top Ten Biggest Men" nine captains of industries and railway magnates. At the time the philosophy of social Darwinism prevailed; it taught that the best naturally succeeded: that survival belonged to the fittest. Successful entrepreneurs believed they prospered because they were virtuous and moral, and that the evidence of their virtue was their wealth. "Prominent businessmen," historian Michael Bliss notes, "were often pillars of their local churches, intensely dedicated Christians who moved easily from board meetings to prayer meetings, eschewed drinking, gambling, dancing, and other frivolities, and tried to apply the golden rule in all their business dealings."[3] To them, wealth and public service went naturally together—out of personal success came public good. Young English-speaking Canadians accepted the theory of the popular American writer, Horatio Alger, that anyone could rise from rags to riches through hard work, thrift, and self-discipline.

152

English-speaking Canadians had numerous successes to model themselves after: Herbert Holt, the billion-dollar recluse who had founded the Montreal Light, Heat and Power Company in 1902 and became president of the Royal Bank; Henry Pellatt, active in the formation of Canadian General Electric and owner of Toronto's Casa Loma, one of the most palatial residences in North America; Joseph Flavelle, president of the William Davies Meat Packing Plant in Toronto, and chairman of the Bank of Commerce and the National Trust Company; Francis H. Clergue, founder of the Algoma Steel Company of Sault Ste. Marie, Ontario; Patrick Burns, owner of the Burns Meat Packing Company of Calgary; Timothy Eaton, whose department stores in Toronto and Winnipeg, factories in Toronto, Oshawa, Hamilton, and Montreal, and buying offices in London, England, and Paris together employed more than nine thousand people; and Max Aitken, Canada's "merger king," who was a millionaire by the age of thirty.

These entrepreneurs built industrial empires worth millions of dollars that employed tens of thousands of workers. Aitken expressed the attitude of these entrepreneurs when he claimed that his satisfaction came not from the success nor from the money, but from the challenge: "I am a builder. ... When the building is finished I do not stay in it but move to build another."

Urbanization

Industrialization accelerated urbanization. Industrial growth required factories, workers, large banks, commercial institutions, and transportation services. During the period 1890–1920, Montreal and Toronto, the two largest and most advanced industrial cities, almost tripled their populations, both surpassing the half-million mark. Winnipeg increased sevenfold and Vancouver twelvefold (growing at a rate of one thousand per month in the peak year of 1910). Calgary's population increased sixteen times. Of all the major western cities, though, Saskatoon eclipsed the rest in the rate of growth, rising from several hundred to nearly ten thousand people in the first decade of the new century. In the decade between 1901 and 1911 alone, the Canadian urban population increased 63 percent. In 1901 Canada had fifty-eight cities with populations over five thousand and by 1911, ninety.

Urban centres controlled the surrounding region, providing the rural inhabitants with manufactured goods and with services, but these centres also became dependents of larger cities beyond. This dependency created a link with Montreal and Toronto, the only two Canadian cities that were not hinterlands of other Canadian cities (although they were dependent on such urban centres outside Canadian borders as London, New York, and Chicago).

153

The dominance of Montreal and Toronto dated back to the mid-nineteenth century and the railway boom. After 1885 and the completion of the CPR, Montreal's and Toronto's influence reached the Pacific Ocean. Their real growth, however, occurred in the 1890s and 1900s, the era of industrialization.

Slower Growth in the Maritimes

The nature and extent of industrial and urban growth varied regionally. In the Maritimes the traditional fish, timber, and shipbuilding industries continued to prosper after Confederation. In the 1870s and 1880s, however, these resource-based economies lost their momentum. The West Indies sugar trade fell dramatically in the 1870s when a world glut of sugar caused prices to collapse resulting in an imbalance of trade between Nova Scotia and the West Indies. In the same decade Britain's demand for Maritime lumber and wooden ships declined, seriously affecting Nova Scotia's and New Brunswick's economies.

Although the resource-based economy was still important in the region, there also developed an industrial economy that fostered significant social and political divisions. Some Maritime entrepreneurs shifted from the traditional staples into a new manufacturing base. Businessmen in Nova Scotia invested in textiles and steel products (such as steel rails and locomotives) to take advantage of the Cape Breton coal fields. Together these developments contributed to an expanding Maritime industrial economy; in fact, in the early 1880s Nova Scotia's industrial growth on a per capita basis actually outstripped that of Ontario and Quebec.

This industrial expansion, in the long run, however, could not keep pace with industrial growth elsewhere in the country. Some historians have pointed out that the region lacked resources as rich or diverse as Ontario's, for instance. Although Cape Breton had coal, timber, iron ore, and fish, agriculture was not as productive as elsewhere. Distance from the large markets of central Canada, high transportation costs, and the small size of the Maritimes' total population meant that factories in the region soon experienced difficulties in expanding. Also, Maritime investors, like their Canadian counterparts elsewhere, saw western and continental development as more potentially lucrative. Led by the banks, they invested their money outside the region, thus depriving the area of much-needed capital.

154
In the end, Maritime industries could not compete with the more efficient Ontario and Quebec rivals, who now also served the Maritime region. Railways like the Intercolonial (completed in 1876) further integrated the Maritimes into the Canadian economy. Both central Canada and the West obtained ice-free ports for export trade, and central Canada also gained another hinterland for its tariff-protected manufactured goods.

As industrialization declined, Maritime cities grew at a slower pace than elsewhere. Halifax increased by only 16 000 between 1871 and 1911, while St. John, New Brunswick actually declined between 1871 and 1891, and then it regained a modest 3500 to bring the population to 42 500 by 1911. These cities remained small, with modest hinterlands of their own. In time they became dependents of larger metropolitan centres, namely Montreal and to a lesser extent, Toronto.

Growth in the West

On the Pacific Coast, British Columbia's economy relied on natural resources—salmon, minerals, and timber. The orientation of trade shifted from a maritime-based economy, connected by the Pacific Ocean to California, Great Britain, and other Pacific Rim points, to a continental-based economy, linked by rail with central Canada.

The Prairies needed B.C. lumber to build homes for new settlers, and the quantity of lumber cut rose by nearly 400 percent between 1900 and 1910. Central Canada provided many of the entrepreneurs who opened up the industry; Britain, the United States, and continental Europe contributed investment capital. Wood-product manufacturing became the major employment sector of the economy. The province's distance from the centre of industrial development in central Canada, high freight rates, and the small regional market ruled out the development of a substantial secondary manufacturing base. Instead, British Columbia, like the Maritimes, became another hinterland region.

RISE OF CITIES IN THE WEST

Two urban centres competed for dominance in west coast trade: Victoria and Vancouver. In the critical period from 1890 to 1914, Vancouver (so named by railway-builder Cornelius Van Horne, vice-president of the CPR at the time of Vancouver's incorporation as a city in 1886) surpassed Victoria as the province's commercial and financial centre. The CPR gave Vancouver its initial advantage by making it the railway's western terminus, and built excellent dock and terminal facilities on Burrard Inlet. Victoria, however, remained the seat of government. By 1914 Vancouver's population had reached 155 000 while Victoria's stood at 35 000. The completion of the Panama Canal in 1914 helped Vancouver to surpass Winnipeg in less than two decades. Prairie farmers could now ship wheat to European markets through Vancouver and the Panama Canal.

On the prairies, wheat was king. Towns and cities were established to service surrounding agricultural communities. Winnipeg was the exception. Thanks to its strategic location as the gateway to the West, it became the third-largest manufacturing city in pre-World War I Canada. Nick-named the "Hub City," Winnipeg joined three transcontinental railways; it processed rural agricultural products and in return sold to settlers construction materials—lumber, bricks, finished steel and cement, as well as a limited number of manufactured goods. The city employed thousands in its rail yards, the largest in the world by 1904, with as many as eighteen hundred freight cars passing through in a single day.

155

Urbanization occurred at a rapid rate on the prairies. When the region was incorporated into Confederation in 1870, no urban centres existed; by 1911, there were seventeen incorporated cities and one hundred and fifty incorporated towns. The urban proportion of the region's population increased from one-fifth to one-quarter between 1901 and 1911. Five dominant cities emerged by 1914: Winnipeg, Saskatoon, Regina, Edmonton, and Calgary, each with a clearly defined hinterland to service. Calgary had the ranching and farming country of southern Alberta; Edmonton, central Alberta; Regina and Saskatoon, the wheatlands of Saskatchewan; and Winnipeg, southern Manitoba. All five had major rail connections with the East, but Winnipeg had the most because all pre-1914 prairie transcontinental trade passed through its municipal boundaries, thus making the entire West its hinterland. Even the major urban metropolises of the prairie region, however, were serviced by eastern cities; ultimately, all western rail lines led to Montreal and Toronto.

Industrialization and Urbanization in Central Canada

At the turn of the century industrial and urban growth occurred largely in Ontario and Quebec. The transition from a commercial to an industrial base in central Canada occurred in two stages—in "two industrial revolutions," according to the Quebec economists Albert Faucher and Maurice Lamontagne.[4] They argue that the first occurred in the late nineteenth century (1866–96), when steel replaced wood as the province's basic product, and the construction of railroads became a major source of economic growth.

Ontario had an advantage over Quebec during this phase because of the province's proximity to the Pennsylvania coal fields and the Minnesota iron ranges. Also, a network of rail lines crisscrossed Ontario, linking towns and cities to the rural countryside and to other urban centres. Furthermore, Ontario already had, by the turn of the century, a host of manufacturing centres scattered from Windsor to Cornwall—London, Berlin (Kitchener), Guelph, and Peterborough, with the largest concentration at the western end of Lake Ontario, including Toronto, Hamilton, Brantford, Grimsby, and St. Catharines. Each of these centres had its own manufacturing base producing such tariff-protected goods as engines, farm implements, stoves, furniture, and canned goods. Hamilton became a steel-producing town as well as the base for extensive rail car shops, while Toronto held the majority of Ontario's largest head offices, financial institutions, factories, and warehouses.

Quebec, by comparison, was dominated by only two major industrial cities: Montreal and Quebec City. A few small textile towns grew in the Eastern Townships—places like Drummondville, Granby, St. Jean, Magog, Coaticook, and Sherbrooke, but most did not develop into manufacturing centres comparable to the smaller towns and cities of Ontario. The province instead concentrated on small-scale manufacturing of shoes, textiles, lumber, and foodstuffs (flour, sugar, dairy products)—light industries utilizing cheap and abundant labour for a limited domestic market. These industries were concentrated near the rail facilities of the two main cities. Montreal had the advantage here, followed by Quebec City.

At the turn of the century a second industrial revolution occurred when hydro-electric power replaced steam as the main source of industrial energy. Pulp and paper, and later minerals, became the new resource products. Quebec had, in the Laurentian Shield to the north, an abundance of water power for electricity and spruce trees for the pulp and paper industry. Thus Quebec's economy accelerated during this period. Nevertheless, the province did not succeed in catching up to Ontario, which also continued to expand greatly during this "second industrial revolution" thanks to mineral production and the pulp and paper mills in the north, and hydro-electric power, especially from Niagara Falls.

In Quebec the development of hydro-electric power also facilitated industrial expansion. Between 1900 and 1910 power production in the province increased by 310 percent. Three companies monopolized the industry by 1914: the Shawinigan Water and Power Company in the St. Maurice valley; the Montreal Light, Heat and Power Company in the Montreal area; and the Southern Canada Power Company in the Eastern Townships.

156

The pulp and paper industry went through a similar period of growth. Increased U.S. demand for newsprint tripled Quebec's pulp and paper industry, from 1900 to 1910. The Laurentide Company, established in 1877, dominated the industry. Initially, the company, along with other smaller ones, produced only pulp to be processed in the United States. Then Premier Lomer Gouin's government (1905–20), at the urging of Quebec nationalists, placed an embargo on exports of pulp from Crown lands, and Quebec pulp mills began producing newsprint for export. Laurentide became Canada's first newsprint-maker, producing 44 500 tons in 1906.

Quebec was thus a leading industrial province on the eve of World War I. More than two-thirds of Quebec's population was engaged in non-agricultural activities (in contrast to the traditional agricultural base of the Quebec economy) and more than 40 percent of its population lived in urban centres. When the French author Louis Hémon published his classic novel *Marie Chapdelaine* in 1913, about a pioneering rural Quebec family, the reality he described was already "ancient history" for many French Canadians.

157

The Uniqueness of Quebec's Industrial Development

For French Canadians, there was, however, one unique and disturbing aspect to Quebec's industrialization: they had almost no control over it. Only 2.4 percent of Canadian entrepreneurs in 1910 were French-speaking; French Canadians were labourers, not owners of industry. There were exceptions—Senator Louis Forget and his nephew Sir Rodolphe Forget, powerful financiers and investors in Quebec industries; Senator Frédéric-Liguori Béique, director of the Banque d'Hochelaga and later president of the Banque Canadienne Nationale; Alfred Dubuc, owner of the Chicoutimi Pulp Company in the Saguenay valley; and Georges Amyot, an influential textile magnate. But these men stood out precisely because they were exceptions.

This imbalance has been blamed on French Canadians' access to a more limited pool of capital than English-speaking Canadians and the Americans. Moreover, since the language of business was English and the ethos of industrialization the Protestant work ethic, French-speaking Catholics faced other obstacles. The church, in particular, has been criticized for failing to encourage technical and scientific education in the school system that it dominated. There were few courses geared towards science or business in the classical colleges. Quebec historians Paul-André Linteau, René Durocher, and Jean-Claude Robert have noted that "education for scientific careers was shockingly neglected."[5]

The provincial government tried to correct this deficiency by offering financial support for the establishment of technical schools. In 1907 Lomer Gouin's government founded two technical schools, one in Montreal and one in Quebec City, "to provide our manufacturers with educated producers, highly skilled overseers, and experienced foremen and elite workers." It also created the Ecole des Hautes Études Commerciales (HEC), a university-level business school. These institutions, however, had difficulty in recruiting French-speaking students and were opposed by the church hierarchy, which feared an encroachment on its jurisdiction.

Recent studies show that the Catholic church did not always oppose industrialization and, in fact, sometimes encouraged it, especially in many urban and one-industry-town parishes as a means to stem emigration and the loss of parishoners. The church did, however, consistently stress that spiritual concerns should be uppermost in life. Official church doctrine held that the real destiny of the French Canadians was in agriculture. The materialism of urban-industrial society was a danger to the faith and to the stability of the family.

158

FRENCH-CANADIAN RESPONSE TO INDUSTRIALISM

French-Canadian intellectuals divided into two camps on how best to deal with the problem of "foreign" ownership of their industries. Some appealed to their fellow French Canadians to turn their backs on industrial development or else run the risk of losing the essence of being French Canadian. Jules-Paul Tardivel, the ultramontane nationalist and editor of the newspaper, *La Vérité*, best expressed such a viewpoint: "It is not necessary for us to possess industry and money. ... We would no longer be French Canadians but Americans like the others. ... To cling to the soil, to raise large families, to maintain the hearths of spiritual and intellectual life, that must be our role in America."

Others, like Errol Bouchette, a French-Canadian economist, urged Quebeckers at the turn of the century to accept industrialization. It was not inherently evil or a danger to survival but had the potential to benefit them as long as they directed its growth within the province. "Emparons-nous de l'industrie" (Let us take over industry) rather than "Emparons-nous du sol" (Let us take over the soil) became his slogan.

"New Ontario"

Industrialization advanced the fastest and the furthest in Ontario. As was noted earlier, the province's proximity to the Pennsylvania coal fields helped, as did the high protective tariff and the extensive railway system tying the province together and linking it to the growing regions outside its borders. But a decisive factor in Ontario's success was the exploitation of timber and mining in the north. Suddenly northern Ontario ceased to be perceived as an unproductive wasteland of rocks, lakes, and muskeg and was recognized instead as "new Ontario," rich in resources waiting to be developed. Sudbury, Cobalt, and Timmins developed as resource centres before World War I. The discovery of silver at Cobalt in 1903 began a mining boom never before experienced in Ontario. More than five hundred Canadian and American companies formed to invest millions of dollars in mining ventures. Cobalt became "the little Bay Street of the Northlands," and Toronto, "the world's biggest mining market."

The environmental cost of development was high, however. Unlike the placer mining in California and the Klondike, where metals were not imbedded in rock and thus were readily retrieved through panning, most mining strikes in northern Ontario required large-scale and sophisticated equipment. In nickel production, for example, the ore had to be mined from the rock and then burned in the open air to concentrate the metal and reduce the sulphur content. The government had no regulations for environmental protection. The land was cleared of trees to fuel the roasting process while sulphur and arsenic fumes escaped from the smokestacks into the atmosphere and poisoned the surrounding vegetation. What counted was production, not the environment.

159

This type of mining meant that companies had to have a great deal of investment capital and technical skill. The Canadian Copper Company was formed in 1886 under the American entrepreneur Samuel Ritchie to mine nickel in the Sudbury district. Full exploitation of the site required a process for separating and refining the nickel content of the ore, as well as the development of markets. Both techniques and markets came in the late 1880s, when it was discovered that nickel could be used in armour plating. By 1890 ore production surpassed 100 000 tons. Sudbury became the world's largest nickel producer and the site of Canada's greatest mines. In 1902 the Canadian Copper Company consolidated with several other smaller American companies to form the International Nickel Company of Canada (INCO).

Consolidation also took place in other mining fields. In the Cobalt and Porcupine districts, three large companies—Hollinger (Canadian-owned), Dome (American-owned), and McIntyre (Canadian-owned after 1915)—controlled 90 percent of the gold production. These became Ontario's golden trio. In its first year Hollinger mined almost $1 million in gold; at peak production Dome produced $1 million in bullion a month. In Sault Ste. Marie, F.H. Clergue, an American-born entrepreneur, built an industrial empire, the Consolidated Lake Superior Company, by using largely American capital.

160

Northern Miner Press.

Hand-rock mining in northern Ontario during the Cobalt silver rush immediately before World War One. Sophisticated equipment became necessary as the miners followed veins more deeply imbedded in the rock.

THE ONTARIO GOVERNMENT DEVELOPS ITS NORTHLAND

The Ontario government played the role of willing provider in the exploitation of its northland (as did other provincial governments of their northern regions). In 1891 the Mowat government, in response to the recommendations of a Royal Commission on Ontario's mineral resources, established the Bureau of Mines in 1891 "to collect and publish information and statistics on the mineral resources and mining industry." The provincial government encouraged the establishment of the School of Mining at Queen's University in Kingston in the early 1890s (it was later merged into the university proper as Queen's Faculty of Applied Sciences). To visiting industrialists and promoters, the provincial government freely handed out loans, railway land grants, timber leases, and mineral rights. When production began, however, the firms had to meet royalty payments. In 1904 one-quarter of the province's revenue came from forestry, and *161* mining soon contributed large sums to the provincial treasury.

MINING TOWNS IN NORTHERN ONTARIO

A host of mining towns accommodated the influx of prospectors and miners in search of valuable deposits. Some of these communities, like Golden City, Elk Lake, and South Porcupine, in northeastern Ontario were little more than extended mining camps made up of shacks and log cabins. Others were company towns, built and owned by the town's only employer; they provided basic services but little else. A few like Sudbury and Timmins became main service or distribution centres for entire regions, giving them a permanence and prominence denied to other towns in the area. All of these northern Ontario mining communities depended on the capricious rise and fall of world metal prices. Moreover, they all fell under the dominance of Toronto—their main supply base, the focus of their rail transport, and the seat of the provincial government that offered financial incentives to the mining companies.

Social Life in the Industrial City

As they became industrialized, cities became more socially stratified. Electric streetcars enabled the middle and upper classes to leave the inner city and to reside in suburban districts away from the congestion and pollution of the downtown core. The city centre became largely working-class. The commission of conservation, established by the federal government in 1909, summed up the situation graphically in its *Annual Report* in 1914:

City of Toronto Archives, DPW 32-259.

Slum courtyards, like this one in Toronto in 1913, served as storage areas, a place to hang
the wash, and a play area for children, often the only play area poor children knew.
These decrepit frame houses with poor water supply and outdoor toilets rented for eight
to twelve dollars a month.

Industrial smoke disfigures buildings, impairs the health of the population, renders the city filthy, destroys any beauty with which it
may naturally be endowed and tends, therefore, to make it a squalid
and undesirable place of residence, and this at a time when economic
influences are forcing into cities an ever increasing proportion of our
population.

LIVING CONDITIONS FOR THE URBAN WORKING CLASS

The average working-class family in the two largest and most industrialized
Canadian cities of Montreal and Toronto lived in poverty at the turn of
the century. Most working-class people rented accommodations in either
boarding or tenement houses—old wooden cottages or two-storey buildings with little or no yards. These tenement houses or cottages abounded
in Toronto's St. John's Ward, a district bounded by College, Queen,
University, and Yonge streets; in Montreal, tenement houses were the
rule in the city's lower town (Griffintown), in the poor English-speaking
area near the dock yards, as well as in the French-Canadian working-class
districts such as St. Henri and Ste. Marie.

An average family of five typically lived in a one- or two-room flat that was damp, unventilated, lighted inadequately, furnished sparsely, and heated poorly. Outdoor "pit privies" were common, as were open sewers. Overcrowding was a constant problem. In Toronto, for example, rapid growth led to a housing shortage, and some families lived in hastily constructed shacks, in tents in backyards, or even on the street.

Each Canadian city had extensive working-class enclaves. Halifax had its north suburbs; St. John, the district on the northeast tip of the harbour; Quebec City its Lower Town, between the promontory and the port; Hamilton its north-end ethnic areas along the waterfront of Burlington Bay. In Winnipeg, the railway divided the city physically and socially between the poorer immigrant areas of the north end and the wealthy districts in the south end. In Regina the railroad also formed the boundary of the working-class area to the south of it and east of the downtown core. In Calgary, the southeast area of the city, near the Ogden railway shops and the brewery, became the working-class district, while in Vancouver, it was the east end, where the largest concentration of Asians lived. Across the country labour camps sprang up where many immigrants—"bunkhouse men"—lived and worked in the construction and lumber industries wherever jobs came available.

163

Industrialization created appalling working conditions. During the peak season the average labourer spent at least six days a week in poorly ventilated, noisy and dirty factories, 10–12 hours a day and upwards of 60–70 hours a week. Foremen often levied fines on workers for being tardy or simply for talking to fellow workers on the job. Industrial accidents and deaths were common because of inadequate safety machinery. One boy, John Gale, reported before the Royal Commission on the Relations of Labour and Capital in 1889 that he had lost an arm while "taking blocks away from a circular saw" that did not have any protective gear around it. When asked whether he knew of other such accidents, he replied: "Yes, about two months after a boy was working in the mill, where I was, and got both his legs and arms taken off."

Job security was non-existent. There was no workman's compensation for victims of industrial accidents or for their families. Furthermore, steady year-round employment was rare. Layoffs, especially during the slower winter months, were frequent. In an age without unemployment insurance (which was not introduced until the early 1940s), layoffs meant months of subsistence without wages.

STANDARD OF LIVING

The cost of living in urban centres was high at the turn of the century and continued to outpace wages. The federal Department of Labour issued "typical weekly expenditure" budgets listing most expenditures necessary for a family of five to enjoy a minimum standard of living. (The modern definition of poverty is any individual or family having to spend more than 70 percent of total income on basic needs such as food, fuel, and shelter.) Though it allowed for only .6 kg of fresh meat per week per person, less than a litre of milk a day for a family of five, and no fresh vegetables or fruit, this minimum was well beyond the reach of most individual bread-winners. At best, the average male worker could, without layoffs, make $425 a year in 1901, or an average of $8.25 a week. But in 1901 the estimated cost of living was $13.38 per week. Thus, many working-class families had to have at least two incomes to survive.

WOMEN IN THE WORK PLACE

Women and children worked as unskilled labourers for low wages. Most women found jobs in "female occupations"—as secretaries, dressmakers, teachers, launderers, milliners, and housekeepers—work that often ena-bled them to stay at home where they could tend their children at the same time. Women and children in factories earned wages one-half to one-quarter of that of an adult male doing the same job. In 1900 young girls commonly worked up to sixty hours a week for eighty cents, or less than two cents per hour.

Female workers predominated in the textile industry. They made up about two-thirds of the work force in 1880 and just less than half in 1900. The majority were between the ages of fourteen (the youngest age per-missable for girls to work after 1885) and twenty-four (the normal marrying age, at which time women were not expected to work). As historian Jacques Rouillard has documented, hours were long and working conditions poor:

> It was not so much the physical effort required by the machines, as the tremendous speeds at which they functioned and the attention they demanded, which taxed the nervous system of the worker. The noise caused by the hundreds of weaving machines as well as the high degree of humidity in the spinning and weaving rooms were especially irritating. This damp atmosphere, maintained to keep the thread from breaking, resulted in fatigue among the workers and often led to loss of appetite and anemia. Many of the young women had to quit their jobs, unable to overcome the tension they suffered in this atmosphere.[6]

Herbert Ames, a philanthropic Montreal businessman, wrote a socio-logical study of a working-class district in 1897 entitled *The City Below the Hill*. He estimated that in an area with 7670 families, 12 500 men, 3265 women, and 460 children below the age of sixteen were employed. The federal census of 1891 reported that about 10 000 children worked

City of Toronto Archives (James 137).

Men, and particularly women, worked long hours for low wages in cramped conditions in textile factories. Mechanization, which was introduced in the late nineteenth century, meant greater efficiency and increased production for the owner, but monotony, a hectic pace and excruciating noise for the workers. Few textile factories were unionized in the early twentieth century.

in Quebec factories, and that women constituted more than one-quarter of the Quebec work force.

Toronto figures were much the same. Although laws forbade girls under fourteen and boys under twelve to work, violations frequently occurred, according to the reports of factory inspectors. Furthermore, some parents kept older children at home to care for younger children while mothers worked. Girls also hired themselves out as domestics or boys as messengers or helpers in the unregulated services.

Frequent illness and a high accidental death rate added to the normal daily problems of living and working. Montreal in particular remained a most unhealthy city in which to live. In the 1860s health conditions had been so bad that two out of five children died before reaching the age of one. They still were atrocious a generation later. At the turn of the century approximately one out of every four infants died before the age of twelve months. City inhabitants still suffered from impure water, unpasteurized milk, and the limited use of vaccines for smallpox, diphtheria, and tuberculosis. Conditions were somewhat better in Toronto. In both cities, however, families had no sick benefits, hospital insurance, or life insurance to protect them.

Charitable and Social Institutions for the Working Class

At the turn of the century, charity was largely in the hands of the churches and of private philanthropic organizations, although the state was being pressured to take on a greater role. Toronto had, early in the century, more than fifty charitable organizations and twenty churches providing relief to the poor. Montreal had nearly thirty shelters for the poor and outdoor relief agencies, as well as about a dozen old-age homes and a dozen orphanages. Between 1900 and 1911, these institutions provided relief for 2000–3000 families in their respective cities each year. Assistance was minimal, however, consisting usually of a meal of soup, bread, and tea, and a bath and a bed.

Charity was stern, designed to be as uncomfortable as possible, because in a society conditioned to *laissez-faire* principles, it was an unpopular concept. Charity went against the idea of individuals making their own way in the world. Generally speaking, society held that—with the exception of the infirm and the aged—the individual alone was to blame for his plight. As a result, however hard they tried, charities were unable to solve the widespread problem of poverty and low living standards. They could only help individuals, not change the system that caused poverty.

Skilled workers in particular looked to fraternal organizations for security (financial and emotional), and for their social functions. Associations and lodges—such as the Orange Lodges, Masons, Oddfellows, and Independent Order of Foresters—as well as sporting clubs for baseball, snowshoeing, rowing, and lacrosse, gave workers (male workers at least, since female workers did not belong) a sense of importance, a feeling of camaraderie, and a sense of pride and dignity. Some associations had mutual aid plans to care for sick members, and for widows and orphans in the event of members' deaths. They also gave workers a means to express publicly and collectively their discontent with industrial capitalism. Association life was, labour historian Bryan Palmer notes, "a realm apart from the troubled conflicts of the workplace,"[7] and an important phase on the road to a working-class consciousness.

UNIONS

A growing number of workers looked to unions to improve their working conditions. There were unions in Canada in the early nineteenth century, but most were local, dispersed across the country, and specialized. Initially, the government had refused to grant them legal recognition or to accept workers' right to collective bargaining. The first victory came in 1872, when the Toronto printers went on strike for a nine-hour day, protesting that "Nine hours a day, six days a week is enough for any man to work." George Brown, the prominent Liberal politician and editor of the Toronto *Globe*, vehemently opposed them. This Father of Confederation had no sympathy for collective bargaining, yet the Typographical society won its case. Prime Minister John A. Macdonald, Brown's archenemy, enacted the Trade Union Act, which recognized the right of unions to exist and to organize without fear of prosecution as illegal associations, although only so long as the unions were registered. This positive measure was offset, however, by the implementation at the same time of the Criminal Law Amendment Act, which imposed severe penalties, including a prison sentence, for most forms of picketing and union pressure.

In the 1870s the Canadian Labour Union, the first national organization of trade unions, was formed, but the depression of the late 1870s undermined its influence. Three other large-scale unions replaced it in the early 1880s: the Knights of Labor, the Trades and Labour Congress (TLC), and the American Federation of Labor (AFL).

The Knights of Labor, an American organization particularly strong in Ontario and Quebec, also had branches in British Columbia, the prairie West, and the Maritimes. The Knights believed in the development of a working-class consciousness through the organization of workers by industry rather than by trade, as well as through education in its labour-oriented newspapers; the best known were the *Palladium of Labour* and *Labour Advocate*. The Knights were also one of the few trade-union organizations that attempted to organize women workers; they even called for equal pay for equal work and were concerned with sexual harassment in the workplace. The movement began a precipitous decline in membership in the late 1880s due to national economic and political pressures: capital was consolidating into powerful organizations, thus putting workers on the defensive, while at the same time the Knights' attempt to influence local politics proved ineffective. The second large union association, the TLC, was founded in 1883 and was composed almost exclusively of skilled workers. Finally, the AFL entered Canada. This organization, begun and dominated by its first president Samuel Gompers, believed that workers should organize by craft in international unions and should shun partisan political activities; instead they would use their economic power (strikes and boycotts) to achieve immediate improvements in wages, working hours, and working conditions. Soon after the AFL arrived, the TLC affiliated with it, thus giving this conservative international organization substantial control over Canada's unionized workers.

Workers who opposed Gompers' philosophy looked to politics or radical unions as the best means of achieving their objectives. Some wanted the creation of an independent socialist party, while others supported such radical unions as the International Workers of the World (IWW), an American-based revolutionary industrial union. The "Wobblies," as they became known, attempted to organize all workers, especially the migrant workers known as blanket-stiffs (because they carried their possessions

167

168

CANADIAN Illustrated News

Vol. V.—No. 23.   MONTREAL, SATURDAY, JUNE 8, 1872.   SINGLE COPIES, TEN CENTS.
$4 PER YEAR IN ADVANCE.

HAMILTON.—PROCESSION OF NINE-HOUR MOVEMENT MEN.—FROM A PHOTOGRAPH.

National Archives of Canada (C58640).

Workers paraded through the streets of Hamilton in the spring of 1872 to demand a nine-hour work day.

rolled up in a blanket), into one large union for the purpose of calling a general strike that would bring down the capitalist system. The first sentence of their constitution emphatically stated: "The working class and the employing class have nothing in common." Neither movement achieved much success, however, except in the West.

The West saw the development of radical labour groups. An economic boom mentality—a belief that if you worked hard you advanced—made trade unions unpopular with the public. The philosophy of the self-made man was strongly entrenched leading to popular opposition to any form of collective action. Yet workers could not escape their condition. Wages were exceptionally low, inflation high, employment sporadic (especially in the primary industries) and working conditions appalling (most notably in the mines of British Columbia, Alberta, and Saskatchewan, and in the western railway work camps). On the one hand, immigration provided a large pool of unskilled workers who posed a threat to the growth of unions by their willingness to work as "scabs" for low wages. On the other, large-scale immigration from Britain and Europe contributed to labour radicalism by leaders—especially from Britain—who were versed in socialist ideas and experienced in union organization.

169

In Quebec, Catholic unions challenged the international unions. The clergy first intervened directly in a labour conflict in the Quebec Shoe Workers' Strike of 1900, thus making employers aware of the workers' position. Then, in 1907, a Catholic union was founded with the guidance of the clergy who feared that the "socialist" and anticlerical leanings of the international unions would destroy the Catholic church's position among the working class.

LIMITATIONS OF UNIONS IN THE PRE-WAR ERA

In general, unions had limited success prior to World War I. As late as 1911, less than one-tenth of the national work force belonged to unions, and this low membership restricted bargaining power. Most unskilled workers and virtually all women were non-unionized. Unions were also divided, and their leaders suspicious of one another, a factor that further reduced their effectiveness. They did organize strikes—one thousand disputes were recorded between 1900 and 1911—but these, too, had limited effect since few ended in successful settlements. Many resulted in physical violence, with the government calling on the militia to end them. Furthermore, employers still had the right to fire immediately workers who belonged to unions or to demand that workers sign contracts stipulating they would not join a union; most refused to acknowledge the legitimacy of workers' complaints. *La Presse* reported one Montreal mill manager in 1908 as having said that "it was not at all his concern whether his employees could live on the wages he paid them. If they don't like it, they can go work somewhere else."

Governments also appeared to be unsupportive of workers. The *laissez-faire* philosophy that government should not interfere in the workplace prevailed, at least in regards to labour. (The same governments, however, assisted employers by means of tariffs or other economic incentives). The Conservative government did establish the Royal Commission on the Relations of Labour and Capital, which in its 1889 report documented the sweeping impact of the industrial revolution in Canada. In 1894 the Conservatives also introduced Labour Day, the first Monday of September, as a holiday. The Laurier government created the Department of Labour in 1900 to help prevent and settle strikes and to enforce a fair wages policy. It also passed in 1907 the Industrial Disputes Investigation Act, which prohibited strikes and lockouts in mines or public utilities until a three-man board had investigated the dispute. The Ontario government under James Whitney introduced the Workman's Compensation Act in 1914, but only after the act had met the approval of employers who benefited as much as workers from government compensation to injured workers. Furthermore, there was no compulsion on either side to accept the Workman's Compensation Board's recommendations. In nearly all labour disputes, management's prerogatives went unchallenged and the demands of the workers unheeded.

170

Development of Canadian Culture

While working-class Canadians often lived in appalling conditions at the turn of the century, middle-and upper-class Canadians enjoyed the country's increased prosperity. A new national confidence surfaced, evident in an emerging Canadian culture. Beginning in the 1880s the "Confederation poets"—Charles G.D. Roberts, Bliss Carman, Archibald Lampman, and Duncan Campbell Scott—wrote about their native regions as well as about Canada as a whole. In Quebec, the Ecole littéraire de Montréal, founded in 1895, received high acclaim for its members' poetry. Emile Nelligan made his reputation on his nostalgic poems, such as "Romance du vin" and "Vaisseau d'or." Other Ecole poets romanticized the rural countryside in this era of urban and industrial growth.

Popular novelists and short story writers also emerged. Ernest Thompson Seton's animal stories were an original Canadian genre. The best Canadian novels had a regional setting. Martin Allerdale Grainger's *Woodsmen of the West* (1908) was set in British Columbia. Robert Service's first collected poems, *Songs of a Sourdough* (1907), won him acclaim as the poet of the Yukon. The settlement of the prairie West provided a subject and an inspiration for several Canadian novelists: Charles Gordon (Ralph Connor), Robert Stead, Nellie McClung, and Emily Murphy (Janey Canuck).

Connor's first novel, *The Sky Pilot* (1899), made his reputation. Before he stopped writing in the 1920s, his books sold more than five million copies worldwide. In Ontario, Stephen Leacock was acquiring international recognition as one of the greatest humorists writing in the English language. *Sunshine Sketches of a Little Town* (1912), a satire on "Mariposa," a typical small Ontario town, and *Arcadian Adventures of the Idle Rich* (1914), a parody on city life, were the best known of some sixty-odd books that earned him a reputation as the Mark Twain of the British Empire. Sara Jeanette Duncan's *The Imperialist* (1904) was set in southern Ontario but dealt with international themes. In Quebec, Gilbert Parker's *The Seats of the Mighty* (1898), a novel about New France, was a bestseller. French-Canadian novelists were reviving the rustic novel. Ernest Choquette's *Claude Paysan* (1899) is one example, but the best known was *Marie Chapdelaine* (1914) by the French author Louis Hémon. Lucy Maud Montgomery's first novel, *Anne of Green Gables* (1908) captured the spirit of her native province of Prince Edward Island. The novel made her and the island world famous. (Today *Anne* is among the three top-selling books in Japan and Poland.) Norman Duncan's *The Way of the Sea* (1903) and Theodore Goodridge Roberts' *The Harbour Master* (1913) were novels set in Newfoundland.

171

Canadian historians and political commentators also captured the national spirit. The *Canadian Annual Review* recorded Canada's political and economic advancements, while *Canada and Its Provinces*, a multi-volume history, chronicled the nation's past. In Quebec, Thomas Chapais wrote the eight-volume *Cours d'histoire du Canada, 1760–1867*. Canadian artists, in particular J.W. Morrice, Maurice Cullen, and Clarence Gagnon, were turning to Canadian subjects in an effort to free Canadian art from an imitation of European models.

POPULAR CULTURE

Popular culture had a wider audience as the wealthy professional and business classes found more time for leisure. Canada's first permanent movie house, the Edison Electric Theatre, opened on Cordova Street in Vancouver in 1902. Five years later, Ernest Ouimet opened an impressive thousand-seat cinema in Montreal. Sports became more popular and more commercial. Football had made its debut in Canada in the late nineteenth century and became a national sport when Governor General Earl Grey donated the Grey Cup in 1909. Canadians already had introduced to their American neighbours the oval ball and the rules of rugby. Lacrosse was considered by many as Canada's national sport, but baseball vied for that title after the Canadian Baseball Association was formed in 1876 and local leagues shortly afterwards. Toronto's Ned Hanlan became the world's

Canadian Football Hall of Fame and Museum.

Football became a popular Canadian sport for middle- and upper-class Canadians in the early twentieth century. Here the two rival universities, the University of Toronto and McGill, compete in a game in 1909.

professional sculling champion from 1880 to 1884. Basketball was invented in Massachusetts in 1892 by James Naismith, who came from the town of Almonte, south of Ottawa.

Hockey already was *the* Canadian sport. The first "world championship," won by McGill University, was held in 1883 in Montreal; the first national association, the Amateur Hockey Association of Canada, was formed three years later. The Ontario Hockey Association was founded in 1890 by a group of colleges, universities, and military and athletic clubs. In 1893 Lord Stanley, Canada's governor general in 1888–93, donated the Stanley Cup to the champion Canadian team. The Montreal Amateur Athletic Association (AAA) was the first team to win the cup in 1894. In 1910, the National Hockey Association, the forerunner of today's National Hockey League, launched its inaugural season.

From 1880 to 1920 Canada underwent an industrial revolution. Manufacturing and large-scale industry grew enormously, resulting in the production in Canada of a variety of goods to service a national and international market. Along with this industrial expansion came urban growth. Across the country new cities developed particularly on the Prairies, where immigration and settlement increased the demand for service centres for the rural agricultural community, and in central Canada, where industrial towns and cities expanded to produce manufactured goods. This urban and industrial expansion meant increased prosperity, a higher national standard of living and growing cultural sophistication, but it also led to the development of a new class of urban poor. Increasingly, workers turned to unions as the best means to improve their living and working conditions. However, in the pre-World War I era—an age of abundant unskilled labour —unions had limited success in improving working conditions.

NOTES

[1] The estimates of the later value of the capitalization appear in Michael Bliss, *Northern Enterprise: Five Centuries of Canadian Business* (Toronto, 1987), p. 374.
[2] H.V. Nelles, *The Politics of Development: Forests, Mines and Hydro-Electric Power in Ontario, 1849– 1941* (Toronto, 1974), pp. 248–49.
[3] Bliss, *Northern Enterprise*, p. 346.
[4] Albert Faucher, and Maurice Lamontagne, "History of Industrial Development" in *French-Canadian Society*, vol. 1, edited by M. Rioux and Y. Martin (Toronto, 1978), p. 258.
[5] Paul-André Linteau, René Durocher, and Jean-Claude Robert, *Quebec: A History, 1867–1929* (Toronto, 1983), p. 467.
[6] Jacques Rouillard, "A Life So Threadbare," *Horizon Canada*, number 25 (1985), p. 594.
[7] Bryan Palmer, *Working-Class Experience: The Rise and Reconstitution of Canadian Labour, 1800–1980* (Toronto, 1983), p. 80.

173

Related Readings

Several articles in R. Douglas Francis and Donald B. Smith, eds., *Readings in Canadian History: Post-Confederation*, 2d ed. (Toronto, 1986), relate to this topic. See Michael Bliss, " 'Dyspepsia of the Mind': The Canadian Businessman and His Enemies, 1880–1914," pp. 204–18; J.T. Copp, "The Conditions of the Working Class in Montreal, 1897– 1920," pp. 218–38; Wayne Roberts, "Honest Womanhood: Feminism, Femininity and Class Consciousness Among Toronto Working Women, 1893–1914," pp. 238–50; J.M.S. Careless, "Aspects of Metropolitanism in Atlantic Canada," pp. 252–63; Paul-André Linteau, René Durocher, and Jean-Claude Robert, "Urbanization," pp. 263–72; and Max Foran, "The CPR and the Urban West, 1881–1930," pp. 273–89.

BIBLIOGRAPHY

Michael Bliss' *Northern Enterprises: Five Centuries of Canadian Business* (Toronto, 1987) provides a comprehensive history of Canadian business. Two chapters—"The Triumph of Enterprise" and "French Canada and the New Industrial Order"—in R.C. Brown and R. Cook, *Canada, 1896–*

1921: A Nation Transformed (Toronto, 1974) deal with industrialization and urbanization in English and French Canada, respectively. On Quebec, also consult Paul-André Linteau, René Durocher, and Jean-Claude Robert, *Quebec: A History, 1867–1929* (Toronto, 1983), and Susan Mann Trofimenkoff, *The Dream of Nation: A Social and Intellectual History of Quebec* (Toronto, 1983), pp. 132–49 and 167–83. Michael Bliss deals with Canadian businessmen's attitudes in *A Living Profit: Studies in the Social History of Canadian Businessmen, 1883–1914* (Toronto, 1974).

On industrialization in the Maritimes, see T.W. Acheson, D. Frank, and J. Frost, *Industrialization and the Underdevelopment in the Maritimes, 1880 to 1930* (Toronto, 1985), and W. Acheson, "The National Policy and the Industrialization of the Maritimes, 1880–1910," in *The Canadian City: Essays in Urban History*, edited by G. Stelter and A.F.J. Artibise (Toronto, 1977; 2d ed., 1984), pp. 93–124. For Newfoundland, see David Alexander, "Economic Growth in the Atlantic Region, 1880–1940," in *Atlantic Canada and Confederation: Essays in Canadian Political Economy*, compiled by E. Seager, L. Fisher, and S. Pierson (Toronto, 1983), pp. 51–78. Major studies in English of industrialization in Quebec include A. Faucher and M. Lamontagne, "History of Industrial Development," in *French-Canadian Society*, edited by M. Rioux and Y. Martin (Toronto, 1964), pp. 257–71; J.H. Dales, *Hydroelectricity and Industrial Development, Quebec 1898–1940* (Cambridge, 1957); and W.J. Ryan, *The Clergy and Economic Growth in Quebec, 1896–1914* (Quebec, 1966); with regards to banks, see Ronald Rudin, *Banking en français* (Montreal, 1985). For Ontario, see H.V. Nelles, *The Politics of Development: Forest, Mines, and Hydro-Electric Power in Ontario, 1849–1941* (Toronto, 1974). Also of importance for Canada as a whole is Christopher Armstrong and H.V. Nelles, *Monopoly's Moment: The Organization and Regulation of Canadian Utilities, 1830–1930* (Philadelphia, 1986).

On urbanization, see J.M.S. Careless's Canadian Historical Association booklet, *The Rise of Cities: Canada Before 1914* (Ottawa, 1978); Richard Preston, "The Evolution of Urban Canada: The Post-1867 Period," in *Readings in Canadian Geography*, edited by R.M. Irving, 3d ed. (Toronto, 1978), pp. 19–46; and the collection of articles in Stelter and Artibise, eds., *The Canadian City* (cited above).

A more detailed study of urbanization in the Maritimes is J.M.S. Careless, "Aspects of Metropolitanism in Atlantic Canada," in *Regionalism in the Canadian Community, 1867–1967*, edited by M. Wade (Toronto, 1969), pp. 117–29. On British Columbia and the Prairies, see Patricia Roy, *Vancouver: An Illustrated History* (Toronto, 1980); Paul Voisey, "The Urbanization of the Canadian Prairies, 1871–1916," *Histoire Sociale/Social History*, 8 (1975): 77–101; A.F.J. Artibise, "The Urban West: The Evolution of Prairie Towns and Cities to 1930," *Prairie Forum*, 4 (1979): 237–62; and A.F.J. Artibise, ed., *Town and City: Aspects of Western Canadian Urban Development* (Regina, 1981). Working-class life in the major industrial city of Montreal at the turn of the century is discussed in T.J. Copp, *The Anatomy of Poverty: The Condition of the Working Class in Montreal, 1897–1929* (Toronto, 1974), and in J. Rouillard, *Les syndicats nationaux au Québec de 1900 à 1930* (Québec, 1979). For Toronto, see Gregory Kealey, *Toronto Workers Respond to Industrial Capitalism 1867–1892* (Toronto, 1980), and Michael Piva, *The Conditions of the Working Class in Toronto 1900–1921* (Ottawa, 1979). On women workers, see J. Acton *et al.*, eds., *Women at Work: Ontario, 1850–1930* (Toronto, 1974), and Wayne Roberts, *Honest Womanhood: Feminism, Femininity and Class Consciousness Among Toronto Working Women 1893 to 1914* (Toronto, 1976).

The labour movement is discussed in Bryan Palmer, *Working-Class Experience: The Rise and Reconstitution of Canadian Labour, 1800–1980* (Toronto, 1983), and in Desmond Morton with Terry Copp, *Working People* (Ottawa, 1980). Also useful is G. Kealey and P. Warrian, eds., *Essays in Working-Class History* (Toronto, 1976).

On literature and art, see Carl F. Klinck, ed., *Literary History of Canada* (Toronto, 1976), and Russell Harper, *Painting in Canada* (Toronto, 1966; 2d ed., 1979). For sports, see Alan Metcalfe, *Canada Learns to Play: The Emergence of Organized Sport, 1807–1914* (Toronto, 1987). Also useful are the relevant entries in *The Canadian Encyclopedia* (Edmonton, 1985).

CHAPTER NINE

Canada at War

In 1914, Canadians entered their first large-scale war. Nearly 10 000 Canadians had fought in the Northwest Rebellion in 1885 and 7000 in the South African War of 1899–1902. Then, between 1914 and 1918, Canadians sent 625 000 men to the battlefields of Europe. This was a tremendous contribution for a nation of only eight million people. More than 60 000—one in ten—never returned.

As a British colony, Canada entered the war automatically when Britain declared war. Once involved, the nation contributed huge quantities of foodstuffs and military supplies, along with large numbers of troops. To co-ordinate Canada's participation, the federal government intervened in the financial, economic, and social life of the nation to an unprecedented extent.

Canadian soldiers fought with distinction in the major battles, but at the cost of high casualties. As the war continued and voluntary enlistments declined, tension increased between English-speaking Canadians, who felt they were bearing to an extraordinary degree the burden of war, and French-speaking Canadians, who did not perceive the war as one of direct concern to Canada. Finally, in the summer of 1917, the Borden government introduced conscription. The prime minister then formed a Union government made up of Conservatives and Liberals in the hopes of putting the entire nation behind the war effort. Such unity was never achieved, however. Conflict continued during the war and in the immediate postwar era between English and French Canadians, and among businessmen, farmers, and workers.

Canada Joins the War Effort

The murder in late June 1914 of the Archduke Ferdinand, heir to the Austro-Hungarian throne, by a young Serbian nationalist began the chain of events leading to World War I. The European powers had created an intricate network of secret alliances and agreements that forced them into war. Austria attacked Serbia, which was allied with Russia. Germany backed Austria, while France came to the defence of its ally, Russia. Britain, the ally of Russia and France, had promised to defend the neutrality of Belgium. When German forces invaded Belgium as part of an attack on France, Britain declared war. As a member of the British Empire, Canada automatically entered the struggle.

Initially, all Canadians supported Britain. When Borden summoned Parliament for a special war session on August 18 he told a cheering House of Commons: "As to our duty, we are all agreed, we stand shoulder to shoulder with Britain and the other British Dominions in this quarrel." He secured unanimous consent for Canadian involvement. Laurier, the leader of the opposition, declared in the same session of the House: "When the call comes, our answer goes at once, and it goes in the classical language of the British answer to the call of duty: 'Ready, aye, ready.' "

Parliament's unanimity reflected the public mood. Throughout the country, loyal demonstrations occurred, involving impromptu parades, flag waving, and, in the streets of Montreal, the singing of "La Marseillaise" and "Rule Britannia." Archbishop Bruchési of Montreal reminded his fellow French Canadians: "England has protected our liberties and our faith. Under her flag we have found peace, and now in appreciation of what England has done you go as French Canadians to do your utmost to keep the Union Jack flying in honour." Even Henri Bourassa, a dedicated anti-imperialist (see chapter 7), initially supported Canadian participation, seeing the survival of France and Britain as vital to Canada. Most English Canadians viewed the war in simple terms: good versus evil; democracy versus autocracy; the Anglo-Saxons versus the "Huns." Recruitment propaganda, including statements by church leaders, reinforced this image. Canadians also believed that the Allies would achieve a quick victory, perhaps before Christmas 1914, and thus could not imagine the sacrifices they would have to make.

177

The Borden government immediately prepared the country for war. Without opposition, Parliament passed in 1914 the War Measures Act. Through orders-in-council, the federal cabinet could, without parliamentary consent, suspend civil liberties and regulate any area of society deemed essential for the conduct of war. The government immediately used the act to control the movement of "enemy aliens," that is, all German or Austro-Hungarian immigrants, who were now suspect because of their place of origin. The act required them to carry special identity cards at all times and to report to the police at regular intervals. Those disobeying and alleged German and Austrian sympathisers could be interned in camps, and eighty-three thousand were before the war ended. Among these interns was a Russian revolutionary seized when the Norwegian ship he was travelling on from New York to Europe, landed at Halifax. After his release

Victoria Park.
Aug. 1914.

Kitchener-Waterloo Record.

In Berlin (renamed Kitchener in 1916), Ontario, anti-German feeling ran high during World War I. A statue of Kaiser Wilhelm of Germany was thrown in a nearby lake and had to be retrieved by divers.

Leon Trotsky joined N.V. Lenin in Petrograd, Russia, to lead the Bolshevik Revolution. During his brief one month detainment at Amherst, Nova Scotia in April 1917, he preached revolution to the eight hundred internees there. In 1918 a further order-in-council forbade the printing, publishing, or possession of any publication in an enemy language without a licence from the secretary of state.

CANADIAN EXPEDITIONARY FORCE

Militarily, Canada was not ready for war. In 1914 its ill-equipped and inadequately trained permanent army numbered only 3000, although it could also call upon 60 000 volunteer militia. At first, recruiting for overseas service went well. Within two months 30 000 Canadian volunteers were training at a hastily built camp at Valcartier, twenty-five kilometres northwest of Quebec City.

Sam Hughes, the 61-year-old minister of militia, believed that volunteer citizens made the best soldiers, and he personally supervised the camp while living in castle-like headquarters on a hill overlooking it. The majority (more than 60 percent) of the troops that made up the First Canadian

Expeditionary Force (known as "Hughes' Boys") were recent British immigrants; they were unmarried, frequently unemployed, and closely tied to the mother country. Next came native-born Canadians of British stock, at 25 percent; the remainder were French Canadians and non-British immigrants. Many of the recruits were in their late teens.

The Canadian Expeditionary Force sailed for England on October 3, 1914 in the largest convoy ever to cross the Atlantic until that time. They trained on Salisbury Plain in southern England. That winter was the wettest in years—over a seventy-five-day period, only five days were dry. Heavy mists and snow on occasion curtailed training. As their army clothing was inadequate, many soldiers became sick and miserable.

Then in February 1915 the 1st Canadian Division, as it became known, left for the front in Belgium and northern France as part of the British army under the command of Lieutenant General E. A. H. Alderson, a regular British officer. There the Canadians faced conditions unimagined back in Canada: mud, vermin, rotten food, and the stench of rotting flesh. The soldiers spent endless hours digging trenches, tunnels, dugouts, and underground shelters, only to have them washed away by the rain and mud or abandoned in haste. Battles that raged for days gained only a few metres of enemy territory. From the time of its arrival at the front in 1915 to the final weeks of hostility, the entire Canadian army fought for an area not much larger than three or four prairie townships. This was a war of attrition, the goal being to kill as many of the enemy as possible.

179

Amid these horrors came a new and unforeseen one—poison gas. The Germans first used chlorine gas, a greenish substance that caused coughing, choking, and burning eyes and skin, on April 22, 1915, at the Battle of Ypres. One Canadian officer described it vividly:

> A great wall of green gas about 15 or 20 feet high was on top of us. Captain McLaren gave an order to get handkerchiefs, soak them and tie them around our mouths and noses. Some were able to do that and some just urinated on their handkerchiefs. Some managed to cover their faces. Others did not.

A British soldier later recalled what he saw when he and his contingent arrived to relieve the Canadians: "We stopped at a ditch at a first-aid clearing station. There were about 200 to 300 men lying in that ditch. Some were clawing their throats. Their brass buttons were green. Their bodies were swelled. Some of them were still alive. Some were still writhing on the ground, their tongues hanging out."

French colonial troops had begun to retreat in the face of the new deadly weapon. On that day the Canadians made their reputation. They held the gap in the French lines and prevented a German breakthrough. By April 25, only three days later, 1850 Canadians lay dead, another 3410 wounded, and 775 taken prisoner, out of a total divisional fighting strength of 10 000.

180

National Gallery of Canada.

At the Second Battle of Ypres in 1915, Canadian soldiers distinguished themselves. The Canadian line held against a German assault in which chlorine gas was used. The war artist Richard Jack recaptured the Canadians' defence of their position.

181

National Archives of Canada (C2533).

These Canadian soldiers catch a few minutes of sleep in the wretched trenches of mud and vermin.

In 1915 and 1916 three more Canadian divisions joined the 1st in France. By this time Lieutenant General Sir Julian Byng, a British regular officer and future governor general of Canada, replaced Alderson as supreme commander of the Canadian Corps. There was also a change of equipment. The Canadian-built Ross rifle, insisted upon by Sam Hughes, proved inefficient in trench warfare, jamming during critical periods of fighting. Soldiers threw their Ross rifles away in favour of the more rugged Lee-Enfields, which they acquired from slain British soldiers. But only after the disastrous battle of the St. Eloi Crater in the spring of 1916 did the Canadian cabinet overrule Hughes and offically replace the Ross rifle with Lee-Enfields.

The Ross rifle affair highlighted yet again the incompetence of Sam Hughes as minister of militia and defence. He had been accused of corruption, of failure to attend to his departmental duties, and of incompetence in handling the administration of the war. Prime Minister Borden later claimed that Hughes ran his department "as if it were a distinct and separate government in itself."

Gradually, other officials assumed his responsibilities. At the end of

1915, the Imperial Munitions Board under the direction of the talented J. W. Flavelle, general manager of the William Davies Packing Company, took on the duty of obtaining munitions in Canada for Britain. By 1917 Flavelle had succeeded in turning the munitions industry from a scandal-ridden and inefficient operation to Canada's greatest industrial effort—the production of shells, ships, fuses, and even airplanes. R. B. Bennett, a Calgary lawyer, wealthy businessman, and Conservative MP, chaired the National Service Board, established in the fall of 1916, to step up recruiting. Sir George Perley, the High Commissioner to Britain, took charge of the newly created Ministry of Overseas Military Forces to handle the war situation in Britain and to control the Canadian Expeditionary Force overseas. In protest, Hughes resigned.

The Interventionist State

The developments leading to Hughes' departure indicated the Canadian government's changed attitude towards the war. Voluntarism was being replaced by government intervention in economic, social, and military affairs as the most efficient means to further the war effort.

The shift began in 1917, when Allied demands for Canadian wheat to feed both civilians and soldiers made it imperative for Canada to step up production and export. The federal government intervened to control wheat production through the Board of Grain Supervisors (succeeded by the Canadian Wheat Board in 1918) and distribution through the Wheat Export Company.

Prairie wheat hectarage almost doubled, and the price per bushel increased by more than 50 percent, during the war years. The government also regulated the production, distribution, sale, and consumption of coal, wood, and gas fuels. According to military historian Desmond Morton: "Canadians learned to live with unprecedented government controls and involvement in their daily lives. Food and fuel shortages led to 'Meatless Fridays' and 'Fuelless Sundays'."[1]

Another controversial move towards intervention came with the government's assertion of control over all the major Canadian railways, except the CPR. Both the Canadian Northern and the Grand Trunk Pacific, the two new railways built during the Laurier era (see chapter 7), had repeatedly asked for private and public money, and independently each had already absorbed $400 million (today's equivalent of $4–$6 billion) by 1915. Sir Thomas White, the finance minister, reminded his Cabinet colleagues: "The collapse of the two railway systems in question, with the involvement of the Grand Trunk, would have a most disastrous effect upon our entire credit, federal, provincial, municipal and industrial."

The government provided aid in 1916 and also appointed a royal commission to examine the situation. Although divided on their recommendations, the commissioners suggested that the Canadian Northern and the Grand Trunk Pacific be consolidated and managed by a board whose members would be appointed by the government. Between 1917 and 1920, the Canadian government brought these rail lines under the control of the government-owned Canadian National Railway.

CANADA'S FISCAL POLICY DURING THE WAR YEARS

The war also altered Canada's fiscal policy. At its outbreak, the government depended on its traditional sources of revenue from the tariff and from the sale of regular federal bonds to finance the war effort. Even here, however, significant changes occurred early in the war. The decline in imports cut custom duties in half, thus undermining tariffs as an important source of government income. In the bond market, New York replaced London as the main source of Canadian securities. For the first time the government sold "Victory Bonds," (so named because funds would support the war effort). More than one million people subscribed to the Victory Loans campaign in 1918. In 1916 the government introduced another important innovation: increased use of direct taxation. First, it imposed a business profits tax to ensure that all Canadians, including the rich, made a sacrifice for the cause. This was followed in 1917 by the first federal income tax, imposed as a temporary wartime measure. A mere one-half of 1 percent of the population paid initially, since the tax applied only to annual incomes of more than $2000.

183

These new sources of revenue were necessary to finance the war. As early as 1915, Canada's military expenditures alone equalled the government's entire expenditures for 1913. Increased demands for raw materials and manufactured goods, along with rising labour costs caused by labour shortages, fed inflation. The government also helped raise inflation through its policy of spending far more money on the war effort than it received in revenue, thus forcing it to borrow vast sums at home and abroad, at high interest rates. The national debt increased five fold from $463 million in 1913 to $2.46 billion by 1918.

The increased cost of living hurt people on fixed incomes and cancelled out the benefits workers received from increased wages. In 1915–18 the average Canadian family budget rose by 50 percent, while the average hourly wage increased only by 44 percent, thus creating a decline in real wages of about 2 percent per year. Workers responded by joining trade unions in an effort to increase their bargaining powers and by staging strikes. The government countered with its "war labour policy" of mid-1918, which forbade strikes and lockouts for the duration of the war.

Women and the War

Women made major contributions to the war effort. Three thousand women served at the front as nursing sisters in the Canadian Army Medical Corps, working at station hospitals, on hospital ships, or on ambulance trains. The nurses came under the command of Margaret Macdonald who, on the eve of the war, had replaced Georgina Pope as matron of the Canadian Nursing Service. Macdonald received the Royal Red Cross from King George V and the Florence Nightingale Medal for her outstanding contribution to the war effort.

Women also gave assistance through voluntary organizations: the Imperial Order of the Daughters of the Empire (IODE), Red Cross clubs, the Great Veterans' Association, the Next-of-Kin Association, the YWCA, Women's Patriotic Leagues, and a host of others. They rolled bandages and knit socks, mitts, sweaters, and scarves for the troops, raised money to send cigarettes and candy overseas, and marshalled support for the cause. They played a large role in the most important organization—the Canadian Patriotic Fund, incorporated by Parliament in 1914 to assist families of soldiers overseas. By 1918 the demands on the Patriotic Fund proved so great that the government stepped in to administer widows' and dependents' pensions directly through its agencies: the Department of Soldiers' Civil Re-establishment, the Women's Bureau, and the Food Board. Thus the war contributed to the government's implementation of a public social welfare programme.

184

Large numbers of women entered the workforce as the demands of recruiting and of war production created labour shortages. On farms, in factories, and in offices, women filled positions previously occupied by men. The Women's Canadian Club organized in 1916 the Women's Emergency Corps to recruit women willing to work in munition production industries in order to free men to enter the armed forces. But women continued to earn wages considerably lower than men doing the same jobs. In addition, they faced discrimination and lacked the support of labour unions, which generally refused to unionize women, seeing them only as temporary workers for the duration of the war. Furthermore, there were no daycare facilities to enable women with children to enter the work force. Despite these drawbacks, by the end of the war tens of thousands of women filled jobs previously closed to them. Women also used their new bargaining position to raise questions about a broad range of social issues: women's suffrage, the use of child labour, conditions of jails and asylums, and female unemployment.

Married women had to keep their families fed, clothed, and educated. Despite the burden of daily and weekly chores, wives of servicemen wrote regularly to their husbands. "I made a habit to write every Sunday," one woman recalled, "because I wanted him to always know that somebody back home cared about him. What made it hard was that I could never be sure he was still alive when I wrote those letters." Women lived the constant fear of receiving a government telegram announcing a death at the front.

Fighting at the Front

As Canadian civilians adjusted to the wartime conditions at home, Canadian soldiers played an increasingly active role on the war front. Their initial involvement had hardened them into effective soldiers. The casualties, though, were enormous, amounting to 8000 during the twelve days of fighting in June 1916 at Mt. Sorrel in the Ypres Salient, a small triangular area around the Belgian town of Ypres.

Mt. Sorrel seemed a minor encounter compared with the Battle of the Somme, which began July 1, 1916. This ill-planned and badly executed attack under Sir Douglas Haig, commander of the British forces, was directed against one of the heavily fortified German strongholds. The co-ordinated assault of the British, French, and Canadians proved no match for the strategically located and well-prepared German army. By the time Haig called off the offensive five months later, there were 600 000 casualties, of which 24 000 were Canadians and Newfoundlanders—all for thirteen kilometres of territory. On the first day of battle, the Newfoundland Regiment lost 720 out of its 1000 officers and men—233 killed, 91 missing, and almost 400 wounded. This loss was the greatest single disaster in Newfoundland's history. Before the war ended, the regiment was accorded the honour, unique in World War I, of being granted the title "Royal." Newfoundland's casualties are believed to have been, together with Australia's, the highest in the British Empire—20 percent.

185

Other Canadian and Newfoundland servicemen contributed to the war on the land, in the air, and on the sea. Approximately four thousand Canadian Indians volunteered and served in Canada's army, a large contribution from a population of only one hundred thousand. Canada did not have an air force during the war, but Canadian flyers (trained in Canada by the Royal Flying Corps after 1917) joined the Royal Air Force (RAF). One RAF staff officer noted in June 1918 that "thirty-five percent of our total strength in pilots is Canadian." Some of them became Canadian heroes, like British Columbia's Raymond Collishaw, Manitoba's "Billy" Barker, Ontario's Ray Brown, credited with shooting down the notorious Baron von Richthofen—the "Red Baron," and the legendary Billy Bishop. The pilot from Owen Sound, Ontario, then in his early twenties, shot down seventy-two German fighters during the war, earning him the coveted Victoria Cross. Canadians who wanted to serve at sea joined the Royal Canadian Navy, under the command of the British Navy. (Nearly two thousand Newfoundlanders also served in the Royal Navy.) These men patrolled Canadian and Newfoundland waters against the German U-boats (submarines) or fought on the high seas.

VIMY AND A SPIRIT OF NATIONALISM

During Easter week, 1917, nearly one year after the Somme offensive, Canadian soldiers fought in the Battle of Vimy Ridge. Here the Canadians, some 70 000 strong, went into combat as a Canadian Corps under their new British commander, Julian Byng. Unlike the Somme, this campaign was carefully prepared; surveillance photographs taken by the Royal Flying Corps had determined the exact location of enemy troops. On Monday, April 9, 1917, the offensive began, as Canadians crossed the no-man's land. The distance which separated them from German lines was, in some cases, as little as thirty-five metres wide. Within hours, the Canadian and British soldiers pushed back the enemy and stood atop the ridge. The cost was high—more than ten thousand Canadian casualties including some three thousand dead, but despite these losses the Canadians had captured the ridge, one of the most important sites on the front. The Americans, who had only just entered the war against Germany on April 6, applauded. In an editorial headlined "Well Done Canada," the New York *Tribune* wrote that "every American will feel a thrill of admiration and a touch of honest envy at the achievement of the Canadian troops. ... No praise of the Canadian achievement can be excessive." Lloyd George, the British prime minister, recalled in his memoirs: "The Canadians played a part of such distinction ... that thenceforth they were marked out as storm troops; for the remainder of the war they were brought along to head the assault in one great battle after another."

Canadian soldiers gained at Vimy a new confidence and reputation. Byng was promoted for his role in the offensive, and General Sir Arthur Currie, a former real-estate agent from British Columbia and commander of the 1st Division, replaced him as the first Canadian commander of the Canadian Corps. Back home, Canadians appreciated the important role that their country played in the "great war for democracy."

"Invite Us to Your Councils"

After Vimy, Canadian politicians demanded a greater voice in Britain's war policy. At the outset of the war, the British government treated Canada as a subordinate rather than as an equal, neglecting to consult with it and the other dominions about war strategy or even to keep them informed on developments. When Prime Minister Borden first requested a larger voice for Canada, Bonar Law, the Colonial Secretary (who by chance had been born in Canada) replied curtly: "I fully recognize the right of the Canadian government to have some share of the control in a war in which Canada is playing so great a part. I am, however, not able to see any way in which this could be practically done."

When Lloyd George became prime minister in 1916, he found a way. He invited the dominion premiers to London to meet as an Imperial War Cabinet, a group consisting of the British War Cabinet and dominion representation. There Borden learned about the Allied position, discussed strategy, and, most important, became involved in the decision-making process.

The Imperial War Conference met simultaneously with the Imperial War Cabinet. The representatives passed a host of resolutions, the ninth of which recognized in theory the equality of the dominions with one another and with Britain. It stated that Britain and the dominions agreed that their new constitutional status "should be based upon a full recognition of the Dominions as autonomous nations of an Imperial Commonwealth."

187

At both the Imperial War Cabinet and the Imperial War Conference, Lloyd George stressed the need for increased contributions to the war effort. He pointed out that the Allies faced the danger of losing the war unless the entire Empire brought all its military power to bear in the struggle.

While in England, Borden visited Canadian soldiers in hospitals and also travelled to the front to see the men. Greatly moved by the tremendous sacrifices they were making for their country, he knew the importance of finding more reinforcements. Realizing that voluntary recruitment had failed, he favoured the only other alternative, conscription.

Recruitment

The problem of recruitment had become critical by the end of 1916 and weighed heavily on the prime minister in 1917. In contrast, during the first few months of war—when everyone believed it would end within a few months—voluntary recruitment had exceeded the government's ability to equip, train, and accommodate volunteers. Borden had confidently pledged in December 1914 that "there has not been, there will not be, compulsion or conscription."

Throughout 1914 and 1915, recruitment went well. By the end of 1915, roughly 160 000 enlisted. This was, however, still 100 000 short of the approved strength (350 000) for the Canadian Expeditionary Force set by Borden after his return from Britain, in October 1915. Despite this shortfall, Borden dramatically announced to a surprised Canadian audience in his New Year's message for 1916 that Canada would send 500 000 men to the war. The prime minister made what became a "sacred promise" without even consulting the cabinet and certainly without prior knowledge of how many recruits were available.

In the first few months of 1916, recruitment was up. Nearly thirty thousand volunteers enlisted in January alone, and by June the total number of enlisted men had surpassed three hundred thousand. Then during the summer months, recruitment dropped off dramatically. Contributing to this decline were the demands of industry and agriculture for manpower to meet the war boom—the opposite of the situation in 1914 and 1915, when unemployment had been an incentive to join the army.

Borden responded by establishing a National Service Board responsible for "determining whether the services of any man of military age are more valuable to the State in his present occupation than in military duties and either to permit or forbid his enlistment." Registration cards were assigned to every male of military age. Out of more than 1 300 000 respondents, 475 000 qualified as soldiers.

188 Borden next established a Canadian Defence Force in the spring of 1917, designed to get men who opposed going overseas to sign up for home defence and thus release those soldiers defending the home front who were willing to serve overseas. It was a last desperate attempt to get more troops without conscription, and it failed miserably. In the first month of operation, fewer than two hundred signed up.

National Disunity

Opposition against the haphazard voluntary system of recruitment now mounted. In particular, resentment grew against the French Canadians who had allegedly fallen behind in enlistment in proportion to English-speaking Canadians.

Several reasons can be given for the lack of enthusiasm on the part of French Canadians. Of all Canadians, they were the most North American in outlook, having little or no emotional tie either to Britain or even to France. Indeed, the war was seen, especially by clerical leaders, as just punishment on the people of France for their secular, liberal values. The conflict was also viewed by many as another British imperial war of no interest to French Canadians. Furthermore, few of the higher officers at the Royal Military College in Kingston, the training school for military officers, were French Canadians, partly because English was the sole language of instruction.

Sam Hughes, the minister of militia and defence, did not encourage French Canadians to enlist and seemed even to discourage them. Strongly anti-French-Canadian in outlook, he placed French Canadians in English-speaking units, seldom appointed or promoted French Canadians to the rank of officer, and prevented French-speaking military units from accompanying religious processions. Apart from the one French-language battalion, the famed "Vandoos" (the Royal Twenty-Second Regiment of Quebec), English was the language of the army. The navy was run completely in English. Furthermore, recruitment in Quebec tended to be done by an English-speaking elite, some of whom were Protestant clergymen with little sympathy for, and even less contact with, French Canadians.

ONTARIO SCHOOLS QUESTION

Most important of all, the question of language again began to poison relations between French-speaking and English-speaking Canadians. By 1910, French Canadians, who had been moving into northern and eastern Ontario since the late nineteenth century, made up 10 percent of Ontario's population. These Franco-Ontarians organized the French-Canadian Education Association to protect bilingual or English–French schools, as they were officially called, and to promote French-language interests.

189

Opposition arose from two groups: the Orange Order and Irish Catholics. The Orange Lodge believed that the English language was an essential bond of the Empire, and thus an extension of French was a threat to British institutions and to Imperial unity. The Irish Catholics feared that concessions to French Catholics on language would allow them to gain control of the separate school system. Furthermore it would encourage Protestant antagonism to the idea of religious schools. They favoured Catholic—but not bilingual—schools. One prominent Irish Catholic summed up the hostility: "Now, no one wants to do the French Canadians an injustice. The British Crown has given them what is actually an empire in the Province of Quebec, but no right or claim have they on this account, or on any other, to all the Provinces of the Dominion." Bishop Michael Fallon of London, Ontario, led the Irish-Catholic opposition. He viewed the bilingual school system as one which "teaches neither English nor French, encourages incompetency, gives a prize to hypocrisy and breeds ignorance."

The Ontario premier, James Whitney, responded by appointing a commission to investigate the bilingual schools. The commissioners pointed out the inadequate training of many teachers in bilingual schools, but they made no specific recommendations to solve the problem. The Whitney government's solution was to bring in Instruction 17, or "Regulation 17," which made English the official language of instruction and restricted French to the first two years of elementary school. Except for its handful of French-speaking members in the Legislature, the Liberal opposition was in fundamental agreement with this policy. In 1913 Regulation 17 was amended to permit French as a subject of study for one hour per day.

Franco-Ontarians and French Canadians in Quebec reacted strongly. Henri Bourassa led the attack. He wrote editorial after editorial in his newspaper, *Le Devoir*, denouncing English-speaking Ontarians as intolerant and a threat to the spirit of Confederation. He warned: "If we let the French minorities which are our outposts be sacrificed one by one, the day will come when the Province of Quebec itself will undergo assault." He compared Ontarians to the Germans, and French Canadians were told that they need not go to Europe to fight the Prussians, since the enemy resided next door.

Bourassa carried this message into Ontario. In Hawkesbury, Ontario, on December 15, 1914, he made a vitriolic speech against English-speaking Ontarians, which no one but the newspapermen around him could hear because of the catcalls. During a speech at the Russell Theatre in Ottawa the next day, a violent demonstration broke out. The secretary of the committee sponsoring Bourassa's appearance was manhandled and shoved through the glass entrance door. A sergeant climbed on the platform and insisted that Bourassa wave a Union Jack. In a momentary hush, Bourassa coolly replied: "I am ready to wave the British flag in liberty, but I shall not do so under threats." The curtain fell as the crowd rushed the stage. Through a back door Bourassa escaped unscathed and calmly finished his speech for his friends and the newspapermen in the lobby of Ottawa's Chateau Laurier Hotel.

Bourassa saw Canada as a dual nation, a bilingual state, a pact between English- and French-speaking Canadians. "The Canadian nation," Bourassa declared at the time, "will attain its ultimate destiny, indeed it will exist, only on the condition of being biethnic and bilingual, and by remaining faithful to the concept of the Fathers of Confederation: the free and voluntary association of two peoples, enjoying equal rights in all matters."

In the Senate a heated argument broke out in March 1915 between a Conservative who proclaimed: "Never shall we let the French Canadians implant in Ontario the disgusting speech they use," and a Liberal member who replied that his fellow senator was "a brutal maniac and ignoramous." At one of the Ottawa separate schools, an army of French-speaking women with hatpins as weapons stood guard, preventing the authorities from entering to remove bilingual teachers. Neither side would yield on the issue of bilingualism.

The Quebec Liberal MP Ernest Lapointe introduced a resolution in the House of Commons in the spring of 1916 urging recognition of the Franco-Ontarians' right to be taught in their mother tongue. Five French-speaking Conservative MPs crossed party lines to vote in favour of the resolution and eleven western Liberals deserted Laurier to defeat the motion. The immediate tension only subsided in September, when Pope Benedict XV appealed for moderation among the Canadian Roman Catholic hierarchy. Two months later the Judicial Committee of the Privy Council ruled that Regulation 17 was constitutional because denominational school guarantees excluded language. But at the same time it ruled that the government's commission appointed to enforce its policy in Ottawa was unconstitutional.

For years the controversy dragged on, with Franco-Ontarians deprived of schooling in their own language. Finally in 1927 Premier Howard Ferguson's Conservative provincial government realized the impossibility of enforcing Regulation 17. It reached a compromise with the Franco-Ontarian population that left each school designated for bilingual education to be considered on its merits by a departmental committee.

Amid the heated debate of 1916, two Toronto Liberals, J. M. Godfrey, a lawyer, and Arthur Hawkes, a journalist, backed by Toronto businessmen, began the Bonne Entente movement, designed to promote understanding between French- and English-speaking Canadians. It arranged for exchanges between Ontario and Quebec to promote good will. Secretly, the leaders hoped to use the movement to win French Canadians over to compulsory military service and a coalition government, both of which they felt were essential for Canada's increased contribution to the war effort, but the movement had little success.

191

Conscription Crisis

Borden consulted with his cabinet about his decision to implement conscription. His French-Canadian ministers, E. L. Patenaude, P. E. Blondin, and Albert Sévigny, warned him that "it will kill them and the party for 25 years." But Borden's English-speaking Canadian ministers strongly favoured conscription. The prime minister decided that the best means to introduce compulsory service would be through a coalition government. Shortly after announcing to the House of Commons on May 18 his government's intention to implement conscription, he approached the leader of the opposition.

Wilfrid Laurier faced the central dilemma of his career. He sympathized with the idea of a coalition government if it were to be composed of an equal number from each party, but he strongly opposed conscription. "I oppose this Bill," he warned at the time, "because it has in it the seeds of discord and disunion, because it is an obstacle and bar to that union of heart and soul without which it is impossible to hope that this Confederation will attain the aims and ends that were had in view when Confederation was effected."

Laurier knew that support for conscription would hand Quebec over to Bourassa and his *nationalistes*, while to oppose it would lose him and the Liberal party the support of his English-speaking Canadian followers. This time there was no room for compromise, and he had to choose one of the two sides. In 1917 Wilfrid Laurier stood with Bourassa and opposed compulsory military service.

OPPOSITION TO THE MILITARY SERVICE ACT

Despite Laurier's opposition, the Military Service Act (the official title of the conscription bill) became law in July 1917, after much impassioned debate in the House. News of conscription was greeted with riots in Montreal throughout the spring and summer of 1917. Crowds marched through the streets yelling "À bas Borden" (Down with Borden) and "Vive la révolution." Canadian troops passing through Quebec in the winter of 1917–18 were pelted with rotten vegetables, ice, and stones when they taunted French-Canadian youth for not being in uniform. Implementation of conscription was followed by more riots in Quebec on the Easter week-end of 1918, which left four dead.

French Canadians were not alone in their opposition to conscription. Many farmers and workers also opposed it. Farmers resented their sons being taken off the farm, where they were contributing to the war effort through food production. (Their opposition succeeded in getting the government to exempt farmers' sons from conscription two weeks before the 1917 election.) Workers saw military conscription as the first step towards compulsory industrial service, forcing them to remain at one job for the duration of the war. Both groups demanded "conscription of wealth" (heavier taxes on the rich and the nationalization of banks and industries) to ensure that financiers and businessmen made their sacrifices. Opposition also came from pacifists. Groups, such as the Quakers and Mennonites, opposed war as inherently evil and immoral and thus refused to enlist to fight. Traditionally, these groups were allowed exemption from military obligations (see chapter 6) and they were free to maintain their pacifism, although not without ridicule from many pro-conscriptionists.

Other pacifists without a direct denominational link opposed fighting in the belief that war was a wasteful and destructive means to settle world problems. This group split during the war years, with one side justifying the war as a means of upholding Christian civilization against German "barbarism," and the other arguing that the war was symptomatic of a deeper malaise in society in general. This latter group which remained opposed to participation advocated non-violent struggle at home to reform society so as to root out the causes of violence and war. The Canadian Women's Peace Party, forerunner of the Women's International League for Peace and Freedom, led the campaign. Leading the group were, ironically, Laura Hughes, cousin of Sam Hughes, and Alice Chown, niece of S. D. Chown, who was superintendent of the Methodist church and a supporter of participation in the war.

192

Union Government and the Election of 1917

With conscription achieved, Borden formed a coalition government pledged to enforce the Military Service Act. Then he implemented two bills to ensure a victory at the polls. The Military Voters Act enfranchised all members of the armed forces, no matter how long or short a time they had lived in Canada. The Wartime Elections Act, passed one month later, gave the vote to Canadian women who were mothers, wives, sisters, or daughters of servicemen; at the same time, it denied the right to vote to conscientious objectors and to naturalized Canadians from enemy countries who had settled in Canada after 1902. Arthur Meighen, the solicitor general, reasoned that these aliens had been banned from enlistment and so should not have the right to vote. But the real reason was that these new Canadians tended to vote Liberal. The Canadian Suffrage Association's president pointed out that it would have been "more honest if the bill simply stated that all who did not pledge to vote Conservative would be disenfranchised."

193

By October Borden had the support of enough English-speaking Liberal defectors and of provincial Liberal leaders (of whom the most prominent were the Alberta premier Arthur Sifton, Clifford's brother, and Newton W. Rowell, leader of the Liberal opposition in Ontario) to announce his Union government aimed at fighting the remainder of the war as a united nation. Some English-speaking Liberals believed that their party would be decimated if they did not "get in" on the war effort by supporting Union government and conscription, that the Conservatives alone would get credit for winning the war. Borden dissolved Parliament and called an election for December 17, 1917.

Both the Union party and the Liberals fought the election campaign largely along cultural lines. One of the Union party's election posters claimed that a vote for Laurier and the French Canadians was a vote for Bourassa, the Kaiser, and the Germans. The Toronto *Mail and Empire* warned that "the hidden hand of the Kaiser lies behind Quebec's desire not to reinforce the troops overseas." A map of Canada depicted Quebec in black, the "foul blot" on the country. On the Sunday before the election, three-quarters of the Protestant ministers across Canada responded to a Unionist circular by appealing in their sermons for support of the Union party as the people's sacred duty. In Quebec, the Liberals painted conscriptionists as a greater danger to the country than the Germans. Bourassa and the *nationalistes*, in a reversal of their stand in the 1911 election (see chapter 7), now urged support of Laurier and the Liberals as the lesser of two evils. They argued that Canada had done enough for the war. "Every Canadian who wishes to combat conscription with an effective logic," Bourassa declared, "must have the courage to say and to repeat everywhere: No Conscription! No Enrolment!"

The outcome of the election was obvious even before voting. The Union

194

Slander!

That man is a slanderer who says that

The Farmers of Ontario

will vote with

Bourassa, Pro-Germans, Suppressors of Free Speech and Slackers

Never!

They Will Support Union Government

Citizens' Union Committee

Killam Memorial Library, Dalhousie University.

This 1917 election propaganda reminded Canadians that Ontario farmers, although they opposed conscription of their sons who were needed on the farm, were still loyal to the war effort. The circular presents the choice as a Union government or a Liberal government, the latter associated with "Bourassa, pro-Germans, and Suppressors of Free Speech and Slackers."

government carried more than two-thirds of the constituencies. It won, though, only three seats in Quebec, all three being in predominantly English-speaking ridings. The Liberals won sixty-two of the sixty-five seats in Quebec but only twenty seats in the rest of the country (ten in the Maritimes, eight in Ontario, and two in the West). The election revealed a nation terribly divided.

In November 1917 the Bolsheviks seized control of Russia. Immediately, Lenin and Trotsky (only a year and a half earlier a detainee in Nova Scotia) sued for peace with Germany, which left the Germans free to shift troops from the eastern to the western front. In October and November, the Allies had lost thousands of men in the last phase of Field Marshal Haig's Flanders' offensive, including sixteen thousand Canadians who fought bravely in the senseless battle of Passchendaele, an attempt to take an insignificant ridge in a sea of mud. Then, in the spring of 1918, came an all-out German counter-offensive, launched before American troops entered the front lines. Once again the Allies faced defeat. Only with the Germans' "black day" at Amiens in August 1918 did the tide turn for the last decisive Hundred Days. On November 11, 1918, the Germans surrendered. The war was over.

195

Few of the Canadian soldiers at the front in the final days of the war were conscripts. While implementation of the Military Service Act did put one hundred thousand more men into the army, only one-quarter of these conscripts reached the front before the Armistice. In hindsight, one wonders whether conscription was worth the price Canadians paid in terms of national unity. Yet, in Borden's defence, no one in late 1917 could forecast that the long drawn-out war would end just one year later.

Advances to Nationhood

Four years of fighting had left over sixty thousand dead. Thousands more returned maimed and disabled. Borden was determined to ensure that Canadians benefited from their major contribution through increased national status at the Paris Peace Conference that met in 1919 to settle the aftermath of World War I. First he pressed for dominion recognition in the Imperial War Cabinet and then in the British Empire delegation at the peace treaty. The United States questioned why Canada should be involved at all in the settlement of European affairs, until it was pointed out by Canadian delegates that Canada had lost more men than the United States in the war. The Big Five (Britain, the United States, France, Italy, and Japan) wanted to make the important decisions, with the "lesser states" involved only in decisions directly affecting them. Borden found this unacceptable, and he won Canada representation as a power in its own right, as well as collectively as a member of the British Empire delegation. Borden also insisted on Canada's right to membership in the League of Nation's General Assembly as well as eligibility for membership in the governing council of the new international body. Although Canada obtained membership in the League, it opposed Article X of the League's charter, the heart of its collective security system, which bound members to come to the aid of other League members in times of attack. Borden feared that this agreement would commit Canadians to involvement in world disputes of no interest to them. In the end, Article X remained.

Canada thus moved from colony to nation as a result of the war effort. Canadians led the way in working out a new relationship of equality between Britain and its dominions that helped to transform the Empire into the Commonwealth, while in the world at large, Canada gained recognition as a nation in its own right.

196   Post-war Unrest

In the early months of peace the country faced a domestic crisis—the Spanish influenza epidemic. The first major outbreak occurred in September 1918 in Quebec, and the illness was almost certainly brought back to the country by soldiers returned from the war. People in some cities were ordered to wear gauze masks in public; in many cities, theatres and schools were closed, public meetings banned, and church services cancelled in an effort to check the deadly disease. Without a known cure, people tried all kinds of home remedies, from camphorated oil on the chest to Epsom salts and even salted herring around the neck, while volunteers fought the dreaded disease in makeshift hospitals.

In the fall of 1919 the federal government established a Department of Health to handle the problem on a national level. In the end, an estimated fifty thousand Canadians died from this "silent enemy"—almost as many as in World War I.

WINNIPEG GENERAL STRIKE

The country faced a second domestic crisis just after the war. Workers upset with post-war inflation, which almost doubled between 1915 and 1919, staged a series of national strikes in 1918 and 1919. The major one took place in Winnipeg in the spring of 1919. On May 1, 1919, metal-working and building unions went on strike to press for better wages and working conditions. Other Winnipeg union workers, including policemen, firemen, telephone and telegraph operators, and deliverymen, joined them on May 15, closing down the city. To provide essential services and to regulate the strike, the organizers created a general strike committee.

Glenbow Archives, Calgary.

With the war behind them, Canadians faced a second crisis—Spanish flu. These employees of the Calgary Bank of Commerce followed the federal government's order to wear surgical masks during the height of the influenza epidemic in the fall of 1918. An estimated 50 000 Canadians died from the epidemic, approximately as many Canadians as died overseas in World War I.

197

Business and government officials saw this committee, with its power to dictate what went on in the city, as usurping their own power and as the first step to a bolshevik state. They countered by creating the Citizens' Committee of One Thousand to maintain public utilities during the walkout.

The federal government intervened by sending Arthur Meighen, minister of justice and of the interior, and Gideon Robertson, minister of labour, to Winnipeg to review the situation. They considered the strike as a conspiracy. Meighen described the strike leaders as "revolutionists of varying degrees and types, from crazy idealists down to ordinary thieves, with the better part, perhaps, of the latter type." He permitted the Royal North–West Mounted Police to arrest ten of the strike leaders on the night of June 16.

In protest, the workers organized a silent parade down Main Street to City Hall on Saturday, June 21. Violence erupted during the demonstration between the strikers and the Citizens' Committee of One Thousand. The mayor of Winnipeg called in the Mounties to disperse the crowd. During the confrontation one man was killed and another wounded. "Bloody Saturday," as it became known, ended in the dispersal of the workers and military control of the city. By Thursday, June 26, the strike committee called off the strike, without the workers gaining any of their objectives. It was some time before labour recovered from this setback.

Canada emerged from World War I well advanced along the road from colony to nation. But the emerging autonomous nation faced serious problems. The war had strained English- and French-Canadian relations to an unprecedented extent, leading for the first time to the formation of national political parties along ethnic rather than political lines. Equally, the war had taxed the nation's capacity both in industrial production and in manpower. Canada had lost a generation of its young men on the battlefields of Europe. At home, such groups as farmers and labourers, who felt that they had made a great sacrifice for the war effort, demanded benefits. Canadians in general hoped that the war would lead to a better Canada by bringing to fruition reforms that had been initiated in the pre-war era. The general post-war dissatisfaction represented, in large part, a growing desire for a better Canada, a social regeneration of the nation.

NOTE

[1] Desmond Morton, "World War I," *The Canadian Encyclopedia*, (Edmonton, 1985), vol. 3, p. 1975.

Related Readings

The relevant articles in R. Douglas Francis and Donald B. Smith, eds., *Readings in Canadian History: Post-Confederation*, 2d. ed. (Toronto, 1986) for this chapter are John English, "Conscription," pp. 337–47; "An Open Letter from Capt. Talbot Papineau to Mr. Henri Bourassa, and Mr. Bourassa's Reply to Capt. Talbot Papineau's Letter," pp. 348–63; Thomas P. Socknat, "Canada's Liberal Pacifists and the Great War," pp. 363–77; and David Bercuson, "The Winnipeg General Strike," pp. 379–405.

BIBLIOGRAPHY

199

For good overviews of Canada during World War I, see R. C. Brown and R. Cook, *Canada: 1896–1921, A Nation Transformed* (Toronto, 1974), pp. 212–94, and the chapter "The Great War," in Desmond Morton, *Canada and War* (Toronto, 1981), pp. 54–81. On Robert Borden, see R. C. Brown, *Robert Laird Borden: A Biography*, 2 vols. (Toronto, 1975, 1980), and John English, *Borden: His Life and World* (Toronto, 1977). For a study of party and politics during the Borden era, consult John English, *The Decline of Politics: The Conservatives and the Party System, 1901–1920* (Toronto, 1977). Joseph Schull's *Laurier: The First Canadian* (Toronto, 1965) and O. D. Skelton's *Life and Letters of Sir Wilfrid Laurier* (Toronto, 1921) deal with the leader of the opposition in the war years.

John Swettenham, *To Seize the Victory* (Toronto, 1965), and Roger Sarty and Brereton Greenhous, "The Great War," *Horizon Canada*, number 85 (1986): 2017–23, describe Canadian involvement at the front. Pierre Berton tells the story of Canada's greatest battle in *Vimy* (Toronto, 1986). G. W. L. Nicholson, *The Fighting Newfoundlander: A History of the Royal Newfoundland Regiment* (Ottawa, 1964) recounts Newfoundland's contribution to the Allied army.

The question of government intervention in the state during the war is discussed in R. Cuff, "Organizing for War: Canada and the United States During World War I," *Canadian Historical Association Report*, 1969, pp. 141–156. On the nationalization of the railway, see T. D. Regehr, *The Canadian Northern Railway* (Toronto, 1976). Women's contributions to the war effort are discussed in D. Smyth, "Women at War: The Origins of the Army Nursing Service," *Horizon Canada*, number 8 (1985): 188–92, and Ceta Ramkhalawonsingh "Women During the Great War," in *Women at Work: Ontario, 1850–1930*, edited by J. Acton *et al*, (Toronto, 1974), pp. 261–308. The conscription crisis is covered in J. L. Granatstein and J. M. Hitsman, *Broken Promises: A History of Conscription in Canada*

(Toronto, 1977; reprint 1985), and in C. Berger, ed., *Conscription 1917* (Toronto, 1969). Mason Wade examines the French-Canadian view of the war in *The French Canadians: 1760–1945* (Toronto, 1955). Students should also consult Elizabeth Armstrong, *The Crisis of Quebec, 1914–1918* (New York, 1938). For the Ontario schools question, see Chad Gaffield, *Language, Schooling, and Cultural Conflict: The Origins of the French-Language Controversy in Ontario* (Montreal, 1987), and the articles by Barber and Prang in R. C. Brown, ed., *Minorities, Schools, and Politics* (Toronto, 1969). The Canadian peace movement is studied in Thomas Socknat, *Witness against War: Pacifism in Canada, 1900–1945* (Toronto, 1987).

On Canadian imperial and foreign relations during and immediately after the war, see Brown's biography of Borden (cited above) and his "Sir Robert Borden, the Great War and Anglo-Canadian Relations," in *Character and Circumstance*, edited by J. S. Moir (Toronto, 1970), pp. 201–24, as well as C. P. Stacey, *Canada and the Age of Conflict*, vol. 1 (Toronto, 1984). On the flu epidemic of 1918, see Eileen Pettigrew, *The Silent Enemy* (Saskatoon, 1983); and on the Winnipeg general strike, see Kenneth McNaught and David Bercuson, *The Winnipeg Strike: 1919* (Toronto, 1974).

200

CHAPTER TEN

An Era of Social Reform: 1890–1925

In both English- and French-speaking Canada, middle-class reformers *201* worried about the impact of urban and industrial growth on Canadian society and on their position within that society. The majority of these social reformers believed that religion should concern itself with contemporary social problems. In English Canada this new view of religion gave rise to the Protestant social gospel movement and in French Canada, to Catholic social action. The religious revival movements in turn inspired other changes. Educational reformers searched for the ideal school system for the new urban and industrial society, while urban planners designed the perfect city for the modern age. Women became involved in the suffrage movement and the struggle for prohibition. In Quebec, Catholic social reformers and the *Ligue nationaliste* sought to preserve traditional Catholic values and French-Canadian institutions by controlling industrialization. These various social reform movements, designed to create an ideal, ordered society, arose at the turn of the century, peaked during World War I, and gradually dissipated in the post-war era. Their influence on Canadian attitudes lingered, however, for a generation or more.

The Social Gospel Movement in English Canada

The social gospel movement was one of a series of religious revival movements aimed at applying Christianity to the collective ills of society to create a perfect "Kingdom of God on Earth." Its basic premise was that people were inherently good. If they erred, it was not because of any basic weakness or maliciousness of character, but because of their environment. Social gospellers believed in environmental determinism and hoped, therefore, to improve social conditions so as to alter people's character for the good and eventually create an ideal Christian society.

Social gospellers wanted the church to be concerned with social problems (prostitution, alcoholism, intolerable living and working conditions, and the plight of immigrants) rather than with such "personal sins" as drunkenness, sex, and slovenliness. The Reverend S.D. Chown of the Methodist church summed up the new attitude in a 1905 lecture on the relation of sociology to the Kingdom of Heaven:

> The first duty of a Christian is to be a citizen, or a man amongst men. We are under no obligation to get into heaven, that is a matter entirely of our own option; but we are under obligation to quit sin and to bring heaven down to this earth.

A second premise followed for social gospellers: that God was immanent in the world and could be found in one's fellow man. Thus the rallying cry of social reformers was "I am my brother's keeper," and their aim was less "to save this man" than "to save this society." This meant creating a humane society based on the Christian principles of love, charity, humanity, brotherhood, and democracy.

202

Many social gospellers—such as J. S. Woodsworth, later to become the first leader of the Co-operative Commonwealth Federation (CCF) party, a third party that pressured the traditional parties to implement legislation to help society's less fortunate (see chapter 12); A. E. Smith, a radical minister expelled from the Methodist church for his communist beliefs; and William Lyon Mackenzie King, future prime minister of Canada—were educated in Britain or the United States, where they had been exposed to similar social reform movements. In Britain, for example, the Fabian Society (a group of social thinkers, labour leaders, and university professors, committed to improving working-class society) was active in creating the British Labour party. In the United States the Progressives, a middle-class reform movement, aimed at exposing social ills in American urban and industrial society. Canadian social gospellers were influenced by these examples and often wed British and American models to design their social reform program.

Social gospellers were united in their aspiration to improve the quality of life, but they were divided on the means to do so. There were as many ways to regenerate and reform society as there were regenerators and reformers.

What one might call the first group of regenerators worked to give immediate and direct assistance to society's destitute through the establishment of missions and settlement houses. In 1890 the Reverend D. J. Macdonnell, a liberal Presbyterian minister, founded St. Andrews Institute to bring the church closer to the working people. Four years later a group of Methodists, with financial assistance from the wealthy Massey family of Toronto, founded the Fred Victor Mission (named in memory of W. E. H. Massey's son who had died of tuberculosis) to care for the downtrodden of Toronto. Sara Libby Carson started the first settlement house in 1902 and was involved in the founding of the Toronto and McGill

National Archives of Canada (C14099).

Christian Indians were mobilized to fight sin and poverty. This photo shows a Christian Indian Band from Fort Simpson, British Columbia, around 1890.

203

University settlements. These were modelled after similar settlement houses in Britain and, especially, Jane Addams' Hull House in Chicago which offered classes in music and art, and provided a gymnasium and day nursery. By 1920 there were at least thirteen settlement houses in Canada offering the basic necessities of food and shelter for their daily visitors and, often, such amenities as night school, and libraries. Many provided medical care. Others included a gymnasium, clubrooms, savings bank, and nursery.

The Army of Salvation, better known as the Salvation Army, started by General William Booth of England, also established centres in Canada after 1882 to help the poor. Using military symbols and trappings (for example, the ministers were called "officers" and the converts, "soldiers"), the army's "field force" enlisted nearly 150 000 in Canada to fight sin and poverty.

A second group of social gospellers believed the way to social reform lay in changing people's attitudes. Because individuals motivated by greed, competition, and materialism caused society's problems, one could, through education, make these people aware of the greater benefits to be derived from living in a society governed by Christian principles of love, charity, brotherhood, and democracy. William Lyon Mackenzie King, at the time a young Canadian labour conciliator, wrote *Industry and Humanity* in 1918 to educate the Canadian populace to moral regeneration. As King explained it, the road to social salvation was to follow the ethical laws of Christianity:

> Abundance of life is to be attained, not through any brute struggle on the part of men or nations in accord with some biological law of survival of the fittest, but through mutual service in accord with the principles of a higher law, the law of human brotherhood which finds its sublime expression in Christian sacrifice and love.

A third group favoured greater governmental involvement in social problems. The concept of *laissez-faire,* or the belief that governments should not interfere to upset the natural laws of the marketplace or in any way to hinder the free expression of the individual, needed to be replaced by a new concept of state intervention. This intervention would insure that all people — and not just a few individuals in society — benefited from the fruits of their labour. These reformers demanded greater governmental involvement in four broad categories: the provision of essential social services; the institution of welfare assistance for the unemployed and the disabled (neither of which, reformers believed, were responsible for their unfortunate circumstances); the regulation of industries so as to make them more socially responsive; and, finally the nationalization of key industries to insure they served the public good.

For a few social gospellers, such as J. S. Woodsworth and A. E. Smith, even these innovative reforms were only a prelude to a more fundamental restructuring of society. They believed that the kingdom of God on earth was a socialist paradise where everyone worked for the well-being of the whole rather than for its individual parts. True social reform meant replacing the profit motive of capitalism with the socialist motive of Christian charity.

IMPACT OF THE SOCIAL GOSPEL MOVEMENT

The social gospel movement had an immediate impact in arousing public consciousness to the ills of urban and industrial society. In their reaching out to help improve society, the social gospellers greatly affected and directed a host of other social reform movements: prohibition, women's suffrage, urban reform, and labour movements. The social gospel gave reformers a religious zeal and a mission that they would not otherwise have had. The social gospel movement also contributed to the passing of the Workmen's Compensation Act in Ontario in 1911, considered the first modern social security measure in Canada, and of the Pensions Act in Manitoba in 1916. The former provided injured workers a regular cash income, while the latter provided a basic allowance to widowed, divorced, or deserted wives with children. Ultimately, the social gospel movement led to the rise of the CCF in the 1930s. In this sense the social gospellers prepared the way for the establishment of our modern social welfare system.

The social gospellers also contributed to the creation of our modern secular society. In their attempts to make religion more relevant to everyday concerns and thus move it away from abstract, theological issues, these reformers, ironically, denied religion its distinctive function as the guardian of men's souls. Religious leaders vied with other social scientists and analysts of society's ills; in essence, they became lay sociologists. The sacred became secular.

Catholic Social Action in Quebec

The origins of Quebec's social reform movements lay in Roman Catholic   *205*
emphasis on personal humanity, and on its principles of social justice and Christian charity. In his 1891 encyclical *Rerum Novarum*, Pope Leo XIII had urged that "some opportune remedy be found quickly for the misery and wretchedness pressing so unjustly on the majority of the working class." Catholic social reformers in Quebec believed that the "remedy" was fundamentally moral and religious, and therefore the family and the church rather than the state could best deal with social problems. The ideal Christian social order, church leaders argued, rested on the family, and on the nation as the cornerstones of society. Thus in Quebec, Catholic values and French-Canadian nationalism became intertwined in social reform.

ROLE OF THE QUEBEC CHURCH IN SOCIAL REFORM

The Catholic church initiated and supported various social reform movements in Quebec. The Jesuits, for example, founded in 1909 the Ecole Sociale Populaire (ESP), an organization responsible for developing a social doctrine for the Quebec church. The ESP published pamphlets, organized retreats, and trained the clergy to become more sensitive to the social needs of their parishioners. Another church-directed reform group, the *Société du parler français*, was established by priests at Université Laval in 1902 to protect the French language from being bastardized by scientific and technical jargon, and from being anglicized in a largely English-language-oriented urban and industrial society.

In the classical colleges, religious instructors under the guidance and inspiration of the young abbé Lionel Groulx of Valleyfield created the *Association catholique de la jeunesse canadienne-française* in 1904 to discover a unique French-Canadian and Catholic response to Quebec's social problems. In 1907 the Quebec diocese started a newspaper, *L'Action sociale* (later renamed *L'Action catholique*), that addressed social problems. It campaigned for the prohibition of alcohol, or at least strict government control of the manufacturing and sale of alcoholic beverages. It also called for the censorship of films, then seen as a potential source of corruption in society.

After 1906 many priests lent their support to the *caisses populaires*, the credit unions begun by Alphonse Desjardins, a journalist who had became the official reporter of the Canadian House of Commons. Desjardins sought to remedy the French Canadians' greatest handicap in business: lack of capital. He established these savings and lending co-operatives to assist strictly French-Canadian enterprises. By 1907 the *caisses* had assets of more than $48 000, certainly not enough to pose a serious threat to the established banks and credit institutions in Quebec, but sufficient to enable other co-operative ventures to get established. At the time of Desjardins' death in 1920, there were more than two hundred *caisses populaires*, chiefly in Quebec but also among French-speaking Canadians in Ontario, Manitoba, Saskatchewan, and among Franco-Americans originally from French Canada in New England. The priests offered their support to the movement.

206

French-Canadian priests worked to promote Catholic unions for Quebec workers. In 1907 Abbé Eugène Lapointe organized forestry and industrial workers in the Chicoutimi area of Lac St. Jean, northeast of Quebec City. His movement expanded, and other unions initiated by priests united in 1921 to reform the *Confédération des travailleurs catholiques du Canada* (CTCC). Church leaders feared that workers in secular-oriented unions, especially American-controlled ones, would become too materialist in their aspirations and socialistic in their outlook. The church, rejecting the idea underlying many unions of organizing workers along class lines, favoured Roman Catholic unions based on a spirit of Christian charity and employer–employee co-operation. The Catholic unions, slow to be established, had a limited effect.

The church also lent its moral support to the *Ligue nationaliste*. The chief members of this middle-class group, founded in 1903, included Armand Lavergne, Olivar Asselin, Jules Fournier, and Omer Héroux; their "patron saint" was Henri Bourassa. These young men worried about the position of Canada within the Empire and of Quebec within the Canadian federal state, but they were also concerned about the problems facing French Canadians as Quebec industrialized (see chapter 7). They formulated a French-Canadian and largely Catholic response based on the premise that French Canadians needed to retain their identity in an increasingly secular society. Like church leaders, the *Ligue nationaliste* believed in the traditional primacy of the family as the fundamental social unit of society and of Christian values as the bulwark of society. Consequently, they opposed any economic or social measures that threatened to undermine these values. While they viewed individual or family businesses as compatible with Christian values and national aspirations, they opposed big business which, they felt, was guided by mercenary concerns. They reacted as well to the individualist nature of the modern North American business community. Instead, they favoured a society based on co-operation and on concern for the public good. The state, they argued, should curtail the excessive monopolization of big business by preventing private control of utilities. Ultimately, however, like the Catholic social action advocates, league members saw the individual, the family, and the church, rather than the state, as the chief instruments for social change.

Educational Reformers

Perceptions of education, like religion, changed during the reform era at the turn of the century. Earlier, educators had concerned themselves with preparing children for the workplace as quickly as possible by teaching good work habits. They viewed children as miniature adults, to be placed into adult society as quickly as possible. By the turn of the century, however, a new generation of educators, strongly influenced by Friedrich Froebel, a European educational philosopher, advocated a child-oriented education that treated children as children (not as miniature adults) by providing them with love and by protecting them from the harsh realities of adult life.

207

One way to do this was through kindergartens. James L. Hughes, a Toronto school inspector (and younger brother of the minister of militia Sam Hughes), and his wife, Ada Marean, established the first Canadian public school kindergarten in 1883 to provide, in Froebel's words, "reverent love for the child, profound respect for his individuality . . .and freedom and self-activity as the condition of most perfect growth physically, intellectually, and spiritually." Four years later, in 1887, Ontario formally incorporated kindergartens into the public school system. The Free Kindergarten Association in Winnipeg advocated the same for Manitoba, arguing that "the proper education of children during the first seven years of their lives" did "much to reduce poverty and crime in any community."

In Montreal and Quebec City, nuns ran *salles d'asile* or day care centres for children of working parents. Between 1898 and 1902, more than ten thousand children were enrolled. In addition to these centres, which offered care on a daily basis, orphanages, provincial asylums, and homes for the poor also provided care for children of destitute families.

Other educational reformers worked for different objectives. Some called for temperance education to warn children of evils of alcohol while others asked for school programmes in public health and in physical and mental hygiene. Educational reformers also advocated "manual training" programs in agriculture, technology, the sciences, and industry, seeing such programs as a means to develop a children's physical skills as well as to prepare them for a vocation. At the turn of the century many provinces introduced manual training through courses in domestic science, school gardening, physical education, and industrial arts.

John Kelso, a young police reporter for the Toronto *World*, became concerned about the street urchins who could not be reached through educational reform. He quit his job to found the Humane Society, and when its members seemed only peripherally interested in the plight of children, he began yet another organization, the Children's Aid Society. The Reverend Alfred Fitzpatrick created in 1901 the Canadian Reading Camp Association, later to become Frontier College, to bring education to immigrant workers in the lumber shanties and railway bunkhouses across northern Canada. These educational reform movements were guided by the Christian belief that the good society was one that operated on moral principles of love and charity and that therefore Christian principles needed to be instilled in children at an early age.

Urban Reform Movement

Urban reformers formed an important part of the social reform movement of the time. Inspired by the City Beautiful movement in the United States and Europe, they believed that reform must begin by first improving the urban environment — the physical structure of the city, its aesthetic nature, or the quality of its municipal government—as opposed to the religious or educational aspects of society. What united urban reformers was "less a single creed and more a common approach to a wide variety of urban problems,"[1] according to historian Paul Rutherford. They worked to mould the urban environment to create humane, aesthetically beautiful, and socially adjusted Canadian cities.

The earliest urban reformers tended to be newspaper editors who concentrated on the miseries and immoralities of urban life. Through their popular, sensational, and inexpensive newspapers (the penny press), among them Montreal's *Daily Star* and *La Presse*, and Toronto's *Telegram*, and *World*, these editors aimed to arouse their readers' emotions over such urban problems as child abuse, slums, prostitution, criminal activity, and political corruption in an effort to initiate action. Seldom, however, did they have concrete solutions to offer to these problems.

Another group of urban reformers who provided an intellectual component to the movement were reform-minded businessmen or concerned laymen: Herbert Ames, a philanthropic Montreal businessman; G. A. Nantel, a former *Bleu* journalist and Quebec cabinet minister; Samuel Wickett, a Toronto academic and later businessman and alderman; and J. S. Woodsworth. As previously mentioned (see chapter 8), Ames financed in 1897 a sociological study of a working-class ward in Montreal,

The City Below the Hill. Nantel wrote *La Métropole de Demain*, a grandiose scheme for better governance for Montreal. Wickett spoke and wrote regularly on the importance of efficient and expert municipal governments as the first step to urban reform, while J. S. Woodsworth wrote the highly acclaimed *My Neighbour* (1911), about the problems of living in the modern city.

A host of professionals—engineers, architects, surveyors, medical people, and urban planners—offered advice on how to create the perfect city. Each group naturally emphasized the importance of its particular discipline. Architects, for example, emphasized stately buildings, while urban planners stressed a city of parks, treed boulevards, and adequate housing. Medical professionals gave precedence to clean water and air, and pasteurized milk.

These urban professionals had limited success in the pre-World War I era because of opposition from vested interests who opposed such expenditures. Developers for example, saw little profit in expensive urban renewal. Nor were badly funded municipal governments prepared to act. Finally even when the reformers succeeded in initiating improvements they often came at a high price in terms of increased taxes which, ironically, fell on the shoulders of the very people that the reformers intended to assist.

209

WILDERNESS CONSERVATION

Although many reformers cared about the beauty of the city, few were concerned about protecting the uniqueness of the wilderness. Canadians had long believed that their nation had unlimited natural resources that did not need conserving, so the idea of conservation emerged slowly. Banff, the first Canadian national park, began in 1885 as a recreation rather than as a conservation park, although the latter would soon become its chief function. Two years later, in 1887, the first bird sanctuary in North America opened at Lake Mountain Lake in present day Saskatchewan. In 1893 the Ontario government established Algonquin Park, south of North Bay, a magnificent wilderness area. Other provinces would later follow Ontario's example and establish provincial park systems. The federal government convened in 1919 the first national wildlife conference to discuss with the provinces how best to conserve Canada's wildlife. Later in the 1930s, the English-born Grey Owl, or Archie Belaney (1888–1938), would become a popular advocate in his books, films, and lectures, for the protection of Canada's wilderness and wildlife.

Women and Social Reform

In the cities a group of middle-class female reformers contributed greatly to social reform. By the 1890s a "new woman" appeared, demanding an active role in society. "Rocking the cradle for the world" was how Nellie McClung, an influential reformer, saw her role. Local, provincial, and national women's organizations, such as the Women's Christian Temperance Union, the National Council of Women, the Young Women's Christian Association (YWCA) and the Dominion Women's Enfranchisement Association, helped these women to unite and to act effectively for reform. By 1912 an estimated one out of every eight adult women—the majority being middle-aged, middle-class, English-speaking Protestants—belonged to a women's group, thus making these organizations influential agents of social change.

The bicycle greatly aided the liberation of the new woman. This amazingly popular vehicle enabled women to abandon their restricting, ankle-length, tight clothing in favour of more comfortable, loose-fitting clothes such as the bloomer (loose trousers gathered at the knees). Unheeded by the young women, churchmen worried about the impact of the bicycle on morals, since women could now go out without chaperones.

Many women accepted the prevailing "scientific" stereotyping of themselves as womanly and motherly. They came to believe that they alone had the ability to reform society. Men had controlled society for ages without making any appreciable improvements; they argued it was women's turn. As Nellie McClung observed:

> Women must be made to feel their responsibilities. All this protective love, their instinctive mother love, must be organized in some way, and made effective. There is enough of it in the world to do away with all the evils which war upon childhood, undernourishment, slum conditions, child labour, drunkenness. Women could abolish all these if they wanted to.

THE WOMEN'S SUFFRAGE MOVEMENT

Increasingly, women reformers saw the vote as the means by which women could obtain the power to improve society. The women's suffrage movement began in Ontario with leaders like Dr. Emily Stowe. Forced into the workplace because of an invalid husband and three children, Emily Stowe wanted to become a doctor. Barred from medical school in Canada because she was a woman, Stowe enrolled in the New York Medical College for Women and graduated in 1868. While in New York City she became

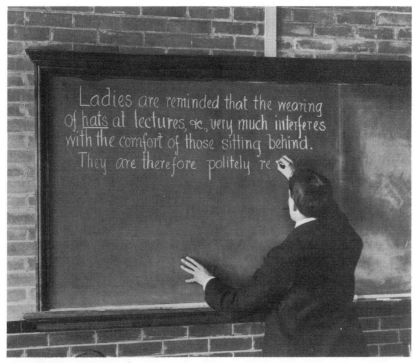

Ladies are reminded that the wearing of hats at lectures, etc., very much interferes with the comfort of those sitting behind. They are therefore politely re...

National Archives of Canada, PA-122876.

A gentle word of advice to the newly-admitted women at McGill. A university lecturer wrote this message on a blackboard in the W.C. Macdonald Physics Building in the late 1890s.

211

interested in feminist causes and advanced feminist ideas upon her return to practice medicine in Toronto as Canada's first woman doctor.

In 1876, she launched the Toronto Women's Literacy Club. Despite its name, the club was a suffrage group. The club issued a magazine, the *Citizen*, and discussed such social concerns as the plight of working women and the problems of the liquor trade. In 1883 the group changed its name to the Toronto Women's Suffrage Society and then in 1889 to the Dominion Women's Enfranchisement Association. It advocated equal suffrage and women's equality in the professions, and invited British and American suffragettes, such as Emmeline Pankhurst, Anna Shaw, and Susan Anthony, to give public lectures. In response, the University of Toronto opened its doors to women in 1886. Almost a decade earlier, Mount Allison University in Sackville, New Brunswick, had conferred a bachelor's degree in science and literature to Grace Annie Lockhart, the first university degree awarded to a woman in the British Empire.

Adelaide Hoodless also assisted women's causes. The daughter of Irish immigrants, Adelaide Hunter married John Hoodless, son of a wealthy furniture manufacturer. Their son died in 1887 at the age of eighteen months, from the unpasteurized milk that farmers delivered in open cans, exposing it to bacterial contamination. Seeing an urgent need to teach women good nutrition and proper health measures, she began domestic science classes through the YWCA and assisted in introducing the subject in the school curriculum and, eventually, in colleges and universities, both at Guelph's Ontario Agricultural College and at McGill University in Montreal. In 1897, she started the first Women's Institute, a female equivalent of the Farmers' Institutes, near Stoney Creek, south of Hamilton, Ontario. The new organization helped women to increase their knowledge of farm and household management. Hoodless also began the Victorian Order of Nurses to offer nursing and housekeeping services for impoverished invalids.

Women reform leaders in the prairie provinces carried on the work begun in eastern Canada. In the newer society of the West, women had found a greater degree of equality. In establishing a homestead and building a farm, women worked alongside their husbands. Early on, they won the support of western farm organizations that were also struggling for national recognition and could, therefore, readily empathize with women's efforts.

The *Grain Growers' Guide*, founded in 1908, added a woman's column to its paper in 1911, while the Grain Growers' Association of Manitoba, Saskatchewan, and Alberta, endorsed woman's suffrage as early as 1912. The presence of a large immigrant population on the prairies also helped the suffrage cause in a somewhat perverse way. Women suffragettes protested against giving recent male immigrants the vote while denying it to long-standing Canadian female citizens. As one suffragette bluntly put it, "What an outrage to deny to the highest-minded, most cultured native-born lady of Canada what is cheerfully granted to the lowest-browed most imbruted foreign hobo that chooses to visit our shores."

The West had several outspoken women who had taken up the cause of female suffrage. The five women who would be involved in the famous "Persons Case" of 1929 (see chapter 11), in which the Supreme Court decreed that women were persons for legal purposes—Emily Murphy, Louise McKinney, Nellie McClung, Irene Parlby, and Henrietta Edwards—lived in the West and at one time resided in the province of Alberta. Perhaps of all five, Nellie McClung with her enthusiasm, energy and wit, epitomizes best the suffrage movement.

Nellie McClung was born in Ontario in 1873 but educated in Manitoba where her family began homesteading in 1880. After attending Winnipeg Normal School and teaching for several years, she married Wes McClung, a pharmacist, in 1896. Early on, she became interested in reform as exemplified in her best-selling novel *Sewing Seeds in Danny*. In 1912 she joined the Winnipeg Political Equality League, whose president was Lillian Beynon Thomas, another reformer. McClung then became involved in the fight to pressure the Manitoba government to grant women the franchise, a struggle Manitoba women won in 1916. Her social commentary, *In Times Like These*, is an eloquent appeal for greater rights for women.

FEMALE REFORMERS IN QUEBEC

Quebec women also participated in social reform in their province. Theirs was a difficult battle, however, since traditional French-Canadian ideology emphasized the role of women as mothers and domestics. Archbishop Bruchési of Montreal defined *féminisme* as "the zealous pursuit by woman of all the noble causes in the sphere that Providence has assigned to her." Then, he added: "There will be no talk in your meetings of the emancipation of woman, of the neglect of her rights, of her having been relegated to the shadows, of the responsibilities, public offices and professions to which she should be admitted on an equal basis with man."

213

Despite such a stern warning, several French-Canadian upper-class women spoke out for the feminist cause. Marie Lacoste Gérin-Lajoie, Caroline Béique, and Josephine Dandurand founded in 1907 the *Fédération nationale Saint-Jean-Baptiste*, the first French-speaking feminist organization aimed at consolidating women's activities in charitable associations, in education, and in the work force. Marie Lacoste Gérin-Lajoie directed the federation's activities for the next twenty years and co-operated closely with local branches of the National Council of Women of Canada, the central women's organization established in 1893. The federation, which was an umbrella organization for religious and secular affiliated associations, offered a forum for women to fight for the pasteurizing of milk to reduce infant mortality, better working conditions for women, and the elimination of alcoholism and white slavery (forced prostitution). It contributed also to the doubling of women teachers' pensions, better lighting in factories, more chairs for women clerks in stores, more domestic science courses, and improved infant feeding through pure milk depots.

In addition, the *Fédération* and the sisters of the *Congrégation Notre–Dame* petitioned Mgr Bruchési to obtain his approval for a classical college that would provide courses for a B.A. degree for women. At first reluctant, the bishop changed his mind when the newspaper *La Patrie* announced the opening of a French *lycée*, a lay-administered classical college for women. Frightened by this, Bruchési then gave the *Congrégation Notre– Dame* permission to establish, in October 1908, the *Ecole d'enseignement supérieur pour les filles*. The *Ecole* would have to wait until 1926 before the title of *collège* was bestowed upon it. In 1910, Marie Gérin-Lajoie, a student at the school and the daughter of Marie Lacoste Gérin-Lajoie, placed first in the provincial university entrance examinations. To the consternation of the examiners, the only female candidate had outclassed all male classical

Courtesy of the Archives of the Institut Notre-Dame-du-Bon-Conseil, Montreal.

Three generations of the distinguished Lacostes: Marie Gérin-Lajoie (left), social worker and founder of a religious order; her mother, Marie Lacoste Gérin-Lajoie, in the forefront of the struggle for women's rights; her grandmother, Lady Lacoste, née Marie Louise Globensky, active in traditional philanthropic causes.

college students in the province. Since women could not attend university, the prize for first place was awarded to the male student who placed second. That discriminatory act was publicly acknowledged only ten years later.

Few French-Canadian women pressed for women suffrage in Quebec, but, here again, Marie Lacoste Gérin-Lajoie, who obtained her education by studying with her father's books and under his supervision, stood out as a notable exception. She was shocked to learn the legal status of women was no more than adjuncts of their husbands, with no personal financial or civil independence, and she considered refusing a marriage proposal in order to devote her life to improving the condition of women. After her liberal-minded suitor promised his support for the cause, she accepted. She spent her early married years writing a legal handbook while raising her children. Together with an English-speaking colleague, she created the Provincial Franchise Committee in 1921 to put pressure on Quebec politicians to grant women the franchise. The committee had no success, and ironically the strongest opposition often came from other women who saw female suffrage as a threat to their identity as wives and mothers. Marie Lacoste Gérin-Lajoie resigned her post as head of the French-language section of the Franchise Committee in 1922.

Prohibition Movement

Throughout Canada women reformers became particularly active in the struggle for prohibition. "Demon drink," they argued, wrecked home life and lead to inefficiency at work. The country, they feared, was drinking itself to death. Prohibitionists argued that the only way to end drinking was to eradicate it. They also maintained that this objective could best be achieved through government regulation. Prohibitionists were willing to use the power of the state for their cause, arguing that governments had a right and an obligation to pass laws for the good of society.

The division between the federal and provincial governments of jurisdiction over alcohol complicated the question. In general terms, the federal government had the power to prohibit the manufacture of, and inter-provincial trade in, alcoholic beverages; while provincial governments controlled retail sales. Thus, prohibitionists had to apply pressure on both levels of government.

They achieved an initial limited victory with the passage of the Canadian Temperance Act (popularly known as the Scott Act) in 1878. The Act allowed for the populace of each municipality or county to decide by a simple majority vote whether it would permit retail sale of alcohol within its boundaries. To prohibitionists, this measure was not sufficient, since it still left open the possibility of "wet" constituencies. They continued to pressure the government to outlaw the liquor trade. The federal Conservative government postponed a decision on this contentious issue to the mid-1890s by establishing a Royal Commission on the Liquor Traffic. During the election campaign of 1896 the Liberals promised a plebiscite on the question if they gained office, and when they won the prohibitionists held them to their promise.

215

The plebiscite results split along cultural lines. Every province except Quebec voted on the "dry" side; Quebec remained solidly "wet." But the voter turnout was low—being only 44 percent. Furthermore, of those who voted, only a small majority of about thirteen thousand had favoured prohibition. Laurier used these indecisive results to avoid enacting legislation that he knew would only divide the country. The Liberals' refusal to follow through on their promise angered the prohibitionists and made them even more resolved to fight for what they believed was a righteous cause.

In that fight, the prohibitionists could count on the support of the churches, especially the more evangelical Protestant churches. The Protestant ministry provided many of the leaders of the prohibition movement. As well, the church lent moral suasion to the cause; prohibition was part of a religious battle. Alcohol, church leaders believed, had to be eradicated to achieve the Kingdom of God on earth. They urged drinkers to sign "the pledge" card by which they promised "by the help of God, to abstain from the use of Intoxicating Liquors."

216

VOTE DRY

HELP US!
WE WOULD CLOSE THE SALOON

HOPE

Glenbow Archives, Alberta.

This Sunday school group in Calgary did their part to rid the city of alcoholism during World War 1. Prohibitionists succeeded in closing the bars in all provinces (including Quebec through federal government legislation) by the war's end.

The Women's Christian Temperance Union (WCTU), formed in Ontario in 1874, identified alcoholism as the greatest single cause of domestic violence and divorce. Initially, the WCTU campaigned for prohibition by issuing petitions, circulating literature, and giving speeches, but members soon recognized the need for political action. They believed that alcohol use could be ended only if women had the right to vote, and thus prohibition and women's suffrage became mutually supportive causes. As Mrs. Jacob Spence, first superintendent of the Ontario WCTU's Franchise Department, noted: "The liquor sellers are not afraid of our conventions but they are afraid of our ballots."

The vision of a purified white Anglo-Saxon society inspired many prohibitionists. Drunkenness became associated with "foreigners," seen by reformers as too liberal in their drinking. Controlling alcohol offered a means of regulating them and of insuring their conformity in an otherwise heterogeneous society. The greatest support for prohibition therefore came from the majority white Anglo-Saxon Protestant population, who believed itself superior to other groups that succumbed to alcohol. Prohibition was, then, a means to get at deeper social problems.

217

Despite these efforts, the prohibitionists remained in the minority prior to World War I. On the eve of the war, only Prince Edward Island had implemented provincial prohibition, while on the national level the federal government had resisted pressure to restrict the production and inter-provincial distribution of liquor.

The Impact of the Great War on Social Reform

Social reform efforts peaked during the war years, as English-speaking reformers harnessed the powerful force of patriotism to their cause. Just as the troops fought for a noble cause on the battle front, so too, reformers argued, should Canadians fight on the home front — against materialism, alcoholism, and corruption. Social gospellers saw the war as the final struggle for bringing God's kingdom to earth. Superintendent S.D. Chown of the Methodist church proclaimed at a church conference on "The Church, the War and Patriotism" that "the war is a divine challenge to build the Tabernacle of God amongst men."

THE SUCCESS OF WOMEN'S SUFFRAGE AND PROHIBITION

Women's suffrage and prohibition both gained support during the war. Women reformers used the war (which they frequently denounced) to great advantage. They argued that the world-wide cataclysm had resulted from man's aggressive nature; if women had the right to vote and the opportunity to rule, then wars would cease. They also pointed out the inconsistency of fighting for democracy abroad when more than half of Canada's citizens were denied the democratic right to vote. As well, women reminded men of their sacrifices for the cause. Wives of servicemen struggled to keep their families together and to support them while their husbands were away. Many women also served in voluntary organizations or filled positions in factories and offices vacated by men who had enlisted. And if women could serve their country, they deserved the right to participate in its political life.

Women suffragettes succeeded in obtaining the franchise. In 1916, the four western provinces granted women the right to vote in provincial elections. Ontario followed in 1917, Nova Scotia in 1918, New Brunswick in 1919, and Prince Edward Island in 1922; Quebec women obtained the provincial franchise only in 1940. Federally, the franchise came in three stages: the Military Voters Act of 1917 gave the vote to women serving in the Armed Forces or as nurses; the Wartime Election Act extended voting privileges to women whose fathers, husbands, or sons were serving overseas; and finally, on January 1, 1919, all women over the age of twenty-one could vote federally.

The war helped the prohibition cause as well. Prohibitionists equated their struggle with that of the men at the front. One prohibitionist advertisement read: "Are we to 'Be British' indeed, and remove a greater enemy than the Hun from our midst? Is the Sacrifice made by our soldiers for us on the battlefield to be the only sacrifice? The Bar or the War? That is the question of the Hour."

The prohibitionists' first victory came in Saskatchewan. In 1915 the provincial Liberal government closed all bars, saloons, and liquor stores and brought liquor under provincially operated outlets. Alberta went further by endorsing outright provincial prohibition the same year. Manitoba followed in early 1916. By the end of 1917 every provincial government except Quebec had implemented prohibition legislation. In 1918 the newly elected Union government imposed prohibition on Quebec and, within a week of its electoral victory in December 1917, moved to prohibit the manufacturing, importation, and transportation of any beverage containing more than 2.5 percent alcohol.

FRENCH-CANADIAN REFORMERS DURING THE WAR YEARS

French-Canadian clerics and laymen continued during the war to press for reform. They did not associate reform with patriotism, as did their English-Canadian compatriots; they instead emphasized the moral need for social action. In 1917 Father Joseph-Papin Archambault, of the *Ecole sociale populaire,* issued a tract, *La Question sociale et nos devoirs de catholiques,* in which he appealed to the church to reach out to the working class. In 1920 he began the *Semaines sociales,* an annual week-long meeting of clerics and laymen to discuss social questions.

Henri Bourassa tried to keep French-Canadian reform linked to Canadian Catholic reform in general, as he believed that French Canadians were first and foremost Canadians. A growing intolerance among English-speaking Canadians towards French Canadians made his work especially difficult. There was arising as well in Quebec a new exclusive French-Canadian nationalism, embodied in the writings of the young Abbé Groulx, that looked at Quebec alone as the French Canadians' state, and the province alone as the field for French-Canadian social reform. This feeling of alienation became more pronounced after the election of the Union government in 1917 (see chapter 9), one without a single French-Canadian member on the government side in the House of Commons from Quebec.

219

ENGLISH-CANADIAN REFORMERS AND THE WAR

English-Canadian reformers, in contrast, regarded the Union government's triumph as their own. They issued a number of books associating the Union government and the war with reform. Salem Bland, a leading figure in the social gospel movement and a professor at Wesley College in Winnipeg, presented his vision of a socialist Canada operating on the Christian principles of love, equality, brotherhood, and democracy, through a new labour Church in *The New Christianity* (1920). Stephen Leacock, the political economist cum humourist, had doubts about the utopian nature of socialism; he favoured instead, in his *Unsolved Riddle of Social Justice* (1920), legislation designed to make the workplace more appealing. In *Wake Up Canada* (1919), C. W. Paterson saw educational reform as the answer to society's ills. The two agrarian reformers, W. G. Good in *Production and Taxation in Canada* (1919) and William Irvine in *The Farmers in Politics* (1920), saw rural values as the ideal of the future. William Lyon Mackenzie King, soon to become leader of the Liberal party (see chapter 11), welcomed the new urban-industrial society in *Industry and Humanity* (1918), provided that "regenerated" men directed it on Christian principles of co-operation and brotherhood.

Post-war Protest and the Decline of Social Reform

The immediate post-war euphoria died quickly. Protest arose first among workers who began a series of strikes in 1918 and 1919 (see chapter 9). These strikes expressed both their dissatisfaction with post-war conditions as well as their utopian dream of a better society. Strikes were a means of demanding higher wages and better working conditions, as well as of regenerating society. J. S. Woodsworth, an active participant in the Winnipeg General Strike (for which he was arrested on charges of seditious libel), described the utopian spirit behind the strike: "The atmosphere was a great religious revival. The movement is a religious revival."

Agrarian protest also was renewed in the reform optimism of the immediate post-war era. Farmers reacted against the new urban and industrial society by opposing it through the Progressive movement, an agrarian-based organization that aimed to re-establish a society based on rural values (see chapter 11). They believed that farmers were God's chosen people and that the family farm was the ideal social unit. "God made the country, man made the city" was the utopian belief underlying agrarian reform.

The disillusionment experienced by workers and farmers in the post-war era was shared by social reform groups. Social gospellers became a minority group in the mainstream churches during the prosperous twenties as a desire to reform society gave way to a search for personal prosperity and an interest in one's own salvation. Equally, the optimism underlying the social gospel ethos seemed out of place in the disillusionment of the early 1920s, when the new millennium promised by reformers had not materialized.

Prohibitionists saw the provincial temperance acts in every province removed one by one, and by the end of the 1920s government-regulated outlets sold liquor in every province except Prince Edward Island. The returned soldiers had taken one of the largest roles in the fight to end prohibition.

The women's suffrage movement had obtained the vote, but it, too, failed to bring about any lasting social changes. Few women were elected to the House of Commons or to the provincial legislatures. Agnes Macphail was the only woman elected in the 1921 federal election, the first open to all women over twenty-one. Edith Rogers was the sole female MP in the Manitoba Legislature in 1920. Furthermore, women refused to vote according to sex and instead divided their votes — as did the men — along class, regional, and ethnic lines. Still, women directed their energy towards improvements in the home and in the workplace. Urban reformers had achieved some of their objectives, such as modern sewage systems in the cities, better public health facilities, and improved architecture, but the ideal "city beautiful" remained a vision.

Nevertheless, much had been done during the first twenty years of the century. The ideas of the social reformers re-emerged in the depression period of the 1930s and in the social welfare state of the post-World War II era.

Between 1880 and 1920, Canada underwent an era of social reform. In response to the rising urban and industrial society, middle-class reformers in both English and French Canada attempted to address social problems in hopes of creating a perfect society. Each group of reformers had a different solution to social problems and its own blueprint for a Canadian utopia. Together, these reformers did bring about important changes, especially during the war years, when they were convinced that the country was about to usher in the new millennium. When it did not, Canadians faced many of the same problems in the 1920s, in addition to new ones.

NOTE

[1] Paul Rutherford, "Tomorrow's Metropolis: The Urban Reform Movement in Canada, 1880–1920," in *The Canadian City: Essays in Urban History*, edited by G. A. Stelter and A. F. J. Artibise (Toronto, 1977), p. 370.

221

Related Readings

The following useful articles supplementing this chapter are found in R. Douglas Francis and Donald B. Smith, eds, *Readings in Canadian History: Post-Confederation*; 2d ed. (Toronto, 1986): Richard Allen, "The Social Gospel and the Reform Tradition in Canada, 1890–1928," pp. 292–307; Carol Bacchi, "Race Regeneration and Social Purity: A Study of the Social Attitudes of Canada's English-Speaking Suffragists," pp. 308–21; and Wendy Mitchinson, "The WCTU: 'For God, Home and Native Land': A Study in Nineteenth-Century Feminism," pp. 322–35.

BIBLIOGRAPHY

Chapters 15 and 16 in R. C. Brown and R. Cook, *Canada, 1896–1921: A Nation Transformed* (Toronto, 1974) provide an overview of the social reform movements.

The social gospel movement is studied by Richard Allen, *The Social Passion: Religion and Social Reform in Canada, 1914–28* (Toronto, 1971), and Ramsay Cook, *The Regenerators: Social Criticism in Late Victorian English Canada* (Toronto, 1985).

Educational reform in the context of social reform is the subject of Neil Sutherland's *Children in English-Canadian Society* (Toronto, 1976). Paul Rutherford's "Tomorrow's Metropolis: The Urban Reform Movement in Canada, 1880–1920," *Canadian Historical Association Report*, 1971, pp. 203–24, and his edited anthology, *Saving the Canadian City, 1880–1920* (Toronto, 1974), deal with urban reform. See as well G. Stelter and A.

Artibise, eds., *The Canadian City: Essays in Urban History* (Toronto, 1977), pp. 337–418. The early conservation movement is discussed by Janet Foster in *Working for Wildlife. The Beginning of Preservation in Canada* (Toronto, 1978).

For women and social reform, see Linda Kealey, ed., *A Not Unreasonable Claim: Women and Reform in Canada, 1880–1920* (Toronto, 1979), and Micheline Dumont *et al. Quebec Women. A History* (Toronto, 1987). The story of Madame Gérin-Lajoie and her daughter is told in Hélène Pelletier-Baillargeon, *Marie Gérin-Lajoie* (Montréal, 1985). On the suffrage movement, consult Carol Bacchi, *Liberation Deferred? The Ideas of the English-Canadian Suffragists, 1877–1918* (Toronto, 1983); Catherine L. Cleverdon, *The Woman Suffrage Movement in Canada* (Toronto, 1950; reprinted 1974); and Deborah Gorham, "Singing Up the Hill," *Canadian Dimension*, 10 (1975): 25–38. Prohibition is examined in the Maritimes in E. Forbes, "Prohibition and the Social Gospel in Nova Scotia," *Acadiensis*, 1 (1971): 11-36; in Ontario, in Gerald Hallowell, *Prohibition in Ontario 1919–1923* (Toronto, 1972); and on the Prairies, in James Gray, *Booze: The Impact of Whiskey on the Prairie West* (Toronto, 1972). On the Women's Christian Temperance Union, see Wendy Mitchinson, "The WCTU" in *A Not Unreasonable Claim* (cited above).

Paul-André Linteau, René Durocher, and Jean-Claude Robert, *Quebec: A History, 1867–1929* (Toronto, 1983), and S. M. Trofimenkoff, *The Dream of Nation: A Social and Intellectual History of Quebec* (Toronto, 1983) discuss social reform in Quebec. Jean Hamelin and Nicole Gagnon, *Histoire du catholicisme québécois; le XXe siècle: tome 1: 1898–1940* (Montréal, 1984) discuss the role of the Quebec church in social reform, while Joseph Levitt's *Henri Bourassa and the Golden Calf* (Ottawa, 1969) analyses the views of the *Ligue nationaliste* on social questions.

For the impact of World War I on social reform, consult John Thompson, " 'The Beginning of our Regeneration': The Great War and Western Canadian Reform Movements," Canadian Historical Association, *Historical Papers*, 1972, pp. 227–45, and his study, *The Harvest of War: The Prairie West, 1914–1919* (Toronto, 1978); for the twenties, see John Herd Thompson with Allen Seager, *Canada, 1922–1939: Decades of Discord* (Toronto, 1985).

CHAPTER ELEVEN

The Twenties: A Decade of Transition

Many new beginnings marked the 1920s. In politics new leaders and forms of social and regional protest emerged. Maritimers united in the Maritime Rights movement to obtain "equality" in Confederation, while prairie farmers turned to the Progressive party to deal with their social and regional problems. In Quebec, the monthly magazine, *L'Action française*, under its new editor, the abbé Lionel Groulx, opposed the evils of urbanization and industrialization. Economically, the nation prospered by mid-decade chiefly due to increased American demand for minerals and pulp and paper, and to growth in secondary manufacturing, particularly in the automobile industry. Many Canadians in the 1920s enjoyed for the first time such modern conveniences as automobiles, telephones, and radios. Women continued their struggle for recognition and rights but in the economic and legal, rather than in the political, spheres.

New Political Leaders

As the twenties opened, two new men replaced veteran national leaders. Mackenzie King succeeded Wilfrid Laurier (who had died in February 1919) as Liberal leader, while Arthur Meighen became prime minister and leader of the Conservatives after Robert Borden's resignation in July 1920.

The Liberals chose Mackenzie King at a leadership convention, the first in the nation's history, in August 1919. On the third ballot the forty-four-year-old bachelor defeated his veteran opponent, W. S. Fielding. King's loyalty to Laurier during the conscription crisis and his progressive views on labour and social questions ensured his victory.

King appeared well suited for his new role. The grandson of William Lyon Mackenzie, leader of Upper Canada's rebellion in 1837, saw himself as a reformer. Graduating from the University of Toronto in 1895, he did graduate work in economics at Chicago and Harvard. While in the United

States between 1896 and 1899 he became involved in social reform movements. Then in 1900, after returning to Canada, the young industrial relations specialist became deputy minister of labour and, in 1908, shortly after his election to the House of Commons, Laurier's minister of labour. Defeated in the election of 1911, King returned to the United States to work for the Rockefeller Foundation as a labour conciliator. He wrote much of *Industry and Humanity* from his own work experience. Although rather convoluted and abstract as a discussion of the labour question in Canada, the book did, nevertheless, establish King as an authority on contemporary social and economic issues. His views became those of his party. At the convention of 1919, party delegates adopted a platform that included such innovative reform proposals as unemployment insurance, old age pensions, mothers' allowances, and an eight-hour working day. Few of these reforms, though, reached the statute books in the 1920s.

224

Almost a year after the Liberal party's convention, the Union party met in caucus (not in convention) in July 1920 to choose a successor to Borden, the prime minister. Borden had wanted Thomas White, his finance minister, to succeed him, but when White declined, Borden accepted the advice of his caucus, which favoured Arthur Meighen. Shortly after graduation from King's *alma mater,* the University of Toronto, Meighen had moved west to Portage la Prairie, Manitoba to practice law. Like King, he first entered federal politics in the election of 1908. He soon earned a reputation as an outstanding parliamentary debater. Borden appointed him solicitor general in 1913 and minister of the interior in 1917.

While in Borden's Cabinet, Meighen became identified with a number of unpopular causes. He had drafted the conscription bill (see chapter 9), and this legislation lost him support in Quebec and among farmers in English-speaking Canada (farmers were exempt immediately before the election of 1917 and then suddenly made eligible after it). He had introduced the Wartime Elections Act, which denied the vote to Canadians who had emigrated from enemy countries after 1902, thus losing him much of the ethnic vote. Against the wishes of the Montreal business community he had nationalized the two bankrupt transcontinental railways; and in 1919, as acting minister of justice, he had intervened in the Winnipeg General Strike against the workers. That the Conservative caucus still chose him as their leader revealed their loss of touch with political reality.

In style, these two new leaders were completely opposites. Mackenzie King constantly spoke in ambiguous generalities. Always, he sought the road of least resistance and the middle path of compromise. There were no right answers in politics, he believed; only answers that seemed better because they offended fewer people. Meighen, by contrast, stated his positions clearly and unequivocally. He upheld principles over compromise and believed that Canadians could be made to see the truth. To him every problem had a solution, and he clearly articulated solutions without regard for the political repercussions.

Regional Protest

King and Meighen, the dominant leaders in federal politics throughout the decade, competed for the support of a divided Canada. A division existed between city and country, which were then roughly equal in population. Secondly, in the cities employers and labour had drawn up in opposing battle lines over wages, working conditions, job security, and the workers' right to debate these questions. Thirdly, regional divisions split the country. Maritimers witnessed in the 1920s a decline in their region's influence in Confederation. Politically, their number of seats in the House of Commons fell by one-quarter (to thirty-one) between 1882 and 1921, partly a result of the depopulation of the Maritimes, as thousands continued to leave the region in search of work. Given that the House of Commons' size had substantially increased during this period, the percentage drop was even greater. Economically, manufacturing companies moved out to establish themselves in the larger markets of central Canada, where they could be more competitive; for example, both the Canadian Car and Foundry of Amherst, Nova Scotia, and the Maritime Nail Company of St. John transferred operations to Montreal in 1921.

225

As well, the region suffered from tariff reductions that had formerly protected Maritime industries. Higher freight rates on the Intercolonial Railway (up to 200 percent and more in the early 1920s) also hurt. When the government-owned Canadian National Railway took over the Intercolonial, it moved the Intercolonial's head office from Moncton, New Brunswick, and later to Montreal. The railway thus ceased to promote regional interests and became part of a national system.

The decline in international demand for Canadian coal and steel hurt Nova Scotia. The conversion to oil for heating and power had lost markets for Cape Breton's coal. Shipbuilding went into decline as Britain, the United States, and Canada, all competed for international sales. The vital Canadian rail market for steel rails collapsed when railway construction ceased in the postwar era. Unemployment became widespread in Cape Breton's heavy-steel industry. The British Empire Steel Company (BESCO) (created from a colossal $500 million merger of all the principal Canadian shipping companies with the Nova Scotia steel and coal companies), which controlled the industry, responded by attempting to cut miners' and steelworkers' wages, with the result that in Cape Breton between 1921 and 1925 occurred the worst industrial warfare ever experienced in Canada.

MARITIME RIGHTS MOVEMENT

Individually, the Maritime provinces seemed powerless to stem the economic decline, but collectively their chances were better. A. P. Paterson led a group of influential businessmen and professionals in launching the

Acadia University Archives.

In the 1920s many Maritimers became concerned about their region's declining position in Confederation. In this cartoon, Maritimers are promised greater wealth if they board the "Maritime Rights train to prosperity." They did elect a number of Maritime Rights advocates to the federal parliament in the election of 1925.

Maritime Rights movement. The New Brunswick grocer from St. John offered a rationale for the movement in *The True Story of Confederation*. Within the pamphlet he put forward his version of the compact theory of Confederation, which he saw as an arrangement under which extra economic costs stemming from a region's geographical location should be borne by all Canadians. Convinced that a study of history could become a weapon in the struggle, Paterson helped to fund the establishment of a department of history at the University of New Brunswick.

The Maritime Rights movement wanted increased annual federal subsidies for the Maritime provinces, the encouragement of more national and international trade through the ports of Halifax and St. John, and improved tariff protection to strengthen the region's steel and coal industries. Their promotion of the tariff separated them completely from the discontented prairie farmers.

Unlike the westerners, the Maritimers worked through the traditional political parties. The movement asked Maritime Liberal candidates in the election of 1921 to swear "to advocate and stand by Maritime rights first, last and all the time." Although taking this pledge helped the Liberals to win all but six of the Maritime constituencies, the MPs could not meet their promises; the Liberal minority government, dependent upon prairie support, could not raise the tariff. Disillusioned, Maritime voters switched to the Conservatives in the election of 1925, giving the party all but three of the thirty-one seats. Unfortunately for Maritimers, the Liberals returned to power in 1926. Mackenzie King diffused the Maritime Rights movement by establishing a royal commission to investigate the group's complaints. The Duncan Commission, as it became known after Sir Arthur Rae Duncan, its head, recommended some major changes to assist the Maritime region, such as a 20 percent reduction in all rail rates, aid to the steel and coal industries, and increased federal subsidies. The Liberal government negated the Commission's recommendations by adapting minor changes only. In the meantime, the Maritime Rights movement had disbanded.

227

THE PROGRESSIVE MOVEMENT

The prairie West launched a strong protest movement in the post-war era. After the defeat of the Liberals and their policy of reciprocity in the election of 1911, many farmers talked openly of creating a third party. But during the war years they remained loyal to the traditional parties as part of their support for the war effort, on the understanding that conditions would indeed improve after the war. Initially, farmers hoped that the Union government, formed in 1917 to unite the country behind the war effort and social reform (see chapter 9), would legislate improvements for farmers, including the removal of the hated tariff. When the Union government failed to do so, Thomas Crerar, a Manitoba farmer, one-time president of the Grain Growers' Grain Company and minister of agriculture in the government, resigned from the federal Cabinet in June 1919. Nine other western Unionist MPs followed. Together they formed a third party, the National Progressive party.

Farmer candidates did well in the provincial elections held immediately after the war. In Ontario, rural depopulation alarmed many farmers, convincing them that they must directly involve themselves in politics. Campaigning on the platform of increased aid to agriculture, the United Farmers of Ontario won the election of 1919, much to their surprise. Neither the premier, E. C. Drury, a farmer from Simcoe County directly north of Toronto, nor most of his party members had any previous legislative experience. In Alberta in the election of 1921, the United Farmers of Alberta (UFA) swept out the Liberal party, in office since 1905. The UFA won considerable support in southern Alberta, where farmers experienced extreme drought conditions as bad, if not worse, than they would experience during the Great Depression of the 1930s. Farmer candidates also did well in Manitoba, New Brunswick, and Nova Scotia. Encouraged by these provincial successes, the federal Progressive party prepared for the fall election of 1921 by supporting farmer candidates in many constituencies.

The results of the election reflected the country's internal divisions. Just under half of the seats (116) went to the Liberals, who won all the Quebec ridings and all but six in the Maritimes. But west of the Ottawa River, the Liberals held only twenty seats. Two-thirds of the Conservatives' fifty seats came from Ontario. The Progressives won sixty-four seats, with thirty-nine of those seats in the West, twenty-four in Ontario, but only one in the Maritimes. Five independents were also elected, of whom two agreed to work together. At the opening of the parliamentary session, Alberta's William Irvine informed the House: "I wish to state that Mr. Woodsworth is the leader of the labour group . . . and I am the group."

Despite its size, the Progressive party was divided. Crerar headed the Manitoba wing, and Henry Wise Wood, an American populist farmer who had come to Alberta in 1905 and had become in 1916 president of the UFA, the Alberta wing. Crerar believed that the Progressives should act as a pressure group to force the minority Liberal government to make important concessions to farmers. He wanted the Progressives to vote as a single unit, in essence as a party.

Wood, in contrast, opposed the very concept of party politics as inherently evil and favoured group government instead. He argued that society naturally divided into several economic interest groups, of which the farmers were one. If each group obtained representation in Parliament, then the laws passed would reflect the interests of all rather than those of the particular group that happened to control the party. Group co-operation would replace party competition.

Unable to resolve their differences, the divided Progressives proved ineffective. They declined the position of official opposition even though, as the second largest party in the House of Commons, they warranted that title. Then in 1922, Crerar resigned as leader, claiming he could not work with Wise Wood. Robert Forke, Crerar's successor, had no better luck at uniting the party. One of his alleged followers commented that Forke "does not control one Progressive vote other than his own, and he is not always sure about that." King compounded the Progressives' problems by courting the Manitoba wing through legislation of special interest to western farmers. The prime minister called the Progressives "Liberals in a hurry," and he worked to convince the moderate Progressives that he could move his party at a faster pace. He reinstated the Crow's Nest Pass reduced freight rates (they had been suspended during the war years), and he slightly lowered the tariff to please prairie farmers. Some Progressives, including Crerar, joined the Liberals, while others, especially the Alberta wing, joined with the labour MPs to form the radical Ginger Group.

Thus, on the eve of the election of 1925, the Progressives were in disarray. Rather than a party, they were a loose federation of regional groups, with only shallow, insubstantial roots in British Columbia, Quebec, and the Maritimes, and with deep divisions within the two regions of strength—the Prairie West and Ontario. In the elections of 1925 and 1926, their numbers declined dramatically, and the party disappeared as an effective political force by 1930.

In many respects, the Progressives had attempted the impossible: to preserve the family farm, to uphold rural values, and to insure the political dominance of agricultural interests in a society that was becoming increasingly more urban and industrial. Still, the spirit of the Progressives lived on in the philosophy of populism and in the tradition of western protest, to be taken up by two new western Canadian-based parties in the 1930s— the Co-operative Commonwealth Federation and the Social Credit Movement (see chapter 12).

229

A "Constitutional Crisis": The King–Byng Affair

Mackenzie King's first administration failed to implement its election promises to reform the Senate, promote immigration, or implement a substantially lower tariff. Historians John Thompson and Allen Seager note that "it is impossible to point to a single conspicuous legislative achievement between 1922 and 1925."[1] William Irvine, the fiery Alberta Labour MP, put it this way: "I have been very much surprised at the agility of their [the government's] movements and their resources in finding excuses to get away from their own promises." As a result, the Liberals lost seventeen seats in the election of 1925, reducing their numbers to ninety-nine; more than half of those seats were from Quebec.

The prime minister lost his own seat in North York, as did eight other cabinet ministers. The Conservatives more than doubled their number to 116, doing exceptionally well in Ontario. The Progressives fell by almost two-thirds to 24 seats. Despite his party's setback, King held on to office, in hopes of winning support from the Progressives and from members of the Maritime Rights Movement, in order to prevent a loss-of-confidence vote. In the throne speech his government promised a farm loan program, the immediate completion of the Hudson Bay Railway, the transfer of three prairie provinces' natural resources to provincial control, and tariff revisions. To gain the support of the J. S. Woodsworth, the Labour MP, he also promised to bring in an old-age pension scheme.

The situation looked encouraging for the Liberals until a Customs Department scandal broke. The opposition discovered a system of payoffs to civil servants for allowing liquor smuggling into the United States, where prohibition was still in force. Sensing that this issue could topple the Liberals, the Conservatives censured the government and demanded a vote of confidence. Realizing that his government faced certain defeat on the motion, King tried to circumvent normal parliamentary procedure by requesting a dissolution of Parliament and an election before a loss-of-confidence vote could be taken in the House. The prime minister had the right to make such a request, but the governor general, Julian Byng, equally had the constitutional right to deny it—and he did. King promptly resigned as prime minister and announced to a surprised House on Monday, June 28, that the country was without a government.

The governor general asked Meighen to form a government, and the leader of the opposition agreed. The Conservative government lasted only three days, giving Meighen the dubious honour of presiding over the shortest-lived government since Confederation. The Conservatives were defeated by a single vote (discovered later to have been cast by a Progressive who, in the confusion, had voted against the government even though he had been paired with a Conservative who was absent from the House— "pairing" is a parliamentary practice by which two voters on opposite sides absent themselves by mutual consent from a vote). The governor general had no choice but to dissolve Parliament and call the election that he had denied King a few days earlier.

In the election of 1926 King argued that the main issue of the election was the governor general's attempt to reduce Canada "from the status of a self-governing Dominion to the status of a Crown Colony" by refusing to take the advice of his elected representative. This allowed him to sidestep the ugly Customs scandal which Meighen emphasized in his campaign. King, the consummate politician, then accused Meighen and the Conservatives of threatening responsible government by taking power unconstitutionally. In the end, King won a majority government, although with a popular vote that was no higher than in the previous year's election.

The Liberals had gained most of their seats at the expense of the Progressives. Meighen lost his seat and the opportunity to form a government—worst of all, to a man that he personally detested. He vacated the prime minister's office on September 25, 1926, and resigned the next day as party leader. King was securely back in power, having succeeded in eliminating the first of what would be a series of political opponents— Meighen on the right and the Progressives on the left.

A Brief Economic Boom

By the time of the 1926 election, Canadians were enjoying an economic boom based, as in the past, on the production and export of raw materials. This boom followed a severe depression between 1920 and 1923, when firms went bankrupt (nearly 4000 in 1922) and unemployment was high.

230

However, new export products, pulp and paper and base metals in particular, together with the traditional staples of wheat and timber, were in demand in international markets.

THE NEW INDUSTRIALISM

After a period of low prices (from $2.37 a bushel in 1919 to less than $1.00 in 1922) and poor yields in the early 1920s, wheat production again regained importance by mid-decade, as a result of increased European demand, lower tariffs, and lower ocean freight rates. Farmers increased their hectarage, established wheat pools to market their crops without having to depend on the middleman in the grain trade, and annually hired more than fifty thousand harvesters from eastern Canada to get their crops to market. The 1928 crop, at 567 million bushels, proved to be the largest on record. Prices also remained high during these years.

231

The wheat boom, however, did not begin another era of expansion; rather, it signalled the final phase in a long cycle of nation-building based on the wheat economy. Canadian farmers now had to compete with other wheat-growing regions of the world, such as Argentina, Australia, and the Soviet Union, for a shrinking world market as wheat consumption declined.

Pulp and paper was Canada's leading new export in the 1920s. At the turn of the century, pulp-and-paper exports had been insignificant but increased phenomenally by the 1920s. In 1920 paper mills in Canada made more than 795 000 tons of newsprint each day; by the end of the decade that had increased threefold to 2 725 000 tons—enough to print forty billion newspapers a year. "By the end of the 1920s," the business historian Michael Bliss observes, "Canada was the leading papermaker and paper-making was Canada's leading industry."[2]

Most of the demand came from the United States, where mass-produced daily newspapers were a lucrative market for cheap newsprint. U.S. paper manufacturers wanted initially to convert unprocessed pulpwood into paper in their American factories. By the mid-twenties, however, they found it more economical to produce the paper in Canadian branch-plant paper mills. Several factors contributed to this decision: the availability of inexpensive pulpwood, cheap hydro-electric power, good transportation facilities, and lower American import duties on Canadian newsprint after 1913. Politics also played a part in increased production of paper in Canada. Provincial governments, especially those of Ontario, Quebec, and British Columbia, placed an embargo on the export of pulpwood from Crown lands or else imposed a stumpage charge on the number of trees cut, which declined if the producers made the pulp in Canada.

Along with increased production came consolidation. By the end of the decade, three giant companies—International, Abitibi, and Canadian Power and Paper—controlled more than half the pulp production, while the next three largest companies controlled another quarter. In this capital-intensive industry, Americans owned and controlled more than one-third of Canada's pulp production.

Mining followed a similar pattern. After a sluggish period in the early twenties, foreign demand for Canadian base metals—copper, zinc, lead, and nickel—revived the Canadian industry. The United States especially needed large supplies to produce such consumer goods as automobiles, radios, and electrical applicances. The Canadian government's decision in 1922 to adopt nickel coinage greatly assisted nickel mining. Prices for base metals rose high enough to encourage exploration and even to reopen some mines with low-quality ore grades. The Americans again provided much of the capital needed to finance purchases of the complex and expensive equipment used in base metal mining. Americanization of the industry did not concern Canadians; on the contrary, provincial governments extended a welcome hand to American investors and did everything they could to help them get established for fear they might invest elsewhere.

Mining increased across the country. In Quebec, mineral production increased nearly thirty fold from 1898 to 1929. Whole new areas, such as Noranda (its name is a combination of the words "North" and "Canada"), Rouyn, Malartic, Val d'Or, and Bourlamaque, opened up with the discovery of copper, zinc, lead, and precious metals. In British Columbia, Cominco developed new flotation techniques to mill base metals, which revived a dying industry. In Manitoba, a Canadian-American group, incorporated as Hudson Bay Mining and Smelting, refined the ore at Flin Flon, about one hundred kilometres north of The Pas, and still farther north at Lynn Lake. Ontario benefited greatly from the rich mineral deposits in its northland. The nickel companies in the Sudbury area doubled production during the decade. Inco (International Nickel Company of Canada) controlled more than 90 percent of world production.

Hydro-electricity provided power for the pulp and paper industry and for the refineries. Production of electricity quadrupled in the 1920s. This energy source was particularly important for the production of aluminum from bauxite ore, which required huge amounts of electricity. Provincial governments realized the importance of hydro-electric power for industrialization and the high cost involved in building hydro-electric plants. In Ontario the industry was nationalized with the blessing of private business, which saw public ownership as an inexpensive way to acquire power. In Quebec, the industry remained in private hands but developed with the provincial government's financial support.

Labour Unions

Labour unions experienced hard times in the 1920s, largely as a result of the new availability of labour after the return of Canadian soldiers from overseas. Business was determined to limit trade unions' effectiveness. Wage cuts, industrial consolidation, and improved technological/managerial methods all worked to the disadvantage of labourers. In retaliation, workers staged a series of strikes to reinforce their demands. Many of these strikes ended in physical violence; almost all failed to improve wages or working conditions. Union membership plummeted by more than one-third, reaching a low of 260 000 by mid-decade.

Unions were also divided. The conservative Trades and Labour Congress (TLC) continued to favour craft unions and to advocate advancement through conciliation and government intervention, if necessary. In opposition, the All-Canadian Congress of Labour (ACCL), created in 1927, began to form industry-wide, or industrial unions, and to support strike action. "What we want," declared president Aaron Mosher at the union's 1929 convention, "is a national union covering each industry in Canada, which will be fully organized and . . . strong enough to take a share in the control as well as the profits of industry."

233

In Nova Scotia bitter disputes occurred in the coal mines and the steel factories. When BESCO, the leading company in the region, attempted to offset declining sales through wage cuts, the workers retaliated with a strike. James B. McLachlan, a militant Scottish immigrant worker who in 1917 helped found the Amalgamated Mine Workers of Nova Scotia, led the strikers. "War is on us, class war," he announced. The company's vice-president responded: "Let them stay out two months or six months, it matters not; eventually they will come crawling to us." In the end, however, the company had to send its security force to break up the strike. The workers won limited concessions but a legacy of hatred remained. Part of that bitterness was directed at the TLC, because it had refused to back the strikers. That is why when Samuel Gompers, the American inspiration behind the TLC, died later that year, McLachlan replied to the invitation to the funeral: "Sorry, duties will not permit me to attend, but I heartily approve of the event."

In Quebec some workers and farmers joined Catholic unions that were guided by priests and sanctioned by the Church. The *Confédération des travailleurs catholiques du Canada* (CTCC) brought twenty thousand workers from a variety of industries and occupations into the CTCC in 1921, while the *Union catholique des cultivateurs* (UCC) in 1924 had a membership of thirteen thousand farmers. These organizations never succeeded in attracting much more than one-quarter of the total Quebec union membership. They did, however, attempt to isolate their members from the secular and often socialistic nature of what they considered were the "foreign" unions, that is, American or English Canadian.

A Revolution in Transportation and Communications

Growth in the primary sector of wheat, timber, and minerals multiplied markets in the secondary sector, the most spectacular secondary growth taking place in the automotive industry. Next to the United States, Canada became "the most motorized country on the globe."[3] The number of cars, trucks, buses, and motorcycles on Canadian roads tripled from 408 000 in 1920 to 1 235 000 a decade later, while the total capital investment in the industry more than doubled from $40 million to $98 million.

Initially, the Dominion produced its own cars—at one time as many as seventy small companies manufactured, assembled, or sold automobiles in Canada. By the 1920s, however, Canadian companies could not keep pace with their automated American counterparts, making mass-produced and less expensive models. Poorly capitalized Canadian car manufacturers sold out to the American giants. In 1904 Gordon McGregor of the Walk-erville Wagon Works obtained a franchise from Ford for Canada and the British Empire and began the Ford Company of Canada. Sam McLaughlin used American technology, expertise, and money to begin producing McLaughlin cars in Oshawa, Ontario, and then sold his company to General Motors in 1918. Chrysler, the last of the "big three" manufacturers to appear in Canada, was created when the American automobile tycoon, Walter P. Chrysler, bought out the ailing Maxwell-Chalmers company of Windsor to establish the Chrysler Company of Canada in 1925. By the end of the decade, the "big three" manufactured three-quarters of the cars purchased in Canada.

Canadians had already begun, in the words of historian Arthur Lower, to worship "the great god CAR."[4] By the end of the decade, one-quarter of all potential owners had an automobile. The car revolutionized the Canadian landscape as the railway had done seventy years earlier. Roads again became important. In the cities, paved streets became commonplace. In 1925 Canada had 75 200 km of surfaced roads; by 1930, 128 000. Tire companies and factories appeared to produce spare parts, service stations sprang up, and tourism prospered. The car also opened the way to wider ownership of summer cottages, making it possible to get to vacation areas— where there were roads.

Aviation also expanded greatly in the 1920s. Veteran World War I flying aces, using surplus war planes, opened up Canada's north. They flew geologists and prospectors into remote areas of the Canadian Shield and provided service to isolated northern settlements. These pioneer flyers travelled by visual flying; lacking proper maps, they had to stay at low altitudes in order to spot landmarks. In 1924 Laurentide Air Services began the first regular air mail service into the Quebec gold fields at Rouyn-Noranda. Other companies followed, and for several years the Canadian government permitted each company to print and issue its own postage stamps.

234

Glenbow-Alberta Institute.

In the 1920s the "great god CAR" still had its problems, many due to the dirt roads. This group of Chatauqua players got bogged down in the prairie mud somewhere in Manitoba. Chatauqua performed in many prairie towns.

Important communications inventions became popular in the 1920s. The telephone, invented about 1875 by Alexander Graham Bell, a Canadian, became a standard household item in Canada. With party lines, eavesdropping (rubbernecking, as it was called then) became a national pastime. Radio, the great communication invention of the twenties, helped to end isolation and loneliness. The first scheduled broadcast in North America took place in Montreal in May 1920, when station XWA (later CFCF) relayed a musical programme to a Royal Society of Canada meeting in Ottawa. Other stations were quick to realize the potential of this new invention. By mid-decade there were numerous stations (most of them small and low-powered) across the country. The Canadian stations found it difficult to compete with the more powerful American stations with their more polished product. By the end of the 1920s an estimated 80 percent of the programmes Canadians listened to were American.

Women in the 1920s

Despite the efforts of women's organizations, Canadian society in the twenties remained male-dominated. Males in all social classes perceived women as homemakers. Birth control measures were not readily available, and social pressure encouraged women to have large families. Although

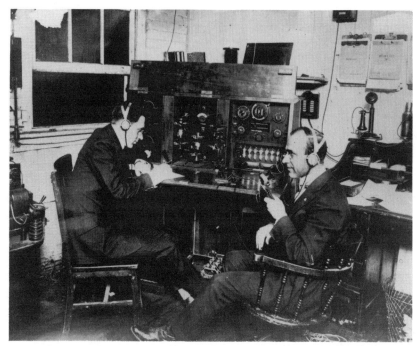

Canadian Marconi Co.

Radio was the greatest communications invention in the 1920s. The very first commercial radio station in the world, Montreal's XWA, broadcasted music, news and weather in 1920 for those fortunate enough to own a crystal radio set.

236

women made up 20 percent of the labour force in 1929 they held traditional female jobs as secretaries, sales clerks, and domestics, or worked in textile or tobacco factories, canneries, or fish plants. If they entered the professions, it was almost inevitably as teachers or nurses; only a handful became physicians, lawyers, or professors. Few women even had the opportunity for a secondary education—by 1929 they made up only one-quarter of the national secondary student body. Moreover, female wages stayed low. The average male earner made nearly $1000 a year by 1929, but the average female had to be content with just over half that amount.

Unions still did little to organize the female-dominated industries and, on occasion, failed even to support women on strike. After a walkout of female workers at the Canada Cotton plant in Hamilton in 1929, for example, the leaders of the TLC apologized to the provincial government for the strike, explaining that 90 percent of the strikers were women and girls who did not know any better. Economic equality—like political equality—remained an elusive goal for women.

In prairie farm homes, women continued to work themselves to early deaths. Farmers could ease their workload through mechanization, but women were expected to perform the traditional tasks of cooking, cleaning,

City of Toronto Archives (James 2534).

Female members of the University of Toronto's class of '28; throughout the twenties increasing numbers of women were graduating, including the first female graduates in engineering.

laundering, and sewing the old-fashioned way, while still caring for children and even working outside at critical times of the year. According to historian Veronica Strong-Boag, prairie women were "pulling in double harness or hauling a double load."[5] Nevertheless, rural women made important advances that helped challenge traditional social barriers. Rural reform leaders made the public aware of the heavy work loads that rural women carried, and also suggested ways to ameliorate those burdens through household science courses, co-operation, and the use of more household appliances.

The middle-class urban women had a higher standard of living in the 1920s. Some middle-class urban women benefited from such modern labour-saving devices as refrigerators, electric stoves, and vacuum cleaners, and from such luxuries as electricity and running water. Outside the home, an increasing number of young, middle-class women were able to stay in school longer or to take a job between school and marriage. Their growing independence was asserted by dressing more freely, smoking in public, and—most daring of all—drinking at parties.

In the late 1920s an important legal definition of women in Canada was changed. Section 24 of the British North America Act stated that "qualified

Trans Alta Utilities Corporation.

The "rotary arm iron" made household ironing easier for women. The iron worked from the power of the drum of the wringer-washing machine.

persons" could become senators. For almost a decade five Alberta women— Emily Murphy, the first woman police magistrate in the British Empire; Irene Parlby, the first woman Cabinet minister in Canada; Nellie McClung, a member of the Alberta Legislature; and two suffragettes and prohibitionists, Henrietta Edwards and Louise McKinney—fought to change the law that held women were not "persons" in the eyes of the law and thus ineligible for appointment to the Senate. Both the Alberta provincial court and the Supreme Court of Canada upheld the statute, but the Judicial Committee of the Privy Council overruled both courts in the famous Persons Case in 1929, calling the exclusion of women from public office "a relic of days more barbarous than ours." In 1930 Cairine Wilson became Canada's first woman senator.

Social and Cultural Changes

In Quebec the church attempted to stem secularization in social and political life. Abbé Lionel Groulx, the editor of *L'Action française* in the 1920s, saw the onslaught of urban and industrial society as anathema to everything French Canadians believed in: the church, the family, and the French-

National Archives of Canada C-54523

The bachelor prime minister William Lyon Mackenzie King looks uneasy amidst the five women who have gathered together to celebrate the fight for legal recognition of women as "persons" in the famous "Persons Campaign." They pose before a commemorative tablet in the lobby of the Senate unveiled in 1938 to honour the original "Famous Five."

239

Canadian nation. He launched an all-out attack—"action française"—on what he perceived to be the anglicization and Americanization of Quebec. The movement gained support in the twenties; through its periodical of the same name (with a circulation of several thousand) raising issues that Groulx believed should concern French Canadians. *L'Action française* for example, warned of the danger to the French-Canadian nation of French Canada's declining population—from 31 percent at the time of Confederation to 27 percent in 1921—in relation to the overall Canadian population. It also opposed the growing urban migration, especially to Montreal. To *L'Action française* this migration threatened the very existence of the French Canadians as a traditionally rural, agricultural people. Historian Susan Mann Trofimenkoff has summarized the movement's outlook: "Cities bred standardization, homogeneity, and ultimately, they suspected, assimilation."[6] To counter this urbanization, *L'Action française* stressed the traditional values of the land, the church, and the nation. Groulx placed a special responsibility on women as guardians of the home and family.

Some English-Canadian Protestants were equally disturbed by the abandonment of prohibition and the increase in immigration. The arrival of almost 1.25 million newcomers in the 1920s fed a xenophobia already well in place. The Ku Klux Klan was responsible for some of the most virulent expressions of the new bigotry. In southeastern Ontario and on the Prairies this American-based organization fostered hatred towards Catholic immigrants, while in British Columbia it attacked Orientals; its traditional animosity towards Blacks was played down only because in Canada there were so few. In Saskatchewan, the Klan had limited success and even temporarily allied itself in the late 1920s with the provincial Conservative party. The Klan's presence reflected the ethnic and racial tensions in Canadian society in the 1920s.

240 AN ENGLISH-CANADIAN CULTURE

English-speaking Canada's culture flourished in the 1920s. The Group of Seven, a new art movement, first exhibited together in 1920; the original members were Frank Carmichael, Lawren Harris, A. Y. Jackson, Franz Johnston, Arthur Lismer, J. E. H. Macdonald, and F. H. Varley — artist Tom Thomson, part of this circle of friends, died in a canoe accident in Algonquin Park in 1917 before the group's formation. The catalogue claimed that art must reflect "the spirit of a nation's growth." To the Group of Seven, the Canadian spirit could be found in nature—in the trees, rocks, and lakes of the Ontario northland. The Algoma region north of Lake Huron became for the group a symbol of the nation similar to the West in the American tradition—a mythical land that became a metaphor for the Canadian people. As well, the "North" represented an escape from the "South," where urbanization, industrialism, and materialism weakened the Canadian spirit.

The group flourished despite some art critics' denunciations of their paintings as belonging to the "Hot Mush School" and of the group as "paint slingers." Norman Brown of the National Gallery arranged to have them represent Canada at the British Empire Exhibition at Wembley, England, in 1924. Soon the group came to symbolize Canadian art, although their best-known paintings depicted only one region of the country—the Laurentian Shield of Ontario—and at that, a section south of the 49th parallel. Other artists also appeared in the early twentieth century. In British Columbia, Emily Carr painted landscape scenes of British Columbia and of West Coast Indian villages. On the prairies, Lionel Lemoine FitzGerald and Illingworth Kerr captured the region's uniqueness on canvas, while in the Maritimes, Pegi Nicol MacLeod painted the New Brunswick landscape in the Group of Seven tradition.

A growing English-speaking literary culture also emerged. Two new

English-language journals appeared: the *Canadian Forum*, which encouraged an interest in Canadian art and politics, and the *Canadian Historical Review*. The Canadian Authors' Association also aided young English-Canadian writers in publishing their works. At McGill a group of young rebellious poets known as "the Montreal group"—F. R. Scott, A. J. M. Smith, A. M. Klein, and Leo Kennedy—helped to change the direction of Canadian poetry by endorsing the modernist movement. They wrote in free verse, discarded the norms of punctuation, and chose their subject material in the modern city. In French Canada, poets like Jean-Aubert Loranger introduced modernist poetry to Quebec. Canadian Clubs were formed across Canada "to foster patriotism by encouraging the study of institutions, history, art and literature of Canada," and to sponsor lecture tours, poetry reading, and art exhibitions.

241

POPULAR CULTURE

In terms of popular culture, however, English-speaking Canadians became more Americanized in the 1920s. They preferred the American-style service clubs like Rotary, Lions, Kiwanis, and Gyro to the elitist Canadian clubs. Canadians who had never set eyes on the *Canadian Forum* or even the mass-circulation *Maclean's* knew about such American magazines as the *Ladies' Home Journal*, *McCall's*, and the *Saturday Evening Post*. These American magazines had a combined North American circulation of more than fifty million copies each issue by 1926. Canadian newspapers adopted an "American" style: glossy advertising, sensational headlines and stories, comic strips, substantial sports sections, and a heavy reliance on American wire services for international coverage. Most English-speaking Canadians close to the international border listened to American stations, with their popular programmes and strong transmitters. The film and movie industry was Americanized to an even greater extent. Lack of capital for production and the control of theatres by American distribution houses, such as Famous Players, weakened the Canadian film industry.

Americans took over another Canadian "industry"—hockey. At the beginning of the 1920s professional hockey was uniquely Canadian; the Pacific Coast League, the Western Canada League, and the National Hockey League all competed for the Stanley Cup. By the end of the decade, however, American entrepreneurs bought out most of the Canadian teams. Only the National Hockey League remained, and even the majority of its teams—with the exception of Montreal's Maroons and Canadiens, and the Toronto Maple Leafs—were American, although almost all the league players were Canadian.

In other sports, however, Canadian amateurs won international attention. Percy Williams and Ethel Catherwood won gold medals at the 1928

Olympics. Williams became known as "the world's fastest human." George Young made a name for Canada in swimming by winning the 32 km race from the California mainland to Catalina Island. In the Maritimes, Captain Angus Walters won the International Fisherman's Trophy three years in succession—in 1921, 1922, and 1923. His sailing ship, called the *Bluenose* after the Nova Scotians' nickname, was later immortalized on the back of the Canadian dime. The famous Edmonton Grads women's team dominated world basketball from 1915 to 1940.

The political, economic, and social changes of the twenties created a society that, by 1929, was different from that of 1919. New political leaders with new political styles emerged. A resurgent Maritime protest movement and rising western agrarian protest added to the complexity of ruling this diverse country. Women continued their battles for legal recognition and for greater rights in the workplace. More Canadians had become urbanized and were enjoying a higher standard of living than ever before, although widespread poverty was still evident. There was a growing cultural sophistication in Canada, while the majority of English-Canadians partook of American popular culture to a greater extent. Few could have predicted, as the decade came to an end, that it would be followed by the worst depression in world history.

242

NOTES

[1] John Herd Thompson with Allen Seager, *Canada, 1922–1939: Decades of Discord* (Toronto, 1985), p. 112.
[2] Michael Bliss, *Northern Enterprise: Five Centuries of Canadian Business* (Toronto, 1987), p. 401.
[3] Quoted in Thompson with Seager, *Canada, 1922–1939*, p. 85.
[4] A. R. M. Lower, *Canadians in the Making: A Social History of Canada* (Toronto, 1958), p. 424.
[5] Veronica Strong-Boag, "Pulling in Double Harness or Hauling a Double Load: Women, Work and Feminism on the Canadian Prairie," *Journal of Canadian Studies*, 21 (Fall 1986): 36.
[6] S. M. Trofimenkoff, *The Dream of Nation: A Social and Intellectual History of Quebec* (Toronto, 1982), p. 223.

Related Readings

The following articles from R. Douglas Francis and Donald B. Smith, *Readings in Canadian History: Post-Confederation*, 2d ed. (Toronto, 1986) deal with the protest in the West and the Maritimes in the 1920s in greater depth: Walter Young, "The Progressives," pp. 406–13; and E. R. Forbes, "The Origins of the Maritime Rights Movement," pp. 413–24.

BIBLIOGRAPHY

For an overview of the 1920s, see John Herd Thompson with Allen Seager, *Canada, 1922–1939: Decades of Discord* (Toronto, 1985). On Mackenzie King's political life in the 1920s, see the latter part of R. M. Dawson, *William Lyon Mackenzie King: A Political Biography*, vol. 1: *1874–1923* (Toronto, 1958), and H. B. Neatby, *The Lonely Heights*, vol. 2: *1924–1932* (Toronto, 1970). A popular study is J. L. Granatstein's *Mackenzie King: His Life and World* (Toronto, 1977). Roger Graham's *Arthur Meighen: A Biography*, vol. 2: *And Fortune Fled* (Toronto, 1963) and his Canadian Historical Association pamphlet, *Arthur Meighen* (Ottawa, 1965) deal with King's political rival in the 1920s.

Maritime protest in the 1920s is discussed in E. R. Forbes, *The Maritime Rights Movement 1919–27* (Montreal, 1979), and in D. J. Bercuson, ed., *Canada and the Burden of Unity* (Toronto, 1977). David Frank, "Class Conflict in the Coal Industry: Cape Breton 1922," in *Essays in Working-Class History*, edited by G. S. Kealey and P. Warrian (Toronto, 1976), pp. 161–84, recounts the story of labour strife on Cape Breton Island. On the Progressive movement, see Walter Young, *Democracy and Discontent* (Toronto, 1969), and W. L. Morton, *The Progressive Party in Canada* (Toronto, 1950). On the King–Byng affair, consult the King and Meighen biographies cited above and Roger Graham, *The King–Byng Affair, 1926* (Toronto, 1967).

On the economics of the 1920s, see the chapter "The Stuttering Twenties," in Michael Bliss, *Northern Enterprise: Five Centuries of Canadian Business* (Toronto, 1987); also, W. L. Marr and Donald G. Paterson, *Canada: An Economic History* (Toronto, 1980); and W. T. Easterbrook and H. G. J. Aitken, *Canadian Economic History* (Toronto, 1956). Consult as well Tom Traves, *The State and Enterprise: Canadian Manufacturers and the Federal Government 1917–31* (Toronto, 1979). For Quebec, see Paul-André Linteau, René Durocher, and Jean-Claude Robert, *Quebec: A History, 1867–1929* (Toronto, 1983).

On women in the 1920s, see S. M. Trofimenkoff and A. Prentice, eds., *The Neglected Majority: Essays in Canadian Women's History*, vol. 1 (Toronto, 1977), and vol. 2 (1985). On Quebec women, see as well Micheline Dumont *et al.*, *Quebec Women. A History* (Toronto, 1987); S. M. Trofimenkoff, *The Dream of Nation: A Social and Intellectual History of Quebec* (Toronto, 1983); and Marta Danylewycz, *Taking the Veil: An Alternative to Marriage, Motherhood, and Spinsterhood in Quebec, 1840–1920* (Toronto, 1987). For Ontario, see *Women at Work: Ontario, 1850–1930* (Toronto, 1974); and for the Prairies, Veronica Strong-Boag, "Pulling in Double Harness or Hauling a Double Load: Women, Work and Feminism on the Canadian Prairie," *Journal of Canadian Studies*, 21 (Fall 1986): 32–52.

S. M. Trofimenkoff's *Action Française: French-Canadian Nationalism in the Twenties* (Toronto, 1975) analyses this French-Canadian group, while

243

W. Calderwood, "Pulpit, Press and Political Reaction to the Ku Klux Klan in Saskatchewan," in *The Twenties in Western Canada*, edited by S. M. Trofimenkoff (Ottawa, 1972) discusses this phenomenon of the 1920s. Canadian culture is dealt with in "The Conundrum of Culture," in *Canada, 1922–1939* (cited above), pp. 158–92, and in Carl Klinck, ed., *Literary History of Canada: Canadian Literature in English*, 2d ed. (Toronto, 1976).

Society and Politics in the Great Depression

The Great Depression dominated the 1930s. The spectacular crash of the   *245*
New York stock market in October 1929 only symbolized the crisis. Heavy
debt burdens throughout the world economy created conditions conducive
to a calamitous downturn. Bank failures caused financial instability in both
Europe and the United States. International trade declined dramatically
as nations implemented "beggar-thy-neighbour" policies of high tariffs in
an effort to protect their own workers and farmers from foreign competition. Worldwide overproduction caused prices of commodities like wheat,
newsprint, and metals—all important Canadian exports—to fall sharply.
Unemployment levels increased substantially as industries cut back production in the face of declining demand. In virtually all sectors of activity,
the world economy plunged downwards in a seemingly endless spiral.

After the United States, Canada experienced the Western world's most
severe decline. Industrial production fell by one-third between 1929 and
1932. During the same years, Canada's gross national product sank by
two-fifths, in current dollars. Imports fell in volume by about 55 percent,
exports by 25 percent. The unemployment rate peaked at 32 percent in
May 1933.

What, though, did the depression signify in human terms? How did
Canadian men and women cope with its effects? In an age when modern
state-sponsored social welfare programmes did not exist, self-reliance counted
most. But it did not suffice. Farm organizations, trade unions, and co-
operatives attempted to defend the interests of their members. Discontented Canadians also came to expect help from their governments, and
listened attentively to the siren calls of a wide variety of opposition parties
and movements.

The Meaning of the Depression

The hundreds of thousands of Canadians who lost their jobs during the depression found it nearly impossible to obtain a new one, at least in the early years of the decade. For them and their families, unemployment meant poverty. Even worse was the psychological impact of depression. Unable to find work, people gradually lost their sense of self-worth. Sometimes family breadwinners left home rather than face the shame of not being able to provide the basic necessities. The jobless had no choice but to fall back on charity, both public and private. Having to seek such aid was humiliating, just as having to support a family on it was barely possible. Even more painful, in many Maritime towns those on welfare had to bear the disgrace of being incarcerated in municipal poorhouses.

Many workers who kept their jobs lived in a state of abject poverty because of abysmally low wages. The Royal Commission on Price Spreads, appointed by the government of R.B. Bennett in 1934 to investigate the buying practices of major department stores as well as labour conditions in certain industries, reported that "the sweat shop still survives in Canada." Existing laws contained loopholes, were unsatisfactorily administered, and frequently ignored. Female employees almost always received lower wages than male workers doing the same job, and companies often attempted to boost profits by replacing older men with young women. Department stores and other mass buyers forced producers to sell at cut-rate prices; the owners then lowered wages.

Wage rates varied significantly among cities and industries. Clerks at Eaton's and Simpson's in Toronto—mostly women—earned $10–$13 a week, while those in Montreal earned much less. Weekly pay for male workers in the furniture industry averaged ten dollars, but "boys" of eighteen or nineteen often earned as little as three dollars. The highly profitable tobacco industry also paid very low wages. Sometimes, on workers' pay envelopes, banks thoughtfully printed the advice: "Think of tomorrow, divide your pay in two. Take what you need to live, put the balance in safety"!

In the textile industry, wage fluctuations were extreme. A Quebec rural home worker, for example, might earn five cents an hour; a Toronto union shop employee could boast of over ten times as much. Employers often established wages in such a complicated fashion that workers could not determine how their earnings were calculated, or at what rates they were paid. Working conditions in the industry were notoriously bad. The work week was longer than in most factories, generally more than fifty hours. The tasks performed required close attention, with constant standing or moving about the machines, which created considerable nervous strain. One woman testified that, when piecework rates dropped, employees tried to work harder to maintain their wages. "You were driven so fast that you were a nervous wreck. The girls cried. I was hysterical myself." Almost

246

all textile workers were non-unionized, and a Royal Commission study of the industry in 1936 described employer attitudes towards bargaining with unions as "strictly negative."

DEPRESSION IN RURAL CANADA

Depression in rural Canada also signified declining living standards or even loss of livelihood. For Prince Edward Island potato growers hit by American tariffs, depression meant that their income fell 75 percent over a five-year period. Atlantic fishermen also became victims of diminishing markets and low prices. Dairy and poultry farmers in central Canada lost their American markets because of high tariffs. Western farmers saw wheat prices fall by 70 percent, to a mere thirty-four cents a bushel in 1932. In an exporting nation like Canada (nearly two-thirds of whose exports were agricultural) such a collapse had catastrophic effects, not only on the farmers but also on the entire national economy.

247

Although farmers across the land were hit hard, probably no group suffered more than those who inhabited what became the Prairie dustbowl, the dry areas of southcentral Saskatchewan and the adjoining corners of Manitoba and Alberta known as Palliser's Triangle. For the biblical seven years, from late 1930 until autumn 1937, almost no rain fell, and during windstorms the bone-dry topsoil blew away. People left their farms, abandoning a lifetime of work, hopes and unfulfilled dreams, their few earthly belongings piled in an old car. They moved farther north, to regions where it still rained, or migrated to the cities in a desperate attempt to find work. Many single men began riding the railroad boxcars from city to city. The plight of single women was equally painful. For example, many immigrants from Britain who had come to Canada to do housework found themselves stranded because of layoffs on farms and in private homes.

Not all Canadians suffered, however. With the decline in prices, those working in white-collar occupations, the professions, and in skilled trades, saw their position improve. Department store owner John David Eaton later recalled: "You could take your girl to a supper dance at the hotel for $10, and that included the bottle and the room for you and your friends to drink it in. I'm glad I grew up then. It was a good time for everybody." The great majority of Canadians, however, did not live as well.

Coping with the Crisis

Many victims of depression sought escape from reality. Window-shopping became a pastime of housewives whose families were on relief. Owners of radio sets in English-speaking Canada listened to *Amos 'n Andy*, the most

Saskatchewan Archives, RA 17005.

The Saskatchewan dust bowl during the mid-1930s. The thin layer of dry topsoil blew away in the windstorms.

popular radio show of the decade, or to *Hockey Night in Canada* with Foster Hewitt. In French Canada, radio stations specialized in live entertainment such as variety shows. They also enjoyed immense success with serials especially written for radio such as *Le curé de village* and *La pension Valder*. Popular magazines, both Canadian and American, featured stories of wealth and glamour, while films from Hollywood portrayed romance and fantasy. The birth of the Dionne quintuplets in May 1934, at Callander, Ontario, attracted wide attention. Between 1934–43 three million people came to stare at them. For a few fleeting moments, it was possible to forget daily worries.

ROLE OF RELIGION

Religion also played a major role, serving as a source of inspiration or allowing for an emotional escape. Some Protestants, notably in associations

Glenbow-Alberta Institute.

Many destitute families fled the drought. They packed all their belongings onto carts and headed north in search of better land.

249

like the Fellowship of a Christian Social Order, founded by members of the United Church, insisted that the realization of the Kingdom of God meant replacing capitalism with socialism. Conservative and fundamentalist groups also flourished, with their promise that if people could not find salvation in this world, they had the opportunity of preparing for it in the next. Spokesmen for the British Oxford Group Movement (a predecessor of Moral Rearmament) toured Canada, delivering a message of "revelation, not revolution," to overflow audiences.

In Quebec the Roman Catholic church saw the depression as evidence of divine punishment for the sins of humankind. It supported a back-to-the-land movement to combat not only unemployment but also "moral decrepitude." It led a crusade against both the evils of communism and the abuses of capitalism. The church also witnessed the growth of a more mystical spiritual element championed by Onésime Lacouture, a Jesuit priest with the charisma of an Old Testament prophet, who urged Catholics—including the clergy—to return to the Gospel and forsake materialism.

IMPACT OF THE DEPRESSION ON MARRIAGE AND FAMILY LIFE

The struggles of daily life had a negative effect on families. The depression put a strain on many marriages and appears to have provoked an increase in wife abuse. Since divorce was generally not possible, victims were told to make the best of matters and to find comfort in their children.

Not surprisingly, marriage rates dropped as young people were forced to put off marriage until times improved. Postponed marriages contributed to a sharp decline in the birth rate. In Quebec, the province with the highest rate, it fell from 30.8 per thousand in 1928 to 25.3 in 1934. In Ontario, the decline was almost as great, while in the Maritimes, birth rates responded little to the hard times of the 1930s, perhaps because that region had experienced depression in the 1920s, too.

For the first time, birth control became a hotly debated issue, and a few clinics were set up to provide information. In one widely publicized case in an Ottawa suburb, police arrested Dorothea Palmer, a social worker who had handed out birth control material, for infringing on the provisions of the Criminal Code on obscenity prohibiting the "advertising and selling of contraceptive drugs and devices." At the trial, the judge acquitted her because he believed that she had acted "for the public good." The poor, he stated, "are a burden to the taxpayer. They crowd the Juvenile Court. They glut the competitive labour market."

Proponents of birth control in English-speaking Canada, notably in Protestant churches or social welfare agencies, extolled its beneficial social effects. With fewer siblings, poorer children would receive better care.

The tiny Eugenics Society of Canada, for its part, favoured birth control as a means of limiting reproduction among what it considered were inferior social groups. Some English-speaking Canadians asserted that birth control would help curtail the extraordinary fecundity of French Canadians, while the latter quite naturally suspected Protestant Anglo-Saxon Torontonians of concocting yet another plot to weaken French Canada. Seldom mentioned throughout the controversy was the right of women themselves to determine how many children to have.

Associations and Trade Unions

Though individualism was still strong in this age of non-interventionist government, the severity of the depression necessitated group action. The Antigonish Movement, launched in the 1920s by liberal Catholics at St. Francis Xavier University in Antigonish, Nova Scotia, spread across the Maritimes, advocating community education and promoting the establishment of credit unions, and consumers' and fishermen's co-operatives. In the West, as the agricultural crisis deepened, farmers fought to save their co-operatives, in particular the Prairie wheat pools that had overextended credit in the booming twenties and now faced bankruptcy. They also promoted the need for more ordered markets, easier credit, and adequate social services through branches of the Canadian Chamber of Agriculture. In Quebec, the *Union catholique des cultivateurs* (UCC) joined with the clergy to organize farmers' wives and compete with the state-sponsored *cercles de fermières*. The UCC also forced the provincial government, at least temporarily, to improve working conditions and wages for woodcutters.

251

Though hit by hard times, labour unions nevertheless were active. Conflicts with management were bitter, especially in the latter half of the decade. The unions' first challenge was to obtain wider legal recognition, but prior to World War II only Nova Scotia's Trade Union Act of 1937 specifically gave them the right to bargain and to collect payroll deductions.

When Canada entered the depression, the country's largest labour organization was the Trades and Labour Congress (TLC) whose members were affiliated with unions in the American Federation of Labour (AFL). These craft unions tended to be conservative in outlook and suspicious of radical reform (see chapter 8). In English Canada the independent All-Canadian Congress of Labour (ACCL), founded in 1927 and bitterly opposed to international unionism, had forty thousand members in various affiliates. More than half of Quebec's union members belonged to the *Confédération des travailleurs catholiques du Canada* (CTCC), the Catholic labour federation whose chaplains unceasingly warned of the dangers of American and non-confessional unions for French-speaking Roman Catholics. All told, the depression would provoke substantial organizational change.

THE WORKERS' UNITY LEAGUE

By 1929 the Canadian Communists' policy of attempting to penetrate existing unions had proven ineffective. Under orders from Moscow, they changed their strategy, and launched their own movement, a "revolutionary trade union centre"—the Workers' Unity League (WUL). It aggressively tried to organize such sectors as mining, textiles, and lumber, as well as among office workers. In practice, WUL organizers quickly signed up workers in mines or shops, then declared a strike that aimed at union recognition and better wages and working conditions. Violent confrontations often broke out between police and strikers, or between strikebreakers and strikers. A bitter walk-out by mineworkers at Estevan, Saskatchewan in 1931 saw three miners killed in a clash with police. In 1934 the league participated in the "foreigners' strike"—so-called because most of the workers were immigrants—against Noranda Mines in Rouyn, Quebec, which the company broke by hiring "scab" or non-union labourers protected by police.

252

In contrast to other unions, the WUL also focussed attention on the jobless by establishing unemployed workers' councils in various cities and by circulating a petition, eventually signed by 300 000 people, calling for a national non-contributory unemployment insurance scheme. Then, when world-wide Communist strategy again changed in 1935 and Moscow adopted a "united front against Fascism" policy, it ordered the Canadian Communist party to disband the league and to tell the WUL unions to join the TLC. An important episode in Canadian labour history thus came to an abrupt end.

THE CIO IN CANADA

Unionism in the new mass-production industries in the United States took a step forward with the formation of the Committee for Industrial Organization in 1935. Soon expelled from the AFL, it showed little interest in Canada, and consequently Canadians almost exclusively financed their own CIO activities.

The lengthy General Motor's strike in Oshawa in 1937, a landmark in Canadian labour history, was a CIO endeavour that got little assistance from Americans. Ontario Premier Mitchell Hepburn resolved to break this strike. Increasingly suspicious of organized labour, he also feared that a CIO success in Oshawa would encourage unionization in northern Ontario mines in which he had investments. Hepburn was supported by his friend George McCullagh whose newspaper, the *Globe and Mail*, roundly condemned "Communism in Canada." When the federal government refused to send in RCMP reinforcements, Hepburn recruited university students and veterans, nicknamed "Hepburn's Hussars" or "Sons of Mitches," as special constables for Oshawa. Thereafter, relations between the Ontario premier and King steadily deteriorated. Hepburn also fired two Cabinet ministers critical of his actions. One of them, David Croll, retorted: "My place is marching with the workers rather than riding with General Motors."

The CIO also attempted to organize Montreal's garment industry workers, most of whom were women. In 1937, in an effort to reach French Canadians, the International Ladies Garment Workers Union (ILGWU) hired Claude Jodoin (later president of the Canadian Labour Congress from 1956 to 1966) as organizer.

In spite of some successes and much publicity, the CIO made little headway in Canada in the 1930s. Opposition came from business which warned, in the *Montreal Star*'s words, that CIO goons would continue to stir up trouble until "each Canadian worker becomes the vassal of the tsars of American unionism." It also came from the conservative AFL which in 1939 pressured the TLC into expelling Canadian CIO affiliates. After the CIO unions merged with the poorly financed and organizationally weak All-Canadian Congress of Labour in September 1940 to form the Canadian Congress of Labour, the Communist presence declined while American influence increased.

Though only a small proportion of female workers were organized, women union members were often as militant as men. During a lengthy strike in the dress industry in Montreal in 1934, for example, the needleworkers defended themselves by sticking pins in the horses' thighs when the mounted police tried to disperse them with whips.

Unions made considerable efforts to organize women, though they usually subordinated women's interests to men's. The CTCC frowned upon working women, whom it saw as endangering family life and morality. Agreements with employers commonly prescribed lower wage scales for women. In some cases, male-dominated unions did demand equal pay—not in order to combat discrimination but rather to ensure that employers would not have a financial interest in replacing women employees with men. Some unions were established by women; a notable example was the *Fédération catholique des institutrices* in Quebec, set up by Laure Gaudreault in 1937 to represent underpaid primary school teachers.

Relief Efforts: From Charity to "the Dole"

Struggling workers' associations could hardly rescue the millions of Canadians who lacked the means to house, feed, and cloth themselves. Until the 1930s, local governments and private religious charities had looked after the destitute (see chapter 8). Private agencies employed a few trained social workers, but the enormous increase in their caseloads at the onset of the depression soon overwhelmed them.

253

On coming to power in 1930 the Conservatives, as promised, passed a bill providing for $20 million—out of a federal budget of only $500 million—in relief. This gesture marked the first grudging recognition that Ottawa did have some responsibility to the unemployed. It was soon called upon to do much more. By 1934 about 2 million Canadians (20 percent of the country's population) depended on relief. Between 1930 and 1938, the federal government had to put nearly $350 million into relief for the jobless and for destitute farmers, while municipal and provincial governments added another $650 million.

Conventional wisdom held that the unemployed should work for relief money to avoid becoming permanent wards of the state. The town of New Toronto, Ontario, for example, had large stones hauled in and placed in vacant lots to be smashed and used for road construction. In Winnipeg, the city hired men on relief to saw wood or to pull weeds along city boulevards. By 1932, however, financial pressures forced governments to cut expenditures. Public works projects often required the purchase of materials and, in any case, the able-bodied unemployed were too numerous for the limited number of projects available. Direct relief—handouts—appeared a less costly measure.

In the framework of what was termed "the dole," federal and provincial governments gave grants to cities and towns which municipal authorities then added to their own welfare budgets. Toronto's budget for relief increased twenty times between 1929 and 1933. In Montreal, 30 percent of whose population was on relief during the winter of 1933–34, Mayor Camillien Houde introduced new business and property taxes, which the largely Anglophone establishment bitterly protested. By the outbreak of war, Montreal's per capita debt load was twice Toronto's. When the province of Quebec, more tight-fisted towards its towns than other provinces, refused to come to Montreal's rescue, the city was forced to declare bankruptcy in 1940.

Western cities did little better than survive the depression. They all sharply curtailed expenses, fired municipal workers, tried to reduce the number of people on welfare through disqualification proceedings, raised taxes, and extended the maturity dates of their borrowings. By 1936, Prairie cities devoted one-third of their budgets to interest. Because of unpaid taxes, they had accumulated thousands of lots and buildings. Cities competed fiercely with one another in fruitless attempts to attract new industry by offering tax exemptions and low rates for utilities. Despite such efforts, urban populations in the West stagnated in contrast to the rapid growth in the decades both prior to and following the depression.

Canada's local governments, faced with diminishing tax revenues, declining federal and provincial subsidies, rising expenses and ballooning debts, were compelled to tighten eligibility criteria for welfare. Towns offering some assistance often had lengthy residence requirements to eliminate drifters and to avoid attracting people living in municipalities where little or no relief was available. Immigrants were particularly unwelcome. As one Toronto suburban newspaper put it: "The taxpayers have enough to do to look after their needy citizens and should be protected against foreigners coming here to seek relief—Deport them at once!" The Immigration Act did provide for the deportation of immigrants on relief, and in 1930–35 Ottawa returned an unprecedented thirty thousand immigrants, largely public charges, to a surely more miserable fate in Europe.

Recipients of relief generally had to be in arrears in rent payments, and to have received notice of discontinuation of electricity and water service, as well as of impending eviction from their lodgings. They might have to turn in their automobile licence plates (the possession of a car was an obvious luxury), prove that telephone service had been discontinued, and ensure that they did not possess a radio set. Some cities gave out vouchers to pay for food, but merchants often had to wait months for reimbursement. Other municipalities made cash payments. In 1933, North York gave families on relief a maximum of $11.60 a week—the Toronto Welfare Council estimated that a family of five needed $28.35 in order to enjoy an adequate living standard. Families of fifteen in Chicoutimi, Quebec, received a meagre $13.08.

255

FEDERAL GOVERNMENT RELIEF PROGRAMME

For most, going "on the pogey" was extremely demoralizing. As historian Michiel Horn put it: "to go on relief was the ultimate indignity to people who saw themselves as being independent."[1] And yet, many middle-class Canadians, more fortunate in that they kept their jobs, charged that the unemployed were lazy. Prime Minister Bennett, himself a millionaire, complained in 1931 that "the fibre of some of our people has grown softer and they are not willing to turn in and save themselves." He hired Charlotte Whitton, head of the Canadian Council on Child and Family Welfare and Canada's best-known social worker, to do a report on unemployment relief in the West. She concluded that 40 percent of recipients really did not need help, that the dole was being abused by large numbers of seasonal workers whose living conditions actually improved, and that local and provincial governments needed stricter control to prevent waste. But she also urged that trained professionals be put in charge of relief administration. Bennett drew his own conclusions: the provinces and the cities were wasting money, therefore Ottawa should give less money. In 1934, announcing Ottawa's intention to reduce direct relief contributions substantially, he complained that people had become "more or less relief conscious, determined to get out of Government all they could."

Governments also disqualified women in some categories from relief. Montreal cut three thousand—"concubines," unmarried mothers, widows with young children, and women whose husbands were in jail—from the list. In response, the women demonstrated in front of City Hall, forcing Mayor Adhémar Raynault to relent. Eventually, they were made eligible for assistance under the Public Charities Act. In 1937 Quebec adopted Aid to Needy Mothers legislation, but it applied only to widows or to women who were invalids or whose husbands were in asylums. In addition, they had to prove poverty, demonstrate their capacity to be good mothers, and provide regularly a certificate signed by a minister or a priest.

RELIEF CAMPS AND THE ON-TO-OTTAWA TREK

Single unemployed persons especially had difficulty finding relief. Towns expected single women to be cared for by their families, and many municipalities initially had no provision for putting them on relief rolls. Many single men had little choice but to seek admission to "temporary" work camps, opened in 1932 by the Department of National Defence. "Inmates" often performed some type of work for which they were paid a modest twenty cents a day. The difficult conditions and the seemingly permanent nature of the camps bred considerable discontent among these "Royal Twenty Centers." In 1935 workers in the "slave camps," as they came to be called, went on strike in Vancouver and, under Communist supervision, organized an "On-to-Ottawa Trek" to make their grievances known to the federal government. In June two thousand Trekkers reached Regina, where they were stopped by police. Only strike leader Arthur Evans and a few others were permitted to continue to Ottawa, where an unsympathetic prime minister met them. Shortly afterwards, during a demonstration in Regina, the police seized Evans. The ensuing riot resulted in substantial destruction, dozens of injuries and the death of a police officer. The trek came to an ignominious end.

New Political Policies and Programmes

The depression forced most Canadians to look to government for help. Soon disappointed at the lack of appropriate remedies, they began to express interest in new political personalities, parties, and movements that claimed to have the answers to the crisis.

Some municipalities elected radical or populist mayors, even though large proportions of the unemployed could not vote since they owned no property. Torontonians put Jimmy Simpson, a socialist, in office in 1935 but many soon found his higher relief spending and increased taxes little to their liking. In Winnipeg, Communist party member Jacob Penner lost a bid for the mayoralty in 1932 but in 1934-35, as alderman, he was able to push for reforms. Other towns were run by charismatic and rather conservative mayors, like Gerry McGeer in Vancouver, Cornelius "Rock pile" Rink in Regina, and "Fightin' " Joe Clarke in Edmonton. But their rhetoric aside, these colourful figures in the end had to exercise financial prudence, since they were financially dependent on banks and other credit institutions, on investors, and on their own taxpayers. Solutions to the crisis, if there were solutions, would have to come from the federal and provincial governments. The cities needed "relief from relief."[2]

BENNETT'S POLICIES

Ottawa saw two shifts of power during the depression, in 1930 and again in 1935. In 1930 worsening economic conditions, the inadequacies of the Liberal government and, in particular, King's election campaign threat not to give "a five-cent piece" for relief to any provincial Tory government, resulted in the election of the combative Conservative leader R. B. Bennett in July 1930. During the campaign, Bennett promised that a Conservative government would "find work for all who are willing to work, or perish in the attempt." Moreover, in the face of the restrictive trading policies that were choking off Canadian exports, he swore to use tariffs to "blast our way" into world markets. Upon election, he immediately increased tariffs on most manufactured goods in a vain effort to boost opportunities for Canadian manufacturers. He also organized an Imperial Economic Conference in Ottawa in 1932. Though he made no progress in forcing up prices, he did, thanks to tough bargaining, obtain some tariff concessions from the British. Yet the downslide continued as commodity exports declined and unemployment increased.

Bennett has never been popular among Canadian historians. In view of the harsh judgment that Canadian voters passed on him in 1935, sympathy might appear misplaced. To some extent, Bennett's reputation as a cold, unyielding, autocratic leader whose own fortune made him oblivious to the misfortunes of others was well deserved. And yet, on a more personal level, the prime minister did respond to many of the hundreds of letters he received from Canadians pleading for a few dollars to buy a pair of shoes, or a wedding present, or a decent meal. Nevertheless, the wealthy Bennett could not himself alleviate the suffering of millions of people.

Moreover, in hindsight, Bennett's policies, when compared with the New Deal of the American president, Franklin D. Roosevelt, appear overly cautious. He was a fiscal conservative quite unprepared for massive governmental intervention in the economy and in social matters generally.

BENNETT'S NEW DEAL

It is in this context that Bennett's New Deal broadcasts should be evaluated. In April 1934, William D. Herridge, Bennett's brother-in-law and Canada's minister to the United States, had pleaded: "We need some means by which the people can be persuaded that they also have a New Deal." In five radio talks in January 1935, Bennett promised to "nail the flag of progress to the mast" and proclaimed, to the surprise and consternation of old-line Tories, "the old order is gone. It will not return." After their initial astonishment had passed, Canadians viewed Bennett's pronouncements as a deathbed conversion made necessary by the upcoming election. The prime minister, they felt, was playing the "politics of opportunism."[3] Professor Frank Scott's lyrics must have echoed the sentiments many less-eloquent Canadians felt:

258

Some glimmering concept of a juster state
Begins to trouble him—but just too late.
His whole life work had dug the grave too deep
In which the people's hopes and fortunes sleep.

Though he was not a great reformer Bennett did adopt several important measures which, over time, were strengthened. In response to the protests of Prairie farmers, he steered through the House the Farmers' Creditors Arrangement Act that, in his words, would "cut both interest and principal down to the productive level of the farm." He set up the Canadian Wheat Board to act as a "buffer between chaotic conditions in the international wheat market and the farmer on the land in Western Canada."[4] The board provided an alternative to the open market for wheat and guaranteed a minimum price. He also brought in the Prairie Farm Rehabilitation Act (PFRA), which addressed erosion control, water conservation, and land reclamation. In journalist James Gray's words, the PFRA became "an effective instrument to contain the desert in Western Canada."[5]

Bennett directed his attention to other sectors, too. After an abrupt about-face, he established the central Bank of Canada with the aim of co-ordinating Canadian monetary policy. He was also converted to the principle of public broadcasting and agreed to set up the Canadian Radio Broadcasting Commission, after strong lobbying by the Canadian Radio League that presented the issue as a choice between "the State or the United States."

By 1934 the Conservative prime minister considered instituting unemployment insurance. The scheme he had in mind was a contributory plan that gave minimal benefits and eliminated large numbers of workers likely to be unemployed. Bennett was sure that such a law would enable Ottawa to reduce spending on welfare. The measure was adopted in 1935, but declared unconstitutional by the Judicial Committee of the Privy Council in London in 1937. (After an amendment to the British North America Act, it was passed again by the King government in 1942.) Bennett also introduced legislation regulating wages and working hours, and the marketing of natural products. The Privy Council, seeing an invasion of provincial authority, struck down these acts as well in 1937. Many of Bennett's reform measures obtained the support of the business community which believed that controlled change was necessary to preserve the capitalist system.

When Bennett called an election in 1935, he had neither a strong campaign platform nor a united party. After the famous New Deal speeches, King had called Bennett's bluff, demanding that the Conservatives present their social reform measures to Parliament. Bennett was unprepared and the Conservatives presented their bills in piecemeal fashion. Nor did the legislation justify the inflated rhetoric of his radio speeches. Then Bennett made no further comment for several weeks. Brother-in-law Herridge mourned: "Our big, beautiful reform child is almost dead."

259

Bennett's response to the depression also seriously undermined Conservative party unity. Strong Tory elements from Montreal's St. James Street lost confidence in Bennett's leadership after his denunciations of the capitalist system. Worse, H.H. Stevens, the prominent head of the Select Committee and then of the Royal Commission on Price Spreads, resigned from the cabinet in October 1934 and began to criticize the government. Before the 1935 elections, he founded the Reconstruction party, promising to "re-establish Canada's industrial, economic and social life for the benefit of the great majority." While Stevens did attract the admiration of middle-class Canadians and small businessmen—one United Church minister assured his flock, "We are looking to Mr. Stevens and he is looking to God,"—the party appeared to be a one-man enterprise. Although it won only 10 percent of the vote in 1935 and then soon disappeared, it did cut into Conservative support.

Ironically, perhaps, victory in 1935 went to the least radical of the federal parties, the Liberals, although the new parties took one in four votes. King won strongly on his slogan "King or chaos," even though his popular vote was less than it had been in 1930 when he had been defeated.

Provincial Politics and the Economic Crisis

These years of crisis witnessed profound political change in the provincial capitals. Dissatisfied with Bennett, the voters were also increasingly critical of provincial governments—some of them, like the Liberals in Quebec and the Conservatives in Ontario, in office for decades—for their inability to come to grips with the economic and social problems of the depression.

NEWFOUNDLAND AND THE MARITIMES

In the East, Newfoundland, then a British dominion, was beset by political corruption, financial ruin brought on by rising public debt, unemployment that affected about half of the labour force in 1933, and economic disaster precipitated by the falling price of fish. In 1932, Sir Richard Squires, the Liberal prime minister, narrowly escaped being lynched by a mob infuriated by new disclosures of scandal. After a royal commission recommended the dissolution of the Legislature, Newfoundland reverted to the status of a British colony until Confederation with Canada in 1949 (see chapter 18).

Maritimers reacted to the ills of the depression by electing Liberal governments and keeping them in office until the 1950s. In Nova Scotia, Angus L. Macdonald, a former law professor, became premier in 1933 and soon asserted his personal ascendancy over party and province. Practising an activist style of government, he implemented old age pensions, paved roads, and denounced what he termed the "deleterious effects" of federal tariffs. Two years later, as Liberals castigated spendthrift Conservatives and promised economic and social reforms, they won elections in New Brunswick and Prince Edward Island as well. Yet all three provinces lacked the money to undertake such projects. By the end of the 1930s, for example, New Brunswick's spending on education and health services was barely half the national average, and illiteracy and infant mortality rates were the highest in the country.

REFORM MOVEMENTS IN QUEBEC

In Quebec, reform was also a major concern. Nationalists, clergy, and reformers bitterly criticized the Liberal administration of Louis-Alexandre Taschereau, premier since 1920. The *Ecole Sociale Populaire,* a Jesuit institution that aimed at applying the Roman Catholic church's social doctrine to Quebec conditions (see chapter 10), elaborated the *Programme de restauration sociale,* which urged a fairer distribution of wealth and various measures to aid workers and farmers; these reforms, it was believed, would correct the obvious abuses of the capitalist system and also diminish the appeal of the Communists, and the newly founded socialist CCF.

Dissident Quebec Liberals led by Paul Gouin, son of former Liberal premier Lomer Gouin, established the *Action libérale nationale* (ALN) in 1933 and borrowed heavily from the Jesuits' *Programme* for their own platform. As the pressures upon his government mounted, Taschereau denounced his political and clerical enemies. Earlier conflicts with the church had led him to be extremely wary of government intervention in social matters and his profound conservatism dictated financial prudence.

The poor judgment of the usually politically astute Taschereau cost him dearly, for an alliance between the ALN and Maurice Duplessis' Conservatives nearly provoked a Liberal defeat in the provincial election of 1935. Duplessis' subsequent exposure of scandal and corruption within the Liberal government soon drove Taschereau from office, and the Union Nationale swept the province in a new election in August 1936.

The Union Nationale government established a system of rural credit at low rates of interest; this measure, along with other forms of aid to farmers and rural Quebeckers later permitted the party to reap handsome political dividends. Yet in most respects the Duplessis government turned out to be as conservative as its predecessor. Its labour legislation, as well as its support of management during a bitter strike at Dominion Textile in 1937, provoked strong protests from the unions. Some prominent Union Nationale MLAs like René Chaloult and Philippe Hamel left the party, denouncing Duplessis as a traitor who had broken his promises. Even business was critical, not of the lack of reforms but rather of the government's financial mismanagement.

261

ONTARIO

In Ontario, the new Liberal leader Mitchell Hepburn, hardly the staid and stolid politician that Ontario has generally seemed to prefer, denounced Tory corruption; yet the province, contrary to Quebec and the Prairies, had no widespread reform movement. During his campaign for the premiership, Hepburn had made the well-publicized remark: "I swing far to the left where even some Liberals do not follow me." Elected handily in 1934, he introduced popular economy measures, denounced the financial barons, and brought in labour legislation designed to equalize and raise wage rates. By 1937, however, the radical rhetoric had disappeared and Hepburn's traditional conservatism had reasserted itself. He opposed unions and personally intervened in the Oshawa strike. His conflicts with Mackenzie King led to poor relations between Toronto and Ottawa. Like Duplessis, he criticized the federal government's decision to establish the Royal Commission on Dominion-Provincial Relations, whose creation he had learned of while reading the morning newspaper over breakfast.

BRITISH COLUMBIA

British Columbia's colourful T. Dufferin Pattullo, also a Liberal, had ambitious plans for reform. After his election in 1933, Pattullo fought with Bennett in an attempt to obtain larger federal loans for his heavily indebted province to fight the "war on poverty." After Bennett's defeat in 1935, Pattullo pressured the King government to help finance public works, hospitals, schools, and welfare. King, wanting to improve Canada's credit and control "spendthrift" provinces, resisted. Nevertheless, Pattullo succeeded in instituting the numerous reform measures that comprised his "Little New Deal."

New Parties, Right and Left

The depression struck the Prairie provinces, especially Saskatchewan and Alberta, more harshly than any other region of Canada. Between 1928–29 and 1932, Saskatchewan's per capita income plummeted by 71 percent, and by 1937 two-thirds of the province's farmers were receiving some form of government assistance. Alberta's per capita income slumped by 61 percent. Widespread Prairie protest gave rise to two new political movements that proposed massive reform: Social Credit and the CCF.

SOCIAL CREDIT MOVEMENT

The Social Credit phenomenon was a mixture of personality, doctrine, and context. Its major spokesman, William "Bible Bill" Aberhart, had become well known throughout Alberta from his weekly religious broadcasts to as many as 350 000 listeners. He showed considerable organizational talent although he had a domineering personality. In late 1932, he began mixing social credit views with religion in his radio presentations. He denounced banks and the world of finance, while affirming that governments should control credit and help boost consumer buying power by issuing monthly dividends of twenty-five dollars to residents.

Aberhart's broadcasts came at a singularly receptive moment. Farmers, heavily in debt because of previous borrowings, were now, with poor markets and the drought, unable to pay even the interest they owed. Foreclosure and seizure of their property appeared imminent. With the collapse of the farm economy, even Albertans who were not farmers could not escape economic collapse.

Aberhart and the Social Credit party won a landslide victory in the 1935 provincial election in Alberta. The new government soon put a moratorium on debt collection and instituted crop insurance and various other reforms, but delayed implementing social credit dividends of $25 a month. Only after a backbenchers' revolt in 1937 did the Legislature adopt the Alberta Social Credit Act which sought to establish provincial control over federally chartered banks. This law, and others of the Social Credit government, were disallowed by the federal government or judged unconstitutional by the courts. Although Aberhart retaliated by depriving Alberta's lieutenant governor (Ottawa's representative in the province) of his staff, his automobile, and his house, social credit remained only a theory and Aberhart continued his pragmatic approach. Social Credit's efforts to organize in Saskatchewan met with complete failure, but a separate group of francophone *créditistes* formed in Quebec in the late 1930s.

THE CCF

Canada's left-wing political groups made few gains during the depression, a fact that seems paradoxical given such difficult economic conditions. Racked by division and unable to gain substantial worker support, the left had a narrow electoral base. Moreover, in the 1920s, farmers had supported their own Progressive party (see chapter 11). Nevertheless, in Calgary in August 1932, a joint meeting of labour parties and farmer groups established a new movement with the rather cumbersome name of Co-operative Commonwealth Federation (Farmer-Labour-Socialist).

263

The new group drew support from university professors in Toronto and Montreal who had already formed the League for Social Reconstruction (LSR), an organization whose goal was political education. They became a kind of braintrust for the CCF; indeed, a committee of LSR members, headed by University of Toronto historian Frank Underhill, prepared the first draft of a declaration that the new CCF adopted as its platform in 1933. The Regina manifesto promised a "new social order," with security of land tenure for farmers, maximum income and leisure for workers, and free health services for all Canadians. Its last sentence, added at the convention, carried a ringing promise: "No CCF government will rest content until it has eradicated capitalism and put into operation the full programme of socialized planning which will lead to the establishment in Canada of the Co-operative Commonwealth."

The CCF immediately provoked intense interest and comment. On the right, Bennett accused the party of wishing to establish a Soviet Canada; one Conservative newspaper, the Toronto *Telegram*, saw CCF policies resulting in "slavery, chaos, misery and terrorism." On the left, the Communist party wanted, in the opinion of one CCFer, to "run it or ruin it." Co-operation with labour in these early years was limited; most unions eschewed political alignment. In addition, as Underhill complained, labour had other preoccupations: "The energy its various factions spend fighting one another would suffice for several social revolutions." Finally, many farmers had doubts about the CCF land policy that originally called for them to lease their land from the state. After a disappointing show in the Saskatchewan provincial election of 1934 and in the federal election the following year under their leader J. S. Woodsworth, the CCF moderated its policies, dropping references to socialism and repudiating any intention to nationalize land.

COMMUNISTS AND FASCISTS

Extreme left- and right-wing movements such as the Communist party and Fascist groups also grew during the depression. Government repression of the Communists was frequent. In one crackdown, leader Tim Buck and other leaders were arrested in Toronto and sentenced to prison terms. Businessmen and conservative political and religious leaders led the battle against communism, with Bennett promising to stamp it out by applying "the iron heel of capitalism." In reality, communism failed to thrive in Canada largely because the great majority of Canadians were not attracted to what appeared to be a foreign ideology. For most reform-minded people, indigenous forms of socialism like the CCF, which pledged democratic change, were a more acceptable alternative. Moreover, the sudden policy reversals imposed by Moscow upon Communist parties allowed the Canadian wing little possibility of formulating its own policies in tune with the Canadian reality. By 1939, the Canadian Communist party supposedly had sixteen thousand members, but the Soviet decision to sign a nonagression pact with Hitler that summer caused many of them to quit the party. Then, in June 1940, the Canadian government declared the Communist party illegal.

The Fascists were even less numerous than the Communists. The Deutscher Bund Canada, founded in 1934 and led by Canadian Germans, never had more than two thousand members; the RCMP would suppress it in the early days of the war. Swastika clubs and a Canadian Nationalist party were founded in English Canada, while in Quebec, Adrien Arcand patterned his National Social Christian Party along Nazi lines. Arcand remained a marginal and somewhat eccentric figure, but the views held by his group, such as its anti-semitism, were prevalent among nationalist movements like the *Jeune-Canada* and the *Ligue d'Action nationale*, and even espoused by many prominent clergymen and politicians. Thus, it was not astonishing that persecuted Jews who were fleeing Nazi Germany found Canada's doors firmly closed, as historians Irving Abella and Harold Troper have shown.[6] Although English Canada was perhaps not as openly opposed to Jewish immigration as French Canada, it was at best indifferent.

264

Limited Economic Recovery

The Liberals returned to power in Ottawa in 1935. Initially they did not put forth any particularly innovative policies; they brought in tax increases to balance the budget and tried to reduce the cost of unemployment programmes. King feuded with all the provincial premiers who demanded federal aid. He did keep his promise to close the relief camps; many from the camps were placed on farms where, isolated, they were not likely to cause trouble.

In 1938, in the midst of a new downturn, the King government launched a modest recovery programme financed by deficit spending that King's finance minister regretfully justified by "sheer social necessity." In 1939, unemployment was still at 10 percent. Only war spending would put Canadians back to work.

King was certainly no Canadian Roosevelt, nor did he set out to become one. The Liberal leader expressed considerable personal admiration for the American president, but he entertained strong doubts about his New Deal legislation and the means he employed; he also worried over the extent to which Roosevelt had "assumed the powers of a dictator." For King, it was not the government's business to regulate the economy or to promote profound social reform. He had few regrets when, in January 1937, the Privy Council declared most of Bennett's New Deal legislation unconstitutional. And he undoubtedly preferred handing over the contentious issues of the day for study by commissions.

265

King's government did take some important initiatives, however. The Canadian Broadcasting Corporation became a national network and C.D. Howe, King's minister of Transport, helped create Trans-Canada Airlines (the forerunner of Air Canada), which began scheduled flights between Vancouver and Seattle in September 1937. Howe himself flew on a "dawn-to-dusk" trial run of "my airline," leaving Montreal early in the morning and arriving in Vancouver nearly eighteen hours later.

The depression changed Canada. Working people, the unemployed, farmers, businessmen, and nationalists, were among those who formed associations to defend their interests. Often powerless to control their individual destinies, people also came to expect more from the state. Governments at all levels began to intervene more widely in the economy and in social affairs, though they usually did so with considerable reluctance. New political parties appeared; one, the CCF (reconstituted as the New Democratic Party in 1961) became a permanent fixture of Canadian politics. Provincial autonomy seemed to take a step forward as strong leaders took power in several provinces. At the same time, the immense financial problems encountered by the provinces made increased federal intervention imperative. Though the majority of Canadians in 1939 had suffered through the most difficult decade of their lives, few probably realized the extent to which the country had changed permanently. Fewer still could antic-ipate the terrible catastrophe that awaited the world in the fall of 1939 when war broke out again in Europe.

NOTES

[1] Michiel Horn, "The Great Depression: Past and Present," *Journal of Canadian Studies*, 11 (February 1976):43.

[2] John Taylor, " 'Relief from Relief': The Cities' Answer to Depression Dependency," *Journal of Canadian Studies*, 14 (Spring 1979):16.

[3] Donald Forster and Colin Read, "The Politics of Opportunism: The New Deal Broadcasts," *Canadian Historical Review*, 60 (1979): pp. 324-43.

[4] T.W. Grindley *et al.*, *The Canadian Wheat Board, 1935–1946*, quoted in Vernon C. Fowke, *The National Policy and the Wheat Economy* (Toronto, 1957), p. 266.

[5] James H. Gray, *Men Against the Desert* (Saskatoon, 1967), p. 34.

[6] Irving Abella and Harold Troper, *None is Too Many: Canada and the Jews of Europe, 1933–1948* (Toronto, 1982).

Related Readings

The following articles from R. Douglas Francis and Donald B. Smith, eds., *Readings in Canadian History: Post-Confederation*, 2d ed. (Toronto, 1986) deal with the Depression era: James Struthers, "Two Depressions: Canadian Governments and the Unemployed in the Thirties and the Eighties," pp. 427–41; H. Blair Neatby, "William Lyon Mackenzie King: The Concilliator in Politics," pp. 442–49; Harold J. Schultz, "Portrait of a Premier: William Aberhart," pp. 450–72.

BIBLIOGRAPHY

John Herd Thompson and Allen Seager's *Canada 1922–1939: Decades of Discord* (Toronto, 1985) contains abundant material on the period. A good brief synthesis is Michiel Horn's Canadian Historical Association pamphlet *The Great Depression of the 1930s in Canada* (Ottawa, 1984). See, as well, the relevant chapters in Robert Bothwell, Ian Drummond, and John English, *Canada, 1900–1945* (Toronto, 1987). A. E. Safarian analyses economic developments in *The Canadian Economy and the Great Depression* (Toronto, 1959). Alvin Finkel, in *Business and Social Reform in the Thirties* (Toronto, 1979), discusses the reactions of business to Bennett's reform proposals.

Labour has been the subject of considerable attention. See, for example, Irving Abella, *Nationalism, Communism, and Canadian Labour: The CIO, the Communist Party and the Canadian Congress of Labour, 1935–1956* (Toronto, 1973), and Evelyn Dumas, *The Bitter Thirties in Quebec* (Montreal,

1975). Much recent research has also been done in social history. In *None is Too Many: Canada and the Jews of Europe, 1933–1948* (Toronto, 1982), Irving Abella and Harold Troper examine Canadian immigration policy towards Jews. On urban development, consult, for example, Alan Artibise's article, "Continuity and Change: Elites and Prairie Urban Development," in *The Usable Urban Past: Planning and Politics in the Modern Canadian City*, edited by Alan F. J. Artibise and Gilbert A. Stelter (Toronto, 1979), pp. 130–54. John H. Taylor explores municipal politics in "Mayors à la Mancha: An Aspect of Depression Leadership in Canadian Cities," *Urban History Review*, 9 (February 1981): 3–14. Ian MacPherson studies co-operatives in *Each for All: A History of the Co-operative Movement in English Canada, 1900–1945* (Toronto, 1979).

On the response of Canadians to the depression, see R. D. Francis and H. Ganzevoort, eds., *The Dirty Thirties in Prairie Canada* (Vancouver, 1980); Michiel Horn, ed., *The Dirty Thirties: Canadians in the Great Depression* (Toronto, 1972); James Gray, *The Winter Years* (Toronto, 1966), and his *Men Against the Desert* (Saskatoon, 1967); and the poignant L.M. Grayson and Michael Bliss, eds., *The Wretched of Canada: Letters to R. B. Bennett, 1930–1935* (Toronto, 1971). How Canada dealt with some "dangerous" immigrants is discussed in Barbara Roberts, "Shovelling Out the 'Mutinous': Political Deportation from Canada Before 1936," *Labour/ Le Travailleur* 10 (1982): 65–85. James Struthers has studied the relief question in *No Fault of Their Own: Unemployment and the Canadian Welfare State, 1914–1941* (Toronto, 1983). In "A Profession in Crisis: Charlotte Whitton and Canadian Social Work in the 1930s," *Canadian Historical Review*, 62 (1981): 169–85, Struthers looks at Canada's best-known social worker of the period. On the issue of birth control, see Angus McLaren and A.T. McLaren, *The Bedroom and the State: The Changing Practices and Politics of Contraception and Abortion in Canada, 1880–1980* (Toronto, 1986).

Politics in the 1930s has been well studied. H. Blair Neatby provides an overview in *The Politics of Chaos: Canada in the Thirties*, (Toronto, 1972). Also see his *William Lyon Mackenzie King, 1932–1939: The Prism of Unity* (Toronto, 1976). On Bennett, consult Richard Wilbur's Canadian Historical Association pamphlet, *The Bennett Administration* (Ottawa, 1969) and, on the New Deal, Donald Forster and Colin Read, "The Politics of Opportunism: The New Deal Broadcasts," *Canadian Historical Review*, 60 (1979): 324–49. Ramsay Cook, ed., *Politics of Discontent* (Toronto, 1967) contains articles on Aberhart, Pattullo, Stevens, and the Leadership League. On Quebec, see Bernard Vigod, *Quebec Before Duplessis: The Political Career of Louis-Alexandre Taschereau* (Montreal, 1986), and Richard Jones' Canadian Historical Association pamphlet, *Duplessis and the Union Nationale Administration* (Ottawa, 1983). Much material on Canada's socialists is available. Walter Young, *The Anatomy of a Party: The National CCF* (Toronto, 1969) is a good analysis. R. Douglas Francis examines Frank

Underhill's socialism in *Frank H. Underhill, Intellectual Provocateur* (Toronto, 1986). On extreme left-wing and right-wing movements, see Jonathan Wagner, *Brothers Beyond the Sea: National Socialism in Canada* (Waterloo, 1982); Lita-Rose Betcherman, *The Swastika and the Maple Leaf* (Toronto, 1975); Norman Penner, *The Canadian Left: A Critical Analysis* (Toronto, 1977); Marcel Fournier, *Communisme et anti-communisme au Québec, 1920–1950* (Montréal, 1979), and Andrée Lévesque, *Virage à gauche interdit: les communistes, les socialistes et leurs ennemis au Québec, 1929–1939* (Montréal, 1984).

CHAPTER THIRTEEN

From Isolationism to Internationalism, 1920–45

During the inter-war period most Canadians were isolationists, determined to keep their distance from the conflicts that developed in Europe, in Africa and in Asia. They obviously did not want war, but neither did they believe that they could do much to prevent one. They only wished that the major powers would succeed in resolving international conflicts and diminishing tension. To ensure that they would not be dragged unwillingly into Britain's wars, most Canadians favoured increased autonomy within the British Empire.

There was never any doubt, however, that once war broke out in September 1939, Canada would participate. But to what degree? And in what form? Those questions would be answered in the course of often stormy debates. In the final months of the war, Canada participated in the creation of new institutions that, it was hoped, would preserve peace. The war and its aftermath thus pushed Canada—not always willingly and enthusiastically—onto the world stage.

Autonomy in International Relations

After 1921 Mackenzie King's Liberal government made significant advances in foreign policy. The prime minister, who also served as minister of external affairs, favoured North American isolation. He appointed O.D. Skelton, whose outlook on foreign affairs parallelled his own, as his adviser and, after 1924, as his undersecretary of state for external affairs, a position Skelton held until his death in 1941.

The Liberal government in the early 1920s reduced military expenditures and the size of the Canadian armed forces. It also consistently opposed (as did the other western democracies) any attempts to strengthen the League of Nations' collective security system. Canada, it might be said, was in the League but not of the League. Canadian delegates continually reminded League members that Canada and the United States had enjoyed more than one hundred years of peaceful relations. Why, therefore, should Canadians pay the heavy price of collective security when their nation was not endangered? As Senator Raoul Dandurand told the League Assembly in Geneva in 1925: "We live in a fire-proof house, far from inflammable materials. A vast ocean separates us from Europe."

THE CHANAK CRISIS AND THE HALIBUT TREATY

In imperial-dominion relations, King moved slowly but consistently towards Canadian autonomy. The Chanak crisis became the first test case. By the Treaty of Sèvres, one of the treaties ending World War I, Britain agreed to maintain troops in Chanak, Turkey, to ensure that the Dardanelles (the strait linking the Mediterranean to the Black Sea) remained neutral waters. Turkish nationalists resented Britain's presence and threatened to attack the British garrison. British leaders saw this menace as a challenge to Britain and to the British Empire. They appealed for a concerted imperial response but did so through a public communiqué rather than through diplomatic channels. This action greatly annoyed King. He also saw the Chanak crisis as another British ploy to embroil the dominions in imperial conflicts of no interest to them. Hoping to delay a decision until the crisis had passed, King cabled Westminster that only Parliament could decide. Opposition leader Arthur Meighen, however, minced no words. "Ready, aye, ready, we stand by you" should be Canada's answer, he claimed in a statement that he would later regret. The crisis ended before King had to take a stand, but the lesson of the exercise remained: that Canada could not be relied upon to come automatically to Britain's aid anywhere and at any time that Britain demanded.

The Halibut Treaty of 1923, a Canadian–American agreement relating to fishing rights on the Pacific coast, was the next step on the road to greater Canadian autonomy. By tradition, only agents of the British government signed treaties affecting the dominions. King resented this "badge of colonialism" and decided to use the treaty to assert Canada's diplomatic independence. He arranged for Ernest Lapointe, Marine and Fisheries minister, to be the sole signator for Canada. Dominion representatives to the Imperial Conference that same year endorsed this procedure, thus making it standard practice thereafter.

THE BALFOUR REPORT AND THE STATUTE OF WESTMINSTER

The treaty-making privilege obtained, King and the other dominion leaders now sought a formal proclamation that recognized the new relationship between Britain and its dominions. That came with the Balfour Report signed at the Imperial Conference of 1926: it termed the dominions "autonomous Communities within the British Empire, equal in status, in no way subordinate to one another in any aspect of their domestic or external affairs, though united by a common allegiance to the Crown, and freely associated as members of the British Commonwealth of Nations." In keeping with its new international status, Canada began to establish legations or embassies in foreign countries.

The Statute of Westminster, signed into law by King George V on December 11, 1931, has been viewed as Canada's equivalent (although it applied to the other dominions as well) to the American Declaration of Independence of July 4, 1776. This act of the British Parliament confirmed Canadian independence and ensured that the nation could develop its own foreign policy.

271

Neutrality

In international forums, Canada used its newly won autonomy to avoid entanglements overseas. When, for example, Japan invaded Manchuria in 1931 and set up the puppet state of Manchukuo, Canada refused to demand punitive measures when the matter came before the League of Nations. Indeed, the Canadian delegate made a speech judged so pro-Japanese that Japan's diplomatic representative in Ottawa thanked the Canadian government! Later, when the League condemned Japan with near unanimity, Canada hid anonymously among the majority. Japan's answer was to withdraw not from China but from the League.

THE ETHIOPIAN CRISIS

In October 1935, Italian dictator Benito Mussolini made a similarly aggressive act, invading the independent African kingdom of Abyssinia (Ethiopia). Canada was in the midst of an election campaign and the two major political leaders, R.B. Bennett and Mackenzie King, showed little inclination to discuss this action, although both agreed that Canada should not get involved. O.D. Skelton commented that Canadians were "immensely more interested in Alberta than in Abyssinia."

Nevertheless, the Canadian government was forced to respond to this major test of the League's ability to curb aggression. Walter Riddell, the Canadian advisory officer at League headquarters in Geneva, personally favoured strong sanctions against Italy, and he proposed including oil and other strategic materials on the embargo list. Moreover, he spoke before receiving specific orders from Ottawa. King, on the advice of Skelton and of Ernest Lapointe, now his minister of Justice as well as his Quebec lieutenant, repudiated the so-called Canada proposal and, in King's words, gave Riddell "a good spanking." Riddell was saved from further embarrassment when Britain and France, in exchange for peace, offered Mussolini the territory he had already overrun in East Africa. The outcry helped turn attention away from Canada. A few weeks later King claimed in the House that Canada had saved Europe from war.

Many Canadians supported a strong League of Nations, however. John W. Dafoe, editor of the *Winnipeg Free Press*, and Newton W. Rowell, former Ontario Liberal leader, both members of the League of Nations Society which sought to promote support for the League in Canada, wanted the country to take a stronger stand against aggression. In general, though, the public shared King's fear of commitments. In English Canada even newspapers approving sanctions were lukewarm in their support, while in French Canada only maverick Jean-Charles Harvey's *Le Jour* endorsed them. Most Canadians probably were relieved when the crisis passed. Even if Canada had demanded vigorous sanctions against Italy, it is doubtful that Britain and France would have gone to war in support of Ethiopian emperor Haile Selassie.

RISE OF NAZI GERMANY

The greatest threat to world peace came from Adolf Hitler, who became chancellor of Germany in 1933. Systematically, the Nazi leader set out to consolidate and to increase Germany's power. Britain and France hoped that German military occupation of the hitherto demilitarized zone of the Rhineland in March 1936, in violation of the Treaty of Versailles and the Locarno agreements, would satisfy Hitler. Then they hoped that the *Anschluss*, the union that Germany forced on Austria in March 1938, would. In their desire to avoid war Britain and France accepted the seizure of the Sudetenland region of Czechoslovakia in the fall of 1938 after the Munich conference, and the annexiation of the rest of Czechoslovakia in March 1939. Canada supported England's and France's policy of appeasement, of making concession after concession to Hitler.

King visited Hitler in 1937, convinced that he was carrying out a divine mission as international peacemaker. The Canadian prime minister described the German führer as "a man of deep sincerity and a genuine patriot," a modern-day Joan of Arc who would deliver his people. King was convinced that Hitler did not want war with Britain or France but was concerned with the spread of communism, just as King himself was. In early 1939, King, still apparently believing that Hitler's appetite could be satisfied, wrote to the German Chancellor to assure him of their mutual friendship and to promise a new visit to Germany once the federal elections were over. Indeed, King seemed to fear that London would do more than Berlin to provoke a war.

Reasons for Appeasement

What was the basis for appeasement of Nazi Germany, this policy denounced so bitterly after it failed to work? Many Canadian supporters of appeasement saw Hitler and Mussolini as bulwarks against the spread of communism, as defenders of order in an era of chaotic revolution. General Franco, the fascist leader in Spain who won a bitter civil war in 1939, was seen to play the same role. To the embarrassment of the Canadian government 1250 Canadian volunteers formed the Mackenzie-Papineau battalion to fight for the Spanish republic against Franco's Fascists. Rodrigue Cardinal Villeneuve, Archbishop of Quebec, reminded his clergy in May 1937 that "dictatorship is better than revolution." Eugène L'Heureux, editorialist at *l'Action catholique*, a Quebec City daily, affirmed in 1936 in a statement that showed how profound anti-semitism was: "We must recognize that [Hitler] has the merit of snatching his country from the Communists by placing his iron fist on the elements of disorder that were, all too often, both in Germany and in Russia, the Jews."

273

There are other reasons for Canada's policy of appeasement. King and some of his foremost advisers, like Skelton, feared that British policies might undermine Canadian autonomy and draw the country into imperial conflicts as in the past. With his sure political instincts, King also knew that another war, just like World War I, risked dividing Canadians in a bitter internal conflict that could destroy national unity as well as his government and the Liberal party.

It was clear, too, that French Canada in particular wanted to keep its distance from Europe. Demographically and sentimentally, French Canadians had long been detached from the Old World; most families had lived in Canada for two centuries. Moreover, there was no attraction to England. The survival of Britain and of its imperial power was hardly a priority for French Canadians.

To some, Quebec had an inordinate influence on Canada's foreign policy and was seen as preventing the country from standing up to a ruthless enemy. Historian C.P. Stacey, for example, has found it "not surprising that a government as dependent on Quebec as King's should shy away from the bold sanctionist policies" of Riddell during the invasion of Ethiopia. "The threat to the country's unity was only too evident. So, of course,

was the threat to the power of the Liberal party."¹ This interpretation
holds some truth, although it fails to explain just why French Canadians
were isolationist. Nor does it take into account the degree of isolationist
sentiment prevalent in English Canada and in the United States. Historian
Frank Underhill said it more bluntly than most when he asserted at the
time that "all these European troubles are not worth the bones of a Toronto
grenadier." Many English-speaking Canadian politicians and professional
policy advisers wanted Canada to take, at most, a "back-seat" position in
the international "lunatic asylum," as Loring Christie, an External Affairs
adviser, described the world.

Did Canada's views matter to the world? In 1933 R.B. Bennett wrote
candidly to a Toronto clergyman: "Canada is not an important member
of the League. ... Our military prowess in the next war is regarded as of
little concern." Concerning his own role, he added: "What can one man
do who represents only ten and a half millions of people?" Little changed
over the next five years. On the eve of war, Canada had only seven diplomatic missions abroad. In 1938–39 the country's total budget for the
armed forces was just $35 million. Years of neglect had weakened Canada's
defences; the country could not defend its own coasts, let alone dispatch
fully equipped and trained forces to Europe. The war, however, was to
have enormous impact upon Canada. It would turn the country into a
major industrial nation, thrust it into the international arena as an important middle power, and profoundly transform its relations with Britain
and the United States.

Canada and the War against the Axis

On September 1, 1939, German troops invaded Poland. Britain and France
declared war on September 3. Canada's declaration came a week later.
The somewhat belated gesture symbolically demonstrated Canada's newly
acquired sovereignty, but there was never any real possibility that Canada
would remain neutral—as the United States chose to do until its naval
base at Pearl Harbor was attacked by the Japanese in December 1941.

Once Canada entered the war, it was not immediately apparent to the
government what the country would—or could—do. The navy had fewer
than a dozen fighting ships, and the air force, at best, only fifty modern
military aircraft. The professional army had just four thousand troops,
the navy three thousand, and the air force only one thousand.

THE BRITISH COMMONWEALTH AIR TRAINING
PROGRAMME

Happily for Canada, the first few months of warfare activity, described as
the "phoney war," made it possible for the government to postpone mak-

ing wrenching decisions. Yet it was during this period that a vitally important part of Canada's contribution to the war got underway: the British Commonwealth Air Training Plan, which eventually trained 130 000 aviators, or nearly half of the Commonwealth's pilots. In 1936, King had refused a British proposal to open and to recruit for Royal Air Force schools in Canada because he felt the plan threatened Canadian sovereignty. Furthermore, British training schools might compete with those that Canada itself could establish. The 1939 plan, much more ambitious than the previous one, gave control of the schools to the Royal Canadian Air Force (RCAF), which had been organized immediately after World War I. The plan had other virtues. For King, this kind of Canadian participation would be acceptable to French Canadians (although most Quebeckers were automatically disqualified because they did not speak English). The plan also gave a tremendous boost to the aeronautics industry and, thanks to the more than $2 billion spent, to the Canadian economy in general. Finally, the air force was a means of preventing the heavy army casualties such as Canada had suffered in the trenches during World War I (see chapter 9).

275

CANADA'S MILITARY CONTRIBUTION

The German blitzkrieg in northern and western Europe during the spring of 1940, culminating in the fall of France in June, transformed the war. Britain and its dominions alone in late 1940 and early 1941 held out against the German and Italian aggressors. Until the German invasion of the Soviet Union in June 1941 and the commitment of millions of German troops to the eastern front, Britain's surrender seemed highly possible. As Britain's chief ally, until Russia's entry into the war and the United States' in December 1941, Canada immediately reassessed its role. It would have to field a much larger army, build dozens of warships and hundreds of aircraft, and convert its economy to war production. In response to Britain's wartime financial needs, Canada lent—and then gave—the country huge sums of money through mutual aid agreements, with no strings attached, although most of the money was spent in Canada.

Canada also made a vital contribution to the defence of the convoys that transported the troop and supply ships to Britain. Allied losses were staggering; by spring 1943, Germany U-boats in the North Atlantic had sunk more than two thousand ships. The Royal Canadian Navy enlisted 100 000 men and some 6500 women. Initially the Canadian navy had few successes in the anti-submarine war, as a result of inexperience, poor crew training, and deficient technical equipment. By September 1942, the danger near Canadian shores had become so great that the government closed the St. Lawrence River and the gulf to shipping. Once properly trained and equipped, however, the Royal Canadian Navy sank, or helped to sink, twenty-nine German U-boats. The Canadians thus played an important role in the Battle of the Atlantic, and contributed 110 ships to the Allied landings in Normandy in June 1944.

It took time, too, for the Canadian Army to be able to boast of successes on the battlefield. While Hitler overran Europe, Canadian troops were relegated to garrison duty in England. Combat action came first in the Pacific theatre, but it brought little cause for pride. The defence of the British colony of Hong Kong, which fell to the Japanese on Christmas Day, 1941, resulted in the death of over 550 Canadians, who died either in the Japanese attack or later under the harsh conditions of the Japanese labour camps. Then, in August 1942, the Canadians received a catastrophic baptism of fire in Europe during the Allied attempt to mount a major raid on the French coast at Dieppe; in the space of a few hours, more than 60 percent of the 5000 Canadian participants were killed or captured.

By late 1942 Canadians were demanding that the country's troops take a more active part in the struggle. As a result of King's pressures on Winston Churchill, the British prime minister, Canadian troops participated as part of Britain's Eighth Army in the Allied landings in Sicily in 1943 where, in British General Montgomery's view, they behaved "magnificently." They also took part in the lengthy Italian campaign that followed, seeing particularly severe action at Ortona where they fought from house to house for control of that strategic village. Nearly 100 000 Canadians of all ranks served in Italy, and nearly 6000 died there.

The year 1944 brought more success, but again the cost was high. Canadians landed in Normandy on D-Day, June 6, and over the next few weeks they suffered heavy losses. In the late winter and early spring of 1945, Canadians participated in the liberation of the Netherlands and then in the final offensive to conquer Germany. A quarter of a million Canadian men and women served in the Canadian army in Europe and the army suffered over 11 000 fatal casualties. In addition, Canadian aviators conducted thousands of perilous night bombing missions over Germany. Over 17 000 of the nearly quarter-of-a-million Canadians who served in the RCAF lost their lives. All told, nearly one million Canadians out of a total population of 11 500 000 saw military service in Canada and overseas during the Second World War. Somewhat more than 40 000 were killed, compared to 60 000 dead in World War I. Worldwide, the bloodbath between 1939 and 1945 claimed the lives of perhaps 60 million civilians and soldiers.

When Canada's heavy economic contribution to Allied arsenals in terms of ships, planes, and tanks is considered, the country's role in the war was substantial. Yet Canada had little success in sharing in wartime Allied decision-making, even when it desired to do so. Canadian military forces outside the United Kingdom were generally under British command and used as the British saw fit, although Canadian officers retained control over organization and administration. Disagreements between Canada and

National Archives of Canada PA-133742.

German soldiers captured by Canadian troops on a Normandy beach in June 1944.

Britain on this matter were frequent, and Canada often complained about lack of recognition for its efforts.

Canadian-American Wartime Relations

Canada did not participate in the basic decisions, taken mainly by the British and the Americans, that determined the direction of the war. As Prime Minister Lester B. Pearson, reflecting on his wartime service at the Canadian Embassy in Washington, put it: "We were not consulted about plans and decisions at high levels unless our agreement was essential, and this was seldom." Pearson had at first worried that Canada might be squeezed between the United States and Britain. As time went on, he became convinced that the main danger Canada faced was simply being squeezed out! Even at the two wartime conferences held in Quebec City that brought the British and American war leaders, Churchill and Roosevelt, together, Canada acted merely as host, and King's presence was largely confined to the official photos.

War inevitably meant closer relations with the United States. In August 1938, President Franklin D. Roosevelt came to Kingston, Ontario, where he pledged that the United States "would not stand idly by if domination of Canadian soil [was] threatened by any other [than the British] Empire." King was pleased by this statement, although Canadian soil was hardly being threatened at that time.

278   OGDENSBURG AGREEMENT

Two years later, in August 1940, King and Roosevelt signed the Ogdensburg Agreement, a declaration creating a Permanent Joint Board on Defence (PJBD) responsible for discussing military questions of mutual interest; this new tie bound Canada and the United States in matters of defence planning. As early as 1938, Canada and the United States had begun to exchange military information. In the summer of 1940 King himself pushed for talks on common defence planning. Many Canadians approved, since they believed Canada could not count either on its own virtually non-existent defences or on Britain's. Thus, when Roosevelt proposed the PJBD, King was delighted (though he apparently had some doubts over making the board permanent), and Canadian newspapers generally supported the plan enthusiastically. Canada was not ready to cede all control over North American defence to the Americans, however. In 1941, for example, Canada forced the United States to back away from its plans for continental integration in favour of a policy based on co-ordination and co-operation.

Historians and political scientists differ in their interpretations of this *rapprochement*. Donald Creighton, always alert to the imperial designs of Canada's southern neighbour, saw the agreement as a major step in the Liberals' surrender of Canadian autonomy: King "behaved like a puppet which could be animated only by the President of the United States."[2] When the prime minister claimed at the time that Canada was fulfilling "a manifest destiny," Creighton noted that King used the very expression that American politicians had used earlier to assert American control of British North America.

In contrast to Creighton, historian J.L. Granatstein has argued that, although the Canadian government's lack of planning was "striking," it seemed, in the circumstances, "prudent and wise to safeguard the Dominion by accepting the protection of the United States."[3] Political scientist James Eayrs, for his part, denies that King was manipulated by the charming Roosevelt, seeing him instead as a shrewd politician who astutely exploited his friendship with the American president for the good of the Allies.[4]

During the early months of war Canada enjoyed some influence in the United States, notably through King's use of quiet diplomacy with the president. For example, King won important modifications to the American Neutrality Act, thus enabling Canada and Britain to purchase military supplies while the United States remained neutral. King knew the limits of his influence, however, and also the limits of an American president's powers in the face of a Congress jealous of its prerogatives.

HYDE PARK AGREEMENT   *279*

King and Roosevelt signed a second agreement, the Hyde Park Declaration, at Roosevelt's Hudson River estate on a "grand Sunday" in April 1941. It proved an even more important milestone in Canadian-American relations than the Ogdensburg agreement.

Canada's wartime economic relations with both Britain and the United States underlay the declaration. Britain was ordering ever-increasing amounts of war supplies from Canada and the United States but lacked the dollars to pay for them, while Canadian trade with the United States was accumulating huge deficits. King stated in early 1941 that, financially, Canada risked being faced with "a greater burden than [its] people ... can be led to bear." Canada had to make enormous defence purchases in the United States for equipment destined for Britain. When in 1941 the United States adopted the Lend-Lease programme eliminating the need for cash payments on British orders, Canada worried that it would lose British business. Britain, for its part, was not averse to using the threat of shifting orders to the United States to pressure Canada into better terms.

Negotiations with the United States were arduous and King feared that Canada would have to pay a high price; perhaps the Americans would insist that Canada sell off investments it had in the United States, just as the British had been compelled to do in order to obtain the benefits of Lend-Lease. He nevertheless managed to get a reasonably satisfactory agreement: the United States promised to increase substantially defence purchases in Canada, enabling Canada to make its own purchases of war matériel in the United States. Britain could continue buying Canadian goods and Canada could even get relief, through Lend-Lease, for its American purchases of war supplies to be sent to Britain. Results were almost immediately evident; most notably, Canada's dollar shortage was over by 1942. Some scholars see the Hyde Park Declaration as another blow to

National Film Board Collection: National Archives of Canada C-22716.

Prime Minister Mackenzie King and Justice Minister Louis St. Laurent announce over the radio, in English and in French, the end of World War II in Europe on May 8, 1945.

Canadian independence, but in view of Canada's precarious situation, the country perhaps could not have obtained better terms.

After Hyde Park, Canada's influence with the United States seriously deteriorated. Relations between the United States and Britain were warming and the American government was becoming more concerned with global rather than hemispheric issues, as it put isolationism behind. The American entry into the war in December 1941 substantially changed American perspectives. Canada lost its special status, becoming the junior partner in the Anglo-American-Russian alliance to defeat the Axis powers from late 1941 to 1945.

Towards a New Internationalism

War ended in Europe when Germany capitulated in May 1945. By September, Japan also surrendered. Peace brought with it new problems and, in particular, the difficult question of how to maintain it. Like the other Allied countries, Canada believed in the necessity of establishing an international organization comparable to, but more effective than, the League of Nations. The Canadian government was kept informed of the discussions at Dumbarton Oaks, near Washington, D. C., in August 1944, where the Great Powers drafted a charter for the future organization. Canada participated in the founding conference of the United Nations at San Francisco in April 1945, where it worked to ensure that both the United States and the Soviet Union became members.

Canada also pushed for world economic and social co-operation. In late 1945 Lester Pearson presided as chairman over the founding meeting of the United Nations Food and Agricultural Organization, in Quebec City. As a member of the United Nations Relief and Rehabilitation Administration, Canada became a major supplier of aid to war-torn countries, though it had great difficulty convincing the Americans of its right to participate in determining the operations of the association. Canada also joined the International Monetary Fund and the International Civil Aviation Organization, whose headquarters came to Montreal. As former External Affairs officer John Holmes commented, Canada "moved with the tide," trying to avoid letting the Great Powers control everything.[5] Conscious of its position as a rising middle power, Canada attempted again, with some success, to get recognition for secondary states. It was willing to recognize that its influence was less than that of the United States, but it wanted the Great Powers to admit that it was more influential than Luxembourg, for example. Whether this kind of activity could be described as evidence of a coming "golden age" of Canadian diplomacy, as some students of Canadian foreign policy would have it, is a matter for debate.

281

The war effectively ended the splendid isolation of the 1930s. Military technology had advanced to the point where Canada could no longer consider itself geographically isolated. Moreover, Canada was caught between the two major combatants in the rapidly developing Cold War and could not escape entanglement.

Involvement in world affairs brought benefits but carried a price. Despite Canada's attempts to develop relationships with multilateral associations of states, this involvement meant closer ties to the United States. For supporters of the *rapprochement*, the closer links brought security and economic prosperity through trade and investments. For critics, the triumphant move towards nationhood in the inter-war years appeared to have abruptly ended, with Canada being relegated once more to colonial status. Canada went from colony to nation and then back to colony. This debate would be fought out, at least in English-speaking Canada, in the late 1960s and 1970s.

NOTES

[1] C.P. Stacey, *Canada and the Age of Conflict, vol. 2: 1921–1948: The Mackenzie King Era* (Toronto, 1981), p. 186.
[2] Donald Creighton, *The Forked Road: Canada 1939–1957* (Toronto, 1976), p. 43.
[3] J.L. Granatstein, *Canada's War: The Politics of the Mackenzie King Government, 1939–1945* (Toronto, 1975), p. 128.
[4] James Eayrs, *In Defence of Canada: Appeasement and Rearmament* (Toronto, 1965), p. 191.
[5] John W. Holmes, *The Shaping of Peace: Canada and the Search for World Order, 1943–1957*, vol. 1 (Toronto, 1979), pp. 235–36.

Related Readings

The following articles from R. Douglas Francis and Donald B. Smith, eds., *Readings in Canadian History: Post Confederation*, 2d ed. (Toronto, 1986) are helpful for this chapter: James Eayrs, " 'A Low Dishonest Decade': Aspects of Canadian External Policy, 1931–1939," pp. 528–43; and R. Cuff and J. Granatstein, "Getting on with the Americans: Canadian Perceptions of the United States, 1939–1945," pp. 475–87.

BIBLIOGRAPHY

Material on Canadian foreign policy in these years is abundant. Among the most useful surveys are vols. 1–2 of James Eayrs' *In Defence of Canada*, vol. 1: *From the Great War to the Great Depression*, and vol. 2: *Appeasement and Rearmament* (Toronto, 1964, 1965), and C. P. Stacey, *Canada and the Age of Conflict*, vol 2: *1921–1948, the Mackenzie King Era* (Toronto, 1981). See also Richard Veatch, *Canada and the League of Nations* (Toronto, 1975). On Canada and League policy towards Mussolini, consult Robert Bothwell and John English, " 'Dirty Work at the Crossroads': New Perspectives on the Riddell Incident," *Canadian Historical Association Report*, 1972, pp. 263–85. On King's foreign policy in the late 1930s, see Norman Hillmer, "The Pursuit of Peace: Mackenzie King and the 1937 Imperial Conference," in *Mackenzie King: Widening the Debate*, edited by John English and J.O Stubbs (Toronto, 1978), pp. 149–72. King's illusions concerning Hitler are dealt with in C.P. Stacey, "The Divine Mission: Mackenzie King and Hitler," *Canadian Historical Review*, 61 (1980): 502–12. On Canadian volunteers in Spain during the civil war, see Victor Hoar, *The Mackenzie-Papineau Battalion* (Toronto, 1969).

For the war years, C.P. Stacey, *Arms, Men and Governments: The War Policies of Canada, 1939–45* (Ottawa, 1970) provides a good analysis. A short summary of Canada and the war by C.P. Stacey appears in "World War II" in *The Canadian Encyclopedia* (Edmonton, 1985), vol. 3, pp. 1975–78. Donald Creighton, *Canada, 1939–1957: The Forked Road* (Toronto, 1976) and especially J.L. Granatstein, *Canada's War: The Politics of the Mackenzie King Government, 1939–1945* (Toronto, 1975) are also useful on foreign policy, as well as the relevant chapters in Robert Bothwell, Ian Drummond, and John English, *Canada, 1900-1945* (Toronto, 1987). W.A.B. Douglas and Brereton Greenhous offer a popular overview in *Out of the Shadows: Canada in the Second World War* (Toronto, 1977). For the story of submarine warfare, see Michael L. Hadley, *U-Boats Against Canada: German Submarines in Canadian Waters* (Montreal, 1985). J.L. Granatstein's *The Ottawa Men: The Civil Service Mandarins, 1935–1957* (Toronto, 1982) deals with a number of high-level civil servants active in this period. J.F. Hilliker examines Canada's role in peace negotiations in Europe in "No Bread at the Peace Table: Canada and the European Settlement, 1943–47," *Canadian Historical Review*, 61 (1980): 69–86. Aspects of Canadian-American relations are covered in R.D. Cuff and J.L. Granatstein, *Ties That Bind: Canadian-American Relations in Wartime from the Great War to the Cold War* (Toronto, 1977).

283

CHAPTER FOURTEEN

The Home Front, 1939–45

Canada escaped the bombs that rained death and destruction upon vast areas of Europe, Africa, and Asia. Yet the war did have an enormous impact upon the country's economy and society. The heavy demands of the wartime economy catapulted the nation out of depression and into rapid industrial growth. In particular, the war had profound, though temporary, implications for Canadian women. The government needed them to participate in war-related activities, to alleviate manpower shortages in the war industries and to support men in the armed forces.

The war also forced Canadians into accepting greater government regulation. As urban migration resumed and people crowded into the cities, the state took an increasingly active role in providing social services. The country thus advanced further towards the modern welfare state. The Canada of 1945 was far different from the country that had embarked on war in 1939.

The war had enduring effects on political life, too. The pendulum of power swung towards Ottawa as the central government mobilized the economy and controlled national finances to further the war effort. As the war approached its end, the federal government found good reasons to enlarge its role. The defenders of provincial autonomy fought back but, more often than not, had to retreat.

Although wars often bring down governments in power, in Canada's case the Liberals successfully weathered war-related problems, including a new conscription crisis. Canadians might not love their pompous and aging prime minister, but they probably recognized Mackenzie King's uncanny skill in sensing change and perhaps even appreciated his typically Canadian prudence; they certainly could not agree on who might do a better job. With the exception of two "accidents" which sent them into opposition in 1957–63 and 1979–80, the Liberals were poised to become the nation's stewards for the next four decades.

The Wartime Economy

On the eve of war Canada's economy was depressed, with more than half a million Canadians—one out of five members of the work force—looking for jobs. Barely a year later, full employment was within sight. Furthermore, the wartime emergency led to a large-scale federal intervention in the economy that a decade of peacetime emergency during the depression had failed to bring. Soon Canada was producing four thousand airplanes a year, as well as ships, tanks, and huge quantities of shells and guns. Investment in industry doubled between 1939 and 1943 as modern factories were built and equipped. War materials had priority over civilian goods, the latter being severely curtailed during the war years. Even though they might have had the money, Canadians had difficulty buying home appliances or automobiles. This was not yet the consumer society whose bywords would be: put aside, discard, and replace; rather, in this era of sacrifice, the depression counsels still held: rebuild, repair, conserve.

285

Just as during World War I (see chapter 9), the burgeoning economy generated inflationist pressures. In the spring of 1941, prices spiralled upwards at an annual rate of over 12 percent. To stem mounting dissatisfaction, the government quickly adopted drastic wage and price controls, for which the Wartime Information Board, the official propaganda agency, tried to build up support. The government also resorted to so-called voluntary measures. It exhorted homemakers to put their savings into Victory bonds and urged merchants to offer customers their change in war savings stamps. Consumers' savings were used to purchase arms and build bombs. And that—as one patriotic poster showed it—was how the very ordinary "Mrs. Morin bombarded Berlin"! Women also established branches of the Consumers Service that, among other activities, denounced merchants who violated the law. Owing to such measures, the cost of living went up very little during the remainder of the war, and the severe inflation associated with World War I was checked.

RATIONING

The relative scarcity of various consumer goods led to rationing. The government issued books of coupons and recruited thousands of female volunteers to distribute them to shoppers. Sugar was the first product to be rationed—modern-day nutritionists would surely have approved; later, tea, coffee, butter, meat, and gasoline were added. Merchants complained of the paper work necessary to administer the coupons. A black market in unused coupons flourished and some farmers sold produce illegally—for a good price. People often hoarded scarce goods, in spite of the threat

National Archives of Canada.

Posters featuring movie stars, like Montreal-born Norma Shearer, urged Canadians to help finance the war by putting their savings in victory bonds.

of fines. Sometimes shortages provoked an outcry. When the brewers could not supply enough of their favourite beverage, Ontario workers threatened to boycott the sale of Victory bonds. "No beer, no bonds!" was their warning.

World War II improved the image of Canadian industrialists, shattered

287

National Archives of Canada PA-108300.

Wartime food shortages brought rationing, as this unilingual English-language sign in Montreal indicates.

during the depression years. War production gave business unparalleled opportunities for expansion, and previously unemployed Canadians re-entered the workforce. Despite wage and price controls, high taxes, and rationing, Canadians were much more prosperous at the war's end than they had been at its beginning.

Businessmen also improved their public image by helping the federal government organize the country's war production. Cohorts of them trooped off to Ottawa, often for a symbolic annual salary of one dollar. Many worked for the powerful C.D. Howe and his Department of Munitions and Supply, the agency in charge of all war procurement. So many came that CCF leader M.J. Coldwell charged that the ministry had become a "concentration point for the Canadian Manufacturers' Association and its friends."

Howe's primary task was to organize war production effectively. The American-born contractor and then MP from Port Arthur, Ontario, set up numerous Crown corporations and adopted the techniques of private enterprise. He also avoided the accusations of graft and profiteering that had so plagued Robert Borden's government during World War I. Business leaders admired Howe's no-nonsense efficiency and were proud to be called "Howe's boys."

288 Women and the War Effort

According to traditional Canadian beliefs and practices, women's place was in the home. War needs, though, encouraged new thinking about the role of women in society. While these changes would by no means be permanent (as the war drew to a close, pressures for women to return to their more usual domestic occupations intensified), they did show what might be and, eventually, what would be.

Many women worked outside the home long before the war, generally in a few low-paying occupations like teaching, office work, and retail sales, and as factory labour in textile and clothing mills, or as domestics (see chapters 8 and 11). In response to the general labour shortage created by the war, women entered the civilian work force, mainly in war-related industries. Through the National Selective Service set up to co-ordinate the mobilization of Canada's labour power, the government vigorously encouraged this recruitment. Department of Labour advertisements urged women to "roll up [their] sleeves for victory," for the men overseas needed support and women had to "back them up—to bring them back." Incentives were necessary, too, because many women had to be transferred from other regions of Canada into the industrial centres of Quebec and Ontario. Salaries for women, particularly in war industries, were relatively attractive; they increased faster during the war years than did men's wages, although they remained substantially lower. Temporary changes in income tax laws made it possible for husbands to continue to enjoy a full married exemption while their wives earned income.

At first, the government sought only unmarried women and married women without children, but by 1943 a chronic lack of "manpower" made it essential to recruit mothers, at least for part-time jobs. Child care often caused problems for working women. Most left their children in the care of relatives and friends, but a modest number of government-funded nur-

National Film Board Collection: National Archives of Canada C-81418.

During World War II, women flocked to work in the factories, like this Winnipeg manufacturer of propellors. Needless to say, working conditions were not always so pleasant.

series began operating by 1943, on a temporary basis, in Ontario and Quebec.

Patriotic appeals drew thousands of women into volunteer work recuperating and recycling such items as paper, metal, fat, bones, rags, rubber, and glass. They also collected clothes for free distribution and prepared parcels to be sent overseas. Together with their unpaid labour in the home, these voluntary efforts, which women often undertook at their own initiative, constituted in the words of historian Ruth Roach Pierson, "far and away the largest contribution made by Canadian women to the war effort."[1]

WOMEN IN THE ARMED SERVICES

For the first time, women served in the armed services, and by the end of the war fifty thousand women were enrolled. However, as Pierson has pointed out, these "Jill Canucks" were not "pistol packing Mommas" and they did not hurl grenades.[2] They were assigned positions considered proper to their sex, were always paid less than males, were subordinate to men of the same rank, and only commanded other women. A special

Canadian Women's Army Corps, created in 1941 and incorporated into the Canadian Army (Active) in late winter 1942, supplied female support staff so that men could be released for more pressing duties. Efforts to achieve fairness and equality did not permeate all aspects of life in the services. Male dominance of the military meant a double standard on sexual morality; for example, literature on venereal disease warned servicemen to beware of "diseased, predatory females," but women received no similar advice regarding "loose men."

In mid-war Ottawa established a special subcommittee to study the role of women in post-war Canada. The members, all women, assumed that many female workers would return to the home. For those who remained employed outside the home, the subcommittee's report recommended expanded employment opportunities, equal pay and better working conditions, and the granting of children's allowances.

These proposals stirred up substantial opposition. Concerned about postwar unemployment, many government planners wanted to get women out of the work force to make room for returning soldiers and workers in shut-down war industries. Also, most Canadians shared traditional ideas about the role of women; one poll showed that 75 percent of men and 68 percent of women wanted women back in the home after the war. The war experience was the exception, not the rule. Moreover, when the report was tabled in early 1944, other more pressing problems had arisen, and according to historian Gail Cuthbert Brandt, the subcommittee's report was "pigeon-holed and forgotten."[3]

In other ways, things returned to normal at the end of the war. The female armed services were demobilized. Many of the formal barriers blocking married women from the work force went back up again. The proportion of women working outside the home plummeted, and it was not until the 1960s that the figure reached the proportion attained in 1944—27 percent.

The Expansion of Unions

Organized labour made significant gains in the war years. The labour glut of the depression years was transformed by the war into a shortage. As employment rose, so did union membership, particularly in the new industrial unions; between 1940 and 1945, union membership doubled to more than 700 000.

Though the war brought higher wages in general and assured jobs, workers had much reason for dissatisfaction. Employers fiercely resisted union attempts to impose collective bargaining, and many bitter strikes resulted from unions' efforts to insure recognition. The government intervened constantly to prevent strikes that could adversely affect war production, and it applied wage controls whose flagrant inequities labour denounced vigorously. As historian Laurel Sefton MacDowell's analysis of wartime labour relations has shown, the government felt it necessary, for political reasons, "to conciliate business, its wartime ally in developing the war economy."[4] Businessmen sat on government policy boards; representatives of labour did not. Compulsory conciliation often involved interminable delays, a situation which favoured employers. The unions soon became convinced that the employers were the real beneficiaries of this imposed co-operation.

INDUSTRIAL CONFLICTS

Workers' growing resentment contributed to a wave of industrial conflicts that peaked in 1943; in that year alone one union member in three went on strike and one million working days were lost. In spite of their organizational rivalries, representatives of the Trades and Labour Council (TLC) and the Canadian Congress of Labour (CCL) united to demand legislative remedies. Labour's increasing support for the CCF party was a matter of great concern to Prime Minister Mackenzie King.

The government responded to labour unrest with Order-in-Council PC 1003, which recognized the right of workers in industries under federal jurisdiction to join unions and to bargain collectively. It established certification procedures, set out penalties for unfair labour practices by which employers commonly interfered with workers' attempts to set up unions, and established a labour relations board to administer the law. After the war the federal government adopted new legislation similar to PC 1003, and most provinces adopted comparable laws.

A strike at the Ford motor plant in Windsor, Ontario, in 1945 also concerned labour insecurity, among other issues. The union wanted an agreement specifying that all employees had to be union members and that the company had to deduct union dues from wage cheques. "Union shop and checkoff" was the workers' demand. Ford adamantly refused, although across the river in Dearborn, Michigan, the company had acquiesced on these issues in 1941. To prevent the company from forcing the picket line, militant strikers set up a massive automobile blockade in the streets around the plant, imprisoning the vehicles of hundreds of commuters. Federal and provincial authorities as well as the CCL itself intervened, without success.

Finally, both sides agreed to accept binding arbitration, and Justice Ivan Rand of the Supreme Court of Canada proposed what became known as the Rand Formula: since all employees benefitted from union activities, all should pay union dues, to be collected by the company and remitted to the union; workers were not obliged to join the union, however. Rand also recommended the establishment of a grievance procedure as well as heavy penalties for unauthorized or "wildcat" strikes. Though he admitted that a strike was not a "tea party" and that strikers were exasperated and provoked, he strongly condemned the motor blockade and also made a vibrant apology for democratic control of unions and for "enlightened leadership at the top."

The late 1940s saw some dramatic confrontations between labour and management, often in provinces whose governments sided openly with employers. Still, unions felt more secure as the war years ended. The relative labour peace of the 1950s was, in part, a result of these wartime gains.

The State's New Role

The war changed Canada in other ways. After the depression Canadians wanted more economic security. Though the war eliminated unemployment and restored a degree of prosperity, it exacted heavy financial sacrifices from the public. As war fatigue set in and increasing Allied success by 1943 pointed the way to the final victory, Canadians reflected on the post–war society they wanted to build. In particular, they wanted governments to introduce measures that would help those in need and would establish greater equality within society.

In 1940 the federal government adopted, with provincial consent, an unemployment insurance plan. An amendment to the British North America Act permitted this. King supported the project because he was "anxious to keep Liberalism in control in Canada [and] not let third parties wrest away from us our rightful place in the matter of social reform." In particular, King felt threatened by the left. In September 1943, as many urban workers endorsed the CCF, the party reached a 29 percent high in the polls, a point ahead of each of the two major parties.

In reaction to the rise of the CCF, Canadian business funded what political scientist Walter D. Young termed "the most extensive and most vicious propaganda campaign ever directed against a single political party in Canadian history."[5] This campaign, along with the King government's move to the left, soon diminished the CCF's popularity. Canadians seemed to become more conservative as well. They wanted consumer goods like refrigerators, automobiles, and houses. And they were optimistic, no longer fearing that the war's end would plunge the country back into depression. There was thus less tendency to heed the CCF's Cassandras who kept warning of impending economic and social doom.

SOCIAL WELFARE MEASURES

Canadians still thought that governments should take better care of them. In 1943, Leonard Marsh, research director for the government's Committee on Reconstruction, presented a report recommending a comprehensive system of social security, including measures to assist the unemployed, a national health insurance scheme, old age pensions, and children's allowances. The report provoked much media interest but the government, fearful of the costs involved, particularly when the country was at war, virtually ignored it. The government's approach was cautious and piecemeal. In 1944, for example, it introduced a family allowance programme which provided monthly payments of $5–$8 to help Canadian mothers support their children. Certain Conservatives, like Ontario Premier George Drew, denounced the project as a "baby bonus" designed to benefit Quebec with its big families and to bring Quebeckers to forgive King for imposing conscription. There is no indication, however, that Ontario mothers refused the allowance cheques when they began arriving.

During the 1945 election campaign, all parties tried to project a new reformist image. The federal Conservatives had worked on a reform platform since December 1942, when they chose John Bracken, Progressive premier of Manitoba, as their new leader, and agreed to his demand that the party's name be changed to "Progressive Conservative." Bracken's main prior connection with the party had been his father's attendance at Sir John A. Macdonald's funeral in 1891! In 1945, he published his "Charter for a Better Canada," which contained proposals for such reforms as a national health scheme. The Progressive Conservatives appealed to their traditional electorate by denouncing socialism and burdensome government interference.

As for the CCF, it called for low-cost housing, hospital and school construction, and jobs. Not to be outdone, King assured voters that "the great natural resources which God has given to all the people are not going to be controlled by a privileged few while great multitudes walk the streets in search of employment." This was his way of justifying a "New Social Order for Canada" which, he reminded voters, the Liberals were already building.

With the support of four out of every ten voters, King won the election, a feat he termed "a miracle." The CCF, in a disappointing showing, won only 28 seats; party sympathizers blamed Liberal and Conservative scaremongers who warned of the demise of liberty and the dictatorship of the state under a CCF government. Regardless of which party won, the election showed that Canadians, with the exception of an extreme Tory fringe, wanted their government to take a firmer hand in directing the economy and in ensuring social security for all citizens.

The War and National Unity

The war had caused innumerable personal tragedies, as thousands of Canadians lost a husband, father, son, brother, or fiancé. Sometimes the sad announcement came brutally; one Canadian girl wrote her soldier boyfriend, and after a few weeks the letter came back stamped "killed in action." Even the return of the soldiers from overseas provoked poignant emotions: time had brought change and lengthy absences had altered perceptions.

Through the strains of war, the government worked to promote support for the war effort. In 1939 it established the Bureau of Public Information to disseminate propaganda promoting patriotism and "Canadianism" among all ethnic groups within English Canada. The need to emphasize Canadian participation was brought home when American newsreels circulating in Canadian theatres showed the Dieppe raid, in which so many Canadians had lost their lives, as primarily fought by Americans. Yet, in historian W.R. Young's opinion, many Canadians "remembered the hysteria of the Great War and remained skeptical of any identifiable propaganda."[6]

One ethnic group in particular—the Japanese Canadians—felt the full brunt of Canadians' animosity. Government policy simply intensified the hatred. The Japanese, like the Chinese, had been victims of racial hostility since their arrival on the West Coast (see chapter 6). In the late 1930s rumours of Japanese espionage had swept British Columbia. Thus, when Japan entered the war on the side of the Axis in December 1941, a hostile public easily convinced federal politicians, notably Pensions and Health Minister Ian Mackenzie, from British Columbia, to act. The federal government quickly evacuated the more than twenty thousand Japanese and Japanese Canadians resident in the province, mainly to detention camps in the interior of British Columbia. It also confiscated their property and auctioned some of it off at giveaway prices. After the war ended, it resettled the Japanese across Canada and even attempted to deport thousands—many of whom were Canadian citizens—to Japan. Although Ottawa abandoned these plans in 1947, hundreds of Japanese Canadians, embittered by life in Canada, did return to Japan.

French Canada posed a special problem. The Wartime Information Board, aided by the stringent Defence of Canada Regulations which provided for censorship of anti-war sentiment in the media, did not significantly raise support for the war in Quebec. Although French Canadians generally accepted participation, they were adamantly opposed to compulsory military service for overseas operations. The Borden government's conscription policy during World War I had disastrous consequences not only for Canadian unity and for the Conservative party, but it also provoked a temporary schism within the Liberal opposition (see chapter 9). With the outbreak of war in 1939, King did not want history to repeat itself.

294

THE CONSERVATIVES AND CONSCRIPTION

Though some imperialistic Tories vociferously urged conscription, the new Conservative leader, Robert Manion, hoping to bring Quebec back into his party's fold, declared repeatedly his opposition to the policy in 1939 and 1940. At the same time, Manion accused King of neglecting the war and in the winter of 1940, advocated the formation of a win-the-war "national government." That idea antagonized Quebeckers who remembered the Union government's imposition of conscription in 1917. Manion attributed his humiliating defeat in the March 1940 election to the fact that both English- and French-speaking Canadians "largely felt that King is doing enough."

After Manion's resignation, old-guard Tories in favour of conscription engineered the return of a somewhat reluctant Arthur Meighen as party leader. Meighen's conscription campaign came to an abrupt halt, however, as voters in a by-election in the supposedly safe Conservative riding of York South, Toronto, preferred Joseph Noseworthy, the CCF candidate, to the extremist Tory.

As the war dragged on and military leaders demanded reinforcements, the majority of English-speaking Canadians began to favour conscription. For one Toronto Tory MP, that was the only way to get the "disloyal bloody French" to fight. When King asked Canadians in a plebiscite in April 1942 if they would release the government from its earlier promises not to impose conscription, 80 percent of Canadians outside Quebec responded in the affirmative.

FRENCH CANADA AND THE WAR

French Canadians held a different view, however. When Quebec voters replaced the vigorously anti-conscriptionist Union Nationale with Adélard Godbout's Liberals in the provincial election of October 1939, they were probably expressing confidence in the federal Liberals' capacity to ward off conscription and heeding the threats of the Quebec ministers in Ottawa to resign if Duplessis were re-elected. Yet King interpreted Godbout's victory as a blanket vote of confidence in Ottawa's war policy.

Events showed that Quebec voters had not written a blank cheque. When the plebiscite was announced, Quebec nationalists formed the *Ligue pour la Défense du Canada* and campaigned energetically for a "non" vote. Although its means were limited (it had little access to the media), the *Ligue* triumphed: Quebec voted 72 percent against. In the fall of 1942, *Ligue* members formed a new political party, the *Bloc populaire*, with both Quebec and federal wings. Although *Bloc* members were unanimous in their opposition to conscription, their unity soon gave way to bitter dissension on other issues as well as on questions of personality: it was a party with too many generals and not enough soldiers. By the 1944 and 1945 elections, it was largely a spent force.

French Canadians' lack of enthusiasm for the war can be partially explained by the sympathy which the clerical elite showed during the 1930s for Fascist leaders, particularly Franco and Mussolini, who portrayed themselves as stalwart opponents of communism (see chapter 12). These same elements rallied to support the very conservative Marshal Philippe Pétain when, after the fall of France in 1940, he took over the leadership of that portion of the country temporarily unoccupied by the Germans.

Nationalists also criticized Ottawa's wartime centralization policies as leading to "another 1837 and the death of Confederation." They denounced the danger of linguistic assimilation by a Canadian army in which the French language was often proscribed. They complained of the dangerous effect military life had on the morals of soldiers who, as a pastoral letter of 1942 stated, all too often tended to pursue "vile pleasures." And many made dire predictions that the war would cause the break-up of families because it brought women into the factories.

296

For the majority, however, the reasons for not wanting conscription were probably simpler. Most French Canadians did not feel immediately concerned. Having been estranged from Europe politically, culturally, and demographically for nearly two centuries, they had few ties with France, and no strong loyalty to England.

THE MANPOWER ISSUE

King's behaviour on this issue pleased few. Many English-speaking Canadians interpreted King's delay in implementing conscription as putting political advantage ahead of the war effort. For them, he was not moving fast enough or going far enough. For many French Canadians, King was going too far too fast, and was betraying his sacred promises.

King did indeed act cautiously, endeavouring constantly to put off the inevitable. In 1940 his government decreed national registration, but for home service only. (Since it applied just to unmarried men, the regulation had the unintended effect of provoking hundreds of instant marriages.) After the plebiscite in 1942, the government amended the National Resources Mobilization Act in order to permit troops to be sent overseas by order-in-council. This action meant "not necessarily conscription but conscription if necessary," and King hoped that conscription would never be necessary.

During the next two years, Canada continued to rely on voluntary enlistments. But in its search for men, the army had to compete with the Departments of Labour, and of Munitions and Supply, which needed

National Archives of Canada C-29452.

Quebeckers voted strongly NON during the plebiscite in April 1942 while English Canada registered a resounding YES.

workers for war industries. By late 1944 officers overseas demanded re-inforcements, particularly the well-trained home-defence conscripts, or NRMA men. Conservatives urged that the government stop appeasing Quebec, while within the Cabinet, Colonel J.L. Ralston, the minister of national defence, who had just returned from a tour of Canadian forces in Europe, pushed for conscription. King, vexed and still not ready, replaced Ralston with General A.G.L. McNaughton, who promised to continue the voluntary system. Then, on November 22, after McNaughton reported that the voluntary system would not produce enough troops, and just as several of his English-speaking cabinet ministers prepared to resign, King yielded. Canada would again have conscription, at least partly: up to sixteen thousand NRMA men could now be sent to Europe. Few conscripts ever served overseas, however, and some deserted. McNaughton became another victim of the crisis, for he was defeated in a by-election in February 1945. Furthermore, conscription ultimately had no effect on winning the war.

298

In spite of the criticism from both supporters and opponents of con-scription, and perhaps because the criticism came from both ends of the spectrum, King was able to portray himself as a moderate. He and the Liberal party managed to survive the struggle and help prevent the ethnic bitterness that had occurred in the conscription crisis in 1917 (see chapter 9).

Federal-Provincial Relations: Towards Federal Supremacy

The depression had restricted the autonomy of the provinces, forcing them to rely increasingly for financial assistance on Ottawa, and the war created conditions that furthered centralization. The federal government now took a dominant role in the organization of the Canadian economy.

THE ROWELL-SIROIS REPORT ON DOMINION-PROVINCIAL RELATIONS

The Rowell-Sirois Commission on Dominion-Provincial Relations, set up by the King government in 1937 (see chapter 12), made public its report in May 1940. With the objective of stabilizing provincial finances and giving equal services to all Canadians, the commissioners recommended that Ottawa collect all income taxes and succession duties and, in return, make unconditional grants to the provinces. Poorer provinces should receive special subsidies to enable them to offer equivalent social and educational services to those of other Canadian provinces without having to tax more heavily than the Canadian average. The federal government should also assume all provincial debts.

Predictably, autonomists condemned the report as a veritable centralizer's "Bible." For them, provincial treasuries would be at Ottawa's mercy, and provincial activities would thus be determined by what the federal government was willing to pay out. Premier Mitchell Hepburn of Ontario—a province that would not benefit from the special adjustment grants—vehemently attacked the report as "the product of the mind of a few college professors and a Winnipeg newspaperman [John Dafoe] who has had his knife in Ontario ever since he was able to write editorial articles."

Most newspapers reacted favourably. Federal ministers and bureaucrats also endorsed the recommendations strongly, particularly those relating to money. Ottawa wanted to ensure control over fiscal policy, not only to pay for the war but also to diminish inflationary pressures. It thus urged the provinces to "rent" their tax fields to the federal government.

299

With no illusions over the outcome, King then invited the premiers in January 1941 to discuss the proposals. Some provinces insisted on the need for further study, but three others—British Columbia, Alberta, and Ontario—rejected the proposals outright. "Don't smash this Confederation," warned Hepburn flamboyantly, accusing Ottawa of wanting to sacrifice Ontario to Quebec and the Prairies. The conference collapsed in deadlock. Ottawa, however, was determined to press ahead. It promised, as a "temporary wartime expedient," that the provinces would be expected to surrender their income taxes only for the duration of the war, and it proposed to compensate the provinces more generously. All the provinces yielded, although some did so reluctantly.

From 1943, the economic planners in Ottawa, many of whom were disciples of British economist John Maynard Keynes, had their eyes upon the immediate postwar era. They feared that depression might result from the reconversion of the economy to peacetime conditions, just as had occurred after World War I (see chapter 9). Moreover, they wanted to make certain that Ottawa could assume the heavy financial responsibilities and the increased debt charges resulting from the war. Ottawa, they urged, should thus act as the "balance wheel" of the economy. If it kept its hand firmly on taxation, it could combat cyclical tendencies, either deflationary busts or inflationary booms; it could maintain high and stable employment; and it could offer costly social security measures to all citizens, thus supporting consumer buying power. For these civil servants, economic, political, and humanitarian objectives dictated that the federal government continue to take charge, although it might consult the provinces in areas of their constitutional jurisdiction, such as social services.

THE DOMINION-PROVINCIAL CONFERENCE ON RECONSTRUCTION

In August 1945, a few days before Japan's surrender, Ottawa convened the Dominion-Provincial Conference on Reconstruction. King assured the provinces that he did not want to weaken or subordinate them but rather wished to ensure their "effective financial independence." He intended to do this by convincing the provinces to continue to allow Ottawa to levy all income taxes in return for increased grants, with no strings attached. The federal government also offered to pay part of the cost of a comprehensive health insurance plan and of old-age pensions, and to expand the coverage of federal unemployment insurance.

Though most provinces reacted positively, the premiers of Ontario, Quebec, and Alberta objected to what they saw as the concentration of financial and administrative powers in the hands of the federal government. For Ernest Manning, premier of Alberta, the federal plans violated "the basic and fundamental principle of effective democratic government." Maurice Duplessis, the Quebec premier, asserted that the federal tax proposals smacked more of confiscation than of a rental agreement. Although the two largest provinces continued to manifest their opposition, Ottawa managed to reach agreement with the others. The federalism of the next decade remained highly centralized. As economist R.M. Burns put it, the 1940s and 1950s were years in which "the central authority reached its zenith."[7]

300

The Provinces in the War Years

The war and the after-effects of the depression fostered the uneven development of regional economies and thus eventually contributed to the growth of regionalism in Canada.

The war had strengthened the economy and diversified its manufacturing capacity, as well as further promoted Canada's resource-based industries. Quebec, British Columbia, and, especially, Ontario made dramatic advances. In Quebec the value of manufacturing increased by 250 percent between 1939 and 1945, and industries like chemical products and aluminum refining expanded rapidly. In Ontario, factory employment increased greatly, and exploitation of the province's huge iron-ore deposits began at Steep Rock Lake north of Lake Superior. On the Pacific coast, the port of Vancouver prospered. Its shipyards and those of Victoria employed thirty thousand workers at their peak. The building of the Alaska Highway, in the face of the threat of a Japanese invasion, proved an impetus to development in the north (see chapter 16), and Prince Rupert became an important supply centre for American bases in Alaska.

By 1943, British Columbians had the highest per capita income of all Canadians.

POLITICAL CHANGES IN QUEBEC AND BRITISH COLUMBIA

The war also brought provincial change. In Quebec, the Godbout government, elected in 1939, formed Hydro-Québec, a publicly owned hydroelectric utility in the Montreal region. To boost educational levels, a law was passed making school attendance obligatory until age fourteen. In the Quebec Labour Relations Act, the province set out the rules governing collective bargaining. The bill, supported by the unions, was supposed to force companies to negotiate with their unionized employees. In 1940 Quebec finally gave women the right to vote provincially, despite the vigorous objections of the church and conservative groups. Suffragist Idola Saint-Jean had argued for this right. "We vote in federal elections as intelligently as women in neighbouring provinces. Why shouldn't we be concerned with problems debated in the Provincial Parliament? Don't housing, public health and education concern us much more directly than the problems of federal politics?" The Legislative Assembly finally agreed.

301

In British Columbia the old political order also changed. Liberal leader Duff Pattullo was sharply criticized for his feuding with Ottawa, his road-building policy, and his abrasive style. When the Liberals failed to gain a majority in the election of 1941, many party members demanded coalition with the Conservatives. Pattullo, who opposed coalition, was ousted. The CCF then formed the opposition to the Liberal-Conservative coalition.

ONTARIO: THE RETURN TO CONSERVATISM

In Ontario, the impetuous Mitchell Hepburn appeared mainly interested in pursuing a vendetta with Mackenzie King. He belittled Ottawa's war effort (which, in January 1940, admittedly deserved little praise) and he denounced federal centralization of finances as reducing the government of Ontario to the status of a county council. Hepburn's tribulations finally drove him, in October 1942, to hand over power to one of his ministers.

At the same time, the provincial CCF was attracting support, largely in urban working-class districts. In the 1943 provincial election, the CCF, with one-third of the popular vote, placed second, after George Drew's Conservatives. While Drew denounced the socialists, he energetically pursued reform policies, notably in health, education, and housing. Provincial planning became important in areas such as forest conservation, industrial development, and water use. Profoundly pro-British, Drew also wanted to boost British immigration, and he even established a War Brides Bureau in London to counsel British wives coming to Canada with their soldier husbands. His enthusiastic salesmanship caused Canadian-born British press magnate, Max Aitken, now Lord Beaverbrook, to comment: "Look George, is Ontario a part of Canada or Canada a part of Ontario?"

The CCF proved much less threatening in the Ontario election of 1945. In decline in the cities and lacking a rural base, it was as well the victim of fierce denunciations of "state socialism." Party leader E.B. Jolliffe's sensational revelations to the people of Ontario that Drew had set up "a paid government spy organization, a Gestapo to try and keep himself in power," backfired. Drew easily won a majority, and Ontario settled into over forty years of Conservative government.

302

THE MARITIMES AND NEWFOUNDLAND

The war was relatively less generous to Canadians in the three Maritime provinces, which benefited little from the enormous federal investments in manufacturing. As historian Ernest Forbes has demonstrated, C.D. Howe was convinced that it was more efficient to develop industry along the St. Lawrence and in the Great Lakes region, a conviction reinforced by the regional prejudices of Howe and his central Canadian political advisers.[8] Nevertheless, the rise in food prices and the growing demand for minerals and pulp and paper did assist the Maritimes, and Halifax became the major port for shipping munitions and other supplies to western Europe. But at the war's end, the region was ill-equipped to undertake industrial expansion.

Newfoundland's case was somewhat special. At the outbreak of war the Crown colony's economy was in dismal shape. Fish prices were low and markets uncertain, the population of the outports lived in appalling poverty, and the relief rolls were overflowing. At first, the war only worsened the situation, resulting in increased taxes and decreased services. Eventually, though, the war created a boom in employment (albeit temporary) through the construction and maintenance of huge defence bases like those at Argentia, Gander, and Stephenville.

THE PRAIRIES

The have-not Prairie region recovered only slowly. As late as 1942, the mayor of Winnipeg complained bitterly that war work employed one million people in the East, but only sixty thousand in Manitoba. By 1944, much-increased demand for wheat, particularly in the newly liberated countries of Europe, led to higher prices, and Prairie farmers were able to increase their incomes substantially. A growing farmers' movement, led by the Canadian Chamber of Agriculture founded in 1935, set out to defend farmers' interests and improve their lot. This was surely necessary: farm incomes had remained much lower than workers' wages, most rural homes had no indoor plumbing or electricity, and farm villages enjoyed few services.

The war (as well as better weather conditions) stimulated agricultural production, although prices rose only slowly. It also boosted crude oil production in Alberta, at least until the Turner Valley field went into decline after 1942. But the war did not create the diversified economy that many Prairie residents felt the region needed.

Politically, third parties on the Prairies grew stronger, although they tended to moderate their ideology. Social Credit in Alberta, led by William Aberhart until his death in 1943 and then for a quarter-century by his protégé Ernest Manning, denounced socialism and centralization, promised able business-like administration, and gently laid Social Credit doctrine to rest.

303

The CCF, for its part, made inroads in all three Prairie provinces, but scored its first victory in Saskatchewan in 1944. Although it had abandoned the socialism of the Regina manifesto, its ambitious programme promised public ownership of natural resources, security of land tenure for farmers, collective bargaining for workers, educational reform, and social services, including a universal socialized health plan. Baptist preacher and CCF leader Tommy Douglas denounced the economic system that he likened to a cream separator: the farmer pours in the milk, the worker turns the handle, and the capitalist, because he owns the machine, "sits on a little stool with the cream spout fixed firmly in his mouth while the farmer and the worker take turns on the skim milk spout." Once in power, the CCF launched major reforms, particularly during its first two years in office, but financial and other factors forced it to make pragmatic policy adjustments.

Wars often accelerate historical trends, and World War II certainly had this effect on Canada's economy and society. The war created an economic boom that lasted until the late 1950s. Trade union organizations made notable gains as governments enacted legislation establishing a new framework for the conduct of industrial relations. The entry of large numbers of women into the work force, though temporary, announced a substantial change in their role. With Canada's new federal social programmes, Canadians took a significant step in the direction of the welfare state.

Important political changes took place as well. Ottawa reasserted a pre-eminence that endured for two decades, until the 1960s. Voters in several provinces elected governments that stayed in office for lengthy periods. There was, however, no change of government in Ottawa: King and the

Liberals survived and even thrived. And yet they elicited little praise. King's highest goal seemed to be to remain in office and set records for political longevity. Perhaps he simply illustrated characteristics of the quintessential Canadian—blandness, self-righteousness, a tendency to the highest ideals while showing that they could always be bent to accommodate pragmatic concerns. Or, perhaps, King succeeded because, in the words of Frank Underhill, he was the leader "who divides us least."[9]

NOTES

[1] Ruth Roach Pierson, *"They're Still Women After All": The Second World War and Canadian Womanhood* (Toronto, 1986), p. 33.
[2] Ruth Roach Pierson, " 'Jill Canuck': CWAC of All Trades, But No 'Pistol Packing Momma'," *Historical Papers/Communications historiques*, 1978, pp. 106–33.
[3] Gail Cuthbert Brandt, " 'Pigeon-Holed and Forgotten': The Work of the Subcommittee on the Post-War Problems of Women, 1943," *Histoire sociale/Social History*, 15 (1982): 239–59.
[4] Laurel Sefton MacDowell, "The Formation of the Canadian Industrial Relations System During World War Two," *Labour/Le Travailleur*, 3 (1978): 186.
[5] Walter D. Young, *The Anatomy of a Party: The National CCF, 1932–61* (Toronto, 1969), p. 200.
[6] W.R. Young, "Mobilizing English Canada for War: The Bureau of Public Information, the Wartime Information Board and a View of the Nation During the Second World War", in *The Second World War as a National Experience*, edited by Sidney Aster (Ottawa, 1981), p. 199.
[7] R.M. Burns, *The Acceptable Mean: The Tax Rental Agreements, 1941–1962* (Toronto, 1980), p. 35.
[8] Ernest R. Forbes, "The Maritimes and the Industrialization of Canada during the Second World War," *Acadiensis*, 15 (1986): 3–27.
[9] Frank Underhill, "The End of the King Era", *Canadian Forum*, (September, 1948), reprinted in F.H. Underhill, *In Search of Canadian Liberalism* (Toronto, 1960), p. 127.

304

Related Readings

Readings related to topics covered in this chapter in R. Douglas Francis and Donald B. Smith, eds., *Readings in Canadian History: Post Confederation* 2d ed. (Toronto, 1986) are: Ruth Roach Pierson, "Canadian Women and the Second World War," pp. 488–507; and W. Peter Ward, "British Columbia and the Japanese Evacuation," pp. 508–25.

BIBLIOGRAPHY

For a general overview of the period with an accent on political aspects, consult J.L. Granatstein, *Canada's War: The Politics of the Mackenzie King Government, 1939–1945* (Toronto, 1975), and the relevant chapters in Robert Bothwell, Ian Drummond, and John English, *Canada, 1900–1945* (Toronto, 1987). On the CCF, see Walter Young, *The Anatomy of a Party: The National CCF, 1932–61* (Toronto, 1969), and on the Conservatives,

J.L. Granatstein, *The Politics of Survival: The Conservative Party of Canada* (Toronto, 1967). On Howe, the "Minister of Everything," see *C.D. Howe: A Biography*, by Robert Bothwell and William Kilbourn (Toronto, 1979). R.M. Burns, *The Acceptable Mean: The Tax Rental Agreements, 1942–1962* (Toronto, 1980) provides a detailed treatment of federal-provincial fiscal relations.

The best study on conscription is J.L. Granatstein and J.M. Hitsman, *Broken Promises: A History of Conscription in Canada* (Toronto, 1977). For Quebec's reaction, see Philip Stratford, ed., *André Laurendeau: Witness for Quebec* (Toronto, 1973); for an explanation of this reaction, see Richard Jones, "Politics and Culture: The French Canadians and the Second World War," in *The Second World War as a National Experience* edited by Sidney Aster (Ottawa, 1981), pp. 82–91. Aster's book also contains relevant articles by John English, "Politics and the War: Aspects of the Canadian National Experience," pp. 52–66; Robert Bothwell, "A Curious Lack of Proportion: Canadian Business and the War," pp. 24–37; and W.R. Young, "Mobilizing English Canada for War: The Bureau of Public Information, the Wartime Information Board and a View of the Nation During the Second World War," pp. 196–212. Social security is examined in a special issue of the *Journal of Canadian Studies*, 21 (Summer 1986) on "Leonard Marsh and Canadian Social Policy." Doug Owram studies the evolution of ideas concerning the role of the modern state in *The Government Generation: Canadian Intellectuals and the State, 1900–1945* (Toronto, 1986). Ernest R. Forbes looks at the effect of the war on the Maritime economy in "The Maritimes and the Industrialization of Canada during the Second World War," *Acadiensis*, 15 (1986): 3–27.

305

On women, see Ruth Roach Pierson, *"They're Still Women After All": The Second World War and Canadian Womanhood* (Toronto, 1986); Geneviève Auger and Raymonde Lamothe, *De la poêle à frire à la ligne de feu* (Montréal, 1981); and Gail Cuthbert Brandt, " 'Pigeon-Holed and Forgotten': The Work of the Subcommittee on the Post-War Problems of Women, 1943," *Histoire sociale/Social History*, 29 (1982): 239–59.

Aspects of union activity are covered in Irving Abella, *Nationalism, Communism, and Canadian Labour: The CIO, the Communist Party and the Canadian Congress of Labour, 1935–1956* (Toronto, 1973); Jacques Rouillard, *Histoire de la CSN, 1921–1981* (Montréal, 1981); Desmond Morton with Terry Copp, *Working People: An Illustrated History of the Canadian Labour Movement* (Ottawa, 1984). On the impact of the war on labour-management relations, consult Jeremy Webber, "The Malaise of Compulsory Conciliation: Strike Prevention in Canada During World War II," *Labour/Le Travail*, 15 (1985): 57–88; Laurel Sefton MacDowell, "The Formation of the Canadian Industrial Relations System during World War Two," *Labour/Le Travailleur*, 3 (1978): 175–96, and by the same author, "The 1943 Steel Strike Against Wage Controls," *Labour/Le Travailleur*, 10 (1978): 65–85. On the landmark Ford strike, see David Moulton, "Ford

Windsor 1945," in *On Strike: Six Key Labour Struggles in Canada, 1919–1949*, edited by Irving Abella (Toronto, 1974).

On the treatment of Japanese Canadians, consult Ann Gomer Sunahara, *The Politics of Racism: The Uprooting of Japanese Canadians During the Second World War* (Toronto, 1981), and Peter Ward, *White Canada Forever: Popular Attitudes and Public Policy toward Orientals in British Columbia* (Montreal, 1978). Another group whose civil liberties were repressed during the war is dealt with in Reg Whitaker, "Official Repression of Communism During World War II," *Labour/Le Travail*, 17 (1986): 135–66.

306

CHAPTER FIFTEEN

The Boom Years, 1945–60

By 1945 Canadians were understandably tired of sacrifices. After a decade of depression and six years of war, they wanted to make up for lost time, forget a bleak past, and look towards the future. Consumers wanted cars, household appliances, and adequate housing. Businessmen wanted to boost profits. Workers demanded jobs and better wages. Canadians also wanted governments to provide a variety of health, educational, and social services as a safety net against misfortune. They took pride in the prestigious role that Canada played in the United Nations, in the North Atlantic Treaty Organization (NATO), and in the British Commonwealth.

Attitudes remained basically conservative, and traditional values and beliefs continued to govern the behaviour of a majority of Canadians. Though more women worked outside the home, traditional beliefs concerning the role of women in society loosened only gradually. By the late 1950s, however, the old mentality was changing. Slower growth with rising unemployment disrupted the post-war boom. Unimaginative politicians who boasted of past successes and talked in platitudinous generalities had few answers to offer. People were ready to welcome new leaders who would put forth new ideas and propose new solutions.

Nirvana in Canada?

Recently, Canadians have looked back nostalgically to the late 1940s and early 1950s as an age when times were good, and people lived together harmoniously and peacefully. By most measures, post-war Canada was indeed prosperous. *Fortune* magazine called it a "businessman's country." Total industrial output went up by half in the 1950s, and productivity soared thanks to technological innovation. With the economies of western Europe devastated by the war, Canada readily found export markets for its goods. The nation's living standard was the highest in the world, after that of the United States. Until the late 1950s, most Canadians who wanted to work were able to do so; unemployment rates were—by contemporary standards—very low: 2.8 to 5.9 percent. University graduates found jobs easily in this seller's market. One university engineering professor boasted in 1952: "This year all my good students have more than five job offers and even my dullest have two!" Canadians could buy a home for $15 000 and then borrow the money to pay for it at a fixed rate of just over 4 percent for twenty-five years. Prices of food and consumer goods increased at barely 2–3 percent annually. Governments rang up surpluses, not deficits.

This may appear to have been nirvana, but appearances were deceiving. Jobs were easy to find for university graduates, but few Canadians had university degrees. Salaries were often low, especially for non-unionized, immigrant, female workers and Canadian Indians, even when one takes into account the fact that the dollar's purchasing power was about five times what it is today. Conditions were difficult for many farmers, too, and thousands of rural Quebeckers and Maritimers, incapable of earning a living, abandoned their land. The less-industrialized Western and Atlantic provinces had low per capita incomes. In Quebec, unilingual anglophones enjoyed income levels twice those of unilingual francophones and one-third higher than those of bilingual francophones. New Brunswick was sharply divided into the impoverished north and east, which was largely Acadian, and the more favoured south, mostly English-speaking. Newfoundlanders in the outports were often victims of extreme poverty. Finally, underprivileged Canadians, whether unemployed or sick, handicapped or elderly, could not count on the array of social programmes taken for granted today.

Canada had many other second-class citizens, too. Women did not enjoy the same employment opportunities as men. Discrimination afflicted Canada's aboriginal peoples as well as Blacks, Jews, and numerous other groups. The French suffered from linguistic inequality, even within Quebec. For many, this Canada was certainly not paradise. Inequalities engendered discontent which, though not much articulated yet, would eventually provoke significant change.

Prosperity and Trade

After demobilization, government policy sought to favour the prevailing climate of "superpush." In 1945 Munitions and Supply Minister C.D. Howe stated that the government should guarantee a "high and stable level of employment and income." To achieve this objective, he wanted to liberalize international trade: only if markets abroad were open, he believed, could a country like Canada, whose economy was largely based on exports, prosper. He also wanted the government to use tax policy to promote investment and to create jobs.

Officials of the Department of External Affairs hoped that new international trade links would help Canada avoid becoming too heavily dependent on the United States and enable it to resist American political pressure. C.D. Howe, described by historian Donald Creighton as the "economic autocrat of the Cabinet,"[1] saw things more simply: "Our best policy is to sell as much as possible wherever possible." To him, the American market represented Canada's great opportunity, and an economic integration of North American resources was a desirable objective.

Although Canada's trade did expand, growth was uneven. From the late 1940s, the country was persistently saddled with a negative trade balance as imports rose faster than exports. In real terms, Canada was exporting less in the mid-1950s than at the end of the war. Most Canadian-made manufactured products were not competitive in international markets; Canadian production costs remained high because Canadian companies manufactured a wide variety of products, but in small quantities. Though it denounced protectionist policies elsewhere that kept out Canadian goods, the government maintained relatively high tariffs on imported manufactured goods; the objective was to reserve the home market for products made in Canada in order to assure more jobs for Canadians. Of course, tariffs meant that consumers paid higher prices, but with more money in their pockets, Canadians bought more imported products.

309

TRADING PARTNERS

Canadian trade with the United States increased steadily. The Conservatives criticized the government during the 1957 election campaign for having "permitted ... trade with the United Kingdom and other European countries to decline while Canada's dependence on trade with the United States has increased alarmingly." In 1957 Canada bought just 9 percent of its imports from Britain and sold the British only 15 percent of its exports; comparable figures for trade with the United States were 71 percent and 59 percent respectively. Opposition leader John Diefenbaker promised that, if his party took office, he would take steps to redress the balance, and even spoke of diverting 15 percent of Canada's imports from the United States to Britain. The Conservatives won in 1957, but nothing changed. Moreover, the Common Market, which was created in that year, posed new threats to Canadian trade with Europe.

The boom of the 1950s did little to help western Canadian farmers. During the war the government had made the Wheat Board into a compulsory marketing agency for all Prairie wheat. It guaranteed farmers a minimum price and eliminated middlemen from the trade. Canada could not control world supply, however, or have much impact on the large variations in world wheat prices. After the war Canada wanted to keep its important British customer and agreed to sell wheat at a lower price. Then, in the early 1950s, as American production increased and the government distributed wheat surpluses through aid programmes, world prices plunged, Canadian farm incomes sank, and huge quantities of wheat piled up in fields, commercial warehouses, pool terminals, and even on discarded lake boats. As the discontent of Prairie farmers grew, the Liberal government tried to assure farmers that their problems were only temporary. When Saskatchewan politician John Diefenbaker became the federal Conservative party leader in 1956 and prime minister in 1957, he demonstrated that he understood the plight of farmers. After he promised new subsidies and found new markets for Prairie wheat, Tory support rose in the West.

Rise of Foreign Investment

310   The post-war years saw a great amount of foreign investment enter into Canada. It tripled between 1950 and 1960, and three-quarters of it was American. To get around the Canadian tariffs, American multinational corporations established more branch plants, especially in central Canada. The Americans also sought Canada's resources. The Paley Commission, reporting to President Eisenhower, warned that, as its own resources were being depleted, the United States would have to look elsewhere. The Korean War in 1950–53 also promoted an investment boom in Canada's resource and defence industries.

ROYAL COMMISSION ON CANADA'S ECONOMIC PROSPECTS

Most Canadians assumed that this trend was good for Canada, and that, despite closer economic links with the United States, their country could maintain its political sovereignty. Nevertheless, the Royal Commission on Canada's Economic Prospects, chaired by Toronto accountant Walter L. Gordon, expressed many reservations about Canada's increasing integration with its southern neighbour. Gordon himself later admitted that for some time he had been worrying about the "complacency" with which Canadians were selling out the country's resources. Not surprisingly, the Gordon Commission recommended in a preliminary report in 1956 that Canada affirm a moderate degree of independence for its economy and that it control foreign investment.

Advocates of North American integration argued that multinationals gave jobs to Canadians and helped the country's balance of payments by reducing imports. Howe protested in a speech in 1956 that, "had it not been for the enterprise and capital from the United States ... our development would have been slower, and some of the spectacular projects of which we are so proud ... would still be in the future." He reacted to Gordon's preliminary report by calling it "manure."[2]

During the prosperous late 1940s and early 1950s, several important development projects were undertaken. Gas pipelines were laid from Alberta to Ontario and American markets, a railway was built north from Sept-Iles, Quebec, to open up ore-rich Labrador, and the construction of the St. Lawrence Seaway and of the Trans-Canada Highway began.

Then the boom ended, and by 1958 growth slowed and unemployment increased to more than 9 percent. Automation had eliminated some jobs. When railroads switched to diesel engines, for example, they needed fewer machinists, blacksmiths, and firemen. Also, the Canadian dollar, which brought a premium when exchanged for an American dollar, was too high, and the high exchange rate hurt exports. Furthermore, some observers maintained that since the jobless tended to have the least education, the country was not investing enough in public education, particularly at *311* higher levels.

A Government of Efficient Administrators

Voters in the late 1940s and early 1950s wanted politicians who would manage the country efficiently and ensure greater prosperity. The Liberal government of businessmen and administrators fulfilled the need; it was a regime that reflected an era.

When William Lyon Mackenzie King retired in 1948, he had been leader of the Liberal party for nearly thirty years and could boast of having been the longest-serving prime minister in the history of the British Empire. Jurist Frank Scott, who objected indignantly to King's being given credit for everything but putting the oil under Alberta, attributed King's success to his blandness: "He will be remembered wherever men honour ingenuity, ambiguity, inactivity, and political longevity."

Yet many observers of Canadian politics—including several of his own cabinet ministers—gave King grudging admiration for his record even though they disliked him personally and found him uninspiring. Liberals could thank him for keeping a host of potentially dangerous opposition groups at bay, from the Progressives in the 1920s to the CCF in the 1940s and including, of course, the usually bumbling Conservatives. Through a war policy that was variously criticized as treasonously insufficient or far too great for Canada's modest capacities, he had avoided most of the shoals on which the Conservatives had so disastrously foundered in 1917. His prudent and politically well-timed social reforms of the war and post-war years had prevented Canada from slipping into the bitter left–right ideological confrontation that characterized European politics. He seemed to follow rather than lead, and to be more concerned with his own and the Liberal party's fortunes than with Canada's well-being, but he had—like Macdonald and Laurier before him—given his name to an era in Canadian political history.

Louis St. Laurent, King's successor, was a former corporation lawyer from Quebec City and the second French-speaking, though fluently bilingual, prime minister. Denounced in his home province during the war for his approval of military conscription, he was clearly no Quebec nationalist. On constitutional questions he opposed the provincial autonomists in Quebec and elsewhere. In foreign affairs, he appeared more internationalist than many Canadians. Then, in August 1948, at what political scientist Reginald Whitaker has described as more a celebration than a convention, Liberals chose him to inherit King's mantle.[3]

THE ST. LAURENT GOVERNMENT

St. Laurent's first government resembled King's. St. Laurent followed his predecessor's "accommodative approach," only acting after consensus had been achieved. This charming, urbane prime minister presided in collegial fashion over a "corporation of provincial chieftains," as political scientist David E. Smith has aptly described his Cabinet.[4] Unlike King, however, St. Laurent took little interest in the Liberal party organization and, by the mid-1950s, had become isolated from constituency opinion.

Some Liberal strategists worried over St. Laurent's possibilities as a vote-getter, because he was politically naive and ill-at-ease with the public out on the hustings. Their fears proved groundless. Before the 1949 election campaign had begun, St. Laurent adopted a relaxed platform style, particularly with small groups. One reporter for a conservative newspaper remarked: "Uncle Louis is going to be hard to beat." The nickname stuck and brought enormous dividends.

Opposition leader George Drew, former Ontario premier, had considerable talent: he was an articulate debater and aggressive in his attacks on the "tired Liberal government" of "socialists in low gear." But historian Frank Underhill's description of him at the time rushing up and down the country "like an enraged bull in a pasture field, snorting and bellowing and tossing his head," was the one that many voters retained. Moreover, it was easy for the Liberals to portray Drew as anti-French and thus to assure continued Liberal domination in Quebec. In addition, the handsome Toronto imperialist (nicknamed "Gorgeous George" by his opponents) was also linked to the rabidly Tory "Bay Street interests," anathema to Canadians in the West and in the East. The result was a spectacular victory for St. Laurent, who won 193 of the 262 seats in the election of 1949; Conservative popular support declined in all provinces west of Quebec.

FEDERAL-PROVINCIAL TENSIONS

The Liberal government's preoccupation with maintaining a buoyant economy had serious implications for Canadian federalism. Civil servants and politicians in Ottawa believed that the federal government should maintain and even strengthen the fiscal and legislative pre-eminence that it acquired during the wartime emergency. But several provinces objected to this policy of centralization. Nova Scotia premier Angus L. Macdonald complained that subsidies destroyed provincial independence and transformed the provinces into "mere annuitants of Ottawa." Ontario insisted on the right to formulate its own economic priorities and programmes. In Quebec, the Duplessis government feuded continuously with Ottawa over federal tax and spending policies, while a provincial Royal Commission of Inquiry on Constitutional Problems (the Tremblay Commission) in 1954 called for an end to federal "imperialism" and a return to "true federalism."

The Liberals' moderate conservatism did not signify a halt in Canada's movement towards a welfare state in terms of health and old age security. In 1948, Ottawa enacted the National Health Programme that provided for separate federal grants to each province in the fields of hygiene and health. In 1952, after all the provinces had agreed to a constitutional amendment, Ottawa began sending old age cheques each month for forty dollars to most Canadians over 70.

313

Federal opposition parties made remarkably little headway against the St. Laurent Liberals before 1957. Diehard Tories blustered about Liberal waste and extravagance. Doctrinaire socialists in the CCF appealed to Canadians to "share the wealth" so that every family could have "a good kitchen sink and a first class bathroom." But the Liberals, promising "a great leader for a greater Canada," occupied the centre of the political spectrum and thus established the consensus so necessary to govern Canada. Undoubtedly prosperity facilitated their task.

Golden Age of Canadian Diplomacy

Some political observers writing in the 1960s and 1970s, like politician Walter Gordon, philosopher George Grant, and historian Donald Creighton, looked back upon the King–St. Laurent years as a period when Canada came increasingly under American hegemony. Most Canadians living in the 1950s probably took pride instead in their country's activities as a middle power in international affairs.

After 1945 Canada had to adapt to a new world power structure. The war had permanently weakened Britain while at the same time giving rise to a new giant in the western world—the United States. To offset growing American power, Canada worked to build strong multilateral institutions. At the same time, it had little desire to let world organizations interfere in its relations with the United States, which it believed it could conduct better alone.

CANADA IN THE COLD WAR ERA

Disappointments were rife in these years as the post-war era rapidly gave way to the cold war. At the Paris Peace Conference of 1946, Canada had hoped to play a role in the European settlement commensurate with its contribution to the war effort. For Canada, though, as J.F. Hilliker has shown, there was "no bread at all;"[5] the country went virtually unnoticed and thus played a much less active role in peacemaking than it had in 1918–19 (see chapter 9).

314 As relations between the Americans and the Soviet Union deteriorated, Canadian foreign affairs officials feared that the often bellicose attitude of the United States would only make matters worse. As External Affairs official John Holmes put it, the Americans refused to negotiate "with the devil" while Canadians wanted only to make him behave.[6]

Events conspired, though, to shake Canadians' faith in the West's capacity to reach some kind of *modus vivendi* with the U.S.S.R. In late 1945 Igor Gouzenko, a cypher clerk at the Soviet embassy in Ottawa, defected and revealed the existence of a Soviet espionage network in Canada reaching into several government agencies. Gouzenko's sensational revelations, made public by the press in early 1946 after arrests (including that of Communist MP Fred Rose) had been made, caused the Soviet threat to appear more dramatic. Dana Wilgress, who headed the Canadian mission in Moscow from 1944 until 1947, denounced the "irresponsible opportunism" that characterized Soviet policies. Within three short years the Soviet Union had succeeded in setting up communist puppet regimes in most of the eastern European states occupied by the Red Army. Then, in 1948, the Soviets organized a *coup d'état* in Czechoslovakia to install a communist government there. Further Russian threats to Turkey and Iran, the communist insurgence in Greece, and the upsurge of the Communist party in France and Italy, all made the danger of communism appear very real indeed.

NORTH ATLANTIC TREATY ORGANIZATION (NATO)

As people lost hope that the United Nations could assure world peace through collective security, the Canadian government pushed for an Atlantic alliance to protect the West against the growing Soviet threat. NATO, established in 1949, was, in the words of Lester B. Pearson, then undersecretary of state for External Affairs, born of "a fear intensified by the failure of every effort to bring about a more friendly and cooperative relationship with Moscow."

Escott Reid, an External Affairs officer, in a speech in the summer of 1947, was probably the first to advocate publicly a collective defence system for the West. Then, in September Louis St. Laurent, as secretary of state for External Affairs, made an address in New York in which he described the United Nations Security Council as being regretfully "frozen in futility and divided by dissension." Dissatisfied democratic and peace-loving member states could be well justified, as a last resort, in coming together and accepting more specific international obligations in return for a greater measure of national security.

The Americans and the British showed interest in the proposal. In the summer of 1948, consultations with the Western European powers proceeded, and by December, work began on a draft treaty. The United States envisaged a purely military pact, but Canada sought co-operation *315* in other sectors that might eventually unite the Atlantic nations into a closely knit community. For that reason, in the treaty that gave birth to NATO, Canada fought for the inclusion of an article indicating general economic and social aims.

Canada's interest was clear. Links with Western Europe would prevent Canada from being left to stand alone and isolated before the militarily dominant Americans. The so-called "Canadian article" did get into the treaty, in spite of the adamant opposition of American secretary of state Dean Acheson to this product of "typical Canadian moralizing." In March 1949 the House of Commons approved the treaty, and on April 4, in a mood of euphoric optimism, NATO came into existence. But the Canadians' hard-won victory soured quickly, for the "Canadian article" soon became a "dead letter."

CANADIAN-AMERICAN RELATIONS

The Atlantic Alliance could not, however, replace Canadian dependence on the United States for the defence of North America. As fears of a U.S.–Soviet confrontation rose, both Canadian and American military strategists realized the importance of Canada's polar regions in North American air defence (see chapter 16). In February 1947 King announced that the military co-operation characteristic of the war years and conducted through the Permanent Joint Board on Defence would continue in peacetime.

Canada also moved to closer economic integration with the United States. In 1947, for example, Canada was beset by a severe shortage of American dollars. One solution was to discuss free trade with the Americans. Discussion led to an agreement on a general plan, but then King became haunted by Laurier's ghost who reminded him of the 1911 election when the Liberal government (of which King himself had been a part) had been defeated by the Conservatives, largely on the reciprocity issue (see chapter 7). King made a decision: "I would no more think of, at my time of life and at this stage of my career, attempting any movement of the kind than I would of flying to the South Pole." Thus Canada either missed a golden opportunity at bringing about free trade or saved its economic independence and political sovereignty by successfully resisting the siren-call of continentalism.

A safer move was to try to convince the Americans to let European countries receiving American aid to use part of it to buy Canadian goods. This Canada succeeded in accomplishing, and the dollar crisis was resolved. Ottawa also hoped that the General Agreement on Tariffs and Trade (GATT) would come to its aid. This multilateral trade agreement, signed in Geneva in 1947, aimed at reducing tariffs and stimulating world trade. It included accords between Canada and its two principal trading partners, the United States and Britain.

In keeping with its desire to balance closer links to the United States with an increased international participation, Canada looked with hope upon the evolving Commonwealth. King, however, strongly opposed the idea of a uniform Commonwealth foreign policy put forth by certain British politicians; to him, such a plan recalled the days of the Empire centralizers. Moreover, the Commonwealth was changing, with the addition of new dominions like India, Pakistan, and Ceylon. Canada would help move the Commonwealth in directions that made it acceptable for these new members. It also supported and contributed to the Colombo Plan set up at a meeting of Commonwealth foreign ministers in 1950 to promote economic development in Commonwealth countries in Asia.

PEACEKEEPING

Canada's attempts at peacekeeping produced mixed results. In 1950, when communist North Korea invaded South Korea and the United Nations Security Council (which the Soviet Union was boycotting) denounced this act of aggression, Canada contributed a brigade to fight alongside mostly American troops, in the name of collective security. As the war moved towards a stalemate, Pearson played a significant role in attempting to restrain the "overzealous" Americans from taking certain risky actions. Then in 1954, Canada agreed, though with considerable apprehension, to join Poland and India in a three-country International Control Commission to supervise the peace in Indochina. Finally, in 1956, came what many considered to be Canada's greatest contribution internationally. In October, despite strong American opposition, Israel, together with Britain

National Archives of Canada PA-110828.

Canadian troops cross a small village during the Korean War, 1951.

and France, invaded Egypt, in response to President Nasser's nationalization of the Suez Canal. Wary of the dangerous split developing in the
Western alliance, Pearson proposed the creation of a United Nations emergency peacekeeping force in the region. For his efforts, Pearson was awarded
the Nobel Peace Prize in 1957.

DAVID FELLS GOLIATH

When Canadians went to the polls in 1957 to select a government, another
Liberal victory seemed likely. The Liberals had been in power for twenty-
two years. The economy was still strong and the Liberals were convinced
that the Canadian electorate was not about "to shoot Santa Claus." In a
post-election issue that went to press before election day, *Maclean's* magazine had editorialized: "For better or for worse, we Canadians have once
more elected one of the most powerful governments ever created by the
free will of a free electorate." *Maclean's*, of course, was embarrassed and
most political observers were surprised, as the Conservatives, under their
new leader John Diefenbaker, a lawyer from Prince Albert, Saskatchewan,
won a narrow victory. Stunned Liberals, as cabinet minister J.W. Pickersgill later put it, wondered why they had to suffer a Tory government
once in every generation. The CCF, which had restated its original aims

MacLean/DND National Archives of Canada C-79009.

CBC journalist Rene Lévesque, future premier of Quebec, interviews Canadian soldiers on the banks of the Imjin River, in Korea, in August 1951.

in less revolutionary fashion in its Winnipeg Declaration of Principles in 1956, was bitterly disappointed over its failure to arrest its decline in popularity.

Political analysts set about attempting to explain the Canadian electorate's unexpected behaviour. Some voters undoubtedly deplored Canada's increasing ties with the United States and the corresponding decline of British influence. Many felt that, during the Suez crisis, the Liberal government should have supported Britain and France whose use of force most countries, including the United States and the USSR, condemned. Canadians in the Prairies and in the Maritimes were discontented with their region's underdevelopment and indignant when Liberal ministers assured them: "You've never had it so good." Many senior citizens agreed with Conservative assertions that old age pensions were scandalously insufficient. Most of all, voters probably wanted a change from what

318

appeared increasingly to be cold, insensitive, uncreative leadership by an aging Liberal gerontocracy.

The electorate also responded to Conservative charges that the Liberals were behaving in an undemocratic, even dictatorial fashion. The culmination of purported Liberal arrogance was the Trans-Canada pipeline affair in 1956. The government had planned to make an important loan to Trans-Canada Pipe Lines, a private company formed by American and Canadian businessmen, to assist in building the western section of a pipeline to carry Alberta gas to central Canadian markets. In a hurry because of a timetable he wanted to respect, Trade and Commerce minister C.D. Howe pushed the bill through Parliament, unamended, by imposing closure (the cutting off of debate) at each stage. In his manoeuvres he was aided by an all-too-helpful Speaker of the Commons. The Liberal Cabinet, as Diefenbaker put it, sat on the front benches, "arrogant, overbearing, condescending ..., sneering at suggestions that they were becoming all-powerful." Many Canadians obviously agreed.

319

THE "DIEFENBAKER PARTY"

Diefenbaker surely played a significant role in the success of what became known as the "Diefenbaker party." The new leader sought to change voters' traditionally negative image of the Tory party. He took control of the party from the hands of the Toronto business élite and gave it to "outsiders," many of whom came from western Canada. Conservatives proclaimed: "It's time for a Diefenbaker government." Diefenbaker, whose oratorical talents far outshone anything the Liberals could muster, proclaimed the message. "This party has a sacred trust," the modern-day Jeremiah thundered to his "fellow Canadians" at Toronto's Massey Hall in April 1957. "It has an appointment today with destiny, to plan and to build for a greater Canada ... one Canada, with equality of opportunity for every citizen and equality for every province from the Atlantic to the Pacific."

The federal election of 1957 was but a dress rehearsal for that of March 1958. The new government barely had time to adopt a few popular measures designed to assist the unemployed, Prairie farmers, and Maritimers before Diefenbaker, anxious to form a majority government, called a new election. The prime minister then presented his "vision of opportunity" for Canada, of the development of resources and of the North. Liberal newspapers like the *Toronto Star* mocked Diefenbaker's admittedly vague programme as "humbug and flapdoodle served up with an evangelistic flourish"; new Liberal leader Lester B. Pearson, whose soporific oratorical style betrayed his diplomatic career, attempted to brush off what he termed the "oracular fervour and circus parades." The result was a Diefenbaker landslide, with the Conservatives taking 208 of the 265 seats in the House of Commons and the Liberals reduced to a rump of 50 members.

From the start, the Conservatives had difficulty governing. So long had they sat in the political wilderness that the new ministers were all inexperienced. In many cases, they were suspicious of the loyalty of civil servants accustomed to a close working relationship with Liberal politicians. For most Quebec Tory MPs, the triumph of 1958 was their first—and last—electoral victory. "The Chief" knew little about Quebec, spoke little French, and entrusted no senior cabinet portfolios to Quebeckers. Diefenbaker's vision of northern development, of "opening Canada to its polar reaches," did not capture the imagination of southern Canadians. Liberals mocked what they called a programme of "roads from igloo to igloo."

The Conservative government's major problem was the country's deteriorating economic situation. It responded by trying to combat rising unemployment with winter works programmes and subsidies, as well as providing benefits for such seasonal workers as fishermen. As expenses increased and government receipts declined, Finance Minister Donald Fleming's budgetary deficits grew, and the business community complained of financial mismanagement. The Conservatives' historic victory of 1958 was fast souring.

The Age of the Consumer

Until the late 1950s, Canadians had been generally disinterested in politics. They wanted more leisure, better wages, and the array of material goods that money could buy. Certainly, the average worker had reason to feel satisfied. Wages in manufacturing doubled between 1945 and 1956. Since prices increased at a much slower rate, workers could count on a steady improvement in their living standards. They also worked less, as the forty-hour week became the norm.

The era of the consumer was underway at last. In towns, the iceman with his horse-drawn cart lost his remaining customers as Canadians equipped their kitchens with electric refrigerators. Coal merchants' sales tumbled as homeowners bought electric ranges and switched to gas and oil heat. Families acquired a variety of new appliances intended to reduce the drudgery of housework. Sales of new automobiles mounted as Canadians bought sleek American Fords and Chevvies, or slim British Morrises and Austins. Subdivisions mushroomed on city outskirts and proud new homeowners hurried to vary the colour of the trim or plant shrubs in order to distinguish their dwelling from the identical constructions on all sides. Roofs acquired an important new use as supports for forests of television antennas.

LIMITED PROSPERITY

The new-found prosperity was far from universal, however. Few rural households could afford the amenities commonly found in town. Before 1950 only a minority even had electricity. The 1951 census revealed that one-half of Canadian families still did not own an electric refrigerator or a vacuum cleaner, 60 percent had no car, 40 percent had no telephone, and 25 percent did not have an electric washing machine. Indeed, one dwelling in three did not have hot and cold running water. By earlier standards, life was better, but prosperity still eluded such groups as small farmers, Atlantic Coast fishermen, department store clerks, coal miners who lost their jobs when the mines closed, and workers, often women, in low-paying industries like textiles: these groups saw no real boom.

Canadians were unhappy, too, when they compared themselves, as they did obsessively, with Americans. Magazines and newspapers featured articles that delved into the revenues and expenses of "typical" Canadian and American families. In 1950 Canadian per capita income was still 40 percent below American levels. Canadians complained that refrigerators at Simpson's costing $400 could be had for only $275 in the United States. Journalist Blair Fraser remarked that, for Europeans still repairing their war-torn economies, second-place Canadians must have appeared like the impoverished tycoon who was down to his last million. Nevertheless, many Canadians of talent, especially entertainers, researchers, and engineers, migrated south, while Canadians who remained behind bemoaned the "brain drain."

321

HEALTH CARE

Canadians who became ill (at least those outside Saskatchewan and British Columbia, which had public health plans) knew the prohibitive cost of health care. One Montreal businessman, after paying the bills pertaining to his wife's serious illness, commented wryly: "There are two things that can send you to the poorhouse: hospital bills and borrowing from loan sharks. And 90 percent of the borrowing from loan sharks is to pay hospital bills!"

Many Canadians called for a national health plan. Anxious doctors warned that a government plan would rob them of their independence, lower their standards, and interfere with the intimate doctor-patient relationship. Finally in 1957, after lobbying by several provincial premiers and some of St. Laurent's own ministers, including Health and Welfare minister Paul Martin, Parliament adopted the Hospital Insurance and Diagnostic Services Act. The act provided federal financial assistance to provinces willing to set up a publicly administered hospital insurance programme with universal coverage.

Labour Relations in Times of Prosperity

Economic growth gave a great boost to the unions. In 1950 membership passed the one-million mark, or 30 percent of the work force. "Elite" unions in sectors like heavy manufacturing disposed of considerable bargaining power and succeeded in negotiating high wages. Other unions were much less fortunate: their workers occupied relatively low-paying jobs in industries like clothing, food, and furniture.

Strike activity was considerable, particularly in the late 1940s: in 1946, one worker in six went on strike and 4.5 million workdays were lost. These strikes aimed at forcing employers to recognize union rights, improve working conditions, and increase salaries. In retaliation, companies frequently hired strikebreakers, and violent confrontations sometimes ensued. Provincial governments supported employers directly by favourable legislation and through the use of the police and the courts.

322

INDUSTRIAL UNREST

Though most workers signed contracts without going on strike, and far more days were lost because of sickness than because of strike activity, certain sensational confrontations earned a place in the annals of working-class history. In one dramatic encounter in 1946, Steel Company of Canada (Stelco) management used airplanes and boats to avoid the picket lines and to transport food and supplies to strikebreakers inside its plant at Hamilton, Ontario. In the same year, textile workers, including large numbers of women, struck in Valleyfield, Quebec. Led by Madeleine Parent and Kent Rowley, the strikers finally obtained recognition for their union after bloody skirmishes with police. In Asbestos, Quebec, workers belonging to the *Confédération des travailleurs catholiques du Canada* (CTCC) struck for five months in 1949 to improve wages and working conditions. The Duplessis government assisted the companies, decertified the union, and sent in special police squads.

Conflict continued into the 1950s. Loggers, fishermen, government employees, and longshoremen in British Columbia, building trades workers in Halifax and Vancouver, gold miners in Ontario and Quebec, automobile workers and employees of the International Nickel Company (INCO) in Ontario, all had major strikes. In August 1950, 130 000 employees of Canada's two major railways left their jobs, but the government, declaring that "the country cannot afford a railway strike," ordered the workers back. In 1952 textile workers at Louiseville, Quebec, were out for ten months. In 1957 copper workers at Murdochville, Quebec, struck for seven months in a violent but vain confrontation. In 1959 Newfoundland loggers, members of the International Woodworkers of America (IWA) went on strike. Average wages were low (about $1 an hour), the workday was long, and camp amenities often non-existent. Violence was rife as the company recruited fishermen to replace strikers. In one skirmish, a policeman was fatally injured. In an effort to break the IWA, Premier Joseph Smallwood set up a union and had the Legislature outlaw the IWA in the province. Although the federal government refused to send the RCMP reinforcements that Smallwood demanded, the strike did fail.

WORKERS VERSUS WORKERS

Workers did not fight only management and governments. They also feuded with each other for political and personal reasons. On the left, Communists and democratic socialists battled one another in fratricidal fury. Both clashed with conservative unionists, who viewed all political links as dangerous for the labour movement.

Anti-communists in the Canadian Congress of Labour (CCL) insisted that "we can't fight the Communists with one hand and the bosses with the other. To fight the boss we must get rid of the Communists." They thus manoeuvred to oust certain affiliate unions whose executives it charged with being "complete vassals of uncle Joe Stalin." The Communist-led Canadian Seamen's Union (CSU) was crushed when the Canadian and American governments combined with the shippers and Trades and Labour Congress (TLC) officers to replace the CSU with the rival Seafarers' International Union (SIU). (After a judicial inquiry later found the SIU guilty of racketeering and of a host of other improper practices, Ottawa placed the union under a government trusteeship; its director, Hal Banks, who had boasted of his ambition to control "everything that floats," forfeited bail and fled to the United States.) For some Canadian unionists, the battle against the Communists merely permitted American unions to reinforce their hold in Canada. As labour historian Irving Abella has written, the Communist purge did little to strengthen the union movement and, in hindsight, was probably "neither necessary nor wise."[7]

Greater labour unity came in 1956 when the TLC and the CCL finally united to form the Canadian Labour Congress (CLC) after a merger in 1955 of the American labour congresses—the AFL and the CIO. The costly raids by TLC and CCL unions on each other, with no total gain in membership, then ended. Claude Jodoin, a well-known Quebec labour leader and president of the TLC, became president of the new million-member CLC. Many of the CLC unions were affiliated with the American AFL-CIO, and they remained subject to American influence. Most Canadian workers, employed by American branch companies, found nothing unusual in belonging to American-dominated unions. This fact was one of the reasons why the Quebec-based CTCC refused to join the congress.

Though unions made major gains in the post-war period, much work remained to be done. Labour legislation had to become more sympathetic to unions. Job security appeared an increasingly serious issue in the face of automation. It was also necessary to make the workplace a safer environment: accidents on the job caused nearly 5 000 000 injuries and more than 12 500 deaths in 1945–59. Moreover, after the mid-1950s, union membership as a proportion of the non-agricultural work force levelled off. Vast numbers of workers, notably in the service sector, remained nonunionized.

324 Status of Women

During World War II, women had entered the work force in great numbers (see chapter 14). Once the war was over, most Canadians, including a majority of women, thought women—especially married women—should return to their traditional occupations in the home. The Montreal nationalist monthly, *L'Action nationale*, accused female factory workers of promoting social and moral disorganization by leaving their children on the streets, where juvenile delinquency flourished. Cultural stereotypes reinforced the "traditional" role of women: surveys of school textbooks showed that interesting, talented personalities described were almost always men, while women were portrayed as staying at home, cooking meals, and scolding children.

THE BABY BOOM

With good times, a higher proportion of young adults married, and they married earlier. Canadian women began, on an impressive scale, to have children, and a veritable "baby boom" set in. By 1947, the birth rate had increased to nearly 29 per thousand. The average family had three or four children. This relatively large contingent of youth, which some demographers described as the "pig in the python," had enormous repercussions on Canadian society. The precise nature of the impact would alter with time, as the baby boomers went through childhood, adolescence, young adulthood, and middle age. The baby boom led to a rapid increase in Canada's population. During the 1950s births exceeded deaths by three million, while immigration brought Canada another one million citizens.

The growth rate exceeded 30 percent, equivalent to that experienced by many third world countries today.

WOMEN IN THE WORK FORCE

For most women, unremunerated housework formed a major part of their economic activity. Slowly, though, female participation in the work force increased. In 1951, one paid worker in four was a woman, usually unmarried. During the 1950s the proportion of married women workers doubled to one in five as mothers rejoined the work force after their youngest children enrolled in school. Most working women were concentrated in occupations where few men could be found, such as secretaries, nurses, sales personnel, and clerks. As late as 1960, only a handful of women were professionals; they accounted for just 7 percent of doctors, 3 percent of lawyers, and a mere 1 percent of engineers.

325

For female workers, evidence of inequality abounded. Men generally received higher wages for performing the same tasks. Universities commonly paid female professors less than male professors of the same rank and experience. Minimum wage rates, fixed by governments, were usually lower for women than for men. Wage parity (equal pay for performing the same task) was only beginning to be an issue as Ontario's Female Employees Fair Remuneration Act of 1951 showed the way in this regard.

Nor did women have equal opportunity for promotions even in female-dominated sectors like teaching; across Canada, men had a far greater chance of becoming school principals. Few women held positions of influence in the business world or in political life in the 1950s. Between 1930 and 1960 the government named seven women senators, at a time when more than 250 men received the coveted lifetime appointment. Only in 1957 did a federal prime minister—John Diefenbaker—choose the first woman federal cabinet minister—Ontario's Ellen Fairclough. While in the opposition in the 1950s, the Hamilton MP had introduced a bill providing for equal pay for equal work, and she had promoted the formation of a Department of Labour Women's Bureau to help fight for equal opportunity for women. For many observers, this was only a modest beginning. Charlotte Whitton, Ottawa's feisty mayor, predicted that women were growing so impatient with "the man-made messes of a man-made world" that they would soon insist on a much larger voice in public affairs.

Women who fought for women's rights faced enormous problems. Thérèse Casgrain, in the forefront of the battle to obtain the right to vote for women in Quebec, was often a candidate in elections; she was never elected, possibly because she was a woman, but more probably because she belonged to the "wrong" party—the CCF. When left-wing Quebec labour leader Madeleine Parent was arrested and charged with seditious conspiracy, the judge reminded the all-male jury that the accused was "a young woman, with a fine education, who belonged to an excellent family, but who got embroiled in activities outside her sphere, and in a milieu that could only destroy her."

Higher Education

Since society perceived a woman's role as very different from a man's, and since many occupations were virtually closed to women, few women attended Canada's universities. In the 1950s, only about one university student in four was a woman. Most being enrolled in programmes in education or the liberal arts, few could be found in the sciences or in the professional schools. In Quebec, classical colleges for women were, until 1960, denied the state funds available to all-male colleges. Quebec women were encouraged to attend "family institutes," nicknamed "schools of happiness," where they would learn to take up the challenges of life in the home. In Toronto, the elite University of Toronto Schools (almost all of whose graduates went on to university) admitted no women, even though it was largely state-supported.

326

The 1950s was not an era of higher education for men, either. In 1951 Canada's colleges and universities had only sixty thousand students, or barely 4 percent of the eligible age group. The Royal Commission on National Development in the Arts, Letters and Sciences (the Massey Commission) judged that Canadian universities "are facing a financial crisis so great as to threaten their future usefulness," and it recommended direct federal financial support.

As the first of the baby boom generation reached high school, the National Council of Canadian Universities warned, in 1956, that enrolments were on the verge of a dramatic increase. The Soviet launching of Sputnik, the first earth satellite, in 1957, proved an unforeseen boon to Canadian universities: the fear of Russian scientific superiority convinced many Canadians that governments should invest much more in higher education. Provincial authorities began to loosen the purse strings and the federal government instituted federal grants. Facilities for higher education expanded and several new universities were built in the late 1950s.

Culture: Canadian versus American

Prosperity enabled many Canadians to spend lavishly on entertainment. They purchased new long-playing records (LPs), often of poor quality and, in terms of current wages, at high cost. In the 1940s, they flocked to the movie theatres which proliferated. The real revolution in the entertainment industry, however, came in the early 1950s with television. Ownership of even the standard ten-inch black-and-white screen was at first a status symbol because of the relatively high cost. Canadians living close to American border cities could receive American television programmes. Then, in 1952, Canada's own commercial television broadcasting began in Toronto and Montreal, and quickly expanded to other cities. The Canadian Broadcasting Corporation (CBC) aired many news programmes, and French-language Radio Canada featured René Lévesque's much-watched current affairs programme, *Point de mire*. Canadian public broadcasting also presented numerous cultural programmes, though such entertainment had a small, but influential, audience.

CANADA COUNCIL

The government also helped to foster culture through the Canada Council, *327* founded in 1957 in response to a key recommendation of the Massey Commission: a multitude of arts organizations—ballet companies, theatre troops (including the Stratford Shakespeare Festival), and orchestras— often pleading imminent bankruptcy, sought millions. Which projects to support proved a formidable problem, since the council had only a few hundred thousand dollars at its disposal. The council also gave grants to writers and scholarships to graduate students.

POPULAR CULTURE

Distinctive Canadian content in popular culture was decidedly limited. Listening to or watching *la Soirée du hockey*, or "Hockey Night in Canada," was a popular pastime of many Canadians on Saturday night. Fans avidly discussed the feats of Syl Apps, Maurice "The Rocket" Richard, and Gordie Howe, and celebrated the Stanley Cup triumphs of the Toronto Maple Leafs in the late 1940s and of the Montreal Canadiens in the late 1950s. English-speaking Canadians enjoyed newspaper supplements like the *Star Weekly* and *Weekend*, while French Canadians read a variety of tabloid newspapers. By the end of the 1950s, however, American mass-circulation magazines, among them *Time, Reader's Digest*, and its French edition, *Sélection du Reader's Digest*, accounted for 75 percent of the Canadian general-interest magazine market.

Most movies were American made, though some came from Britain or, in the case of the Quebec market, from France. The Canadian National Exhibition in Toronto always imported American talent, like Danny Kaye or Jimmy Durante, as the major attractions for its grandstand shows. Television brought in American variety shows like *The Ed Sullivan Show*, and American comedies like *I Love Lucy* and *The Jackie Gleason Show*. Canadian shows often imitated American cultural forms. French-language television had more native content: while it beamed a French-speaking Hopalong Cassidy, and many other programmes dubbed in French into Quebec living rooms and kitchens, it also carried original productions, like the series adapted from novelist Roger Lemelin's *La famille Plouffe*.

ENGLISH-CANADIAN LITERATURE

Canadian literature in both languages came into its own in the post-World War II era. In Montreal Hugh MacLennan published the celebrated novel *Two Solitudes*, with its theme that Canada's two major nationalities needed to demonstrate more mutual tolerance. In Vancouver, Earl Birney, an English professor at the University of British Columbia and part of a new generation of Canadian poets, acquired considerable renown for his collection of poems, *Now Is the Time*. W.O. Mitchell interpreted the struggles of a small-city Saskatchewan boy with Prairie realities in *Who Has Seen the Wind*, while Ernest Buckler, in *The Mountain and the Valley*, examined the dilemma faced by a brilliant and ambitious Nova Scotian boy who finds his creativity stifled by his deep attachment to rural life.

328

Mordecai Richler's *The Apprenticeship of Duddy Kravitz*, a portrait of a young Montreal Jewish entrepreneur, established the Montreal native as a successful novelist. Adele Wiseman's first novel, *The Sacrifice*, was strongly influenced by the experiences of her Russian-Jewish parents. In 1951 Morley Callaghan's highly acclaimed *The Loved and the Lost*, set in Montreal, appeared. Robertson Davies published a trilogy that examined the difficulty of sustaining a cultural life in Canada. Poet Dorothy Livesay won Governor General's awards for *Day and Night*, in 1944, and *Poems for Peace*, in 1947, while the versatile and flamboyant Irving Layton produced numerous volumes of love poems and prose.

FRENCH-CANADIAN LITERATURE

At the same time, an "esthetic thaw" came slowly to Quebec. In a manifesto entitled *Refus global*, artist Paul-Emile Borduas condemned asphyxiating orthodoxy and proclaimed the right to freedom of expression: his criticism cost him his teaching job and resulted in his departure from Montreal for New York and Paris. Novelists cast aside traditional themes of religion and rurality. Some, like Gabrielle Roy in *Bonheur d'occasion* and Roger Lemelin in *Les Plouffe*, used urban working-class settings. Others, like Anne Hébert in *Le Torrent* and André Langevin in *Poussière sur la ville*, forcefully portrayed personal dramas. Yves Thériault won international fame with *Agaguk*, a novel on the Inuit. Professional theatre troops proliferated, with some of their repertories supplied by Quebec playwrights. The play *Ti-Coq*, by Gratien Gélinas, encountered spectacular success and the film that followed attracted three hundred thousand spectators. Quebec culture seemed to have attained new vibrancy, despite the province's tiny market, few public libraries and bookstores.

Canadians generally continued to cherish conservative values. Books were often censored, particularly when they described sex scenes too explicitly. Movie censorship in all provinces regulated what movies Canadians saw. The British Columbia Moving Pictures Act, for example, outlawed films "considered injurious to morals or against public welfare, or which may offer evil suggestions to the minds of children." Alberta's censors watched carefully for "any materialistic, undemocratic, un-Christian propaganda disguised as entertainment." Sometimes the cuts produced films probably more objectionable than the original version. One Quebec film featured a scene in which a married man obtained a divorce so that he could pursue a love affair with his girlfriend; the censors in this still very Catholic province cut out the divorce scene—and the couple thus appeared to go on living happily ever after in unwed bliss!

329

RELIGION

The majority of Canadians still attended church or synagogue regularly. Religion was present in most schools across the country, even in so-called public schools. Pious Quebeckers knelt around the radio after supper for the "Family Rosary," and also read the *Annales de Sainte-Anne* or other religious material. Nevertheless, the times were changing. Less pious Quebeckers bought a million copies each weekend of sex-and-crime tabloids like *Allo Police*, which flourished in spite of—and possibly because of—the opposition of the Catholic church.

The quiet Sundays of English Canada (supposedly conservative Quebeckers managed to have fun on Sundays), also came under attack. It was said that, in Toronto, one could harmlessly fire a cannon ball down Yonge Street on Sundays, and the local press editorialized in favour of the maintenance of Toronto's "typically Canadian" Sunday. But the citizens of "Toronto the Good" voted in favour of Sunday sports in a plebiscite and, in December 1951, elected as their mayor Allan Lamport, a churchgoer who had pledged to make it possible to watch double-headers on Sundays at Maple Leaf Stadium. Across English-speaking Canada, provincial drinking restrictions that determined who could drink, where, and under what conditions, were increasingly challenged.

The late 1940s and 1950s were prosperous years for many Canadians. Consumers had more money to spend and new products to spend it on. Most workers easily found jobs and, in general, pay scales increased substantially. Governments went about the task of managing economic growth. Yet prosperity and the prevailing climate of optimism camouflaged the poverty and inequalities that were the lot of many Canadians. By the late 1950s, as the post-war boom appeared to have run its course, it was clear that attitudes and aspirations were evolving. Canadians in general now seemed convinced that it was time for a change. A new era was at hand.

NOTES

[1] Donald Creighton, *The Forked Road: Canada, 1939–1957* (Toronto, 1976), p. 185.
[2] Actually, Howe used a more earthy synonym; see Robert Bothwell and William Kilbourn, *C.D. Howe, A Biography* (Toronto, 1979), p. 320.
[3] Reginald Whitaker, *The Government Party: Organizing and Financing the Liberal Party of Canada, 1930–58* (Toronto, 1977), p. 175.
[4] David E. Smith, "Party Government, Representation and National Integration in Canada," in *Party Government and Regional Representation in Canada*, ed. by Peter Aucoin (Toronto, 1985), pp. 21–23.
[5] J.F. Hilliker, "No Bread at the Peace Table: Canada and the European Settlement, 1943–7," Canadian Historical Review, 51 (1980): 69–86.
[6] John W. Holmes, *The Shaping of Peace: Canada and the Search for World Order 1943–1957*, (Toronto, 1982), p. 36.
[7] Irving Abella, *Nationalism, Communism, and Canadian Labour: The CIO, the Communist Party, and the Canadian Congress of Labour, 1935–1956* (Toronto, 1973), p. 221.

Related Readings

Students interested in further readings related to topics covered in this chapter should consult in R. Douglas Francis and Donald B. Smith, eds., *Readings in Canadian History: Post Confederation*, 2d ed. (Toronto, 1986) the following articles: S.D. Clark, "Movements of Protest in Postwar Canadian Society," pp. 578–91; Edgar McInnis, "A Middle Power in the Cold War," pp. 544–60; and Kenneth McNaught, "From Colony to Satellite," pp. 560–68.

BIBLIOGRAPHY

General studies of this period include Donald Creighton, *Canada, 1939–1957: The Forked Road* (Toronto, 1976); J.L. Granatstein, *Canada 1957–1967: The Years of Uncertainty and Innovation* (Toronto, 1986); and Robert Bothwell, Ian Drummond, and John English, *Canada since 1945: Power, Politics, and Provincialism* (Toronto, 1981).

Among the works on prime ministers, see Dale C. Thomson, *Louis St. Laurent, Canadian* (Toronto, 1967); *One Canada: The Memoirs of the Rt. Hon. John G. Diefenbaker* (Toronto, 1975–77); and Peter Newman's very critical *Renegade in Power: The Diefenbaker Years* (Toronto, 1963). On the "Minister of Everything," read Robert Bothwell and William Kilbourn, *C.D. Howe: A Biography* (Toronto, 1979). J.M. Beck, *Pendulum of Power: Canada's Federal Elections* (Scarborough, Ont., 1968), and John Meisel, *The Canadian General Election of 1957* (Toronto, 1962), are also useful. Reginald Whitaker examines the Liberals in *The Government Party: Organizing and Financing the Liberal Party of Canada 1930–58* (Toronto, 1977). Walter D. Young studies the CCF in *The Anatomy of a Party: The National CCF, 1932–61* (Toronto, 1969). J.L. Granatstein looks at the role of federal bureaucrats in *The Ottawa Men: The Civil Service Mandarins, 1935–57* (Toronto, 1982).

On Canadian foreign policy of the late 1940s and 1950s, see James Eayrs, *In Defence of Canada: Growing Up Allied* (Toronto, 1980). Contemporary accounts by members of the Canadian foreign service include Escott Reid, *Time of Fear and Hope: The Making of the North Atlantic Treaty, 1947–1949* (Toronto, 1977), and John W. Holmes, *The Shaping of Peace: Canada and the Search for World Order, 1943–1957*, 2 vols. (Toronto, 1979, 1982). The first two volumes of Lester B. Pearson's memoirs, *Mike* (Toronto, 1972, 1973), are pertinent to the period. On the Korean War, see Denis Stairs, *The Diplomacy of Constraint: Canada, the Korean War and the United States* (Toronto, 1974). Post-war Canadian-American relations are discussed in R.D. Cuff and J.L. Granatstein, *Ties That Bind: Canadian-American Relations in Wartime from the Great War to the Cold War* (Toronto, 1977), and in their *American Dollars/Canadian Prosperity: Canadian-American Economic Relations, 1945–50* (Toronto, 1978); see as well Joseph T. Jockel, *No Boundaries Upstairs: Canada, the United States, and the Origins of North American Air Defence, 1945–1958* (Vancouver, 1987).

On union life, consult Charles Lipton, *The Trade Union Movement of Canada, 1827–1959* (Montreal, 1968); Gad Horowitz, *Canadian Labour in Politics* (Toronto, 1968); Irving Martin Abella, *Nationalism, Communism, and Canadian Labour* (Toronto, 1973); and Irving Abella, ed., *On Strike: Six Key Labour Struggles in Canada, 1919–1949* (Toronto, 1974). William Kaplan chronicles maritime labour strife in *Everything that Floats: Pat Sullivan, Hal Banks, and the Seamen's Unions of Canada* (Toronto, 1987).

On women, see the *Report of the Royal Commission on the Status of Women in Canada* (Ottawa, 1970); Micheline Dumont *et al.*, *Quebec Women. A History* (Toronto, 1987); and Pat Armstrong and Hugh Armstrong, *The Double Ghetto: Canadian Women and their Segregated Work* (Toronto, 1984). Patricia T. Rooke and R.L. Schnell, *No Bleeding Heart: Charlotte Whitton, A Feminist on the Right* (Vancouver, 1987) examines the evolution of this famous person.

CHAPTER SIXTEEN

Aboriginal Canada and the North since 1945

332   Over the past half-century Canada's native peoples have assumed much greater national importance, including a recognized place in the country's constitution. As late as the 1930s it was commonly believed that Canada's Indians were a vanishing people. In his *Indians of Canada* (1932), Diamond Jenness, the respected Canadian anthropologist, wrote: "Doubtless all the tribes will disappear. Some will endure only a few years longer, others, like the Eskimo, may last several centuries."[1] Far from biologically disappearing, however, Canada's native peoples are now increasing at a rate faster than the general population. Moreover, throughout much of the area termed the North by Canada's southern inhabitants, the native population predominates. The Inuit, Dene, and Métis constitute a numerical majority in the Northwest Territories. The Indians and Métis are also a sizeable minority in the Yukon Territory, in the northern sections of the four western provinces, and in Ontario, Quebec, and Labrador. Southern Canadian cities, such as Regina, Winnipeg, Edmonton, Saskatoon, Calgary, Vancouver, and Toronto, have large native communities.

For more than a century the federal government regarded Canada's native societies as transitory, rather than enduring. Ottawa worked after 1867 to change the southern Indians' traditional values and to assimilate them into the dominant society. It began applying assimilation policies in the Yukon and the Northwest Territories after 1945. Then, in the 1980s, the federal government—with wide public support—revised its policy. Owing to a dramatic native political renaissance in the 1960s and 1970s, and to the re-definition of Canada as a multicultural country, the native peoples in 1982 won formal recognition in Canada's new constitution. Instead of terminating special status, the Constitution Act of 1982, acknowledges and affirms existing treaty and aboriginal rights, and it defines the Indians, Métis, and Inuit as the aboriginal peoples of Canada.

Canada's Indians since Confederation

To understand the evolution in Canadian Indian policy and in Canadians' perception of their native peoples since 1945, a brief historical review is necessary (see chapter 3). Canadian politicians from the mid-nineteenth century onward regarded the Indians in the settlement areas as "foreigners," to be Christianized, "civilized" (educated in the ways of European society), and then assimilated into white society. One decade after Confederation, federal politicians consolidated all the laws pertaining to Indians in the Indian Act of 1876, as amended in 1880, which still governs Canada's Indians today.

THE RESERVE AND ENFRANCHISEMENT

The reserve became the central institution in southern Canadian Indian policy, a sort of temporary halfway house for the native trainees to stay while *en route* to the larger society. No provision was made for an increase in reserve size, because it was felt that the Indians would soon be assimilated or would simply die out. The mortality rate was indeed extraordinarily high. From 1881 to 1915 the registered Indian population in Canada actually declined from roughly 108 500 to 103 750. The outbreak of the Spanish flu epidemic in 1918 was responsible for the deaths of 3700 Indians, or more than 3 percent of the total population. The declining population at the turn of the century led a number of the Indian agents to pressure for surrenders of the reserve land to open it up to non-native farmers.

Attempts to assimilate Indians continued. To help introduce the values of the dominant society the Indian agents sent children from six to eighteen to church-run boarding schools where parents had no authority over their own children. The agents and missionaries also worked to change the Indians' native spiritual practices and to introduce Christianity. Yet this coercion failed, and an Indian identity survived even within native Christian congregations.

Throughout Canada most bands opposed enfranchisement, or the provision in the Indian Act that allowed those adult Indian males (deemed of good character, free of debt, and fluent in English or French) to apply to become British citizens with the right to vote and to have all other legal privileges. The "enfranchised" Indians in return lost their legal Indian status, and with it the right to live on a reserve. To speed up the process the federal government amended the Indian Act during World War I, making it easier for Indians living off the reservation and for Indian women married to non-Indians to renounce their Indian status. In the 1920s and 1930s the pressure on the Indians to assimilate increased to the point that the government altered the Indian Act, giving the Indian Department the power to end the Indian status of all Indians that it judged ready for enfranchisement (in force 1920-22; 1933-51). Ottawa never implemented its policy of forced enfranchisement, however, due to Indian protests.

CANADA'S NEW ATTITUDES TOWARD THE NATIVE PEOPLES AFTER 1945

Immediately after World War II Canadian attitudes towards the native peoples changed for several reasons. First, social scientists completely discredited the pseudo-scientific race theory, thus removing any basis for regarding Indians, Métis, and Inuit as inferior peoples. Second, the contribution of more than three thousand Indian volunteers to the war effort led many Canadian servicemen and citizens' groups to argue for better treatment of the native peoples. They urged the extension of the services of Canada's new post-war welfare state to its original citizens. Many more Canadians supported such an extension when, through the press and radio (and later in the 1950s through television), they learned of the impoverished health and living conditions of the Indian and Inuit. Finally, Canada's Indians underwent a political renaissance, and demanded change.

334

The Indian Association of Alberta, founded in 1939 and reactivated in 1944, took a leading role, for example, in the agitation for a review of the Indian Act. It participated with other provincial Indian organizations in the subsequent hearings of the Joint Committee of the House of Commons and the Senate on the Indian Act which sat in the late 1940s. The committee's recommendation that the Indian band councils be given more powers was eventually incorporated in the new Indian Act of 1951. While eventual assimilation still remained the government's goal, no longer would it be forced upon the Indians.

Throughout the 1950s and 1960s Canadians became more aware of contemporary native concerns. Minority rights became national and international issues. The civil rights movement in the United States led many Canadians in the 1960s to re-examine their own attitudes and treatment of Canada's native peoples. The Indian-Eskimo Association (now the Canadian Alliance in Solidarity with Native Peoples) was organized as a non-native support group in southern Canada in the early 1960s.

THE WHITE PAPER OF 1969, AND ITS AFTERMATH

The Liberal government of Pierre Trudeau inadvertently made the greatest contribution to a native resurgence in Canada. In 1969 the newly elected prime minister proposed a White Paper on Indian Affairs, a discussion document prepared without talks with native leaders. It called for the end—within five years—of the Department of Indian Affairs, the repeal of the Indian Act, the elimination of the reserves, and the transfer to the provinces of many of the responsibilities the federal government performed for Indians. Canada's Indians feared that they would immediately become citizens, their special status would end, and they would be pushed into the non-native Canadian society. The prime minister also announced his government's rejection of land settlements for that half of the country not under treaty. Overnight, young educated Indian leaders joined with native elders to oppose the government's position paper. The native leaders protested so vigorously that the Liberal government withdrew the White Paper. The opinion of six of the seven Supreme Court judges in the Nishga case of 1973 (that aboriginal rights still existed) also led the federal government to accept comprehensive claims in the areas of Canada not covered by treaties. Between 1970 and 1983 the federal government provided $96 million for Indian claims research, much of it in the form of loans. Native land claims are now underway in many parts of the country, particularly in British Columbia, the Yukon, and the Northwest Territories.

335

CONTEMPORARY LIVING CONDITIONS ON THE RESERVES

Much of the present urgency felt by Canada's 330 000 registered Indians for new agreements over land claims and over self-government has arisen from conditions on the reserves, and in urban communities (where 30 percent of Canada's Indians now live). Bands have sought economic development on the reserves and greater educational opportunities. Many Indians have left reserves (some with unemployment rates in the 1970s reaching 80 percent) to seek jobs in the city. While a number adjusted successfully, others did not. Many who arrived without any marketable skills found that they had simply traded unemployment at home for unemployment in the city.

Canada's native peoples stand at the very bottom, economically and socially, of all ethnic groups in Canada. Incomes among the average Indian family are only one-half to two-thirds of those of the average Canadian family. According to federal government statistics, the average Indian's life expectancy is approximately ten years less than that of the average Canadian. The high school completion rate for the Indian population has risen greatly since the 1950s, but it remains at one-quarter of the national average. The elders realize that to survive economically, the young need to acquire a knowledge of the ways of the larger society.

Many of the reserves are small and cannot economically support their population. A recent federally imposed change in the Indian Act would possibly add as many as 100 000 more people to the number of status Indians in Canada. Under the previous Indian Act, as revised in 1951, any status Indian woman marrying a non-status Indian, a Métis, or any other non-Indian automatically became enfranchised, which meant she ceased to be a status Indian. (Indian status gave the individual the right to live on a reserve, to participate in band government, to be exempt from taxes, and to have free medical services and post-secondary education.) In 1985 those who had been enfranchised were allowed to reapply for their Indian status.

In response Indian leaders have protested that the addition of thousands of newly registered Indians to band membership lists will create chaos on reserves, that the already crowded reserves cannot accommodate an influx of reinstated women, their non-Indian husbands, and children. The bands need more land, and increased funds. The federal government, they argue, should have left the membership procedure as it was, until Ottawa had completely overhauled the Indian Act with full Indian consultation, or until it had granted Indian self-government—for the Indian leaders contend that the Indian people themselves are in the best position to decide their own membership.

336

CURRENT INDIAN POLITICAL DEMANDS

The definition of aboriginal rights and the demand for self-government have become the major constitutional questions for Indian people today. Canada's new constitution of 1982 recognizes existing treaty and aboriginal rights, such as those outlined in the Royal Proclamation of 1763. Yet, at a series of four subsequent meetings (in 1983, 1984, 1985, and 1987), the prime minister, the provincial premiers, and native representatives failed to reach an agreement on both a definition of the meaning of the phrase "aboriginal rights " and of native self-government. A special House of Commons Committee on Indian Self-Government in 1983 endorsed the concept of full Indian control over matters such as education, child welfare, health care, and band membership. It reported: "Ending dependency would stimulate self-confidence and social regeneration." At the last constitutional conference in 1987, however, the objections of four provincial premiers to the lack of a definition of self-government prevented the addition to the constitution of a clause on the right to self-government.

CANADA
Northern perspective (computer-generated outline)

337

National Film Board of Canada.

A look at Canada's ten million square kilometres from "the North." The proposed territory of Nunavut appears in the centre and Denendeh is to the right.

The Métis, the Inuit, and the Federal Government

The Métis position differs from that of the registered Indians. The federal government has maintained that Canada's obligations to the Métis ended after Ottawa had dealt with the land claims under the Manitoba Act, and after it had issued land allowances (or a money equivalent) in the Northwest Territories in 1885 and 1899–1900. The federal government contends that the provinces have responsibility for the Métis. Even the total number of Métis in Canada is itself unknown, as an accurate count of mixed-blood people and non-registered Indians has never been taken; estimates vary between 200 000 and 800 000. The Métis reached the high point of their political struggle for recognition with their identification in Canada's new constitution as an aboriginal people. The Métis National Council, the political organization for the Prairie Métis, argues that this means they have a right to a land base and to self-government.

Of the three native groups, the twenty thousand Inuit have perhaps the best chance of achieving control of their remaining lands, for they still constitute the overwhelming majority of the population in the Arctic. The Inuit Tapirisat, a political organization which represents the people of the central and eastern Arctic, has evolved the idea of Nunavut as a territory where the predominantly Inuit population would be responsible for governing a quasi-province with power over the administration of justice, education, housing, land use planning, and wildlife management. The federal government has accepted Nunavut as a distinct possibility.

The Yukon and the Northwest Territories in the Early Twentieth Century

Over the past century the nature of native-white relations in Canada, and especially in the Yukon and the Northwest Territories, has changed enormously. Here the federal government only applied its full assimilationist policy after 1945, and here it has failed.

338

Three main native groups occupied the Yukon and the Northwest Territories in the early twentieth century: the Dene (pronounced "de-ne," or "de-nay," meaning, "the people" in the northern Athapaskan languages), the Métis, and the Inuit. The Dene lived in the Yukon and the Mackenzie River valley. The Métis moved into the Great Slave Lake area in the early nineteenth century and trace their ancestry to relationships between fur traders and Indian women. Others moved north after the Rebellion of 1885 and settled in the Mackenzie River valley. North of the tree line dwelt the Inuit, whose ancestors had migrated eastward across the Canadian Arctic several thousand years before the arrival of Europeans. Like the Dene, their name for themselves means "man" or "human being."

The History of the Dene to 1939

Originally the Dene obtained all their food and clothing from fish and game. They moved frequently, in winter travelling together in groups of a few families, then forming larger bands in the warmer months. While they had no concept of private land in the European sense, each group recognized distinct tribal areas. The Dene had established extensive trading among themselves, and therefore when European traders arrived in the late eighteenth century, they naturally bartered their furs for iron goods and weaponry. By the early twentieth century many Dene in the Mackenzie River valley had abandoned much of their own technology and had come to rely on the traders' iron products, textiles, tobacco, and tea.

In the mid-nineteenth century Christian missionaries had reached the Mackenzie River valley (Northerners often joke that the Hudson's Bay Company's initials literally stand for "Here Before Christ"). Two churches, the Roman Catholic and the Anglican, simultaneously launched and maintained missionary campaigns for nearly a century. The Roman Catholic church was favoured by the availability of the numerous priests and lay brothers of the Oblate order, and the assistance of nuns, particularly the Sisters of Charity, or Grey Nuns, a Canadian order. They established, as part of their work, permanent mission stations with schools, churches, and other buildings. The Anglicans had fewer helpers but they benefited from the support given them by the Hudson's Bay Company's English directorate. By the beginning of the twentieth century a rough division of Roman Catholic and Anglican spheres of influence had evolved in Dene country. The Anglicans predominated in the Yukon, the Oblates along the Mackenzie and Liard rivers and around Great Slave Lake. Further north the Anglicans arrived first among the Inuit. As in the Dene country to the south, a fierce denominational struggle soon broke out, waged between the Anglicans and Roman Catholics who followed their Protestant rivals northward.

More newcomers arrived at the turn of the century, when the introduction of steamboats on the Mackenzie and Yukon rivers brought sports hunters and prospectors north. As the land was generally unfavourable for agriculture, it remained free of settlers. Native northerners could still travel, hunt, trap, and fish without obstruction.

339

IMPACT OF THE KLONDIKE GOLD RUSH

The North-West Mounted Police arrived in 1894, just before the discovery of gold was made in 1896. After the gold rush began, the police and the Yukon Field Force, a contingent of two hundred Canadian regular soldiers, imposed law and order in a territory largely inhabited by American miners. The policemen's attitude towards the Dene was similiar to that of most other Canadians. Charles Constantine, the commander of the first mounted police expedition to the Yukon, described the Indians along the Yukon River as " ... a lazy, shiftless lot ... content to hang around the mining camps. They suffer much from chest trouble and die young."

Ottawa had no intention of signing a treaty with the Yukon Indians, as it did not want to confirm the Indians' possession of any potentially valuable lands in the west-central Yukon. Moreover, Ottawa believed that the gold rush would be transitory and, when it ended, the non-natives would leave. To save government expenditures, the Indians were encouraged to remain as hunters and trappers. In contrast to the policy in the south, Indians were not encouraged to live in settlements or to send their children to school. The assimilation policy was not applied in the North until after World War II.

After the collapse of the gold rush the Yukon's population continued to drop. The native peoples of the Yukon had immediately become a minority in their own homeland during the gold rush years, but after the economic bust the Indians re-emerged. They numbered 2000, or approximately one-half of the Yukon's diminished population in 1921. In the areas remote from the gold fields, they continued their old way of life of hunting and trapping, once again relatively undisturbed until the early 1940s.

Treaties with the Northern Indians

To the east of the Klondike gold fields the federal government did make treaties with the Indians. The passage of several thousand Klondikers through present-day northern Alberta and northeastern British Columbia on their way north had led to friction with the local Indians. The potential wealth of the Athabaska tar sands, as well as the need to avoid conflict with the Indians, had led the government to propose Treaty Eight in 1899–1900, by which the Indians surrendered present-day northern Alberta, northeastern British Columbia, and the area of the present-day Northwest Territories south of Great Slave Lake. Similarly, Imperial Oil's significant oil strike at Norman Wells in 1920 led the Indian Department to sign Treaty Eleven with the Indians north of Great Slave Lake in the Mackenzie River valley in 1921. Both treaties were hastily drafted and poorly explained to the Dene. In 1973 Mr. Justice William Morrow of the Supreme Court of the Northwest Territories expressed his opinion that neither treaty constituted a genuine cession of Indian land.

340

After the creation of Alberta and Saskatchewan in 1905, the federal government neglected what remained of the Northwest Territories. Only in 1921 did it establish a Northwest Territories branch within the Department of the Interior to oversee and administer the territories, with an office at Fort Smith on the Northwest Territories–Alberta border. The branch's activities were greatly curtailed in the 1930s with the onset of the depression. Anxious to cut expenditures, Ottawa adopted a "hands-off" policy and left the missionaries to continue providing most of the education and health services.

The native peoples suffered in the 1920s and 1930s from an influx of non-native trappers. Other newcomers also arrived. Aerial prospecting led in 1930 to the discovery of ores on the eastern shores of Great Bear Lake, where a silver-radium mine went into production at Port Radium. A gold-mining boom also began at Yellowknife Bay on Great Slave Lake, with several gold mines in operation in the late 1930s. But while some Indians obtained work in the mines, the Dene benefited little from the great mining discoveries.

THE HISTORY OF THE INUIT TO 1939

To the north of the Dene and Métis, the Inuit of the Arctic had developed over a period of several thousand years a highly specialized technology that used such local materials as stone, bone, skins, animal oils, and snow to make housing, clothing, light and heat, tools, and means of transport. In winter they lived in camps near the sea and in summer usually in inland hunting communities. Since the late sixteenth century the Inuit in the eastern Arctic occasionally met with European explorers searching for the Northwest Passage. In the late seventeenth and eighteenth centuries the Inuit in the Hudson Strait (leading into Hudson Bay) had made casual contact with the Hudson's Bay Company supply ships.

INUIT–WHITE RELATIONS

Since the eighteenth century a growing number of Europeans, particularly Englishmen, became interested in the maritime wealth of the Arctic waters. The Arctic bowhead whale arrived early each spring to feed on minute shrimps, or brit, that lived off the plankton. The whale's twenty-metre frame carried tons of blubber, desired for its oil to be used for fuel, for lighting, and as a lubricant. The merchants also prized the baleen, or plastic-like fibre found in its mouth, with which the whale strained the brit from the seawater. Until plastics were developed in the late nineteenth century, few substitutes existed for baleen.

341

Brief, dangerous, but highly lucrative voyages began from British ports to Davis Strait and to Baffin Island. The introduction of steam power after 1850 allowed the ships to penetrate farther and farther into the Arctic Archipelago. From mid-century British and American whalers faced a scarcity of whales in the Atlantic and thus began operating in Hudson Bay. Seeking a longer season and a second summer in the Arctic, many wintered over.

An economic interdependency arose between the Inuit and the whalers in the eastern Arctic as the Europeans began to rely on them as suppliers of fresh meat (to avoid scurvy) and as boat crewmen. The Inuit, glad to work for the new goods, particularly the guns and whaleboats, came to the whalers' settlements, sometimes in groups of as many as 200–300. These *Kabloonamiut*, as they were called in the Inuit's language, performed traditional jobs for the whalers: the men as hunters, and the women as seamstresses, making the whalers' winter clothing. The whaling master exercised only a loose authority, leaving the Inuit free to come and go as they pleased, as long as they brought in meat and skins.

Negative aspects for both the *Kabloonamiut* and the *Nunamiut* (those Inuit who stayed on the land) followed. Communicable diseases, against which the Inuit had no natural immunity, struck after contact with the whalers. In the western Arctic, around Herschel Island off the Yukon's northern coast where whaling developed in the 1890s, nine out of ten Inuit died from smallpox, tuberculosis, and measles. Losses were not always as great in the eastern Arctic, but they were high.

The *Kabloonamiut*'s dependency on the whalers' trade goods also became pronounced. Rifles had greater accuracy, range, and killing power than bows and arrows; iron kettles were lighter and more durable than those of stone; metal blades were sharper and stronger than ivory ones. A generation of *Kabloonamiut* grew up without mastering their parents' ancient skills and hunting lore. Many Inuit could not, for example, track down the breathing holes of the seals in the ice; fewer still could harpoon a seal from a kayak or approach it within harpoon range as it slept in the sun or lay on the surface of the ice. High-powered rifles had led them to forget the art.

When the whole population declined and as plastics replaced baleen in the early twentieth century, the whalers abandoned their Inuit helpers. Fortunately, trapping saved the Inuit during this crisis, providing them with the needed economic base. Natural furs still had an excellent market—fur farming remained in its infancy and synthetic furs had not yet been developed. Thanks to the growing middle classes, a rich southern clientele existed for the furs of the white fox and the muskrat, which was plentiful in the Mackenzie River Delta. Shortly after the whalers left, the Hudson's Bay Company and its great rival in the 1910s, Révillon Frères, moved north. The fur traders immediately reversed the trend toward population centralization, regular employment, and close cultural contact with whites. As the *Kabloonamiut* were not needed around their posts, the traders sent them back onto the land to trap.

342

THE CANADIAN GOVERNMENT AND THE INUIT TO 1939

The Canadian Government did little to protect its sovereignty in the Arctic, or to assist the Inuit before the outbreak of World War II. Canada had acquired Rupert's Land in 1870, and Britain had completed the transfer of Britain's Arctic Islands by an order-in-council in 1880, but apart from establishing police posts in the Arctic in the early twentieth century, Canada did little until the late 1940s to maintain its northern sovereignty. It left the Arctic and its Inuit population under the control of the police and, as in the Yukon and the Mackenzie River valley, avoided making extensive expenditures. This made it very difficult for the Inuit to survive during the depression, when the price of a silver fox pelt, which had brought sixty-nine dollars in 1929, fell to eight dollars in 1934. The Canadian Inuit expected that the white newcomers who had destroyed their old way of life would help them to get on their feet again, but they were mistaken.

Impact of World War II on the Territories

The outbreak of World War II had a great impact on both the Yukon and the Northwest Territories. Although the Americans had not yet formally entered the war, they helped Canada and Britain covertly before December 1941. After Denmark fell to the Nazis in the spring of 1940, the Americans assumed control of Greenland, while Britain occupied Iceland. The three powers co-ordinated their efforts to build an effective air-staging route to fly warplanes to Britain, via Greenland and Iceland. The major air base became Goose Bay at the head of Lake Melville in Labrador.

AMERICAN PRESENCE IN THE CANADIAN NORTH

With the Japanese surprise attack on the U.S. Navy fleet at Pearl Harbor in December 1941, Japan momentarily gained mastery of the Pacific and even captured two of the western Aleutian Islands in Alaska. The Americans rushed through a series of small airfields—a Northwest air staging route to Alaska—then they began plans for an all-weather highway. In 1942, the United States Army Corps of Engineers co-ordinated the construction teams that built the 2500 km highway from Dawson Creek in northeastern British Columbia to Fairbanks, Alaska. The next year the Public Roads Administration, an American civilian agency, directed the transformation of the rough military road into a permanent civilian highway, widening it, extending branch roads to the airstrips, and completing a telegraph line along this American highway built on Canadian soil. (Canada obtained control in 1946 after paying $120 million for the highway's various installations and services.)

343

The disaster at Pearl Harbor also led American defence planners to worry about the threat to energy supplies in the Northwest. The United States shipped all of Alaska's oil in slow and scarce oil tankers; these ships were now suddenly vulnerable to Japanese submarine attack. Could Imperial Oil's operating oil field at Norman Wells on the Mackenzie River be expanded? The Canadian Oil (Canol) project began as a proposal to make greater use of the Norman Wells oil field. Large-scale expenditures were made to build a pipeline to Whitehorse, a refinery, and a whole host of subsidiary facilities: an improved port on the Pacific, air strips, new roads, and winter trails. So anxious were the Americans to begin that they issued a contract for the construction of the pipeline two weeks before the Canadian government agreed to the project. For three years thousands of men worked on this second American project on Canadian soil. By 1944, General MacArthur had reversed the Japanese advance and the American navy controlled the eastern Pacific. Now totally unneeded, the completed Canol pipeline was shut down and the Whitehorse refinery dismantled and shipped south.

Developments continued simultaneously in the eastern Arctic. The Americans rushed through the construction of huge airfields at Churchill, Fort Chimo (now Kuujjuaq), and Frobisher Bay (Iqualuit) to ferry warplanes to Britain. By the time of completion, however, the greatly increased range of aircraft, and the growing success of transporting aircraft by sea convoy, eliminated the Allies' urgent need of these bases.

All of these sudden developments had an impact on the native peoples. In the Yukon the consequences of the building of the Alaska Highway proved as substantial as those of the Klondike Gold Rush. It meant the entry of approximately 30 000 men into the southern Yukon in 1942. Due to the Alaska Highway and Canol, Whitehorse's population rose temporarily in the early 1940s from 750 to 20 000. This influx of outsiders completely disrupted the Indians' way of life in the areas close to the highway, as the newcomers hunted and trapped along it.

The highway shattered the isolation of once remote Indian villages that now lay along its route. John Marchand, a doctor with the Public Roads Administration, noted that within less than one year of the Alaska Highway's completion, successive epidemics of measles, German measles, dysentery, jaundice, whooping cough, mumps, tonsillitis, and meningitis swept the area. When the boom finally ended after the war, many natives lost their low-paying jobs at a time when fur trade prices had declined. They became dependent on the newly available income from federal family allowances and old-age pensions introduced in the late 1940s.

344

Federal Policy after 1945

Seeing that the fur trade would not return to its former prominence after the late 1940s, the federal government began a policy of encouraging the Dene in both the Yukon and the Northwest Territories to move into settlements, find wage employment, and send their children to schools to learn the skills of an industrial capitalistic society. Ottawa provided new housing, better medical services, and new schools. A coercive element entered later. In the late 1950s school attendance became compulsory, and in many districts family allowance payments were tied to attendance. In order to remain with their children and obtain cash payments, Dene parents had to move permanently into town.

Like the Dene, the Inuit benefited very little from the massive American defence spending in the Northwest Territories in, and immediately after, the war years. Some Inuit around the new airfields obtained jobs as day labourers, work which was financially more rewarding than hunting and trapping; the drivers of the airfield garbage trucks, for instance, earned more than the best trappers. When defence spending fell immediately after the war, however, many of the jobs disappeared.

With the development of the Cold War in late 1940s the Canadian North again became an area of vital strategic interest to both Canada and the United States. Acting together the two countries worked to provide a warning system in the event of a Soviet nuclear attack on Canadian and American cities. The Soviet bomber threat led to the creation of some native employment around the new Joint Air Weather Stations (JAWS) and the chain of several dozen Distant Early Warning (DEW) Line stations built in the 1950s across the Arctic from Alaska to Baffin Island. The DEW Line allowed for four to six hours of warning of a manned Soviet bomber attack across the North Pole. Begun in 1954 and completed in 1957, the system remained in full operation for nearly a decade, until intercontinental ballistic missiles largely replaced the bomber threat. With warning time now calculated in minutes, rather than hours, the DEW Line lost much of its effectiveness.

In the 1950s the Canadian government also used a number of Quebec Inuit to affirm Canadian sovereignty. The Americans' intrusion into the Yukon and the Northwest Territories to build the Alaskan Highway and the Canol pipeline, and then their role in building the DEW Line system, had raised fears about Canada's sovereignty in the North. Recognizing that one of the surest grounds for Canada's claim of sovereignty in the Arctic is what is called "effective occupation," the federal government in the 1950s pressured Inuit groups in northern Quebec to relocate nearly 2000 km from their home. The migrants that established settlements on Cornwallis and Ellesmere Islands in the High Arctic lost contact with their own relatives and, the government's promises aside, found themselves in a much more inhospitable environment than that which they had left behind.

345

INUIT HEALTH AND EDUCATION AFTER 1945

The Canadian government made large-scale expenditures on Inuit health and education after World War II. In 1939 the Supreme Court of Canada had ruled that, for constitutional purposes, the Inuit were Indians and that therefore they were a federal responsibility. (Up until that point the federal government had argued that they were already Canadian citizens and, hence, not Ottawa's responsibility.) In the post-war era the federal government, anxious to eliminate economic want throughout Canada and to establish the structure of a modern welfare state, greatly expanded spending in the Arctic. This bound the Inuit to the settlements, as the government (as with the Dene) compelled them to send their children to school as a condition of obtaining the baby bonus. Then the government began a campaign against tuberculosis by x-raying and by immunizing as many Inuit as possible with anti-tubercular vaccine. Federal officials also sent hundreds of Inuit south by plane or by boat, if their condition demanded immediate hospitalization. The introduction of modern drug treatment for tuberculosis had miraculous results; by the 1950s the Department of Health and Welfare had lowered the high mortality rate.

Education became as important a concern as health and living conditions, with a system of state schools replacing those run by the missionaries. Each year the government flew hundreds of native children to centralized boarding schools and hostels. Eventually, day schools were opened in smaller centres, permitting many children to remain in their settlements. At first, the teachers taught the children in English (only in the 1960s was French introduced in northern Quebec), and provided little instruction about native ways. They used the basic southern Canadian curriculum and encouraged the native children to renounce their own culture, believing that they would assimilate more easily into the dominant society if they acquired its language and attitudes.

The federal government also constructed and staffed governmental nursing stations in each of the twelve widely separated Inuit settlements, from which the nurses could then visit fourteen other outposts. During the 1960s and 1970s, in both the Yukon and Northwest Territories, Ottawa also provided public housing and municipal services (water, power, fuel delivery, and waste disposal). The state left virtually no aspect of Inuit or Dene life untouched. The health and housing improvements throughout the Yukon and the Northwest Territories helped enormously. The native population in the Yukon almost tripled from 2200 in 1951 to 6000 in 1976 (out of a total population of about 20 000). In the Northwest Territories the Indian, Métis, and Inuit population nearly doubled in the same twenty-five-year period, from 13 000 to 24 000 (out of a total population of about 40 000). While the federal government had finally acted to help the Inuit and Dene in the North, there was a negative side to this intervention. Rarely, for example, did federal officials bother to consult the native peoples as to their wants or needs. They simply assumed, for instance, that the native peoples wanted to live in settlements and that they wanted to abandon their old culture and traditions.

Political Renaissance of the Dene and the Inuit

Political changes came to both the Yukon and the Northwest Territories after World War II. Whitehorse, the new transportation centre of the Yukon, became the territorial capital, replacing Dawson in 1953. Fourteen years later the federal government named Yellowknife as the new capital of the Northwest Territories, and it became the administrative centre for the Mackenzie River valley and the western Arctic. The federal government built Inuvik in the 1950s and made Frobisher Bay (Iqualuit) the administrative centre for the eastern Arctic. Hundreds of non-native southerners came north to run the new bureaucracies of the two territories. Others came north to work in the new resource industries. In both the Yukon and the Northwest Territories, non-natives controlled both territorial assemblies in the 1960s and early 1970s. While the natives still

347

National Archives of Canada PA-114838.

Prime Minister John Diefenbaker (in the centre) with four Inuit in Ottawa to attend a meeting of the Eskimo Affairs Committee, May 1959. The Eskimo Affairs Committee played an important role in initiating new federal policies for the Inuit in the years 1952 to 1962. The four visiting Inuit are: George Koneak from Fort Chimo (now Kuujjuaq), Quebec; Shinuktuk from Rankin Inlet on Hudson Bay; Jean Ayaruark from Rankin Inlet; and Abraham Ogpik from Aklavik in the Mackenzie Delta. The men are shown pointing out their settlements to the prime minister on a map of northern Canada.

constitute a majority in the Northwest Territories, they are outnumbered three to one by non-natives in the Yukon.

The natives were assigned a peripheral role, economically and politically, without any real voice in the administration of their country. A native political awareness arose in the Yukon in the late 1960s. Elijah Smith, an Indian leader in the Yukon, urged his people to start looking for guarantees to their rights to their homeland. A new generation of bilingual native leaders, men and women in their twenties—ironically, themselves products of the Indian boarding schools which had been established to assimilate them into the dominant society—came forward to help him with their aboriginal claims and to preserve the native cultures. In 1973 the Yukon Native Brotherhood (to become the Council of Yukon Indians later that year) began formal talks with the federal government about unsurrendered aboriginal rights in the Yukon.

The claims process began in the Mackenzie River valley in the late 1960s. As part of Canada's centennial in 1967, the federal government brought communities in the Mackenzie River valley together to celebrate the event. In effect, these gatherings helped to bring about a new political awareness and Indian pride. Discussions began in 1968 to form the first territorial organization, and in the following year sixteen chiefs from sixteen villages founded the Indian Brotherhood of the Northwest Territories (now the Dene Nation). In 1970 the Committee for the Original Peoples' Entitlement (COPE) was formed in Inuvik to protect the interests of the Inuit in the Mackenzie Delta, or Inuvialiut as the Inuit in the Western Arctic term themselves. Later, in 1973, the Métis formed their own association.

THE MACKENZIE VALLEY PIPELINE PROPOSAL

348 All native groups faced the possibility in 1972 that a Canadian pipeline carrying American oil and gas from the vast Prudhoe Bay discovery on the northeastern coast of Alaska would be built along the Mackenzie River valley. The major Christian churches and southern support groups offered assistance to the Indians and the Inuit to fight the project's immediate implementation.

The development of the multi-billion dollar Mackenzie valley pipeline seemed a certainty until 1973, when three events occurred in quick succession. First, the Supreme Court of Canada in the Nishga case in January 1973 recognized that aboriginal title existed. Second, Justice Morrow of the Supreme Court of the Northwest Territories accepted, in a decision of September 1973, that "notwithstanding the language of the two Treaties [Eight and Eleven], there is sufficient doubt on the facts that aboriginal title was extinguished." Third, in November 1973 the Cree Indians of James Bay momentarily secured an injunction halting the multi-billion dollar James Bay hydro-electric project, which had been begun before a native land claims settlement had been negotiated.

These important developments led Prime Minister Pierre Trudeau to reconsider immediate federal approval. Moreover, public pressure and the fact that the minority Liberal government depended upon NDP support in the House of Commons, made it politically imperative that Trudeau appoint a royal commission to investigate the pipeline project. In March 1974, he selected Thomas Berger, a former leader of the NDP in British Columbia and a legal expert on native and civil rights questions, as the commissioner.

No one expected Berger to undertake the massive study he then began. The federal government had hoped that the royal commission, like so many before it, would bury the issue, with its hearings held in Yellowknife far from the national media. Instead, Berger prepared to undertake a free-ranging, comprehensive environmental, social, and cultural impact study.

When pressured, he refused to be rushed, and even obtained $2 million of federal money to help special-interest groups prepare their submissions to the commission. The commissioner encouraged wide media coverage of the proceedings, with his staff contacting radio, television, newspapers, and even the National Film Board to ensure their presence at the hearings. The coverage swung public opinion in favour of the native and environmentalists' concerns. Berger himself held the community hearings, not just in Yellowknife but in thirty-four other settlements potentially affected by the pipeline. A thousand people participated, with sessions lasting at times from early afternoon until after midnight. The commissioner also held hearings in the major southern cities from Halifax to Vancouver.

Berger's final report in 1977 called for the prior settlement of native land claims and a ten-year delay on the development of the Mackenzie Valley pipeline. The report eloquently articulated in its pages the native peoples' concern that the North was their own distinct homeland, and not simply a resource frontier for southern Canada. The National Energy *349* Board in Ottawa, the national regulatory body, also rejected the proposed development in the Mackenzie River valley. For the first time in Canadian history, the native peoples had been fully consulted on a major resources development project. Their concerns about it contributed to the final decision to postpone the pipeline.

Nunavut and Denendeh

Since publication of the Berger Report, the idea of dividing the Northwest Territories has preoccupied native politicians. The government of the Northwest Territories submitted a plebiscite on the issue in 1982, one in which 56 percent of the votes cast favoured division. Later that same year the federal government accepted the proposal in principle. An Inuit constitutional forum representing Nunavut ("Our Land"), and a second the Western district, or to use the term most frequently used to describe the territory, Denendeh, a Dene word meaning "Land of the People," were formed to discuss how division might be accomplished. A major stumbling block became the proposed border between the two jurisdictions. To whom would the Inuvialiut, the Inuit of the western Arctic, adhere?

Despite blood ties with their fellow Inuit in the east, the Inuvialiut decided to keep their economic links with the west. The adherence of the western Arctic, rich in newly discovered oil and gas potential, to their proposed jurisdiction greatly pleased the Dene and the Métis. The addition of the Inuvialiut also helps to raise the native population in Denendeh to near-equality (15 000) with that of the non-natives (17 000). On January 15, 1987, leaders of the two constitutional forums confirmed in Iqaliut the decision to divide the Northwest Territories. If approved by the Northwest Territorial Legislative Assembly, in a Northwest Territories-wide plebiscite, and by the federal government, then division could occur by 1991.

Nunavut might well strengthen Canada's sovereignty in the Arctic, as its claims to the Northwest Passage are based largely on the Inuit's use and occupancy of the area. The voyages through the waters of the Canadian Arctic archipelago of the *Manhattan*, an American oil tanker in 1969, and the *Polar Sea*, an American ice-breaker, in 1985, have awakened Canadians to the uncertain status of their northern waters. Yet, as Gordon Robertson, a former deputy minister of northern affairs and national resources and secretary to the federal cabinet, has written: "The application of the laws of a Canadian Inuit government to an ice and water region used by them would be a valid and genuine form of occupation. "[2]

350

One other recent development deserves mention. In 1984 COPE, the political organization of the 2500 Inuvialuit in the Western Arctic, signed the first comprehensive settlement with the federal government in the Yukon and the Northwest Territories. In return for surrendering approximately 345 000 km² of land, they obtained title to about 90 000 km² (an area greater than the size of New Brunswick) and 13 000 km² of this includes the sub surface mineral rights. They also received $107 million. Both the Dene and the Inuit in the Central and Eastern Arctic have themselves refused similar offers, holding out for a complete territorial jurisdiction.

Just as one can speak of a "Quiet Revolution" in Quebec in the early 1960s, a similar transformation has begun in aboriginal Canada. The federal government has officially abandoned its assimilationist model. The native peoples have taken advantage of Ottawa's new openness to have their aboriginal rights and treaty obligations entrenched in the new Canadian constitution. No longer are the natives the passive victims of a paternalistic federal government. Throughout Canada, and particularly in the Northwest Territories, the original Canadians are currently striving to obtain self-government and economic control over their destinies.

The example of the Northwest Territories and, to a lesser extent, that of the Yukon, best illustrate the recent changes in the relationship between the Canadian government and the native peoples. Ottawa began to make major expenditures in the Northwest Territories and the Yukon in the 1940s. World War II changed southern perceptions of the North's military importance and of its economic potential. The government intervened in the late 1940s, 1950s and 1960s, by promoting development, establishing a military presence, and building new settlements. The wishes of the area's original inhabitants received little attention, however, until the mid-1970s. The Berger Commission on the economic, social, and environmental consequences of building a pipeline down the Mackenzie River valley marked the first occasion in which the government genuinely consulted the native peoples of northern Canada about their future.

The Dene and Métis of the Mackenzie valley and the Inuit of the eastern Arctic have recently made known their aspiration to form two new political jurisdictions. In 1982 the federal government accepted the proposal in principle, one which could lead eventually to provincial status for De-nendeh in the western part of the territories, and Nunavut in the eastern. If partition or even quasi-provincial status is achieved, Nunavut will have an overwhelming Inuit majority, and Denendeh would be roughly one-half native. Today the Northwest Territories already has the only native-dominated legislature in Canada.

NOTES

[1] Diamond Jenness, *The Indians of Canada* (Ottawa, 1932), p. 264.
[2] Gordon Robertson, "Nunavut and the International Arctic," *Northern Perspectives*, 15 (May–June 1987): 9.

Related Readings

R. Douglas Francis and Donald B. Smith, eds., *Readings in Canadian History: Post-Confederation* 2d ed. (Toronto, 1986), has an article on the North: see Richard J. Diubaldo, "The North in Canadian History: An Outline," pp. 594–605.

BIBLIOGRAPHY

For a review of Canadian Indian policy in the early twentieth century see E. Brian Titley, *A Narrow Vision. Duncan Campbell Scott and the Admin-istration of Indian Affairs in Canada* (Vancouver, 1986). Two important summaries of federal Indian policy are included in *As Long as the Sun Shines and Water Flows*, edited by Ian A.L. Getty and Antoine S. Lussier (Vancouver, 1983): George F.G. Stanley, "As Long as the Sun Shines and Water Flows: An Historical Comment," pp. 1–26; and John L. Tobias, "Protection, Civilization, Assimilation: An Outline History of Canada's Indian Policy," pp. 39–55.

Other valuable introductory studies of the Canadian Indian in the twen-tieth century include Hugh Dempsey *The Gentle Persuader. A Biography of James Gladstone, Indian Senator* (Saskatoon, 1986); Harold Cardinal *The Unjust Society. The Tragedy of Canada's Indians* (Edmonton, 1969)—a Cree Indian's indictment of Canadian Indian Policy; and Edgar Dosman's *Indians:*

The Urban Dilemma (Toronto, 1972). For an overview of native health, see G. Graham-Cumming, "Health of the Original Canadians, 1867–1967," *Medical Services Journal of Canada*, 23 (1967): 115–166. George Jasper Wherrett, "Tuberculosis in Native Races," in *The Miracle of the Empty Beds: A History of Tuberculosis in Canada* (Toronto, 1977), pp. 98–120, is also useful.

A great deal of work remains to be done on the history of the Métis in the twentieth century. D. Bruce Sealey and Antoine S. Lussier provide one of the few historical overviews in the final chapters of *The Métis: Canada's Forgotten People* (Winnipeg, 1975), pp. 143–194. Murray Dobbin reviews the Métis' political struggle in western Canada in *One-And-A-Half Men: The Story of Jim Brady and Malcolm Norris. Métis Patriots of the 20th Century* (Vancouver, 1981).

The literature on the native peoples of the Yukon and the Northwest Territories is extensive. Ethnographic background is provided in the following volumes of the *Handbook of North American Indians:* vol. 5, *The Arctic*, edited by David Damas (Washington, 1984); and vol. 6, *The Subarctic*, edited by June Helm (Washington, 1981). *Denendeh: A Dene Celebration* (Yellowknife, 1984) introduces the Dene of the Northwest Territories; Rene Fumoleau's *As Long as This Land Shall Last: A History of Treaty 8 and Treaty 11, 1870–1939* (Toronto, 1973) reviews the Dene's land claims. An overview of the Inuit in the early twentieth century is supplied by Diamond Jenness in *Eskimo Administration*, vol. 2: *Canada* (Montreal, 1964). William R. Morrison's *A Survey of the History and Claims of the Native Peoples of Northern Canada* (Ottawa, 1983) reviews that important topic. For a discussion of federal Indian policy in the Yukon, see Ken Coates, "Best Left as Indians: The Federal Government and the Indians of the Yukon, 1894–1950," *Canadian Journal of Native Studies*, 4 (1982): 179–204. The situation of the Dene in the Northwest Territories is reviewed by Michael I. Asch, "The Economics of Dene Self-Determination," in *Challenging Anthropology*, edited by David H. Turner and Gavin A. Smith (Toronto, 1979), pp. 339–51. Donald Purich *Our Land: Native Rights in Canada* (Toronto, 1986) deals with the topic of native rights nationally.

Several general studies of the North include Peter J. Usher, "The North: Metropolitan Frontier, Native Homeland?" in *Heartland and Hinterland: A Geography of Canada*, edited by L.D. McCann (Scarborough, 1982), pp. 411–56; and Morris Zaslow, *The Northwest Territories*, Canadian Historical Association Booklet no. 38 (Ottawa, 1984). An historical study is Morris Zaslow's *The Opening of the Canadian North, 1870–1914* (Toronto, 1971). Gurston Dacks emphasizes political developments in *A Choice of Futures: Politics in the Canadian North* (Toronto, 1981). Kenneth Coates provides a popular history of the North in *Canada's Colonies: A History of the Yukon and Northwest Territories* (Toronto, 1985).

Specific aspects of northern history are reviewed in W. Gilles Ross,

Whaling and Eskimos: Hudson Bay, 1860–1915 (Ottawa, 1975); William R. Morrison, *Showing the Flag: The Mounted Police and Canadian Sovereignty in the North, 1894–1925* (Vancouver, 1985); Kenneth Coates, ed., *The Alaska Highway: Papers of the 40th Anniversary Symposium* (Vancouver, 1985); Stanley W. Dziuban, *Military Relations Between the United States and Canada, 1939–1945* (Washington, 1959); Robert Page, *Northern Development: The Canadian Dilemma* (Toronto, 1986); and John Honderich, *The Arctic Imperative. Is Canada Losing The North?* (Toronto, 1987).

Two useful collections of articles are William C. Wonders, ed., *Canada's Changing North* (Toronto, 1971), and Morris Zaslow, ed., *A Century of Canada's Arctic Islands, 1880–1980* (Ottawa, 1981). A short survey of the Alaska Highway's construction is provided in William Morrison's "Uncle Sam's Warpath," *Horizon Canada*, number 76 (1986): 1820–24. William Stephenson writes of Canol in "Pipe Dreams," *Horizon Canada*, number 88 (1986): 2108–12. Two valuable overviews are K.S. Coates and W.R. Morrison, "Northern Visions: Recent Writing in Northern Canadian History," *Manitoba History*, 10 (1985): 2-9; and Bruce W. Hodgins and Shelagh D. Grant, "The Canadian North: Trends in Recent Historiography," *Acadiensis*, 16 (1986): 173–88.

353

CHAPTER SEVENTEEN

Quebec since 1945

Quebec has long fascinated historians, social scientists, journalists, and other observers of contemporary Canada. Developments since 1945 within Quebec help explain this interest. Here was a society, culturally and linguistically different from the rest of Canada and, indeed, North America that appeared to have been stagnating since World War II. Then, in 1960 it began to change dramatically when the Liberals took power and inaugurated what became known as the "Quiet Revolution." The Québécois talked about catching up with the "rest of North America" (though they usually made the comparisons with Ontario). Nevertheless, many of the reforms possessed considerable Quebec content and were not simply imitations of what was being done elsewhere. This era of change continued until 1980, though not always at the rapid pace of the years 1960–64.

What really attracted attention to Quebec was the development of a new nationalism within the province that had profound implications for the rest of the country. When Québécois complained of being second-class citizens in Canada and demanded increased recognition for the French language within the federal government and for the French-speaking minorities in the rest of the country, English-speaking Canadians had to respond. When various political movements and parties vied with one another in claiming greater political autonomy for Quebec—or even demanded outright independence—the future of Canada as a political entity appeared in doubt.

Quebec under the Union Nationale

Maurice Duplessis and the Union Nationale (UN) party first took power in Quebec in 1936, on the heels of the depression (see chapter 12). Defeated in 1939 by an electorate that believed that the Liberals could best prevent conscription, Duplessis made a surprising comeback in 1944.

Although the Liberal government of Prime Minister Adélard Godbout adopted a number of important measures while in office from 1939 to 1944—women gained the right to vote in provincial elections; a publicly owned hydro-electrical company, Hydro-Québec, was created; and school attendance was made compulsory until age fourteen—they lost support over issues linked to the war and to the federal Liberals, such as conscription and provincial autonomy. With Duplessis' return, the Union Nationale began an unbroken sixteen-year reign.

During the period 1945–60, Quebec changed in many respects. The province's population, like Canada's, increased rapidly, by 30 percent in the 1950s. Montreal alone gained 750 000 inhabitants, and the population of the city's suburbs mushroomed. Although 400 000 immigrants settled in the province, most of the population increase stemmed from a sharply higher birth rate.

Quebec also underwent rapid economic growth as investment—much of it foreign—increased greatly. The United States provided a market, along with development capital for resource industries like mining; as a result, vast new areas of the province, such as the North Shore, opened up. Employment in the principal manufacturing industries—food and beverages, clothing, textiles, iron and steel products—also rose significantly, but the major gains in jobs came in the tertiary sector, or the service industries.

355

Quebeckers, like other Canadians who had endured the sacrifices of depression and war, began to enjoy relative prosperity. Unemployment rates were low by contemporary standards, and wage gains outpaced inflation. Hourly wages for a seamstress in the cotton industry, for example, nearly tripled to $1.36 over the period 1945–60, while the salary of a day labourer in the construction industry more than doubled. Federal transfer payments, like family allowances and old-age pensions, also put more money in consumers' pockets, helping them to buy automobiles, kitchen appliances, televisions, and other goods. After having lived for so long in cramped quarters, a good number of Quebeckers were at last able to purchase a house; the less-fortunate majority could at least hope to rent a more modern and spacious apartment. Construction boomed; by 1960 nearly half of the housing in Quebec had been built since the end of the war.

The very conservative Duplessis, in office throughout this period, emphasized the importance of religious values and of respect for the established order. His government favoured private enterprise, encouraged the entry of foreign (largely American) capital, and kept taxes and provincial debts low. It built roads and bridges, especially in election years, and aided agriculture.

National Archives of Canada C-53641.

Quebec Premier Maurice Duplessis with Msgr. Joseph Charbonneau, Archbishop of Montreal. Relations between the two potentates became strained when Charbonneau sided with the workers during the Asbestos strike of 1949. Charbonneau was transferred to Victoria, B.C. soon afterwards.

Union Unrest in the Duplessis Era

Duplessis perceived militant union activity as a deterrent to investment and to further economic development. Union membership increased in 1945–60 from 25 to 30 percent of the labour force, and many strikes occurred, despite government regulations and the pro-employer bias of provincial labour boards. The government occasionally used the provincial police to protect strikebreakers or break up demonstrations.

One strike in particular—in the asbestos mines in 1949—took on great symbolic value—sociologist Jean-Charles Falardeau viewed it as a "quasi-revolution."[1] It lasted nearly five months and involved five thousand workers. The clergy, including Archbishop Joseph Charbonneau of Montreal, sided openly with the strikers (one of whose supporters was a young Montreal lawyer, Pierre Elliott Trudeau). Police intervention resulted in dozens of injuries and hundreds of arrests. The strike settlement, achieved thanks to the mediation of Archbishop Maurice Roy of Quebec, gave workers only a psychological victory; they made no significant material gains.

Non-unionized workers generally enjoyed less favourable working conditions than unionized employees. The government set a low minimum

357

National Archives of Canada PA-151688.

Montreal's slums in 1949, home to thousands of the city's disadvantaged citizens.

wage, which especially affected large numbers of working women and immigrants. Other glaring inequalities, which the government did little to alleviate, also cast a pall over the general atmosphere of prosperity. Thousands of Montrealers with incomes below the poverty line lived in the tenements of St. Henri. Inhabitants of outlying regions like Abitibi and the Gaspé peninsula had per capita revenues only half of Montreal levels. Average wages of French Canadians as a group were inferior to those of most other ethnic groups within the province.

The educational system did little to promote equality among Quebec's citizens. The government spent heavily on school construction, but in 1951, fully 70 percent of the schools had only one room; most had neither electricity nor running water. The great majority of primary school teachers were women, and wages—the minimum was six hundred dollars a year—did nothing to attract qualified personnel into the profession. The few high schools that existed were poorly equipped. Church-managed classical colleges, which offered an eight-year course after elementary school, were twice as numerous for boys as for girls; their task was to educate the elite. Few students went on to university: in 1960, Quebec's universities had only twenty thousand full-time students, with half of them from Quebec's English-speaking minority. A mere 15 percent were women.

OPPOSITION TO DUPLESSIS

In the 1950s, Duplessis' opponents became increasingly vocal. They included political opponents, union leaders, some members of the clergy, the newspaper *Le Devoir*, as well as intellectuals like Pierre Trudeau who, with Gérard Pelletier, published a left-wing magazine, *Cité libre*, which was uncompromisingly hostile to the Union Nationale. Several university professors, among them Dominican priest Georges-Henri Lévesque, dean of the faculty of Social Sciences at Université Laval, also criticized the government. These critics wanted a more liberal, modern Quebec. They differed considerably, as historian Michael Behiels has recently shown, in their views on nationalism.[2]

Duplessis' adversaries attacked the Union Nationale's corrupt political and electoral behaviour. They showed how the party machine shamelessly extorted money from nearly every commercial establishment and entrepreneur in the province, and then used it to buy political support so as to ensure re-election. Election day witnessed such abuses as stuffed ballot boxes, police intervention in favour of government candidates, and "telegraphs," whereby electors voted under false identities. These practices demonstrated clearly, as journalist Pierre Laporte pointed out in a series of articles after the election of 1956, that elections are not "won by prayers alone."

The church was also denounced for its generally uncritical support of Duplessis in return for subsidies for church schools, hospitals, and social agencies. As well, critics censured the government for unprogressive attitudes in areas such as labour relations, education, and health. They denounced incompetent civil servants chosen primarily for their political loyalty. They claimed that the government's economic development policies resulted in a virtual giveaway of the province's natural resources to foreigners. They blamed Duplessis for his obstinate refusal to accept federal money to finance necessary social, educational, and other programmes.

They decried the Union Nationale's neglect of urban Quebec, a failure symbolized by the government's refusal to revamp an outdated electoral map that blatantly favoured rural areas. By 1956, some urban ridings had more than 100 000 voters, while many rural districts counted fewer than 10 000.

Anti-Duplessis forces also deplored *le chef*'s vendetta against opposition groups. Duplessis had sought to discredit left-wing opponents by linking them with communism, in a blatant effort to make easy political capital at a time when anti-Soviet sentiment in the West was strong. His government went even further by applying the notorious "padlock law" of 1937 that authorized police to lock premises from which alleged communist activities were conducted. In other attacks on civil liberties, the government brought hundreds of Jehovah's Witnesses before the courts for distributing brochures on the streets, and had them fined and imprisoned. Moreover, Duplessis often ran the Legislative Assembly as a personal fiefdom, with total disregard for parliamentary procedure.

359

RE-EVALUATION OF THE DUPLESSIS ERA

Nevertheless, in their harsh appreciation of the Duplessis record, the critics do ignore certain important factors. Patronage, though rife, was hardly limited to Quebec (although in certain other provinces it was carried on more subtly). Duplessis' refusal of federal funds for roads, universities, and other programmes appeared negative (although it probably brought dividends from nationalist voters on election day), but this was his means of blocking Ottawa's aggressive incursions into areas of provincial jurisdiction. Duplessis welcomed foreign capital, just as prime ministers Lomer Gouin and Louis-Alexandre Taschereau had done before him (see chapters 8 and 11). Such investment provided jobs and opened up new areas of the province for development. The government's spending policies were conservative, but they kept down the public debt and taxes.

Perhaps more telling is the fact that the UN enjoyed very substantial public support while it was in power. Fifty percent of Quebeckers and more than 60 percent of French-speaking electors voted for it. Although the over-represented rural counties were its base of support, the UN carried most of the urban districts as well, with the exception of the English-speaking areas of the island of Montreal. Even in 1960, a tiny shift of votes would have assured the Union Nationale's re-election. Yet by this time not only Duplessis but also Paul Sauvé, his popular successor, were dead, and the once-powerful UN appeared a spent force compared to the Liberals with their capable new leader, dynamic team, and revitalized programme. Perhaps many of those who later viewed the Duplessis era as Quebec's *grande noirceur*, or "Dark Ages," tended to compare the sombre realities of the Union Nationale years to their own heady visions and ambitious aspirations—not surprisingly, they found the Union Nationale regime wanting.

Jean Lesage and the Quiet Revolution

The term "Quiet Revolution" was coined by a journalist to describe the years 1960–66 during which Liberal leader Jean Lesage and his *équipe du tonnerre* brought rapid but non-violent change to Quebec. Actually the major changes had taken place by 1964. Nevertheless, some observers with a mind to historical continuity point out that the Union Nationale, when it returned to power in 1966, continued the reforms, as did the Liberals under Robert Bourassa after 1970; the Parti Québécois also had an agenda of reform which it implemented in 1976–80. Thus, it might be said that the Quiet Revolution, in spite of pauses, lasted for two decades.

360

Although the Liberals came to power with numerous reforms in 1960, they had little idea of how much they would be able to accomplish. Lesage's Cabinet contained a few forward-looking personalities like René Lévesque and Paul Gérin-Lajoie, and Lesage added others later. It harboured as well many solid conservatives who, while they accepted the need for change, did not want to revolutionalize Quebec society. When, for example, the UN attempted in 1960 to discredit its opponents by pointing out that the Liberals threatened the Roman Catholic church's role in Quebec life, the Liberals countered by publishing biographical sketches of their own candidates that emphasized the numbers of priests, nuns, and brothers among their relatives. Jean Lesage was described as having fought for Catholic schools for the "Eskimos" and as having had an audience with Pope Pius XII.

LIBERAL REFORMS

Once in power the Liberals ended electoral corruption; they also cleaned up much of the petty patronage practised by the Union Nationale, though in so doing they alienated many supporters who wanted a share in the spoils now that their party was at last in power. Early in its mandate, the government also set up a royal commission, presided over by Monseigneur Alphonse-Marie Parent of Université Laval, to examine Quebec's educational system. Then it established a ministry of Education to oversee educational concerns. Paul Gérin-Lajoie, the minister, set about regrouping the province's hundreds of school commissions into fifty-five regional districts. The government built large, "polyvalent"—or comprehensive—secondary schools, improved teacher training, revised curricula, and broadened access to educational facilities. The church retreated. Actually it had little choice, since Quebec's post-war population explosion meant that increased human and financial resources—resources that the church simply did not possess—had to be devoted to schooling. As well, recruitment into the orders had slackened noticeably during the 1950s.

Though educational reforms constituted a very important part of the Quiet Revolution, change pervaded all sectors of Quebec society. In 1962, after heated Cabinet debate, René Lévesque convinced Lesage to nationalize the province's private electrical power companies and to merge them with the Crown corporation, Hydro-Québec. That giant company contributed enormously to the development of the province over the next two decades. The government also set up the *Société générale de financement* to serve as a holding company that would acquire small companies in difficulty. This was but one example of the government's active intervention in the province's economy. In addition, such steps served to promote a more dynamic francophone presence in an economy dominated by capital from outside the province.

361

The government improved the financial situation of Quebec's municipalities and established the ministry of Cultural Affairs, though the new minister, former Liberal leader Georges-Emile Lapalme, protested bitterly the paltry budget given the department. In the important sector of labour relations, the government revised the labour code and, significantly, gave the right to strike to most employees in the public sector, with the exception of police and firemen. Progressive measures in the field of health care included the establishment of a provincial hospitalization insurance plan—this had been one of the Liberals' major electoral promises in 1960. Their campaign literature presented a cartoon in two segments comparing hospital care in the Union Nationale era to what the Liberals pledged. On the left, the bad old days: the patient arrives at the hospital, bounced around on his stretcher by two uncaring orderlies, as a hand is thrust forth from the admissions window. Beneath is the caption: "How much do you earn?" To the right, the Liberal future: the patient is reclining comfortably in bed, a celestial smile on his face, while a nurse standing beside him inquires gently: "What can we do to help you?"

QUEBEC-OTTAWA RELATIONS

Finally, in relations with Ottawa, Lesage took an aggressive autonomist stance. He created the department of Federal-Provincial Affairs and named himself minister. Shortly after arriving in power, he promised to end the conditional subsidies by which the federal government paid part of the cost in return for determining the conditions of the programmes, and Lesage demanded financial compensation for those federal programmes

Courtesy Gilles Savoie.

Contemporary Montreal features skyscrapers which dwarf the tallest structures that old Montreal boasted: church steeples.

362

in which Quebec did not participate. As the spectre of separatism raised its head, he also insisted that Ottawa turn over more tax money to Quebec in view of the "prior needs" of that province. Ottawa, he asserted, was taking in more money than it needed, leaving the provinces financially starved. After the Pearson government in Ottawa unveiled its proposals for the Canada Pension Plan in 1963, Lesage responded (successfully, as it turned out) with his own plan that gave the province enormous sums of money that it could invest. To keep a watchful eye over all such questions, Lesage also took on the financial portfolio.

The Quebec government established the *Caisse de dépôt et placement du Québec* to administer funds from Quebec's own pension plan. Particularly in the late 1970s the *Caisse* sponsored the expansion of a number of francophone-controlled firms in Quebec, and purchased shares in Canadian corporations. It used its ownership role to advance the promotion of French Canadians to the boards of directors of these corporations, thus increasing francophone involvement.

The Quiet Revolution thus changed dramatically the face of Quebec. Sociologist Guy Rocher sees these years as a "cultural mutation," signifying that, beyond the structural reforms, Quebeckers' basic attitudes and values changed.[3] The transformations announced the end of what remained of traditional clerical society as the influence of the Roman Catholic church waned.

Québécois also acquired a new confidence in themselves that brought them to challenge the inequalities they faced as French-speaking Canadians. They denounced a Canada in which the federal bureaucracy spoke only English, in which French enjoyed no official recognition in nine provinces, and in which the economy functioned—even within Quebec—largely in English. Here indeed were the makings of a new nationalism.

Revolution and Reaction

Perceptions of the Quiet Revolution have varied considerably. Many in the urban middle class viewed it as the birth of a modern Quebec or, as sociologist Marcel Rioux expressed it poetically, "the reappearance of a spirit of independence that had frozen in the course of the long winter that had endured for more than a century."[4] For this group, the Quiet Revolution signified needed reforms in the important sectors of education, political life, the social services, the civil service, and the economy. A more modern Quebec offered obvious advantages to both them and their children.

The breathless pace of change upset many conservative Quebeckers. Rural Quebec felt ignored and grew nostalgic for the Duplessis era. Disadvantaged citizens in French-speaking districts of Montreal also felt bypassed by the major thrust of the Quiet Revolution, as large-scale spending on higher education and the rapid growth of the civil service failed to benefit them. Other Quebeckers were unhappy with the seemingly perpetual structural changes in education. For some, the arrival of the state in the schools meant that religion was being ruthlessly driven out. "Give Jean Lesage breeches and a beard and he'll be a Castro," Union Nationale Opposition Leader Daniel Johnson warned. In rural Quebec, where hundreds of small schools had been closed and children were being bussed long distances to large impersonal institutions, discontent was rife. After his defeat in 1966, Lesage complained that "education beat us," and his biographer Dale C. Thomson found much evidence that change in this sector "generated more discontent than satisfaction."[5]

The Lesage era was also a time when big government and bureaucracy, coldly technocratic and often insensitive to the needs of the individual, came to Quebec. Higher spending and increased taxes won Lesage the politically disadvantageous nickname of "Ti-Jean LaTaxe." In the realm of labour, public-sector unions became more demanding and began to use their newly acquired right to strike. Lesage was being increasingly criticized for his "arrogance," a characteristic that came to the fore during the election of 1966, when he campaigned virtually alone. Conservatives felt that there must be pause in the implementation of change.

Lesage was also attacked by a small but vocal minority on the left. Some urban Quebeckers doubted the government's continuing commitment to

363

reform, especially after 1964. The marxists and socialists who wrote for magazines like *Socialisme* and *Parti pris* went further and called for the overthrow of capitalism. Militant left-wing nationalists viewed Lesage's objective of greater autonomy for the province as insufficient. They favoured separation, with the creation of an independent French state, as outlined in the programme of Pierre Bourgault's *Rassemblement pour l'indépendance nationale* (RIN). The RIN and a right-wing separatist group, the *Ralliement national*, managed to win 8.6 percent of the votes in the election of 1966. Presuming that the RIN took votes from the Liberals, its very presence enabled the UN to win in several close races.

RETURN OF THE UNION NATIONALE TO POWER

364   The Union Nationale regained power in 1966, thanks to strong support in rural Quebec and to Lesage's failure to redraw the electoral map. Indeed, though it won the largest number of seats, the UN received 7 percent fewer votes than the losing Liberals. People wondered what would become of the Quiet Revolution, whether Johnson would attempt to undo the reforms the Liberals had put in place. In fact, the Union Nationale under Johnson (and then his successor, Jean-Jacques Bertrand, who became premier after Johnson's sudden death in September 1968) neither proposed spectacular new reforms nor attempted to turn back the clock. In the field of education, Johnson proceeded to apply the recommendations of the Parent commission and began implanting the *Collèges d'enseignement général et professionnel* (CEGEPs), junior colleges where Quebec students enrolled in occupational programmes or prepared for entrance into the universities. It also established the public Université du Québec, which opened campuses in several regional centres.

During the late 1960s Quebec society became increasingly polarized between left and right over issues like labour–management relations. Strike activity, notably in the public sector, increased dramatically, and as elsewhere in the Western world at this time, protests shook institutions like the colleges and universities.

In Quebec the protest movements took on a distinct national and cultural colouration. Tension within the province, as well as between English and French Canada, and Ottawa and Quebec, accordingly grew. Before winning power, Johnson had published a manifesto, *Egalité ou indépendance*, in which he warned that if French Canada could not achieve equality within Canada, there would be no choice but to seek independence. Johnson set out his claims for equality for French Canadians during the Confederation of Tomorrow Conference organized by Ontario Premier John Robarts in Toronto in November 1967.

Johnson sought more than linguistic equality for French Canadians. In keeping with Quebec's time-honoured political tradition, he also wanted greater autonomy for the province. He argued that Quebec, as the home of more than 80 percent of French-speaking Canadians, represented one of Canada's two major ethnic communities or "nations," and that a new constitution should recognize this fact through an appropriate division of powers. Ottawa and most of the other provinces stated that they were ready to discuss the issue, but Pierre Elliott Trudeau, Canada's prime minister after 1968, warned that he would not allow federal authority to be diminished. (Some English-speaking Canadians had vigorously denounced his predecessor, Lester B. Pearson, for appeasing "greedy" provinces and thus helping to "balkanize" the country.) Moreover, to Pierre Trudeau, the federal government represented all Canadians—not just English-speaking Canadians— and he believed Ottawa could and should act to further linguistic equality across the country.

The Debate on Language

Conflict over language was inevitable in Quebec after the Quiet Revolution. Many *Québécois* felt that their language did not occupy the position it deserved in the province. The great majority of English-speaking Quebeckers knew little French, and thus communication between French- and English-speaking Canadians was, of necessity, in the language of the minority. The powerful Montreal business establishment was English-speaking, and included few French Canadians. In the stores of downtown Montreal, service in French was frequently unavailable. Commercial signs in Montreal were often in English only.

Quebec's English-speaking community possessed its own institutions, including schools, universities, newspapers, hospitals, and municipal councils. This was the only province where the linguistic minority—in this case, English-speaking—could function entirely in its own language; no French-speaking minority in the English-speaking provinces came close to occupying such a position. Moreover, census statistics confirmed that French Canadians outside Quebec were, except in eastern Ontario and northern New Brunswick, fighting a losing battle with assimilation. Only in certain areas could they be assured of getting at least part of their education in French. In addition, most jobs required a knowledge of English.

Since Confederation, Quebec residents had enjoyed the right or privilege to choose whether their children would be educated in French or English. In practice, however, the great majority of immigrants to Quebec since World War II, seeing little reason to learn French, had enrolled their children in English-language schools to assure their integration into the English-speaking community. Demographers warned that if current trends continued, francophones in Montreal would constitute a minority by the year 2000. For Québécois worried about the survival of their language, "free choice" of the language of education represented a serious threat.

CONFLICT OVER ENGLISH-LANGUAGE SCHOOLS

The first conflict over the language of education erupted in the Montreal Island community of St. Leonard, where the Catholic school board's French-speaking majority voted in 1967 to convert an English-language school, attended mainly by children of Italian origin, into a French-language school. The crisis symbolized the determination of many French-speaking Quebeckers to ensure that children of non-English origin enrolled in French schools, but it also demonstrated to the English-speaking community that the traditional free choice of the language of education was in jeopardy.

366   Both groups pressured the government to support their positions. The UN adopted legislation to preserve the status quo, thereby generally satisfying the non-French population. But among French-speaking Quebeckers, the legislation unleashed storms of protest. Language became a full-fledged political issue, although Quebeckers were divided over what should be done.

A Polarized Quebec

The 1970s constituted a difficult period for Quebeckers as issues like language, Quebec's future political status, union unrest, inflation, and other economic problems divided the province. In 1970, in the midst of an economic downturn, the Liberals led by youthful economist Robert Bourassa returned to power.

The new government soon stumbled from crisis to crisis. Shortly after assuming power, the Liberals were confronted with the "October crisis." Since the 1960s, a terrorist fringe group, the *Front de libération du Québec* (FLQ), had been placing bombs in mailboxes and stealing sticks of dynamite. The climax of the FLQ's activities occurred in October 1970, when extremists kidnapped James Richard Cross, a British trade representative in Montreal, and then Pierre Laporte, a Quebec Cabinet minister, and murdered the latter. The federal government now intervened, relegating the Bourassa government to a secondary role. It invoked, for the first time in peacetime, the War Measures Act, which enabled police to arrest several hundred citizens on suspicion of being sympathetic to the revolutionaries. Nearly all of these people were eventually released with no charges being laid against them.

Bourassa appeared equally hesitant in 1971 when, after lengthy discussions on the constitution, he finally said no to the Victoria Charter, a

367

National Archives of Canada PA-129838.

These young spectators must have been impressed as the army was deployed in Montreal during the October Crisis of 1970.

package of constitutional proposals, including an amendment formula and a bill of rights, assembled by the federal government. Hopes for a renewed federalism then dissipated. The Liberals also had to face growing animosity from public sector unions, whose leaders spoke ominously of the need to overthrow the regime and to replace the capitalist system with socialism. Contract negotiations with the unions led to painful public service strikes and even, in 1973, to the arrest and imprisonment of the three major union leaders.

BILL 22

Nor could Bourassa escape from dealing with the complicated language question. His solution was Bill 22, which aimed at increasing the use of French in the work place mainly through persuasive measures. In regard to the language of education, the bill gave access to English-language schools only to children of English mother tongue and to other children of non-French origin who could pass a language test. It also created enrollment quotas for English schools in each school district. Bourassa may have hoped to satisfy the moderates, but on the language question this group was small. In the end, Bill 22 pleased no one. Nationalists com-

Canapress Photo Service.

Charles de Gaulle, President of France, making his famous "Vive le Québec libre!" speech in Montreal during the Centennial celebrations in 1967.

plained that the law was ineffective and that Protestant school boards interpreted it with the greatest possible latitude in order to boost enrollment in English schools. The English-language community and ethnic groups denounced the law bitterly as arbitrary and even totalitarian. The issue cost Bourassa support in the election of 1976, when he lost to the Parti Québécois.

Perhaps historians will judge the first Bourassa regime more kindly than contemporary observers. It has been argued by the defenders of the multi-billion dollar James Bay hydro-electric project that, despite the damage it has caused to the livelihood of Quebec's native peoples as well as to the northern environment, it has proven economically successful. The Bourassa government also introduced a provincial medicare programme and adopted a provincial charter of human rights one of whose articles made Quebec the first Canadian province to protect homosexuals from discrimination.

The Rise of Nationalism

In the late 1960s nationalism appeared on the rise, with calls for constitutional reform, language legislation in Quebec, more bilingualism in the federal government, and an increased French presence in Quebec's economy. Some English-language journalists blamed a few individuals for this new and worrisome trend. They accused Jean Lesage and Daniel Johnson of undermining Quebeckers' loyalty through their aggressive stances in relations with Ottawa. In particular, they censured French President Charles de Gaulle for the support he gave to the cause of independence by his celebrated cry of "Vive le Québec libre," uttered from the balcony of Montreal's City Hall during the Expo 67 celebrations.

Politicians may have deliberately adopted nationalist slogans to gain votes in elections. Yet the real roots of protest went much deeper; nationalism had been a force in Quebec since at least the early nineteenth century, and it was thus not a new phenomenon in the 1960s.

Contemporary nationalists, however, tended to be members of the new middle class—teachers, civil servants, and journalists, and even, in some cases, of the business and professional communities. Cynics have delighted in pointing out that this group had a vested interest in nationalist causes. A bilingual civil service in Ottawa, for example, would create job openings for francophones. But these nationalists also resented the inferior position that francophones occupied in Canada and, to a certain extent, in Quebec itself. Nor were they insensitive to events elsewhere in the world. The movements of national liberation in Africa and Asia, and the struggle of American Blacks for civil rights, reminded many French Canadians of what they perceived to be their own condition. In one poignant autobiographical account, *White Niggers of America*, journalist and FLQ theorist Pierre Vallières portrayed French Canadian workers as cheap labour, as exploited second-class citizens who had no control over society and the economy.[6]

369

It was one thing to advocate nationalist causes, and quite another for a nationalist party to take power and use the provincial government to promote these causes. For this to happen, nationalists—and especially independentists—had first to join forces in a single movement. Unification proved relatively easy: René Lévesque, who left the provincial Liberal party in 1967 and established the *Mouvement Souveraineté-Association*, had the prestige and stature needed to rally the great majority of nationalists. The instrument he used was the new Parti Québécois (PQ), founded in 1968.

RISE OF THE PARTI QUÉBÉCOIS

The rise of the Parti Québécois was little short of meteoric. Quickly realizing that only a small minority of Quebeckers considered themselves to be unconditional independentists, party leaders set out to convince more moderate nationalists that independence would make it possible to implement reforms that would greatly improve their lot. While in opposition, the Parti Québécois succeeded in linking nationalism to a variety of social causes, and was thus able to build a relatively broad coalition of supporters.

The rising percentage of *péquiste* votes confirmed the success of this strategy. The party won one-quarter of the vote in the election of 1970; in that election economic problems, particularly a high unemployment rate, brought Quebeckers to favour the Liberal party whose leader, Robert Bourassa, promised to create 100 000 jobs. Three years later, although the Liberals took virtually all the seats in the National Assembly, PQ support nevertheless increased to one-third. Then, in 1976, with slightly more than 40 percent of the vote, the Parti Québécois won an election contested by three major parties.

Many *péquistes* saw their victory as a vote for independence, the first step in the march towards national liberation. Certainly, the "happening" in the Paul Sauvé Arena in Montreal on the night of November 15, as party militants savoured victory, proved that hopes were high. Other observers, however, saw the PQ success simply as a vote for good government, a vote against the scandal-ridden Bourassa regime. The PQ after all had promised that it would not try to separate Quebec from Canada until the decision was approved in a referendum. Most voters therefore believed that they were voting only for a change in government.

Quebec under the Parti Québécois

The new PQ government pursued reforms that continued the Quiet Revolution of the 1960s. In order to democratize Quebec politics, it overhauled the electoral law to prohibit large—mainly corporate—contributions to political parties, thus preventing powerful interests from "buying" favourable legislation. The government also introduced a no-fault system of automobile insurance, covering all personal injuries sustained; private companies continued to insure drivers for damage to vehicles. It brought in agricultural zoning legislation designed to protect inceasingly scarce good farm land, much of which had been gobbled up by urban sprawl since World War II. It set up a dental health care plan for children, adopted new legislation to protect consumers, and froze tuition fees for university students at the lowest levels in Canada. It also supported unions through an anti-strikebreaking law, which management bitterly opposed.

In contrast to Bourassa's vacillation on the language question, the Parti Québécois appeared much more uncompromising. Yet, on many occasions after 1968, that issue threatened party unity. René Lévesque frequently had to intervene against militant hardliners who favoured the elimination of publicly financed English-language schools. Then, in 1977, the gov-

370

ernment adopted a charter of the French language, Bill 101, with the intention of making Quebec as overwhelmingly French as Ontario was English. The bill specified that English-language schools would be open only to children who had at least one parent educated in English in Quebec. The language of the work place was (with a few exceptions) to be French, and professionals were required to have a knowledge of the French language. Most signs were to be posted in French only.

Though the legislation proved popular among the province's francophone majority, Quebec's English-speaking minority expressed deep resentment. Between 1976 and 1981, nearly one-fifth of Quebec's anglophones, including one-quarter of the adults aged 20 to 34, left the province. At the same time, a large number of corporate head offices in Montreal, complaining of language legislation, high taxes, and poor relations with unions, moved westward, mainly to Toronto. The added pressures in favour of French in the work place forced many of the anglophones who remained in Quebec to become bilingual. (The courts also considerably moderated several parts of Bill 101.)   *371*

It is of course difficult to measure the full impact of Quebec's controversial language legislation. Nevertheless, by the mid-1980s, a majority of immigrant children were enrolled in French schools. More workers could earn their living in French, and more francophones held upper-level positions in business. The stipulations concerning the language of signs assured that Montreal "looked" more French than in 1970. Adversaries of Bill 101 warned that the legislation would hurt economic development in the province; and it may have. At the same time, perhaps no other solution existed to the language problem during these years. It would have been impossible to promote aggressively the use of French while not undermining the important, even dominant, role of English in Quebec, particularly in the province's economy.

THE REFERENDUM DEBATE

Of greater interest to Canadians than the language question, which was basically an internal Quebec issue, was Quebec's referendum on political sovereignty that was to decide Quebec's—and Canada's—future. The Parti Québécois shrewdly worded the question by which it asked Quebec voters for a mandate to negotiate political sovereignty together with an economic association with the rest of Canada. In the hope of getting majority support, the government appealed both to Quebeckers' desire for change and to their more conservative instincts by asking only for the right to negotiate. There was to be no unilateral declaration of independence. The campaign debate was fierce, dividing families and friends, but without violence. Claude Ryan, Robert Bourassa's successor as the Quebec Liberal leader, led the *non* forces. Prime Minister Trudeau intervened late in the campaign, and promised unspecified constitutional change if Quebeckers voted *non*.

On May 20, 1980, Quebeckers defeated the referendum proposal by a 60–40 margin. While almost all non-French-speaking Quebeckers voted no, the French-speaking population divided virtually down the middle. Analyses of the vote showed that anglophones, Quebeckers of non-French and non-English origins, the older age groups, the economically disadvantaged, and those with relatively little education tended to vote *non*, while the *oui* received support from younger age groups and from people with more education and higher incomes.

A Difficult Decade

372   The mood of the early 1980s in Quebec was pessimistic. The 1981–82 recession dramatically cut employment in the resource and manufacturing industries. Unions suffered membership losses as well as rising unpopularity among a public weary of strikes and agitation. Quebeckers complained about the declining quality of education and, as in other provinces, the universities bitterly condemned the government's stringent cutbacks in financing.

Nor did the outcome of the constitutional debate cause much rejoicing in Quebec. The federal government's proposals for a new constitution gave Quebec none of the powers that its provincial governments had consistently claimed since 1960, and that a discussion paper issued by Claude Ryan's provincial Liberal party urged during the referendum campaign. Moreover, Ottawa managed to isolate Quebec by playing it off against the other nine provinces. During the celebrations on April 17, 1982, when Queen Elizabeth II proclaimed Canada's new constitution, neither Premier Lévesque nor Liberal Opposition leader Claude Ryan was present. The enormous energy expended by Quebeckers on debating constitutional issues since the early 1960s appeared to have had few lasting effects.

Perhaps Quebeckers were looking for balance when they re-elected the Parti Québécois in 1981: they had said no to the separatist government's constitutional proposition in May 1980; in 1981 they said no to the strongly federalist provincial Liberal party. Some *péquistes* regretted the victory, warning that the PQ needed a spell in opposition and that the portents were unfavourable for a second mandate; they turned out to be right. The government had to face an economic slowdown as well as a severe budget crisis that forced reductions in services and increases in taxes. Its draconian measures to recover part of the salary increases granted to the public sector alienated the unions that had so enthusiastically endorsed the Parti Québécois while it was in opposition before 1976. Moreover, the years of social and economic reform seemed far in the past as a new conservative mood gained strength throughout the Western world, including Quebec.

The national question, however, would not go away. After all, the first article of the PQ programme stipulated that the party would work towards sovereignty-association. René Lévesque's decision to put the issue aside for the foreseeable future provoked a dramatic revolt within the party in late 1984 and early 1985; several veteran Cabinet members, among them Camille Laurin, the father of Bill 101, and Jacques Parizeau, the minister of Finance, resigned. As the party's popularity fell, pressures increased to force René Lévesque to quit. His resignation in June 1985 perhaps helped clear the air; it did not, however, repair the split in the party. Even with the new leader Pierre-Marc Johnson, son of the former Union Nationale premier Daniel Johnson, the party was not in a position to wage a strong campaign in the election of December 1985. The result was a return to power of the Liberals under their reincarnated leader, Robert Bourassa. Continued discontent in the party led to the resignation of Johnson, a moderate on the sovereignty-association issue, in late 1987.

373

CURRENT CHALLENGES IN QUEBEC

Today, Quebec faces several challenges. Unemployment stands significantly higher than in neighbouring Ontario, which has much more heavy industry and a more rapidly expanding service sector. Poor markets for many minerals have hurt the province's resource industry. Inefficient tariff-protected industries like textiles and furniture have come under considerable competition from imports. Protection abroad, especially in the important American market, threatens some exports. Montreal, once Canada's premier city, searches for ways to restore some of its past greatness.

Potentially more dangerous for Quebec's future are demographic trends. Should the province's low birth rate continue to drop or even stabilize at present levels, Quebec's population will begin declining early in the next century. In addition, relatively few immigrants now choose Quebec as their new home because of linguistic and especially economic factors. Quebec's declining share of Canada's population obviously portends declining political weight as well, especially in comparison to Ontario.

Finally, although Quebec in the foreseeable future will remain French-speaking, the French language will continue to be spoken only by a minority in Canada and by an infinitely smaller minority in North America. The threat of assimilation will continue to weigh heavily, and the French-speaking community will be forced to continue to search for ways to give their language and culture new vitality.

By the late 1980s Quebec seemed destined to evolve for a time in a less-dramatic fashion. The politicization of Quebec society, a phenomenon that marked the 1960s and early 1970s, faded away; the now middle-aged champions of yesterday's nationalist causes appeared disillusioned, while younger Quebeckers worried about finding jobs. The once hotly debated constitutional issue became simply a question of finding a suitable compromise that would enable Quebec to adhere to the Canadian constitution. When the federal government and all the provincial premiers, including Quebec's Robert Bourassa, reached agreement on this question at Meech Lake in 1987, and when the Quebec National Assembly became, in June, the first legislature to approve the accord, opposition within Quebec was restrained. As for language, while the subject was far from dead, it stirred up less tension than in the 1970s, as English-speaking Quebeckers adapted to a Quebec that was more French and French-speaking Quebeckers espoused less radical positions.

374

NOTES

[1] J.-C. Falardeau, *Bulletin des Relations industrielles*, 4 (1949): 68, quoted in Fraser Isbester, "Asbestos 1949" in *On Strike: Six Key Labour Struggles in Canada 1919–1949*, edited by Irving Abella (Toronto, 1974), p. 163.

[2] Michael D. Behiels, *Prelude to Quebec's Quiet Revolution: Liberalism versus Neo-Nationalism, 1945–1960* (Montreal, 1985), pp. 84–120.

[3] Guy Rocher, *Le Québec en mutation* (Montréal, 1973), p. 18.

[4] Marcel Rioux, *La question du Québec* (Paris, 1969), p. 104.

[5] Dale C. Thomson, *Jean Lesage and the Quiet Revolution* (Toronto, 1984), p. 309.

[6] The original French title is *Nègres blancs d'Amérique* (Montréal, 1968).

Related Readings

For this chapter, consult the following article from R. Douglas Francis and Donald B. Smith, eds., *Readings in Canadian History*, 2d ed. (Toronto, 1986): Richard Jones, "English-Canadian Attitudes to French Canada, Yesterday and Today," pp. 617–25.

BIBLIOGRAPHY

Chapters 17 to 20 of Susan Mann Trofimenkoff's *The Dream of Nation: A Social and Intellectual History of Quebec* (Toronto, 1982) review this period. Recent research on modern Quebec is summarized in Paul-André Linteau, René Durocher, Jean-Claude Robert, and François Ricard, *Histoire du Québec contemporain– II : Le Québec depuis 1930* (Montréal, 1986). A good general interpretation in English is Kenneth McRoberts and

Dale Posgate, *Quebec: Social Change and Political Crisis* (Toronto, 1980). Michael Behiels, ed., *Quebec Since 1945* (Toronto, 1987) contains useful essays and documents.

On the Duplessis years see Conrad Black, *Duplessis* (Toronto, 1977); Herbert F. Quinn, *The Union Nationale: Quebec Nationalism from Duplessis to Lévesque* (Toronto, 1979); and, for a brief sketch, Richard Jones' Canadian Historical Association booklet, *Duplessis and the Union Nationale Administration* (Ottawa, 1983). Michael Behiels, *Prelude to Quebec's Quiet Revolution: Liberalism versus Neo-Nationalism, 1945–1960* (Montreal, 1985) examines the ideological conflicts among Duplessis' opponents.

Dale C. Thomson studies the early 1960s in *Jean Lesage and the Quiet Revolution* (Toronto, 1984). Ramsay Cook evaluates the Quiet Revolution in "Has the Quiet Revolution Finally Ended?", in *Canada, Quebec, and the Uses of Nationalism* (Toronto, 1986), pp. 105–118. This volume also contains several other important articles on modern Quebec. For an account by a journalist of the Bourassa years, see L. Ian MacDonald, *From Bourassa to Bourassa: A Pivotal Decade in Canadian History* (Montreal, 1984). Henry Milner reviews the 1960s and early 1970s in *Politics in the New Quebec* (Toronto, 1978). On the separatist movement in general, consult William D. Coleman, *The Independence Movement in Quebec, 1945–1980* (Toronto, 1984). On the Parti Québécois, see Graham Fraser, *PQ: René Lévesque and the Parti Québécois in Power* (Toronto, 1984); Peter Desbarats, *René: A Canadian in Search of a Country* (Toronto, 1976); and René Lévesque, *Memoirs* (Toronto, 1986). Dominique Clift explains the decline of nationalism in *Quebec Nationalism in Crisis* (Montreal, 1982).

The constitutional question is examined extensively by Edward McWhinney, *Quebec and the Constitution 1960–1978* (Toronto, 1979), and in his *Canada and the Constitution 1979–1982: Patriation and the Charter of Rights* (Toronto, 1982). John R. Mallea, ed., *Quebec's Language Policies: Background and Response* (Quebec, 1977) analyses the language question. Ronald Rudin provides an excellent study of Quebec's Anglophone community in *The Forgotten Quebecers: A History of English-Speaking Quebec, 1759–1980* (Quebec, 1985). Georges Mathews has written a provocative analysis of population trends: *Le choc démographique* (Montréal, 1984). Jean Hamelin chronicles the recent evolution of the Roman Catholic Church in *Histoire du catholicisme québécois: le XXe siècle: II—De 1940 à nos jours* (Montréal, 1984). The experience of women in Quebec is covered in Micheline Dumont *et al.*, *Quebec Women. A History* (Toronto, 1987). Denis Monière's *Ideologies in Quebec* (Toronto, 1981) is a useful intellectual history. Jacques Rouillard examines the history of one major union federation in *Histoire de la CSN, 1921–1981* (Montréal, 1981). The most famous strike of the Duplessis years is analysed by Pierre Elliott Trudeau, ed., *The Asbestos Strike* (Toronto, 1974)—originally published in French as *La grève de l'amiante* (Montréal, 1956).

375

CHAPTER EIGHTEEN

The English-speaking Provinces since 1945

376   The intense discussion of the Canada–Quebec question after 1960 tended to obscure two important realities. First, English Canada was not a monolith; and, in fact, the bonds of inter-regional and inter-provincial unity within English Canada were not really as cohesive as proponents of a "dual Canada" seemed to believe. Second, in spite of the substantial coverage that the media gave the dramatic events in Quebec, important changes were transforming the other provinces as well.

A history textbook, *Canada: Unity in Diversity*, published in the mid-1960s, acknowledged the importance of the regions and devoted separate chapters to their study.[1] Provincial politicians have also strongly affirmed their region's distinctive character and special problems. Many commentators supported this cause. In a book that set out the discontent of the West, Alberta civil servant Owen Anderson asserted that "Quebec has its own distinctive brand of nationalism rooted in a distinctive cultural milieu, but no more so than Western Canada."[2] Those who championed the interests of the Atlantic provinces, the Prairies, British Columbia, or the North, bitterly noted that central Canadian observers labelled expressions of western and Maritime discontent with the slightly disparaging term "regionalism"; at the same time, journalists and academics in Toronto and Montreal elevated Quebec regionalism to the level of nationalism. The implication was that Quebeckers were battling for collective rights while other Canadian malcontents were selfishly demanding more attention and financial help from Ottawa.

Substantial economic differences, with political, social, economic, and cultural ramifications, do exist among the nine provinces with English-speaking majorities. They mould regional identities and protect local interests, especially against encroachment by the federal government; they also contribute to friction among the regions and with Ottawa. Regionalism has been a theme throughout Canadian history and no less so after 1945 and particularly after 1960.

The Atlantic Provinces

Canada's four easternmost provinces—Newfoundland, Nova Scotia, New Brunswick, and Prince Edward Island—are often considered as one unit. Their combined population is less than one-tenth of Canada's total. Few immigrants settle there, and out-migration has often been substantial. During the period 1951–71, for example, fully 15 percent of Atlantic Canada's inhabitants left the region. Since representation in the House of Commons is determined by population, slow growth has meant a declining voice in Ottawa and limited political influence.

As early as 1949, Newfoundland Premier Joseph R. Smallwood proposed a union of the four eastern provinces (an idea that dates back to Confederation) (see chapter 2) which would enable them to increase their bargaining power in Ottawa. In 1970 the Deutsch Commission on Maritime Union recommended "full political union as a definite goal." But grassroots support for such a step was lacking, and only four years later Nova Scotia Premier Gerald Regan pronounced Maritime union "as dead as a door nail." A number of regional programmes and bodies, like the Council of Maritime Premiers, were created, but co-operation did not signify union. In 1977 Premier Alexander Campbell of Prince Edward Island could still complain: "We are four separate, competitive, jealous and parochial provinces. ... [We] do not have a regional identity. ... Our only common rallying points are poverty and a regional inferiority complex, self-destructive negative attitudes, and a belief ... that Ottawa has all the answers, all the power and all the money."

377

PROBLEMS OF THE ATLANTIC ECONOMY

The major problems of this region have historically been economic. The provinces' economies remain relatively undiversified and rely heavily on agriculture, forestry, fishing, and mining. Export prices for products of the primary sector often fluctuate wildly in international markets. Few manufacturing industries locate in this area, since distances from major markets are too great and local markets too small. Consequently, unemployment remains high, afflicting 10–20 percent of each province's workforce in the mid-1980s.

Not surprisingly, inhabitants of the Atlantic provinces have ceaselessly decried the regional disparities of which they are the major victims. Before World War II central Canadians largely ignored Maritime discontent. Residents of Canada's more favoured regions blamed Maritime problems on their inhabitants' alleged unprogressiveness. A comment in 1935 by R.L. Calder, a well-known Montreal lawyer, was all too typical: Maritimers prefer "to sit on the country store steps ... chew apples and talk politics."

More recently, as historian David Alexander put it, many central Canadians continued to dismiss Atlantic protest as "an illogical and petty resentment of the inexorable march of industry into southern Ontario."[3]

Atlantic complaints and demands have had some impact since the 1960s. Through the Atlantic Development Board, which funded economic development projects, equalization grants, and other subsidies, the federal government has helped create jobs and ensure that the area can offer its citizens services similar to those provided by wealthier provinces. Federal transfer payments comprise about 50 percent of provincial revenues in the region. Also, in 1969, the newly established federal Department of Regional Economic Expansion began offering incentives to encourage companies to locate in less-favoured areas, such as the Atlantic provinces, to alleviate regional inequalities. In practice, however, gains were modest. Rick Desbrisay, chairman of the Atlantic Provinces' Chamber of Commerce, contended in 1986 that the hundreds of millions of dollars pumped into the region by Ottawa simply "kept the gap from widening."

378

FEDERAL-ATLANTIC RELATIONS

For many residents of Atlantic Canada, the problem has been how to ensure generous and continued federal aid. Since 1930 the region has not experimented in any substantial way with third parties to convey protest, and Maritime MPs have been more concerned with maintaining party solidarity than with safeguarding provincial interests. Though Maritimers appeared to have little impact in determining how Canada's great national issues should be resolved, federal elections helped direct some federal monies eastward in the pre-1957 era. As political scientist Reginald Whitaker noted, the elections were a "means whereby cash from St. James St. [Montreal] could flow into the hands of [Liberal] party workers and voters in a chronically depressed region."[4] In 1957, however, protest in Atlantic Canada led many to support Diefenbaker's Conservatives. At the provincial level, Atlantic Canada either elected Liberals who strongly defended provincial interests, like Joey Smallwood in Newfoundland, Louis Robichaud in New Brunswick, and Angus Macdonald in Nova Scotia, or they chose Conservative governments during the long years of Liberal rule in Ottawa under Pierre Trudeau.

Historian George Rawlyk defines Maritime attitudes towards the federal government as "ambivalent."[5] Confederation has yielded obvious benefits for the Maritime provinces, but most Maritimers believe that Ottawa's policies have brought far more prosperity to central Canada. Despite perennial manifestations of economic discontent, Atlantic Canadians have generally defended the principle of a strong federal government, even in the 1960s and 1970s when many Canadians elsewhere sought to weaken federal authority. Maritime discontent—as strong as it has been and still is—has not, since the turn of the century, been able to find a vehicle in local separatist movements, mainly because few Maritimers could argue convincingly that the region would be better off without Canada.

The region's problems can be seen from another point of view. Though federal spending has brought needed funds into provincial treasuries and individuals' pockets, economist Thomas Courchesne contends that such transfers have made the four provinces "wards of the [federal] state."[6] The provinces have been encouraged to pressure Ottawa to increase federal transfers, thus ultimately deepening their dependence on Ottawa. Federal funds for economic development have reinforced regional disparities, destroyed incentives for local rehabilitation, and damaged Canada's international competitiveness. For Courchesne, the cycle of dependence can be broken if the provinces are given greater autonomy to pursue their own economic strategies. The Atlantic Economic Council has suggested that the region invest heavily in human capital and in organizational structures rather than in industrial plants, and that it work to favour regional economic integration.

379

NEW BRUNSWICK

Speaking of Atlantic Canada as a whole belies the very real differences among the four provinces comprising it. New Brunswick's major difference with the other three provinces lies in the ethnic and linguistic mix of its population, one-third of which is French-speaking. Long at a disadvantage both economically and linguistically, the French-speaking Acadians have sought and, to some extent, achieved greater equality. In the early 1970s, Acadians confronted Moncton's mayor, Leonard Jones, an adamant opponent of bilingual municipal services. Jones' obstinacy—which students from the Université de Moncton underlined by depositing a severed pig's head on the mayor's doorstep—probably served as a catalyst for the Acadians' struggle. The Parti Acadien, formed in 1972 to promote Acadian interests, never succeeded, however, in drawing Acadians' loyalty from the established parties.

In 1968 New Brunswick adopted an Official Languages Act that was largely an affirmation of rights that did not yet exist in reality. Then, through the 1970s, the provincial government cautiously proclaimed and applied the various clauses of the legislation. Attitudes changed but slowly. A 1978 survey showed that more than half of New Brunswick's francophones saw themselves as victims of discrimination, while three-quarters of the province's anglophones denied the existence of such discrimination.

In the 1960s New Brunswick underwent a period of rapid social change under the Liberals led by Louis Robichaud, the province's second Acadian premier. Robichaud's Equal Opportunity programme aimed at improving the lot of the province's poorer citizens who lived mainly in rural areas in the north and east; in particular, the government greatly expanded health, social, and educational services. This activity generated fierce opposition among anglophones in the south, who regarded it as proof of a costly Liberal plot to "rob Peter to pay Pierre."

A major opponent of Robichaud's Equal Opportunity plan was the powerful K.C. Irving. A biographer claimed that "surely no individual in any single Canadian province ... ever held so much raw economic power."[7] In addition to three thousand gas stations, the Irving family's business interests include trucking and bus lines, shipbuilding, huge forest reserves, paper and saw mills, the province's English-language daily newspapers, and radio and television stations.

380

In the 1970s Conservative Premier Richard Hatfield attempted several experiments designed to stimulate New Brunswick's economy and to compensate for the decline of the agricultural sector. Forest and mining industries did expand, and the federal government made substantial grants. But one notable industrial venture, the Bricklin automobile project, in which the provincial government invested heavily, failed totally. Premier Hatfield came under increasing attack in the 1980s for government plans to extend bilingualism, for his flamboyant lifestyle (Liberal critics nicknamed him "Disco Dick"), and for some ministers' personal use of public funds. In October 1987, New Brunswick's voters elected the first Liberal government in that province since 1970. The Liberals won all fifty-eight seats in the legislature, only the second time in Canadian history that a provincial party has done so. (In 1935 the Liberals won all 30 seats in the Prince Edward Island legislature).

NOVA SCOTIA

Nova Scotia, the most populous and prosperous of the four Atlantic provinces, has the most diversified economy. Fishing is the most valuable primary industry, but agriculture, mining, and forestry are also significant. Tourism is an important source of income, and the service sector is more developed than in the other three provinces. Secondary industry is frequently linked to the processing of primary products. Some areas of the province, mainly Cape Breton Island, have suffered chronically high unemployment as local industries such as coal, steel, and heavy water (a compound of hydrogen and oxygen), have declined. Nor have federal incentives been able to attract large numbers of new companies to the province. The discovery of gas and oil off the Atlantic coast, together with an agreement on offshore oil development in 1982, raised hopes for new revenues. But the federal government's decision to reduce funding for drilling, as well as a general shift in interest to Newfoundland's more promising oil fields and a decline of oil prices in the mid-1980s, have left these hopes unfulfilled.

Economic issues have dominated provincial politics in Nova Scotia. According to political scientist J. Murray Beck, the Liberals and the Conservatives have alternated in power partly because urbanization and in-migration have broken down traditional party loyalties.[8] Each party has produced major personalities like the Liberals' "All's well with Angus L." Macdonald (the election slogan proved highly successful) and the Conservatives' Robert Stanfield, often considered the builder of modern Nova Scotia. Although his government improved education and paved roads, Stanfield's priority was economic development. He created Industrial Estates Limited to invest in local enterprises, but serious losses followed its initial successes. Gerald Regan's Liberal government in the 1970s also planned many development projects, including an oil refinery complex on the Strait of Canso that was to strengthen Nova Scotians' industrial base, but the harsh economic realities of the late 1970s brought the Conservatives, led by John Buchanan, back to power.

381

PRINCE EDWARD ISLAND

Political scientist Frank MacKinnon has somewhat facetiously described Prince Edward Island as having one of the largest governments in the world, measured by the "number of politicians and civil servants per population, per square mile, and per dollar earned or spent."[9] Of course, the province's tiny population—127 000—explains this situation.

The island has undergone substantial change since World War II. Poor prices for potatoes, the largest single crop, have often hurt the agricultural sector, and the number of farms has dropped by more than two-thirds since 1951 as farms have been consolidated and small farmers have left the land. High energy costs and transportation difficulties have also hindered growth of the private sector. In 1959 federal politicians began promising to build a causeway to the mainland; a start was eventually made on the project but rising costs forced its cancellation.

Yet there have been successes—rising tourism, for example, has given a needed boost to the island's economy. A Comprehensive Development Plan of social and economic change, largely financed by Ottawa, brought some positive results amid much controversy in the 1970s. Numerous income support programmes and other grants have improved living standards—but at the cost of greater dependence on the federal government.

NEWFOUNDLAND

Newfoundland, which entered Confederation in 1949, has had the region's most distinctive political history. The long and bitter battle waged by supporters and opponents of Confederation was one between those attracted by union with an incomparably richer country, and those Newfoundlanders wanting to keep their independence from the mainland. Joey Smallwood, leader of the confederate forces, campaigned tirelessly, at times from an old seaplane equipped with loudspeakers, to prove that, under Confederation, Newfoundlanders "would be better off in pocket, in stomach, and in health." Anti-confederates denounced those who would "lure Newfoundland into the Canadian mousetrap"; they called Smallwood a "Judas" who was belittling Newfoundland's good name and lamented that at least Iscariot had had the decency to hang himself.

382 A referendum held in June 1948 allowed Newfoundlanders to choose among Confederation (favoured by both Britain and Canada); responsible government or dominion status, perhaps leading to economic union with the United States; and the unpopular existing system by which a commission of British appointed officials governed Newfoundland. Responsible government won; Confederation placed second. Since there was no clear majority, however, a second referendum was held in July in an atmosphere of sectarian bitterness. Most Catholics, fearing loss of their denominational schools, spoke against Confederation, while many Protestants favoured it. In general the commercial classes opposed Confederation, fearing the competition of the big Canadian department stores (like Eaton's) and the mail order companies. The mere thought of the high Canadian federal income tax also frightened many of the well-to-do. This time, however, the confederates won narrowly, and Canadians and Newfoundlanders set about negotiating the final terms of union. Union became official a few minutes before midnight on March 31, 1949, rather than on April 1, as originally planned, because Smallwood, Canada's most recent Father of Confederation, objected: "I didn't want to spend the rest of my life listening to taunts that Confederation had come on All Fools' Day."

Historian David Alexander sees the decline of the fishing economy as having "led Newfoundlanders reluctantly into Confederation."[10] By 1949, the island's citizens had incomes only one-third of those of Canadians, and death rates for diseases associated with poverty were two or three times higher than in Canada. Yet, as historian David Mackenzie points out, Canada, or at least some federal civil servants and politicians, also wanted Newfoundland. During World War II Canada had discovered the island's strategic and economic interest; Canadians also worried that the United States might seek to strengthen its ties with the island.[11]

Joey Smallwood, Newfoundland premier for more than two decades, hoped to carry out an industrial revolution that would create thousands

National Archives of Canada PA-128080.

Joey Smallwood signs the agreement by which Newfoundland entered Confederation on March 31, 1949.

383

of new jobs, stem emigration and, as he said, drag the province "kicking and screaming into the twentieth century." Foreign investment was encouraged because Smallwood believed that local businessmen, rather than seeking to invest in basic production industries, were "scrambling around, like henhawks eyeing a chicken-coop, for their share of the millions of family allowances and other cash pouring in from Ottawa." Many of Smallwood's costly ventures ended in bankruptcy, however. Smallwood also sponsored projects to develop the province's natural resources, such as iron and pulpwood, as well as Labrador's vast hydro-electric potential at Churchill Falls. Despite the failures, the Smallwood revolution, aided by federal contributions, totally transformed life in the hitherto isolated outports.

The Smallwood government also reformed education. In 1949 two-thirds of Newfoundland's schools had only one room and lacked electricity and running water. Few teachers had a university diploma, while annual salaries were below one thousand dollars. Students usually left school at age fourteen. Over the next two decades the government built new schools, trained teachers, and transformed Memorial College into a modern university. The largest Protestant denominations agreed to amalgamate their school systems.

The Conservatives took over Newfoundland's government in 1972. Brian Peckford's stewardship since 1979 has been marked by acrimonious confrontations with the federal government over offshore oil rights and fisheries, with Quebec over electric power sales regulated by a contract that brought immense windfall profits to Hydro-Québec, and within the province, with labour, especially the public service unions. The province's economy continues to depend largely on primary industries, of which fishing still employs the largest number of workers. Serious problems in that industry, brought on by overfishing and extensive competition from European fleets, especially French fleets off St. Pierre and Miquelon, have helped keep the island's official unemployment rate at about 20 percent of the work force. The eventual development of the Hibernia oil field could, however, bring needed cash resources into the province.

384

British Columbia

British Columbia constitutes a separate region. Its population (which in 1986 exceeded that of Atlantic Canada), its high per capita incomes, and its rich resource base make it a "have" region; enthusiastic newcomers from other Canadian provinces have called it a "lotus land." As Premier W.A.C. Bennett told the Constitutional Conference in Ottawa in 1969: "With the population of British Columbia growing at twice the rate of the rest of Canada, the presence of British Columbia as an economic region of its own is more obvious as each day passes." Turned towards the Pacific and the U.S. West Coast, it is, in both its geography and attitude, quite distant from Ottawa. Political scientist Martin Robin points out that British Columbians' attitudes are influenced immensely by the Rocky Mountains.[12] R.M. Burns of Queen's University used the expression "disinterested detachment" to characterize British Columbia's relations with Ottawa, a sort of "acceptance of the Canadian idea but without any great sense of responsibility for it or feeling of need to make a contribution toward it."[13]

Resource-based activities (forestry and mining, especially coal and copper, but also oil and gas) are the main components of the province's economy. The declining international markets of the early 1980s hurt this sector and contributed to high unemployment, up to 15 percent. Hydroelectric developments on the Columbia and Peace rivers provide inexpensive energy. The province has a relatively weak industrial structure, and many primary products undergo little or no processing before export, a situation that economist Thomas Gunton attributes to managerial preferences and to the provincial government's traditional policy of encouraging resource investment.[14] In 1986 the Vancouver World's Fair was held amid the government's hopes that it would "put the city and the province on the map"; it did have a positive impact on tourism and gave a temporary boost to the economy of the Lower Mainland.

POLITICS IN BRITISH COLUMBIA

Politically, the province's recent history has been different from that of other provinces, with Social Credit and the CCF–NDP as the two major parties. General political disillusionment and resentment of the old-line Liberals and Tories led the hitherto small Social Credit party to a victory in 1952. After the election, the caucus chose as its leader W.A.C. Bennett, who had broken away from the Conservatives and who adjusted Social Credit to his own brand of conservatism. Eventually, traditional Liberal and Tory supporters rallied to Social Credit, seeing the party as the new standard-bearer of free enterprise. Bennett governed for the next twenty years, keeping the "socialist hordes" at bay and, as Bennett himself once said, "making policies for the hour." Social Credit votes came mainly from outside metropolitan Vancouver, though the party did manage to build significant support among the urban middle class as well.

385

During the Bennett years, British Columbia's economy developed rapidly. The state played a considerable role despite Social Credit's much-vaunted dedication to private enterprise. It nationalized the giant B.C. Electric Company, and it undertook hydro-electric projects and improved highway, rail, and maritime transportation. Bennett battled with the federal government over the terms of the Columbia River Treaty signed between Canada and the United States in 1961—Bennett wanted to sell British Columbia's power allotment from the Columbia dam to the United States while Ottawa opposed the sale. Victoria and Ottawa also clashed over resources and on constitutional and fiscal questions. Why should Ottawa treat British Columbia as "a goblet to be drained" and then redistribute its wealth among the less successful provinces, asked Bennett, suggesting that cheques go directly to low-income citizens throughout Canada rather than to provincial governments.

The CCF (later the New Democratic Party, or NDP) opposition denounced government corruption and Bennett's alleged dictatorial tactics as well as the government's hostility to labour. Having succeeded in becoming a respectable alternative party, and in the face of disenchantment with Bennett's policies on education, health care and welfare, the NDP finally won power in 1972. Under combative leader Dave Barrett, it initiated many controversial reforms—its opponents accused it of "legislating by thunderbolt"—including public automobile insurance, a new innovative labour code, and an attempt to preserve agricultural land. Barrett's reforms and new taxes led conservative forces to unite in reaction. Thanks largely to an economic downturn, this new coalition brought the Social

Credit party back to power in 1975, under W.R. "Bill" Bennett, W.A.C. Bennett's son. Critics mocked Bennett's broad coalition of supporters by calling it the "united vegetable party."

The recession of the early 1980s was particularly hard on the province's exports of natural resources and led to high unemployment. The government's attempts to curtail spending provoked confrontation with the public-sector unions, and Social Credit's popularity fell to new lows. But the climate of optimism brought on by Expo 86 and the "sunshine offensive" of William Vander Zalm, Social Credit's charismatic new leader who took over from Bennett in 1986, enabled the party to win an easy victory in the fall of 1986, though the NDP won more than 40 percent of the popular vote.

The West

The term "West" is probably more appropriate than "Prairies" for the region comprising Manitoba, Saskatchewan, and Alberta. The latter term evokes an image of immense fields of golden wheat with grain elevators on the horizon, sticking up into the azure-blue sky. Such may be the easterner's stereotype of the West, but it is no longer how many westerners view their region.

The wheat economy has contributed greatly to the region's conflict with central Canada (see chapter 7). Farmers railed against protective tariffs, and denounced grain traders, and the banks and railroads headquartered in Montreal and Toronto. Over time, grievances have changed but they have become no less intense. Westerners complain bitterly of what might be called their "hinterland status" that applies to culture as much as it does to politics and economics and means an absence of control over decisions that affect them.

Since World War II all three provinces have undergone considerable change and their economies have lost much of their previous similarity. Oil has replaced agriculture as the leading component of the Alberta economy, with revenues reaching a peak of $20 billion in 1985—five times the value of farm cash receipts. Agriculture occupies a greater position in Saskatchewan, while Manitoba has a more diversified economy. What has remained the same is the region's dependence on outsiders—especially on the federal government's policies on energy and other resources, on railway transportation, on the marketing of Prairie wheat, and on assistance to farmers heavily in debt or whose crops have failed.

Conservative leader John Diefenbaker, a lawyer from Prince Albert, Saskatchewan, showed sympathy for western grievances when, during the 1957 federal election campaign, he promised better crop insurance, cash advances on farm-stored grain, and, most important, a system of flexible support prices to ensure a fair price-cost relationship. Once elected, his government quickly introduced the Agricultural Stabilization Act and found new markets for Prairie wheat, largely in the Communist bloc.

WESTERN ALIENATION

During the prosperous 1970s, western dissatisfaction grew as the federal government in general, and Prime Minister Pierre Trudeau in particular, seemed to ignore the West's needs. A survey in 1976 showed that three-quarters of Albertan respondents felt that their province's politicians were not taken seriously in the East as the federal political parties depended upon Ontario and Quebec for most of their votes, Alberta had little influence in national politics. Discontent peaked in 1980 when the increasingly unpopular Trudeau announced the National Energy Programme. The suddenly respectable separatist parties urged westerners "to take to   *387* the lifeboat of independence before it's too late."

In Alberta, Elmer Knutson, an elderly millionaire from Calgary, founded West-Fed, a movement stressing provincial autonomy. West-Fed's political rivals included the Western Canada Concept (WCC) set up by British Columbian Doug Christie. Aspiring to establish a unitary state across the Prairies and British Columbia it enjoyed its greatest success in Alberta. Gordon Kesler, a separatist WCC candidate, won a provincial by-election in February 1982, but was defeated in the following Alberta provincial election late that same year. All of the separatist movements spawned in the early 1980s shared a common enmity for Pierre Trudeau, whom Knutson described as "this little yahoo down there on the left... who says we have to be bilingual," and denounced what they termed the federal government's subservience to Quebec.

Western separatism began to wane in 1982 and 1983 with much internal wrangling and splits in the WCC. The arrival of the federal Conservatives in power in 1984, with a strong western contingent, caused western discontent to recede, but falling prices for agricultural commodities, oil, and other resources soon provoked new frustrations.

ALBERTA

The three western provinces have developed along separate paths particularly in the last half-century. The discovery of oil in the Leduc Valley in Alberta in the late 1940s signalled massive changes for that province's economy. By the late 1950s petroleum revenues from sales in the United States and eastern Canada enabled the Alberta government to spend more money per capita than any other province. The completion of the national

388

Provincial Archives of Alberta.

Imperial Oil's Leduc No. 1 well blew in on Feb. 13, 1947, signalling the beginning of a new era for Alberta.

pipeline system had allowed Alberta producers to reach eastern Canadian markets. In 1961 the Diefenbaker government acted to prevent Montreal refineries, using less expensive crude from Venezuela, from entering the Ontario market; Ontario had to buy oil from Alberta and Saskatchewan, produced at a slightly higher cost. The Diefenbaker oil policy resulted in increased production in Alberta. Many Albertans felt, however, that imported crude should also have been excluded from Montreal, and that Ottawa gave too much consideration to pressures from Quebec and the multinational petroleum companies.

The sharp increase in international oil prices in the mid-1970s gave Alberta a new sense of independence and self-confidence, and provoked a bitter crisis in Edmonton–Ottawa relations. The federal government imposed a "made-in-Canada" oil price that allowed central Canadian consumers to pay prices lower than the world price. The producing provinces resented federal price controls which deprived them of billions of dollars, and they held that they deserved the best deal possible before their diminishing reserves were depleted. At one point, the Alberta government threatened to shut off the flow of oil east, and some Alberta automobile bumpers sported stickers that belligerently proclaimed: "Let the Eastern bastards freeze in the dark." Alberta also vigorously opposed the Trudeau government's policy of Canadianization of the oil industry and blamed it for declining investment in the oil fields.

389

The expanding oil industry promoted rapid population growth in Alberta in the 1970s as eastern and central Canadians arrived in search of high-paying jobs. Construction boomed and dozens of new office towers sprang up in Calgary and Edmonton. The residential home market resembled the stock exchange in its headiest moments: prices skyrocketed and speculators sold dwellings at immense profits within days of purchase. In enviable financial health, the Alberta government placed oil royalties in the Heritage Fund, a future financial reserve whose assets by the mid-1980s surpassed $13 billion. Albertans have thus been able to enjoy high-quality social services while paying the country's lowest income taxes, no sales tax, and, until 1987, no tax on gasoline.

The decline in demand for oil during the 1982 recession, followed by sharply lower oil prices in 1986, checked Alberta's growth and clearly showed the basic fragility of its resource-based economy. Construction on the huge synthetic-oil production and heavy-oil upgrading projects ceased. The jobless rate matched eastern Canadian levels; unemployed workers left the province and many returned to eastern and central Canada. Real estate values fell sharply. Two major Albertan bank ventures collapsed resoundingly, though the federal government agreed to finance a costly bailout. The oil industry called upon both Edmonton and Ottawa for assistance; Ottawa was urged to apply a floor price to provide some stability to the industry and to keep the Alberta economy from plunging into a new and deeper downturn. At the same time, agriculture faced serious difficulties, as drought afflicted hundreds of farmers in the province's southern region, and declining world prices and increased costs wiped out profit margins.

Politically, Albertans have favoured one-party dominance. For thirty-six years, until 1971, they supported the Social Credit party. After World

War II the party provided conservative and, by most accounts, good government in a climate of general prosperity and rising oil revenues. In the late 1960s, Calgary lawyer Peter Lougheed revived the provincial Conservative party. Strongly supported by urban Alberta, the Conservatives won power in 1971 and established a new political dynasty. The immense amounts of oil money flowing into the Alberta treasury greatly facilitated the Lougheed government's tasks. Its hope was that the money would permit industrial diversification.

Lougheed's successor as Conservative leader was Montreal-born Don Getty, one of his former Cabinet ministers, who had come west from the University of Western Ontario in London, Ontario, thirty years earlier to play for the Edmonton Eskimos. Although Getty won a comfortable majority in the provincial election of 1986, the opposition parties, notably the NDP, accomplished a rare breakthrough.

390

SASKATCHEWAN

Neighbouring Saskatchewan's political development was quite different from Alberta's and substantially more competitive. In 1944 the moderately socialist CCF gained office under Baptist preacher Tommy Douglas and began implementing a series of social and economic reforms, including a pioneering hospital services plan that offered hospital care at public expense. The province was also the first to enact medicare in 1962. In the mid-1960s, the Liberals defeated the CCF (now the NDP) but they did not dismantle the political reforms. Their quarrels with the federal Liberals over natural resources development and federal fiscal measures were notorious. The NDP regained power in 1971 under Allan Blakeney. Saskatchewan's economy improved substantially in the late 1970s and the province, in contrast to the early 1970s, gained in population. Then, in 1982, the Progressive Conservatives led by Grant Devine came to power and formed a new government, although political divisions between Conservative rural Saskatchewan and the NDP urban areas became important.

Economically, agriculture (the province's largest industry) has been subject to violent swings, depending on world wheat prices, export markets, and weather conditions. For farmers, the mid-1980s were depressing years: not only were prices low, driving many close to bankruptcy, but also drought and grasshoppers prevented successful harvests. The province also possesses immense resources of potash, whose commercial exploitation began in the late 1950s, and Canada's second-most important deposits of oil and uranium. Like agriculture, the health of these resource industries is subject to factors beyond the province's control, in particular, world prices, and the necessity of access to the American market.

MANITOBA

Manitoba's diversified farming industry occupies a relatively small area in the southwestern portion of the province. There is more manufacturing than in Saskatchewan, while mining and hydro-electricity have undergone considerable development in the north since the mid-1950s. Exploitation of the West's non-agricultural resources at first generated new markets for Winnipeg manufacturers, but the rise of Calgary and Edmonton meant new competition. Winnipeg suffered, too, from the decline of old industries; the relocation of CP Air to Vancouver in 1948 and, later, of Air Canada's repair and overhaul base to Montreal, also cost the city many jobs.

Politically, the major forces since the 1950s have been the Conservatives and the NDP, the latter particularly strong in the poorer north and central districts of metropolitan Winnipeg. Duff Roblin's Progressive Conservative government of the 1960s proved more progressive than conservative, spending heavily on health, welfare, and education. When NDP leader Ed Schreyer defeated Roblin's Conservative successor, Walter Weir, in 1969, his government adopted major social reforms in order to "open a new way to those who have previously known only disparity and discrimination." Conservative critics denounced the NDP's public automobile insurance plan, its higher taxes, and, in general, state intervention, warning that Manitoba was moving towards socialism. After 1977 the new Conservative government of Sterling Lyon proceeded with a programme of restraint and lower taxes, but in 1981 cutbacks and economic problems contributed to a return to power of the NDP, led by Howard Pawley. In the 1980s the question of the linguistic rights of the Franco-Manitobans—about 5 percent of Manitoba's population—generated fierce debate, with the Conservatives adamantly opposed to new "concessions." Their stand on this question caused the NDP to retreat from its plan to extend French-language services.

391

Ontario: The "Province of Opportunity"

In a country marked by profound economic imbalances, Ontario has traditionally been Canada's major "have" region. More than one-third of Canadians live there, assuring the province a major role in determining national policy. Half of Canada's new immigrants choose Ontario and the province also attracts substantial in-migration from other less-favoured provinces. Immigration has made Toronto Canada's largest city and also transformed it into a sophisticated, cosmopolitan cultural centre. Benefiting from the post-war decline of Montreal, Toronto has become Canada's financial capital. It also has more than 40 percent of the country's head offices, and three-quarters of the members of journalist Peter Newman's "Canadian national business establishments." In the mid-1980s, unemployment rates in the province were usually the lowest in Canada. Manufacturing, including 95 percent of the huge automobile and parts industries, is concentrated here. The power, the people, and the money reside in this "province of opportunity."

Ontario's material success and political power have inevitably coloured the manner in which other Canadians view the province and its citizens. For example, westerners and Maritimers have suspected central Canada of using Confederation to cement its economic mastery over the rest of the country, especially through protective tariffs.

They were also convinced that the economic nationalism of the 1970s fostered by the *Toronto Star* and Ontario university professors, among others, contained little promise for them. They judged that most regions outside Ontario, which were afflicted with relatively high unemployment, could not enjoy the luxury of picking and choosing among investors. Joey Smallwood had affirmed in his typically colourful manner that he would not hesitate to deal with the devil if that gentleman had money to invest. Westerners furiously denounced Ottawa for an oil policy that favoured Ontario, while Quebeckers pointed to the striking difference in the jobless rates between the two provinces as proof that central Canada's weight really meant Toronto's power.

To Ontarians, the outsiders' views are largely unjustified, the product of envy, resentment, and frustration. The province has prospered but there have been periods of adversity. Southern Ontario has also benefited from a favourable geographical location. Ontarians point out that their taxpayers pay a large portion of the cost of the equalization grants, unemployment insurance, farm subsidies, and industrial development projects that the federal government gives poorer regions. The province, they insist, has done its share to shoulder the "burden of unity."

ONTARIO'S ECONOMIC DEVELOPMENT

The 1940s and 1950s were prosperous years for Ontario. The government's major objective was economic growth, and demand for a wide variety of goods stimulated industrial expansion, especially in the south. By 1951, 10 percent of the Canadian labour force had jobs related to motor vehicles, and most of these jobs were in southern Ontario. Services—banking, merchandising, educational, health, governmental—multiplied. The province budgeted large sums for improving and expanding higher education; between 1950 and 1975, the number of publicly supported universities increased from three to fifteen. The construction industry prospered thanks to heavy demand for housing. Governments invested heavily in the construction of highways and urban expressways, built watermains and sewers, promoted urban transit, sponsored electric power projects including nuclear power plants, and completed work on the St. Lawrence Seaway. This intense activity explains why the unemployment rate generally stayed below 4 percent from 1945 until 1970. It rose slightly after the mid-1970s but remained below the national average. These were indeed, as economist Kenneth Rea has termed them, the "prosperous years."[15] But Rea adds that while the Ontario government might take credit for permitting growth to occur and even, on occasion, stimulating it, it was not the cause of growth.

Ontario found the 1970s more difficult as jobs, capital, and people moved west and energy prices skyrocketed. In response, the provincial government tried to control public spending. In the field of higher education, increasingly the subject of intense public criticism, Queen's Park moved to get, in the words of historian Paul Axelrod, "more scholar for the dollar."[16] The severe recession in the dominant automobile industry in the early 1980s also hit Ontario hard. After 1984, however, recovery was rapid and manufacturing boomed, giving Ontario Canada's lowest jobless rate and its citizens the country's highest income levels.

393

Politically, the Conservatives dominated Ontario throughout the period until the Liberal victory of 1985. Three premiers in particular made their mark: Leslie Frost, who co-operated with the federal Liberals in many development projects; John Robarts, who oversaw expansion of the education system and adopted a conciliatory attitude to Quebec's calls for constitutional reform; and William Davis, a pragmatic politician who proved Trudeau's strongest ally in the patriation of the Canadian Constitution.

Davis's much less popular successor, Frank Miller, lost the provincial election of 1985. Liberal Premier David Peterson came into office thanks to an agreement reached with the provincial NDP that allowed his minority government to survive non-confidence votes. Also, the province's economic health helped boost the new government's popularity. Its defence of Ontario's interests led to frequent conflict with Prime Minister Brian Mulroney's government, especially over free trade with the United States and proposals to bring Quebec to accept the Constitution of 1982. Like the Davis government before it, the Peterson government also took steps to extend the linguistic rights of the Franco-Ontarian minority. In an election in September 1987, Peterson won an overwhelming majority of seats, while the NDP became the official Opposition.

Since Confederation, Canada has been an often uneasy association of regions and sub-regions. Differences in geography, culture, language, and population contribute to the strength of regionalism, but within English-speaking Canada, economic issues have probably been most significant. The nature of the Canadian economy has meant that the nation's wealth has been concentrated in relatively small areas of the country. Such profound imbalances, though inevitable, create tension. Canadians in the more privileged areas have attempted to increase their affluence, while those in the country's more disadvantaged sections battle for a fairer share of the national wealth.

In the course of the debates over the distribution of national wealth and the determination of national policy, the federal government plays the role of arbiter. The party in power may seek to alleviate regional conflict since dissatisfaction risks alienating voters, but no federal budget is ever sufficient to satisfy all demands upon it. Influential lobbies seek measures which necessarily favour certain regions over others. Each major federal decision will provoke the anger of regions that, rightly or wrongly, blame Ottawa for being overly attuned to the needs and interests of other regions.

Canada's history both early and recent demonstrates the strength of regionalism within the country, the power of regional interest groups, and the intensity of regional problems. In this regard, the future will likely resemble the past, and regionalism will thus remain a major challenge to Canadian unity.

NOTES

[1] Paul Cornell, Jean Hamelin, Fernand Ouellet, and Marcel Trudel, *Canada: Unity in Diversity* (Toronto, 1967).

[2] John Barr and Owen Anderson, *The Unfinished Revolt: Some Views on Western Independence* (Toronto, 1971), p. 56.

[3] David G. Alexander, *Atlantic Canada and Confederation: Essays in Canadian Political Economy* (Toronto, 1983), p. 45.

[4] Reginald Whitaker, *The Government Party: Organizing and Financing the Liberal Party of Canada 1930–58* (Toronto, 1977), p. 387.

[5] G.A. Rawlyk, "The Maritimes and the Problem of the Secession of Quebec, 1967 to 1969," in *One Country or Two?*, edited by R.M. Burns (Montreal, 1971), p. 212.

[6] Thomas J. Courchesne, "Avenues of Adjustment: The Transfer System and Regional Disparities," in *Canadian Confederation at the Crossroads: The Search for a Federal-Provincial Balance*, edited by Michael Walker (Vancouver, 1978), p. 158.

[7] J.E. Belliveau, *Little Louis and the Giant K.C.*, quoted in Rand Dyck, *Provincial Politics in Canada* (Scarborough, 1986), p. 171.

[8] J. Murray Beck, "The Party System in Nova Scotia: Tradition and Conservatism," in *Canadian Provincial Politics: The Party Systems of the Ten Provinces*, edited by Martin Robin (Scarborough, Ont., 1972), 168–97.

[9] Frank MacKinnon, "Prince Edward Island: Big Engine, Little Body," in *ibid.*, p. 240.

[10] David G. Alexander, *Atlantic Canada*, p. 32.

[11] David MacKenzie, *Inside the Atlantic Triangle: Canada and the Entrance of Newfoundland into Confederation, 1939–1949* (Toronto, 1986).

[12] Martin Robin, "The Politics of Class Conflict," in Robin, *Canadian Provincial Politics*, p. 27.

[13] R.M. Burns, "British Columbia and the Canadian Federation," in Burns, *One Country*, p. 269.

[14] Thomas I. Gunton, "An Economic Strategy for British Columbia," in *After Bennett: A New Politics for British Columbia*, edited by Warren Magnusson et al. (Vancouver, 1986), p. 63.

[15] K.J. Rea, *The Prosperous Years: The Economic History of Ontario, 1939–75* (Toronto, 1985).

[16] Paul Axelrod, *Scholars and Dollars: Politics, Economics, and the Universities of Ontario, 1945–1980* (Toronto, 1982), pp. 141–78.

Related Readings

Topics in this chapter can be examined in greater depth in the following articles from R. Douglas Francis and Donald B. Smith, eds., *Readings in Canadian History: Post-Confederation*, 2d ed. (Toronto, 1986): Gerald Friesen, "The Prairie West Since 1945: An Historical Survey," pp. 606–16; and D. Alexander, "Canadian Regionalism: A Central Problem," pp. 625–31.

BIBLIOGRAPHY

On the economic inequalities afflicting Canada, see the Economic Council of Canada, *Living Together: A Study of Regional Disparities* (Ottawa, 1977); Paul Phillips, *Regional Disparities* (Toronto, 1982); and O.F.G. Sitwell and N.R.M. Seifried, *The Regional Structure of the Canadian Economy* (Toronto, 1984). A useful anthology is David Jay Bercuson and Phillip A. Buckner, eds., *Eastern and Western Perspectives: Papers from the Joint Atlantic Canada/Western Canadian Studies Conference* (Toronto, 1981). David Jay Bercuson, ed., *Canada and the Burden of Unity* (Toronto, 1977) also treats regional development in the post-war period. For studies of provincial politics, see Martin Robin, ed., *Canadian Provincial Politics: The Party Systems of the Ten Provinces* (Scarborough, 1972), and David Bellamy et al., eds., *The Provincial Political Systems* (Toronto, 1976); Rand Dyck, *Provincial Politics in Canada* (Scarborough, 1986) offers a substantial bibliography. Other useful collections are R.M. Burns, ed., *One Country or Two?* (Montreal, 1971), and Richard Simeon, *Must Canada Fail?* (Montreal, 1977).

David MacKenzie looks at Newfoundland's entry into Canada in *Inside the Atlantic Triangle: Canada and the Entrance of Newfoundland into Confederation, 1939–1949* (Toronto, 1986). S.J.R. Noel examines political issues in *Politics in Newfoundland* (Toronto, 1971). James K. Hiller and Peter Neary, eds., *Newfoundland in the Nineteenth and Twentieth Centuries: Essays in Interpretation* (Toronto, 1980) has material on the post-war period. David G. Alexander, *The Decline of Trade: An Economic History of the Newfoundland Saltfish Trade, 1933–1965* (St. John's, 1977) is an excellent study of a major economic issue; his *Atlantic Canada and Confederation: Essays in Canadian Political Economy* (Toronto, 1983) contains several articles bearing on underdevelopment and dependence. Among the biographical works on Joseph Smallwood are Richard Gwyn's *Smallwood, the Unlikely Revolutionary* (Toronto, 1972), and former minister Frederick W. Rowe's *The Smallwood Era* (Toronto, 1985). On English-French relations in New Brunswick, see Stephen H. Ullman, "The Political Attitudes of New Brunswick's Acadians and Anglophones: 'Old Wine in New Bottles'?" *American Review of Canadian Studies*, 16 (1986): 161–80. J.M. Beck, "The Maritimes: A Region or Three Provinces?" *Proceedings and Transactions of the Royal Society of Canada*, 15 (1977): 301–13 is a useful piece on a little-studied subject.

For a general survey of Ontario, Joseph Schull, *Ontario since 1867* (Toronto, 1978) is highly readable, as is Robert Bothwell, *A Short History of Ontario* (Edmonton, 1985). An excellent study of Ontario's economy is K.J. Rea, *The Prosperous Years: The Economic History of Ontario, 1939–75* (Toronto, 1985); D.C. MacDonald, ed., *The Government and Politics of Ontario* (Toronto, 1980) also contains several pertinent articles on that province. On higher education in Ontario, consult Paul Axelrod, *Scholars and Dollars: Politics, Economics, and the Universities of Ontario, 1945–1980* (Toronto, 1982). Politics in the 1960s is examined in A.K. McDougall, *John P. Robarts: His Life and Government* (Toronto, 1986).

396   Western Canada has been widely studied and thus only a few titles can be mentioned here. Gerald Friesen, *The Canadian Prairies: A History* (Toronto, 1984) provides a highly original synthesis that emphasizes social and economic history. John Archer, *Saskatchewan: A History* (Saskatoon, 1980), also has material on the post-war period. A good urban study is Ruben Bellan, *Winnipeg: First Century; An Economic History* (Winnipeg, 1978). Roger Gibbins, *Prairie Politics and Society: Regionalism in Decline* (Toronto, 1980) offers an overview of the contemporary West. On the political history of Alberta, consult John J. Barr, *The Dynasty: The Rise and Fall of Social Credit in Alberta* (Toronto, 1974), and Carlo Caldarola, ed., *Society and Politics in Alberta* (Toronto, 1979). John Richards and Larry Pratt, *Prairie Capitalism: Power and Influence in the New West* (Toronto, 1979) also includes Saskatchewan. For a review of the NDP activity in Manitoba, see James McAllister, *The Government of Edward Schreyer* (Montreal, 1984). Western discontent is examined in John Barr and Owen Anderson, eds., *The Unfinished Revolt: Some Views on Western Independence* (Toronto, 1971), a kind of manifesto for separation, and in the more recent and scholarly work by Larry Pratt and Garth Stevenson, *Western Separatism: The Myths, Realities and Dangers* (Edmonton, 1981). Also, on Western alienation see Kenneth H. Norrie, "Some Comments on Prairie Economic Alienation," *Canadian Public Policy*, 2, 2 (1976): 211–44.

Among works on the recent history of British Columbia the following provide strongly contrasting views: David J. Mitchell, *W.A.C. Bennett and the Rise of British Columbia* (Vancouver, 1983); and Martin Robin, *Pillars of Profit: The Company Province 1934–1972* (Toronto, 1973). J. Terence Morley et al., *The Reins of Power: Governing British Columbia* (Vancouver, 1983) examines politics in the province. Paul Knox and Philip Resnick, *Essays in B.C. Political Economy* (Vancouver, 1974) is an analysis of the B.C. economy from a socialist perspective. Works critical of the Bennett government policies in the 1980s include Warren Magnusson *et al.*, *The New Reality: The Politics of Restraint in British Columbia* (Vancouver, 1984); Warren Magnusson *et al.*, *After Bennett: A New Politics for British Columbia* (Vancouver, 1986); and Robert C. Allen and Gideon Rosenbluth, *Restraining the Economy: Social Credit Economic Policies for B.C. in the Eighties* (Vancouver, 1986).

Several journals specialize in regional history: BC *Studies*, *Alberta History*, *Saskatchewan History*, *Ontario History*, and *Acadiensis*.

397

CHAPTER NINETEEN

Post-war Immigration and Ethnicity

During the 1960s and 1970s, both the aboriginal and the French-speaking communities in Canada voiced strong dissatisfaction with cultural inequalities of which they had long been victims and demanded fairer treatment (see chapters 16 and 17). At the same time, members of Canada's other ethnic minorities, who comprised nearly 30 percent of the country's population in 1971, expressed considerable reservations with the concept of two nations or founding peoples that was increasingly popular among Canadians of French and English origin. The federal government's multiculturalism policy announced in 1971 gave ethnic groups an official status they had not enjoyed in the past, and served as recognition of how Canada, in one century, had become a multi-ethnic and multicultural society (see chapter 6).

The history of immigration since 1945 involves three closely intertwined elements: the Canadian government's immigration policy; Canadians' response to immigration and to the various groups of immigrants who have made Canada their new home; and the experience of the immigrants themselves. This final topic gives rise to several more specific questions: where have the immigrants come from, and why? How have they reacted and adapted to their new environment? How have immigrant communities been transformed, and what impact have they had on Canadian society?

The European Refugees

In 1946 millions of destitute refugees from war-torn areas remained crowded in camps while awaiting a permanent haven. Canada, however, was in no hurry to come to the rescue and risk being swamped by a flood of humanity for whose problems it felt no responsibility. The country had received virtually no immigrants during the preceding fifteen years and, as historians Irving Abella and Harold Troper have compellingly demonstrated,

Canada seems to have distinguished itself primarily by keeping the doors firmly closed to Jews fleeing Nazi persecution.[1] Canadians were tired of being told to "do their part," and most probably agreed that the country had other, more urgent priorities to attend to; Canada had its own children, as well as its injured soldiers and veterans, to look after. And economists were worrying that the war's end would bring on another depression, like the one following World War I (see chapter 9). A wave of new arrivals risked swelling the ranks of the unemployed.

Displaying his unusual intuition about the nation's mood, Prime Minister William Lyon Mackenzie King was well aware of Canadians' hesitations over immigration and saw little electoral advantage to be gained by opening the country's doors to Europe's homeless. Pressure, however, continued to mount. In the House of Commons, MPs like Alistair Stewart, a CCF member from Winnipeg North, denounced the government's "shameful" vacillation and Anthony Hlynka, a Social Credit member from Vegreville, Alberta, insisted on Canada's "moral and Christian duty" towards the unfortunates of Europe. A few Liberals like David Croll objected that Canada could not be satisfied with sending "old clothes and surplus food" across the ocean, and pleaded for the launching of a coherent immigration programme. Such religious groups as the Catholic Immigrant Aid Society and the Canadian Council of Churches also spoke in favour of the refugees, and ethnic associations campaigned for a loosening of restrictions.

Pressure came from outside Canada as well, as international organizations told External Affairs personnel that Canada should "do something." Finally, after holding hearings in the spring of 1946, the Senate Committee on Immigration and Labour concluded that Canada needed immigrants as long as they did not take jobs from Canadians or reduce Canadian living standards. It recommended that immigration offices be opened in Europe to process as many displaced persons and refugees as the country could absorb. The Canadian government decided to move forward cautiously.

Refugees trickled in with the arrival, in 1946, of some 4000 Polish veterans who had fought in Western Europe and who now refused to return home to a Poland occupied by the Red Army. Hugh Keenleyside, deputy minister of Mines and Resources (the department that had responsibility for immigration), believed that Canada had to do more. If it did not hurry, he warned, other countries would select the best immigrants, and Canada would have to settle for whoever remained. By admitting a few thousand displaced persons immediately, Canada could obtain good candidates, improve the country's international image, and encourage other nations to follow suit.

Humanitarian motives were combined with other less noble or pragmatic interests. John Holmes, an External Affairs officer, claimed that Canada selected refugees "like good beef cattle, with a preference for strong young men who could do manual labour and would not be encumbered by aging relatives."[2] A token 5000 refugees immigrated in June 1947 and, by the fall of 1948, 40 000. The numbers then began to decrease: many of the remaining refugees were sick, elderly, or handicapped, and Canada did not want them. By 1953, about 165 000 refugees had come to Canada. Many of them, after arrival, applied to bring in their close relatives.

Many refugees in war-ravaged Europe were ethnic Germans expelled from territories formerly belonging to Hitler's Reich. Others came from the now communist countries of Eastern Europe. At the end of the war, thousands of Eastern Europeans had been forced into boxcars and repatriated behind the "iron curtain," often to prison, persecution, and even death. Some of those who escaped this fate eventually reached Canada with barely a suitcase containing their meagre belongings. Many were well-educated professionals or highly skilled workers. Often, they concealed their training in order to better their chances with Canadian officials, who were seeking manual labourers. Industries in need of unskilled labour sponsored many of the refugee immigrants, who readily accepted almost any job, salary, and working conditions. Once in Canada, they fulfilled their contractual obligations on farms, in lumber camps, in mines, and often, in the case of women, in domestic service, then usually moved on to more suitable occupations.

400

REFUGEE LABOUR

Some refugees and other new immigrants were exploited by their employers. One notorious scheme involved Ludger Dionne, an MP and owner of the Dionne Spinning Mill Company at Saint-Georges-de-Beauce, south of Quebec City. In 1947 Dionne obtained government authorization to recruit one hundred Polish girls for his mill. *Time* reported that he paid his workers twenty cents an hour; after deductions of $6.00 a week for board, the women were left with $3.60 weekly. Dionne assured parliamentarians that girls from Quebec City did not want to work in the small towns and that his working conditions were better than those found in Toronto. For good measure, he also accused his detractors of being propagandists for communism.

Most refugees had no familiarity with Canadian attitudes and customs. Few spoke either English or French. Naturally, various groups attempted to build a cultural life in their new homeland, particularly in such cities as Toronto, Montreal, and Vancouver. Often, they lived in the same urban neighbourhoods, and joined or established ethnic associations and parishes.

Economically, many refugees progressed rapidly. By 1971, Latvians and Estonians, for example, had incomes that were 25 percent higher than the Canadian average. As political scientist Karl Aun has shown, this evolution can be explained in part by the fact that such groups included unusually large numbers of educational, community, cultural, and political leaders.[3] Yet stories abound like that of the poor Estonian fisherman who, after settling in southern Ontario, spent as little and saved as much as possible from the earnings of all family members. With the help of a loan from the Estonian Credit Union, he then bought a house with several apartments, continued saving and purchased a second apartment house, moved into the best unit and eventually sent the children to university. Many prospered in the booming business climate of the 1950s. A drive to succeed, the encouragement and mutual support of the community, and the relative youth of the newcomers were all factors that helped these immigrants adjust to their new environment.

Ottawa's Immigration Policy

Most prospective immigrants to Canada, even in the early post-war years, were not refugees, and the country needed a general immigration policy. King finally formulated the government's position in a much-commented speech to the Commons on May 1, 1947. Typically, the prime minister attempted to satisfy partially both supporters and opponents of immigration. He said that Canada would benefit by boosting its population, and that immigration would make the country more prosperous and secure. At the same time he put forth the notion of Canada's "absorptive capacity," promising that the government would "ensure the careful selection and permanent settlement" of only as many as could "advantageously be absorbed in our national economy." How many immigrants might that signify? Well, the number admitted could vary from year to year, in a turn-on-the-tap, turn-off-the-tap manner. *401*

King's comments also reveal Canadian racial attitudes of the era. Responding to those who denounced racial distinctions in immigration policy as "contrary to all principles of humanity, morality and social welfare," King asserted Canada's right to choose its future citizens. The government did repeal the blatantly discriminatory Chinese exclusion law of July 1, 1923. Nevertheless, it continued to apply severe restrictions on Asian immigration since, in King's words, "massive immigration of Orientals would alter the fundamental composition of the Canadian population" and "give rise to social and economic problems."

Despite King's public willingness to welcome immigrants, his government did not intend to endorse large-scale immigration. Political scientist Gerald E. Dirks describes the Immigration Branch of the late 1940s as "unimaginative" and "plodding"[4]; nor were other departments eager to provide the money and the resources necessary to carry out an effective programme. Three departments manoeuvered to obtain control of immigration. The Ministry of Labour wanted to link immigration to business needs, while Immigration personnel talked in terms of long-range policy, and External Affairs officers were subjected to international pressures to accept more immigrants.

Canadian Attitudes to Immigration

Canadians could not agree on how many immigrants the country needed and who should be admitted. Business and financial leaders lobbied for substantial immigration, maintaining that a larger population would be good for the economy and yield per capita savings in areas such as transportation and administration. Ethnic associations and several religious groups also favoured increased immigration.

Many Canadians were reluctant to receive a sizeable influx of immigrants, however. A poll in 1947 found that only 51 percent thought the country needed more immigrants. By 1954, just 45 percent of Canadians thought immigration a good thing, while 48 percent disagreed. This opposition to immigration may be explained partly by workers' fear for their jobs and their view of immigrants as competitors willing to work for lower wages. Unions, while complaining that the government seemed more attuned to employers' needs than to labour's, cautiously supported bringing in "only those immigrants quickly assimilable to the Canadian way of life," as long as their arrival did not mean a reduction in Canadian living standards, an increase in unemployment, or the weakening of the trade union movement. The unions wanted immigrants to be carefully selected and preferably to occupy unattractive jobs in remote regions that Canadians did not want.

Other Canadians, historian Arthur Lower among them, were convinced that immigrants displaced high-quality native Canadian workers, who headed for the United States. Many Canadians of British origin feared that immigration would weaken the British element in Canada. The Orange Order, for its part, resisted the admission of Catholic immigrants, preferring Protestants from Britain and the Nordic countries, who were considered "most helpful in time of war"; other nationals would "clog the wheels of defence."

FRENCH IMMIGRATION

French Canadians undoubtedly had reason to feel deep anxiety over immigration. They were afraid that a flood of new immigrants would undermine their already insecure and unequal minority position in Canada. Many nationalists unhesitatingly accused the federal government of deliberately encouraging immigration to weaken French Canada. Did not immigrants who settled in Montreal tend overwhelmingly to integrate into the English-speaking community? By 1960, as birth rates declined in Quebec, many French-speaking Canadians feared that the immigrants' preference for English would ultimately make French speakers a minority in Montreal.

In the fall of 1948 the federal government, in hopes of satisfying French-speaking members of the Liberal caucus as well as French-Canadian opinion in general, put French nationals on an equal legal footing with British subjects and American citizens for purposes of entry into Canada. Civil servants, however, immediately slowed down the new policy for "security" reasons, arguing that a large proportion of would-be French immigrants were either Communists or former Nazi collaborators.

All told, Ottawa's new policy on French immigration had a limited effect: between 1946–50, fewer than five thousand French immigrants came to Canada. Although the French authorities did not encourage emigration, prospective immigrants besieged Canadian consular offices in Paris. While the Canadian consul made urgent requests for more staff and office space, Keenleyside advised the deputy minister of Labour to channel "all efforts in the same direction, that is to say, the encouragement of British immigration to Canada."[5]

French immigration did increase in the 1950s and 1960s before declining again. In spite of the entry of francophones from such countries as Belgium and Haiti, their proportion of total immigration has remained low. Between one-half and two-thirds of immigrants to Canada have been English-speaking, whereas French speakers have numbered about 3 percent and bilinguals, 4 percent. The remainder, speaking other languages, soon learned English. Immigration, then, has indeed tended to reinforce the numerical strength of English-speaking Canada linguistically, although diversifying it ethnically and culturally.

An Evaluation of Post-war Immigration Policy

This first wave of immigration, which brought some 1.7 million immigrants to Canada, ended in the late 1950s when rising unemployment led the Canadian government to reconsider its policy. The year 1957, however, proved a sort of boom before the bust, with 282 000 arrivals (a figure that still pales in comparison with the 400 000 immigrants who came in 1913 (see chapter 6). Some 37 500 of these new arrivals were mainly young and often highly skilled Hungarians who in 1956 fled their homeland as Soviet armies crushed the Hungarian revolution. Among them were the entire student body and faculty of a Hungarian school of forestry, which was transported across Canada on a "freedom train" and relocated at the University of British Columbia. In general, the resettlement of the Hungarian refugees proceeded smoothly.

BASIS OF IMMIGRATION POLICY

Such major movements of people gave rise to myths and half-truths. Officially, Canadian policy was inspired by humanitarian ideals and a sense of international responsibility. Canadians saw themselves as generously offering liberty and opportunity to victims of persecution and of political and military turmoil.

In practice, however, economics usually dictated which immigrants and how many of them came to Canada. Ottawa sought immigrants possessing certain skills, and initiated bulk labour schemes. Industries as well as the Ministry of Labour sent representatives to Europe to select suitable immigrants. Federal authorities directed many immigrants, once in Canada, to outlying regions and to farms in order to fulfil perceived national needs. Once here, however, many immigrants soon left for the cities.

Political questions also influenced immigration policy. For example, recent arrivals could assist relatives to come to Canada. By the late 1950s the sponsorship provisions had created substantial backlogs of prospective immigrants from Europe. As Canada sank into recession, the Diefenbaker government, concerned about the influx of unskilled "sponsored" workers, acted without warning in 1959 to restrict the admission of relatives to immediate family members. The anger of the ethnic communities concerned, mainly southern Europeans, as well as of members of the Liberal opposition with strong immigrant populations in their constituencies, led the Conservatives to rescind the order hurriedly.

Racial bias explains why few immigrants were admitted from outside Europe and the United States. In one celebrated case in 1952 that involved a prospective black immigrant from Barbados, the granddaughter of a Canadian citizen, the minister responsible justified his refusal on grounds of climate: "It would be unrealistic to say that immigrants who have spent the greater part of their life in tropical or subtropical countries become readily adapted to the Canadian mode of life." Critics were convinced that "climate" could only mean race. Immigration from the Indian subcontinent was limited by the application of tiny quotas. The location of immigration offices also ensured that the great majority of immigrants would come from Britain and the European continent, as well as the United States, and the government confined its promotional activities to these areas.

BRITISH IMMIGRATION

Of all groups, Canada preferred British immigrants. J.W. Pickersgill, minister of Citizenship and Immigration, stated in 1955: "We put forth much more effort in the United Kingdom than in any other country. We have the goodwill of the government and we are allowed to do active promotion." It was only natural, he asserted, that Canada favour British immigration since it was easier to transplant individuals into "similar soil." (Nevertheless, statistics showed that British immigrants were in no hurry to take out Canadian citizenship.) In the summer and fall of 1947 the province of Ontario airlifted with much fanfare ten thousand British nationals to Canada. The province also advertised for immigrants in the United Kingdom and elsewhere in Europe, sometimes at the risk of upsetting foreign governments unhappy at seeing their skilled labour depart.

In the face of large-scale British and European immigration and of the economic slowdown of the late 1950s, many Canadians thought some restrictions should be imposed. Senator David Croll, an enthusiastic advocate of higher immigration a decade before, joked: "If you put pants on a penguin, it could be admitted to this country." Pickersgill admitted that the massive influx of new arrivals in 1956–57, 40 percent of whom were British, was "too big for Canada to digest." Nevertheless, he added candidly that any attempt to stem the tide of British immigration "would be the finish of the Liberal party in many Anglo-Saxon constituencies."

405

EMIGRATION

During the economic downturn of the late 1950s and early 1960s, the unwelcome reverse side of the immigration coin came to the fore. Disappointed with the lack of opportunities in Canada and embittered by what they considered were false promises on Canada's part, thousands of immigrants, particularly British, returned home. There they contributed to tarnishing temporarily Canada's image. From the early 1950s to the early 1970s, one in every three or four immigrants either returned to their country of origin or moved to the United States. Even more worrisome to many Canadians was the movement southward of eight hundred thousand native-born Canadians in the period from 1952 to 1971. Perhaps one-tenth of this group were professionals or managers, constituting the much-publicized "brain drain." *Maclean's* estimated in 1963 that eight thousand graduates of the University of Toronto were living in the United States, and that eight hundred of these were teaching in American colleges. Historian Arthur Lower conjectured that this loss of talent helped keep Canada "in that state of low water which has always been the object of the Yankee's good-natured scorn."[6] After a temporary reversal of the brain drain in the 1960s at the time of the Vietnam war and race riots in the United States, the movement south resumed again in the late 1970s and 1980s. By the mid-1980s, fifty thousand Canadians were departing annually, attracted largely by the dynamism of the American economy and, perhaps, southern sunshine. The media gave particular attention to the case of scientists who left Canada for better career opportunities and higher levels of government funding in the United States.

Immigration and the Conservatives

Due to an economic slowdown, the Diefenbaker years witnessed a slump in immigration. Fewer agents staffed Canadian immigration offices abroad. Unions exerted pressure to decrease immigration, and most MPs were at best indifferent. Even Diefenbaker, despite favourable public pronouncements in speeches aimed at ethnic groups, appeared to have little interest in the question.

Sometimes immigration made sensational headlines. For example, the press urged the government to stop foreign seamen from jumping ship in Canadian waters and then hurriedly marrying Canadian women in order to remain in Canada. Large-scale illegal Chinese immigration, promoted by a Hong Kong-based industry that bought and sold false identities, also appeared to overwhelm the government. Ottawa promised to accord amnesties to most illegals who would come forth and declare themselves—and many thousands did so—but the programme did not eliminate the illegal immigration rings.

The Conservatives did introduce new regulations in 1962 that ended race or national origin as reasons for exclusion from Canada. The old discriminatory provisions appeared anachronistic and unacceptable in an era when racism was discredited. In 1960 Diefenbaker had proudly presented a Bill of Rights that rejected discrimination by reason of race, national origin, colour, religion, or sex. Economic factors also brought about a reversal of the policy: Canada could simply no longer get the labour it needed from the "old countries." For a time, southern Europe had supplanted Britain and northern Europe. Then, immigration diminished from these countries, too, and Canada turned towards Asia and the Caribbean.

New Wave of Immigrants

The return of economic prosperity in the early 1960s heralded a steep rise in immigration. The Liberal government also instituted structural changes. In 1966 it established the Department of Manpower and Immigration, a move that showed the government's intention to relate immigration to the needs of the labour market. The Department of the Secretary of State obtained responsibility over the integration of immigrants into Canadian society.

New immigration regulations effective in October 1967 completely elim-

407

Courtesy Jean-François Gratton.

Many immigrant workers, like this Haitian woman in Montreal, found employment in the textile industry.

inated the old discriminatory provisions. It also became more difficult for sponsored dependents and particularly for non-dependent relatives to be admitted. Independent applicants were to be selected through a system of points based on such criteria as education and training, personal qualities, occupational demand, as well as age and linguistic capacity. In addition, the government set up an independent Immigration Appeal Board, which was almost immediately overwhelmed with appeals from alleged "visitors" who had applied to stay but had been refused and ordered deported.

The elimination of racial discrimination from Canada's immigration policy, the decline of European sources of immigrants, and the expansion of the network of immigration offices around the world, transformed the ethnic mix of Canadian immigration. In 1966, for example, fully 87 percent of immigrants were of European origin; only four years later, 50 percent came from new regions. The West Indies, Haiti, Guyana, India, Hong Kong, the Philippines, and Indo-China have all figured among the major suppliers of immigrants in the 1970s and 1980s. Visible ethnic and racial minorities became part of Canada's social fabric. For example, while just 12 000 West Indians lived in Canada in 1961, this figure climbed to 200 000 in 1981. The number of Canadians of Chinese origin went from 60 000 to nearly 300 000 in the same period.

RECENT IMMIGRANT SETTLEMENT

The new immigrants, like those of the 1950s and 1960s, did not spread evenly across the country. They came mainly to metropolitan areas like Toronto, Montreal, and Vancouver and, in the oil boom years of the late 1970s, Calgary and Edmonton. Big-city Canada thus became much more cosmopolitan. Newcomers to major cities usually settled in ethnically segregated neighbourhoods; studies by sociologist Warren E. Kalbach indicate that such concentrations have declined "only in the case of a few ethnic populations of British and other western and northern European origins."[7]

The major pole of attraction since 1945 has undeniably been Ontario, especially the south, with more than half of all immigrants choosing that province as their destination. Good employment opportunities and the region's prosperous image attracted immigrants as did well-established ethnic communities with religious centres, clubs, welfare organizations, newspapers, and professional and other services. Quebec, with one-quarter of Canada's population, has received fewer than 15 percent of new arrivals—about the same proportion as British Columbia. The Atlantic provinces and Saskatchewan have experienced little immigration.

ADAPTATION

For most Third World immigrants, their new life in Canada was a considerable material improvement over the past. Moreover, political conditions prevented many immigrants from returning home, even if they had so desired. They did, however, face a much greater cultural shock than earlier British and European immigrants. To an extent, provincial governments and community associations have attempted to assist the new arrivals. Mutual aid and support among families has also been important. Still, it has often been difficult to find jobs to match past occupational experience, especially in times of economic slowdown.

Immigrants have also faced the upsetting necessity of coming to terms with Canadian customs. Anthropologist Norman Buchignani has shown in his study of East Indians or South Asians (to adopt the term now used to refer to those from India, Pakistan, Bangladesh and Sri Lanka) that only a small proportion of homeland cultural practices survive the settlement process.[8] Eating habits and cultural celebrations tend to be maintained in those cities where immigrant groups are sufficiently numerous, but it is more difficult to retain religious practices: Hindu parents, for example, often find that children know far more about Christianity than about Hinduism.

Furthermore, the clash between Canadian values and mores and accepted values and attitudes in the country of origin has frequently caused serious problems for immigrants. For example, the extended family, common in many cultures and providing an extensive support system, has been gradually transformed into the North American nuclear family. The role of women in the family, particularly in southern European and South Asian cultures, has generally been defined very rigidly, with male authority supreme and male financial supremacy to back up that authority. Contact with Canadian mores in this regard has often provoked conflict within the family; parental authority has weakened in the much more permissive society. In South Asia, for example, parents tend to choose marriage partners for their children, and dating is a "foreign" practice. In Canada, the generation gap between immigrant parents and their children has often deepened into a gulf as children become Canadianized through the schools, television, and contacts with Canadian friends.

409

DISCRIMINATION

Many immigrants, especially visible minorities, have suffered discrimination. In one widely publicized case, white and South Asian members of a railway crew in Daysland, Alberta, clashed with bottles and axes. In numerous instances in the late 1970s, Sikhs were attacked and had their turbans forcibly removed. Blacks were frequently harassed or assaulted physically. In Montreal, taxi companies threatened to fire their Haitian drivers, complaining they were losing business to companies employing only white drivers. Also in Montreal, the fatal shooting of an unarmed black youth by a police officer in 1987 sparked widespread demands for an inquiry into racism within the Montreal urban community police force.

Most complaints about discrimination have concerned employment and housing. South Asians and Caribbean Blacks have frequently been victims of racism. A 1985 study at the University of Toronto found that when members of these groups, with the same qualifications as white applicants, applied for job openings, they were told, in two cases out of five, that the opening no longer existed. In some cases, the same employer on the same day then interviewed white candidates for the same position. A survey of complaints filed with the Alberta Human Rights Commission after 1974 showed that several dozen Blacks and South Asians claimed to have been victims of discrimination. Sociologist Jennifer K. Bowerman believed, however, that most victims failed to report incidents to relevant bodies, believing that nothing would be done or, worse, fearing retaliation.[9] Human rights defence groups have indeed criticized the courts for their slowness and their leniency and denounced existing laws for their lack of severity. In 1984, the Special Committee on Visible Minorities in Canadian Society, established by the federal government, published *Equality Now*, a report recommending affirmative action programmes to combat discrimination in the workplace.

"Established" Canadians have had mixed reactions to the new arrivals of the 1970s. Religious and civic groups have strongly urged the admission of refugees, such as the Indochinese "boat people," but public-opinion polls have shown substantial opposition to greater immigration from Third World countries. Asked to rank immigrant groups by order of acceptability as neighbours or marriage partners, Torontonians named Americans as the most acceptable group, Blacks as the least desirable, with "Hindus" and Japanese also at the bottom of the list. Peter S. Li's study of Saskatoon found over 40 percent of respondents opposed to South Asian immigration.[10] In the early 1980s, three-quarters of West Indians judged employment discrimination in Toronto to be "very serious"; reports on eleven other Canadian cities confirmed this same finding. Various studies have shown that many Canadians dislike immigrants speaking their home languages in public, or wearing traditional dress, like the sari. They tend to see immigrants as ignorant of Canadian cultural practices and unwilling to "act like Canadians."[11]

Recent Trends in Immigration

In the early 1980s—with the economic downturn—immigration again declined and economic problems contributed to an anti-immigrant backlash. Many Canadians saw immigrants as competitors for scarce jobs or believed they were crowding the welfare rolls.

Studies on the relation between immigration and employment tend to demonstrate that immigrants do not increase unemployment among indigenous workers but rather help to create a larger, more flexible and adaptable labour force. Immigrants often do work that Canadians cannot or will not do. For some time after arrival, they may require more social services, but eventually, through their need for housing, food, clothing, and other consumer goods, they increase the size of the domestic market and thereby assist in boosting growth. A report in 1982 by Joel Clodman and Anthony Richmond of York University's Institute for Behavioural Research concluded: "The objective evidence does not support the view that the relation between immigration and unemployment is a major problem."[12] Other studies have shown that most immigrants have been able to obtain suitable jobs soon after arrival, although Third World immigrants, despite high education levels, usually earn less than other immigrants.

The presence of immigrants lined up outside employment offices in times of recession has surely influenced public opinion far more than sociological studies. Thus, in 1982, the government felt it necessary, in view of Canada's economic problems, to enact new restrictions. Three years later, barely six thousand independent applicants were admitted. All told, as the government revised each year's projections downward, according to its vague predictions of what the economy could bear, immigration declined to its lowest levels in more than two decades. The government did facilitate entry into Canada, however, of several hundred "business-class" immigrants, wealthy entrepreneurs who declared that they were prepared to invest their capital in Canada, set up businesses, and thus create jobs for Canadians.

Some critics of Canadian immigration policy have expressed concern over the downward trends, and urged the government to put long-term goals ahead of short-term considerations. Immigration Canada warned in 1985 that, if present low fertility and immigration rates were maintained, the country's population would begin to decline early in the next century; to maintain future population growth at 1 percent annually, Canada would need 275 000 immigrants a year—triple the current rates. Some middle-aged Canadians began to worry over who would pay their old-age pensions and future health care, and suggested that more young immigrants be brought in. In 1987, the federal government announced that the ceiling would be raised to 125 000 immigrants, a figure higher than that of preceding years but still very modest compared to the peak years of the 1960s and 1970s, when more than 200 000 persons arrived. It also launched a three-year demographic study to analyse, in particular, the economic and social aspects of immigration.

411

Critics of the federal government's policy towards refugee immigrants have become increasingly voluble. They judge quotas to be unreasonably low in some areas of the world, such as Central America, while the quotas have gone unfilled in other areas, like Africa and the Middle East. Within Canada, procedures for studying the cases of persons claiming refugee status proved so cumbersome that it was estimated in 1985 that forty years would be necessary to clear up the backlog. The *Globe and Mail* noted the paradox that, in a world awash with eleven million refugees, Canada devoted its energy "not to the resettlement of those who desperately need a new home, but to the adjudication and removal of those who advance counterfeit claims to refugee status." Immigration officials complained of having their hands tied in their attempts to find an estimated 50 000 illegal immigrants, often brought in by unscrupulous immigration "consultants." Public opinion led the Mulroney government to take measures against illegal immigration in 1987, but religious and ethnic groups feared that the legislation would make it much more difficult for political refugees to come to Canada.

The "Cultural Mosaic"

Canadians have often taken pride in the image of their country as a "cultural mosaic" (or a "tossed salad," in writer Arnold Edinborough's words) rather than as an American-style "melting pot." Official policy no longer favours rapid assimilation, and social scientists prefer to speak of integration or of acculturation. In his first speech in the Senate in 1964, Senator Paul Yuzyk, Manitoba-born of Ukrainian origin, discussed the emergence of what he termed a "third force," comprised of Canadians of neither French nor British descent.

In October 1971 Prime Minister Trudeau told the House of Commons that the government "accepts the contention of other cultural communities that they, too, are essential elements in Canada and deserve government assistance in order to contribute to regional and national life in ways that derive from their heritages." Multiculturalism—but not multilingualism—was to be encouraged.

Politicians were well aware of the potential electoral benefits from recognizing the contributions of the other ethnic groups. Journalist Richard Gwyn put it bluntly: the programme was "a slush fund to buy ethnic votes." Also, the Liberal government hoped that recognition of multiculturalism would attenuate hostility to bilingualism and biculturalism, and appeal to English-Canadian nationalists who wanted a distinct Canadian identity.

412

Support for Multiculturalism

By 1984 the federal government was providing more than $23 million annually for its multicultural programme, including aid to day care centres, heritage-language classes, and cultural festivals, and the preparation of histories of major Canadian ethnic groups. The policy has also focussed on changing Canadians' attitudes towards immigrants. Some provincial governments were also given financial support to multiculturalism, and many school boards have set up courses in non-official languages. Edmonton public schools, for example, began offering immersion schooling in Arabic, Chinese, Hebrew, Ukrainian, and German. Such policies have practical relevance: by the 1980s, half of children enrolled in Toronto public schools, and 40 percent of those in Vancouver's schools, did not have English as their mother tongue.

The federal government's support of ethnic diversity has given rise to the question of who really speaks for the ethnic communities and thus of which associations to support. Twenty organizations, for example, represent eight thousand Edmontonians of various Asian origins. In Vancouver the well-established Chinese Benevolent Association feuded with newer, more activist organizations like the Chinese Cultural Centre over local issues such as a plan to build a freeway through Chinatown. West Indians have a multitude of often competing organizations whose membership is determined by an immigrant's island of origin.

Also, the ethnic communities themselves have questioned whether the

Multicultural History Society of Ontario, S.I. Sugunasiri Collection.

The cultural mosaic in Canada: here a Sinhalese drummer leads a Sri Lankan parade in Toronto, 1983.

right programmes are being supported or whether Ottawa has not preferred short-term, highly visible manifestations of what has been termed "ethnic exotica." Perhaps rather than keeping immigrants "singing and dancing and talking their own language," as journalist Caitlin Kelly put it, the federal government should address "real" problems such as ethnic inequality. Certain groups like the Ukrainians have vigorously proposed the recognition of minority linguistic rights. Other students of multiculturalism doubt that English-French dualism and ethnocultural pluralism can really be reconciled or that the vastly diverse multicultural third force has the power to assure changes in the traditional bases of Canadian society. Further attempts to foster ethnic and linguistic heterogeneity might facilitate national unity or, contrarily, make it more difficult to attain. Agreement over such issues presently appears impossible.

Although heritage language programmes have emphasized retention of the mother tongue, immigrants in order to integrate into Canadian society have had to learn English or in Quebec (to a much lesser degree), French. Although such groups as the Portuguese, the Greeks, and the Chinese have had considerable success in retaining the language of the country of origin, assimilative trends become more pronounced over time and the retention of non-official languages diminishes sharply, notably between the first and second generations.

Fewer than 20 percent of Ukrainian Canadians, for example, speak Ukrainian on a regular basis, and inter-marriage has hastened the pace of assimilation. Historian Varpu Lindstrom-Best views second- and third-generation Finns as having become an "indistinguishable part" of Canadian society, though they will still glue a Finnish flag to their bumper or, after relaxing in the sauna, "demonstrate their legendary 'sisu' (tenacity) by jumping for a refreshing dip in an icehole"![13] In a study of Poles in Canada, Henry Radecki concludes that ethnic identification will have to depend upon knowledge of Poland's culture and history rather than on rapidly declining mastery and use of the language in Canada.[14] Of Toronto's half-million-strong Italian community, historian Robert Harney estimates that fewer than 150 000 (belonging generally to the original immigrant generation) are "active in Italian institutions."[15] In his opinion, large numbers of Italians have deliberately broken their ethnic links and taken refuge in "Anglo conformity" because of the prejudice they have faced. Studies carried out by sociologist Jeffrey Reitz and others have shown that "language retention is at best temporary"[16] and suggest strongly that linguistic assimilation leads to destruction of the cohesive ethnic community.[17] The prognosis for linguistic survival appears bleak indeed, particularly for those ethnic communities no longer being replenished by immigration.

IMPACT OF IMMIGRATION

Immigrants have had an immeasurable impact upon Canada's economic, political, social, and cultural life. The contributions of entrepreneurs such as the Reichmann brothers (born in Hungary), and Thomas Bata and Stephen Roman (both born in Czechoslovakia), journalist Peter Newman (born in Austria), Montreal publisher Alain Stanké (born in Lithuania), and politician David Lewis (born in Poland), are well-known. But many other more recent immigrants have distinguished themselves within various ethnic communities, in business, in the academic world, and in arts and letters. The Canada of tomorrow will likely reflect the presence of the Asians, Latin Americans, West Indians, and other immigrants who came to Canada in the 1970s and 1980s.

The presence of immigrants has brought new political questions, not least of which is immigration policy, to the fore, and the ethnic vote is significant in many constituencies. Though immigrants traditionally favoured the Liberals, to whose immigration policies they owed their arrival in Canada, their descendants' political loyalties have proven much more volatile. Immigration has also enabled Canada to acquire a much more diverse and vibrant cultural life. Demographically, immigration boosted Canada's population by a full 8 percent in the decade of the 1950s, and to a considerably lesser extent in more recent years. With immigration, the importance of both the British and the French elements has declined while, from a linguistic point of view, the fact that the great majority of immigrants have adopted English as their new language has contributed to weakening the relative position of Canada's francophone population.

415

Immigration also brought much of the blue-collar labour the country needed for large-scale industrial and resource development in the 1950s. By 1961, 12 percent of the country's work force, and fully one fifth of Ontario's, was composed of post-war immigrants. Immigration also provided many of the skilled workers and professionals that the country needed. In the 1960s, for example, hundreds of American university professors entered the country, permitting the rapid expansion of the Canadian university system but also setting the stage for the nationalist outcry against American domination in the early 1970s. Bringing in educated immigrants has helped ease the pressure on an already overburdened educational system in Canada, which has had a much higher proportion of young people than the United States and most European nations. Ironically, for a country that has often complained of a brain drain to the United States, Canada has been criticized by some Third World states for attracting the highly qualified manpower these developing nations need.

Immigration will likely remain a much-discussed issue. There is little prospect that Canadians—themselves all former immigrants or descendants of immigrants, except for the native peoples—can ever agree on how many immigrants the country needs, how many refugees it should welcome, where immigrants should come from, and what role they should play in Canadian society. Nevertheless, there can be no doubt that, partly because of immigration, the Canada of the 1980s is very different from the country that emerged from World War II.

NOTES

[1] Irving Abella and Harold Troper, *None is Too Many: Canada and the Jews of Europe, 1933–1948* (Toronto, 1982).

[2] John W. Holmes, *The Shaping of Peace: Canada and the Search for World Order, 1943–1957*, vol. 1 (Toronto, 1979), p. 101.

[3] Karl Aun, *The Political Refugees: A History of the Estonians in Canada* (Toronto, 1985).

[4] Gerald E. Dirks, *Canada's Refugee Policy: Indifference or Opportunism?* (Montreal, 1977), p. 148.

[5] The subject of post-war French immigration is examined in Richard Jones, "Spécificités de l'immigration française au Canada au lendemain de la deuxième guerre mondiale," *Revue européenne des migrations internationales*, 2 (1986): 127–43.

[6] Quoted in Christina McCall Newman, "The Canadian Americans," *Maclean's*, July 27, 1963, p. 10.

[7] Warren E. Kalbach, *Ethnic Residential Segregation and its Significance for the Individual in an Urban Setting* (Toronto, 1981), p. 61; Anthony H. Richmond and Warren E. Kalbach, *Degré d'adaptation des immigrants et leurs descendants* (Ottawa, 1980), pp. 177–214.

[8] Norman Buchignani and Doreen M. Indra with Ram Srivastiva, *Continuous Journey: A Social History of South Asians in Canada* (Toronto, 1985), p. 163.

[9] Jennifer K. Bowerman, "East Indians in Alberta: A Human Rights Viewpoint," in K. Victor Ujimoto and Gordon Hirabayashi, eds., *Visible Minorities and Multiculturalism: Asians in Canada* (Toronto, 1980): pp. 181-91; J. Rick Ponting and Richard A. Wanner, "Blacks in Calgary: A Social and Attitudinal Profile," *Canadian Ethnic Studies*, 14 (1983): 57–76.

[10] Peter S. Li, "Prejudice Against Asians in a Canadian City," *Canadian Ethnic Studies*, 11 (1979): 70–77.

[11] For example, Josephine C. Naidoo, "East Indian Women in the Canadian Context: A Study in Social Psychology," in Ujimoto and Hirabayashi, eds., *Visible Minorities ...* (Toronto 1980): pp. 193–218; and John W. Berry, Rudolf Kalin and Donald M. Taylor, *Multicultural and Ethnic Attitudes in Canada* (Ottawa 1977), p. 107.

[12] Quoted in Henry Aubin, "Do immigrants steal jobs or create new ones?" *The Gazette* (Montreal), January 10, 1985.

[13] Varpu Lindstrom-Best, *The Finns in Canada* (Ottawa 1985), p. 18.

[14] Henry Radecki with Benedykt Heydenkorn, *A Member of a Distinguished Family: The Polish Group in Canada* (Toronto, 1976), p. 106.

[15] Quoted in Margot Gibb-Clark, " 'Italian community' a myth, historian says," *Globe and Mail*, October 20, 1984, p. 14.

[16] Jeffrey G. Reitz and Margaret A. Ashton, "Ukrainian Language and Identity Retention in Urban Canada," *Canadian Ethnic Studies*, 12 (1980): 39.

[17] Jeffrey G. Reitz, "Language and Ethnic Community Survival," in *Ethnicity and Ethnic Relations in Canada*, edited by Jay E. Goldstein and Rita M. Bienvenue (Toronto, 1980), p. 122.

BIBLIOGRAPHY

Post-war immigration policy has been studied by David C. Corbett, *Canada's Immigration Policy* (Toronto, 1957) and, more recently, by Freda Hawkins in *Canada and Immigration: Public Policy and Public Concern* (Montreal, 1972). On refugees, see Gerald E. Dirks, *Canada's Refugee Policy: Indifference or Opportunism?* (Montreal, 1977) and, for a solid monograph on one group of refugees, Milda Danys, *DP: Lithuanian Immigration to Canada After the Second World War* (Toronto, 1986). Alan Green provides an economist's point of view in *Immigration and the Postwar Canadian*

Economy (Toronto, 1976). Warren E. Kalbach and Wayne W. McVey, *The Demographic Bases of Canadian Society*, 2d ed. (Toronto, 1979) contains useful statistical material.

The Department of Manpower and Immigration published a review of post-war immigration, *Immigration Policy Perspectives* (Ottawa, 1974). One volume of the report, *Three Years in Canada*, contained the results of a survey of the economic and social adaptation of immigrants in Canada. Among the many publications on multiculturalism and ethnicity, see Howard Palmer, ed., *Immigration and the Rise of Multiculturalism* (Toronto, 1975); Leo Driedger, ed., *The Canadian Ethnic Mosaic: A Quest for Identity* (Toronto, 1977); Jean L. Elliott, ed., *Two Nations, Many Cultures: Ethnic Groups in Canada*, 2d ed. (Scarborough, 1983); Alan B. Anderson and James S. Frideres, *Ethnicity in Canada: Theoretical Perspectives* (Toronto, 1981); and Jay E. Goldstein and Rita M. Bienvenue, eds., *Ethnicity and Ethnic Relations in Canada* (Toronto, 1985).

Howard Palmer and Tamara Palmer, eds., *Peoples of Alberta: Portraits of Cultural Diversity* (Saskatoon, 1985) is a good study of one province's ethnocultural groups. On Asians in particular, see Norman Buchignani and Doreen M. Indra with Ram Srivastiva, *Continuous Journey: A Social History of South Asians in Canada* (Toronto, 1985), and K. Victor Ujimoto and Gordon Hirabayashi, eds., *Visible Minorities and Multiculturalism: Asians in Canada* (Toronto, 1980). Language retention is discussed in K.G. O'Bryan, J.G. Reitz, and O.M. Kuplowska, *Non-Official Languages: A Study in Canadian Multiculturalism* (Ottawa, 1976), and in Ronald Wardhaugh, *Language and Nationhood: The Canadian Experience* (Vancouver, 1983). Jorgen Dahlie and Tissa Fernando, *Ethnicity, Power and Politics in Canada* (Toronto, 1981) contains essays on the political behaviour of ethnic groups. Henry Radecki has studied the voluntary organizational structure of one ethnic community; see *Ethnic Organizational Dynamics: The Polish Group in Canada* (Waterloo 1979).

Barry Broadfoot, *The Immigrant Years: From Europe to Canada, 1945–1967* (Vancouver, 1986) presents interviews bearing on the immigrant experience. Racial discrimination is briefly studied in James W. St.G. Walker, *Racial Discrimination in Canada: The Black Experience* (Ottawa, 1985). An ongoing series published by the Canadian Historical Association, with the support of the Canadian government's multiculturalism programme, provides useful syntheses; brochures have thus far appeared on the Scots, the Portuguese, the Japanese, the Poles, the East Indians, the West Indians, the Jews, the Finns, the Chinese, the Ukrainians, and the Germans. For book-length studies of various ethnic groups, see the "Generations: A History of Canada's Peoples" series, published by McClelland and Stewart in conjunction with the *Multiculturalism Directorate*, which includes histories of the Portuguese, the Poles, the Japanese, the Scots, the Norwegians, the Greeks, the Arabs, the Hungarians, the Estonians, the Ukrainians, the Croatians, the Chinese, and the South Asians.

417

CHAPTER TWENTY

Economic Development: Prosperity and Problems

Opinion polls clearly reveal Canadians' intense preoccupation with economic questions. In most elections, such issues are the dominant themes: jobs, interest rates, government spending, inflation, the devalued Canadian dollar, and taxes. Moreover, the major social concerns of our time—relations between management and labour, women's rights, native rights, social programmes, the environment, education—are all inextricably linked to the economy.

Economic historian O.J. Firestone, using W.W. Rostow's model of the stages of economic growth, has described the years since World War II as the "age of high mass consumption."[1] During most of this time Canada has seen at least moderate economic growth, enabling most of its citizens to acquire enviable living standards. Nevertheless, since 1960, Canada has had to face increasingly hard-to-solve problems. Creating jobs has become more difficult: with each slowdown of the economy, the general unemployment rate has tended to remain at a higher plateau than after the previous recession. A resurgence of inflation in the 1970s and early 1980s moved the cost of living up sharply. Canadians have also been concerned about mounting foreign, especially American, investment. The fluctuations in the value of the Canadian dollar in terms of American currency also made headlines at many moments throughout the period; in the decade after 1976, in a climate of waning confidence, the Canadian dollar sank steadily to record lows.

Since the 1960s the Canadian economy has undergone substantial structural changes. Indeed, one can argue that Canada has entered the post-industrial society, one in which services, such as banks, governments, schools, and hospitals are the largest sector of employment, followed by industry and, at the bottom, agriculture—a reversal of the Canada of 1867 (see chapter 1). Canadians have had to face the need for painful adjustments as many traditional "soft" industries like footwear and textiles have lost their markets and reduced their work force, while other sectors, such as transportation and communications, have benefited from new technologies. Natural resources industries have also been confronted with increasingly severe competition from foreign sources. Finally, profound inequalities in development among Canada's diverse regions have stimulated widespread discontent and at times even endangered the very survival of the country.

Bust and Recovery, 1960–67

The great post-war economic boom ended in the late 1950s as Canada entered its most serious recession since the Great Depression of the 1930s. The economy began to decline in 1956, as Canadians encountered more difficulty in selling goods to foreign markets. Worldwide overproduction and diminishing prices hit farmers particularly hard. A pronounced downturn in the Canadian economy took hold in the spring of 1960, and the winter of 1961 proved especially harsh; 11 percent of Canada's workers found themselves jobless—a very high figure for those years. *419*

The Diefenbaker government, first elected in 1957 and then re-elected in 1958 with an overwhelming majority, tried to attack unemployment through budget deficits, increased tariffs, and a devalued Canadian dollar. Government spending was intended to stimulate the economy. Higher tariffs made it more expensive for consumers to buy American-made products, while a lower dollar was supposed to make Canadian exports more attractive. In general, the business and financial community reacted negatively to these economic policies. The Canadian Chamber of Commerce judged the nearly $800 million deficit in 1961 to be "staggering," and investors were said to be "as nervous as cats in a dog pound." The Liberal opposition maintained that Canada's standing abroad was declining and quoted financial publications like *Barron's Magazine*, which warned that because of large deficits, exchange rate manipulation, and reckless spending policies, Canada was "headed for serious trouble."

In the spring of 1962, shortly after announcing why it was inappropriate to peg the Canadian dollar, the government fixed it at 92.5 cents (U.S.). This measure provoked a wide range of reactions, from outright condemnation by importers to enthusiastic approval by exporters. Most Canadians were simply bewildered. The Liberals, however, protested noisily that devaluation would mean higher prices for consumers. They printed thousands of so-called "Diefenbucks" (92.5 cent dollars adorned with the prime minister's likeness), which they used effectively during the election campaign of June 1962.

National Archives of Canada PA-114895.

420 INFLATION

By 1963, recovery seemed well underway as unemployment dropped to about 5 percent. Even the usually despondent *Globe and Mail* expressed optimism: "Where gloom and doom about the future of Canada has been the governing mood in recent years, there is now buoyancy and optimism." By 1966, however, a new, worrisome trend was becoming evident: prices were moving up more quickly and the monthly price indexes confirmed consumers' suspicions. Angry shoppers launched boycotts of supermarkets, accusing them of price gouging. Prime Minister Lester B. Pearson's Liberal government raised some taxes in an effort to lessen demand, but most Canadians disagreed vigorously with economists' explanations that inflation was caused by the fact that consumers had too much money to spend. The Conservative opposition also denounced the new taxes, with the party's financial critic even going so far as to compare the minibudget to miniskirts: "Taxes are getting higher and higher and covering less and less."

Canadians battled inflation in various ways. The members of strong unions in key sectors of the economy like transportation won massive pay increases. Seaway workers demanded a 35 percent raise over two years and obtained 30 percent; railway workers struck and won 24 percent spread over three years; Air Canada's machinists went out in support of their demands for 20 percent in one year. A disquieting trend was being established that risked provoking serious social conflict. Worse, in 1967, while inflation showed no signs of abating, the economy slowed down noticeably. Economists coined a new word to describe the phenomenon: stagflation, that is, inflation at a time of slow economic growth. First-year economics textbooks insisted that this combination could not occur—but it did, in Canada and throughout much of the world. The stage was set for the economic miseries of the 1970s.

The 1960s did bring some good news as Canada's first century drew to a close. Canada's trade balance on goods improved in spite of a growing deficit on finished products. Early in the decade, the Diefenbaker government finally found markets—in Communist China, the Soviet Union, and Eastern Europe—willing to purchase hundreds of millions of bushels of Canada's surplus grain. These new sales improved the incomes of many western farmers. At the same time, many eastern farmers made little gains; their farms were too small, their soil too poor, their costs too high. Many abandoned the land that their families had farmed for generations.

Trade Relations with the United States

Despite this progress, Canada still registered deficits in its dealings with the United States. Canadian subsidiaries sent back dividends to the United States and Canadian visitors spent heavily there. Some economists stated that such deficits were "more often molehills than mountains" but others viewed them as a serious problem. The Diefenbaker devaluation did stimulate exports, but the Conservative government failed to divert more trade towards Britain.

421

Indeed, various measures further increased trade with the United States. In 1959 Canada and the United States renewed their defence production treaty, thereby stimulating the arms trade between the two countries. Then, in 1965, the Liberals signed the Automotive Products Agreement with the United States. The "Auto Pact" provided for free trade among the manufacturers; Canadian drivers could not, however, bring back automobiles duty-free from the United States. The pact also contained safeguards protecting Canada's share of production. Most economists agree that the pact (and more recently a lower Canadian dollar as well) has had substantial economic advantages for Canada, especially for southern Ontario where most of the automobile industry is located. Manufacturers were able to rationalize their production and Canadian plants could specialize in producing relatively few models.

American Ownership of Canadian Industries

American ownership of a large portion of Canadian industry became a passionately debated issue in these years. The Diefenbaker government applied a tax on interest, dividends, and profits sent to non-residents, a measure designed to make investment in Canada somewhat less attractive; in practice, it had little effect. Ironically, in 1963, President John F. Kennedy, in an attempt to find a solution to American balance of payments problems, put a 15 percent tax on purchases by Americans of stocks and bonds in foreign countries, including Canada. As the *Globe and Mail* noted, the measure hit Canadian markets "with all the delicacy and force of a wet mocassin across the face"; Canada protested and eventually obtained an exemption. Perhaps Canadians were proclaiming a double standard by demanding restrictions on American capital but then condemning similar limits imposed by the Americans. For Canadians, *they*—not the Americans—should decide how much foreign capital should come to Canada.

Even when the supposedly pro-American Liberals returned to power in 1963, the problem of foreign investment refused to go away. Walter Gordon, Liberal finance minister, announced a tax on takeovers of Canadian firms by foreigners, but the ensuing outcry forced him to retract the proposal. Undaunted, Gordon in 1966 published *A Choice for Canada*: the country would have to choose between political and economic independence, or colonial status within the American empire. He also set up a task force on the structure of Canadian industry, chaired by University of Toronto Professor Mel Watkins, to study "the significance—both political and economic—of foreign investment in the development of our country, as well as ways to encourage greater Canadian ownership of our industrial resources while retaining a climate favourable to the inflow of foreign investment, as required, for Canada's optimum development."

422

At this time, however, the Liberal government had very few economic nationalists. Mitchell Sharp, named minister of Finance in 1965, did not even want to publish the task force report, while Trade and Commerce minister Robert Winters assured a San Francisco audience that "Canada welcomes foreign capital regardless of doubt-provoking remarks to the contrary from time to time." Canadians were thus still far from reaching a consensus on the issue.

Inflation in the 1970s

Older Canadians had previously lived through periods of inflation, notably at the beginning of World War II as well as in the late 1940s and early 1950s. Then, in 1973, inflation returned. The ten-cent coffee, the dime newspaper, the nickel postage stamp, and the 25-year fixed-rate mortgage belonged to the past. Until 1972, prices crept up at between 4 and 5 percent annually. In 1973, led by a 17 percent rise in food prices—which pleased farmers but vexed urban Canadians—the increase in the cost of living reached 9 percent. That year Canadians paid 30 percent more for meat, 40 percent more for poultry, 40 percent more for eggs. Younger Canadians were also being pushed out of the housing market as prices for homes jumped upward by as much as 20 percent in Vancouver, Toronto, and Ottawa, and by 10 percent in other urban communities.

Prices were even higher in 1974 as Canadians endured double-digit inflation. The cost of food again soared by 17 percent. Although the cash registers displayed dismal news for all Canadians, some suffered more than others. Low-income families, who had to spend three-quarters of their income on food and housing, were hardest hit because prices of these two components of the cost of living index were increasing the fastest.

Politicians were quite naturally tempted to blame outside forces for these substantial price increases. After all, inflation was plaguing most other countries, in particular the United States, where it was fed by the war in Vietnam. Moreover, world food prices, in the face of insufficient production, moved sharply upward. The cost of wheat, for example, more than doubled in just one year, from 1973 to 1974. The Organization of Petroleum Exporting Countries increased oil prices substantially too, in 1973 and again in 1979.

Nevertheless, Canada had domestic causes of inflation. Unions were accused of making unrealistically high wage demands that forced companies to raise their prices. In turn, labour blamed rising prices on excessive corporate profits. Inflation was conditioning Canadians to expect more inflation and to act accordingly. This attitude, though understandable, assured that the problem would persist.

FEDERAL ANTI-INFLATION POLICY

As inflation set in, Canadians, convinced of the government's responsibility to manage the economy, demanded that Ottawa do something. At the outset, the federal government had declared its intention to fight inflation vigorously. Such strong words were followed by the establishment of the ineffective Prices and Incomes Commission, which searched vainly for a workable formula for voluntary restraints on wage increases. Not unexpectedly, management was in favour of such restraints. Equally predictable was labour's refusal to co-operate when the commission called for a freeze on prices and for guarantees that non-wage income would be controlled.

As the bout with "foodflation" provoked an even greater public outcry, a skeptical André Raynauld, chairman of the Economic Council of Canada, commented: "The public believes the government has a magical formula but is too weak to use it." The magical formula turned out to be the creation of the Food Prices Review Board, chaired by Beryl Plumptre. While the board diligently conducted studies, issued reports and made recommendations, prices continued their relentless ascent. Nevertheless, from the government's point of view there was an advantage—shoppers vented their wrath upon the board rather than on the government.

New and bolder strategies appeared necessary. Robert Stanfield's Conservatives called for a freeze on wages and prices, which Liberals repudiated as unworkable. However, on Thanksgiving Day, in October 1975, a year after winning an election partly on that very issue, the Trudeau government imposed controls. These controls, which affected the public sector and large private companies, were to last three years. The rate of increase in prices did slow, but it took more than controls and guidelines to defeat inflation.

Ottawa also followed the American lead in boosting interest rates to slow down the economy. Economists warned the government that if it overreacted in the fight against inflation, higher unemployment could well ensue. The costs of living with inflation, they suggested, might be much less than the costs of avoiding it. Unemployment did rise, as during the 1973–75 recession, but Canadians told pollsters that inflation was the major issue of the day. Unemployment affected the unemployed and their families, but inflation concerned all Canadians.

The government also announced measures to alleviate the effects of inflation. Tax exemptions, family allowances, and old-age pensions were indexed to the cost of living. "Indexed" Canadians thus found some inflation protection. Unfortunately, such measures contributed to ensuring that inflation would continue and also had catastrophic effects on government finances. Government expenses began to spiral out of control and annual budget deficits swelled.

424

Problems over Trade

For Canada, which exported one-quarter of its production, trade continued to be an area of great concern. To ensure that jobs remained in Canada, the government kept tariffs, especially on manufactured products, among the highest in the industrialized world. In 1971 the Gray Report on foreign ownership of Canadian industry (named for Herb Gray, an economic nationalist who had recently joined the Liberal Cabinet) concluded that the tariff "provides sufficient protection to a wide range of industries to enable them to compete in the domestic market even when they are less efficient than foreign producers." Canadians were also told that they were 20 percent less productive than Americans, even though their wage rates were similar. The slide of the Canadian dollar after 1976, when it reached $1.04 U.S., helped compensate for these inefficiencies and gave a needed boost to Canadian exports; it also meant that imports cost more.

As in the late 1950s, Canada's wheat farmers in the 1970s had to contend with mounting world surpluses of wheat and sagging prices. Frustrated farmers exhorted the federal government to act, while a frustrated Prime Minister Trudeau asked rhetorically: "Why should I sell your wheat?"

ATTEMPTS TO DIVERSIFY TRADE

Throughout the 1970s, as the proportion of Canadian trade with the United States crept higher, Canada insistently proclaimed its belief in diversification. It appeared increasingly risky to rely on a single country for almost all Canada's imports and exports. In 1970 the Department of External Affairs prepared a White Paper (actually six brightly coloured booklets) on Canada's international relations, entitled *Foreign Policy for Canadians.* Called the "Trudeau Doctrine" by political scientist Peyton Lyon, it proposed strategies for developing relations with Latin America, Europe, and East Asia.[2] Europe, in particular, was supposed to serve as a counterweight to American influence. Some academic and parliamentary critics regretted the Paper's denigration of Canada's traditional image of the world's "helpful fixer." Like the *Globe and Mail*, they viewed the new emphasis on economic growth as having "tipped the scale towards the dollar and away from diplomacy." Canadian nationalists noted that there was no booklet on Canada-U.S. ties, and wondered when Canada was going to come to grips with the American relationship. For the moment, the government was not ready to commit itself beyond stating piously: "The United States is Canada's best friend and ally and will remain so."

Then, in 1972, immediately after U.S. President Richard Nixon instituted draconian protectionist measures, the Canadian government published *Canada–U.S. Relations: Options for the Future.* The study offered Canadians three options. It was apparent that concerned, patriotic Canadians should dismiss options one (the status quo) and two (continental integration), in favour of the so-called Third Option, which implied less dependence on the United States and stronger links with other countries, such as the European states.

Canadian trade with Britain continued to decline, particularly after Britain entered the Common Market in 1974. Nor did the Europeans express much interest in buying Canadian manufactured products; they were much more preoccupied with selling their own. Numerous Canadian trade missions did visit Third World countries peddling Canadian goods, and Canada tied its aid to African states on the condition that they spend their credits in Canada. Far from becoming diversified, however, Canada's trade became increasingly concentrated on the United States: by the late 1970s, about two-thirds of Canada's exports were going there, and 70 percent of its imports originated there.

Periodic multilateral trade negotiations in the framework of GATT discredited protective tariffs. But in the 1960s, Canada, like many other countries, threw up a host of non-tariff barriers in an effort to impede the entry of imports and keep jobs at home as well as to subsidize industries that exported their production. Government purchasing—Canada's governments at all levels spent nearly $70 billion in 1981—favoured products made in Canada and even, as interprovincial trade wars heated up, within a particular province.

As both employers and employees in such industries as clothing and footwear lobbied to prevent the entry of inexpensive foreign goods, the federal government began imposing quotas on imports and urging "guilty" East Asian countries to apply "voluntary" restraints on their exports to

Canada. In many cases, these declining industries in Canada had little hope of ever competing with similar industries in the so-called low-wage countries. Still, the federal government attempted to exact promises from these companies that they would restructure and modernize.

Such non-tariff measures were designed to save Canadian jobs, but they also signified higher prices for Canadian consumers and risked inciting other countries to erect similar barriers to Canadian exports. The Canadian strategy had its winners; it also had many losers.

Rise and Fall of Economic Nationalism

In the late 1960s, many Canadians, particularly in Ontario, expressed concern about American ownership of Canadian industry. In 1968, the *Report of the Task Force on the Structure of Canadian Industry* acknowledged the benefits of foreign investment for economic growth and living standards but warned of the costs in terms of "possible impediments to the creation of a more independent national economy." The report concluded: "The nation has been built, but its sovereignty must be protected and its independence maintained. A diversified economy has been created, but its efficiency must be improved and its capacity for autonomous growth increased." There was little immediate reaction. The *Globe and Mail* commented simply that the report, "heralded as a potential bomb, has fluttered to earth with a gentle plop."

By 1970, though, the campaign against foreign investment had gained ground. Nationalist authors published books with provocative titles: *Silent Surrender*; *Close the 49th Parallel*; *Canada Ltd.*; *The Precarious Homestead*; *Partner to Behemoth*; and *The Elephant and the Mouse*. These works portrayed Canada as a satellite of the American metropolis. To journalist Peter Newman, Canada seemed on the road to economic union with the United States, and "the end of the Canadian dream" was imminent.

Some critics did offer solutions to the dilemma of foreign ownership. The militantly socialist and nationalist Waffle group within the New Democratic Party (NDP) urged large-scale nationalization of foreign-owned businesses and resources. More moderate nationalists called for a gradual buying back only of large enterprises. Still others believed that actual ownership mattered little if Ottawa exercised stronger control over giant foreign-owned corporations operating in the country. In 1971 the Gray Report had recommended several measures to control foreign investment. Two years later, in response to political pressures, the federal government set up the Foreign Investment Review Agency (FIRA) to screen takeovers to determine whether they were of "significant benefit" to Canada. Yet, by 1980, according to political scientist Stephen Clarkson, FIRA had shown itself to be a "paper tiger" that had not noticeably prevented American investment in Canada.[3] U.S. Ambassador Thomas Enders confirmed this

426

analysis by expressing satisfaction with the agency's 90 percent approval rate.

NATIONAL ENERGY PROGRAMME

To the federal Liberals, one area needing Canadianization was the energy sector, and they created a new Crown corporation, Petro-Canada, in 1975. Then, five years later, Trudeau launched the National Energy Programme (NEP): its objectives were to make Canada self-sufficient in oil by 1990, gain a greater share of huge oil revenues for Ottawa, and reduce the role of American oil companies in Canada to less than 50 percent. In 1982, Canadian control in the oil and gas sector reached 55 percent. Still, Ottawa's timing could not have been more inappropriate: just as it spent billions of dollars purchasing foreign oil companies and assisting oil exploration by Canadian companies, oil prices crashed dramatically. Canada's biggest corporate liability became Dome Petroleum, a creation of Liberal energy policies that had accumulated a debt of over six billion dollars by the mid–1980s.

427

American opposition to the NEP was vehement. U.S. Trade Representative William Brock warned of retaliation: "We have a quiver full of arrows and we are prepared to shoot them in self-defense if we must." The hostile reaction, not only in the United States but also among the western Canadian business community, probably convinced Trudeau to back down from his pledge in 1980 to "expand and strengthen FIRA, not weaken it." Ottawa hoped that the use of Canadian government purchasing to force American subsidiaries to expand manufacturing and research and development spending in Canada, as well as the application of moral suasion, would bring better results without the glare of publicity.

With the election of the federal Conservatives to office in 1984, the NEP was quickly dismantled. Announcing that Canada was again "open for business," the Mulroney Conservative government defanged what it called "the FIRA tiger," transforming it into a new agency, Investment Canada, whose mandate was to encourage foreign investment. By the mid-1980s, a wave of foreign takeovers of Canadian companies led economic nationalist Mel Hurtig, a book publisher and chairman of a nationalist group called the Council of Canadians, to comment that matters have " ... gone from being open for business to selling out the country." Most Canadians appeared unconcerned.

Recession and Recovery

Recession hit Canada, as it did the rest of the world, early in the 1980s. Partly it was the result of policies for fighting inflation, as no apparent solution existed that would enable governments to combat inflation and unemployment simultaneously. It also stemmed from worldwide over-production in the resource industries, in agriculture, and in secondary manufacturing. In 1981–82 production in Canada declined by 5.5 percent, making this the most severe post-war recession. Frequent magazine articles evoked the Great Depression of the 1930s. The daily press offered a sombre litany of factory closings, layoffs, cutbacks, and countless austerity meas-ures. Canada's Roman Catholic bishops solemnly pinned the blame for unemployment upon a structural crisis within international capitalism. But the economic crisis did bring the inflation rate down from 12.5 percent in 1981 to 5.8 percent in 1983, and then even lower.

By 1983, some regions of Canada were well on the road to recovery. With the return to health of the auto industry and of manufacturing in general, southern Ontario prospered. Other regions of the country, af-flicted by low oil prices (like Alberta and Nova Scotia), by poor weather as well as financial and sales problems in agriculture, or by limited markets for resources, did not fare as well; unemployment levels remained high and even increased. Young people found it especially difficult to break into the job market.

SIGNS OF ECONOMIC RECOVERY

The recovery improved the public image of business leaders. Although bank failures did shake Canadians' confidence in their supposedly solid banking system, gone (at least temporarily) was former NDP leader David Lewis's 1972 election campaign image of "corporate welfare bums" who had unjustifiably benefited from government subsidies and tax privileges. Polls showed that Canadians feared big government and, in Quebec, big unions far more than big corporations. Popular interest was rekindled in a new group of businessmen, such as the Belzbergs, the Bronfmans, the Reichmanns, Conrad Black of Toronto-based Argus Corporation (whom Peter Newman presented rather heroically as the new prince of the Ca-nadian establishment), Pierre Desmarais of Montreal's Power Corporation, and Pierre Péladeau, President of Quebecor in Montreal, whose empire grew from a tiny periodical he bought in 1950 with a loan of $1500, to a $450 million press and printing empire.

As the recession eased, better economic conditions led to an increase in imports while the prices of many Canadian exports, like forest products, minerals, and grain, stagnated or—as in the case of gas and oil—decreased. Canada's major exports and imports (close to one-third of the total) re-mained autos and auto parts. Canadians still sold more goods abroad than they bought, but the country ran a large deficit in the flow of investment income and the services trade.

428

At the same time Canadians could no longer count on assuring their prosperity simply by developing their natural resources. In the opinion of two hundred prominent community leaders polled in early 1987, Canada was "a second-rate economic power moving towards third-rate status." Cut-throat worldwide competition contributed to the decline of many of Canada's resource towns like Sudbury; Schefferville, Quebec; and some other mining towns in northern Quebec and northern Ontario. If Canada wanted to boost its share of world trade, it had to increase sales of manufactured goods abroad. A 1982 Conference Board survey warned that "Canada's relative lack of diversification has contributed to a fall in our share of world trade," from 4.7 to 3.6 percent in 1955–79. Canada has had some brilliant successes in conquering outside markets, in areas like telecommunications and rapid transit, but it had to do much more—and it has had to do it in the face of rising worldwide protectionism.

429

The Great Free Trade Debate

In this context, a new chapter in the perennial debate over trade relations with the United States began. Brian Mulroney's Conservatives promised during the election campaign of 1984 to work for free trade and increased investment. Actually, their ultimate objective appeared uncertain. Conservative Trade minister James Kelleher defined the goal as "the removal of tariffs and non-tariff barriers on substantially all bilateral trade" with the United States. Others talked more prudently of enhanced trade or simply of freer trade. Who could be affected? What would be the costs and benefits? It was obviously difficult to answer these questions with any degree of certitude.

The government defended its proposal by invoking the need to boost Canada's share of world trade to create jobs and to preserve living standards. Prime Minister Brian Mulroney told Canadians that "a comprehensive trade agreement with the U.S." was an essential step towards lowering the unemployment rate to manageable proportions. During the first Commons debate on the subject in 1987, Mulroney argued that free trade would benefit Canada's have-not regions, so that "Newfoundlanders and British Columbians and Albertans and others ... get their chance. They must be given the opportunity to trade their way to prosperity."

Free trade advocates were numerous. The Royal Commission on the Economic Union and Development Prospects for Canada, chaired by Donald Macdonald, endorsed it. Many sectors of the business community had long favoured it; polls showed that, in the early stages of the debate, a solid majority of Canadians backed it, too. Consumers were generally convinced that free trade would bring lower prices, and more efficient Canadian industries.

OPPOSITION TO FREE TRADE

As the debate gathered force, public support for the project began to cool. American protectionist measures contributed to weakening Canadian enthusiasm. Labour unions, farmers, the federal NDP and Liberal parties, some provinces (especially Ontario) and several businesses warned that free trade would cost thousands of jobs, that entire indigenous industries could disappear. Canada's breweries, for example, inefficient because of their small local markets, affirmed that they could not compete with the American giants. Also U.S. companies might close their higher-cost branch plants in Canada and serve the Canadian market from their more productive American base. Remaining subsidiaries could find their autonomy ever more circumscribed by parent firms interested in rationalizing production. Canada could lose control over the pricing of resources like fish and lumber and be forced to abandon transport subsidies in the agricultural sector.

430

It was also argued that Canada's trade relationship with the United States was working well and only needed maintenance from time to time, and that although Canada's share of world export trade was declining, its trade share with the United States was increasing. Indeed, in 1985, Americans bought nearly 80 percent of Canada's exports—an historical record. What was really necessary was to boost declining exports to the rest of the world.

Anti-free traders further warned that Canada might be forced to curtail its social programmes, and might even have to sacrifice control over its own cultural industries, the vehicles of Canada's elusive, hard-to-define identity. Worst of all—here were shades of the 1911 election and the reciprocity debate (see chapter 7)—was the possibility that free trade could jeopardize Canada's political sovereignty. Free traders insisted they would not sacrifice the Canadian identity. While admitting that dislocations were inevitable, they warned that Canada had ultimately to face worldwide competition. Some branch plants might close but others would specialize in producing large runs of a small number of products, thus overcoming one of the major causes of Canadian inefficiency.

As Canadians hotly debated the issue, trade negotiations moved forward arduously, culminating in the conclusion first of a preliminary agreement in October 1987, then of a detailed accord in December. Very serious obstacles remained however: in the United States, the agreement had to be ratified by the Senate, while in Canada, its future appeared to depend on the outcome of the next general election.

The 1980s: Charting New Courses through Troubled Waters

The 1980s also demonstrated the necessity of other painful readjustments. "Reaganomics" came to Canada (though in milder form) as conservative-minded Canadians vigorously criticized the role of government in the economy. During the 1984 summer election campaign, the Conservatives promised to reduce the size of government by getting rid of regulations and cutting civil service staff and by privatizing Crown corporations.

One major reason underlying the campaign for smaller government was cost. During the late 1970s, public finances deterioriated and deficits greatly increased. New or improved social programmes introduced in the 1960s and early 1970s, as well as vastly improved educational and health services, became more expensive. Inflation greatly increased costs. Higher unemployment levels drove up expenses and caused revenues to fall.

Solutions were not easy to find. It was difficult to reduce services upon which Canadians had come to rely. Politicians naturally feared that drastic tax increases would bring them electoral ruin. The painless, though admittedly short-term, remedy was to borrow more, even at historically high interest rates, in the hope that conditions would somehow improve and that the problem would resolve itself, or that it would be bequeathed to tomorrow's politicians and taxpayers.

431

THE FEDERAL DEFICIT

Public finances reeled under the heavy blow of the recession of the early 1980s, and recovery did little to alleviate the situation. In 1985 the government had a record shortfall of more than $38 billion. Newspaper stories depicted a wailing infant with the caption: "Already $8000 in debt." That was each Canadian's share of the $200 billion-and-growing national debt. By 1987, the baby owed nearly $14 000 when rising provincial indebtedness was taken into account, and Ottawa was devoting about one-quarter of its revenues simply to paying interest on its borrowings. Some economists contended that the federal debt was not a genuine burden since it was owed to Canadians and interest payments remained within the country. But most economists and business leaders saw the deficit as a "time bomb, ticking away." Brian Mulroney, speaking in Toronto in February 1986, promised Canadians: "Our determination to reduce it or eradicate it is, and will be, unyielding and successful."

Canadians generally agreed that governments had to control their budgets and cut back waste, many examples of which came to light in the annual reports of auditors general. Governments at all levels did reduce hiring and practiced some restraint. Capping expansion of the public sector was perhaps acceptable to most Canadians because they were not employed by the state; yet such measures were only part of the solution.

Canadians wanted governments to reduce expenditures but without ruthlessly cutting services. They had become used to government intervention and were not about to forego appeals to the politicians in times of need. They wanted the health services that the state provided, and family allowances, and old-age pensions. When the Mulroney government expressed its intention to index old-age pensions only partly to the rise in living costs, senior citizens mobilized and forced the government to retreat. The less-organized family lobby vainly urged inflation-proof family allowances.

After two western banks crashed resoundingly in 1985, investors successfully demanded reimbursement of their losses. When refineries closed in Montreal, taking away more jobs in the city's hard-hit east end, pressures mounted for Ottawa to take corrective measures. When oil prices declined, that hard-hit industry urged the government to set a price floor. Struggling western grain producers pleaded for financial support. In areas of high unemployment, local potentates sought an array of subsidies and low-cost loans to help create new jobs or save threatened ones. Industry and the universities denounced Canada's low spending levels on research and development. Provinces claimed more money from Ottawa for education and health care. Municipalities demanded more money from provinces for sewers, roads, libraries, and public transport. Few Canadians, it seemed, really wanted the state to wither away.

The Mulroney government's substantial tax increases, concerning not only the so-called "sin taxes" on cigarettes and alcohol, but also sales taxes, excise taxes, and income taxes, dissatisfied many Canadians, particularly when they looked at the cheap gasoline and low income taxes south of the border. Moreover, although two-thirds of Canadians believed that their country's tax system was unfair, they regarded Conservative plans to reform it by reducing income taxes (while extending the federal sales tax to cover food and services like haircuts and automobile repairs) as quite unacceptable. By 1987, the federal deficit still hovered above $30 billion, while the financial health of many provincial governments deteriorated.

By most criteria, Canadians in the 1980s generally live better than their parents did in the "prosperous" 1950s. At least until 1978 wages advanced more quickly than prices, making it possible for Canadians to buy more. A 1986 survey by the Organization of Economic Co-operation and Development showed Canada in second place, behind the United States, in terms of the industrial worker's take-home pay and the number of hours an individual must work in order to purchase a range of basic goods and services. Higher education has become widely available. One-third of Canadians now have at least some post-secondary education; in the 1950s very few of their parents had been to university. Canadians travel far more than in the past. Social programmes provide a security blanket offering at least minimal protection from the cradle to the grave. In 1987, the Population Crisis Committee in Washington, D.C. judged Canada sixth best in the world for its quality of human life; Switzerland placed first, and the United States, fifth.

Paradoxically, economic problems have multiplied. The late 1980s are presenting Canadians with challenges of great magnitude. Trade relations and the restructuring of the Canadian economy will remain important issues. The unequal economic development of Canada's regions will need constant attention. Environmental issues have become matters of increasingly grave concern, as Canadians discover the true costs of maintaining clean water, clean air, and clean soil. The coming years will show whether Canada can successfully meet these formidable new challenges.

433

NOTES

[1] O.J. Firestone, *Industry and Education: A Century of Canadian Development* (Ottawa, 1969), p. 124.
[2] Quoted in Bruce Thordarson, *Trudeau and Foreign Policy: A Study in Decision-Making* (Toronto, 1972), p. 5.
[3] Stephen Clarkson, *Canada and the Reagan Challenge: Crisis in the Canadian-American Relationship* (Toronto, 1982), pp. 87, 90.

Related Readings

The following reading from R. Douglas Francis and Donald B. Smith, eds., *Readings in Canadian History: Post-Confederation*, 2d ed. (Toronto, 1986) presents one side of the economic debate of the 1960s on American ownership of Canadian natural resources and industries: Kari Levitt, "Regression to Dependence," pp. 570–78.

BIBLIOGRAPHY

Two general syntheses cover parts of the period since 1960: J.L. Granatstein, *Canada, 1957–1967* (Toronto, 1986), and Robert Bothwell, Ian Drummond, and John English, *Canada since 1945: Power, Politics, and Provincialism* (Toronto, 1981). The *Canadian Annual Review* published since 1961, contains a wealth of information. Statistics on all aspects of the economy are available in F.H. Leacy, ed., *Historical Statistics of Canada*

(Ottawa, 1983). An excellent synthesis of business history is Michael Bliss, *Northern Enterprise: Five Centuries of Canadian Business* (Toronto, 1987).

R.C. Bellan and W.H. Pope, eds., *The Canadian Economy: Problems and Options* (Toronto, 1981) discusses economic issues. Some government economic policies are studied in W. Craig Riddell, *Dealing with Inflation and Unemployment in Canada* (Toronto, 1985). James Laxer, *Canada's Economic Strategy* (Toronto, 1981) examines the rise of Western Canada's economy in the 1970s.

A large number of studies by economic nationalists deal with Canadian-American economic relations. See, for example, Kari Levitt's oft-quoted *Silent Surrender: The Multinational Corporation in Canada* (Toronto, 1970); and Abraham Rotstein and Gary Lax, eds., *Independence, the Canadian Challenge* (Toronto, 1972); as well as the same editors' *Getting it Back* (Toronto, 1974). For a biography of economist nationalist Walter Gordon, see Denis Smith, *Gentle Patriot* (Edmonton, 1973). One recent provocative survey bearing on many economic aspects of Canadian-American relations is Stephen Clarkson's *Canada and the Reagan Challenge* (Toronto, 1985).

On the free trade debate, see Nuala Beck and Richard Krystak, *Free Trade: A Comparative Analysis of Economic Policies and Industrial Competitiveness in Canada and the United States* (Toronto, 1985); Duncan Cameron, ed., *The Free Trade Papers* (Toronto, 1986); James Laxer, *Leap of Faith: Free Trade and the Future of Canada* (Edmonton, 1986); Richard G. Lipsey and Murray G. Smith, *Taking the Initiative: Canada's Trade Options in a Turbulent World* (Montreal, 1985); and John Whalley, res. coord., *Canada–United States Free Trade* (Toronto, 1985). Canadian-American economic relations in general are examined in Denis Stairs and Gilbert R. Winham, *The Politics of Canada's Economic Relationship with the United States* (Toronto, 1985).

Peter C. Newman's biography of Conrad Black, *The Establishment Man* (Toronto, 1982) is a readable account of a leading Canadian businessman. On the families controlling the Canadian economy, also see Diane Francis, *Controlling Interest* (Toronto, 1986). Books on the energy question include Philip Sykes' highly critical *Sellout: The Giveaway of Canada's Energy Resources* (Edmonton, 1973); James Laxer, *Canada's Energy Crisis* (Toronto, 1975); and G. Bruce Doern and Glen Toner, *The Politics of Energy* (Toronto, 1984). Western agriculture is covered in C.F. Wilson, *A Century of Canadian Grain* (Saskatoon, 1978).

CHAPTER TWENTY-ONE

Politics since 1960

Historians' growing predilection for social and economic themes since the   *435*
1960s has usefully enlarged the field of study of the profession. The resulting de-emphasis on politics, however, surely does not reflect any marked
decline of concern for such questions among the population. Indeed, since
the late 1950s, Canadians have shown passionate interest in some of their
political leaders, and politicians have frequently kindled voters' expectations. The realities of government has usually meant, however, that these
hopes have led to disappointment. As Prime Minister Brian Mulroney,
back from a trip to the West, remarked to voters in Baie Comeau, Quebec:
"Canada is a difficult country to govern!"

In earlier chapters we have seen the difficulties that Macdonald, Laurier,
King, and other political leaders encountered in attempting to satisfy the
conflicting demands emanating from Canada's regions, ethnic communities, and interest groups. The problem is thus not new, but in the past
quarter-century it has become more difficult to build and especially to
maintain a workable political consensus. Old loyalties have broken down,
and voters have become more volatile. As Canadian society has become
more complex, lobbies seeking to influence government policy have multiplied. Increased state intervention has made citizens more dependent on
governments, and thus more demanding of them.

Politics in the Age of Mass Media

Since Confederation, Canadian politics has been largely focussed on personalities. Political scientists have explained this tendency by the assertion
that the two major parties have not differed significantly on questions of
basic principle, and that "longstanding and well-understood ideological
differences do not emerge during campaigns."[1] What parties have offered

is different leaders, and leadership thus becomes a significant asset or a liability.

The advent of television undoubtedly increased this focus on the leader. Television has been a rapid and effective means of communicating information, and through the news and televised events such as leadership conventions, it has brought the politicians into the homes of Canadians. At the same time, as political scientist Frederick J. Fletcher has pointed out, television has inhibited thoughtful exposition of policies and promoted "simple and flashy promises and one-line put-downs of the opposition."[2] Though John Meisel, chairman of the Canadian Radio-Television and Telecommunications Commission from 1980 until 1984, admits that television has provided "a matchless opportunity to witness the party game," he is convinced that "politics and politicians are filtered by a medium in which the primary concern is often not enlightenment, knowledge or consciousness-raising but maximal audiences and profits."[3] Finally, television now plays a major role in moulding images—sometimes favourable, sometimes unfavourable—of politicians.

436

Diefenbaker: A Prophet Outcast

Conservative leader John Diefenbaker (1957–63) benefited in 1957 and again in 1958 from a remarkably positive image (see chapter 15); by 1960 he was fast acquiring a very negative one. Diefenbaker's victory in 1958, after nine months of minority government, was paralleled only by his fall from grace in 1962, when he barely managed to retain power with a minority government. A year later he was in opposition. It took but five short years to destroy the boundless confidence that Canadians had placed in "Dief the Chief."

One reason for this rapid change was that much of Diefenbaker's support in 1958 had been weak, notably in Quebec where party organization had long been deficient. Diefenbaker's French was dreadful and often the subject of ridicule. His royalism, his ferocious loyalty to the Union Jack during the Flag debate of 1964, his championing of so-called unhyphenated Canadianism—in Quebec these aspects were reasons *not* to vote for him. Moreover, Diefenbaker understood little of the awakening that that province was experiencing; indeed, the Conservative party would struggle unsuccessfully for two decades to deal with the complex "Quebec question." As for the urban-rural or centre-periphery division in Canada, it had long plagued Canadian political parties when they debated such issues as tariffs and railways; it would continue to torment politicians long after Diefenbaker had left the stage.

The government itself seemed disorganized and rife with dissension: Diefenbaker complained that enemies from within were plotting to "deliver up my head on a silver platter." Most to blame, in journalist Peter Newman's opinion, was Diefenbaker himself, a "renegade in power" who had conquered a generation and brought only disillusionment.[4]

To some extent, the controversial prime minister was a victim of circumstances. After twenty-two years in opposition, the Conservatives had no experience with the art of governing, nor could they count on the support of many Ottawa bureaucrats whose loyalties lay with the Liberal party. The severe recession of 1960–61 was not Diefenbaker's fault any more than the Great Depression had been of R.B. Bennett's making. Still, the bad times inevitably had deleterious effects on Conservative budgets and considerably reduced the government's ability to launch new policies. Instead of development proposals, the minister of Finance had to resort to austerity measures and to arrange credits with the International Monetary Fund.

Many Canadians charged Diefenbaker with economic mismanagement. After 1960, the Canadian economy showed serious weaknesses: budgetary deficits rose (although they were trifling by contemporary standards), the Canadian dollar fell, and unemployment grew steadily. Atlantic and western Canada continued to endorse the Conservatives. But Ontario and Quebec, and especially the cities, opposed him. By 1962, even traditionally Conservative newspapers like the Toronto *Globe and Mail* and the Montreal *Gazette*, evoking the business community's loss of confidence in Diefenbaker, were calling for a Liberal government to "get us out of the abyss."

437

STRAINED CANADIAN-AMERICAN RELATIONS

Others deplored strained Canadian-American relations and what they felt was Canada's deteriorating international image. Diefenbaker had promised to divert more trade to Great Britain; he hoped to control American investment in Canada. As well in 1962–63 he refused (thereby reversing himself) to accept the nuclear warheads that the Americans wanted to install in their anti-aircraft missiles on Canadian soil, even though shortly after the 1957 election he had without cabinet scrutiny committed Canada to NORAD — the North American air defence plan by which Canadian and American officers would jointly administer an integrated air defence force under supreme American command. Moreover, he intensely disliked President Kennedy. Nor did Kennedy have any liking for the Canadian prime minister; the briefing notes he received on Diefenbaker were highly negative. Lawrence Martin, at the time the *Globe and Mail*'s Washington correspondent, wrote that Canadian-American relations were plunged into what was, up until then, their "worst state of disrepair in the century."[5] In these years of incipient Canadian nationalism, Canadians began to agonize over the kind of relationship they wanted with their southern neighbour.

Diefenbaker's somewhat clumsy attempts to re-orient Canadian policy reflected the will of part of the electorate, but they also provoked the disgruntlement of many other Canadians, including several Conservative cabinet ministers.

Federal Third Parties, Right and Left

The rapid decline of federal Conservative strength in Quebec coincided with the rise of a third party in that province. Social Credit was strong in Alberta, but in Quebec, though present since the late 1930s, it remained a fringe group. Then, in 1962, to the surprise and even stupefaction of most observers, it won one-quarter of the popular vote and twenty-six seats—one-third of the province's total. In evaluating the *créditistes*, the *Montreal Star* recalled a comment by the Duke of Wellington, the British general of the Napoleonic era, who welcomed a battalion of new recruits of doubtful quality with the remark: "I don't know how Napoleon will find them but, great God, they frighten me!"

438

POPULARITY OF THE CRÉDITISTES

Social Credit's success in the election may be explained partly by Quebeckers' obvious desire for change. For some, a vote for the *créditistes* was a way of striking back against the establishment. Leader Réal Caouette, an automobile salesman from Rouyn who had joined Social Credit in 1939, carried his crusade through rural and small-town Quebec. He promised a national dividend to all citizens to raise consumers' buying power. He pledged help for the aged, the unemployed, and large families, and most of all he assured voters that they had nothing to lose by trying Social Credit. Caouette delivered the same message to weekly television audiences. No one could ignore the fiery orator's own contribution to his party's success; to journalist Peter Gzowski, Caouette was a "demagogue" who combined in his personality something of Alberta Social Credit leader William Aberhart, French right-wing politician Pierre Poujade, Argentine dictator Juan Peron, and the American Dale Carnegie, author of the bestseller *How to Win Friends and Influence People*.

Political scientists Maurice Pinard and Vincent Lemieux have examined other dimensions of Social Credit's success. Pinard demonstrated that its support was strongest in regions where the Liberals' backing was traditionally weakest. Lemieux studied the formidable organizational work carried out by party members, often in the kitchens of ordinary citizens far from the prying eyes of curious journalists.[6]

Whatever the reasons for Social Credit success, the impact on federal

Liberal fortunes was considerable: it seriously reduced the party's strength in the province, probably costing it the election in 1962 while ensuring that it could form only a minority government in 1963 and again in 1965.

A RECONSTITUTED CCF

Less spectacular was the reconstitution of the national CCF. After its very poor showing in the federal election of 1958, the CCF decided to co-operate with the Canadian Labour Congress and with left-wing organizations to form a broad-based movement for social reform. The result was the launching in 1961 of the New Democratic Party and the choice of Tommy Douglas, then premier of Saskatchewan, as its leader. The party programme called for jobs, health insurance, free education and, in a break with the CCF's past tendency to favour a powerful central government, a policy of "co-operative federalism." Financial and organizational difficulties quickly put an end to the euphoria of the new party's first moments, and electoral results during the 1960s at both the federal and provincial levels proved disappointing.

439

Third parties contended that the "old-line" parties had identical policies and were both devoted to serving the interests of business. Only third parties offered a real alternative and showed concern for the plight of the ordinary citizens. John Diefenbaker and Lester Pearson often seemed to do their best to reinforce claims that not much difference existed between the old parties' national leaders.

POLITICS IN DISARRAY

Politics in the early 1960s promoted cynicism among many voters. The problems that the country faced were grave indeed: at the beginning of the decade, more Canadians were out of work than at any time since the Great Depression, and the country was incurring large deficits in foreign trade. Prices were moving up, too, and provoking costly demands from some unions. Relations with the provinces were strained, while growing discord also characterized ties with the United States. All the while, the Conservatives' leader John Diefenbaker and the Liberals' Lester B. Pearson appeared to have no vision or long-term plan about what could be done.

Four times, these two knights in tarnished armour faced each other on the electoral battlefield; only at the first encounter, in 1958, were they greatly mismatched. In 1962, 1963, and again in 1965, neither was able to win enough seats in the House to form a majority government. Each made numerous—and costly—promises in attempts to rally enough voter support. Some of their techniques, borrowing heavily from Madison Avenue, elicited mockery and disdain. The Liberals published colouring books portraying Diefenbaker riding backwards on a rocking horse, and they formed a "truth squad" whose purpose was to pursue the Conservatives relentlessly across the country and make sure they told the truth (the squad lasted all of three days). Once elected, Canada's parliamentarians then devoted themselves to discussing a seemingly endless succession of alleged scandals. In his memoirs, Lester B. Pearson gave the title "Politics in Disrepute" to a chapter on the years 1964 and 1965.

The Pearson Years

While in office from 1963 until 1968, Pearson did attempt to solve new problems. He sought to conciliate the provinces and initiated a series of federal-provincial conferences on the Canadian constitution. In answer to French Canadians' claims for linguistic equality, he set up the Royal Commission on Bilingualism and Biculturalism to study the issue. His government adopted numerous social measures, such as the Canada Pension Plan and universal medicare. After weeks of debate, it gave Canadians a national flag.

LIBERAL CRITICS

Yet his critics were numerous. Most reproached the Liberal prime minister for his failure to give the country firm and sure leadership. Business thought his election promises impossibly costly and blamed him for surrendering too easily to the unions, while labour portrayed itself as the victim, not the cause, of inflation. Canadian nationalists accused him of doing little to counter the Americanization of Canada; in cultural matters, for example, legislation designed to assist Canadian magazines contained important exemptions for the two biggest American magazines in Canada, *Time* and *Reader's Digest*. To protect Canada, Pearson authorized nuclear warheads for American missiles in the country. Canadians hotly debated the issue of American ownership of the Canadian economy but the Pearson government did little to control American investments. Although Finance minister Walter Gordon did include proposals to limit foreign investment in his budget in 1963, he was obliged to back off ignominiously.

Quebec nationalists thought Pearson was resisting their province's legitimate demands, while at the same time strong centralists declared that his vacillation was balkanizing the country. Monarchists censured him for tolerating creeping republicanism while French Canadians and new Cana-

National Archives of Canada C-90482.

Prime Minister Lester B. Pearson visits President John F. Kennedy at Hyannisport on Cape Cod. Pearson's relationship with the American president was far more cordial than Diefenbaker's had been.

dians favoured a loosening of Canada's ties with the British monarch. Unhappy residents of the Atlantic provinces thought he was doing little to alleviate regional disparities, and westerners judged him ill-attuned to their region's interests. In sum, Pearson endeared himself to really none of the regions or major interest groups.

Perhaps Pearson and his Liberal administration should not have been expected to build a consensus on the major questions of the day when Canadians themselves could not agree on the answers. The 1960s were a time of increasing polarization, and in that climate Pearson manoeuvred with some skill. The policy of "co-operative federalism," by which Ottawa showed greater sensitivity to provincial concerns, was perhaps the best that could be hoped for in a climate of confrontation between Ottawa and the provinces, particularly Quebec. In regard to French-English relations, the establishment of a royal commission, though hardly a solution, appeared a logical step to take. As for the economy and the growing problem of inflation, the long-term solutions were hardly apparent. Also, even though the Pearson government did have more than its share of scandals, the prime minister's own conduct was above suspicion.

Finally, concerning American-Canadian economic and cultural relations, perhaps delay was necessary while Canadians debated options. American participation in the Vietnam War certainly poisoned relations between the North American neighbours. After Pearson made a speech in Philadelphia in April 1965 urging Americans to stop bombing North Vietnam, President Lyndon B. Johnson invited him to Camp David. There, greatly irritated, he seized Pearson by the shirt and told him in earthy language what he thought of this speech delivered in Johnson's own "backyard." As the war escalated, so did Canadian criticism of American actions in Vietnam. The American government could only express regret for the lack of support from its northern ally.

Many Canadians have viewed the Diefenbaker–Pearson years as the culminating point of a bygone and increasingly repugnant brand of politics. The public longed for a new style, a new type of leadership, an imaginative and refreshing approach to the complex issues of the day. In 1968, many believed they found all this with Pierre Elliott Trudeau.

442

From Trudeaumania to Trudeauphobia

It was not apparent who might succeed Pearson when the Liberal leader announced his resignation in late 1967. Journalists like Claude Ryan of *Le Devoir* wrote that the Liberal party was in need of as profound a transformation as the American Democratic party had undergone with Kennedy. A number of central Canadian intellectuals, like historian Ramsay Cook, actively promoted Trudeau's candidacy. Trudeau, as Justice minister, attracted much attention at the Constitutional Conference in early 1968, where he jousted with Quebec Premier Daniel Johnson over the role of the federal government.

TRUDEAU'S BACKGROUND

Trudeau had been elected for the first time in 1965, when Pearson had convinced him, along with labour leader Jean Marchand and journalist Gérard Pelletier, to enter the House of Commons to help renew Quebec's presence in Ottawa. Prior to that period, Trudeau had generally favoured the NDP and its predecessor, the CCF. During the Duplessis years, Trudeau had been a bitter critic of the Union Nationale regime and, with Pelletier, had established a small-circulation review called *Cité libre* to give a voice to liberal-minded Quebeckers. He had also studied at Harvard and at the London School of Economics and obtained a law degree. And he had been a globe trotter. But was he the leader the Liberals needed? Quebec nationalists had no liking for this intellectual who incessantly stigmatized separatism. Business did not have confidence in a candidate who had lacked

443

National Archives of Canada C-25003.

Prime Minister Lester B. Pearson recruited Quebec stars Pierre Elliott Trudeau, Gérard Pelletier and Jean Marchand—John Diefenbaker called them "the Three Wise Men"—to run for the Liberal party in 1965.

experience in the corporate world; indeed, the business community had its own candidate at the 1968 leadership convention—Robert Winters, one of St. Laurent's appointees to the federal cabinet.

Nevertheless, Trudeau's style and his background intrigued delegates at the Ottawa leadership convention. His image was of a wealthy bachelor surrounded by beautiful women. He was athletic, drove a Mercedes sports car, and often dressed flamboyantly. As the *Globe and Mail* put it: "He is the man we all would like to be: charming, rich, talented, successful." This image was certainly at the base of the wave of "Trudeaumania" that broke out during the Liberal leadership race and reached its zenith during the election in June 1968, which the Liberals won easily.

TRUDEAU'S PROGRAMME

444

Trudeau's programme was surely not of the same order as Pearson's or Diefenbaker's had been. In the 1968 election campaign, he made few specific promises designed to buy blocks of voters with their own money. Rather he expressed a number of general priorities. He attempted to define the "just society" that he wanted Canadians to build: a society whose personal and political liberties were ensured by a Charter of Rights, a society in which minorities would be sheltered from the caprices of majorities, in which regions and social groups who had not participated fully in the country's material abundance would have greater opportunities. He wanted to discuss with Canadians their country's future; this emphasis on participatory democracy was what appealed to and attracted many electors. Trudeau also promised a complete revision of Canada's foreign policy in an effort to re-orient and reinvigorate Canadian activity abroad.

Trudeau had much to say on the constitutional question as well. When he asked for a strong mandate to oppose the Quebec government's ambitions to play a role in international affairs, the *Globe and Mail* congratulated him for his "firmness." He vigorously attacked new Conservative leader Robert Stanfield's implicit support for the "two nations" doctrine of a more decentralized Canada. For advocates of a strong central government, here was someone who would stand up to the provinces, which they viewed as continually encroaching upon Ottawa's authority. Trudeau could also promise Quebec that he would promote bilingualism in Canada, notably in the federal civil service, and that he would give Quebec and French Canada a major role to play in federal politics. Moreover, like Laurier and St. Laurent before him, he was a French-speaking Canadian.

TRUDEAU'S RECORD

The Trudeau years were replete with paradoxes. Trudeau had promised to strive for national unity—he championed this trusty Liberal theme at

445

National Archives of Canada/D. Cameron.

Trudeau savours his fourth-ballot victory at the Liberal Party's leadership convention in April 1968.

election after election—but during his term in office the country faced probably the most serious threats to its existence that it had ever confronted, especially in Quebec and in the western provinces. He had insisted on the need to defend Canadians' political liberties; yet perhaps at no moment was that need more graphically expressed than during the FLQ crisis of October 1970, when the government, by invoking the War Measures Act, in effect suspended civil liberties and the police arrested hundreds of individuals and held them incommunicado for several days without laying charges against most of them (see chapter 17). When advocates of civil liberties protested, his response was to call them "weak-kneed bleeding hearts."

Trudeau had also frequently denounced the dangers of nationalism, but after the legislation controlling foreign investment and foreign magazines, as well as his National Energy Programme of 1980, Americans were convinced that they were dealing with a strident nationalist. He had promised, in the name of justice, to expand the role of the French language in Canada and to place French-speaking Canadians on an equal footing with English-speaking Canadians. His government adopted the Official Languages Act in 1969 to ensure that government services would be more widely available in French. But, while many French Canadians despaired of ever attaining genuine equality, many English-speaking Canadians complained that they were now the victims of unfair treatment. Finally, Trudeau had promised to battle regional imbalances. With this objective in mind, he set up the Department of Regional Economic Expansion, and increased equalization payments and other transfers to the provinces. But, as economist Paul Philipps has stated, these measures, while important in reducing disparities, had little effect on their root causes, that is, an industrial structure favourable to the central regions of Canada, and the dependence on resources of most parts of the Canadian hinterland.[7]

Even though Trudeau held office for fifteen years—as long as Laurier—his government frequently had to weather substantial voter disaffection. By 1972, Trudeaumania had been transformed into Trudeauphobia, as the seemingly modest Trudeau of 1968, who had said that he wanted to listen to Canadians, was now transformed into an arrogant, remote, temperamental personality. As political scientist John Meisel put it: Trudeau "appeared increasingly unable to suffer not only fools but also critics, gladly."[8] The trademark rose in Trudeau's lapel had changed into a thorn. The election results in 1972 signalled near disaster: 109 Liberals, 107 Conservatives, 31 New Democrats, and 15 *Créditistes*. Canadians were surely reacting negatively to the new Trudeau image. But questions of policy were also important considerations. In a few districts, the backlash against bilingualism and French power cost the Liberals dearly. The government's apparent inability to handle economic questions—not only inflation but also unemployment, welfare, strikes, and high taxes—also weighed very heavily in any explanation of voter disaffection. Only the New Dem-

446

ocrats could feel jubilant: they increased their popular vote to 18 percent and prepared to enter a short but sweet era of "performance."[9]

Liberal Ups and Downs

During the two-year minority government that followed the election of 1972, the prime minister and his Cabinet took several measures to win back voter approval. The government greatly increased public spending on social programmes and indexed income tax brackets and exemptions to protect taxpayers from inflation. A multiculturalism programme was announced in an effort to attract ethnic voters. To win support in central Canada, the government promised to keep oil prices, which were increasing rapidly, to levels substantially below world levels, a policy which, however, hurt the oil producing western provinces. In the hope of appeasing nationalist discontent, it established the Foreign Investment Review Agency (FIRA). When, in 1974, Opposition leader Stanfield promised a wage and price freeze, labour hesitated, then gave its support to Trudeau who declared his opposition to such a freeze. "Zap! You're Frozen!" he mocked in one notorious repartee. Trudeau won re-election in 1974 with a majority; the next year the Liberals reversed themselves and adopted a wage and price freeze.

447

Between 1974 and 1979, the polls showed Liberal support fluctuating wildly; at one point in 1976 it sank lower than any governing party had known since polling had begun in the early 1940s. By 1979, with Canada again in a severe inflationary crisis and the government lacking ideas on how to right the economy, support was at best shaky. The business community in particular was worried over the foundering economy and the rapidly rising federal deficit. Ontario resented the fact that its representation in the Cabinet was weak. The West, embittered against the Liberals for more than twenty years, lamented that Trudeau was insensitive to its grievances. With the notable exception of Quebec, the Trudeau consensus thus largely broke apart, with the result that the Conservatives, under their new leader Joe Clark, won a fragile mandate in the election of May 1979.

JOE CLARK'S CONSERVATIVE GOVERNMENT

Clark's unfavourable image, though largely undeserved and based on a superficial appreciation of the individual, was nevertheless a heavy yoke for the Conservatives to bear, both in and out of power. The morning after his victory in the 1976 Conservative leadership race, a *Toronto Star* headline read "Joe Who?" The gibe remained to haunt Clark even after he became prime minister. Journalist Jeffrey Simpson concluded that the Tories won the election of 1979 not because of Clark but in spite of him. As a leader, Clark was never a match for Trudeau. While not afflicted with Trudeau's arrogance and addiction to power, Clark lacked the Liberal leader's qualities of intellect and vision as well as his enviable international reputation.

The energy question, which divided producing provinces and consuming provinces, was the issue that brought the collapse of Clark's brief government. Promoting a policy of "short-term pain for long-term gain," Finance Minister John Crosbie instituted an immediate eighteen cents per-gallon excise tax on gasoline (about four cents per litre) designed to bring billions of dollars into the federal treasury in order to attack the rising deficit. In the House, the opposition parties combined to defeat the government and thereby provoke its resignation. The new tax, which former-and-new Liberal leader Pierre Trudeau promised to revoke, proved immensely unpopular with the Canadian public. During the ensuing election campaign Joe Clark continued to suffer from his strongly negative image of a weak and indecisive prime minister, as Liberal organizers encouraged Trudeau to adopt a low profile in order not to revive public antipathy towards him. The outcome was a Liberal victory in February 1980 and the return to power of Pierre Trudeau.

TRUDEAU'S FINAL YEARS IN POWER

Trudeau's final mandate was probably more difficult than any other. True, the danger of Quebec separatism seemed remote after the referendum in May 1980, even though Quebeckers returned René Lévesque and the Parti Québécois to power a year later (see chapter 17). True, too, Trudeau did succeed against fairly formidable odds in repatriating the constitution in April 1982 and in attaching to it the Charter of Rights and Freedoms and an amendment formula. But voters were primarily interested in economic questions, and the deep recession of 1980–82 (see chapter 20) with the extremely high rates of unemployment that accompanied it provoked new animosity. Other economic issues, like the declining value of the Canadian dollar in terms of American currency, the growing federal deficit, and escalating interest rates, led to continued accusations of economic mismanagement. Finally, the constantly unfavourable polls and the selection by the Conservatives of businessman Brian Mulroney to replace Joe Clark as party leader convinced Trudeau that it was time to resign. His successor as leader, John Turner, former Finance minister who had been out of Parliament for nine years, went into the election campaign of the summer of 1984 having to justify the Trudeau government's failures. Canadians reacted by voting for what appeared to be real change: they gave the

Conservatives 211 seats, the largest number in Canadian history. For the first time since 1958, the Conservatives even won a majority of seats in Quebec.

Politics in the Mid-1980s

The Canada of the mid-1980s was, in many respects, a very different place from that of the late 1960s and 1970s. As in the United States the electorate was in a conservative mood, as many Canadians voiced their opposition to high levels of government spending, to rising taxes, and to many aspects of state interference in the economy.

Conservative rhetoric in the early 1980s lent much credence to the notion that the party had an agenda of the political right to carry out. It seemed that the two old-line parties had at last adopted separate ideological stances. While the Liberals continued to support state intervention and insisted that the federal government's strategic role in the economy and in other sectors should not be relinquished to the provinces, the Conservatives endorsed free enterprise and a vision of a more decentralized Canada, a "community of communities."[10]

449

THE MULRONEY GOVERNMENT

At first, conditions appeared favourable for the Mulroney government to "set things right." Mulroney had promised an "era of national reconciliation" in federal-provincial relations. In 1984–85, regional dissensions seemed to have diminished: Mulroney appeased the West by dismantling the National Energy Policy; he pleased Nova Scotia and Newfoundland by yielding them control of offshore mineral resources; and he satisfied the Quebec government simply by not being Trudeau. He also promised to negotiate Quebec's acceptance of the Constitution of 1982, a promise that was kept in 1987 when, in meetings at Meech Lake, the federal government and the ten provinces reached agreement on constitutional amendments. The Conservatives had also blamed the Liberals for Canada's poor relations with the United States and promised to improve them. Again, they were assisted by changing opinions within Canada, as the support for economic nationalism declined. On economic issues, the strong recovery, in full swing before Mulroney even took power, came to the aid of the Conservatives. Unemployment declined from the heights attained during the recession. Inflation also appeared to be under control and interest rates fell. Certainly, the omens appeared favourable for the construction of a new consensus.

CONSERVATIVE MISFORTUNES

The Conservative honeymoon proved brief, however. The Mulroney government's apparent disorganization and frequent bouts with scandal deeply hurt its public image and, by 1987, helped drive it down into third place in the polls, after the front-ranked NDP and the Liberals.

Regionalism had not gone away; in fact, it rose phoenix-like on the heels of a flagrantly unequal economic recovery. While metropolitan Toronto and southern Ontario attained virtual full employment, the cities of Quebec, the North, the West, and the Atlantic provinces struggled with continued high jobless rates. The decline of oil and resource prices, coinciding with a severe farm crisis, dealt a heavy blow to the economies of the western provinces. Canada seemed more divided than ever into areas of wealth and regions of stagnation.

Mulroney's plans to control spending and reduce the deficit were hampered by the political necessity of more federal expenditures. Moreover, Canadians began having second thoughts about spending reductions that might affect them adversely. They prevailed upon the government to reaffirm its somewhat wavering faith in the universality of social programmes like old-age pensions, so that all Canadians—rich, poor, and, especially, the worried middle classes—would continue to be covered. After a study of unemployment insurance in 1987 recommended substantial changes in order to reduce costs, labour and the poorer provinces rallied to the defence of the much-maligned programme. "Rattlesnakes get warmer welcomes," said the Montreal *Gazette* of the government's reaction to the report. When Ottawa proceeded with the planned reduction of grants to the provinces, especially those directed to higher education and medical care, provincial governments accused it of pushing its deficit on them. Beleaguered farmers asked for more subsidies to shield them from declining world grain prices, Alberta's oil industry sought financial assistance, and cities and provinces across the country urged Ottawa to make grants that would encourage new industries to locate in their territory. Few Canadians believed that their government was doing enough.

Mulroney did enjoy some success in managing government spending. But his major effort to reduce the massive and growing annual deficit handed to him by the Trudeau government involved substantially higher income taxes and particularly sales taxes. When the government did reduce some taxes through measures such as a lifetime exemption on capital gains, up to a specified limit, critics accused Mulroney of robbing the poor to pay the rich.

Even Canada's foreign relations deteriorated. Mulroney continued Trudeau's efforts to forge closer links with *la francophonie* and his government asserted Canada's belief in sound multilateral institutions and in arms control. It continued to dispense aid to the Third World, but at levels substantially below those recommended by the United Nations. It also stressed human rights and attacked racial discrimination in South Africa.

Canadians, though, were especially concerned by relations with Canada's next-door neighbour. Hopes were high at first as Mulroney struck up a close personal relationship with Ronald Reagan when the American president met the Canadian prime minister in Quebec City in early 1985. As negotiations over free trade with the United States got under way, Canadians pondered the implications, and as time went on, doubts over the advantages of such an agreement began to grow. Nor did a series of American protectionist measures reassure many Canadians over the possibility of simply maintaining the status quo. Canadians also complained bitterly over American reluctance to clean up acid rain, whose harmful effects on the Canadian environment were becoming increasingly evident. A frustrated Brian Mulroney complained during a speech in Chicago that "tinpot dictators" commanded infinitely more attention in the United States "than a tremendous ally and friend like Canada." He had wagered that he could improve Canadian-American relations, but was less and less certain that he would win his bet.

451

Again, an attempt to build a new harmony, in an era of promise, with a solid mandate, a new style, and an updated message appeared to have come to nought. The positive images of the Conservatives and especially of their leader had been transformed virtually over night. Diefenbaker, Pearson, Trudeau, Clark, Mulroney: Canadians relentlessly criticized all of them, and many judged them failures. An innocent bystander might wonder if it were possible for anyone to succeed. Perhaps the complexity of Canada's problems and the expectations of its citizens simply made consensus impossible.

NOTES

[1] William P. Irvine, "The Canadian Voter," in *Canada at the Polls, 1979 and 1980: A Study of the General Elections*, edited by Howard R. Penniman (Washington, D.C. 1981), p. 67.

[2] Frederick J. Fletcher, "Playing the Game: The Mass Media and the 1979 Campaign," in *ibid.*, p. 319.

[3] John Meisel, "The Decline of Party in Canada," in *Party Politics in Canada*, edited by Hugh G. Thorburn, 5th ed. (Scarborough, 1985), p. 104.

[4] Peter C. Newman, *Renegade in Power: The Diefenbaker Years* (Toronto, 1963).

[5] Lawrence Martin, *The Presidents and the Prime Ministers: Washington and Ottawa Face to Face: The Myth of Bilateral Bliss. 1867–1982* (Toronto, 1982), p. 193.

[6] Maurice Pinard, *The Rise of a Third Party: A Study in Crisis Politics* (Englewood Cliffs, N.J., 1971), pp. 21–35; Vincent Lemieux in *Papers on the 1962 Election*, edited by John Meisel (Toronto, 1964), pp. 33–52.

[7] Paul Phillips, *Regional Disparities* (Toronto, 1982), pp. 97–119.

[8] John Meisel, *Working Papers on Canadian Politics*, 2d ed. (Montreal, 1975), p. 229.

[9] Desmond Morton, *The New Democrats, 1961–1986: The Politics of Change* (Toronto, 1986), p. 145.

[10] John Courtney, "Campaign Strategy and Electoral Victory: The Progressive Conservatives and the

1979 Election," in Penniman, *Canada at the Polls*, p. 148, and M. Janine Brodie, "Tensions from Within: Regionalism and Party Politics in Canada," in Thorburn, *Party Politics*, pp. 74–75.

BIBLIOGRAPHY

As in the preceding chapter, J.L. Granatstein, *Canada 1957–1967: The Years of Uncertainty and Innovation* (Toronto, 1986), and Robert Bothwell, Ian Drummond, and John English, *Canada since 1945: Power, Politics, and Provincialism* (Toronto, 1981) are useful. The *Canadian Annual Review* (Toronto, 1961–) also contains considerable material on political developments.

Canadian politicians have been thoroughly studied by political scientists, journalists, and historians, as well as by themselves. On Diefenbaker, one can read journalist Peter C. Newman's *Renegade in Power: The Diefenbaker Years* (Toronto, 1963); also, the more scholarly Peter Regenstreif, *The Diefenbaker Interlude: Parties and Voting in Canada* (Toronto, 1965); or the chief's autobiography, *One Canada: Memoirs of the Right Honourable John G. Diefenbaker*, 3 vols. (Toronto, 1975–77). Newman also offers a "strip-tease contribution" (in the words of Lester B. Pearson) on the Diefenbaker–Pearson rivalry in *The Distemper of Our Times* (Toronto, 1968). On Pearson, one can consult Pearson's own *Mike: The Memoirs of the Right Honourable Lester B. Pearson*, 3 vols. (Toronto, 1972–75); Robert Bothwell, *Pearson: His Life and World* (Toronto, 1978); as well as Peter Stursberg's two volumes of oral history: *Lester B. Pearson and the Dream of Unity* (Toronto, 1978), and *Lester B. Pearson and the American Dilemma* (Toronto, 1980).

Journalistic accounts of the Trudeau years abound. Consult, for example, George Radwanski, *Trudeau* (Toronto, 1978); Richard Gwyn, *The Northern Magus: Pierre Trudeau and Canadians* (Toronto, 1980); and Christina McCall Newman, *Grits: An Intimate Portrait of the Liberal Party* (Toronto, 1982). Geoffrey Stevens has studied Conservative Opposition Leader Robert L. Stanfield in *Stanfield* (Toronto, 1973). On the brief Clark months, see Jeffrey Simpson's well-documented study, *Discipline of Power: The Conservative Interlude and the Liberal Restoration* (Toronto, 1980). The Mulroney government is taken to task in David Bercuson, J.L. Granatstein, and W.R. Young, *Sacred Trust? Brian Mulroney and the Conservative Party in Power* (Toronto, 1986). Another challenging analysis of the 1980s is Ron Graham, *One-Eyed Kings: Promise and Illusion in Canadian Politics* (Toronto, 1986).

The Social Credit phenomenon in Quebec is analysed in Michael B. Stein, *The Dynamics of Right-Wing Protest: A Political Analysis of Social Credit in Quebec* (Toronto, 1973), and in Maurice Pinard, *The Rise of a Third Party: A Study in Crisis Politics* (Toronto, 1975). On the NDP, suc-

452

cessor to the CCF, see Desmond Morton, *The New Democrats, 1961–1986: The Politics of Change* (Toronto, 1986). The elections of the 1960s are covered in J.M. Beck, *Pendulum of Power: Canada's Federal Elections* (Scarborough, 1968); those of 1968 and 1972 in John Meisel, *Working Papers on Canadian Politics*, 2d ed. (Montreal, 1975); those of 1974, 1979, and 1980 in two books edited by Howard R. Penniman: *Canada at the Polls: The General Election of 1974* (Washington, D.C., 1975), and *Canada at the Polls, 1979 and 1980: A Study of the General Elections* (Washington, D.C., 1981). Among numerous works on political parties, see Hugh G. Thorburn, *Party Politics in Canada*, 5th ed. (Toronto, 1985), and Joseph Wearing, *The L-Shaped Party: The Liberal Party of Canada, 1958–1980* (Toronto, 1981). William Christian and Colin Campbell challenge the traditional thesis of brokerage politics in *Political Parties and Ideologies in Canada: Liberals, Conservatives, Socialists, Nationalists* (Toronto, 1974).

Federal-provincial relations, in particular the perennial constitutional question, have interested scholars. Consult, for example, Richard Simeon, *Federal-Provincial Diplomacy: The Making of Recent Policy in Canada* (Toronto, 1972); Donald V. Smiley, *Canada in Question: Federalism in the Eighties*, 3d ed. (Toronto, 1980); Garth Stevenson, *Unfulfilled Union: Canadian Federalism and National Unity*, rev. ed. (Toronto, 1982); and David Milne, *Tug of War: Ottawa and the Provinces Under Trudeau and Mulroney* (Toronto, 1986); also, Robert Sheppard and Michael Valpy, *The National Deal: The Fight for a Canadian Constitution* (Toronto, 1982); and the highly critical Keith Banting and Richard Simeon, eds., *And No One Cheered: Federalism, Democracy and the Constitution Act* (Toronto, 1983). Material on a variety of political issues can be found in Ronald Manzer, *Public Policies and Political Development* (Toronto, 1985).

453

On aspects of Canada's international relations, see Arnold Smith, *Stitches in Time: The Commonwealth in World Politics* (Toronto, 1981); Peyton V. Lyon and Tareq Y. Ismael, eds., *Canada and the Third World* (Toronto, 1976); and, on the early Trudeau years, Bruce Thordarson, *Trudeau and Foreign Policy* (Toronto, 1972). Several volumes in the series *Canada in World Affairs* are available for the post-1960 period: Peyton V. Lyon, vol. 12: *1961–1963* (Toronto, 1968); Charlotte S.M. Girard, vol. 13: *1963–1965* (Toronto, 1980); Peter C. Dobell, vol. 17: *1971–1973* (Toronto, 1985). On the conduct of foreign affairs during the Diefenbaker years, see John F. Hilliker, "The Politicians and the 'Pearsonalities': The Diefenbaker Government and the Conduct of Canadian External Relations," *Historial Papers/Communications Historiques*, 1984, pp. 151–67.

Much has been written on Canadian-American relations. Two good accounts are Stephen Clarkson, *Canada and the Reagan Challenge*, 2d. ed. (Toronto, 1985); and Lawrence Martin, *The Presidents and the Prime Ministers* (Markham, 1982). Canada's relations with the United States over Vietnam are discussed in Victor Levant, *Quiet Complicity: Canadian Involvement in the Vietnam War* (Toronto, 1986).

CHAPTER TWENTY-TWO

Evolving Canadian Society

454   The pace of change in Canada accelerated after 1960 as the nation experienced profound social and cultural upheavals. Youth in particular protested against authority in all its forms. By the late 1970s and early 1980s,
though, the era of rapid transformations had run its course, and in a far
different climate, many Canadians reasserted more conservative attitudes.

Population: From Boom to Bust

Demographically, the baby boom of the late 1940s and 1950s tapered off
into a "baby bust" during the 1960s. In just one short decade, the rate
of growth of Canada's population was nearly halved. Newfoundland's birth
rate remained the highest; its decline came in the 1970s. Quebec, traditionally reputed the province with the largest families, went from having
one of the highest rates in 1960 to having the lowest rate of the ten provinces
in 1970. At the beginning of the decade the average Quebec family had
four children; by its end, the two-child family—the minimum needed to
replace the population—had become the norm.

By the mid-1980s, though babies were not yet on the endangered species
list, the average Canadian family had shrunk to a mere 1.6 children.
Demographers warned ominously that only large-scale immigration could
assure a growing or even stable population. Quebec in particular, with
just 1.4 children per family and a victim of substantial out-migration,
appeared at the point of actually declining in population. Moreover, slow
growth was the norm across the country, except in Ontario, where a
vigorous economy attracted newcomers both from abroad and from other
Canadian provinces. During the 1970s Alberta and British Columbia had
been the country's major poles of attraction, but economic problems stifled
the call of the West in the 1980s. By the end of 1986, the population of

TABLE: Live births per 1 000 population, selected years

Year	Nfld	PEI	NS	NB	Que	Ont	Man	Sask	Alb	BC	Can
1951	32.5	27.1	26.6	31.2	29.8	25.0	25.7	26.1	28.8	24.1	27.2
1960	33.9	26.5	26.3	27.7	27.5	26.1	25.6	26.3	30.2	25.0	26.8
1965	30.2	23.1	21.9	23.0	21.7	20.9	20.7	21.6	22.5	18.7	21.3
1970	24.3	17.8	18.1	18.4	16.1	17.8	18.6	17.5	20.0	17.3	17.5
1976	20.0	16.4	15.5	17.4	15.5	14.8	16.4	17.3	18.0	14.5	15.7
1981	17.8	15.5	14.3	15.1	14.8	14.2	15.7	17.8	19.1	15.1	15.3
1985	14.8	15.8	14.1	14.1	13.1	14.6	16.0	17.8	18.6	14.9	15.0

Source: Statistics Canada, *Vital Statistics*, Cat. No. 84-204 (Ottawa, 1987).

Canada was about 25 700 000 and was growing by less than 1 percent a year. Most Canadians residing within densely populated urban areas said they were content with a population of that magnitude.

As birth rates plummeted and advances in medicine enabled Canadians to live longer, Canadian society began to age. The relative size of the younger age groups diminished sharply, while those over age sixty-five increased to one in ten by the mid 1980s—a figure well over the 8 percent criterion used by the United Nations to signify an aging population.

455

REASONS FOR THE DECLINE IN THE BIRTHRATE

It was one thing for demographers to identify a demographic revolution; it was quite another to explain it. Canadians were behaving like citizens of other industrialized countries, though the statistics varied significantly from one country to another. Quebeckers might attribute the decline of the birth rate to the secularization of Quebec society, but the trends were the same in all the provinces. Many observers emphasized the availability of better contraceptive methods: birth control pills, for example, came onto the market in the early 1960s and, since the early 1970s, thousands of men and women in their thirties have undergone voluntary sterilization. An increase in abortions also played a role: in Ontario, by the early 1980s, one out of five pregnancies terminated voluntarily. That issue has provoked bitter and sometimes violent conflict between supporters and opponents of abortion-on-demand.

Obviously, Canadians wanted fewer children, if they wanted children at all. In earlier times, larger families had been an economic asset—on farms, for example, and when elderly parents needed assistance. In Canada's modern consumer society, one that also provided extensive social programmes, large numbers of children were no longer necessary; in fact they were often a liability. The difficulty of juggling children and careers brought an increase in yuppie-style marriages that sociologists called "dinks"—dual-income, no kids. Often, conscious choices to delay temporarily having a family evolved into permanent decisions, as the biological clock ticked on.

MARRIAGE UNDER ATTACK

The decline in the birth rate was but part of a broader revolution in traditional family patterns. Conservative-minded Canadians had long looked askance at the phenomenon of marriage breakdown in the United States and complacently congratulated themselves for living in a more stable society. After 1968, when federal law was changed, divorce became frequent in Canada, too. By the 1970s Canada registered one divorce for each three marriages. The trend was particularly apparent in Quebec where, as in Newfoundland, divorce procedures had previously been exceedingly complicated. The number of divorces in Quebec went from about 600 in 1968 to 12 000 in 1974, reaching a peak of 19 000 in 1981. Actually, Quebec was only catching up with the other provinces, where divorce rates had been consistently much higher.

As traditional sexual taboos relaxed, younger Canadians experimented with different types of living arrangements. Homosexual relationships became more open and the government, promising to stay out of the nation's bedrooms, legalized homosexual practices between consenting adults. For a time, communes were popular, although few lasted for long.

More popular and more durable was the phenomenon of cohabitation, or common-law marriage. Canadians who practised these arrangements were thus excluded from the marriage statistics when they moved in together, and from the divorce statistics when they moved out. Many women involved in such relationships denounced marriage as a form of economic servitude disguised by the myth of romantic love but serving mainly to force women to work without pay. In most cases, for both men and women, convenience probably provided the basis for these relationships. The phenomenon was most common among young adults; by 1981, about 10 percent of Canadians in their early twenties were partners in a common-law relationship.

Marital instability—indeed, questioning of the entire institution of marriage—resulted in the formation of large numbers of single-parent families, the great majority of them headed by women. A study produced by the National Council of Welfare in 1984 showed that half the families led by single women, many of them poorly educated, had incomes below what Statistics Canada defined as the poverty line. In comparison, only one in ten of Canada's two-parent families was classed as poor.

Revolt and Protest

As traditional moral values came under attack, their defenders appeared to be in retreat. In Quebec the Roman Catholic church's influence waned as the church largely abandoned its historic role in the schools and in social institutions, and as religious observance declined precipitously. Elsewhere in Canada, the major Protestant denominations also lost ground. At first, they attempted to combat practices that appeared un-Christian: in the 1950s, as the champions of beer parlours and Sunday movies made more and more converts, United Church moderator James Mutchmor outspokenly denounced the new trends. Mutchmor's critics mocked: "Let's have much less of Mutchmor!"

Then in the 1960s and the 1970s the churches attempted to come to terms with the social changes that appeared inevitable. Liberal Roman Catholics found church teaching on doctrinal questions too conservative. Conservative adherents of the United Church and other mainstream Protestant churches denounced their leaders' teachings as spineless liberalism. One Toronto newspaper wondered whether there was not an opportunity here for a measured swap of members. Many members of all denominations, seeing the church as irrelevant, lapsed into outward religious indifference. In 1981, one British Columbian in five claimed no religious affiliation. By mid-decade only three Canadians in ten attended a religious service weekly, or half of the 1957 figure. Numerous Canadians wishing to practise religion joined the more conservative fundamentalist sects like the Pentecostals that grew prodigiously. Others, particularly in the late 1960s and early 1970s, were attracted by a wide variety of cults. Immigration from Asia in particular introduced sizeable communities of Moslems, Buddhists and Hindus to Canada.

457

Much of the revolt against established social and cultural patterns was of a superficial nature. High school boys put away the Bryll Cream and let their hair grow, while their mothers remonstrated with them in vain. College students and non-students began sporting mustaches, sideburns, and beards. Flower children dressed in fringes and beads and young women displayed psychedelic colours. Blue jeans became the uniform of a generation. Youth denounced age and experience, and promised to stay young. A drug culture also flourished, as did sexual experimentation.

Young Canadians swung to the rhythm of rock (including, in the 1970s, a Toronto rockband called *Rush*), enthusiastically fell victim to Beatlemania, and empathized with the messages of folksingers such as Americans Bob Dylan and Joan Baez; English-speaking Canadians Gordon Lightfoot, Joni Mitchell, and the duo Ian and Sylvia; and Québécois Félix Leclerc, Gilles Vigneault, Claude Léveillé, and Pauline Julien. Robert Charlebois, who sang in *joual*, or Quebec slang, broke sales records with his albums. Paul Anka, son of an Ottawa Lebanese restaurant owner, emerged as a teenage sensation in the late 1950s, and Anne Murray from Nova Scotia won international acclaim in the 1970s. Still, American songs dominated the market, both in English- and in French-speaking Canada.

CAMPUS UNREST

The revolution of the late 1960s and 1970s also challenged established authority. The universities were a focus of protests, with many demonstrations taking place on campuses. Infused with the spirit of "peace and love," English-speaking university students, like Americans and Western youth in general, picketed against the war in Vietnam as well as on behalf of a wide range of reformist causes. Québécois staged rallies in favour of the French language and of national independence.

458

Abandoning classes and occupying administrative offices, students also demonstrated for more active participation in the university community and for the recognition of students' rights. Perhaps the universities had grown too quickly—enrollments doubled during the 1950s, then nearly tripled over the 1960s and 1970s. The parents of baby boomers, many of whom had never been to university, preached the virtues of a college diploma to their progeny who flocked to the halls of higher learning that were supposed to deliver the key to a bright future. Across Canada provincial governments, convinced that higher education would bring enormous economic benefits to society, dramatically increased spending on university education, and established a multitude of new institutions. The federal government, which had been making grants directly to the universities since 1951, began in 1966 to make contributions directly to provincial governments.

One particular problem the universities faced was finding adequately trained staff. English-speaking universities looked largely south and recruited on American campuses. By 1968, fewer than half of the university professors in Canada were Canadians. In that year, only one of every eight positions filled went to a Canadian, and critics accused universities of ignoring the presence of Canadian university graduates in their hiring policies. Celebrated Canadian author Hugh MacLennan who, years earlier, had been unable to find a teaching position even with degrees from Oxford and Princeton, lamented that Canadian universities had embarked on a "programme of national suicide."[1] Carleton University professors Robin Mathews and James Steele compiled statistics on university hiring policies and called for the Canadianization of faculties, but by the late 1970s the universities no longer had many positions to fill.

Canadian universities also became the fertile soil in which nationalist protest took root and prospered. Academics in the social sciences, particularly in Toronto, prepared studies that proved how much Canada had become an American colony and proposed means for buying or taking it back. In Quebec universities equal fervour was applied to proving how much Quebec had become a Canadian colony and to showing how it could be liberated. Canadians outside these two areas debated how their regions had been subjugated by central Canada.

University protest had profound repercussions on politics: in Quebec, the Parti Québécois, strongly supported by intellectuals, came to power in 1976. In Ottawa, some of the causes that Pierre Trudeau had championed in 1968 enlisted support from academe, and nationalist outcry caused the Liberals to question the continentalism they had espoused during the 1950s and to adopt more firmly nationalist policies.

During this era of change many protesters saw the state, at all levels, as a necessary tool for reform. Municipal governments, they believed, should use their power to improve the quality of life within cities, controlling the heights of buildings and curtailing expressway expansion, fighting urban blight, and protecting established neighbourhoods; provincial governments should concentrate on improving the quality of—and the access to—education as well as expanding social services. By the beginning of the 1970s, Canada had a relatively comprehensive national health scheme or, rather, it had ten provincial health plans funded largely by the federal government. Provincial governments were also urged to legislate to protect consumers, promote the equality of women, and combat discrimination against minority groups. As for Ottawa, reformers wanted it to take measures to protect society's weaker elements—the unemployed and citizens of the disadvantaged regions, for example, and to assist Canadian cultural development.

459

A Canadian Cultural Revolution

The Canada Council along with federal and provincial grant agencies gave considerable assistance to cultural endeavours, funding both organizations and individual artists. Such subsidies, however, were only part of the cultural revolution that Canada underwent after 1960. Universal education greatly increased the potential market for cultural products, and higher disposable incomes made it possible for people to buy them. Most provinces also invested substantially in libraries, museums, theatres, and concert halls.

CANADIAN LITERATURE

Most important in the development of culture were the creators and their creations. In Quebec, the 1960s and 1970s saw the rapid growth of a vibrant and diverse literature. Quebec French-language publishers quadrupled the number of novels published. Notable authors from among a lengthy list included Anne Hébert, Marie-Claire Blais, Antonine Maillet, Roch Carrier, Victor-Lévy Beaulieu, and Yves Beauchemin. Playwrights such as Marcel Dubé and Michel Tremblay brought effervescence, and a considerable public, to the theatre. Works in history and the social sciences proliferated, too, thanks to the intense political and social debate that characterized the era.

Canadian literature in English experienced a renaissance as well, and several authors won international recognition. Margaret Atwood's trenchant nationalist and feminist critiques, in such novels as *Surfacing* and *The Handmaid's Tale*, secured her reputation in Canadian fiction; Margaret Laurence and Alice Munro also won acclaim, as did outspoken poet Irving Layton. Mordecai Richler and Robertson Davies continued to write for a growing readership in Canada, the United States, and Britain. Self-taught poet Al Purdy evoked Canada's past in such works as *In Search of Owen Roblin*. Rudy Wiebe, Timothy Findley, and Jack Hodgins, all winners of Governor General's awards, were among the host of new voices making themselves heard. Many works dealt with minority groups such as the native peoples and immigrants, or focussed on political themes or moral issues. Non-fiction also blossomed, to a large extent the result of massive investment in research in Canada's rapidly growing universities.

460

Changing Status of Women

The age of protest brought to the fore the question of women's rights as women's groups demanded state intervention, at both the federal and provincial levels, to promote equality. In 1967 the Pearson government created the Royal Commission on the Status of Women in Canada, chaired by Florence Bird. The commission received nearly five hundred briefs and held hearings across Canada. The commissioners believed that women should be free to decide if they wished to work outside the home. Their view was that society had particular responsibilities in view of women's childbearing function and childbearing was thus a task to be shared by the mother, the father, and the state. The commission report called for a change of attitudes towards women and proposed dozens of recommendations bearing on women in the economy, in political life, in education, and in family life. Three of the seven commissioners expressed reservations with the report, however, notably on the question of abortion; a fourth, John P. Humphrey, one of the commission's two male members, disagreed with so many recommendations that he wrote his own minority report.

Radical feminist movements in Canada, inspired by theorists such as the American Kate Millett and the Australian Germaine Greer, demanded a quick end to male domination over females in all sectors of society; for them, the Bird report was far too conservative. In Quebec, feminists organized the short-lived *Front de libération des femmes*, which attempted to link the struggle for women's liberation with national liberation. Growing pressure brought governments to set up advisory councils on the status of women; a federal council was established in 1973. Colloquiums on questions involving women were organized during 1975, which the United Nations decreed International Women's Year.

In part, the battle for equality of the sexes was waged in the home, where women traditionally took primary responsibility for domestic work, but change came slowly. Polls suggested that Canadians in general wanted men to take a greater share in the housework. One study in Vancouver in 1975 revealed that husbands in childless families had increased their housework time by a full six minutes since the beginning of the decade, while in homes where there were children, men furnished an extra hour. As in the past, responsibility for child care continued to fall mainly to women. A federal government poster published during International Women's Year attempted to extol the virtues of homemaking by linking women's jobs to prestigious occupations: nurse, teacher, accountant, plumber, chef. Women criticized it for failing to mention less-prestigious occupations that also occupied a large portion of a homemaker's time: janitor, laundress, dishwasher, waitress, "taxi driver," and maid.

461

Sociologists examined the role of women as moderators of tension in the home during hard times. Women, as well as children, have often been victims of such tension. In 1982 a House of Commons standing committee produced a report on violence in the family that showed that wife-beating had become widespread. As many as 10 percent of wives were directly concerned, and the report noted that the numbers of victims appeared to be increasing. Such social problems did not lend themselves to easy resolution.

WOMEN IN THE WORK FORCE

Male-dominated parliaments did adopt some laws that improved the lot of women in many respects. Divorce became simpler, child-care expenses were made tax-deductible, and maternity benefits became more generous. The major demands for change—and indeed, the changes themselves—came in the workplace. During the 1950s and 1960s large numbers of women entered the labour force. Many were single, but increasing numbers of married women also sought jobs outside the home. In 1971, one married woman in three was in the labour force (though often in part-time employment). By the mid-1980s, an overwhelming majority of Canadians thought that women without young children should work outside the home. Moreover, half of those polled believed that even married women with young children should be in the work force. When Gallup pollsters first asked that question in 1960, only 5 percent of Canadians had approved of the idea.

Sex segregation in the workplace remained the norm. As retail stores proliferated in a consumer-oriented society, women found jobs as salespersons. The expansion of health care and education also created employment for women. Clerical work, too, was considered "women's work," and expanding governments hired large numbers of women. Indeed, by the late 1960s, the federal government was the largest employer of women in Canada. Eighty percent of its female employees worked in office or administrative support jobs; men dominated the higher-level better-paying managerial positions.

Unionization did improve working conditions and pay in some traditionally female occupations, particularly in the hospitals, in education, and in the public-service sector. Nevertheless, many women criticized unions for failing to organize large groups of female workers, for not dealing with the specific problems of women such as equal pay or child care, and for not according women a significant role in union executives. By 1985, still fewer than one-third of female workers were unionized—a rate about 25 percent lower than that for men. Many of the unprotected majority worked in banks or restaurants, in offices or retail sales, and often they worked part time.

Throughout the 1960s and 1970s, the principle of equal pay for men and women performing the same job gained wide recognition, in part because of anti-discriminatory legislation. Yet even by the 1980s, the average woman's wage remained only about 65 percent of the average man's. The difference could partly be explained by women's lesser work experience and generally lower educational levels, but the continued concentration of women in low-pay occupations appeared the major factor.

As a partial solution, Judge Rosalie Abella, the head of a one-woman federal Commission on Equality in Employment, recommended in November 1984 mandatory "employment equity" programmes, to be implemented through affirmative action: employers under federal jurisdiction, such as the federal civil service, banks and national transportation companies, would be obliged to give women and minorities better job opportunities. These initiatives appeared all the more necessary because the difficult economic situation of the early 1980s had meant that, instead of hiring, companies had laid off personnel. Women, being the last hired, were often the first fired.

Women did make slow progress in the nation's boardrooms. In 1976 a statement by W. Earle McLaughlin, chairman of the Royal Bank of Canada, that the bank had been unable to find a qualified woman to serve on its board of directors, provoked an outcry by women's groups. (Two months later, the bank discovered one.) By 1984, 20 percent of Canada's 640 leading companies had women directors. Very few of these companies had more than one, however, so that of the total number of directors, women constituted a meagre 2.5 percent. Moreover, only one of the com-

462

panies was headed by a woman. Since two of every five students enrolling in commerce or business administration programmes are now women, the percentage of women in managerial positions is expected to rise substantially within a few years.

It was also apparent that women were being paid less than men for jobs requiring similar skills, effort, responsibility, and entailing similar working conditions. This became the battleground of the late 1980s: equal pay for work of equal value, or pay equity. The federal government and the governments of Manitoba and Quebec instituted pay equity laws, but the Ontario government went much further by forcing both public and private sector employers to compare the value of work in their male- and female-dominated work categories, and then to increase the wages of lower-paid women. Mary Cornish, head of the one-million member Equal Pay Coalition, described the measure as "a law with half a heart"; it was a step forward, even though it did not cover casual workers or women working in establishments where there were no men with whom to make comparisons. The business community, however, expressed considerable hostility to what the president of the Canadian Federation of Independent Business termed "a radical social experiment doomed to fail."

Business and Labour

Women were not alone in their criticisms of business. The enemies of the establishment and "the system" in the 1960s and 1970s pointed the finger at business, especially the large multinational corporations, as being the principal villains and prime forces of conservatism. They were accused of thinking only of increasing profits and displaying no social conscience; of destroying old urban neighbourhoods by building high-rise apartment buildings and office towers; and of "gouging" consumers by ceaselessly raising prices, thus fanning the flames of inflation. In Canada's case, corporations were largely foreign-owned, thus virtually by definition unresponsive to Canadian needs.

Attacks on business came partly from left-wing political parties, like the Parti Québécois, with its initial pro-worker bias, and the New Democratic Party, beneficiary of considerable union support. Criticism also came from the universities, where student movements espoused socialism and various left-wing causes. The major assault on business, however, came from the unions.

UNIONS

The 1960s brought new challenges to the union movement. Inflation made it imperative to obtain higher wage settlements, and the increasingly militant union rank and file rebelled frequently against conservative union establishments, launching wildcat strikes (illegal work stoppages). Declining membership meant that the unions had to organize new sectors, especially the public service—federal, provincial, and municipal employees—as well as hospital workers and teachers.

Many governments, at all levels, legalized strike activity to place public sector employees on an equal footing with those in the private sector, and as in the private sector, public employees went out on strike in support of their demands. Lengthy work stoppages in the post office, for example, became notorious. In Quebec, where bargaining was centralized, two hundred thousand provincial government employees struck in 1972 seeking, among other benefits, a minimum weekly wage of one hundred dollars. In order to conduct negotiations, the province's three major labour bodies established a Common Front. The talks quickly reached an impasse and the largest strike in Canadian history began. Finally, the Quebec government adopted special legislation ordering strikers back to work. Three years later, history virtually repeated itself.

464

Strikes in the public sector everywhere brought significant discomfort, and public opinion turned against the unions. Two of every three Canadian workers remained ununionized, and many resented unions' attempts to secure a greater share of the national wealth. When public sector unions were involved, taxpayers quickly realized that they would have to foot the bill for what many began to view as excessive government generosity. Canada acquired a negative image for its strike activity—only Italy had a worse record. Yet, although eleven million workdays were lost to strikes in 1975, a particularly bad year, that figure was barely 1.5 percent of total working time. Accidents, illness, and general absenteeism caused far more loss of time.

In most cases, the union militancy of the 1970s aimed at obtaining higher salaries and better working conditions. Many unions, of course, denounced politicians and governments for their failure to yield. In some cases, however, particularly in Quebec, unions attacked the capitalist and federal system, seeking to replace it with an independent and socialist Quebec. "The State is our exploiter," proclaimed a Quebec Labour Federation manifesto. "We [the workers] are our own strength. Let's stop selling ourselves," urged a document published by the *Confédération des syndicats nationaux*. Here indeed was the high point of labour's confrontation with management.

465

Toronto Telegram, York University Archives.

Inflation brought rising demands from the unions in their efforts to catch up with, and stay ahead of, price increases. Here, an episode from a brief but violent illegal strike at the Stelco plant in Hamilton, Ontario, 1966.

National Archives of Canada C-30085.

A spectacular event in Canada's centennial celebrations, Expo 1967 drew 50 million visitors.

An Era of Great Celebrations

The 1960s and 1970s were a time of celebration as well as confrontation. In 1967, the year of the Canadian centennial, provinces and municipalities organized various festivities to mark the event. Typically subdued, Canadians gave vent to few of the effusions of American-style patriotism, and many wondered whether the country was going to succeed in holding itself together.

One activity was not restrained: Expo 67, staged on an island in the St. Lawrence River at Montreal, brought more than sixty nations together to celebrate the theme "Man and His World." Fifty million visitors passed through the turnstiles; governments, both federal and provincial, spared no expense (perhaps unfortunately for the taxpayers).

A second great international gathering took place in Canada in 1976: the twenty-first summer Olympic Games, hosted by Montreal. Taxpayers were uneasy at the prospect of new budget deficits but Montreal Mayor Jean Drapeau assured them there was no more possibility of incurring a deficit than there was of his becoming pregnant. Nevertheless, it soon became evident that the Olympic lottery, the Olympic coins, the Olympic stamps, and the other promotional paraphernalia would not be enough to prevent a massive deficit; delighted cartoonists thereupon drew sketches of a pregnant mayor. The games themselves provided much excitement (though Canadian prowess would be much greater at the Los Angeles Olympics in 1984). Then the athletes departed, and Montrealers and Quebeckers began getting the true picture of the financial disaster that had been created; it would prove much more durable than the glamour of the competitions.

Between these two events the 1972 Canada-Soviet hockey series took place. Watched by the largest Canadian television audience on record, Team-Canada managed to win the series in the last seconds of the dramatic final encounter. One Canadian university president suggested that the series probably did more to create a Canadian identity than did ten years of Canada Council fellowships.

Return to Conservatism: the 1980s

After a lengthy period of constant and often unsettling change that shook the industrialized world, the pendulum seemed to swing back from liberalism and experimentation to moderation and conservatism. It did not swing as far right in Canada as it did in the United States, but neither had the protest movements been as radical above the border as below it.

The recession of the early 1980s aided in moderating the protests of the 1960s and 1970s. Many workers, particularly in the manufacturing industries, lost their jobs; many others feared for theirs. This was no longer a time for radicalism. Even students appeared to think the same way; a more docile mood reigned on campus, with students seemingly more concerned about their future in a tight and competitive job market than with defending social ideals.

The causes that so many Canadians had believed in fell on hard times. In Quebec, the *indépendantiste* tide ebbed under the double blows of the referendum defeat in May 1980 and the economic crisis. In English Canada, economic nationalists again retreated. After huge anti-nuclear marches of earlier years, at best a few hundred participants turned out to protest against Cruise missile tests on Canadian soil in the early 1980s. The socialists had shrunk in number while the more extreme marxists simply disappeared. As the women's rights movement became institutionalized, radical feminists toned down their rhetoric, too. A *Winnipeg Free Press* survey of teenage women found that most simply wanted a suburban home, children, and a "prince charming." Those who aspired to careers saw sexism in the workplace as an issue of the past. For most Canadians, it was time to restore the "peaceable kingdom."

FINANCIAL RESTRAINTS

The recession of 1981–82, as well as high spending levels of the 1970s, provoked severe financial crises for many governments. It forced them not only to avoid new, expensive commitments but also to attempt to escape old ones. Governments no longer had the means to pay for new reformist policies unless they reordered priorities.

Economic difficulties also battered the unions, particularly the American-based internationals. Membership declined as plants laid off workers or simply shut down, and governments cut back personnel. As many of the old manufacturing industries declined, it seemed as if unions might be weakened permanently. Some unions adapted aggressively to the new conditions. They denounced free trade, fought for job security, and signed up workers outside their original jurisdictions. The steelworkers' union, for example, enrolled security workers, restaurant workers, and employees of fish-processing plants, promising: "If it moves or eats with a knife and a fork, we'll organize it." By 1986, such efforts had brought union strength back up to where it had been in 1975: 37 percent of the non-farm work force. Yet unions' popularity had waned; since the 1960s, there had been too many strikes, too much inconvenience, too much violence, at too great a cost. Indeed, in the mid 1980s, polls showed that businessmen had regained public confidence while union leaders had become as unloved as politicians.

The counterrevolution—if that is what the reaction of the 1980s may be termed—was provoked in part by what many Canadians perceived to be the excesses of the preceding two decades. In most ways, however, it did not seek to turn back the clock but rather to put a halt to rapid change. Few Canadians, for example, wanted to curtail access to educational institutions, though many thought it necessary to improve the quality of education. Few Canadians wanted to limit availability of health care through extra-billing by doctors and hospital user fees, but many realized that steps had to be taken to avoid a financial catastrophe. Most Canadians also believed that bilingualism was a good thing, that women's role in the workplace should continue to be expanded, that provincial and federal charters of rights were necessary to protect minority groups, and that governments should not divest themselves of their major activities. Nor did Canadians seem to want to return to an era of large families.

Finally, although sexual practices did remain far more liberal than they had been in the 1950s and most of the old taboos were gone, there were indications of a new moderation. Concerned citizens pressured governments to take measures against pornography. A *Maclean's* poll in late 1985 revealed that fidelity was much more in vogue than promiscuity: the woman from rural Nova Scotia who claimed 110 different sex partners during the year was an exception. Self-styled Casanovas were becoming outmoded. Seventy percent of Canadians claimed only one partner and another 10

468

percent claimed none. A 1987 poll of Montrealers over the age of fifteen found that only 4 percent had had more than one partner, while more than 20 percent had none. An epidemic of sexually transmitted diseases, and especially the spread of the fatal disease AIDS, were major factors in provoking the return of more conservative attitudes. AIDS attracted enormous publicity and, though its incidence was much higher in the United States, it had already killed five hundred Canadians by 1987. Epidemiologists predicted that thousands more would die within a decade, and health authorities launched campaigns promoting safe sex or abstinence.

The late 1970s and 1980s produced other disappointments for Canadians. High inflation and high unemployment together yielded a high "misery index," misery further compounded by high interest rates and low dollars. By the middle of the decade, conditions improved in general, though job seekers outside southern Ontario and prospective homeowners in cities like Toronto, where housing prices spiralled, faced difficulties. English-speaking Canadians in particular regretted the gradual change *469* from the Imperial system of measurements to the metric—or what was often bitterly termed "the French"—system. The media did assist, through appropriate translations, those who felt that Celsius temperatures were colder because they were more often "below zero" than Fahrenheit temperatures, but few gas station owners dared advertise their prices in expensive gallons even when the federal goverment backtracked and made it possible to do so. Other Canadians, railway buffs who had lamented over the demise of the steam locomotives in the 1950s, began to fear that cabooses would soon be diverted to their final siding.

CANADIAN HEROES

Despite these disappointments, the 1980s also brought a new set of heroes that Canadians could admire and, in some cases, even worship. Many of them, particularly in the field of popular music, were Americans, but Canada did produce Bryan Adams and Corey Hart. Some singers, though, tended to be meteors who would streak over the landscape and burn out almost immediately in a blaze of pyschedelic light. Athletes enjoyed more staying power, as long as they continued to score or hit, or win races on the slopes, in the water or on the speedways. Hockey, of course, produced Wayne Gretzky, the Edmonton Oilers' superstar, who attained the crowning glory of being pictured on *Time*'s front cover. As befit the times, space produced Marc Garneau, a Canadian astronaut who was part of the Challenger space shuttle expedition in 1984 and could describe his experience in both languages. Religion brought Pope John Paul II, whose tour across Canada in September 1984 gave rise to unbridled enthusiasm and fervour. Finally, touching the hearts of almost all Canadians, there was Terry Fox, top newsmaker for two years who courageously made his way halfway across Canada in a "marathon of hope" for cancer research but was then forced to abandon his project at Thunder Bay, as the deadly disease to which he had already lost a leg, returned to destroy him.

Concerns of Tomorrow

The 1980s seemed to define Canadians' future challenges. News stories on environmental pollution were increasingly common: PCBs spilled on a highway in Ontario, pollution of the Great Lakes and of British Columbia rivers, acid rain killing lakes and threatening forests in central and Atlantic Canada, cancers caused by environmental factors. The very struggle to survive dictated that Canadians contribute to finding and implementing solutions to these problems.

470   Canadians also appeared more conscious of the need to take preventive measures to ensure personal good health. Non-smokers' lobbies and governments took aim at cigarette users, dieticians underlined the importance of healthy low-fat high-fibre diets, automobile associations and victims of drunk drivers pressured governments into taking measures to reduce highway fatalities. Again, Canadians' survival and the quality of their lives were at stake.

Poverty remained a problem despite what was, except in the early 1980s, a growing economy. Canada's numerous social programmes had not brought the poor and the rich any closer in terms of income. The National Council of Welfare calculated that the poorest fifth of Canada's population received 6.1 percent of national personal income in 1951 and only 5.9 percent in 1984. The World Bank reported that, in this regard, Canada's performance was the worst in the entire Western world. Unemployment, coupled with the remarkable rise in single-parent families, most headed by women, helped explain the increased poverty. In contrast, at the other end of the scale, the wealthiest fifth increased their share from 41.4 to 42.5 percent. Indeed, six Canadian families each possessed assets of more than $1 billion; the Irving family's wealth reputedly surpassed $17 billion. Some politicians and many social workers called for a redirection of federal transfer payments and an overhaul of the tax system. This issue would be on the agenda of the future.

Rising crime had become a serious social problem in the 1970s, although American statistics for such violent crimes as murder and armed robbery were far higher. Statistics Canada calculated in 1982 that virtually all Canadians were destined to be victims, at some time in their lives, of a "silent insidious" property crime. Crime rates in Canada varied from one province to another, but in general they increased steadily from east to west. Perplexed criminologists blamed a "frontier mentality" or higher alcohol consumption in the West. Some westerners blamed imported Torontonians. Nevertheless, Canadians wanted the courts to hand down more severe sentences, and most even desired the return of capital punishment. Parliament, however, voted against the restoration of the death penalty in 1987.

The aging of the country's population is another factor that will inevitably have an enormous impact on Canadian society and require radical institutional and social adjustments. As the baby boomers embark upon a collective midlife crisis and the younger age groups diminish in their size, flower power can only yield to grey power, forcing politicians to heed the concerns of the elderly. Education, emphasized so strongly in the 1960s and 1970s as the baby boomers passed through the system, will have to share the attention with health care, pension reform, and other issues of particular interest for older Canadians.

On July 1, 1987 Canada celebrated its 120th birthday. In the preceding chapters we have seen how gradually, in the nineteenth century, then more rapidly in the twentieth, the country evolved into the complex society it *471* has become today. The nation's population diversified ethnically and culturally. Material progress and improving living conditions, though by no means continuous, were generally apparent. The role of the state increased greatly, especially after 1930, as governments came to play a role in virtually all aspects of human existence. Interest groups of all types proliferated, as Canadians sought to counter the powerlessness of individuals acting alone.

Although Canada has changed greatly, in many respects the basic themes of the country's early history remain true today. Canada in 1867 was a nation of regions; to a large extent, despite modern transportation and communications systems, it remains so today. By the 1880s, federal-provincial relations had become acrimonious; one hundred years later conflict continues to pervade inter-governmental contacts. French-English relations were the source of bitter controversy in the nineteenth century; intercultural relations in the twentieth century have continued to generate debate. In 1867 British and American influence weighed heavily upon the new nation; a century later, the impact of the United States upon Canada, culturally, politically, and economically, is even more apparent. Finally, despite the rise of the middle class and of government efforts, flagrant social inequalities distinguish Canadians from one another as they did in the past. Constant change, but equally apparent continuity: these two themes reflect Canada's past as the country prepares to enter the twenty-first century.

NOTE

[1] "Address by Hugh MacLennan to the Montreal Symposium on de-Canadianization," in *The Struggle for Canadian Universities*, edited by Robin Mathews and James Steele (Toronto, 1969), p. 148.

BIBLIOGRAPHY

There are few books bearing directly on many of the subjects examined in this chapter; for that reason, many newspaper and magazine articles have been consulted. The final volume of the Canadian Centenary series does, however, offer some useful material: J.L. Granatstein, *Canada 1957–1967: The Years of Uncertainty and Innovation* (Toronto, 1986). Robert Bothwell, Ian Drummond, and John English, *Canada since 1945: Power, Politics, and Provincialism* (Toronto, 1981) also touches on several of these questions and in particular captures the spirit of the 1970s. The *Canadian Annual Review*, appearing annually since 1961, contains a wealth of material.

Population questions are treated in David K. Foot, *Canada's Population Outlook: Demographic Futures and Economic Challenges* (Toronto, 1982). On attitudes towards birth control, see Angus McLaren and Arlene Tigar McLaren, *The Bedroom and the State: The Changing Practices and Politics of Contraception and Abortion in Canada, 1880–1980* (Toronto, 1986). Allan Moscovitch looks at social spending in "The Welfare State Since 1975," *Journal of Canadian Studies*, 21 (Summer 1986): 77–94.

472

On women, the *Report of the Royal Commission on the Status of Women in Canada* (Ottawa, 1970) is a good survey of the question as it was posed in the late 1960s. One can also consult its sequel, *Ten Years Later* (Ottawa, 1979), by the Canadian Advisory Council on the Status of Women. The relations of women and labour is the subject of a Canadian Advisory Council on the Status of Women publication by Julie White, *Women and Unions* (Ottawa, 1980). On women and work, see Pat Armstrong and Hugh Armstrong, *The Double Ghetto: Canadian Women and their Segregated Work* (Toronto, 1984) as well as Pat Armstrong, *Labour Pains: Women's Work in Crisis* (Toronto, 1984). On women in Quebec, Micheline Dumont, *et al.* offer a detailed synthesis in *Quebec Women. A History* (Toronto, 1987). On political aspects of the feminist movement, see Sandra Burt, "Les questions féminines et le mouvement féministe au Canada depuis 1970," in Alan Cairns and Cynthia Williams, res. coords., *The Politics of Gender, Ethnicity and Language in Canada* (Toronto, 1985), pp. 125–91.

For a brief synthesis on the labour movement, consult Jack Williams, *The Story of Unions in Canada* (Toronto, 1975). See also the final chapters of Desmond Morton with Terry Copp, *Working People: An Illustrated History of the Canadian Labour Movement* (Toronto, 1984); Robert Laxer, *Canada's Unions* (Toronto, 1976); Walter Stewart, *Strike!* (Toronto, 1977); and John Anderson and Morley Gunderson, eds., *Union-Management Relations in Canada* (Don Mills, 1982). On the public sector in particular, Jacob Finkelstein and Shirley Goldenberg, *Collective Bargaining in the Public Sector* (Toronto, 1983) is useful.

Index

473

475

477

484

487

488

489

491

To the owner of this book:

We are interested in your reaction to Francis/Jones/Smith, **Destinies: Canadian History since Confederation**. With your comments and suggestions, we may improve this book in future editions.

1. What was your reason for using this book?

____ university course   ____ continuing education course
____ college course   ____ personal interest
                                    ____ other (specify)

2. Which school? _____

3. Approximately how much of the book did you use?
    ____ $\frac{1}{4}$ ____ $\frac{1}{2}$ ____ $\frac{3}{4}$ ____ all

4. What is the best aspect of the book?

5. Have you any suggestions for improvement?

6. Is there anything that should be added?

Fold here

— — — — — — — — — — — — — — — — — —

Business
Reply Mail
No Postage Stamp
Necessary if Mailed
in Canada

43652

POSTAGE WILL BE PAID BY
SUSAN LILHOLT
Publisher
College Editorial Department
HOLT, RINEHART AND WINSTON
OF CANADA, LIMITED
55 HORNER AVENUE
TORONTO, ONTARIO
M8Z 9Z9

Tape shut